TUTORIAL TUTORIAL TUTORIAL TUTORIAL TUTORIAL TUTORIAL

# DATABASE MANAGEMENT

JAMES A. LARSON

# data-base management

IEEE Computer Society Order Number 714
Library of Congress Number 86-45873
IEEE Catalog Number EH0252-7
ISBN 0-8186-0714-9

IEEE THE INSTITUTE OF ELECTRICAL AND ELECTRONICS ENGINEERS, INC.

IEEE COMPUTER SOCIETY PRESS

Published by IEEE Computer Society Press
1730 Massachusetts Avenue, N.W.
Washington, D.C. 20036-1903

COVER DESIGNED BY JACK I. BALLESTERO



IEEE Computer Society Order Number 714
Library of Congress Number 86-45873
IEEE Catalog Number EH0252-7
ISBN 0-8186-0714-9 (Paper)
ISBN 0-8186-4714-0 (Microfiche)

Order from: IEEE Computer Society
Post Office Box 80452
Worldway Postal Center
Los Angeles, CA 90080

IEEE Service Center
445 Hoes Lane
Piscataway, NJ 08854

IEEE Computer Society
Avenue de la Tanche, 2
B-1160 Brussels,
Belgium

THE INSTITUTE OF ELECTRICAL AND ELECTRONICS ENGINEERS, INC.

# Preface

A Database Management System (DBMS) maintains and integrates data in a computer on behalf of one or more computer users. Computer users everywhere now use DBMSs on a daily basis. DBMSs have become one of the most frequently used software systems today.

When should you use (or not use) a DBMS? How can you communicate with a DBMS? How do you design a database? How does a DBMS work? What will future DBMSs be like? This tutorial is designed for systems analysts, programmers, and computer system managers who need answers to these questions.

This book is organized in the following manner.

Chapter 1 is an introduction to database management. The papers reprinted here contain descriptions of the advantages and disadvantages of database management, describe the environment for a database management system, and characterize useful database management systems.

The papers in Chapter 2 focus on user interfaces to database management systems. The traditional interfaces (file, CODASYL network, and relational) are reviewed. The more recent two-dimensional languages and graphic interfaces are described. The chapter ends with an evaluation of query languages.

Chapter 3 deals with database design. The papers here cover the four main steps in designing databases: view design, schema integration, accommodation, and physical data design.

Chapter 4 describes the nuts and bolts of database management system design. Topics in the papers include transaction processing, backup and recovery, and concurrency control.

Chapter 5 overviews recent developments in database management systems. The papers reprinted in this chapter characterize the commercial database management systems of tomorrow.

This book and the papers included in it are used as reference material in professional development seminars and in an introductory course in database management systems which was conducted by the author at the University of Minnesota. Please forward to the author any suggestions for improvements, especially recommendations for papers to reprint in the next edition.

*James A. Larson*
Honeywell Computer Science Center
1000 Boone Avenue North
Minneapolis, Minnesota 55427

# Table of Contents

# Chapter 1: Introduction

## 1.1: Why Database Management?

People form enterprises to accomplish goals that may be impossible for a single person to accomplish alone. An *enterprise* is a group of people working toward a goal by using resources and tools held in common. An educational institution, a police force, a hospital, an airline company, and a toy manufacturer are all examples of enterprises that involve people using common resources working toward goals.

Keeping track of all the resources of an enterprise can be a problem, especially for large enterprises. Fully using resources and people often may mean the difference between a successful organization that meets its goals and an unsuccessful organization that does not reach its goals. Most enterprises have an organization of managers to deal with the utilization of resources and people. Tools have been developed to help managers perform the tasks of identifying the locations and amounts of resources and analyzing alternative uses of resources. Such management tools include electronic computers.

Computers can be used to store information of interest to the enterprise. This information may be organized, summarized, extracted, and interpolated by the computer and presented to managers of the enterprise who use these results to make decisions for directing the enterprise. Information, represented as data in the computer, can be considered to be a resource of the enterprise just as equipment, capital, and employees are also considered resources. Access to information represented as data in a computer is frequently vital in an enterprise's pursuit of its goals. Such information is needed in making decisions regarding the future of the enterprise. Many enterprises need such information on a day-to-day basis to function effectively. The availability of such information when it is needed is a great asset to an enterprise and may very well determine the difference between success and failure.

## 1.2: The Database and Database Administrators

The collection of data representing information of interest to an enterprise is called the enterprise's *database.* The database consists of data representing objects, concepts, and events of interest to the enterprise. The database thus consists of objects, concepts, or event extensions that can be retrieved, modified, inserted, or deleted by users of the database management system. A database is more than just a collection of data stored in a computer. As Wiederhold explains in his paper, "Databases," reprinted in this chapter, "Information, the desired product of having a database, is generated by relating facts and situations that were previously separate." The true power of a database becomes apparent when you can obtain new insights by detecting trends and discovering relationships among previously separated data.

Information does not always need to reside on electronic or magnetic storage devices that can be quickly accessed by a computer. For example, a recipe card file, a library of books, a cave with prehistoric paintings on the wall, or an elderly person's recollections and stories about childhood are not usually stored in a computer. However, to quickly and effectively retrieve data, the data need to reside on a medium that can be accessed electronically. As we will see in Chapter 5, some database management systems can maintain graphics, voice, and video information; however, most can deal only with tabular types of data.

The data stored in a database must be organized to promote ease in locating any desired piece of datum. Just as the books in a library are arranged on shelves, data in a computer must be organized and arranged systematically. The person responsible for the organization of data in the database, the *database administrator,* determines not only how data are stored in the database, but also what data are to be stored and who may access the data. *Database users* use the database management system to insert, delete, modify, and retrieve data in the database according to the rules specified by the database administrator.

Database administrators need tools to help them manage the data in the database. One such tool is a *database management system,* which is a collection of computer software used to describe, insert, delete, modify, and retrieve data in the database. Some database management systems are designed to manage data from a single application domain and are carefully tailored to the particular requirements of that application. Other database management systems can be used across a wide range of domains. These general database management systems are designed and implemented so that a database administrator can easily define and implement new databases by using the software tools of the database management system. In this tutorial we will consider only general purpose database management systems that maintain databases for several domains.

As users insert, delete, and modify data, the data in the database changes. When designing a database, the database administrator does not have on hand the complete collection of data for the lifetime of the database. Thus, a design based solely upon the data to be initially placed into the database does not produce results of lasting value. It is better for the database administrator to view an enterprise more abstractly by identifying classes of enterprise objects, concepts, and events called data types. For example, the data instances TONSILLITIS, HERNIA, and INFLUENZA can be abstracted to the data type ILLNESS. A data model is used to describe the types of data in the database and the relationships between the data types.

### 1.3: The Data Model

A *model* often refers to an abstraction of a real-world system. For example, economists develop *theoretical models* that describe portions of the economy. Such models isolate certain aspects of the system being modeled and attempt to explain those aspects, perhaps even allowing the forecasting of future events. These theoretical models may involve complex equations that simulate or model a real-world system. Although computers frequently may be used to process such theoretical models, this book deals with another kind of model, the *data model.*

Unfortunately, the term, data model, is used in several different ways in the area of database management systems. One use refers to the description of a specific database. For example, the EMPLOYEE model refers to the PAYROLL, ADDRESS, and JOB-HISTORY record types of the EMPLOYEE database. In this book we will not use the term, data model, in this way. Instead, we will use *schema* to refer to a description of a specific database. We will use a more general definition of *data model.*

*Data model* will refer to the style of describing and manipulating data in a database. Many formal definitions of data models are based on mathematical constructs, such as relations, sets, and graphs. Some formal definitions include operations that may be performed on these mathematical constructs, while others do not describe any data manipulation commands. Because database management systems are used to modify the database, we will consider data manipulation to be an important aspect of the data model.

Data models differ in the style in which data objects and relationships between data objects are described. They also differ in the style in which constraints on data objects are expressed and in which operations upon the database are expressed.

Many data models have been proposed, each with its own concepts and terminology for specific modeling capabilities to express the semantics and structure of data. Each is appropriate for a limited range of applications, but no one data model seems to be suitable for all applications.

Data models are used for several reasons. Data models aid in communicating ideas. Computational problems can be specified by using a data model. The solution may involve description of data by using the data model. Examples can be defined by using the data models. Data models help to express the intent, the scope, and the boundaries of the problem area. They enable ideas to be passed between people and between people and machines. They clarify what can (and what cannot) be understood. Finally, data models help people to be thorough and rigorous in problem statements. Just as a mathematician uses special symbols to define an area of analysis or an accountant uses standard bookkeeping entries to record transactions, the computer user describes the database access problem to be solved by using a data model.

One data model is the *file data model* used by COBOL, FORTRAN, and other programming languages, where data are described by a declaration in the source language listing the names of the fields of data in each record of a file. The declaration also describes the type and length of each field. Data manipulation commands include READ, which transfers data from the file to the program work space, and WRITE, which transfers data from the program work space to the file.

In the *hierarchical data model,* records of data are arranged in a hierarchy or tree structure (Figure 1.1). A superior-subordinate relationship may exist between records in this data model. In addition to the READ and WRITE commands

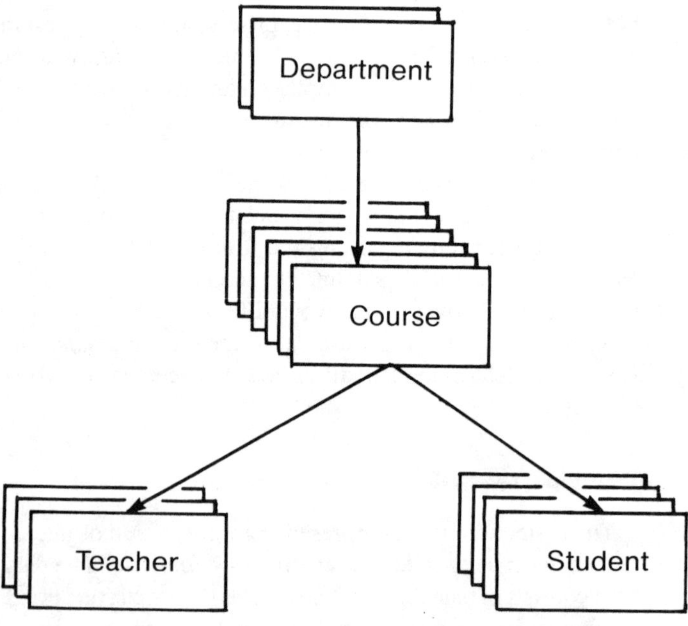


**Figure 1-1. Hierarchical Data Model**

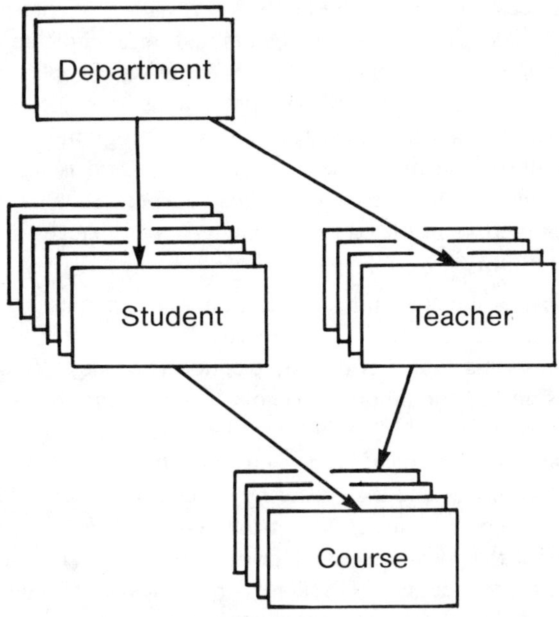


**Figure 1-2. Network Data Model**

used to transfer data between the database and the program work space, there are commands to traverse the relationships between the records. A record may be directly subordinate to at most one other record in the hierarchical data model. The *network data model* (Figure 1.2) removes this restriction. In this data model, records of data are arranged in a network of relationships. A record may be directly subordinate to several other records in the network. Because a hierarchical data structure also can be considered a network data structure, the hierarchical data model can be considered to be a submodel of the network data model. No record is subordinate to another record in the *relational data model* (Figure 1.3). Special relational data model commands can be used to coordinate records and select records for retrieval and update.

The file, hierarchical, network, and relational data models are similar in that each can be used to describe entities, attributes, and relationships of data in a database. The relative merits of each kind of model are hotly debated. Such arguments make sense only when the application environment is considered; only when the use of the data model is known, can an appropriate data model be chosen.

The concept of a data model as used here is somewhat different from that of a programming language like FORTRAN or COBOL. One major difference between a data model and a programming language is where the manipulated data resides. In our use, a data model is a style for describing and manipulating data in a database and transferring data between the database and the program work space. A *programming language* is a collection of rules for using words and phrases to describe and manipulate data in the program work space. Frequently, programming languages are extended to include data model commands that transfer data between the program work space and the database. While FORTRAN and COBOL were originally developed with the READ and WRITE commands of the file data model, more recently they have been extended to include data manipulation commands for other data models. When data model commands are embedded into programming languages, the data model is extended to conform to the syntax conventions of the programming language. For example, a data model command embedded into COBOL may end with a period, while the same data model command ends with a semicolon when embedded into PL/1.

In some data management systems, data manipulation commands can be entered directly into the computer by using a terminal and without being embedded into a programming language. Such languages are called *query languages,* which may range from the very complex (for use by computer experts) to the very simple (for use by individuals without training in computer usage). An important factor in selecting a database management system is its query language. Some database management systems support more than one query language.

Data models are used to describe schemas, which in turn describe data in the database. A database management sys-

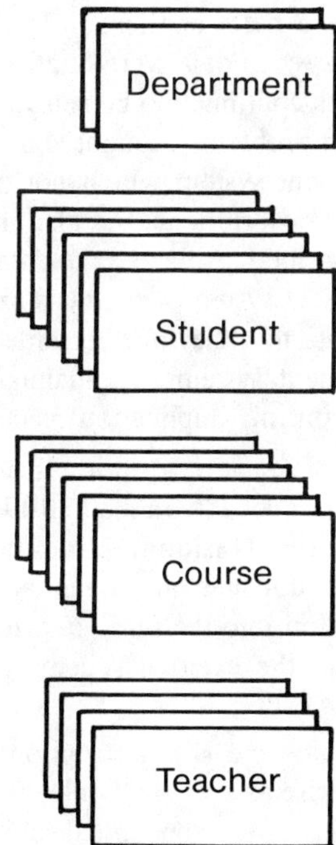


**Figure 1-3. Relational Data Model**

tem may have several schemas, each describing a different aspect of the database. The collection of schemas in a database management system is called the *information architecture* of the database management system.

## 1.4: The Information Architecture for a Database Management System

There was a time when an application program could be regarded as a self-contained unit. Data processing merely involved the execution of application programs against a set of files. The structures of the files would be declared within application programs, and the program statements would be tightly bound to those definitions. Programs quickly became unmaintainable and the coordination of executing update programs became a nightmare. Such problems triggered the migration of some functions common to application programs into database management systems.

It became clear that file definitions should be controlled centrally rather than be dispersed and replicated throughout many application programs. A facility was introduced to COBOL for incorporating file definitions into a central library. The file definitions were copied from the central library into the application program during program compilation. In this way, conflicting descriptions of files could be eliminated and naming conventions could be enforced.

The migration of data definition to a central library was not a universal panacea because it was difficult to restrict program access only to parts of files; little could be done to ensure consistency when data were duplicated across many files; and programs continued to be sensitive to data definition changes. Such problems brought about the birth of the database management system which not only maintains a repository for data descriptions, but also maintains one for the data being described. All access to data is made via the database management system, which ensures that processes access only the data that they are permitted to access. The database management system also maintains relationships among data and controls duplication of data.

The functions of data description have been defined thoroughly in the past decade. In the mid-1970s, a committee of the American National Standards Institute, ANSI/X3/SPARC, published an influential report that separated data description into the three interrelated levels: the conceptual schema, the external schema, and the internal schema (Figure 1.4).

The *conceptual schema* is a description of types of data useful to the enterprise as a whole, while the *external schema* represents a masking of the conceptual schema and presents a description of the types of data and their interrelationships of interest to one or more applications within an enterprise. Many external schemas can be defined for a single conceptual schema, each for use with a different set of applications. External schemas ensure that applications have access only to data relevant to those applications. A program perceives data only in terms of the external schema and is insulated from many types of changes to the conceptual schema; thus, programs are insulated from many types of changes in data definition.

Neither the conceptual nor the external schemas describe how the data should be represented in computer storage because this aspect of data description is prone to frequent revision and should not be visible to most users. In particular, programs should not be dependent on how data are stored on secondary storage. Storage considerations, such as indexing techniques and the clustering of records on second storage devices, are described in the *internal schema,* which ensures that data described in the conceptual schema are stored and accessed efficiently; revisions to the internal schema should not require changes in the conceptual or external schemas.

Data description functions, therefore, have evolved from application programs and have been stratified into different types of data description called *schemas.* The types of schemas and their interrelationships are called an *information architecture.* The ANSI/X3/SPARC information architecture is a three-level information architecture. A schema type may be defined by using any of several data models; for example, the external schema type might be defined by using any of the file, network, hierarchical, or relational data models.

Many different data architectures have been suggested for database management systems depending on the intended use. Different classes of users may require different schema types determined by a variety of factors, including the roles of the users. For example, the role of a person might reflect the individual's degree of sophistication or workload. Another criteria is time dependencies. The data administration task might be fragmented into a sequence of subtasks that need not be performed at the same point in time; a schema type can be created for each subtask. Some aspects of the data administration task might need more frequent revision than other aspects; schema types can be created according to the volatility of an aspect.

It is possible to justify many separate schema types. For example, schema types might be envisaged to cope with security considerations, the geographical distribution of data, and backup and recovery. It is apparent that an information architecture relevant to one enterprise might not be so appropriate to another enterprise or even for the same enterprise at a later date. For example, a small enterprise might need only external schemas and a conceptual schema. As the

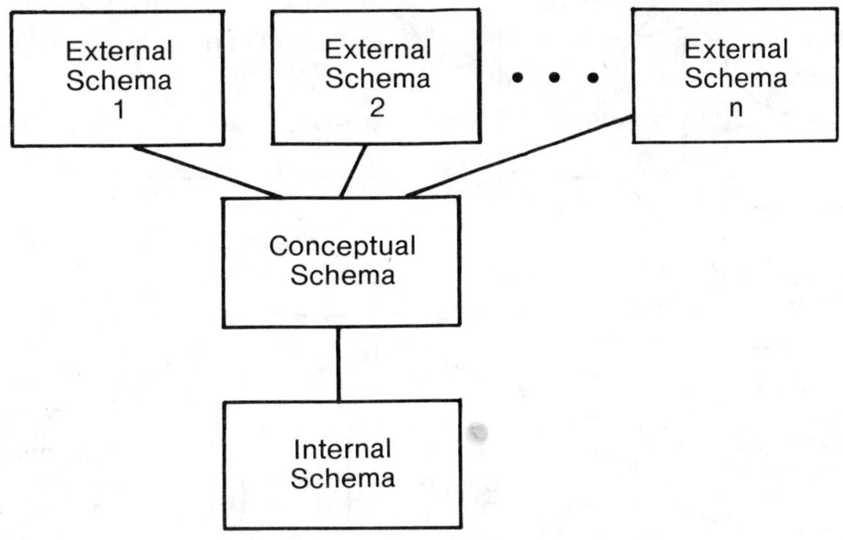


**Figure 1-4. Information Architecture**

organization expands, it might identify a need for one schema type to cope with data distribution and another, such as an internal schema type, to increase control over the structure of stored data. Thus a rigid architecture appears to have significant drawbacks; a database management system should provide a flexible information architecture. Unfortunately, most existing commercial database management systems have only a fixed information architecture.

The various software processes and modules of a database management system and their interrelationship is called the *system architecture*, which is described in the next section.

## 1.5: System Architecture for Database Management Systems

Database management systems are popular because they provide useful features for maintaining and accessing data. These features include multiple user interfaces, concurrency transparency, program data independence, and transaction atomicity. The three processors, user command translator, canonical command translator, and runtime support processor (Figure 1.5) are responsible for supporting these features.

1. *Multiple user interfaces:* Different database management system users may access the database by using different user interfaces. Several user interfaces to database management systems are described in Chapter 2. Just as programmers may choose from various programming languages, database users may choose from various interfaces. There may be several *user command translators,* each accepting user requests expressed using a different interface and converting these commands into a canonical format. The external schema, the conceptual schema, and the external schema-to-conceptual-schema mappings guide the user command translator in converting user commands into canonical commands.
2. *Program-data independence:* Some changes to a database require that application programs that access the database be modified by a programmer, which is frequently an expensive task. An application program has *program data independence* (sometimes simply called data independence) if it does not require modification when the database is restructured or reorganized. Program data independence is provided by hiding the physical placement and organization of data in the database from the application program. The *canonical command translator* support program-data independence. The canonical command translator converts the canonical commands into physical commands to be executed by the runtime support processor. The canonical command translator is responsible for choosing an optimal or nearly optimal access path to the physical data. If the physical data structures or access paths are changed, the canonical command translator must be invoked to choose a new optimal or nearly optimal access path. Thus, physical data structures and access paths can be fine tuned to make the overall DBMS perform as efficiently as possible without having to modify existing application programs or queries. The conceptual schema, the internal schema, and the mappings

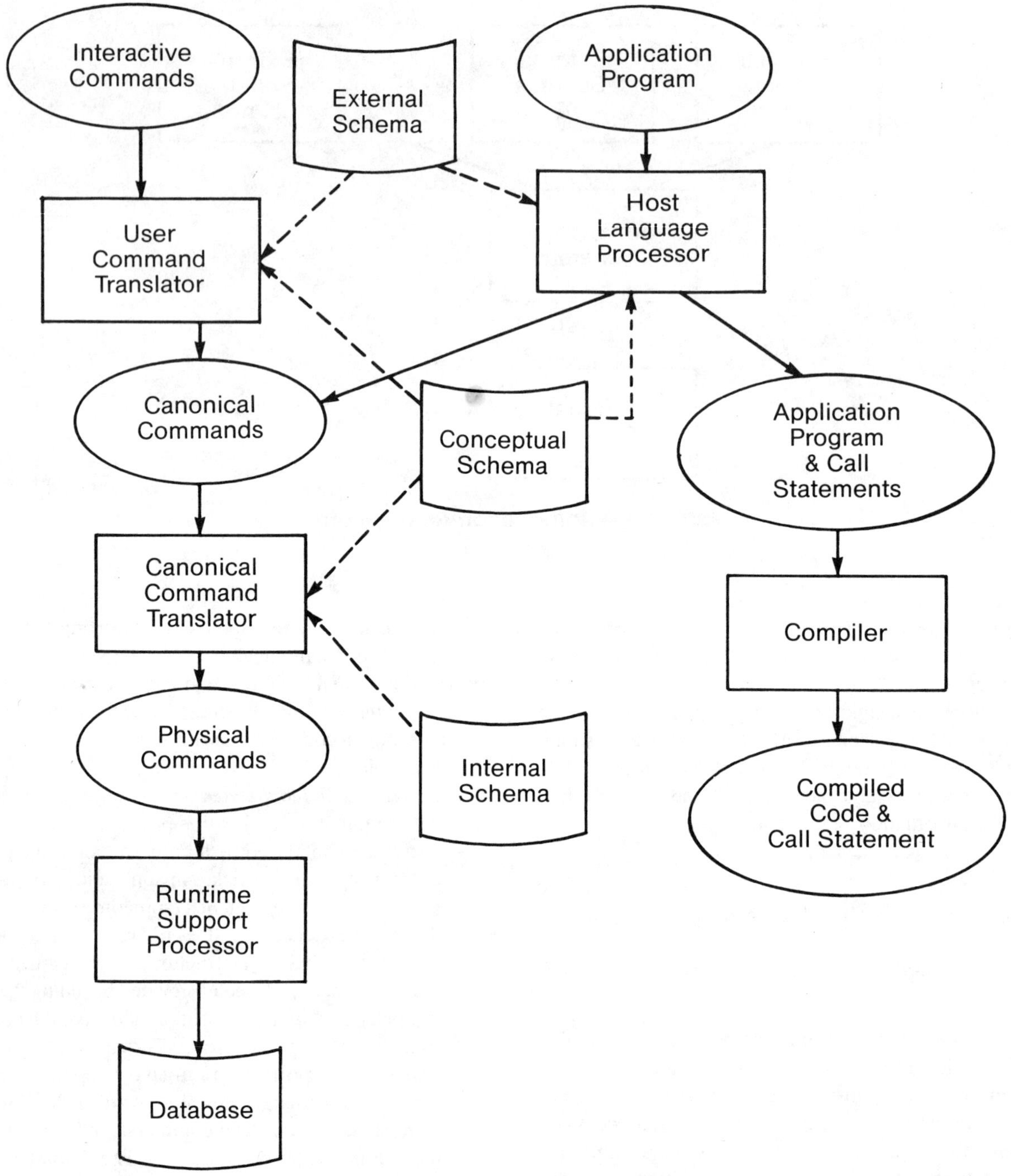


**Figure 1-5. System Architecture**

between these two schemas guide the canonical command translator in choosing the optimal access path and in converting the canonical commands into the appropriate physical commands.

3. *Concurrency transparency:* Concurrency transparency enables users to believe that each one has sole access to the database even though the DBMS can support several users simultaneously. Occasionally, two or more users may attempt to access the same portion of the database at the same time. Concurrent access presents a special problem in that the value of data objects may change unexpectedly or worse, an update may be lost. The *runtime support processor* is respon-

sible for accepting several requests, scheduling the processing of those requests, and returning the results. It resolves the problem of concurrent updates. It provides concurrency transparency in that each user believes that he/she has sole access to the database and is isolated from the actions of other concurrent users. Chapter 4 discusses approaches for concurrency control.

4. *Transaction atomicity:* Transaction atomicity means that each transaction is either completely executed with any modifications made to the database permanently recorded or the transaction is aborted with no permanent change to the database. When transaction atomicity is supported, the user does not have to restore the database if a transaction aborts. The runtime support processor is also responsible for guaranteeing that the changes to the database made by a transaction are made permanent in the database. If for some reason a transaction aborts, the runtime processor is responsible for guaranteeing that any database changes are removed from the database. Chapter 4 discusses how to achieve transaction atomicity.

To integrate database commands into a programming language for developing sophisticated applications, a special kind of user command translator is needed. In Figure 1.5, this special user command translator is called a *host language preprocessor.* It accepts an application program written by using a programming language (such as COBOL or FORTRAN) and database manipulation commands. It extracts the database manipulation commands from the program, replacing them with calls to the runtime support unit. The extracted database manipulation commands are converted into canonical commands, which are then passed to the canonical command translator. The physical commands are saved and executed by the runtime support processor when the compiled application program is executed.

Other processors may exist in the system architecture of a database management system. Special processors may accept data description from the database administrator and convert the data description into the internal representation of any of the schemas (external, conceptual, or internal). The internal representation of the schemas is often stored in a special database, called a data dictionary. A *data dictionary* is a database that contains data about other data. The contents of the data dictionary is sometimes called *meta data.*

Now that we have seen both the information architecture and the system architecture of a database management system, let's review what database management systems can do.

## 1.6: Job Description for Database Management Systems

Database management systems are popular because they provide features that are useful and convenient for people dealing with a database. Such features include data independence, data semantics, control of redundancy, backup and recovery, security, and enforcement of standards, and sharing.

### *Data Independence*

When a database is *reorganized,* data in it may be moved from one location to another. Data structures such as indexes may be adjusted or rebuilt. Sometimes data may be moved from one device type to another, such as from magnetic tape to magnetic disks. A database may be reorganized to make better utilization of existing storage resources or to migrate data to storage devices that can be accessed more rapidly. Reorganization normally should allow programs that worked correctly before the reorganization to continue to do so after the reorganization.

From time to time it becomes necessary to add new types of data to an existing database; for example, when an enterprise expands into new areas and needs to store new information in the database or as more and more noncomputerized applications become computerized. Sometimes it is also desirable to remove existing types of data from the database (perhaps when the enterprise shrinks or when a single database is divided into two or more separate databases). As the enterprise itself changes, so do the types of data required in the database.

A database can be *restructured* by adding or deleting from the database description a type of data or a relationship between types of data. Restructuring a database may cause existing software to become invalid. For example, deleting an enterprise data type may result in a program abnormally terminating when it attempts to access the missing data.

A program has *data independence* or, more accurately, *program-data independence,* if it does not require modification as a result of a database reorganization or restructuring. There are several degrees of data independence. Some changes to the database require that a programmer modify statements in a source program, which is very expensive in terms of programmer and computer-testing time. Other changes do not involve changes to the source program but involve recompiling it instead. Some changes to the database involve only relinking or remapping a program. Plus, some database changes do not require any program changes. Complete data independence can never be achieved; however, a large degree of data independence can be realized. Data independence is one of the primary goals of a database management system.

To optimize both overall storage utilization and computer performance for critical database applications, the database administrator may vary the physical format of data, its placement, and data access technique. A database management system provides data independence by isolating the program from the format of data, the physical placement of data, and the techniques used to access data. If any of these change, the program logic remains unaffected and the program does not need to be modified. However, the execution speed may be affected.

A cost is associated with data independence. The database management system resolves the differences between the way a program perceives the data and the way the data are actually stored on the physical storage devices of the computer. The correlation between the program's perception of the data and the actual storage determines the number of transformations to be performed by the database management system. With computer processing costs decreasing and maintenance costs increasing, applications require more data independence. Database management systems can provide a cost savings by reducing costly program maintenance at a smaller cost in increased execution costs.

*Data Semantics*

At one time, application programs performed all data validation and manipulation resulting in duplication of code across many application programs, fertile territory for inconsistencies. A modification to a single update program could have a profound and unexpected effect on many other programs. It became clear that some mechanism had to be interposed between programs and their data. A stopgap measure, which reduces the amount of replicated code, is to place file access and data validation routines in a library that is accessible to application programs. With the advent of the database management system, it became clear that such routines were one aspect of data description. It should be the responsibility of the database management system, not the programmer, to call validation routines prior to storing a record.

Data description languages can specify a lot of the data meaning, or semantics. Semantics can be described in terms of what can and cannot be done with the data. Statements that in the past would have appeared in application programs are now found in the data descriptions. For example, the CODASYL data description language includes validation statements, which provide for range checking and data consistency checking (such as CHECK HEIGHT <WIDTH); record selection expressions that contain criteria for selecting individual record occurrences from a database (application programs merely initialize parameters and trigger the predefined record selection expressions); and database procedures, which can be associated with data description to perform many types of tasks previously performed by application programs.

Many of the decisions about how to access data can be removed from application programs and placed into the database management system. An application program describes the data to be retrieved and stored, and the database management system determines how the data are accessed in the database. A typical data manipulation statement might retrieve a single record occurrence from the database; the database management system must (1) determine whether access should be granted to the record occurrence, (2) traverse the database to locate the required record, and (3) reformat the stored record to the form required by the application program.

*Redundancy*

Applications based on file systems often involve more than one file. To avoid expensive file coordination, identical data elements appear on each file. For example, both a payroll and a personnel file may contain EMPLOYEE NAME and CURRENT WAGE data fields. Although the cost of storage is becoming less expensive, there is still a cost associated with storing the same data in two places. There is also the cost of updating both files in order to keep the files consistent. (Redundancy breeds inconsistency.) A database management system can be used to minimize inconsistency between duplicate copies of the same data field by storing the data field only once, reducing storage costs as well.

*Backup and Recovery*

The big nightmare for programmers in charge of a payroll system is to be told, "The master file is lost." With perhaps thousands of people expecting checks that can be generated only from the data on the master file, losing any portion of that file and not being able to recover and restore those data is serious. Any programmer who has faced such a problem is careful to make duplicate copies of all files used by the payroll system.

It seems to be an unwritten law in the world of data processing that a backup copy of a file is never needed unless one does not exist. If this unproven law is true, it is worth making a backup copy just so it is never needed. If this law is not true, a backup copy of a file will be needed when the original master file is lost. In any case, there should always be a backup copy of critical files.

A database management system can be used not only to produce a backup copy of all data in the database but it also records all changes made to the data after the backup copy was created. If the database becomes invalid because of human, program, or mechanical error, the backup copy can be loaded and brought up to date by using the *transaction log*, which contains the changes made since the backup was created. For some applications, the backup and recovery features can be one of the most important benefits of a database management system.

*Security*

To support security a database management system provides mechanisms designed to prevent unauthorized users from accessing data in the database. Anyone who wishes to access data must first identify himself or herself to the database management system. The system then determines whether that person may gain access to a specific piece of datum. It is also important to prevent unauthorized modification of data either maliciously or unintentionally. To fail to do so may result in loss of data integrity, which may be very costly in terms of both dollars and prestige.

*Standards*

The main virtue of consistency is that it is easier for concerned individuals to understand what is being done. If all programs refer to the same data field by the same name, then a programmer working with one program can more easily understand the programs written by others. Programs that conform to such standards are usually less costly to modify. A database management system can be used to ensure that all programs in the same application system use the same names for the same data fields. It can also provide a consistent view of the structure of data to all programs.

*Sharing*

Database management systems also make it easier for different programs to share data by allowing separate programs accessing the same data to execute simultaneously. The database management system is responsible for guaranteeing that updates to shared files are processed correctly and that no updates are lost. This problem, called *concurrency control,* is discussed in Chapter 4.

*Other Criteria*

In his paper reprinted at the end of this section, Wiederhold identifies four unique database characteristics: logging, database modeling, schemas, and nonprocedural access. The last criteria needs some explanation. The data manipulation languages associated with most data models can be divided into two groups, called procedural and nonprocedural.

A *procedural data manipulation language* is one in which the programmer can specify that objects in the database be located and manipulated one at a time. The READ and WRITE commands of the file data model are procedural data manipulation languages. Each time a READ command is invoked, a single record is retrieved from a file; each time a WRITE command is invoked, a record is written into the file. Usually procedural data manipulation commands require the use of IF-THEN-ELSE, DO, and other programming language control constructs.

A *nonprocedural data manipulation language* is one in which a single command can manipulate many objects in the database. When using these languages, programmers specify what objects to access rather than how to access the objects. Usually, these languages do not require the use of IF-THEN-ELSE and DO control constructs of programming languages. A single command of a nonprocedural data manipulation language can be equivalent to a sequence of procedural data manipulation commands. For this reason, writing requests using nonprocedural rather than procedural languages is both faster and easier.

Some very important database management systems support only procedural data manipulation languages. The CODASYL network database management systems originally only supported a procedural data manipulation language. However, with the increasing popularity of relational databases and their nonprocedural data manipulation languages, many CODASYL network database management systems have been extended to also support nonprocedural data manipulation languages. The popular trend is certainly to database management systems that support nonprocedural access. However, there are some very good database management systems that support only procedural access.

### 1.7: System Characteristics

A good system is more than a system that works correctly. Any software system, including a database management system, should provide a number of characteristics.

*System Documentation*

Each component of the system must be documented carefully, a practice that can be of great help to the individuals responsible for the system.

*User Documentation*

Without good user documentation, users will have to ask constantly how to use the system or, more likely, will not use the system at all. If the system is not used, it is worthless, and all of the time spent designing and implementing it is wasted.

*Ease of Use*

Complexity is the breeding ground of errors. Complex interfaces to systems result not only in errors by users of the system, but also in frustration. Systems should be easy to use and also easy to install. They should be flexible and able to handle new applications easily.

*Meaningful Error Messages*

System users appreciate knowing if the system will not deliver an answer and also if the answer may be incorrect because of some kind of system error. Every error deserves a message, one that is understandable. For example, the error message "3147" would not seem a satisfactory explanation for why a computer request went awry.

*Not Error Prone*

It is possible for a data request to destroy the database completely. Thus users must be protected from themselves. The user interface should be carefully designed to avoid errors. For example, the commands for delete should bear no similarity to commands for deliver.

*Easy to Maintain*

System use changes over time as people conceive of new and better ways of doing things. No system is static; no system will last forever unchanged. With the increasing cost of programming time, it is important to design a system for easy adaptation and change. Good documentation is necessary, but a designer can and should do more to ease future maintenance costs. By careful partitioning of the system, future modifications may be isolated to a few modules that can be easily modified and tested.

It is important to design any system so that different individuals may design, create, and modify subcomponents independently of the system. These modules can be tested and debugged separately before being integrated into the overall system.

*Reliability*

Any system that does not perform as advertised should be considered a fraud. A system that performs incorrectly is even worse. The system should be completely debugged by a series of carefully designed tests and by potential users who purposely attempt to break the system.

*Good User Response Time*

Results supplied by the system will be worthless if they are not available when needed, and users need them when they make a request for the information. A simple request should not take longer than a couple of seconds.

*Efficiency*

The software must execute rapidly, and the data structures must minimize storage space. These are important parameters, which need to be carefully chosen to make a system efficient. However, the principal parameter in the efficiency of every system is the system user. Personnel costs are becoming more expensive while machine costs are becoming less expensive. Systems should be designed first to minimize personnel costs and second to minimize computer time and computer storage.

## 1.8: Other Problems

*Problems Not Solved by a Database Management System*

Many attempts at implementing database management systems have failed because the implementors expected too much of the database management system. There are some problems that cannot be solved by a database management system. In fact, database management systems sometimes make these problems more severe.

A database management system cannot identify and remove redundant data. A database administrator must do this. Most database management systems have no way of detecting and removing redundant data. On more than one occasion, existing files have been loaded directly into a database management system without removing data. Inconsistencies are then discovered in the database and the database management system gets blamed.

A database management system cannot improve poor application system design and implementation. It does not improve poorly stated requirements nor does it correct ill-defined office procedures. A database management system is not a substitute for good system analysis.

*Problems Created by a Database Management System*

A database management system is a set of complex programs. With any complex software, there is a risk of failure. The software may not function properly. It may not solve the enterprise's problems as expected. Some problems created by the database management system should be resolved:

1. Converting existing data and loading it into the database.
2. Converting existing software so that it accesses data in the database.
3. Training users and programmers to use the database management system.
4. Adding hardware needed to run the database management system.
5. Adding personnel, especially database administrators, to manage the database management system.
6. Changing the organizational structure of the enterprise.

Most major problems created by a database management system can be foreseen. Plans to deal with these problems should be made well before the database management system is implemented.

## 1.9: Alternatives to Database Management

Several alternatives to database management systems should be considered. They include file systems, data dictionaries and directories, report generator, and application generators.

*File Systems*

File systems available with almost every operating system provide great efficiency of computer resources. Most programmers are familiar with file systems. There are a few enhancements that you may want to make to your file system to make it more like a database management system. These enhancements cost very little:

- Remove all of the file descriptions from application programs, and place a copy of each file description in a library. Replace the file description with a COPY (COBOL) or INCLUDE (PL/1) or similar command so that when the compiler processes the application program, the file descriptions are automatically retrieved from the library and inserted into the application programs. This has two effects: (1) All applications must use the same naming standards for files and fields in files. This is a type of naming standard enforcement. (2) When a file must be extended to include a new field, just add the new field description to the file description in the library and recompile all of the application programs. This is a form of program-data independence.
- Replace I/O commands in application programs by CALLs to subroutines placed into a library. If the file structure changes (for example from a hashed to a keyed file), change the I/O routines in the library and re-link-edited the application programs. This is another form of program-data independence.
- Implement backup and restore utilities. Make sure the backup utility is scheduled periodically.
- Combine files with redundant data. This will require modifying the application programs that updated the original files. This will decrease the data inconsistency that occurs with redundant data.
- Implement and enforce a password protection scheme with each file.

These few extensions can make your file system much like a database management system with a modest investment in time.

*Data Dictionary and Data Directory*

Data dictionaries and directories provide another alternative to database management systems. A list of all of the data elements (fields) and the files in which they appear can be very useful. Users can refer to the list to determine what data elements are available. Programmers can refer to the list to obtain the correct spelling of the data element names.

The list can be expanded to include an English description of the contents of each data element. The dates when values of the data item are current help in scheduling report programs. The meaning of all codes and symbols help data entry personnel. An indication of who is responsible for keeping values up to date helps improve data integrity.

This list can be maintained manually in a printed form with periodic revisions being issued to reflect changes and enhancements. An online data dictionary would alleviate many problems from using an outdated list, while an online copy could be used to generate file descriptions used by application programmers, thus increasing the use of naming standards. Software programs are available that make the creation, update, and reporting of data dictionary information easy. Most database management systems come with a built-in data dictionary, although sometimes available only as an extra cost option.

Other features of dictionary systems are found in the reprinted paper, "The Integrated Dictionary/Directory System," by Allen, Loomis, and Mannino in this chapter.

*Report Generators and Application Generators*

Other alternatives to a database management system are report and application generators. A *report generator* is a software program that accepts a description of the format and contents of a report and causes that report to be produced. Data are selected according to prespecified selection criteria from one or more files (which may or may not be maintained by a database management system). Data is sorted and displayed as a report that may be either displayed on a video screen or printed on a printer. Specifications for data selection and report formatting are nonprocedural.

An *application generator* is a software program that accepts a specification expressed in a nonprocedural language and generates an equivalent procedural programming language program. The program may access one or more files. Usually the types of programs generated by an application generator include:

- Report programs (of the type produced by report generators),
- Update a master file from a transaction file (with data validity checking), and
- Simple transaction generation.

The paper, "A Survey of Application Generators," by Horowitz, Kemper, and Narasimhann, reprinted in this chapter, further describes application generators.

Report generators and application generators can go far in helping solve some data processing problems. The greatest advantages occur, however, when they are used in conjunction with, rather than in place of, a database management system.

File systems, data dictionaries and directories, report and application generators, and database management systems can all be used to solve various data management problems. It is important to use a database management system only if the intended application warrant its use. The next section provides guidelines for deciding when to use a database management system.

### 1.10: When to Switch to a Database Management System

If you have several of the following data management problems, you should consider switching to a database management system.

- Application needs are constantly changing.
- Frequent data access for ad hoc requests.
- Many data elements are shared by several users.
- Backlog in developing applications, especially reports.
- Inconsistencies exist among the redundant copies of the same data.
- Different departments need to share and relate data.

Unlike the snake oil salesman of the old traveling medicine show, I will not promise that all problems can be solved by one simple treatment of database management system magic. There is no magic in a database management system. It is only a tool. Its success depends upon how it is used.

### Additional Readings


Bradley, James, *File and Data Base Techniques,* Holt, Rinehart and Winston, New York, 1982. Excellent review of file techniques and CODASYL, hierarchical, and relational database systems, primarily for the computer science student.

Bradley, James, *Introduction to Data Base Management in Business,* Holt, Rinehart and Winston, New York, 1983. Overviews the basic database concepts and systems from the viewpoint of business students. Instructor manual is available.

Bray, Olin H., *Distributed Database Management Systems,* Lexington Books, Lexington, Massachusetts, 1983. An easy-to-read book with overviews of distributed database management systems, data communications, distributed processing, data and function distribution, update synchronization, and request decomposition.

Cardenas, Alfonso F., *Data Base Management Systems,* Second Edition, Allyn and Bacon, Boston, Massachusetts, 1985. Describes the fundamental technology and practice of database and data management system design, implementation, and application. The emphasis is on fundamental, practical, and generally applicable matters. Contains chapters on CODASYL network, Total, IMS, System 2000, SQL/Data System, and Query-by-Example systems in addition to normalization, data dictionaries/directories, and database machines.

Ceri, Stefano and Giuseppe Pelagatti, *Distributed Databases: Principles and Systems,* McGraw-Hill, New York, 1984. A complete and thorough review of distributed DBMS issues. Chapters are devoted to distributed transparency, distributed database design, query decomposition, concurrency control, and reliability. Each chapter has an extensive annotated bibliography.

Date, C.J., *An Introduction to Database Systems,* Volume 1, Fourth Edition, Addison-Wesley, Reading, Massachusetts, 1986. The standard introductory text for database management systems for computer science students. The fourth edition is divided into six major parts: basic concepts, a sample relational system, relational database management, the database environment, nonrelational systems, and current developments. The text emphasizes relational systems and their user languages. Lacks guidelines for designing databases (other than a mathematically oriented chapter on normalization). Volume II (1982) covers a range of aspects related to implementing database management systems.

Goldstein, R.C., *Database Technology and Management,* John Wiley and Sons, New York, 1985. An introductory text divided into two parts: database design and database administration. It does a nice job of first describing technology and then applying the technology.

Gray, Peter, *Logic, Algebra and Databases,* Ellis Horwood Limited, Chichester, England, 1984 (distributed by John Wiley and Sons, New York). Examines the applications of logic programming and application programming to databases through the database query language. It has a heavy emphasis on the Fifth Generation logic programming language Prolog.

Kent, W., *Data and Reality,* North-Holland, New York, 1978. Recommended reading describing the nature of information and how it is represented in the conceptual schema. This book reviews the problems of using record-like structures for representing information.

Larson, James A. and Saeed Rahimi, *Tutorial: Distributed Database Management,* IEEE Computer Society, Washington, D.C., 1985. Introductions and reprinted papers covering the following aspects of distributed database management: transforming database commands, semantic integrity constraints, distributed query optimization, distributed concurrency and replication control, and distributed execution. Several case studies of distributed database management systems are presented.

Maier, David, *The Theory of Relational Databases,* Computer Science Press, Rockville, Maryland, 1983. For the serious student with a mathematical background, this text provides an in-depth description of the theoretical bases for relational databases and provides a firm basis for understanding current research papers in the area.

Martin, James, *Application Development Without Programmers.* Prentice-Hall, Englewood Cliffs, New Jersey, 1982. Describes tools and techniques for efficiently developing applications.

McFadden, Fred R. and Jeffrey A. Hoffer, *Data Base Management,* Benjamin/Cummings, Menlo Park, California, 1985. An excellent text for an introductory course for business students in database management systems with lots of case studies and examples. This text provides a nice balance between managerial and technical issues. The emphasis is on how to use database management systems. Also available are an instructor's guide and a case study book.

Schmidt, Joachim W. and Michael L. Brodie (eds.), *Relational Database Systems: Analysis and Comparison.* Springer-Verlag, New York, 1983. A feature analysis of several relational database management systems, including ASTRAL, IDAMS, the IDM, University INGRESS, MRDS, MRS, NOMAD, ORACLE, PASCAL/R, PRTV, QBE, RAPID, RAPPORT, and System R.

Teorey, Toby J. and James P. Fry, *Design of Database Structures,* Prentice-Hall, Englewood Cliffs, New Jersey, 1982. This book is for the professional database analyst, designer, database administrator, and application programmer. It establishes a consistent framework for multilevel database design, defines a workable methodology, and describes a set of general principles, tools, and techniques for database design at each level and it includes chapters on conceptual design, implementation design, physical design, and special design issues. This book gets to the nuts and bolts issues of designing an efficient database.

Tsichritzis, D.C. and A. Klug (eds.), "The ANSI/X3/SPARC DBMS Framework: Report of the Study Group on Database Management Systems," *Information Systems,* 3, 1978. This report, written by the Standards Planning and Requirement Committee (SPARC) of the American National Standards Committee on Computers and Information Processing, suggests the three schema levels (external, conceptual, and internal) as well as identifying several interfaces.

Ullman, Jeffrey D., *Principles of Database Systems,* Second Edition, Computer Science Press, Rockville, Maryland, 1982. An excellent in-depth description of both practical and theoretical database management, with strong emphasis on the theory. Suitable for the serious student with a mathematical background.

Vasta, Joseph A., *Understanding Data Base Management Systems,* Wadsworth, San Francisco, California, 1985. A "shop manual approach" to database management systems. It includes a balanced coverage of the three data models (hierarchical, network, and relational), database design, direct comparison of important features, on-line systems, and practical experience. Also available is a project workbook.

Weldon, Jay-Louise, *Data Base Administration,* Plenum Press, New York, 1981. This book provides a practical description of the DBA function.

# Databases

**Gio Wiederhold**
**Stanford University**

**Once a database had only to provide input-output programs and to manage multiple user interactions. Today, it must be easy to use, error resilient, and capable of reasonable performance.**

Although Vannevar Bush described most of what was required for today's databases as long ago as 1945,[1] database technology is relatively new to the computer science field. The primary reason for its delayed entry is that database concepts could not be implemented until computer technology had become sufficiently sophisticated. Before examining the "prerequisites" of databases, however, we need to understand what a database is and what requirements it must meet.

The objective of a database is to collect and maintain data so that it will be available for operations and decision making. Databases must satisfy a number of technical requirements: for example, data must be accessible to a variety of users, it may be collected far away from where it will be used, and it may be stored for long periods before its use; update and read data access may be concurrent; and data has to be organized so that relationships among the data can be explored.

Information, the desired product of having a database, is generated by relating facts and situations that were previously separate. This process may involve extensive data processing or simple retrieval of stored facts from the database, either to access unfamiliar facts in remote sources or to refresh the user's memory.

Good hardware is a primary prerequisite. To keep data accessible, storage devices with adequate performance and reliability are needed. Because many database applications require large quantities of data, the capacity and cost of storage was a significant factor in the emergence of databases. "Large" in this sense means more data than we can conveniently manipulate in primary memory, although long-term storage facilities are always needed for data permanency and sharing. The boundary of memory and storage capabilities is always changing and with it the scope of a true database.

Operating systems, another prerequisite for databases, handle the simultaneous processing that arises when many users access data at unpredictable times. *On-line* databases require more services than those provided by early timesharing systems. A successful timesharing system isolates competing users, keeping them from interfering with each other, even while they are using the same storage devices. Since a database is generally shared, its operating system has to permit cooperative access to selected data while protecting the database from





Reprinted from *Computer*, October 1984, pages 211-223. Copyright © 1984 by The Institute of Electrical and Electronics Engineers, Inc.

users who, operating independently, could inadvertently destroy it. Since now both interaction and isolation are required, the problem is compounded. Modern operating systems may include *transaction support* to aid the management of the often short-lived processes that share database access, and some systems provide transaction support without timesharing.

The last prerequisite for a successful database is adequate file services. File-management software exploits the capabilities of storage devices, which permit random access. It must support a number of functions, including retrieval and insertion of data records anywhere in the files. Unfortunately, data updates cause the number of records to grow, which makes insertion into the original sequence difficult. Even today, many operating systems provide only rudimentary random access capabilities for files, but database systems may circumvent these limits by incorporating a substantial amount of file-handling software.

## Memex: the first concept of a database

The following quotations are taken from "As We May Think," an article by Vannevar Bush published in the January 1945 edition of *Atlantic Monthly*. Bush was describing Memex, a name given to the first study of databases.

(1) "Our ineptitude in getting at the record is largely caused by the artificiality of systems of indexing. When data of any sort are placed in storage, they are filed alphabetically or numberically [sic], and information is found (when it is) by tracing it down from subclass to subclass. It can be in only one place, unless duplicates are used; one has to have rules as to which path will locate it, and the rules are cumbersome. . . ."

(2) "The human mind does not work that way. It operates by association. With one item in its grasp, it snaps instantly to the next that is suggested by the association of thoughts, in accordance with some intricate web of trails carried by the cells of the brain. . . ."

(3) ". . . Selection by association, rather than by indexing, may yet be mechanized. One cannot hope thus to equal the speed and flexibility with which the mind follows an associative trail, but it should be possible to beat the mind decisively in regard to the permanence and clarity of the items resurrected from storage."

(4) "Consider a future device for individual use, which is a sort of mechanized private file and library. It needs a name, and, to coin one at random, "memex" will do. A memex is a device in which an individual stores all his books, records, and communications, and which is mechanized so that it may be consulted with exceeding speed and flexibility. It is an enlarged intimate supplement to his memory."

(5) "It consists of a desk, and while it can presumably be operated from a distance, it is primarily the piece of furniture at which he works. On the top are slanting translucent screens, on which material can be projected for convenient reading. There is a keyboard, and sets of buttons and levers. Otherwise it looks like an ordinary desk. . . ."

(6) "When the user is building a trail, he names it, inserts the name in his code book, and taps it out on his keyboard. Before him are the two items to be joined, projected onto adjacent viewing positions. . . ."

(7) "It is exactly as though the physical items had been gathered together from widely separated sources and bound together to form a new book, it is more than this, for any item can be joined into numerous trails. . . ."

(8) ". . . There is a new profession of trailblazers, those who find delight in the task of establishing useful trails through the enormous mass of the common record. The inheritance from the master becomes, not only his additions to the world's record, but for his disciples the entire scaffolding by which they were erected."

"Thus science may implement the ways in which man produces, stores, and consults the record of the race. . . ."

(9) ". . . ignored are means yet unknown which may come any day to accelerate technical progress as violently as did the advent of the thermonic [or vacuum] tube. . . ."

## Unique database characteristics

When we users are sharing a common, long-term information resource, we can expect the system that provides that capability to have several unique features. These include *schemas; logging; nonprocedural access;* and, though not part of the database itself, *database modeling,* which aids data management by providing conceptual tools to abstract the complexity of a database. Models aid in the interaction of database users, designers, and implementers. Figure 1 shows database components and the database environment in an overall computer system.

**Schemas.** Schemas distinguish database management from the traditional use of files. Schemas contain machine-processable descriptions of the database contents. The description allows users to learn the names and definitions of data elements, but its primary function is to control input/output operations for files that hold data.

A schema is used to retrieve data from the database. To access data, the user gives the name of the data element; all accesses are indirect, mediated through information in the schema. Invariably, after some time, additions must be made to the database structure either to satisfy a user or to support some system enhancement. These changes are reflected in the schema, and most applications should continue to operate undisturbed.

Information in the schema is made available in a variety of ways, all of which relate to the organization of the database management system, or DBMS:

- Schema tables are interpreted at execution time. A schema translator precompiles the tables into a suitable format. The processor time needed for interpretation may not be great relative to file access times.
- Schema information is compiled into a suite of programs that apply the basic append, read, and update operations to the data elements. Such an approach speeds up execution time. To eliminate the need for large numbers of programs, related elements may be grouped into segments.
- Schema information can be bound into transaction programs, then referenced during program compilation, and finally incorporated into the application code. Changes to the schema require that user programs be recompiled. These programs will be kept in a library associated with the DBMS to ensure that any required changes are incorporated.

In all cases, the symbolic names given by the user are translated to addresses within the appropriate file. The schema also includes other specifications, such as the format of the data, its type, its relation to data in other files, and information about access structure, necessary for locating data rapidly. A schema may also contain information on access privileges, which simplifies the sharing of the database. A schema provides a single interaction point for each user, although many distinct users access the database. The only drawback is that the schema interface increases the processor load.

**Logging.** Logging consists of writing all the effects of user-database interaction into an auxiliary file to provide an historical record. This record, called a log, protects the database as a common resource. If the computer system fails, a backup copy can be combined with recent log entries, so that no records are lost.

The log also provides an audit trail that allows users to undo any errors made in interactions with the database. Without this ability, users—often far from the database and thus unaware of all activities—would soon be frustrated and give up on the system.

Logging also helps database sharing since it keeps errors and failures from interfering with operations. The only disadvantage is that logging

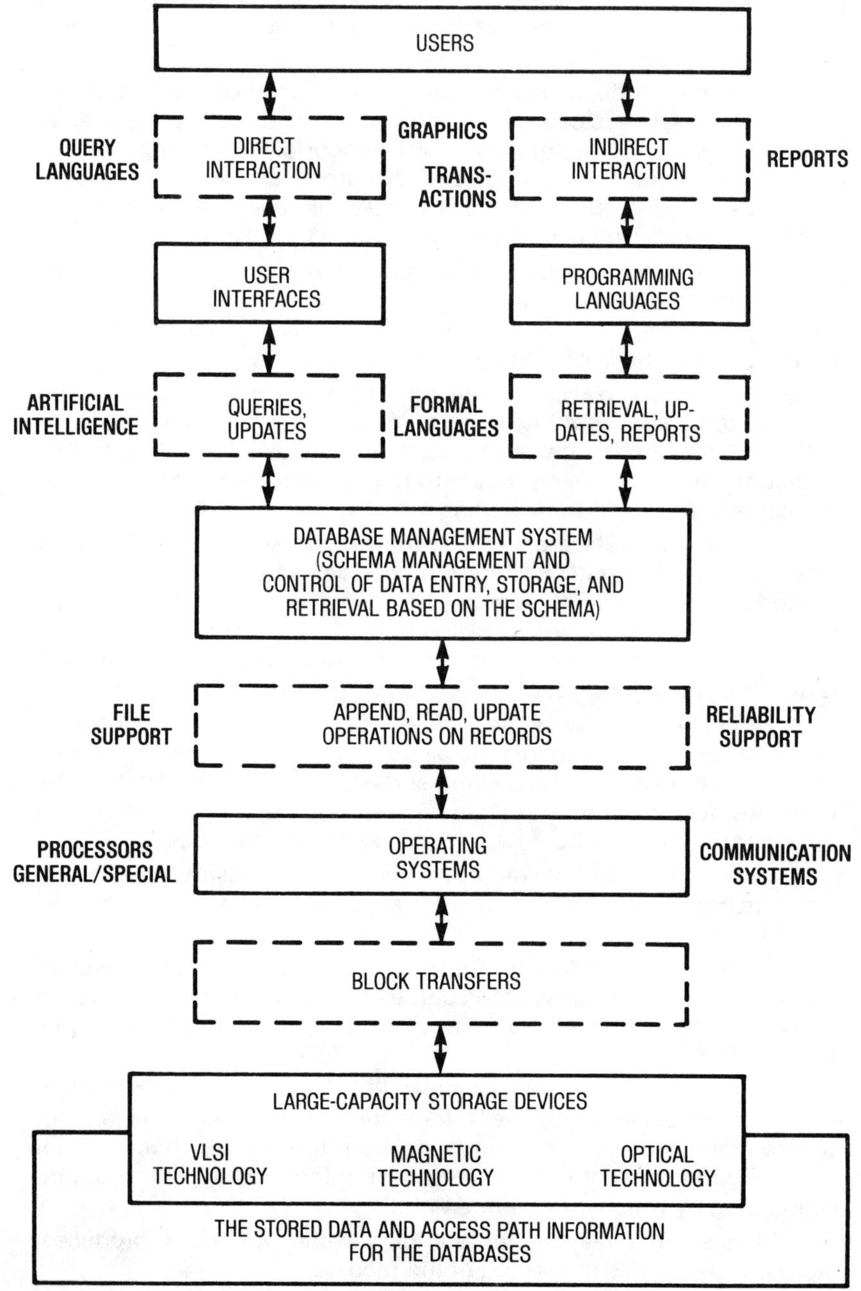


**Figure 1. The place of databases within computer systems.**

places additional demands on storage resources.

**Nonprocedural access.** Since clerical and management personnel want to access databases directly, many higher level, problem-oriented languages for database interaction have been developed. Today database management has joined word-processing and spreadsheet programs in the microcomputer market, appealing to those with little or no programming experience. The use of high-level languages also increases processing requirements, and since most interaction involves display terminals, high-bandwidth communications and effective graphics interfaces are also required.

## A word about DBMSs

An integrated collection of computer programs that provides the services required to manage a database is referred to as a database management system. Several DBMSs had their origin in the sixties and are still in use today, although a substantial body of new knowledge and techniques has since emerged. Certain older systems assimilated some of these advances but became quite complex in the process. However, personnel able to deal with this complexity find that these systems provide a high level of performance and reliability.

In the last 10 years, many newly developed DBMSs have exhibited a simpler structure. The problem of their acceptance seems to mirror the problem of the acceptance of new programming languages: As simpler and more powerful approaches challenge older systems, those experienced in the more established procedures fear disruption, and discourage the investment needed to replace existing systems. In newly established settings, the more modern systems dominate.

## The history of databases

Database development began in industry and was triggered by advances in storage techniques. Industrial successes, which are analyzed and formalized in research institutions and universities, follow a sequence that has dominated all computer science advances: namely, technology triggers industrial development and universities follow with generalization and education.[2] Figure 2 depicts the major events in database development from 1945 to the present.

**Early industrial developments.** Data was first externally stored on data processing cards and paper tape. Magnetic tape became available after 1945 and was the first medium to permit automated data searching. However, because of the sequential nature of the tape, processing had to be performed in cycles, with data read from front to end during one phase. Any input was sorted into the same order, and if the data had to be modified, another complete tape had to be written. Applications that could not be scheduled into a processing cycle simply suffered.

Sharing meant access to tapes and required users to describe the contents of the tapes. The need to generalize access to files led McGee to propose the schema concept.[3]

Some very early computers had rotating magnetic memories, but these were not available for permanent storage. In 1959, the IBM Ramac with the first moving-head disk units appeared, featuring 20 magnetic recording platters and a single pair of read/write heads that moved up and down and in and out between the disks. These units enabled nonsequential access to data, and when combined with hashing techniques, enabled random access as well.[4] Random access, however, could not replace sequential data processing, since random retrieval is substantially slower than access to the next physical block. Operating systems of that era did not support interactive access, in which random access is essential.

Data processing problems were prevalent in parts management and inventory applications. As is true today, data about parts and subassemblies had to be accessed for a variety of products and managed by part location and supplier. Hashing, though it provided rapid file entry, did not solve the problem of retrieving the related subsets for these tasks. A novel multilist structure that provided a network of access paths was described in a 1959 proposal by Prywes and Gray.[5]

The earliest implementations of linked lists in databases were supported by General Electric. Initially, hashing was used only to access the header of a list. Eventually GE computers included a hashing function in their instruction set. Soon papers describing these structures started appearing.

The first generalized DBMS, GE's Integrated Data Store, or IDS, included schemas and logging. Used for a manufacturing application in 1961,[6] the system was further developed and saw wide distribution by 1964. The IDS system provided mainly an interface for programmed operations to ensure that complex data structures were being manipulated correctly.

Graphic techniques, later called Bachman diagrams, were developed to explain the underlying structure at a high conceptual level. Eventually a terminology that called a collection of similar records a *record type* and the linkages between records of two types a *set* became accepted in that community.

When General Electric's computer operations were taken over by Honeywell, the work on IDS continued. Important extensions were made to the system at the Weyerhauser Lumber Company. Since IDS applications require many simultaneous transactions to access the same integrated database, interference was occurring when the same element was accessed. To solve the problem, the IDS logging mechanism was used to roll back and restart transactions that led to conflict. The ability to proceed with a transaction, optimistically expecting that it will not cause a conflict and being able to roll it back if it does, greatly increased the capability to handle multiple users.

In another method to ensure that no conflicts arise, portions of the database are locked during update and are kept inaccessible to other users during the length of the transaction. This alternative pessimistic approach is preferred when critical sections of the transactions are short or when few data elements have to be locked.

George Dodd of General Motors Research Laboratory conducted work on a database system called the Associative Programming Language, which provided similar facilities on IBM equipment.[7] In 1969, impressed by the power of these systems, the Committee on Data Systems Languages, or Codasyl for short—the organization that had earlier developed Cobol—sponsored an analysis of database features. The analysis by Codasyl included database systems such as the IBM GIS and IMS, GE IDS, Informatics Mark IV, IBM FFS, Western Electric SC/1, System Development Corporation TDMS, and RCA UL/1. A subsequent report in 1971 provided a more detailed feature analysis for these systems.

Codasyl also established the Database Task Group in 1969 to develop a proposal for a database description language and additional programming facilities within Cobol to manipulate databases. Some systems were built

**EVENTS**

YEAR | DISK CAP. | HARDWARE | STUDIES | FUNDAMENTALS | APPLICATIONS | SYSTEMS

1945 MEMEX
1946 MAGNETIC TAPE TECHNOLOGY
1947
1948 INFORMATION THEORY
1949 DIGITAL MAGNETIC RECORDING
1950
1951 DEVELOPMENT OF
1952 SCIENTIFIC COMPUTERS
1953 USE OF ELECTRONICS
1954 IN DATA-PROCESSING
1955
1956 128KB SMALL FIXED-HEAD DISKS
1957
1958 4MB MOVABLE HEAD DISKS HASHING
1959 MULTI-LISTS SCHEMA INVENTORIES INDEXED RETRIEVAL
1960 AIRLINE RESERVATION SABRE
1961 BILL-OF-MATERIALS INF. RETRIEVAL STUDIES IDS MIACS
1962 42MB INFORMATION ALGEBRA
1963 MEDLARS
1964 7MB REMOVABLE DISK-PACKS. GE IDS NORTH AM. ROCKWELL IMS
1965 SEMAPHORES SDC SURVEY SYMP.
1966 GM APL
1967 DM-1/SC-1 SDC TDMS
1968 FIRST COURSES SET MODEL IBM IMS
1969 CODASYL DBTG
1970 29MB SHARE DB COMMITTEE B-TREES RELATIONALS MODEL
1971 TRANSACTION SUPPORT
1972 PRIVACY COURANT CONFERENCE
1973 58MB DATA MANAGEMENT BOOKS SHARE CONF. SYSTEM 2000
1974 AND PAPER COLLECTIONS IBM SYSTEM R PROJECT ADABAS
1975 NEW DBTG REPORT VLDB STARTED QBE ANSI-SPARC REPORT
1976 100MB ACM TODS BEGUN DATABASE TEXTBOOKS DATABASE MACHINES
1977 INTENSE DISCUSSIONS: NETWORK VS. HIERARCHICAL VS. RELATIONAL
1978 200MB CODASYL INTERNAL SCHEMA PRIVACY LEGISLATION
1979 CONCURRENCY CONTROL SEVERAL RELATIONAL
1980 2.5GB ACTIVITY UNIVERSAL DATABASE SYSTEM.
1981 1.2MB FLOPPY DAPLEX RELATION MODEL IBM SQL/DS
1982 DISKS FOR MICRO-COMPUTER RELATIONAL STANDARDIZATION
1983 100MB HARD MICRO-COMPUTERS ACCESS TO LARGE DBMS
1984 OPTICAL DISCS. LOCAL COMMUNICATING DATABASES

**Figure 2. Events in database development.**

according to this 1969 definition, although most current Codasyl database systems follow the revised definitions provided in 1971. The work of the committee continued, and a major revision was produced in 1975. The specifications permitted the construction of a network of linkages between record types.

Most manufacturers began developing a DBMS using these specifications. An exception was IBM. Users of IBM equipment who needed the Codasyl capabilities depended mainly on IDMS, a system initially developed at B.F. Goodrich and, since 1972, developed and marketed by Cullinet Corporation.

At the same time, the inventory, or bill-of-materials, problem was being addressed by industry directly. An early IBM system, Bomp, and its successors—Dbomp in 1969, Total in 1971, and Image in 1974—provided a simple two-level network. The concept found many applications, and Total became available for a large variety of machines.

Engineers at North American Rockwell faced a massive problem of material management in the early sixties. The work on vehicles for rapidly expanding space-exploration projects caused their parts and assembly list to grow to 18 reels of tape. With the advent of disk storage, several disk-oriented file systems were developed to manage hierarchically organized segments of data records. The move to 360 equipment in 1964 was used to coalesce these systems, with help from IBM system engineers, into what became IBM's Information Management System, or IMS.[8] IMS maps the data segments sequentially into files using a generalization of the master-detail record concept or preorder sequence.[9] In this technique, data representation is compact and hence access within the hierarchy is rapid. IBM gradually distributed IMS to 360 other users and eventually greatly enhanced the system.

An important addition to the original IMS structure was the provision for multiple logical hierarchies within one physical hierarchy. The alternative logical hierarchies were established by pointer linkages. The secondary internal structures resembled the network structures in a Codasyl system. In IMS, related data elements are located near each other when they are obtained according to the physical hierarchy. Because this grouping was not possible in logical hierarchies, the retrieval performance of the IMS depended greatly on which hierarchy was chosen.

**A system that experiences high-speed transactions is the Credit Reporting System operated by TRW.**

An early application, begun in 1959 at IBM, was the Sabre airline reservations system for American Airlines. This system is noteworthy because it dealt for the first time with the problems caused by high-volume simultaneous access, and because it included a large communications network. Eventually the system was generalized so that it could be marketed to other airlines. The more recent version permits one computer system to serve multiple airlines and reflects the distinct views of each on the priorities to be applied when reserving seats. This version, called the Programmed Airline Reservation System, or PARS, is in wide use and permits high transaction rates.

In the late sixties, a number of other database systems were developed in industry, often emphasizing some set of applications. Auerbach developed the SC-1 system for Western Electric inventories. A system that experiences high-speed transactions, which it accommodates by using a simple file structure, is the Credit Reporting System operated by TRW. Recently, the decision was made to convert this application to the IMS DBMS.

Parallel developments in indexing took place under the rubric of information retrieval. At a 1961 conference at Princeton, 20 projects were identified.[10] *Indexed access* techniques were first used for bibliographic retrieval, an example being Medlars at the National Library of Medicine.[11]

Information retrieval and database systems developed virtually independently. Database systems ignored interactive usage and variable-length textual data, while information retrieval systems ignored update and processing. The split, although less distinct, continues.

Indexing was generalized at System Development Corporation to provide fully inverted access in the TDMS, an unusual system in that it was developed not just for a particular family of applications but for truly general data retrieval. Indexes provided good locality for access, since the keys were replicated in the index blocks and could be rapidly scanned. The replication increased the storage and update costs. Storage costs were still an important consideration at that time, but the perceived complexity of TDMS may have been the reason it was not widely adopted commercially.

Updates were typically handled through overflow linkage structures within the files. When the linkages became too long, the file was copied and new indexes created. The need for periodic reorganization of indexes was overcome with the invention of the B-tree at Boeing and other sites in 1970.[12] In general, problems associated with rapid shared access to large files were being solved.

**The seventies: a period of rapid growth.** The term "management information system" became popular, and much greater capabilities were promised than the underlying technology could deliver—a conflict that raised concern in the data processing community. Eventually, in 1970, the IBM user groups, Share and Guide, published requirements documents that defined notions of user interfaces, program independence, and privacy protection.

These developments encouraged thinking about standardization of databases and schema languages. To consider the issue, a committee chartered by ANSI, called Sparc/DBMS, was established. No standard proposals were found acceptable, but a very influential report identifying weaknesses in existing systems was published in 1975.[13] An important contribution of this report was the partitioning of the schema into three distinct levels:

- a central *conceptual* schema describing the data requirements and relationships for the entire enterprise;
- an *internal* schema describing the mapping of the conceptual schema to physical storage units for the implementation; and
- an *external* schema describing the data as seen at the user-interface level.

The conceptual schema reflected the importance of the database as an essential resource for its target enterprise. As production and distribution facilities became more automated and effective, decision making on allocation and investment became increasingly critical, and the information hidden in the database provided the basis for consistent and rapid action. This is still true today.

Several external schemas could exist for the same database, providing different views for the different users. Views can support alternative programming languages as well as alternative modeling perceptions and can also incorporate the access privileges of the user. External schemas had been envisaged in the earlier Codasyl proposals, though merely as simple subschemas of the overall database.

The Sparc proposals were not sufficiently detailed to lead to implementation, but the proposed concepts were partially implemented and appear in many current database systems. In 1978 Codasyl proposals, the overall schema is partitioned into a high-level schema that avoids the specification of access path implementation and an internal schema. The specifications for the internal schema language have not yet been formally accepted by Codasyl. Since the internal schema level has to interface with operating systems of different manufacturers, agreement within the committee is difficult to obtain. Some Codasyl 1975 implementations, for instance IDMS, already provide a distinct section for the mapping of the data structures to storage.

The attractiveness of the Codasyl proposals has always been that manufacturers view their implementation as feasible. Users of Codasyl systems can hope that programs and programmer training on one system will be at least partially applicable to another manufacturer's system. The schemas and data, however, are rarely portable. To date, no complete systems appear to be following the 1978 Codasyl proposals, although many of the 1978 concepts are recognizable in the IPAD system, an Air-Force-sponsored project at Boeing to support aircraft design.

**The attractiveness of the Codasyl proposals has always been that manufacturers view their implementation as feasible.**

Meanwhile, also during this period, IBM was working on IMS, including its adaptation to a B-tree-based file management system. This approach replaced the previous strategy of providing file support with four underlying file organizations, each of which had unique advantages and liabilities. A very high performance version of an IMS (now available) keeps a large fraction of the database in memory. Today, many installations using IBM and IBM-compatible computers spend a large fraction of their resources on supporting IMS and its applications. Special hardware features, called accelerators, have been developed to support IMS operational requirements.

## Research contributions

As we stated earlier, the interaction of industrial and research development has followed a familiar path: initial contributions are made in industry—often by people with very respectable academic backgrounds—and when the scope and problems become significant, researchers in academia and a few industrial research laboratories step in to formalize these contributions.

The formalization process leads to generalization and permits problem modeling, which, in turn, enables the evaluation of better and cleaner solutions to problems. These solutions are published as research papers and eventually the body of material on the subject becomes large enough to be taught to those outside the field. Teachers first use collections of papers, and, later, books written specifically as course texts. Finally, the field gains respectability and is integrated into the curriculum.

A Codasyl-sponsored development committee attempted in 1962 to formalize the underlying concepts of files, attributes, and mappings.[14] Later, an Air-Force-sponsored study at IBM Research led to the development of access path models.[15] Because these models were so complex, they had little impact.

The most significant formalization was provided by Ted Codd of IBM research in 1970.[16] The relational model he presented and extended in papers at the 1971 Courant Computer Science Symposium on databases[17] enabled us to understand the essential issues of database systems. The model formalized a simple tabular view of the database and some well-defined operations. Data describing entities is *normalized* into the tabular structure so that operations can deal with data as relations. Relations, an extension of the mathematical concept of sets, provided an abstraction that linked database concepts to a body of existing theory. The applicability of relational theory, in turn, kindled interest by mathematically oriented scientists.

The relational model, still used today, does not attempt to include relationships and semantics between them, nor does it consider the database performance. This simplicity helps increase its acceptability.

**Dissemination.** The relational model rapidly generated attention. Conference series were expanded and established to deal exclusively with databases. Of note was the ACM special interest group on file definition and translation (now renamed SIG, Management of Data, or Sigmod) and, later, the Database Working Group 2.6, a part of the IFIP TC-2 committee. Problems specific to very large databases were the focus of a conference series by that name initiated in 1975. Soon after proceedings from these conferences were published, many practitioners became aware of relational concepts and began incorporating them in their thinking and implementations.

The concepts provided by the relational model also made it easier to teach courses on databases. Notes were developed from those courses, and the first database textbooks incorporating abstract notions were published in 1976. Authors of early books were associated with IBM, but later authors came from academia as well as from industry.

Database performance depends greatly on the adequacy of the algorithms used to implement the system. An awkward access method can easily increase response times by a factor of 1000. The performance of searching and sorting strategies was effectively summarized by Knuth[9] in a book that forms the foundation for on-going work in the development and analysis of algorithms for database organization and access.

**A new wave of DBMSs.** Database research projects, often stressing generality and simple query interfaces, were started at several universities. Research at the University of Texas in Austin led to the development of a portable hierarchical database system. This work, which entered the commercial marketplace rapidly, is now available through Intel Corporation as System-2000. Many systems stressed simplicity to obtain ease of use and fairly high performance. An example is the TOD system and its descendants (Clinfo, Prophet, RS/1, CPIS, Medlog, and CDBS at Duke), which provide a simple relational view oriented toward statistical data analysis.[18]

European contributions were Socrate from France and Adabas from Germany. Socrate distinguishes itself by having an elegant schema language in a Pascal-like style. Developed at the University of Grenoble in 1970 on IBM 360/67 equipment, it was available only on French CII and related Roumanian hardware. Recently, this software has become available in the US for the IBM 360 under the name Cleo. Adabas, developed with assistance from the Technical University of Darmstadt, employs complex hashing techniques for rapid access; it has enjoyed substantial acceptance in the US.

As research projects clarified the issues of relational databases, complete relational systems began to appear.[19] Today derivatives of relational database systems that started in research laboratories and universities are marketed by a large number of companies. The term *relational* has become so popular that Codd has had to restate what a relational database should include[20]—criteria that many systems offered today fail to meet. A standardization effort for relational databases is in process.

In 1984, a count showed that more than 120 distinct database management systems are being offered. Many of the new relational and pseudo-relational systems include desirable user-oriented features and extensive semantics. The relative value of these additional features, however, is hard to assess. Users who attempt to select a database by trying to match their requirements with what is available find the selection process nearly impossible. Before they can complete even one analysis, some new system enters the market or another loses support.

## Models and modeling

The relational model describes database contents as a collection of independent relations. Its clarity has motivated a widespread interest in relational implementations.

An alternative approach to database implementation includes linkages, implementation of connections between relations. To clarify their approaches, developers of systems relying on linkages started explaining their work in model terms as well. *Network models* are now used to describe Codasyl-oriented and related systems, while *hierarchical models* are used to describe IMS and approaches like System-2000.[21]

Several other model types have been defined and promoted, and as discussions among modelers became more intense, the confusion increased. Why couldn't database researchers agree on a single model to describe databases and the data contained in them? Let us consider this issue.

When devising a model, we need a trade-off between simplicity and power. The number of primitive concepts in a model must not be greater than the user can easily comprehend. At the same time, the model has to describe all essential features of the problem being addressed. There is no ideal unifying model that does everything for everybody, and the search is likely to be as fruitless as the search for the ideal programming language. Recent data models concentrate on representing relationships among conceptual entities and on mapping these conceptual structures to files and linkages. Relations and connections may be used as an important formal, but intermediate, concept.

In the *entity-relationship* model, the specifications of user needs and logical requirements are supported.[22] (See Chen's discussion in the box on the following page.

In the *functional* model, relationships are modeled by functions to help formalize procedural constraints in programs that operate on the database. It may be implemented directly.[23]

In the *structural* model, relationships are defined as formal connections between relations. This model supports transformations, permitting diverse user views to be integrated and quantitative factors for database design decisions to be specified.[24]

In the *universal relation* model, the entire database is viewed as a single relation, and all relationships are described through a family of dependencies. While dependencies in the relational approach are used to allocate attributes to appropriate distinct relations, dependencies remain unbound in the universal model, and the user no longer has to visualize the assignment of attributes to relations. The conceptual simplicity of the model greatly enhances the formal analysis of data semantics—an area that has become an academic subdiscipline in its own right.[25]

Transformations between all these model types are possible. Whenever one model does not express some concepts of another model, some semantics are lost. Conversely, the converted model is incomplete. Some concepts will always translate awkwardly, so the clarity of expression is lost for those concepts. For a casual user the choice of models is not always obvious, since model builders rarely state what their models will *not* represent.

In developing models, we can deal with realistic applications abstractly. Database tasks are often complex;

## ER—the user's view of the database problem

Peter P. Chen

The concept of entity and relationship, or ER, is simple and natural for modeling our perceptions of the real world. Although this concept has been used informally in the computer field for a long time, it was not seriously studied until the mid-1970's.

Interest in the ER concept stems from the need for a modeling tool that can specify user needs and requirements better than implementation-oriented data models. In the early seventies, people debated the relative merits of the hierarchical model, the network model, and the relational model. In the mid-seventies, it became apparent that each of these tends to emphasize the structures of data as represented in computers rather than the structures of data as perceived by users. The entity-relationship model was motivated by the need for a conceptual data model suitable for specifying user views and logical requirements. The original ER model was based on the following primitive concepts: entity, $n$-ary relationship, attribute, and values. A diagramming technique, the ER diagram, permits us to visualize entity, relationship, attribute, and value types. Many who are not data processing specialists find the ER concept easy to understand and suitable for specifying their views of the database problem.

**Recent developments.** There is now considerable interest in modifying the original ER model or proposing new models. Almost all these models use the concept of entity and relationship, but they differ in how many and which primitive concepts to have and how to represent them. There are possibly hundreds of variations of the ER approach. The models and methodologies differ, for example, on whether $n$-ary relationships are allowed, or whether the model has explicitly represented the concept of attribute. A framework for classifications of ER models is presented elsewhere.[1] Three conferences on the ER approach have been held, and many extensions of the original ER model as well as new ER-like models can be found in the proceedings.[2-4]

**Applications and future directions.** The ER approach can be applied to several areas including user requirement specifications and database design and DBMS design, user interface, distributed databases, and conceptual schema. In the first area, ER models and diagramming techniques have been used successfully in many organizations. In the near future, automated tools will be available to assist users and database designers.[3,4]

In the second area, ER models can be used as underlying data models for a new type of DBMS. Several prototype DBMSs have been developed using the ER model as a basis; a few commercial systems have appeared on the market or are in development. Other possible uses of ER models include developing DBMS languages that are based on the ER concept,[1,5,6] data translation in heterogeneous distributed databases,[7] and the construction of conceptual schema,[8] following the ANSI-Sparc report.

In summary, the ER concept provides an important basis for specifying a user's view of the database problem. It can be applied to many areas of database management and to areas outside computers.[9]

### References


1. *Entity-Relationship Approach to Information Modeling and Analysis,* P. P. Chen, ed., North-Holland, Amsterdam, 1983.
2. *Entity-Relationship Approach to Systems Analysis and Design,* P. P. Chen, ed., North-Holland, Amsterdam, 1980.
3. *Entity-Relationship Approach to Software Engineering,* C. Davis et al., eds., North-Holland, Amsterdam, 1983.
4. R. Reiter, "On Closed World Data Bases," in *Logic and Data Bases,* H. Gallaire and J. Minker, eds., Plenum Press, New York, 1978.
5. C. Parent and S. Spaccepietra, "An Entity-Relationship Algebra," *Proc. IEEE Int'l Conf. Data Engineering,* Apr. 1984.
6. C. Zaniolo, "The Database Language: GEM," *Proc. ACM 1983 Sigmod Conf.,* May 1983, pp. 207-218.
7. A. Cardenas and M. H. Pirahesh, "Database Communication in a Heterogeneous Data Base Management System Network," *Information Systems,* Vol. 5, 1980.
8. A. Dogac and E. A. Ozkarahan, "A Generalized DBMS Implementation of a Data Base Machine," *Proc. ACM 1980 Sigmod Conf.,* May 1980.
9. W. E. McCarthy, "An Entity-Relationship View of Accounting Model," *Accounting Review,* Vol. 54, Oct. 1979.

detailed specifications for some applications require sets of documents many inches thick. At the same time, many actual DBMSs are so complex that even a description of their features does not provide us with enough understanding of their capabilities. The notion of modeling is likely to become important in other areas of computer science that deal with complex systems.

Models also enable us to integrate diverging user requirements and subsequently match requirements to DBMS capabilities. A clear model permits the user to be involved in the conceptual design process. The effectiveness of a model is limited, of course, to areas in which its abstractions are relevant. A major effort to develop a complete set of modeling procedures for database design has been supported by the Italian research establishment.[26]

## The database of today

Today, databases are ubiquitous. Early databases required a high level of expertise from their users—typically programmers who had to understand data management concepts, be able to program the interface, and understand the potential application. The only services provided by these DBMSs were a suite of input/output programs and the management of multiple user interactions. Now, however, database users are not expert programmers, so the required services must extend to ease of use, an intelligent interface, resiliency to errors, and a reasonable level of performance.

**Technology**. The hardware needed for database systems is now commonly available. Storage costs are a fraction of the cost of data collection, unless data is acquired automatically. Some database applications still require too much storage to be feasible, but in general, the volume of data that can be handled continues to increase. For example, disk units can now handle several gigabytes, a more than thousandfold increase over what early devices could process. Unfortunately, access speeds have not increased proportionally.

The access speeds on modern devices are in a narrow range. Floppy disks, an economical technology common to personal computers, can now store more than a megabyte, and the drives access a block of data stored on disk in about 250 ms. Costly gigabyte units require about 25 ms, not much improvement, when we consider the increased price.

Research into database machines is oriented toward improving access speeds. Simple but effective database machines now provide up to an order of magnitude speed-up, but do not deal well with multifile operations on large files—a problem that cannot be handled with simple algorithms.

Great aggregate processing power is available in distributed systems, but scheduling database processing so that activities actually take place in parallel is difficult. Also, operating in a distributed environment adds communication delays so that transactions often take longer. Moreover, distribution adds considerable complexity to design and execution algorithms.

For large databases sophisticated software remains essential in coping with the volume of data and user response expectations. Performance optimization during database design can be effective if common access patterns are known. The design procedures are becoming well understood, and tools that help make allocation and access-path decisions are available with many DBMS products.

**Interfaces**. Today's users can deal with an abstract conceptual view of the database they are accessing, using the model provided by the DBMS. A request for information can be submitted using some matching formalism. Query statements describe *what* information should be obtained, avoiding instructions that state *how* it should be done. In short, DBMSs have satisfied the conditions required to bring computing capabilities to the public. Database queries, one of the few areas in which *nonprocedural languages* are regularly used, are successful because the simple models describe what is relevant and hide underlying details.

The easiest interface provided by database systems is to present *menu choices*, which are automatically created from the information provided in the data description. Such an interrogative style is apt to be frustrating for the experienced user, especially if the menus are not extremely reactive. In familiar menu sequences, even nonclerical users will try to make several selections per second.

For regular use, we need to be able to interact with the system. With *command-style query languages* the user has to supply the commands and the names of the relations and their attributes. It is too much to ask that the user have complete knowledge of the entire database content and structure, as well. Prewritten transaction programs restrict users to a narrow and well-defined view and are the main path for clerical database interaction.

In advanced systems, the user can query through informal *natural language* statements, or make a request through *form-oriented interaction* on a display terminal. The use of forms is based on a simple metaphor that calls on the user's experience in a nonautomated, traditional environment of file cabinets, folders, and documents. Implementations of such database services are now available on professional workstations. Some of these take the metaphor to the extreme by actually providing icons—small illustrations of file cabinets, folders, and documents—for the conceptual units. Figure 3 shows a sample display from Visicorp's Visi On system.

Natural language interaction has been quite successful, particularly in demonstration systems. Since having a specific database defines the domain of discourse, the set of terms used to describe entities and attributes is limited. Within this set completeness can be expected. These features remove much of the ambiguity so difficult to resolve in the general processing of natural language. They also permit the use of queries that involve negation and quantification, whereas these operations become unmanageable when the system has to deal with an unlimited world.[27]

Techniques that are classified under the query-by-example approach to database retrieval display a partial layout of the database model on the screen and then permit rapid selection. Microprocessor technology permits major improvements in the style of interaction, since the heavy computation required to produce an attractive and effective visual display can now be carried out locally.

**Database administration**. When performance is a major concern, a database administrator can be used to control the quality and performance of the database. The administrator arranges the structure of the database and selects access paths from the choices provided by the DBMS, such as linkages and indexes, so that performance criteria can be met. In many small organizations, no database administrator is involved and the principal user can define the schema simply and often interactively. If later the schema is found to be inadequate, it can be revised. Some DBMSs will automatically readjust existing programs and the storage layout to match schema changes; others require the user to copy the contents of affected parts into the new format.

## The database of tomorrow

It is always risky to predict the future: the importance of the developments just described was not always obvious at first, and some technological innovations that did raise high expectations fizzled. To be on the safe side, I will concentrate on issues that appear to have some momentum right now.

**Hardware.** The cost curve for storage is still declining. Storage for microprocessors now has costs similar to those for large devices, although the performance is lower. With the reduction of storage costs, the biggest limitation of database growth becomes the cost of data entry and the maintenance of data correctness. Database performance remains an issue, since the access performance of new devices does not appear to be increasing at the same rate as storage capability.

Optical storage can be economical in the distribution of reference databases. Read-often, write-once optical storage can take off once the file support software becomes available.

**Data storage organization.** The availability of ever greater and less expensive storage devices has removed the impediment that prevented keeping very detailed or extensive historical information in on-line databases. Optical disk technology, though it cannot rewrite previously recorded information, provides storage capacities greatly exceeding those of current systems. The voluminous data will need more identification, so data timestamping and the recording of contributor and user will be common.

An immediate effect of these changes will be the retention of past data versions over long periods. A new problem is the maintenance of large indexes on optical disks needed to manage the storage capacity and provide access to past versions of data.[28] Version maintenance will simplify the reliability algorithms now in use, as well as avoid logging.

Having past versions permits queries and some updates to proceed in parallel—avoiding mutual interference and increasing the performance of highly loaded systems. In distributed systems, past versions can be used to restore consistency after synchroni-

Figure 3. Database display using a mouse and Visicorp's multiwindow Visi On system on a personal computer.

zation is lost because of failures in the communication network.

**Distribution and personal computing.** Most personal computers contain individual databases, but to benefit from the power of shared data we need distributed data access. With good communication, the personal computer becomes a workstation within an institution.

Databases are viewed by managers of enterprises as an institutional resource and hence a prime candidate and even a reason to install centralized computing. With the advent of remote workstations, administrators of computing facilities are making read-access to the centralized database available. Many believe that update from remote personal workstations should be avoided to prevent database "pollution."

As computing becomes more distributed, however, it will be hard to constrain remote database updates. The person with the operational responsibility for a certain segment of some enterprise will want to maintain and update relevant data on the local workstation. Hard disks on personal workstations already have an adequate capacity to handle many requirements and can handle most of them if mutual remote database access over a high-bandwidth network is available.

The danger of conflicts from distributed data maintenance is not as great as data-center management might fear. The operational rules in most institutions already grant update privileges to specific organizational units and avoid granting them simultaneously to conflicting departments.

The distribution of facilities reinforces a parallel distribution of authority and responsibility. The notion that only a central site can maintain correct data has already been invalidated in many practical situations. The actual update documents do come from many remote locations, and the quality of a centralized database still depends on the cooperation, the quality control, and the enthusiasm of remote users.

I believe that data quality can be improved in distributed systems if the responsibility for data maintenance of specific elements is allocated throughout the organization. The tight local feedback loops possible in a distributed environment can contribute greatly to database quality. When central facilities are sluggish, remote users rely on local copies of the data for immediate service. The difference is that local copies, once paper files, are now local computer files. Consistency is improved if these become visible to the entire enterprise.

**Many believe that update from remote personal workstations should be avoided to prevent database "pollution."**

The issue of data distribution among autonomous distributed nodes in an institutional network has not yet been adequately or formally dealt with, although many industrial examples are available. In the medical field, distribution of clinical data for speciality practice is already a reality; the need to have data on the local computer for immediate clinical decisions has forced the issue. As better models of distributed computing are developed, we can expect improved solutions to be found.

**Interfaces.** This review has stressed the important function of database interfaces; undoubtedly much further development will take place, making the actual use of databases in the future as easy as their conceptual use today.

Which new technology will dominate is not clear. We now find menu selection by keyboard, joysticks and mice, touch-screen, and voice commands. Probably all of them will find their niche, and database systems will have to support them all.

To make databases appear smarter to users, the semantic content of database schemas will have to increase. Techniques from artificial intelligence are effective here and do not apply solely to natural language query processing. With powerful heuristics, we can intelligently abstract retrieved results, automate inferencing, and effectively present information. Some of the required knowledge can be automatically obtained from the database and the user's interactions with it.[29]

**Privacy.** Protecting the privacy of information stored in databases has been a long-standing concern. Although congressional investigations have taken place, and some countries have passed comprehensive protective legislation, it does not appear that privacy of data is easily assured. Research in database protection is further frustrated by the gaping holes in today's operating systems. Encryption appears to provide the best solution but thwarts a major objective of databases, namely, sharing.

For now, and in the immediate future, truly sensitive data is best excluded from databases, and we should adopt a relaxed attitude about the data collected. Protection schemes that are only partially effective may be worse than none, providing access to a selected few, while excluding many others that need access. □

## Acknowledgments

This review can present only some high points in the development of databases. I have cited a few significant papers, including some that are particularly novel and not commonly known. An extensive bibliography on possible future directions is available on-line.

This article, supported in part by DARPA contract N39-82-C-250 for research into knowledge-based management systems, has benefited from careful reading by Thanasi Hadzilacos and Peter Rathman, and information supplied by the, unfortunately anonymous, reviewers.

The views expressed are those of the author and should not be interpreted as representing any agency of the US Government.

## References


1. V. Bush, "As We May Think," *Atlantic Monthly,* Vol. 176, No. 1, Jan. 1945, pp. 101-108.
2. *Roles of Industry and the University in Computer Research and Development,* M. Hammer and M. E. Rose, eds., National Academy Press, 1982.
3. W. C. McGee, "Generalization— Key to Successful Electronic Data Processing," *J. ACM,* Vol. 6, No. 1, Jan. 1959, pp. 1-23.
4. W. P. Heising, "Methods of File Organization for Efficient Use of IBM RAMAC Files," *Proc. AFIPS,* Vol. 14, 1958 FJCC, AFIPS Press, Reston, Va., pp. 194-195.
5. N. S. Prywes and H. J. Gray, "Outline for a Multilist Organized System," *Proc. ACM Nat'l Conf.,* 1959.
6. C. W. Bachman, "MIACS—User of the First Generalized Data Base System?" *Proc. Intercon 74,* IEEE Press, New York, 1974.
7. G. G. Dodd, "APL—a Language for Associative Data Handling in PL/1," *Proc. AFIPS,* Vol. 29, 1966 FJCC, AFIPS Press, Reston, Va., pp. 677-684.
8. R. R. Brown and P. Nordyke, Jr., "IMS Development," *Proc. FID-IFIP 1967,* North-Holland, Amsterdam, 1968, pp. 637-660.
9. D. E. Knuth, *The Art of Computer Programming: Sorting and Searching,* Vol. 3, Addison-Wesley, New York, 1973.
10. *Comm. ACM,* papers from the 1961 Princeton Conference on information retrieval, Vol. 5, No. 1, Jan. 1962.
11. S. Adams, "The MEDLARS System," *Fed. Proc.,* Vol. 22, 1963, pp. 1018-1021.
12. R. Bayer and E. M. McCreight, "Organization and Maintenance of Large Ordered Indexes," *Acta Informatica,* Vol. 1, No. 3, Feb. 1972, pp. 173-189.
13. T. B. Steel, "Interim Report of the ANSI-SPARC Study Group," *ACM Sigmod FDT,* Vol. 7, No. 2, 1975.
14. R. Bosak et al., "An Information Algebra," *Comm. ACM,* Vol. 5, No. 4, Apr. 1962, pp. 190-204.
15. M. E. Senko, V. Y. Lum, and P. J. Owens, "A File Organization Evaluation Model," *Proc. 1968 IFIP Congress,* pp. C19-C23.
16. E. F. Codd, "A Relational Model of Data for Large Shared Data Banks," *Comm. ACM,* Vol. 13, No. 6, June 1970, pp. 377-387.
17. *Data Base Systems,* R. Rustin, ed., Prentice-Hall, Englewood Cliffs, N.J., 1972.
18. G. Wiederhold, J. F. Fries, and S. Weyl, "Structured Organization of Clinical Data Bases," *Proc. AFIPS,* Vol. 44, 1975 NCC, pp. 479-486.
19. M. Stonebraker, "Retrospection on a Data Base System," *ACM Trans. Database Systems,* Vol. 5, No. 3, Sept. 1980, pp. 225-240.
20. *Relational Database Systems,* J. W. Schmidt and M. L. Brodie, eds., Springer-Verlag, New York, 1983.
21. *ACM Comm. Surveys,* special issue on database management systems, E. H. Sibley, ed., Vol. 8, No. 1, Mar. 1976.
22. P. P. Chen, "The Entity-Relationship Model—Toward a Unified View of Data," *ACM Trans. Database Systems,* Vol. 1, No. 1, Mar. 1976, pp. 9-36.
23. D. W. Shipman, "The Functional Data Model and the Data Language DAPLEX," *ACM Trans. Database Systems,* Vol. 6, No. 1, Mar. 1981, pp. 140-173.
24. G. Wiederhold, *Database Design,* 2nd ed., McGraw-Hill, New York, 1983.
25. R. Fagin, A. O. Mendelzon, and J. D. Ullman, "A Simplified Universal Relation Assumption and Its Properties," *ACM Trans. Database Systems,* Vol. 7, No. 3, Sept. 1982.
26. S. Ceri, ed., *Methodology and Tools for Data Base Design,* North-Holland, Amsterdam, 1983.
27. R. Reiter, "On Closed World Data Bases," in *Logic and Data Bases,* H. Gallair and J. Minker, eds., Plenum Press, New York, 1978.
28. P. Rathman, "Dynamic Data Structures on Optical Disks," *Proc. IEEE Int'l Conf. Data Engineering,* Apr. 1984, pp. 175-180.
29. G. Wiederhold, "Knowledge and Database Management," *IEEE Software,* Vol. 1, No. 1, Jan. 1984, pp. 63-73.

**Gio Wiederhold** is an associate professor of medicine and computer science (research) at Stanford, where his research includes the application of artificial intelligence techniques to database problems. His book *Database Design* stresses a quantitative approach.

Wiederhold started programming in Europe in 1957 and, after coming to the US in 1958, worked for a number of companies, as well as for the University of California, Berkeley, and Stanford University as a programmer, project leader, manager, division director, and consultant. In 1976 he obtained a PhD from the University of California, San Francisco, where he focused on the design of medical databases. After obtaining his PhD, he joined the faculty at Stanford University.

Wiederhold's address is Dept. of Computer Science, Stanford University, Stanford, CA 94305.

# The Integrated Dictionary/Directory System

FRANK W. ALLEN, MARY E. S. LOOMIS, AND MICHAEL V. MANNINO

*Department of Management Information Systems, University of Arizona, Tucson, Arizona 85721*

The concept of an integrated Dictionary/Directory (D/D) System is discussed in detail, and the state of current systems in both the centralized and distributed database environments is surveyed. For the centralized database environment, three aspects are emphasized: (1) the *software interfaces* between the D/D System and other software packages, (2) the *convert functions* of the D/D System, and (3) the *environmental dependency* between the D/D System and a Database Management System (DBMS). For the distributed database environment, the article elucidates the necessary extensions to the centralized D/D, the additional software interfaces required, and the use of the D/D as a distributed database. An example of a commercial D/D System that is integrated with a distributed DBMS is presented.

Categories and Subject Descriptors: C.2.4 **[Computer-Communication Network]**: Distributed Systems—*distributed databases*; H.2.5 **[Database Management]**: Heterogeneous Databases; H.2.7 **[Database Management]**: Database Administration—*data dictionary/directory*

General Terms: Documentation, Languages, Management

## INTRODUCTION

The concept of information resource management (IRM) is that information is a vital corporate asset that should be invested in, controlled, and used like other resources. Management's ability to measure performance, to create bonds with the consumer, to gauge competitors' actions, and to rapidly shift tactical plans depends on accurate, timely, and understandable data. In recognition of the IRM concept, many firms have acquired data management software, such as database management systems (DBMS), and have created a data administration function.

The data administration function generally is responsible for the firm-wide inventory and control of data. Data inventory management requires pertinent facts and relationships about the various data objects, processes, users, and equipment in the data-processing environment. Data administration's internal control procedures restrict access to data, manage development of new types of data, and protect data from erroneous update and system failure. The focus of this paper is one of the data administrator's important tools: a Dictionary/Directory (D/D) System.

Vendors provide D/D support to information systems under a variety of names. Some packages are called dictionary/directories, or simply dictionaries, while others are characterized as information resource managers. We refer generically to all of these as D/D Systems.

The heart of a D/D System is a database, called the D/D. If data are defined by {attribute, value} pairs, then the D/D is defined to be the set of all data attributes, hereafter referred to as metadata, that describe entities such as information, processes, users, and hardware. For the data

CONTENTS



element NO-OF-DEPENDENTS, the D/D might contain attributes such as length, type, and value range, but not the actual number of dependents. The distinction between data values and metadata is not totally exclusive if a data value for one entity is metadata for another entity. For instance, the value of NO-OF-DEPENDENTS could be metadata to define the range of the data aggregate NAMES-OF-DEPENDENTS.

The D/D System provides two primary functions. It facilitates understanding and communication about the relationship between system applications and system data usage, and it assists in achieving data independence by permitting system applications to access data without knowledge of the location or storage characteristics of the data in the system. An illustration of the first function is end-user access to a D/D System to determine the names, descriptions, and sources for data in their applications. The typical D/D System provides reporting capabilities that disclose data element definitions for each application program. An example of the D/D System's utility in achieving data independence is its participation in the conversion of a data request by a system application into appropriate physical access calls, verification of the authorization of the data request, and the return of the requested data in a suitable format for use by the system application.

The extent to which a D/D System qualifies as being "integrated" is a relative notion determined by the scope of its metadata and the way that it interfaces with other software. Today, the most common use of the term "integrated" is with reference to a D/D that is the sole source of metadata in the system. The integrated D/D is accessed for all references to metadata. In reality, however, most D/D Systems have not reached this level of integration with their environments. Many software packages use their own, internally generated metadata, resulting in multiple sources of descriptors within the systems. The D/D System permits these systems to access the D/D indirectly and convert the metadata of each system to the format required by the D/D. For example, a D/D System might communicate with a compiler in either of two ways: (1) by generating file and record definitions that the compiler accepts via copy statements, or (2) by reading source programs and creating transactions to load the D/D with descriptions of files, records, and elements.

This paper explains the concepts of D/D Systems with varying degrees of integration with their environments. It surveys the state of current D/D Systems in the centralized and distributed database environments. Section 1 presents background information about D/D Systems including definitions, statement of objectives, classification of users, structure, content, and functions of the typical D/D System. Section 2 proposes a generalized framework for studying integrated D/D Systems in a centralized database environment and relates this model to commercially available systems. Three aspects of integrated D/D Systems in the centralized database environment are emphasized: (1) software interfaces, (2) convert functions, and (3) the environmental dependency between the D/D System and a DBMS. Section 3 introduces the distributed database environment, and describes a commercial D/D

System that is integrated with a distributed DBMS. Section 4 draws conclusions and identifies future directions of work. The series of charts that comprise the appendix highlights salient features of commercial D/D Systems.

We assume that the reader has a general knowledge of business data processing and database management. Many examples here utilize terminology common to COBOL, to CODASYL database management systems, and to the relational data model. No background is necessarily assumed in the areas of D/D Systems and distributed data management.

The survey presented here results from extensive review of the literature of D/D Systems, distributed database management, and related topics, and of manuals, product bulletins, and other technical information from vendors of D/D Systems and distributed DBMSs. The vendors' information was compiled into charts and confirmed by each source.

## 1. D/D SYSTEM BACKGROUND

This section introduces D/D Systems and defines terminology used throughout the paper. Readers who want additional background on aspects not included here, such as the selection and evaluation of a D/D System, should consult papers by Uhrowczik [UHRO73], Lefkovits [LEFK77], Lomax [LOMA77], Leon-Hong [LEON77], Elbra and Hardy [ELBR80], Ross [ROSS81], Curtis and Dieckman [CURT81a], and Auerbach publications [PLAG77a, PLAG77b, PLAG78]. A reader already familiar with D/D Systems can consult Figures 1 and 3, which summarize key terms and ideas, and then proceed to Section 2.

### 1.1 Definition, Objectives, Users

A D/D System is an automated information system composed of

- a *database*, called the D/D, that contains data describing the data, processes, users, and processors of an organization, that is, metadata;
- *retrieval and analysis capabilities* that assist a wide range of user groups in application development;
- *management tools* that help ensure the security, validity, recoverability, integrity, and shared accessability of the D/D;
- *functional interfaces* that permit other software modules to access the D/D and that convert metadata into the format required by the D/D System.

A D/D System has three primary objectives:

(1) It helps to achieve control of the data resource, by providing an inventory of that resource, including data names, definitions, locations, storage formats, sizes, and other characteristics. With this repository of information, standards for names, access, storage, and validation can be more easily implemented and enforced.

(2) A D/D System helps to control the costs of developing and maintaining applications. A D/D System can provide accurate and complete data definitions for use in application programs and in program generators such as report writers and query processors. The program maintenance function can also be facilitated by D/D System reports of program data usage.

(3) A D/D System can provide for independence of metadata across computing environments, improving resiliency to the effects of hardware and software changes. Standards bodies, such as ANSI [WILS80] and NBS [APPL80], consider persual of this objective to be very important.

Six groups of users are direct beneficiaries of a D/D System: (1) *data administrators*, who use the system as a major tool for inventorying the data resource, implementing standards, and designing, monitoring, and restructuring databases; (2) *application personnel*, such as analysts and programmers, who use the system to reduce program coding efforts, store the designs of evolving systems, and support analysis of system changes; (3) *operations staff*, who retrieve information about jobs from the D/D; (4) *data-processing management*, who receive high-level impact and summary reports about data usage from the D/D; (5) *end users*, who obtain descriptions

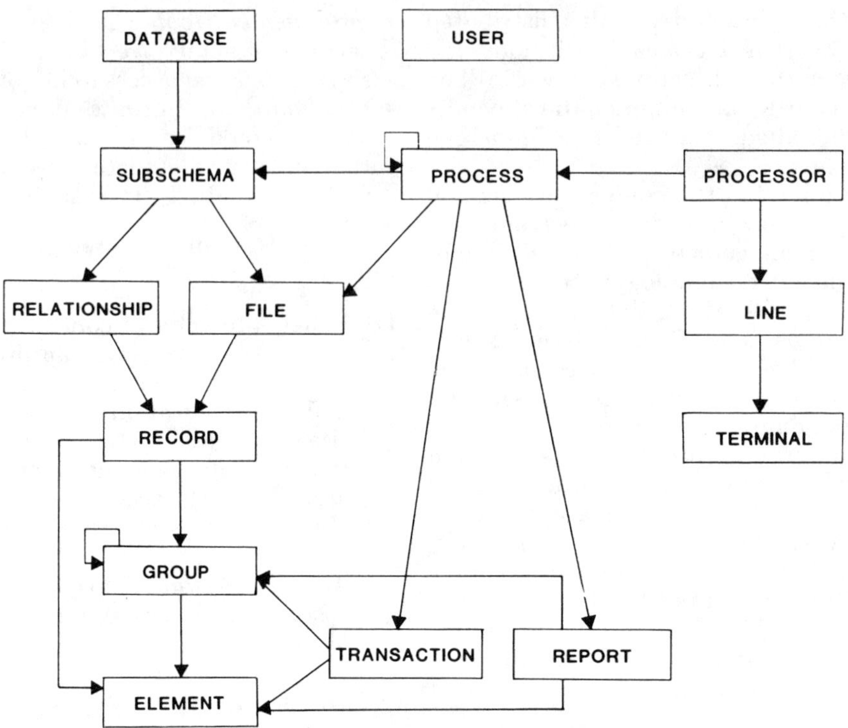


**Figure 1.** Logical structure of a typical D/D.

of their data views from the D/D; and (6) *auditors*, who examine system documentation provided through the D/D.

### 1.2 D/D Structure and Content

The D/D System's database can be represented by a network data model of entities, relationships, and attributes. An entity is an object of interest about which information is collected; a relationship is an association between one or more entities; an attribute is a characteristic relating to an entity or relationship. Nearly all commercial vendors represent the logical structures of their D/Ds with network models.

Figure 1 illustrates the entities and relationships of a typical D/D. The entities in the diagram can be classified as (1) Internal data consisting of the Database, Subschema, Relationship, File, and Record entities; (2) Atomic data consisting of the Group and Element entities; (3) Input–Output data consisting of the Transaction and Report entities; (4) User data; (5) Equipment data consisting of the Processor, Line, and Terminal entities, and (6) Process data describing the program (Process) entities.

The relationships shown in Figure 1 are shown in minimal form, as some D/Ds also include many-to-many links between entities. Although not shown here, the User entity may be related to nearly all the other entities, thereby representing, for example, the User–Subschema, User–Process, User–Terminal, User–Transaction, and User–Report relationships.

Numerous attributes can be used to describe the entities and relationships shown in Figure 1; some D/D Systems permit definition of over 500 separate attributes. Many of these attributes correspond to clauses found in data definition languages (DDLs) and in programming languages such as COBOL. Table 1 shows representative attributes for the Element entity. Note that in this example, 6 of the 11 attributes have analogous COBOL clauses.

A turnkey D/D System may not meet the specific requirements of a particular organization, and so an extensibility feature is often available. Extensibility allows an

**Table 1.** Typical Attributes for the Element Entity

| Attribute | Meaning |
|---|---|
| Type | Data type, e.g., integer, real, alphabetic |
| Range | Minimum and maximum allowable values |
| Length | Number of bytes |
| Unit of Measure | Characteristic, e.g., dollars, meters, tons, seconds |
| Usage | Value of the USAGE clause in COBOL, e.g., COMP, COMP-1 |
| Language Names | Names used in languages such as COBOL, PL/I, and assembler |
| Repetitions | Number of occurrences |
| 88 Levels | Names and values of any 88-level entries in COBOL |
| Key | Names of the files or database records for which the element is a key |
| Default value | Initial value |
| Display format | Format of the element when it appears on reports |

organization to tailor its D/D structure by defining additional entities, relationships, and attributes. Extensibility can be provided in two ways. In the simplest method, the vendor supplies *optional* sets of objects, for example, those required for a structured design methodology or message-formatting environment. With this method the vendor can more easily control the update transactions, reports, and queries for the optional objects and the upward compatibility with new releases of the D/D System.

In the more dynamic approach to extensibility, the D/D System accommodates *user-defined* entities, relationships, and attributes. User-defined entities are generally subject to constraints; for instance, a new entity must assume the relationships of a predefined entity. In Figure 2, the new entity named Job is a special case of the Process entity [TSI80a]. With user-defined entities, compatibility with future releases of the D/D System may be difficult to ensure.

The extensibility of a D/D System becomes increasingly important as it evolves into a means for coordinating software development tools at each stage of the application life cycle. D/D Systems traditionally have supported primarily the implementation and maintenance phases of application development; most D/D Systems today furnish interfaces with at least one language compiler and one DDL Processor. More recently, however, D/D Systems have been integrated with the design and operation phases of application development. Design aids such as DBDA [IBM80], INFO-DESIGN [CINC80], and ADF [BRYC79] can reference the vendor's D/D dynamically. Several vendors also provide query processors and report writers that utilize the D/D as a directory to user databases.

The potential to interface the D/D to other functions in the operational phase of systems, such as to performance monitors, performance optimizers, and database validators, is at present unexploited in commercial systems. The D/D is a natural repository for performance information about storage utilization and access frequencies. Researchers at the University of Aberdeen recently demonstrated the feasibility of statically interfacing a D/D to a performance monitor [JOHN80a, JOHN80b]. System R stores population statistics in the system catalogs (the System R D/D) for use in optimizing access paths [BLAS81]. The typical D/D also contains validation criteria that can be utilized by the DBMS to ensure database quality. Some of this information, for example, data type and length, is currently utilized by the associated DBMS; however, other criteria, such as value ranges and comparisons with other data elements, are commonly ignored. In the near future, the D/D System will become more active in supporting performance monitoring, optimization, and database validation functions.

Another important characteristic of a D/D is the ability for entity occurrences to exist in different states, for example, test, production, and historic. *Test* status information is used to document evolving systems and uncompleted changes to productional systems. The file descriptions for a new program of an existing system have test status until the program is thoroughly tested. *Production* status occurrences in the D/D are reflections of operational systems. Because the security of productional status information is paramount, update access is usually reserved for the data administrator. *Historic* status reflects superseded metadata, thus providing an audit trail of changes to the D/D. Version

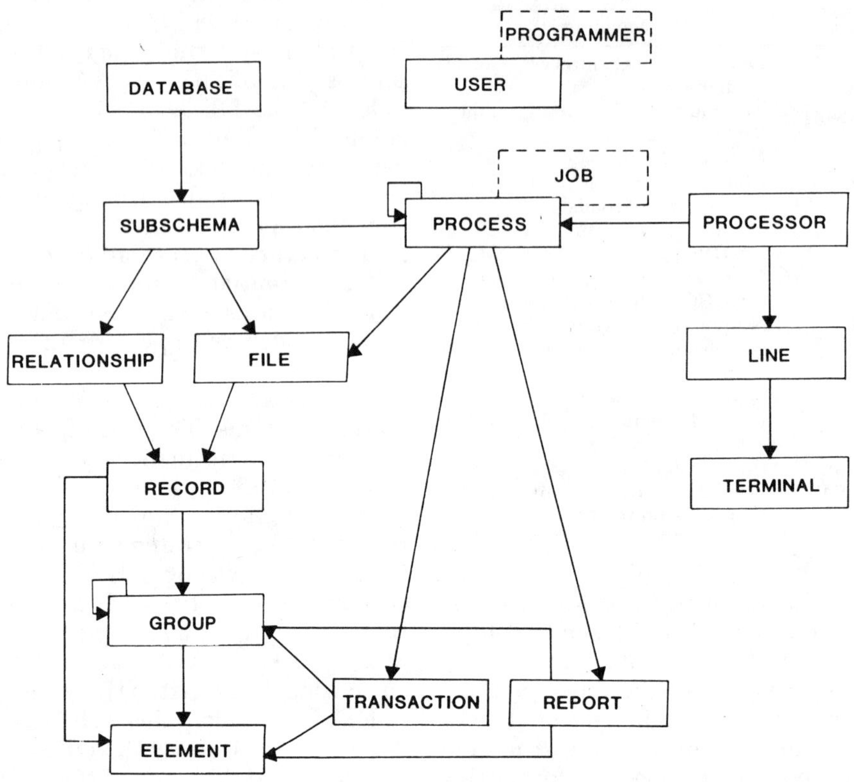


**Figure 2.** Extended logical structure of a D/D.

numbers allow multiple occurrences of the same entity to exist with the same status.

### 1.3 D/D System Functions

Figure 3 shows the functions of a typical, commercial D/D System. The *D/D Maintenance* function interprets and processes requests to add, change, or delete contents of the D/D. The prevalent maintenance methods include (1) a keyword-driven language, (2) a position-sensitive transaction format, (3) interactive, prompted input, and (4) interactive, preformatted screens of menus. Figure 4 illustrates the first three methods. For a more thorough presentation of these maintenance methods, consult LEFK77.

The *Extensibility* function of a D/D System enables the D/D structure to be extended by the definition of additional entities, relationships, and attributes. For example, a "clone" transaction could be used to alter the D/D structure to include the Job entity shown in Figure 2 [TSI80a]. Other types of extensions may require more elaborate specification. For example, to add a totally new type of entity, it may be necessary to (1) create the specification for a new transaction type, (2) create a file of occurrences of the new entity, and (3) create specifications for additional relationships to be included in the D/D.

The *Report Processor* function of a D/D System provides predefined reports, the ability to customize the reports, and a user-defined reporting capability. Common predefined report types include (1) name listings such as keyword-in-context (KWIC) and keyword-out-of-context (KWOC) reports; (2) relationship reports, for example, all the elements contained in a database; (3) detail reports, for example, descriptions for all elements with a common keyword; (4) summary reports such as the compilation date, change description, number of source lines, and the responsible programmer for all programs in a recent version; (5)

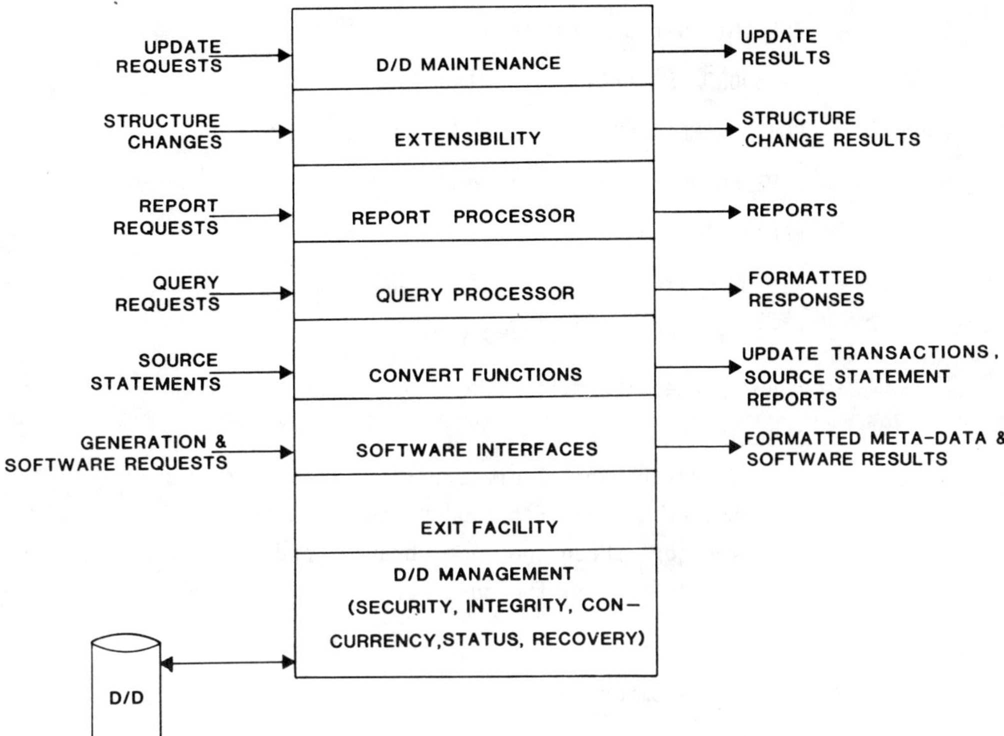


**Figure 3.** D/D System functions.

matrix reports, such as type of access (input, output, input–output) to all files within a program; and (6) graphical reports, for example, showing the hierarchical structure of a program. Figure 5a and b displays examples of relationship and detail reports. The vendor often furnishes a method to change report formatting parameters. Sometimes the user can define new reports using the vendor's report writer. For example, users of Cullinane's Integrated Data Dictionary (IDD) can define new reports using the CULPRIT report writer [CULL78].

The *Query Processor* function of a D/D System allows English-like queries of the D/D. This query function for the D/D is analogous to the corresponding function in DBMSs for access to databases and is used for low-volume retrieval. A query might be

```
SELECT report-name
  WHERE column = "Supplier Name"
    AND frequency = "monthly"
```

The *Convert Function* of a D/D System reads application programs, libraries, and schemata and generates for the D/D Maintenance Function input transactions that describe the detected metadata. This automated conversion facility alleviates some of the problems of initially loading the D/D from the variety of sources of metadata that exist in an organization.

The *Software Interface* function provides a formatted pathway, enabling the D/D System to provide metadata to other software systems such as compilers and DDL processors, and enabling these systems to retrieve and update information in the D/D. A software interface component might generate file descriptions for storage in a program library; another might accept a user's identification code and then generate a copy of that user's database view.

Section 2 further details software interfaces and convert functions because these two functions are fundamental parts of an integrated D/D System.

The *Exit Facility* of a D/D System enables the vendor-supplied routines to be extended. For example, the user organization might code additional validation con-

(a)
```
ADD ELEMENT Customer-Number
    PASSWORD IS "XYZA";
    COBOL-NAME custnum;
    TYPE numeric;
    LENGTH 10;
    KEY OF custrec;
    DISPLAY-FORMAT "99-999-99999";
    USAGE packed-decimal;
    DESCRIPTION
        Customer-Number uniquely identifies each account
        holder.  The first two digits identify the district,
        the next three the local branch, and the final five
        digits specify the customer;
```

(b)
```
+ADD Customer-Number
    'XYZA', custnum, num, 10, 'custrec',
    '99-999-99999', pdec,
        Customer-Number uniquely identifies each account
        holder.  The first two digits identify the district,
        the next three the local branch, and the final five
        digits specify the customer.
```

(c)
```
GIVE FUNC (FUNCTION = NAME)
    ADD ELE = Customer-Number
GIVE PASSWORD
    'XYZA'
GIVE COBOL-NAME
    custnum
GIVE TYPE
    numeric
GIVE LENGTH
    10
```

**Figure 4.** Examples of D/D maintenance methods: (a) keyword-driven language; (b) position-sensitive transaction format; (c) prompted input.

```
                                   D/D SYSTEM              DATE:  3/15/81
                                INDENTED REPORT            PAGE:        1

ENTITY-TYPE   NAME               VERSION  STATUS   DESCRIPTION

DATABASE      Customer-Account      1       T      Credit customer database
  FILE          CFILE               1       T      CFILE contains identifying customer
                                                   information
   RECORD         Cust-Rec          1       T      One Cust-Rec per account
    ELEMENT         Customer-Number 1       T      Customer-Number uniquely identifies
                                                   account holder.
    ELEMENT         Customer-Name   1       T      Last name, middle initial, first name.
    ELEMENT         Customer-Address 1      T      Street, City, State, Zip Code
    ELEMENT         Customer-Date   1       T      Expiration date of credit card
    ELEMENT         Customer-Limit  1       T      Maximum credit amount
```

(a)

```
                                   D/D SYSTEM                    DATE:  3/15/81
                                  DETAIL REPORT                  PAGE:        1

ENTITY-TYPE:  ELEMENT              NAME:  Customer-Number   (ØØ1) TEST
AUTHOR:  John Doe                  ORGANIZATION:  DBA
DATE-ADDED:  3/15/81               LAST-DATE-CHANGED:
ATTRIBUTE                          ATTRIBUTE-VALUE
COBOL-NAME                         custnum
TYPE                               numeric
LENGTH                             10
KEY                                Cust-Rec
DISPLAY-FORMAT                     99-999-99999
USAGE                              Packed Decimal
                  TEXT
..................  ......................................LINE NO

Customer-Number uniquely identifies each account holder.  0000001
The first two digits identify the district,               0000002
the next three the local branch, and the final            0000003
five digits specify the customer.                         0000004
```

(b)

**Figure 5.** SAMPLE reports of the D/D System: (a) indented report (format similar to DATADICTIONARY by ADR); (b) detail report (format similar to DATADICTIONARY by ADR). (From APPL79a. Adapted with permission of Applied Data Research, Inc.)

straints to be applied prior to deletion of a particular entity from the D/D. A new security check might be coded for use upon access to an attribute. An Exit facility is not available in all D/D Systems because of the possible side effects that its use may introduce. A user-written routine could be incompatible with a new release of the D/D System or the routine might not be thoroughly tested before implementation, raising a potential conflict between the vendor and user over responsibility for any ensuing problems.

The *D/D Management* function of a D/D System performs database management tasks such as security, integrity, concurrency control, and internal access for the D/D. Many D/D Systems utilize the services of an existing DBMS to provide aspects of this function. However, one special subfunction, Status Maintenance, generally is not provided by a DBMS. This subfunction, which we introduced in Section 1.2, permits an entity occurrence to exist in multiple states and to change states (e.g., from test to production).

## 2. INTEGRATING THE D/D SYSTEM

A D/D System is integrated with other software packages by facilities that (1) allow direct and indirect access to the D/D and (2) automatically capture the metadata used by other systems. The previous section identified these two capabilities as software interfaces and convert functions, respectively. Sections 2.1 and 2.2 fully explicate the options and variations of these capabilities. Section 2.3 explains the environmental dependency of the D/D System and a DBMS in terms of three approaches. Section 2.4 surveys the software interfaces, convert functions, and environmental dependency of several commercial D/D Systems.

### 2.1 Software Interfaces

A software interface permits another system to access the D/D either statically or dynamically. First, we consider the static interface, which links the D/D with another system *indirectly* via the extraction of a file of formatted metadata. For example, consider the static interface of a D/D System and a DBMS. The data administrator enters into the D/D System all pertinent transactions to describe the database. After reviewing the accuracy of this database description, the data administrator activates a D/D System command, for example, GENERATE, that uses this description to produce a file containing DDL. The DBMS's DDL Processor then translates this generated DDL into a schema file that the run-time unit of the DBMS can access. No run-time connection between the D/D System and the DBMS exists here; the DBMS's DDL Processor is not executing during the D/D System's DDL-generation process.

Static interfaces differ somewhat, depending upon whether they interface the D/D System with user-written programs or with vendor-supplied software packages. Static interfaces for programs written in languages such as COBOL and PL/I produce file, record, and database descriptions for the user programs from the D/D. These interfaces sometimes feature edit capabilities, format options, and various other functions to make the interface more flexibile. Figure 6 depicts some of these options. Edit capabilities may include being able to add prefixes and suffixes and even to replace entire names. Format options may control indentation, level-number increments, sequence numbers, and line identifiers. Inclusion of various clauses such as comments, condition names, and initial values also may be allowed.

Static interfaces for software packages, such as DDL processors, communication monitors, and query processors, produce formatted statements for those packages or create specially encoded control files for their use. For example, a software interface of UCC's D/D System, UCC TEN, generates message and terminal description statements from its D/D for use by IBM's Message Format Service, while Cullinane's IDD creates from its D/D the control file utilized by the IDMS–DC communications monitor.

The options for customizing the interface with these types of software packages are more limited than are the options provided for interface with user-written programs; the packages generally have more rigid lan-

(a)
```
GENERATE PAYMENT-FILE
     INSERT "PAY" BEFORE "CUST"
     REPLACE "NUMBER" WITH "NUM"
     INCLUDE COMMENTS
     INCREMENT LEVEL-NUMBERS BY 2
     INDENT 3 SPACES.
```

(b)
```
FD IN-PAYMENT-FILE
 RECORD CONTAINS 50 CHARACTERS
 BLOCK CONTAINS 20 RECORDS
 VALUE OF ID "PFILE ØØ1"
***This is a transaction file for the
***Customer Credit System
 Ø1 PAYMENT-RECORD.
   Ø3 PAY-CUST-NUM                    PIC 9(10) COMP-2.
   Ø3 PAY-CUST-NAME.
      Ø5 PAY-CUST-LNAME               PIC X(20).
      Ø5 PAY-CUST-FNAME               PIC X(10).
      Ø5 PAY-CUST-INIT                PIC X.
   Ø3 PAY-CUST-DATE                   PIC X(6).
   Ø3 PAY-CUST-AMOUNT                 PIC 9(6)V99.
```

**Figure 6.** Generate function example: (a) GENERATE command for COBOL; (b) generated COBOL file description.

guage formats and the interface statements are usually used only by the data administrator. Some D/D Systems have an extended file extraction capability that enables metadata to be formatted and saved in a sequential file. A user program can then process this file for specialized analysis of the data resource.

Static interfaces are prevalent because of their utility, compatibility, and efficiency. With powerful static interfaces, the data administrator can quickly change formatted metadata or create new formatted definitions from existing D/D entities for use by both user-written applications programs and vendor-supplied software packages. The static D/D can be made compatible with many versions of other software packages (e.g., several different DBMSs) and can be developed independently of the source code of particular software packages. This is definitely attractive to the independent vendor of D/D Systems.

A disadvantage to the user of a static interface is the extra effort that may be required to generate and catalog metadata for the D/D. More significantly, the static interface itself has no capabilities of updating the metadata of the systems with which it interfaces. Without adequate synchroni-

**Table 2.** Types of Software Packages I D/D Systems

| Module | Descriptions |
|---|---|
| DDL Processor | Creates a schema file |
| Database Control System (DBCS) | Run-time unit of a DBMS |
| Preprocessor | Translates data manipulation language (DML) into CALL statements |
| Query/Update Processor | Provides direct end-user access to stored databases |
| Batch-Code Generator | Reduces the time to develop a standard function (e.g., report writer, input processor) as compared to a compiler-level language |
| Source-Program Manager | Provides security protection, data compression, and editing capabilities for source programs |
| Teleprocessing (TP) Monitor | Provides the capability of interactive computing to remote terminals |
| Test-Data Generator | Creates test files and databases according to user specifications |
| Design Aid | Analyzes and generates designs of databases or information systems |

zation and controls, the metadata in the D/D System and the metadata in other systems can become inconsistent. By comparison, dynamic interfaces provide increased potential for data control.

Dynamic interfaces provide *direct* access of the D/D to other software modules. This direct access is commonly achieved via high-level interface commands that shield the software package from the physical details of the D/D. The commands activate standard D/D System functions, so as to select all entity occurrences that satisfy a particular condition. Some D/D Systems provide a facility that makes commands available through call statements; any program can then access the D/D without knowledge of its physical structure.

Dynamic interfaces provide consistency control and capabilities for both update and retrieval. Changes to the D/D are automatically reflected in the next execution of any software packages to which the D/D is interfaced; no intervening procedures are required as are with static interfaces. A software package can directly retrieve and update metadata stored in the D/D. For example, a COBOL preprocessor can retrieve file descriptions from the D/D and update the D/D to reflect the new compilation date in the identification of invoking modules. All requests by software packages for metadata are routed through the D/D System by a dynamic interface function. Thus the security and validity checks of the D/D System are always applied.

Use of a dynamic interface incurs significant overhead due to the size and complex structure of the typical D/D. Application-development support aids, such as preprocessors, source program managers, and design aids, generally can afford this overhead because response time is not critical. On the other hand, efficiency *is* critical for transaction-processing systems that reference the D/D. For example, a query processor, which is a transaction-processing system, can control access to user databases by retrieving from the D/D information about data access privileges, external (user) and internal names, and available access paths. To reduce the potential overhead, common queries may be precompiled and stored in the D/D. This approach is used in System R [CHAM81]; the access modules for precompiled SQL statements are part of the broad D/D contents. Retrieval of a precompiled query includes all the necessary metadata. Another technique used to reduce overhead is for the software package to retrieve all the metadata required for a transaction at once; thus future accesses for this transaction are all memory lookups.

Some of the types of software that presently interface with D/D Systems are described in Table 2.

### 2.2 Convert Functions

In addition to software interfaces, the integration of a D/D System into its environment is provided by convert functions.

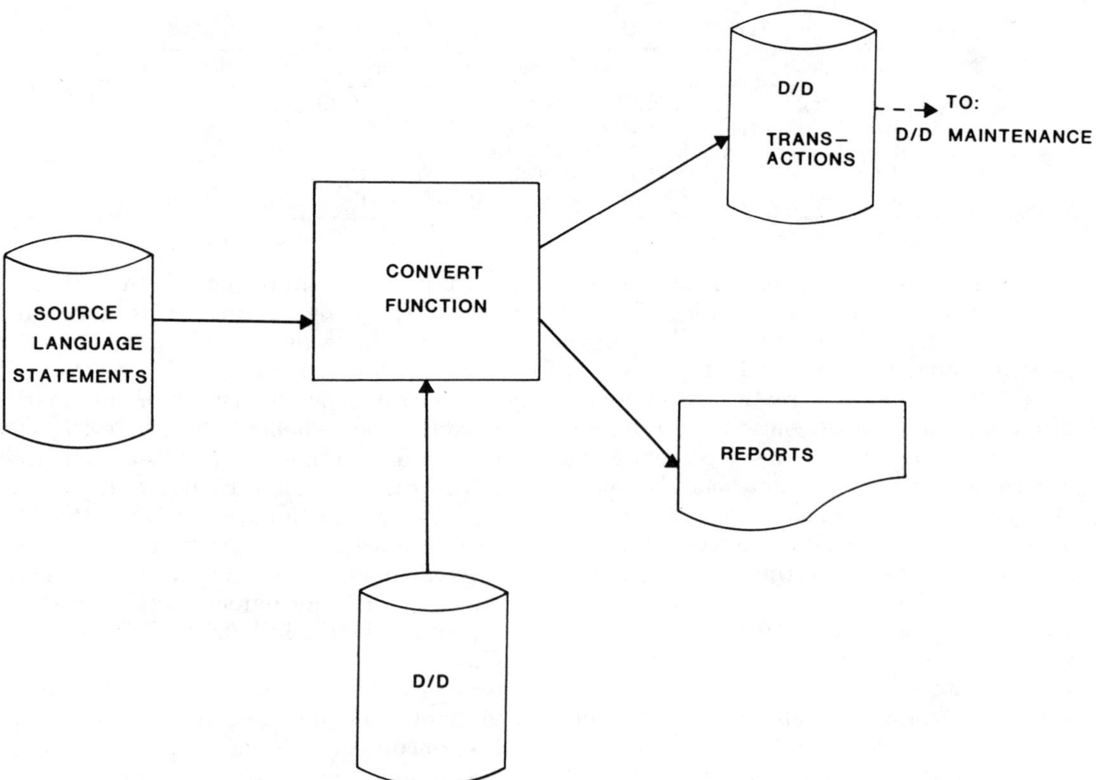


**Figure 7.** System flow for a Convert function.

These functions alleviate some of the problems encountered in initially populating a D/D. A typical organization that acquires a D/D System has hundreds of programs, reports, and files to manage. The data administrator must encode thousands of maintenance transactions to capture the metadata of all these applications. The convert functions of a D/D System scan source programs, database descriptions, and teleprocessing environment descriptions and automatically produce maintenance transactions, thus sparing the data administrator many hours of manual effort. Actually, the data administrator must scrutinize these generated transactions for the possibility of redundant and nonstandard entries. For example, if the naming conventions used in source programs are uncontrolled, then the data administrator will find it necessary to change details in many of the transactions in order to impose standardization.

Figure 7 illustrates the flow of data through a typical convert function. Inputs include the source language statements and the D/D; outputs are a file of transactions to be input to the D/D Maintenance module and a report. The D/D Maintenance transactions include descriptions of databases, files, records, groups, elements, and programs. The report lists the transactions and possibly includes some analysis of source statements.

Convert functions are offered to convert metadata from both user-written programs and from a DBMS and its related components. For example, a D/D System may furnish conversion facilities for several programming languages (e.g., COBOL, PL/I, assembler), as well as for the DDL Processor and report writer of a given DBMS. Table 3 summarizes the ways in which metadata of various types of modules relate to the logical structure of the typical D/D (recall Figure 1).

Convert functions have four significant

**Table 3.** D/D Convert Function Transactions

| Module type | Transactions generated by the Convert function |
|---|---|
| Programming (e.g., COBOL, PL/I) | ELEMENT, GROUP, RECORD, FILE, and sometimes SUBSCHEMA and PROCESS |
| Database Description (DDL) | DATABASE, FILE, SUBSCHEMA, RELATIONSHIP, RECORD, GROUP, ELEMENT |
| Teleprocessing | TERMINAL, LINE, PROCESSOR, TRANSACTION |

characteristics: (1) the content of the generated transactions, (2) the input file, (3) the command options, and (4) the source program analysis. The D/D maintenance transactions that are created by a convert function usually also contain the relationships between data entities (e.g., between a record and an element) and most language clauses. For example, Element transactions generated by a COBOL convert function capture metadata for the D/D from the program's OCCURS, PICTURE, and USAGE clauses. A convert function is considered to be generation equivalent if the D/D System can regenerate the input source data description from the D/D's metadata.

The input file to a convert function can be a source program or a library file. If the input is a source program, then the convert function can capture information about data usage by that program (e.g., the way a file is opened). If the input is a library file, then only the data descriptions that actually reside in the library file can be converted to the D/D format.

Options for a convert function may include the ability to change names, select lines to scan, select types of transactions to create, and to override generation of some types of metadata. The following hypothetical conversion command demonstrates these options:

```
CONVERT COBOL
  DELETE "PAY"
  REPLACE "CUST" WITH "CUSTOMER",
        "NUM" WITH "NUMBER"
  SCAN 100-1000, 2000-3000
  CREATE RECORD, GROUP, AND
    ELEMENT TRANSACTIONS
  OVERRIDE ELEMENT TRANS-
    ACTIONS
```

The DELETE and REPLACE clauses here permit the entity name generated for the D/D to differ from the entity name used in the COBOL program. The SCAN clause instructs the convert function to generate metadata from only certain lines of the program. The CREATE clause grants the user control over the types of metadata transactions spawned by the convert function. In this example, only transactions for the Record, Group, and Element entities of the D/D are specified. The OVERRIDE clause enables the convert function to create an Element transaction even though an entity with the same name and type already exists in the D/D [TSI80a, MSP80b].

The ability to analyze the metadata of source programs can make the D/D System a valuable tool for auditing adherence to software control techniques. The D/D System can detect and disclose inconsistencies in the names, formats, and clauses (e.g., comments, initial values) of the record definitions used in several programs and the corresponding standard record definitions in the D/D.

### 2.3 Environmental Dependency

The environmental dependency characteristic of a D/D System is determined by its reliance on a specific hardware configuration, an operating system, a DBMS, or a teleprocessing monitor. Ideally, the D/D System can operate in all environments with no loss of efficiency and functionality. However, at present this ideal is far from attainable.

The extent of environmental dependency between a D/D System and a DBMS is determined by the degree to which the D/D System relies on the DBMS for data management services and the source of metadata used by the DBMS for access to stored databases. The DBMS may provide the D/D System with management services such as internal access, recovery, and concurrency control. In a completely integrated D/D System, the DBMS accesses

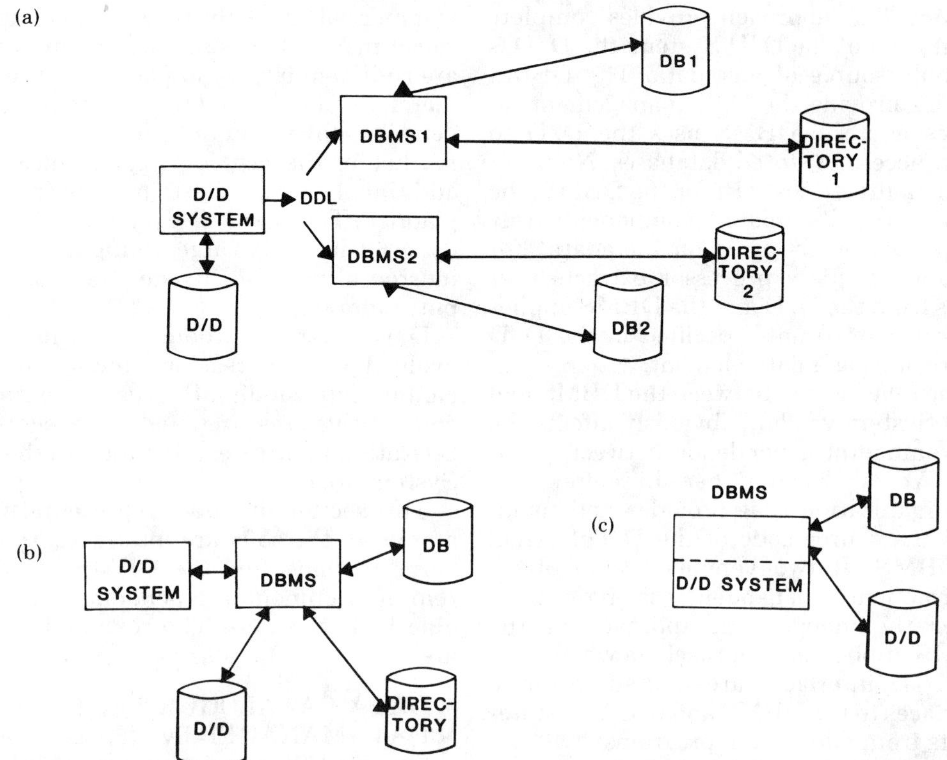


**Figure 8.** D/D System: DBMS relationships. (a) Independent approach; (b) DBMS—application approach; (c) embedded approach.

stored databases via the D/D. In less integrated systems, the DBMS may maintain its own directory file for accessing stored databases. Figure 8 illustrates three variations of the environmental dependency, which we denote as independent, DBMS-application, and embedded. The terms free standing, dependent, and in-line have also been used [LEFK77, FIPS77, Ross80].

In the *Independent* approach, the D/D System is autonomous; it does not rely on any particular DBMS. The DBMS maintains its own source of metadata; the D/D System uses none of the DBMS utilities for providing D/D Management functions. One benefit of this approach is that one D/D System may provide description facilities, convert processors, and software interfaces in a variety of environments with different DBMSs or no DBMS at all. The DBMS software interfaces in this approach are generally limited to generate formatted data descriptions from the D/D for use by the DDL Processor. Interfaces are not usually provided for other DBMS-related components, for example, a query processor. However, dynamic interfaces may be provided to the other software packages offered by the D/D System vendor, such as to design aids and test-data generators.

In the *DBMS-application* approach, the D/D appears to the DBMS as just another database. The DBMS maintains its own metadata for each database; these metadata are separate from the D/D. The DBMS utilities provide most of the D/D management functions, but metadata are defined separately for the DBMS and for the D/D System. In this approach, the D/D System interfaces dynamically with only one DBMS and its related components, but there may be static interfaces to other DBMSs that operate with the same hardware.

In the *Embedded* approach, the D/D System is actually a component of the

DBMS. This approach provides complete integration of the D/D System; the D/D is the only source of metadata. The DBMS utilities provide the D/D management facilities and the DBMS uses the D/D to direct access to stored databases. No other internal directories exist for the DBMS; the DBMS and its related components rely completely on the D/D for metadata. For example, a query processor extracts user views from the D/D and the DBMS applies integrity constraints specified in the D/D before storing a data element.

The relationship between the DBMS and D/D System vendors obviously affects the environmental dependency between products. We use "vendor" here in reference to the organization that provides and maintains the source code of the D/D System or DBMS. If two vendors are involved, environmental dependency is a result of either the independent approach or the DBMS-application approach, in which case the D/D interfaces are limited to static interfaces to the DBMS and to CALL statements from application programs.

If both the DBMS and D/D System are from one vendor, then environmental dependency is a result of either the DBMS-application approach or the embedded approach. The choice of approaches is influenced by considerations such as the development effort required and the vendor's marketing strategy. Development of a D/D System with the DBMS-application approach may be simpler than with the embedded approach if the vendor already has a fully developed DBMS and related software that rely on schema files. The marketing strategy represented by the two approaches differs; the two systems can be sold as separate products with the DBMS-application approach, but are bundled with the embedded approach.

### 2.4 State-of-the-Art Review

The demand and supply of D/D Systems today are indicative of their growing significance. The 15 largest vendors have installed approximately 2000 D/D Systems, primarily in large organizations. Many other organizations utilize D/D Systems that were developed in house; may even use manual systems. The potential demand for commercial D/D Systems seems vast because many of these home-grown systems are rudimentary in comparison to the commercially available D/D Systems. Many vendors have entered the D/D System market in the last few years, and several additional D/D System offerings are planned. Today's D/D Systems are primarily used in fairly large configurations; tomorrow's will also invade the small computer market.

D/D System product offerings have evolved with increasing functionality, including extensibility. Because of continuing competitive pressures, vendors are even accelerating their research efforts in the D/D System area.

This section discusses representative examples of the software interfaces, the convert functions, and the DBMS–D/D System environmental dependencies in available D/D Systems. The reviewed systems are

- DATA CATALOGUE 2 by TSI Inc.;
- DATAMANAGER by Management Systems and Programming, Ltd. (MSP);
- Integrated Data Dictionary (IDD) by Cullinane Database Systems, Inc.;
- DATADICTIONARY by Applied Data Research, Inc. (ADR);
- TIS DIRECTORY by Cincom Systems, Inc.;
- Integrated Data Dictionary (IDD) by Intel, Inc.

Our discussion of these particular systems does not signify their commercial superiority over others. These systems were chosen as illustrative of the functions identified in Sections 2.1–2.3. The evaluation and selection of a D/D System involve many factors that are beyond the scope of this paper. The series of charts (Tables 4–9) included in the appendix of this paper serves to summarize all the commercial D/D Systems that we reviewed in the course of preparing this survey.

#### *2.4.1 Software Interfaces*

This section describes the following functions of commercial D/D Systems for generic classes of interfaces to various types of software:

(a)

```
$GENERATE COBOL
OPTIONS DATASET = NO, IDEN = 'TRANS'
SELECT  TRANSACTION-FILE
```

(b)

```
          1   1   2   2   2           4              7    8
1......8...2...6...0...4...8...........0..............3....0

000000*TRANSACTION-FILE *DEFINITION CREATED FROM DC2  TRANS
000010IDATE OF GENERATION: 02/10/82                   TRANS
000020*MASTER FILE REVISION NUMBER =   1              TRANS
000030*DATE OF LAST REVISION = 02/10/82               TRANS
000040*                                               TRANS

000050 FD  TRANSACTION-IN                             TRANS
000060     RECORD CONTAINS   92 CHARACTERS            TRANS
000070     RECORDING MODE IS F                        TRANS
000080     LABEL RECORDS ARE STANDARD                 TRANS
000090     BLOCK CONTAINS 1840 CHARACTERS             TRANS
000100     DATA RECORDS ARE                           TRANS
000110         INVOICE-RECORD                         TRANS
000120         PAYMENT-RECORD.                        TRANS
000130 01  INVOICE-RECORD.                            TRANS
000140     03  CUSTOMER NUMBER  PICTURE XXXXXXX.      TRANS
000150     03  INVOICE-NO       PICTURE 9(7).         TRANS
000160     03  INVOICE-DATE     PICTURE 9(6).         TRANS
000170     03  TX-CODE          PICTURE 99.           TRANS
000180     03  INVOICE-NUMBER-AMOUNT                  TRANS
000190                    PICTURE S9(11)V99  COMP-3.  TRANS
000200     03  FILLER     PICTURE X(63).              TRANS
000210 01  PAYMENT-RECORD.                            TRANS
000220     03  CUSTOMER-NUMBER  PICTURE XXXXXXX.      TRANS
000230     03  TX-CODE          PICTURE 99.           TRANS
000240     03  PAY-AMOUNT                             TRANS
000250                    PICTURE S9(11)V99 COMP-3.   TRANS
000260     03  INVOICE-NO    PICTURE 9(7)             TRANS
000270                    OCCURS FROM  1 TO 9 TIMES   TRANS
000280                    INDEXED BY CALC.            TRANS
000290     03  FILLER     PICTURE X(13).              TRANS
```

**Figure 9.** DATA CATALOGUE 2 generated file description: (a) GENERATE command; (b) listing. (From TSI80b. Reprinted with permission of TSI, International.)

- the COBOL GENERATE command of DATA CATALOGUE 2;
- the DML Processor interface to Cullinane's IDD;
- the Query Processor interface to TIS DIRECTORY and to Intel's IDD;
- the Source Program Manager interface to DATADICTIONARY;
- the User Interface facility of DATAMANAGER.

These examples depict both static and dynamic interfaces to application-development and transaction-processing systems.

The *COBOL GENERATE* command of DATA CATALOGUE 2 creates from the D/D fully formatted file and record definitions that can be stored in a library file. Included are most COBOL clauses such as 88 Levels, INDEX BY, SYNCHRONIZED, REDEFINES, and OCCURS. The OPTION clause of this command permits name changes, the designation of sequence numbers, level numbers and identifiers, and the inclusion of program comments. Figure 9 demonstrates a GENERATE command and the corresponding output file listing. The generation date, last

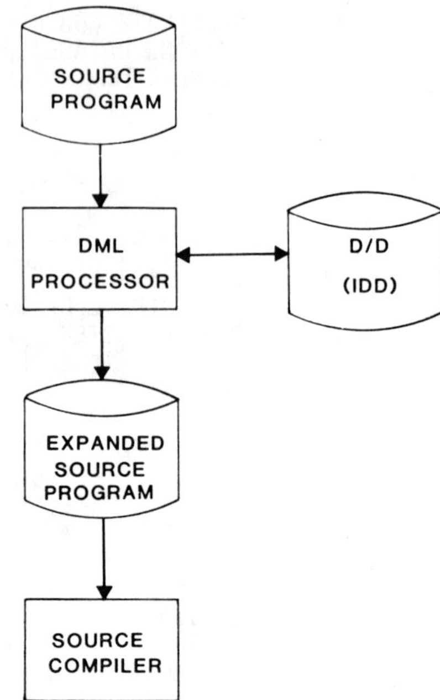


**Figure 10.** Software interface to Cullinane's DML processor. Note: D/D retrieval—(1) record description, (2) module source code, (3) IDMS DML statements translated into CALLS; D/D update—(1) language, (2) estimated lines, (3) programs(s) called, (4) module(s) copied, (5) file use (input, output, I—O), (6) subschema used, (7) area activity, (8) record activity, (9) set activity, (10) date compiled, (11) number of compiles. (From CULL80. Adapted with permission of Cullinane Database Systems, Inc.)

revision date, and revision number are automatically recorded in both the listing and in the D/D.

The COBOL GENERATE command also may contain job control statements to be included on the output file. The output file then can be executed as a job that creates and catalogs the COBOL metadata as a member of a library under control of any of the various source program managers, for example, PANVALET, LIBRARIAN, COPYLIB. In Figure 9, job control statements are not included because the option for production of an output file was not specified (i.e., DATASET = NO) [TSI80a].

Cullinane's *DML Processor* dynamically retrieves and updates information in the IDD as depicted in Figure 10. A COPY-like statement in a source program triggers the retrieval of file and subschema descriptions and other appropriate source code from the IDD. The DML Processor records control information and data usage information in the IDD. Updating of the IDD by the DML Processor can be suspended through an optional parameter [CULL78, CULL80].

The dynamic interface of Cincom's TIS DIRECTORY to its *Query Processor* controls the operation of that component. Three types of statements are provided by Cincom's Query Component: Help, Control, and Define. The *Help* commands permit a user to browse through relevant parts of the DIRECTORY. The user can examine the headings and formats of external fields, the descriptions of fields used in subschemas and in equations, and the names of other user-created queries. The *Control* statements direct Query component to perform some action, such as to delete a query, to execute a query, or to access the DIRECTORY. The SAVE statement catalogs a compiled query in the DIRECTORY, while the RECALL statement retrieves a defined query from the DIRECTORY. The LET statement provides the user with a means of defining an Expression Equation occurrence in the DIRECTORY. An Expression Equation is any TIS Query syntax, from single words to complete phrases. The set of *Define* statements specifies query logic and data to retrieve. In parsing and executing Define statements, the Query Processor references the DIRECTORY to determine access privileges, to create access paths to files, to determine headings and display formats, and to restrict resource usage, for example, the maximum number of displayed lines and database calls [CINC80].

Intel's IDD supplies a file-extraction interface to its Query Processor: Query Update By Example (QBX). This static interface creates the QBX run-time directory that contains user views, internal record and item names, user identifications, and access paths between records and items. Any time a user view is changed by IDD, a new directory is generated. QBX uses this directory to display user views and to map from requests on user views to DML-level requests [INTE80].

ADR's *Source Program Manager,* LIBRARIAN, dynamically interfaces with its DATADICTIONARY. A COPY-like statement extracts data definitions from the DATADICTIONARY and inserts them into source code during the LIBRARIAN's execution. However, LIBRARIAN cannot retrieve data definitions unless the proper authorizations are stored in the DATADICTIONARY. That is, the appropriate relationship between Program and File entity occurrences must exist. After a compilation, LIBRARIAN records in the DATADICTIONARY the date compiled and the files accessed by the source program [APPL79b].

The *User Interface Facility* of DATAMANAGER allows any program written in COBOL, PL/I, or assembler to activate dynamically any DATAMANAGER commands. Invocation of the User Interface Facility is by a standard CALL statement with parameters that specify (1) control information and DATAMANAGER commands; (2) a buffer area in a user program to receive the output from the CALL; and (3) a dynamic storage area used by DATAMANAGER. The buffer area (second parameter) is backed up by an access work file, which catches overflow. DATAMANAGER applies the same security and validity checks to requests from a program's CALL statement as to requests from a user at a terminal. Some applications of this facility by DATAMANAGER users include a dynamically interfaced precompiler and input edit programs that dynamically extract validation criteria from the D/D [MSP80c].

### 2.4.2 Convert Functions

This section describes the convert functions of DATA CATALOGUE 2 and of DATAMANAGER for COBOL metadata. In both systems, the D/D System examines a COBOL source program and creates a generation-equivalent set of transactions for construction of the D/D. The functions in the two systems differ with respect to command options and types of transactions generated. Neither system analyzes procedural statements.

Figure 11 illustrates the DATA CATALOGUE 2 Convert command. Some of the options are (1) inclusion of the program's REMARKS statement as part of the generated program transaction, (2) deletion of prefixes from data names, (3) renaming of data names, (4) specification of version numbers for transactions, (5) selection by data name, and (6) designation of the transaction types to be created. In Figure 11, all of the components of the file IN-MAST-FILE are converted to transaction types: Element, Record, File, and Program for the D/D. No Group transactions are specified [TSI80a].

Figure 12 displays an example of the DATAMANAGER convert function (known as Automation of setup) for the same partial COBOL program (Figure 11). The DATAMANAGER command differs from the DATA CATALOGUE 2 command with respect to (1) selection by line numbers as well as by data names, (2) inability to generate program definitions, (3) the use of more robust editing options (REPLACE, INSERT, DELETE), and (4) the inclusion of an override option that causes the definitions created by the convert function to replace matching definitions in the DATAMANAGER source file. In the example, the DATAMANAGER command overrides any ITEM definitions in the source program that match the generated ITEM definitions in name and version number [MSP80b].

### 2.4.3 DBMS–D/D System Environmental Dependencies

This section includes examples of the three approaches to environmental dependency: (1) the independent approach of DATAMANAGER, (2) the DBMS-application approach of DATADICTIONARY, and (3)the embedded approach of DIRECTORY. In each case, files of the D/D and

(a)

```
000100 IDENTIFICATION DIVISION.
000200 PROGRAM-ID.  PROGRAM-1.
000300 REMARKS.  THIS PROGRAM CALCULATES THE REORDER
000400           AMOUNTS FOR ALL OUT-OF-STOCK ITEMS.
000500 ENVIRONMENT DIVISION.
000600 INPUT-OUTPUT SECTION.
000700       SELECT     MASTFILE
000800                  ASSIGN TO SYS005-UR-1403-S-IN-MASTFILE
000900                  ACCESS IS SEQUENTIAL.
001000 DATA DIVISION.
001100 FILE SECTION.
001200 FD  IN-MASTFILE
001300     LABEL RECORD OMITTED
001400     DATA RECORD IS MASTRECORD.
001500 01  IN-MASTRECORD.
001600       05  IN-STOCKDATE   PIC 9(6).
001700       05  IN-STOCKPLACE  PIC X(24).
001800       05  IN-STOCKVALUE  PIC 9V99  COMP SYNC RIGHT.
```

(b)

```
CONVERT COBOL
MODULE NAME PROGRAM-1 INCLUDE NOTES
       CATNAME IS CALCULATE-REORDERS
CREATE ELEMENTS RECORD FILE PROGRAM
SELECT IN-MASTFILE
       AT LEVEL FD
       STRIP PREFIX 'IN'
RENAME IN-MASTFILE TO INVENTORY-MASTER-FILE
RENAME IN-MASTRECORD TO INVENTORY RECORD.
```

**Figure 11.** DATA CATALOGUE 2 Convert example: (a) partial COBOL program; (b) DATA CATALOGUE 2 command. (From TSI80a. Reprinted with permission of TSI, Inc.)

the dependency on the DBMS and related products (e.g., TP monitor) are emphasized.

DATAMANAGER exhibits an independent approach. The DATAMANAGER D/D comprises five IBM VSAM or BDAM files: the Source file, the Data Entries file, the Index file, the Error Recovery file, and the Log file. The Source file contains the DATAMANAGER command statements exactly as input except for compression of spaces. The Data Entries file contains encoded data definitions and pointers that establish the interrelationships between entity occurrences in the D/D. The Index file has the name and address of each entity occurrence in the other two files; thus the Index file permits the fastest access to source and encoded entity occurrences. The Error Recovery file accommodates the before- and afterimages used by the recovery system. The Log file is a record of activity against the D/D and is primarily used for audit purposes and checkpoint recovery processing. DATAMANAGER is compatible with nine TP monitors including CICS, IMS/DC, and ROSCOE [MSP80a]. DATAMANAGER generates schema and subschema definitions for five DBMSs.

DATADICTIONARY exhibits a DBMS-application approach to environmental dependency. The DATADICTIONARY is a database controlled by ADR's DATACOM/DB. Figure 13 shows the files in the DATADICTIONARY. Each entity type (e.g., Database, System) and support category is stored in a separate file; a separate schema file is maintained for each database. Utilities are provided to dump, recover, and load the D/D. DATADICTIONARY furnishes a software interface that creates a schema file for DATACOM/DB from the information contained in the database, area, file, key, and element entity types. DATADICTIONARY operates in a variety

(a)
```
CONVERT COBOL FROM PROGRAM1
ITEM-OVERRIDE
USING ENTERED-AS
STARTING WHEN LINE = 100
DROPPING '-IN' WHEN ANY = 'IN'
REPLACING 'MAST' WITH 'INVENTORY-MASTER-'
```

(b)
```
PRINT OF STOCKDATE
ITEM
ENTERED AS
NUMERIC-CHARACTER       6
END OF PRINT

PRINT OF STOCKPLACE
ITEM
ENTERED AS
ALPHANUMERIC           24
END OF PRINT

PRINT OF STOCKVALUE
ENTERED AS
BINARY     1.2
END OF PRINT

PRINT OF INVENTORY-MASTER-RECORD
ENTERED AS
CONTAINS       STOCKDATE
               STOCKPLACE
               STOCKVALUE     ALIGNED
END OF PRINT
```

**Figure 12.** DATAMANAGER Convert example: (a) DATAMANAGER command; (b) partial transaction listing. (Revised from MSP80b.)

of on-line environments and interfaces with DATACOM/DC, CICS, and ROSCOE [APPL79a, APPL79b].

Cincom's TIS DIRECTORY exhibits the embedded approach to environmental dependency. The DIRECTORY is the controlling element for the other components in a Cincom Total Information System (TIS) that includes a database manager (DBM), a query processor, a report writer, and a TP monitor. The DIRECTORY database is the system's only source of metadata for information about databases, users, queries, and reports. The DIRECTORY is a standard TIS database with two master files and three variable files.

Access to the TIS DIRECTORY by all TIS components except the utilities occurs via high-level directory-interface commands. Figure 14 illustrates this process. A component such as the query processor issues requests, for example, to access an element or to validate a user's access privileges. These requests are received by the DBM Control Program and routed to the Directory Interface Manager (DIM), which interprets the requests and calls the appropriate DBM functions, such as to read a record. The DBM function accesses the stored TIS DIRECTORY via a standard access method of the operating system. The DIM is an embedded component of the DBM [CINC80].

## 3. D/D SYSTEMS IN THE DISTRIBUTED ENVIRONMENT

Thus far we have been addressing the roles and structures of D/D Systems in centralized environments. In this section, we consider the design and function of D/D Sys-

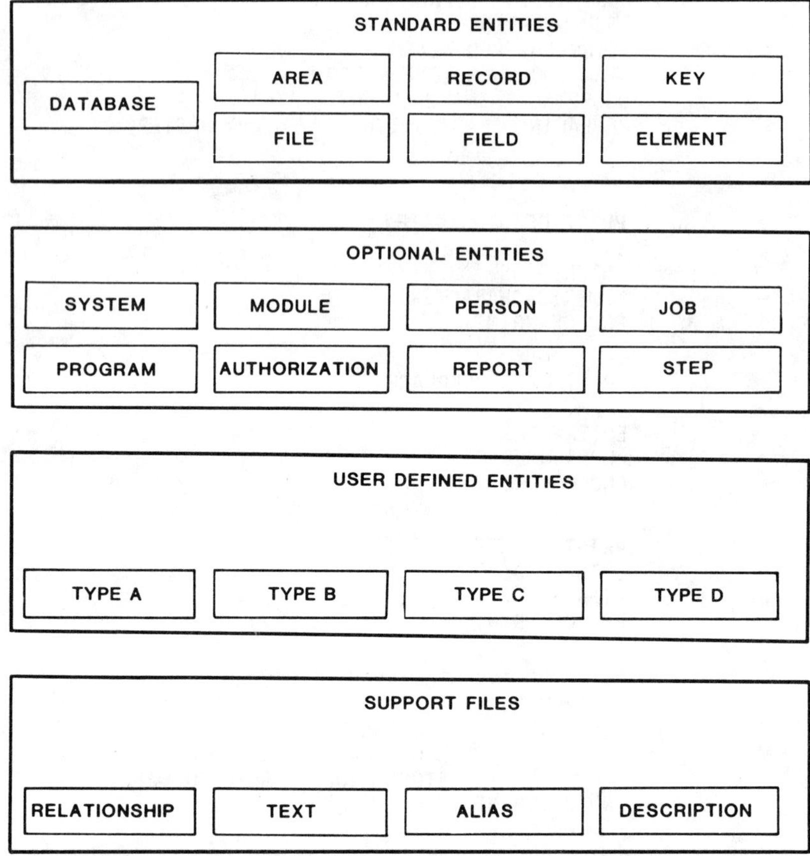


**Figure 13.** Files in the DATADICTIONARY database. (From APPL79b. Reprinted with permission of Applied Data Research, Inc.)

tems in the distributed database environment. Section 3.1 establishes a common framework for discussion of distributed DBMS (DDBMS) and distributed D/D Systems. Section 3.2 proposes extensions to the centralized D/D to enable it to function effectively in a distributed environment. Section 3.3 discusses additional software interfaces that need to be provided by a distributed D/D System, and Section 3.4 considers the D/D as a distributed database. Section 3.5 reviews one commercial D/D System that is integrated with a DDBMS.

### 3.1 Distributed Data Management

A distributed database is a consistent, logically interrelated collection of data stored at dispersed locations. The major advantages of distributing rather than centralizing a database are potential for improved performance, increased reliability, and easier incremental growth. Performance may improve because of reduced communication volumes, smaller transmission delays, and less congestion. Reliability may increase because the entire database is not rendered inaccessible when one of the networked computers fails. Incremental growth may be easier because a new node can be added without incurring excessive down times. A distributed database is particularly useful to applications that involve extensive processing in different locations. Such applications include the airlines, banking, retail, and military command and control [ROTH77].

A distributed database can be allocated among the nodes of a network according to

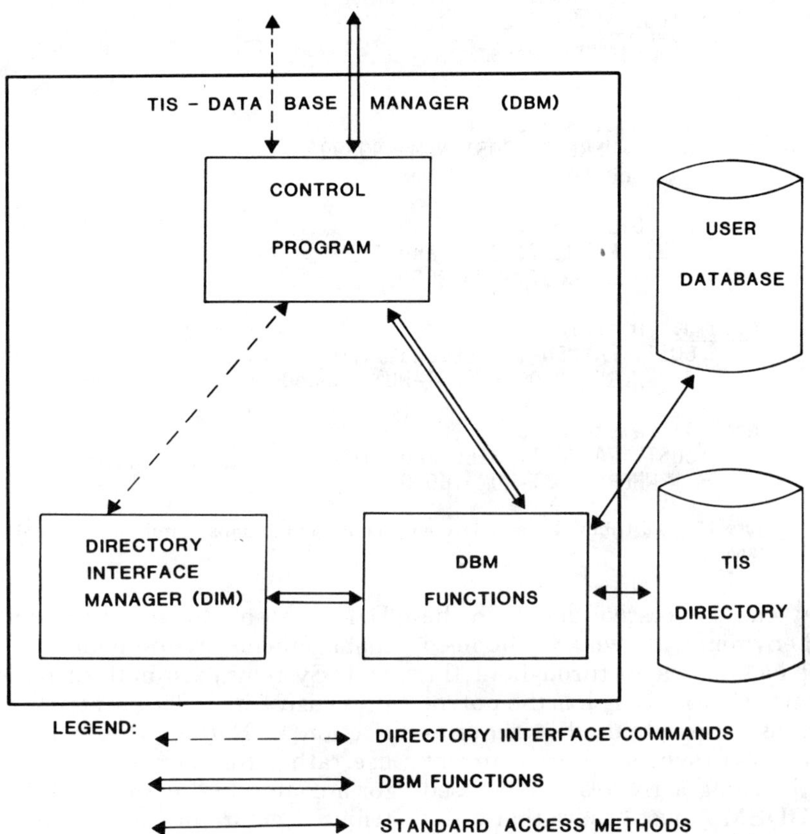


**Figure 14.** TIS Database Manager component. (From CINC80. Adapted with permission of Cincom Systems, Inc.)

various criteria for fragmentation. A distinction is useful between a *partitioned* database, which consists of nonoverlapping subsets, and a *replicated* database, which has some data redundancy. Replication may enhance the availability and locality of the database, but it requires that the DDBMS provide more sophisticated concurrency and recovery procedures. It may be reasonable to prohibit or severely restrict data replication in an effort to control data management overhead.

Figure 15 shows an example of fragmentation criteria in a distributed Customer Credit database on four nodes. The global database contains four relations: CUST, PAYMENT, BILL, and ITEM. These data are allocated such that CUST is completely stored at node 1; CUST, PAYMENT, BILL, and ITEM data are allocated over nodes 2, 3, and 4 according to a CUST–NUM criterion. The local databases in this example are restrictions of the global database by tuples (i.e., rows). The global database instead could be split by projections (i.e., by columns). For example, a local database might contain the relation CUST–NUM, CUST–NAME, and CUST–ADDR, which is a projection of the CUST relation.

The major problems in development of good techniques for managing a distributed database are due to communication volumes and delays and to potential for parallel processing. Communication requirements may cause some centralized database management solutions to work poorly in the distributed environment. For example, the traditional use of locks by a centralized

```
(a)  CUST (CUST-NUM, CUST-NAME, CUST-ADDR, CUST-DATA, CUST-LIMIT)
     PAYMENT (CUST-NUM, PAYDATE, PAYAMT)
     BILL  (CUST-NUM, BILL-DATE, BILL-AMT)
     ITEM  (CUST-NUM, BILL-DATE, ITEM-NUM, ITEM-AMT, ITEM-DESC)


(b)  Node 1:  National Office
          CUST WHERE 0 < CUST-NUM < 99999
          (All customers)

     Node 2:  District 1
          CUST, PAYMENT, BILL and ITEM
             WHERE CUST-NUM < 30000

     Node 3:  District 2
          CUST, PAYMENT, BILL and ITEM
             WHERE 30000 ≤ CUST-NUM ≤ 60000

     Node 4:  District 3
          CUST, PAYMENT, BILL and ITEM
             WHERE CUST-NUM < 60000
```

**Figure 15.** Distributed customer credit database: (a) global database; (b) local databases.

DBMS may cause excessive delays in the distributed environment owing to the need to transmit lock messages throughout the network. Parallel processing has the potential to increase throughput, but requires complex controls to synchronize concurrent reading and writing activities at dispersed sites. The DDBMS must ensure that operations executed in parallel have the same net effect on the database as an equivalent set of serially executing transactions.

There are five basic problems that must be addressed in distributed data management: (1) coordination of the DDBMS with the data transmission network such that reliable delivery of messages can be ensured; (2) decomposition of transactions into atomic parts, selection of nodes to execute those parts, and control of any movement of data between sites necessary to process transactions; (3) synchronization of logically related updates and retrievals that are processed at different nodes; (4) detection and resolution of conditions where a part of the database becomes inaccessible due to node or line failure; and (5) management of metadata describing the distributed database and environment. It is on the last problem that we focus our attentions here.

First, we consider the D/D of the distributed environment; later we discuss the full D/D System. In present distributed data management environments, no distributed D/D Systems exist in the sense of the comprehensive metadata systems described in Section 2. Rather, the available DBMSs use rather rudimentary D/Ds. A proposal for a comprehensive D/D System in a distributed environment can be found in papers by Martella and Schreiber [SCHR79, SCHR80].

Before considering extensions to these basic directories that are necessary for evolution to distributed D/D Systems, we give an example of the role of a D/D in transaction processing for the distributed database described in Figure 15. Consider the following query:

```
SELECT ITEM-NUM, ITEM-AMT,
        ITEM-DESC,
        AND CUST-LIMIT
  WHERE CUST-NUM = (28150 OR 55560)
    AND BILL-DATE = "3/26/82"
```

Assume that the query originates at node 1. The query is parsed at node 1 into a tokenized form. Because the query cannot be processed by the part of the database stored at node 1 (note ITEM information is only at nodes 2, 3, and 4), some parts of the query need to be handled remotely. If there is a directory stored at node 1 of what data are stored where, the transaction man-

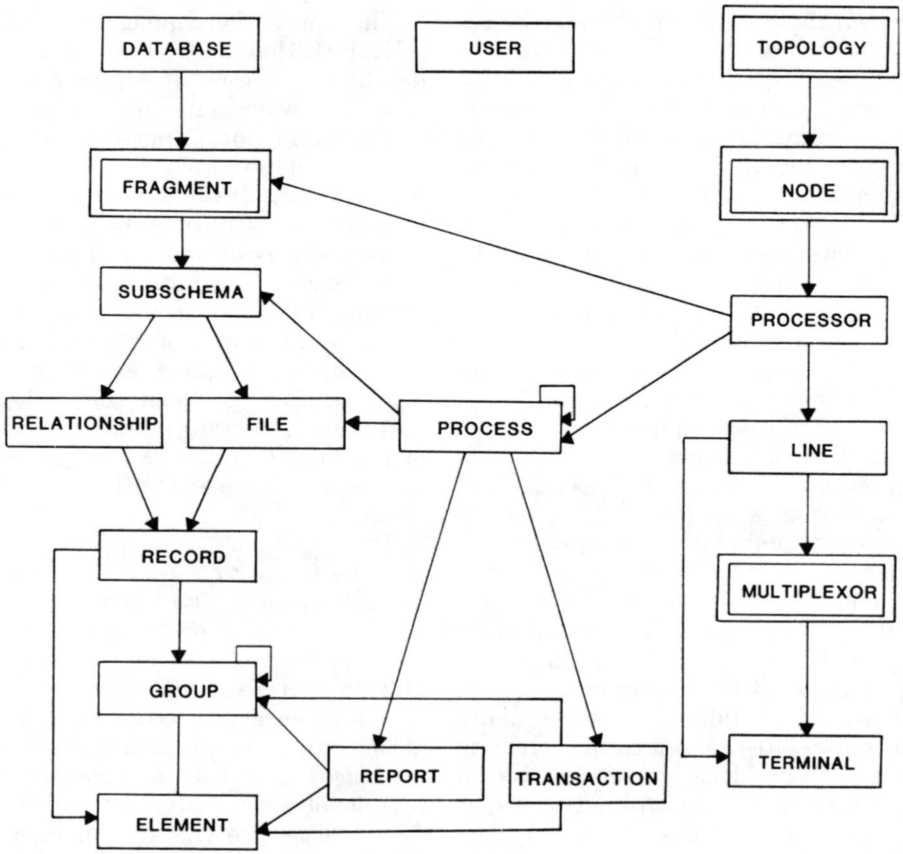


**Figure 16.** Logical structure of a D/D in a distributed database environment. Note: Entities in double boxes are additions to the D/D of Figure 1.

ager can match the WHERE clause restrictions of the query and the fragmentation criteria of the database, and determine that data are needed that are stored at nodes 2 and 3. The Query Processor could either request that the entire ITEM relation at nodes 2 and 3 be shipped to node 1, or that nodes 2 and 3 select the qualifying ITEM-tuples and send them to node 1. Of course, any conflicting demands on resources would have to be resolved and it would have to be ensured that no partially updated data are accessed.

Thus the D/D plays a significant role in transaction management. It is used to determine where data are located, to plan transaction execution strategies, to coordinate multiple-site updates, and to ensure adherence to validity and security criteria. In the distributed environment, the D/D itself becomes a distributed database; we investigate this idea further in Section 3.4.

### 3.2 Extensions to the D/D

Understanding of the significant role of the D/D in a distributed database environment suggests that the D/D should contain metadata describing the database distribution, the characteristics of the nodes, and some aspects of the data communications network. Figure 16 depicts the logical structure of a hypothetical D/D in a distributed database environment. There are four entity types that did not appear in the logical structure of a typical D/D in the centralized environment (Figure 1); four entity types are enhanced. The terminology used here is for a distributed database that uses the relational model.

The *Database* entity in the distributed environment describes the global view of the database. This entity includes attributes for relation and attribute names, validity constraints such as length, type, and dependency requirements, and the identification of local databases.

A *Fragment* entity describes portions of the local databases. The entity includes the names of relations and attributes and the fragmentation criteria. It may also include population estimates and the numbers of occurrences within ranges of attribute values. These size estimates are useful in optimization of transaction handling.

A *Topology* entity describes the physical configuration of network components and the links between nodes. A *Node* entity describes the combination of network subcomponents at a particular site of the network. The *Terminal, Line, Multiplexor,* and *Processor* entities include common attributes that describe a network design. For example, a cost attribute specifies a cost per month or a cost table. An error attribute records error statistics. A location attribute specifies a physical location, for example, in terms of standard map coordinates. A reliability attribute includes the mean time between failures and the mean time between repairs [BRAC80].

### 3.3 Enhancements to the D/D System

The contents and structure of a D/D must be altered to reflect the distributed environment. The software interface capabilities of a D/D System must also be enhanced to function effectively with distributed data management systems. The distributed D/D should interface with the DDBMS's DDL Processor, its transaction management routines, and its control functions, as well as with various design aids for the distributed environment.

The DDL of a DDBMS may include specification of both global and local schemata, and requires some additional clauses over a centralized DDL. The D/D System may interface with the DDBMS DDL Processor in an indirect way by generation of files of DDL statements or in a more active way by responding directly to interface commands from the DDL Processor.

The transaction management routines of a DDBMS handle both nonlocal and local database requests. We have already seen that when processing nonlocal requests, the transaction manager needs to reference the D/D to determine (1) the location of needed data; (2) the access privileges associated with users of remote data; (3) the current status of addressed nodes; (4) the user's view of remote data; and (5) the number of data occurrences at remote nodes. The last type of information is useful in planning the query execution strategy. The interface between the D/D System and the transaction management routines of the DDBMS can be dynamic or static, just as we discussed for the centralized environment.

The D/D may also contain metadata that are useful to the DDBMS transaction control routines. The distributed D/D System should facilitate this interface and enable the control routines to reference the D/D to determine data locations and to assess a transaction's concurrency and synchronization requirements. This software interface may be implemented through high-level commands, but the need for efficient access to this concurrency control information suggests that the interface be implemented by file extraction from the D/D. This type of interface is similar to the one used in Computer Corporation of America's developmental SDD-1 [ROTH80a] DDBMS. SDD-1 modularizes the transaction control data as a file separate from other directory-oriented information.

There is an evident need for a D/D System to provide software interfaces to various distributed database design packages. However, work on these design aids is still primarily in the research phase. The complex interactions of factors in the distributed environment make development of realistic design aids difficult. It appears that the D/D could be a useful resource to support these design tools.

### 3.4 The D/D as a Distributed Database

The D/D in the distributed environment itself becomes a distributed database. Contents of the D/D may reside at various locations; replication of parts of the D/D across nodes may or may not be desirable, depending upon characteristics of its usage. Thus the designer of the distributed D/D encounters the same basic problems as does the designer of a distributed database. Additionally, the designer must determine the appropriate extent of environmental dependency between the D/D and the DDBMS. As in the centralized environment, the distributed environment exhibits three basic variations to the type of relationship between a D/D System and a DDBMS: (1) Independent Distributed, (2) DDBMS-Application, and (3) Embedded Distributed. In the *independent distributed* approach, the D/D System vendormust develop any distributed capabilities of the D/D System. The distributed D/D has no run-time connections to any portions of the DDBMS, and hence is not actively or directly used in transaction processing by the DDBMS.

In the *DDBMS-application* approach, the D/D is just another distributed database to the DDBMS, and so the D/D System vendor does not need to develop separate data management functions to handle the distributed D/D. For performance reasons the DDBMS may manage its own run-time directory that is separate from the D/D. The location and size of the D/D would then have no effect on the transaction handling performance of the DDBMS.

In the *embedded distributed* approach, the D/D provides the run-time directory for the DDBMS. All the components of the DDBMS would obtain their metadata from the D/D. Because of the close ties between the D/D System and DDBMS, the size and location of D/D fragments would have significant effects on the performance of the DDBMS. The D/D size, location, and content also would affect the performance of other D/D System functions such as D/D maintenance, reporting, and query.

### 3.5 State of the Art

Until recently, most development in the distributed database area was directed toward solution of difficult control problems such as synchronizing distributed updates. Results from prototype systems such as SDD-1 [ROTH80b] and distributed INGRES [NEUH77] are leading to the viability of commercially available DDBMSs. Many vendors will undoubtedly integrate their D/D Systems with their new distributed data management capabilities. We survey the DATACOM/D-NET System from Applied Data Research here as an example in the context of the framework used in the rest of this paper.

The software components that participate in this DDBMS are shown in Figure 17. D-NET is the controlling module and is located at each node of the network. D-NET performs the following functions: (1) interception of all data requests and determination of whether the data are locally or remotely available; (2) verification of the accessibility of remote data; (3) routing of requests to remote nodes; (4) control of transactions; and (5) recovery of portions of the database in case of problems. D-NET interacts with the other pictured components to accomplish these functions. These other ADR systems are resident at each node where their functions are required. For example, the DBMS DATACOM/DB is necessary at any node with a local database, and the Teleprocessing (TP) monitor is required at any node with connected terminals [MILL80].

Two types of D/Ds exist in this distributed environment, one for D-NET use and one for DATACOM/DB use. Each local DATACOM/DB DBMS maintains a D/D (called a Database Control File) describing the local database and processes transactions that it receives from D-NET just as if D-NET were a user in the centralized environment. Each copy of D-NET utilizes a DATADICTIONARY database. Recall that DATADICTIONARY was one of the example D/D Systems covered in Section 2. DATADICTIONARY describes one logical network location, including attributes such as the site identifier, communications capabilities, and database fragmentation criteria.

Three alternatives are possible for locating the DATADICTIONARY D/D in a D-NET environment. In the *local* approach, each site contains its own partition of the D/D; there is no replication across nodes.

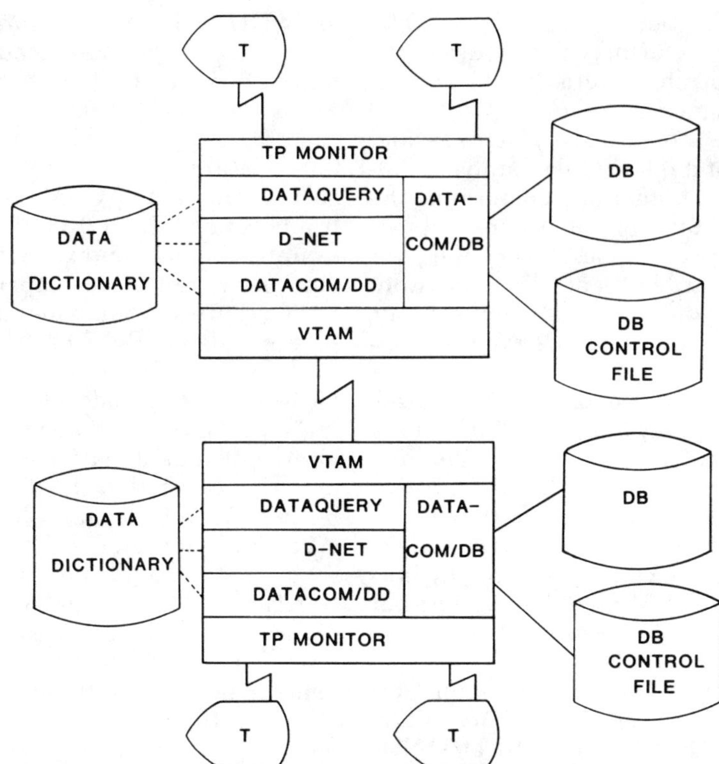


**Figure 17.** D-NET environment. Note: DATAQUERY, D-NET, and DATACOM/DD logically access the DATADICTIONARY database. DATACOM/DB performs the physical accesses. (From MILL80. Reprinted with permission of Applied Data Research, Inc.)

In the *central* approach, a master D/D is constructed that contains all the metadata for the global database. This D/D can be located at a single site or can be replicated at multiple sites. In the *hybrid* approach, any combination of master, local, and partially replicated D/Ds that reflect overlapping metadata can exist [SLOA81].

D-NET interacts with its DATADICTIONARY D/D in three situations: (1) node initiation, (2) transaction initiation, and (3) D/D update. During the initiation of a node, D-NET constructs a local in-core directory that contains the identification of all participating nodes and databases and reduces access to the D/D for skeletal details about the network. Transaction initiation causes an access to the appropriate node's DATADICTIONARY for more detailed information, for example, about the descriptions of fields within a record. If the local D/D cannot provide this information, or if a local D/D does not exist, then D-NET routes the request to another node either by broadcasting the request to all nodes or by sending the request to a specific node based upon knowledge of fragmentation criteria. Update of a local DATADICTIONARY affects only one site. Update of a master or hybrid DATADICTIONARY must be reflected in all copies containing affected data [SLOA81].

## 4. CONCLUSIONS AND FUTURE DIRECTIONS

D/D Systems will play increasingly important roles in tomorrow's information resource management environments.

Integrated D/D Systems thus have important roles in controlling both centralized and distributed information resources. The benefits of a D/D System include increased control over the data, reduced cost and time requirements for application development, and enhanced independence of metadata across computing environments. However, the effective use of a D/D System depends on a strong data administration commitment. Typically, a data administration group needs several years of experience before being able to use a D/D System effectively. The data administration group must have the support of top management in the form of a corporate charter, as well as high visibility in the organization. This support is difficult to obtain in many organizations. Application of a D/D System is facilitated when standards are already fully in place, for example, standards pertaining to names, change control, program logic, and system design.

Even with a strong organizational commitment, an organization faces difficulties because of the limitations of commercially available D/D Systems. The command languages of most D/D Systems are not suitable interfaces for most users. Many organizations are clamoring for interfaces that a naive user can easily grasp. Organizations also are requesting more support from D/D Systems for system development methodologies [CURT81b]. Few D/D Systems today provide the reports, consistency checks, and graphics capability required by the commonly used methodologies for systems design and development.

In the near future, development in eight related areas seems likely.

(1) Vendors will release distributed DBMSs that are connected to their D/D Systems. Independent vendors will upgrade their D/D Systems to interface statically with other vendors' DDBMSs.
(2) D/D Systems will support the prevalent systems' development methodologies via graphics and enhanced reporting and control features.
(3) Improved interfaces will be developed to accommodate naive users.
(4) D/D Systems will evolve to support a DBMS-independent view of the information resource.
(5) Design aids and performance evaluation software will interface with D/D Systems.
(6) Standards for D/D Systems will emerge.
(7) D/D Systems will have the ability to manage multiple D/D.
(8) Vendors will develop D/D Systems for use on small computers, and D/D System functions will migrate into operating systems of some of the small machines.

## APPENDIX. COMMERCIAL D/D SYSTEMS

### Explanation of Chart Elements (Tables 4–9)

The charts (Tables 4-9, pages 276-286) contain selected facts about existing D/D Systems that are designed for large mainframes. Each vendor verified the enclosed information. Where applicable, the most recent commercial developments (prior to July, 1982) are listed in the Comment column of Table 4 (Basic Facts chart).

#### *Basic Facts (Table 4)*

(1) System: Name of the D/D System.
(2) Vendor: Name of firm that developed the D/D System.
(3) First release: First year of commercial availability.
(4) Installations: Vendor's estimate of current installations.
(5) Other product types: Other software packages provided by the vendor. Complete product line means that the vendor offers most of the software packages defined in Section 2.3. Also, whether the vendor also offers a DBMS.
(6) Comments: Miscellaneous remarks related to the D/D System's history or the vendor's plans.

#### *Architecture (Table 5)*

(1) System: Same as in Basic Facts chart (Table 4).
(2) Hardware: Manufacturer and model numbers of the hardware.
(3) Source language: Language in which the D/D System is written.
(4) Architectural dependency: Independent, DBMS-application or Embedded, as described in Section 2.1.

(5) Dependent DBMS or File Organization: DBMS or file organization required for the D/D.
(6) Comments.

*D/D Characteristics (Table 6)*

(1) System: Same as in Basic Facts chart (Table 4).
(2) Entity names: Entities furnished as part of the basic system.
(3) Extensibility: Brief description of any extensibility capability.
(4) Status capability: Status names and version numbers.
(5) Comments.

*Selected Capabilities (Table 7)*

(1) System: Same as in Basic Facts chart (Table 4).
(2) Maintenance methods: The methods to change the D/D as mentioned in Section 1.3 (keyword-driven, fixed-format transactions, prompted-tutorial input, and preformatted screens).
(3) On-line query: Availability of on-line query.
(4) Security levels: Security protection as stated by the vendor.
(5) User-defined reports: The ability to alter existing reports and to define new ones.
(6) Comments.

*Convert Functions (Table 8)*

(1) System.
(2) Source language: Languages analyzed.
(3) Entity types: Entity types created in the transactions as stated by the vendor.
(4) Detailed information: Complete or limitations in the attributes captured.
(5) Command options: Name changing, scanning, overriding (consult Section 2.2).
(6) Comments.

*Software Interfaces (Table 9)*

(1) System.
(2) Software Package: Proprietary name and function, such as DDL. Processor and preprocessor (consult Section 2.3). The function is in parentheses.
(3) Interface method: File extraction (static) or Interface commands (dynamic).
(4) Options: Options pertaining to source language generation such as syntax checking and name editing.
(5) Comments: Brief description.

## ACKNOWLEDGMENTS

We gratefully acknowledge the cooperation of representatives from all the firms listed in the Appendix. Without their help, this study would never have been possible. We especially thank TSI, Cincom Systems, Sperry-Univac, ICL, ADR, MSP, Cullinane Database Systems, and Intel for the use of their manuals, and Kathy Todd, who patiently and skillfully typed this manuscript.

This research was partially funded by Electric Power Research Institute Grant No. 1603 and NSF Grant No. MCS77-24234.

## REFERENCES

APPL79a APPLIED DATA RESEARCH, INC. *DATA-DICTIONARY User Reference Manual*, Sept. 1979.

APPL79b APPLIED DATA RESEARCH, INC. *DATA-COM/DD System Reference Manual*, 1979.

APPL80 APPLICATION SYSTEM DIVISION. "Prospectus for data dictionary system standard," NBS Special Pub. 80–2115, Washington, D.C., 1980.

BLAS81 BLASGEN, M. W., ET AL. "System R: An architectural overview," *IBM Syst. J.* **20,** 1 (1981), 41–62.

BRAC80 BRACKER, W., AND KONSYNSKI, B. "An overview of a network design system," in *Proc. AFIPS NCC Nat. Computer Conf.*, 1980, AFIPS Press, Arlington, Va., pp. 41–48.

BRYC79 M. BRYCE & ASSOCIATES. *PRIDE–Logik Information Systems Resource Manager*, Cincinnati, Ohio, 1979.

CHAM81 CHAMBERLIN, D. D., ASTRAHAN, M. M., KING, W. F., LORIES, R. A., MEHL, J. W., PRICE, T. G., SCHKOLNIK, M., GRIFFITHS SELINGER, P., SLUTZ, D. R., WADE, B. W., AND YOST, R. A. "Support for Repetitive Transactions and ad-hoc Queries in System R," *ACM Trans. Database Syst.*, **6,** 1 (March 81), 70–94.

CINC80 CINCOM SYSTEMS, INC. *TIS A Technical Overview*, Cincinnati, Ohio, 1980.

CULL78 CULLINANE DATABASE SYSTEMS, INC. *IDD User's Guide*, Westwood, Mass., 1978.

CULL80 CULLINANE DATABASE SYSTEMS, INC. *Introduction to IDD: Classroom Aids*, Westwood, Mass., 1980.

CURT81a CURTICE, R., AND DIECKMAN, E. "A survey of data dictionaries," *Datamation* **27,** 3 (March 1981), 135–158.

CURT81b CURTICE, R. "Data dictionaries: An assessment of current practice and problems," in *Proc. 7th Int. Conf. Very Large Databases* (ACM) (Cannes, France, 1981).

ELBR80 ELBRA, R., AND HARDY, N. "Cost justification of data dictionaries," *Comput. Bull.* (Sept. 1980), 12–14.

FIPS77 FIPS TASK GROUP 14C. "A Survey of Eleven Government-Developed Data Element Dictionary/Directory Systems," NBS Special Pub. 500-16, U.S. Dept. of Commerce, Washington, D.C., Aug. 1977.

IBM80 IBM, INC. *DB/DC Data Dictionary General Information Manual,* GH20-9104-3, 1980.

INTE80 INTEL CORP. "QBX, Query/Update by Example," Product Support Manual, Austin, Texas, 1980.

JOHN80a JOHNSTON, C., AND STONE, A. "Monitoring CODASYL database management systems," University of Aberdeen Computing Centre, Aberdeen, Scotland, June 1980.

JOHN80b JOHNSTON, C., AND STONE, A. Personal notes, 1980.

LEFK77 LEFKOVITS, H. *Data Dictionary Systems,* QED Information Sciences, 1977.

LEON77 LEON-HONG, B., AND MARRON, B. "Technical Profile of Seven Data Element Dictionary/Directory S tems, NBS Special Pub. 500-S, Natio Bureau of Standards, Washington, D.C., 1977.

LOMA77 LOMAX, J. "*Data dictionaries,*" National Computing Centre, Manchester, England, 1977.

MILL80 MILLSAP, E. "DATACOM/DNET: DATACOM distributed network," Product Support Bull. DNPS-80-01, Applied Data Research, Dallas, Texas, May 1980.

MSP80a MSP, LTD. "DATAMANAGER user's guide," MSP Tech. Documentation, London, England, 1980.

MSP80b MSP, LTD. "DATAMANAGER automation of setup," MSP Tech. Documentation, London, England, 1980.

MSP80c MSP, LTD. "DATAMANAGER user interface facility," MSP Technical Documentation, London, England, 1980.

NEUH77 NEUHOLD, E., AND STONEBRAKER, M. "A distributed version of INGRES," in *Proc. 2nd Workshop on Distributed Processing* (Berkeley, Calif., May 1977), National Technical Information Service, Springfield, Va., pp. 19–36.

PLAG77a PLAGMAN, B. "Criteria for the selection of data dictionary/directory systems," *Auerbach Ser. on DBMS* 22-04-01, 1977.

PLAG77b PLAGMAN, B. "Data dictionary/directory system: A tool for data administration and control." *Auerbach Ser. on DBMS* 22-01-02, 1977.

PLAG78 PLAGMAN, B., AND MOSS, C. "Alternative architectures for active data dictionary/directory systems," *Auerbach Series on DBMS* 22-04-02, 1978.

ROSS80 ROSS, R. "Data management for the 80s," *Computerworld Extra,* CW Communications, Sept. 17, 1980, pp. 36–47.

ROSS81 ROSS, R. *Data Dictionaries and Data Administration,* AMACOM, New York, 1981.

ROTH77 ROTHNIE, J., AND GOODMAN, N. "A Survey of Research and Development in Distributed Database Management," in *Proc. 3rd Int. Conf. Very Large Databases* (Tokyo, Japan, Oct. 6–8), 1977, pp. 48–62.

ROTH80 ROTHNIE, J. B., JR, BERNSTEIN, P., A., FOX, S., GOODMAN, N., HAMMER, M., LANDERS, T. A., REEVE, C., SHIPMAN, D. W., AND WONG, F. "Introduction to a System for distributed databases," *ACM Trans. Database Syst.* **5,** 1 (March 1980), 1–17.

SCHR79 SCHREIBER, F., AND MARTELLA, G. "Creating a conceptual model of a data dictionary for distributed data bases," *Database* (ACM SIGBDP) **11,** 1 (Summer 1979), 12–18.

SCHR80 SCHREIBER, F., AND MARTELLA, G. "A Data Dictionary for Distributed Databases," in *Conf. on Distributed Databases,* C. Delobel and W. Litwin (Eds.), North-Holland, New York, 1980, pp. 17–33.

SLOA81 SLOAN, K. Private communication, 1981.

TSI80a TSI. *The DATA CATALOGUE 2 System Standard Facilities Manual,* TSI International, Bedford, Mass., 1980.

TSI80b TSI. *DATA CATALOGUE 2 Examples,* TSI International, Bedford, Mass., 1980.

UHRO73 UHROWCZIK, P. "Data dictionary/directories," *IBM Syst. J.* **12,** 4 (1973), 332–350.

WILS80 WILSON, T., ED. "ANSI/X3/SPARC database systems study group—Standing paper 1," Version 1.1, Aug. 1980.

Received April 1981; final revision accepted March 1982.

**Table 4.** Basic Facts Chart

| System | Vendor | First release | Approximate users | Other products | Comments |
|---|---|---|---|---|---|
| ADABAS DATA DICTIONARY | Software AG of North America, Inc. | 1978 | 1000 | Complete product line | Revised system in development |
| DATA CATALOGUE 2 | Synergetics Corp. | 1974, 1977 | 250 | Complete product line | Early version released in 1974; completely revised system released in 1977 |
| DATA CONTROL SYSTEM | Cincom Systems, Inc. | 1976, 1980 | 130 | Complete product line | Formerly known as DATA DICTIONARY; Revised version released under current name in 1980 |
| DATA CONTROL SYSTEM (DCS) | Haverly Systems, Inc. | 1976 | 5 | Variety of software and consulting services | |
| DATA DICTIONARY SYSTEM (DDS 1100) | Sperry Univac | 1981 | 30 | Complete product line | |
| DATA DICTIONARY SYSTEM (DDS) | International Computers, Ltd. (ICL) | 1977 | 70 | Complete product line | |
| DATADICTIONARY | Applied Data Research, Inc. (ADR) | 1979 | 100 | Complete product line | |
| DATAMANAGER | Management Systems and Programming, Ltd. (MSP) | 1975 | 600 | Manager products (test data, project, source program) | |
| DB/DC DATA DICTIONARY | IBM | 1974 | N/A | Complete product line | |
| DICTIONARY/204 | Computer Corporation of America | 1982 | 35 | DBMS and related products | Completely new version released Jan. 1982 |
| EDICT | Infodata Systems, Inc. | 1976 | 150 | Complete product line | Revised system in development |
| Integrated Data Dictionary (IDD) | Cullinane Corp. | 1977 | 100 | Complete product line | |
| Integrated Data Dictionary (IDD) | Intel Corp. | 1980 | 40 | Complete product line | |
| PRIDE-Logik | M. Bryce & Associates | 1974 | 300 | PRIDE system development methodology, Design Aid | |
| TIS DIRECTORY | Cincom Systems, Inc. | 1979 | 10 | Complete product line | Integrated precompiler planned |
| UCC TEN | University Computing Center (UCC) | 1970 | 300 | Tape management, direct access management, job scheduling, and others | |

**Table 5.** Architecture

| System | Hardware[a] | Source language | DBMS–D/D System relationship | Dependent DBMS or File Organization | Comments |
|---|---|---|---|---|---|
| ADABAS DATA DICTIONARY | IBM 360, 370, 30XX, 43XX | Assembler, COBOL, NATURAL | DBMS-application | ADABAS | |
| DATA CATALOGUE 2 | IBM 360, 370, 30XX, 43XX, Univac 1100, Honeywell 66 series | COBOL | Independent | COBOL relative files | |
| DATA CONTROL SYSTEM (Cincom) | IBM 360, 370, 30XX, 43XX, NCR Century and Criterion | COBOL and MANTIS | DBMS-application | TOTAL | |
| DATA CONTROL SYSTEM (Haverly) | Univac 1100 | COBOL | DBMS-application | DMS-1100 | |
| DDS 1100 | Univac 1100 | PLUS | DBMS-application | DMS-1100 | |
| DDS | ICL 2900 | COBOL | DBMS-application | IDMS (ICL version) | |
| DATADICTIONARY | IBM 360, 370, 30XX, 43XX | Assembler | DBMS-application | DATACOM/DB | |
| DATAMANAGER | IBM 360, 370, 30XX, 43XX, FACOM M series, Siemens 7.000 | Assembler | Independent | VSAM or BDAM | |
| DB/DC DATA DICTIONARY | IBM 360, 370, 30XX, 43XX | Assembler | DBMS-application | IMS or DOS PL/I | Some modules written in compiler-level language |
| DICTIONARY/204 | IBM 360, 370, 30XX, 43XX | Model 204 user language | DMBS-application | Model 204 | |
| EDICT | IBM 360, 370, 30XX, 43XX | Primarily PL/1 | Independent or DBMS-application | Sequential File or INQUIRE DBMS | User selects the physical implementation |
| IDD (Cullinane) | IBM 360, 370, 30XX, 43XX | Assembler | DBMS-application | IDMS | |
| IDD (Intel) | IBM 360, 370, 30XX, 43XX, CDC 6000, 70, 170, Univac 1100 | Assembler | DBMS-application | System 2000/80 | |
| PRIDE/Logik | IBM 360, 370, 30XX, 43XX, Burroughs Medium and Large Systems, Honeywell Series 60 and 6000, HP-3000, CDC 6600, DEC 10, 20, and VAX, Univac 1100, ICL 1903, Cyber 175, Prime 750 | COBOL | Independent | COBOL relative files | |
| TIS DIRECTORY | IBM 360, 370, 30XX, 43XX | Assembler | Embedded | TIS-DBM | |
| UCC TEN | IBM 360, 370, 30XX, 43XX | 90% COBOL, 10% Assembler | DBMS-application | IMS HIDAM databases | |

[a] IMB plug-compatible mainframes are not listed.

**Table 6.** D/D Characteristics

| System | Entity names | Extensibility | Status capability | Comments |
|---|---|---|---|---|
| ADABAS DATA DICTIONARY | Fields, relationships, files, databases, field verification procedures, owners/users, programs, modules, systems, reports, response codes, user views | Define additional entities, attributes, and relationships | No status codes or version numbers | Status capability via separate D/Ds; Extensibility via changes to the D/D schema |
| DATA CATALOGUE 2 | Element, Group, Record, File, Form, Task, Resource, Report, Module, System, User | Define additional entities, relationships, and attributes | Status codes (Existing, Proposed, Obsolete, and user defined) and version numbers | Additional entities used with IMS, TOTAL, ADABAS, DMS, OMS-1100 S2000/80, and IDMS |
| DATA CONTROL SYSTEM (Cincom) | User, Report, Program, System, Source Document, Element, File, Data Base, Transaction, Physical Logical Element | Additional entities, attributes, and relationships supported through MANIS | Test and production versions for the program and system entities | Entity support for structured analysis planned |
| DATA CONTROL SYSTEM (Haverly) | Schema, Set, Area, Record, Field, Program, Subschema | Additional attributes | None | |
| DDS 1100 | Module, Run unit, DBA, Analyst, Application Schema, Subschema, Area, Record, Group, Data-Item, Data-Name, Set, Database-Procedures, Run stream, File, Record-Relation | Define additional entities, relationships, and attributes | Status codes (Proposed, Test, All, Approved, Active, and Obsolete) and versions (Test, Training, Production, All, and user defined) | |
| DDS | Entity, Relationship, Attribute, File, Virtual File, Record, Group, Item, Operation, Event, System, Program, Module, PMAP, DMAP, DUSE, Area, Schema, Subschema, Set | None | Status codes (Operational and user defined) and version numbers | Conceptual and implementation entities |
| DATADICTIONARY | Database, Area, File, Key, Element, Record, System, Person, Authorization, Job, Step, Module, Program, Report | Define additional entities, relationships, and attributes | Status codes (Test, Production, and History) and version numbers | |
| DATAMANAGER | System, Program, Module, Database, File, Group, Item, Segment, PCB | Three additional entity structures supported; additional entity types, relationships, and attributes based on existing ones | Version numbers; status facility allows partitioning by time, project, status, etc. | Additional entity types for each DBMS it supports |
| DB/DC DATA DICTIONARY | Database, Segment, Element, PCB, SYSDEF, System, Job, Program, Module, Transaction, PSB, DDUSER | Define additional entities, relationships, and attributes | Status codes (Test, Production, Installed, and user defined) | |

| | | | | |
|---|---|---|---|---|
| DICTIONARY/204 | File, Group, Record, Field, Procedure | Define additional entity types, relationships, and attributes | None | |
| EDICT | Element, Database | None | None | |
| IDD (Cullinane) | Basic Entities: User, System, Program, Entry Point, Module, Element, Record, File, TP Entities: Task, Queue, Map, Panel, Line, Physical Terminal, Logical–Terminal, Destination, Message | Define new attributes; full extensibility planned | Status codes (Test, Production, and Historic) and version numbers | |
| IDD (Intel) | Application, Work Unit, Program, File, Work Area, Work Structure, Data Base, Schema, Subschema, Item, User | Define additional entities, attributes, and relationships; some reporting not applicable | Status codes (Production, Test, Obsolete, Development, and Load) and version numbers | |
| PRIDE-Logik | System, Subsystem, Procedures, Programs, Modules, Files, Inputs, Outputs, Call Arguments, Records, Data Elements | None | One status for each of nine development phases, modification, improvement, active | All metadata relates to the PRIDE methodology |
| TIS DIRECTORY | System Data: Component, Edit Mask, Reserved Word, Translate Table; Schema Data: Environment, Buffer Pool, File, Environment File, Internal Record, Physical Field, Subschema, Access Set, External Field, User Data: User, Procedure, Expression Equation | None | User-defined statuses | |
| UCC TEN | Database, Shared Secondary Index, Data Set Group, Index Data Field, Segment, Index Data Field List, LChild, Field, PSB, Application, Job, Program, Module, and 21 more for message formatting and communications | None | Test and Production status with 256 sides | Metadata that describes an environment with IMS/DC, MFS, and ADF |

**Table 7.** Selected Capabilities

| System | Maintenance methods | On-line query | Security levels | User-defined reports | Comments |
|---|---|---|---|---|---|
| ADABAS DATA DICTIONARY | Fixed format, preformatted screens | Yes | Entity, attribute, attribute value, and function (read and write) | Via NATURAL | NATURAL is a program development facility. |
| DATA CATALOGUE 2 | Keyword driven, prompted-tutorial input, preformatted screens | Yes | Entity type and command | Customization via macro routines; additional reports via call and file extraction capabilities | New reports require user software. |
| DATA CONTROL SYSTEM (Cincom) | Preformatted screens | Yes | Passwords for Element entity occurrences, user password profiles | Through the Socrates report writer | |
| DATA CONTROL SYSTEM (Haverly) | Fixed format | Yes via QLP (Sperry-Univac product) | None | Report options | |
| DDS 1100 | Keyword driven | Yes via QLP | Command and entity occurrence | Via QLP | |
| DDS | Keyword driven | Yes | Entity type, function, user, and operational status | Report options via the SELECT clause | |
| DATADICTION-ARY | Fixed format | Yes | Entity occurrence | Through DATAREPORTER | |
| DATAMANAGER | Keyword driven | Yes | D/D creation, sign on, commands, user, and entity | Customization via macro routines; additional reports via Call and File Extraction capabilities | New reports rely on the User-Interface facility. |
| DB/DC DATA DICTIONARY | Keyword driven, preformatted screens | Yes | Sign on, status, and entity type | Via GIS | |
| DICTIONARY/204 | Fixed screens | Yes | Login | Via User Language | Security levels planned |
| EDICT | Fixed format | Yes | Entity type and others via user-defined security routine | Via the User-Defined Language | |
| IDD (Cullinane) | Keyword driven, fixed and variable screens | Yes | User view and record level | Customization through changing of parameters; new reports via CULPRIT | |
| IDD (Intel) | Keyword driven, preformatted screens | Yes | Element entity and command | Via Report Writer | |
| PRIDE-Logik | Keyword driven, fixed format and fixed screens | Yes | Function, entity type | Via Extract facility | |
| TIS DIRECTORY | Preformatted screens | Yes | Command | Via Comprehensive Retrieval Component | |
| UCC TEN | Fixed format, preformatted screens | Yes | Command | Report parameters | Additional security can be added via security tables. |

**Table 8.** Convert Functions

| System | Source language | Entity types | Detailed information | Command options | Comments |
|---|---|---|---|---|---|
| ADABAS DATA DICTIONARY | 1. Loader definitions (database description) | 1. File, Fields | 1. Complete | 1. None | |
| DATA CATALOGUE 2 | 1. COBOL | 1. Element, Group, Record, File, Program | All complete | 1. Renaming, deleting prefixes, selecting transactions, including comments | 1. Source program input |
| | 2. DBD and PSB of IMS and DDL of DMS-1100 | 2. Database, Segments, Fields, LChilds, XDFields | | 2. Rename, including comments | |
| DATA CONTROL SYSTEM (Cincom) | 1. COBOL/COBOL-XT | 1. Program Database, File | 1. Identifies identity occurrences only | 1. None | 1. Element must previously exist in the D/D. |
| | 2. DDL of TOTAL | 2. Database, File, Element | 2. Identifies identity occurrences only | 2. Rename | |
| | 3. SOCRATE Dictionary | 3. Element | 3. Integrates the report and data dictionaries | 3. None | |
| DATA CONTROL SYSTEM (Haverly) | 1. DDL of DMS-1100 | 1. Schema, Set, Area, Record, Field | 1. Complete | 1. None | |
| | 2. COBOL with Schema section | 2. Program | 2. All the information about the schema usage | 2. None | |
| DATADICTION-ARY | 1. COBOL | 1. File, Record, Field, Element | 1. Complete | 1. Renaming | 1. Library file input |
| DATAMANAGER | 1. COBOL, PL/I | 1. File, Group, Item | 1. Complete except for selected PL/I clauses | 1. Replace, Insert, Delete, Line Scanning, Override | 1. Source program input; no File definitions for PL/I |
| DB/DC | 1. COBOL, PL/I | 1. SEGMENTS, ELEMENTS | 1. Complete except for certain PL/I clauses | 1. None | 1. Library file input |
| | 2. DBD, PSB of IMS | 2. Element, Segment, PSB, PCB | 2. Complete | 2. None | |

*(continued)*

| | | | | | |
|---|---|---|---|---|---|
| DICTIONARY/204 | 1. Model 204 files | 1. File, Procedure, Field | 1. Complete | 1. None | 1. Directly updates the dictionary |
| IDD (Cullinane) | 1. COBOL, PL/I | 1. Record, Element | 1. Complete except for some PL/I clauses | 1. None | 1. Library file input |
| TIS DIRECTORY | 1. DDL of TOTAL | 1. File, Internal Record, Physical Field | 1. Complete | | 1. Facilitates conversion from TOTAL to TIS |
| UCC TEN | 1. COBOL, PL/I | 1. Segment, Field, Program | 1. All are complete | None | 1. Automatically computes an 8-character D/D name; library file input |
| | 2. DBD and PSB of IMS | 2. Data Base, Segment, Field, PSB, LChild | | | |
| | 3. MFS Macro | 3. Field, Device Page, Division, Device, Format, Table, Message, If, Logical Page, Message Segment, Message Password | | | |
| | 4. Stage 1 Sysgen | 4. Logical Terminal, Physical Terminal, Pool, Idlist, Control Unit, Station, Type, Line, Line Group, Configuration | | | |
| | 5. ADF (Application Development Facility) | 5. ADF system, Segment, Field, Transaction, Screen Image | | | |

**Table 9.** Software Interfaces

| System | Software package | Interface method | Options | Comments |
|---|---|---|---|---|
| ADABAS DATA DICTIONARY | 1. COBOL, PL/I, Assembler | 1. File extraction | 1. Prefixes, alternate functions, sequence numbers | 1. File definitions and JCL for library update |
| | 2. ADAWAN (DDL Processor) | 2. File extraction | 2. None | 2. File and field definitions for ADABAS |
| | 3. ADAMINT (Preprocessor) | 3. File extraction | 3. None | 3. File definitions |
| | 4. ADASCRIPT (Query Processor), ADACOM (Report Writer), NATURAL | 4. File extraction | 4. None | 4. Data definition modules (Files, Fields) |
| DATA CATALOGUE 2 | 1. COBOL, PL/1 | 1. File extraction | 1. Prefix, suffix, level numbers, sequence numbers, and line identifier, include comments and initial values | 1. File and Record descriptions |
| | 2. IMS, TOTAL, ADABAS, IDMS, DMS-1100, IDS II, MARK IV (DDL Processors) | 2. File extraction | | 2. Schema and Subschema definitions |
| DATA CONTROL SYSTEM (Cincom) | 1. TOTAL (DDL Processor) | 1. File extraction | | 1. DDL input for DBGEN |
| | 2. COBOL | 2. File extraction | | 2. COBOL DATA DIVISION and some PROCEDURE logic |
| | | | | 3. More direct interaction if used with other Cincom products |
| DDS 1100 | 1. DMS-1100 (DDL Processor) | 1. Interface commands | | 1. Add the database and subschema structure to the D/D |
| | 2. DMLP (Preprocessor) | 2. Interface commands | | 2. Add the Run-Unit-Subschema relationship and entities |
| DDS | 1. IDMS (DDL Processor) | 1. File extraction | 1. For both functions: renaming capability, syntactic check on names, inclusion of comments, initial values, and condition names, and prefix and suffix capability; other options with DDL generation | 1. Schema, Subschema, and virtual file translation |
| | 2. COBOL | 2. File extraction | | 2. File descriptions inserted into the source code |
| | 3. COBOL programs | 3. Dynamic | | 3. Retrieve entity occurrences via a CALL statement |
| DATADICTIONARY | 1. DATACOM/DB (DDL Processor) | 1. File extraction | | 1. Database control file |

(*continued*)

Table 9 continued

| System | Software package | Interface method | Options | Comments |
|---|---|---|---|---|
| | 2. DATAREPORTER (Report Writer) and COBOL | 2. File extraction | 2. Include comments | 2. File description |
| | 3. DATAQUERY (Query Processor) | 3. Interface commands | | 3. User views, logical to physical mapping |
| | 4. DATACOM/DL (Preprocessor) | 4. Interface commands | | 4. Extract user views and restrict access to views |
| | 5. LIBRARIAN | 5. Interface commands | | 5. Extract data descriptions, add the data compiled to the D/D, and restrict access to data definitions |
| DATAMANAGER | 1. COBOL, PL/I, assembler | 1. File extraction | 1. Replace, delete, and insert editing options, include comments, initial values, and condition names | 1. File and record descriptions |
| | 2. ADABAS, IDMS, IMS, S2000, PL/I, TOTAL (DDL Processors)' | 2. File extraction | | 2. Database and Subschema descriptions |
| | 3. Methodology interface | 3. Interface commands | | 3. Activate DATAMANAGER commands via the User Interface facility |
| DB/DC DATA DICTIONARY | 1. COBOL, PL/1, Assembler Mark IV | 1. File extraction | 1. Prefix, suffix, level numbers, and include comments | 1. File and record descriptions |
| | 2. IMS (DDL Processor) | 2. File extraction | 2. Segment lengths and field start positions recalculated via the RECALCULATE-SEGMENT function | 2. DBD, PSB, and partial macro for Stage 1 Sysgen |
| | 3. DBDA (Design Aid) | 3. Interface commands | | 3. Receives database specifications and stores the design results |
| | 4. GIS (Report Writer) | 4. File extraction | | 4. DDT (Data Description Table) |
| | 5. Other software | 5. Interface | | 5. Activate certain retrieval commands via the Program Access facility |
| EDICT | 1. INQUIRE (DDL Processor) | 1. File extraction | | 1. Create a Data Definition Table |
| IDD (Cullinane) | 1. IDMS (DDL Processor) | Interface commands for all | | 1. Generate database descriptions, record schema compilations |
| | 2. DML Processor (Preprocessor) | | | 2. Generate Subschema, file, and record descriptions; update the D/D with compile date, number of compiles, estimated lines, file and subschema usage, and modules called |

*(continued)*

| | | | | |
|---|---|---|---|---|
| IDD (Cullinane) (*continued*) | 3. CULPRIT (Report Writer) | | | 3. Extract and save report parameters |
| | 4. OLQ (Query Processor) | | | 4. Extract and save queries, retrieve access privileges |
| | 5. IDMS-DC (TP Monitor) | | | 5. Generate IDMS-DC control file, retrieves error messages at run time |
| IDD (Intel) | 1. SYSTEM 2000/80 (DDL Processor) | 1. File extraction | | 1. Database description |
| | 2. COBOL and COBOL PLEX (Preprocessor) | 2. File extraction | 2. Sort the generated data descriptions, select structures within views, renaming | 2. File, record, subschema, and logical views |
| | 3. QUBE (Query Processor) | 3. File extraction | | 3. QBX Directory |
| PRIDE-Logik | 1. COBOL, PL/I | 1. File extraction | | 1. COBOL FDs and PL/I structures |
| | 2. ADF (Design Aid) | 2. Interface commands | | 2. Accepts D/D input and records design results in the D/D |
| | 3. JCL | 3. File extraction | | 3. JCL library entries |
| | 4. IDS II, IMS DL/I | 4. File extraction | | 4. Schema descriptions |
| TIS DIRECTORY | 1. DBM (DBCS) | 1. Interface commands for all | | 1. Physical database descriptions |
| | 2. QUERY COMPONENT (Query Processor) | | 2. Examine and update user views | 2. User views, query constraints, access paths, physical mapping, display formats |
| | 3. COMPREHENSIVE RETRIEVAL (Report Writer) | | 3. Save the RDL statements in the D/D | 3. Print formats, access paths, physical mapping, user views |
| UCC TEN | 1: IMS (DDL Processor and System Generator) | File extraction for all | | 1. DBD, PSB, macros for Stage 1 Sysgen and Terminal Security Blocks |
| | 2. MFS (Terminal Monitor) | | | 2. Message and device descriptions (MID, MOD, DIF, DOF) |
| | 3. COBOL, PL/1, assembler | | 3. Suffix, prefix, and replace editing options, indentation and level number control, include comments, condition names, and initial values | 3. File, record, PCB, RSA, and SSA |
| | 4. GIS (General Information System) | | | 4. Data Description Table (DDT) |
| | 5. ADF (Batch Program Generator) | | | 5. ADF statements (i.e., Rule-Generator, Generate, and |

# A Survey of Application Generators

**Ellis Horowitz, Alfons Kemper, and Balaji Narasimhan**
**University of Southern California**

**By encouraging the unsophisticated computer user to develop his own data-intensive programs, application generators can significantly improve software productivity.**

The past quarter century has witnessed an amazing improvement in our ability to fabricate sophisticated hardware devices. The growth in the number of active elements per chip has been doubling every few years for the past 25 years. But this exponential growth has in no measure been matched by productivity improvements at the software level.[1] One result of this fact is that the cost of a computer system has shifted from being almost entirely hardware related to being almost entirely software related. The distribution of software cost versus hardware cost of a typical system was given by Boehm[2] and is shown in the diagram of Figure 1.

As pointed out by McCracken,[3] today's software developers are facing the following challenges:

(1) increased demand for new applications;
(2) increased complexity of new applications; and
(3) increased cost and decreased availability of skilled people.

It is extremely unlikely that these demands can entirely be met by the careful application of conventional software engineering methodologies and tools. What we need are techniques that gain us *orders of magnitude* improvements in productivity. A recent IEEE meeting on software productivity[1] said it this way:

> Every panel observed that major increases in productivity for software engineering will come about only through elimination of the number of skilled man-hours required to produce new software. This reduction can occur by: (a) reducing the cost of each step in the development/maintenance life cycle, (b) eliminating the need for a step in the life cycle, (c) reducing the number of iterations back through life-cycle steps, or (d) reducing the cost of the impact of change.

One approach to meet these challenges, which we investigate in this article, is to use application generators. Application generators, sometimes abbreviated AG, are software systems geared primarily to support data-intensive application development. AGs provide a very high level, special-purpose "programming" language with a user friendly syntax. Therefore, AGs can easily be applied by the end-user, who is usually not sophisticated in computer skills.

Conventional wisdom holds that the software development process can be viewed as a series of steps, consisting of system specification, architectural design, detailed design, coding, testing and debugging, documentation, and maintenance. When using an application generator, the user begins by specifying a very limited prototype of the desired application, and then incrementally extends and modifies the prototype until it meets all of the requirements. This methodology has several implications on the conventional life-cycle process.

One, there is no coding phase in the usual sense. The software specification is literally turned into an executable program. Two, testing and maintenance are significantly reduced because the programmer returns to the specification when changes have to be made. This specification is expressed as an application generator program, and as such it is at a level much higher than a program written in a conventional programming language. Therefore, the testing and maintenance phases are simplified. Three, documentation is aided by the fact that the program is easily readable. Four, the high-level nature of the language permits less sophisticated end-users to program directly. For all of these reasons, people have observed that application generators, where appropriate, offer large degrees of improvement in software development time.[4]

But can the success of application generators in the world of EDP be brought to other environments? This sentiment was suggested recently by the DoD Software Initiative,[5] which cited application generators as one means for improved DoD software productivity. In this article, we intend to look closely at some of the existing application generators to see precisely what facilities they offer and in what form. We will describe the basic components that most of the existing systems share. Then we hypothesize a generic application generator. Using this generic system, we discuss the language features it offers, and write several programs as demonstrations. Finally, we contrast application generators to general-purpose programming languages, and discuss how programming languages can be extended to support the development of data-intensive applications.

## Today's application generators

Application generators have their origin in the early report-generator systems, such as IBM's RPG.[6] These software packages let the user generate reports at a very high level of description, permitting him to avoid having to deal with low-level issues such as page layout and data representation. Today's application generators are substantial extensions of these report generators. They address the need of the business world to have a uniform approach to data-intensive applications —database management, data manipulation, and data retrieval—in the form of simple database queries, as well as in the generation of sophisticated reports. Contemporary application generators may also make use of the more recent hardware developments facilitating graphics support. In addition, some AGs include software modules for very specialized applications, such as financial modeling or statistical analysis packages. In summary, application generators typically consist of the following modules:

- database management system,
- report generator,
- database query language,
- graphics package, and
- special-purpose software.

**Commercially available application generators.** In order to get a better idea of the current state of application generators, we investigated the following systems: Nomad, Ramis, Focus, ADF, and Dbase II. Of course, this list of application generators is not exhaustive. In particular, some database management systems have to be considered as application generators, since they have added high-level features for report and forms generation, for example, Ingres.[7] In this section we briefly summarize the attributes of the systems that we investigated in detail.

*Nomad.* Nomad[3] was developed by National CSS, starting in 1973. Recently Nomad has been extended and is now available as Nomad2.[8] Nomad2 supports three kinds of database structures:

- relational
- hierarchical, and
- hybrid combinations of hierarchical and relational structure.

The hybrid database structure incorporates both hierarchical as well as relational features. This was done in order to combine the efficiency of the hierarchical model with the flexibility of data access of the relational system. In order to provide efficient and flexible data retrieval for a variety of applications, Nomad supports a wide range of access methods such as keyed access, balanced tree indexing, table look-ups, etc. Thus, Nomad has the full capabilities of a database management system, including data manipulation, data integrity, and data security features.

In Nomad, the end user can generate reports from the database using the **list** command. The underlying data records of the report can be sorted, screened, and totalled by applying some very high level language constructs such as the "**select...where...**" command for data screening. NCSS has added high-level graphics features to Nomad2 to generate graphics reports on the screen. Most of the scaling is done automatically by the system, but, if the user wishes, he can choose his own scaling factors, thereby overwriting the predefined system parameters. Also, the user-specified headings and legends are automatically put into place by the system.

*Focus.* Focus,[9] developed by Information Builders, Inc., is one of the most extensive application generators available. It is based on a hierarchical database management system, and provides an interactive data entry language, called FIDEL. Besides the high-level report generator and a sophisticated terminal graphics package, it has built-in a wide range of special-purpose software for business applications. This covers statistical analysis functions and a financial modeling language.

For the more experienced user, Focus has a host language interface to facilitate the access to Focus files from a general-purpose programming language, like Fortran or Cobal. Also, the user can redefine the syntax of Focus to suit his needs.

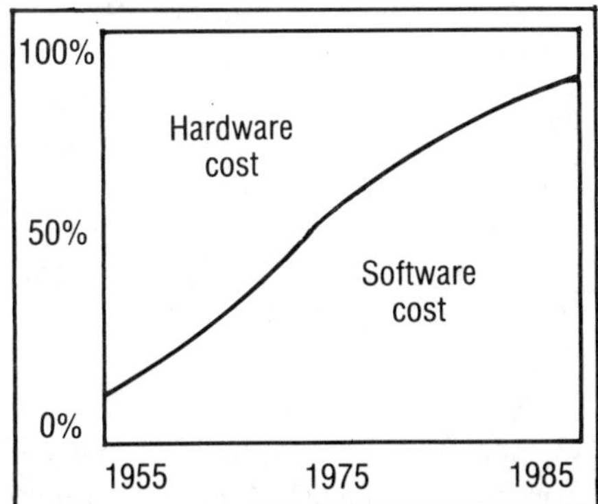


**Figure 1. Distribution of software versus hardware cost for a typical computer system.**

*Ramis.* Ramis[10] was developed by Mathematica Products Group, Inc. Ramis is designed specifically for IBM mainframe computers. The Ramis database is structured as a network of data segments, where the segments can be in different files. In addition, Ramis supports a purely hierarchical data model. Besides its own files, Ramis can also interface to DL1 and IMS files. The records management system provides the user with a nonprocedural language for retrieving and processing data records. The report preparation system of Ramis is designed in the form of an English-like language and lets the user retrieve, sort, calculate, and format data into tabular or graphic reports. In Ramis, the report generator and the graphics language were designed to have a unified syntax.

*Dbase II.* In recent years, several systems for application generation have been designed for personal computers.[11] One of these systems is Dbase II,[12] which is a relational database system for microcomputers. It was developed by Ashton-Tate in 1980, and runs under CP/M and MS-DOS. In addition to the database operations such as addition, deletion, and update of records that the user can perform using the data manipulation language of Dbase II, reports from one or more databases can also be generated. The report generation facility is very concise, and consists of a set of prompts from the system to the user about the different aspects of the report, such as report heading, column headings, totals on columns, etc. The command language of Dbase II has the syntax of an Algol-like language. The Dbase II system also provides a full-screen editor to set up a screen format for use as a data entry facility. Note that this entire system costs significantly less than $1000.

*Application Development Facility.* Application Development Facility[13] was developed by IBM as an "installed user program" to be used with their IMS database management system. Applications developed using ADF have a common overall structure. Such an application is produced as a set of program modules tailored by the applications developer to suit his specific application. The modules contain the program logic for the following tasks:

- dialog management,
- data access,
- application logic, and
- control of the interaction of the above modules.

A transaction driver directs the execution of the application program so that the menus, data displays, and messages are joined to produce a complete application. ADF also supports nonconversational and batch mode applications.

**Several systems for application generation have been designed for personal computers.**

An application developer tailors the modules to suit his application by supplying a set of rules using a simple, English-like language as input to a component of ADF, called the *rule generator*. These rules are used internally by the transaction driver to control the functions of the modules at execution time. Where programming is required by the special nature of an application, the programming can be interfaced with the above modules.

**Basic components of application generators.** In this subsection, we will investigate in detail the basic components of an application generator that are present in most of the commercial systems.

*Database management.* All commercially available AGs have their own DBMS, and in addition support access to external files as well. Typically, the underlying data model is either hierarchical or relational. A database usually consists of two files: the master file and the data file. The master file contains user-entered data format information describing a particular database, that is, type definition of fields, field names, relationship among different segments, etc. Creation of this master file is usually done interactively, such that the system displays some skeleton form for the master file, and the user, in this case the database administrator, has to fill in the blanks.

The data file contains the actual data, which is entered and modified via the database query language. In order to make access to this data as efficient as possible, the user can specify in the corresponding master file what access method is to be used, and he can also specify the key fields of the database, if any.

*Report generator.* One of the essential features of all application generators is the report generator feature. The facilities are provided in the form of a special-purpose sublanguage. The language of the report generator is often characterized as *nonprocedural.* This, however, does not mean that there are no subroutines; later in this article we will actually show an example of the use of a subroutine in report generation. The characterization of the report generator as nonprocedural is used in the sense of *very high level.* This means that the programmer has to specify only the major steps of the computation, but is not concerned about the low-level details, such as data representation or the exact sequence of computation. In the literature, notably Leavenworth and Sammet[14] and Leavenworth,[15] nonprocedural languages are often characterized by the fact that the user has to specify *what* he wants to be done. But he can leave out the details of *how* the system is to accomplish this task. For this reason, the term *goal-oriented language* might be more appropriate to define the nature of these nonprocedural languages. Sammet pointed out that all these terms are relative and depend on the state of the art. For example, the first high-level programming languages like Fortran and Algol60 were considered very high level with respect to assembly languages, which again were viewed as high level relative to machine languages.

To get a better understanding of the difference between using a nonprocedural language and a conventional general-purpose programming language, let us look at the program fragments of Figure 2. Both programs accomplish the same task, that is, generating a list of all employees of the CSCI department and their respective salaries from the EMPLOYEES database. Figure 2(a) shows the program as it would appear in an application generator whereas the much longer version, shown in Figure 2(b), outlines the basic steps of the program written in some conventional Pascal-like programming language. Note that the program in Figure 2(a) is complete whereas Figure 2(b) only shows an outline of the program to be written.

(a)

```
file EMPLOYEES
list NAME SALARY
WHERE DEPT = "CSCI"
```

(b)

```
<open file EMPLOYEES>
for i: = 1 to MaxNumOfEmpl do
      begin
        <retrieve ith data record using
          some existing retrieval path>
        <extract NAME and SALARY fields>
          if DEPT[i] = "CSCI" then
          begin
               writeln(NAME[i],SALARY[i])
          end
        end
<close file EMPLOYEES>
```

**Figure 2. Program fragments in (a) report generator, and (b) conventional programming language.**

Two major low-level details that are removed from the programmer's concern when he uses an application generator are the specification of explicit iteration over all data records and the specification of the retrieval paths to obtain the data fields (for example, NAME and SALARY) from all data records. In a report generator, the user can rely on *associative referencing*. This is a term describing the accessing of data based on certain characteristics associated to it, like field name or range of possible values. This is in contrast to explicitly traversing some existing retrieval path or performing a search over all possible elements in a certain data set, like a database relation. The user of an application generator is not concerned with how the system is actually managing to retrieve the data. Furthermore, the details of the report layout and conversion of the data to the appropriate output format are left to the system.

In summary, we can say that in a conventional programming language we have to specify the program more in terms of how the system is supposed to do the computation. In an AG, the user writes more in terms of what the outcome of the program should look like.

The syntax of the report generator sublanguage is typically very much like natural English. The reason for this is twofold. One, the report generator is mostly used in business applications where Cobol was, and still is, the primary programming language. It was felt that the English-like syntax would ease the transition from Cobol to an application generator for most programmers in that application domain. Two, application generators were designed to be used by the end user, that is, a business person with no, or very little, data processing experience. The English-like syntax was expected to help these users adapt to the new system more quickly.

*Graphics package.* Recently, application generators have begun to include a sophisticated graphics package that, just like the report generator, interfaces to the DBMS. The graphics package is actually a special form of the report generator, with the distinction that a *graphical report* is produced rather than a tabular output. For ease of use, the syntax of the graphics language is basically the same as for the report generator. The main difference is that the user has to specify in what kind of a graph he wants the information to be reported. Typically, application generators provide the following five kinds of graphs: connected point graphs, histograms, bar-charts, scatter diagrams, and pie-charts.

With the growing development of graphics hardware and software, we can foresee that the graphics software in an application generator will become more sophisticated. One important development on the horizon is automatic scaling and headings for graphs. Also, color graphics and three-dimensional representation of the information is already possible. Optimally, an application generator is connected to a graphics display terminal as well as to a plotter to provide interactive output on the screen as well as hardcopy output. We further explain the graphics package below.

*Database manipulation language.* Ideally, the database manipulation language should use the same syntactical structure as the other modules of the AG, namely, the report generator and the graphics package. The database manipulation language must provide for interactive as well as batch processing of the needed database modifications. It has to include functions for the following operations:

- inserting data,
- deleting data records,
- updating data,
- retrieving and listing of data records,
- statement of consistency constraints, and
- statement of authority constraints.

If the user wants to interactively edit the database, the easiest syntactical way seems to be one in which the system prompts the user for the necessary

```
schema

table CUSTOMER key(CUST#)
        field CUST#             number          heading'CUSTOMER, number'
        field CUSTNAME          text            heding'CUSTOMER,NAME'
        field CUSTADDR          text            heading'CUSTOMER,ADDRESS'
        end table definition

        table PRODUCT key(PROD#)
        field PROD#             number          heading'PRODUCT, number'
        field PRODNAME          text            heading'PRODUCT,NAME'
        field LSTPRICE          money           heading'LIST,PRICE'
        field UCOST             money           heading'PRODUCT,COST'
        end table definition

        table SALES key(INVOICE#,PROD#)
        field INVOICE#          number          heading'INVOICE,NUMBER'
        field DATE              date            heading'SALE,DATE'
        field CUST#             number          heading'CUSTOMER,NUMBER'
        field PROD#             number          heading'PRODUCT,NUMBER'
        field UNITS             number          heading'UNITS, SOLD'
        define CUSTNAME   pointer CUSTNAME   in table CUSTOMER   key CUST#
        define CUSTADDR   pointer CUSTADDR   in table CUSTOMER   key CUST#
        define PRODNAME   pointer PRODNAME   in table PRODUCT    key PROD#
        define LSTPRICE   pointer LSTPRICE   in table PRODUCT    key PROD#
        define UCOST      pointer UCOST      in table PRODUCT    key PROD#
end table definition
end schema definition
```

**Figure 3. Database definition.**

information that needs to be specified for the corresponding operation. This can be done by displaying a skeleton table of the corresponding database and letting the user fill in the blanks or modify the existing entries. This approach was taken in the design of Query-By-Example, which was developed at IBM.[16] The data manipulation language is mostly menu driven, that is, the possible operations supplied by the system are being selected via a menu. This eliminates the need for the user to memorize the complete syntax of the system.

In addition to editing the data, the user also has the possibility of modifying the definition of the database. In this case, he has to edit the master file, that is, the file with the type definition of the corresponding database. If the modification of the master file leaves the database in an inconsistent state, the user will subsequently be prompted to edit the data in the corresponding database.

*Other components.* Many application generators include some special-purpose software packages that create very specialized applications more easily. Like the other modules of an AG, the special-purpose software interfaces to the DBMS. The functions of this module are very often initiated via a menu, just like the data manipulation language.

Two such packages that are commonly found in AGs for business applications are a software package for statistical analysis and another for financial modeling. The spectrum of statistical tools covers means and standard deviation, correlation coefficients, analysis of variance, exponential smoothing and forecasting, and the like. To make the use of these tools more user-friendly, they have been designed as interactive tools. The user selects the desired operation, and then the system will automatically prompt him for the appropriate parameters. This makes the system more suitable for the casual user, for he does not have to memorize all the details.

The financial modeling language is an extension to the report generator with the purpose of creating financial statements, such as balance sheets or income and expense tables. It also supports the creation of financial models, for example, projected capital needs and budget consolidation. The financial modeling language lets the user specify in an easy way how the particular columns of a report are to be computed. This is very much like spreadsheet programs,[17] except that the financial modeling language of application generators interfaces with the database management system. Personal computer software has yet to achieve this level of integration.

## A generic application generator

In this section we describe a generic application generator. This AG has essentially all the components described in the previous section. The syntax of this generic application generator has been chosen to be similar to one of the AGs introduced before, Nomad. We will now explain the following modules of the AG:

(1) database management system,
(2) report generator,
(3) data manipulation language, and
(4) graphics package.

**Database management system.** As was pointed out before, application generators are based on a database management system, which either employs a relational[3] or a hierarchical data model.[9,10] In this presentation, we have chosen a relational DBMS. Relations (tables) are defined by the database administrator in the way shown in Figure 3.

In this schema definition, the three tables CUSTOMER, PRODUCT, and SALES are declared. For each relation a key is specified, which consists of one or more fields (attributes). A field is specified by its name, its type, and its heading. In our generic application generator, there are four built-in types, which are **number** (an integer), **money** (decimal number), **date** (in the

```
report
file SALES
title 'UNITS SOLD PER CUSTOMER'
        list
          by CUSTOMER
          across YEAR
          sum(UNITS)
          rowtotal
          columntotal
        where YEAR in 1980 . . . 1982
end report
```

**(a)**

UNITS SOLD PER CUSTOMER

| CUSTOMER | 1980 UNITS | 1981 UNITS | 1982 UNITS | TOTAL |
|---|---|---|---|---|
| COMPUTER DEVELOPMENT, LTD. | 23458 | 34563 | 43210 | 101231 |
| ENGINEERING ASSOCIATES | 5979 | 19820 | 9983 | 35782 |
| BIGMONEY, INC. | 98877 | 54438 | 78945 | 231260 |
| BLACKMARKET, LTD. | 23451 | 9983 | 32564 | 65998 |
| SOFTTEST ASSOCIATES | 76590 | 65094 | 43679 | 185313 |
| TOTAL | 228355 | 183898 | 208381 | 619584 |

**(b)**

**Figure 4. Program to generate a report (a), and the resulting output (b).**

```
report
    file <FILE NAME>
  [title <'TITLE TEXT'>]
  <VERB>
    by <OBJECT> [as <'TITLE'>] {<OBJECT>[as <'TITLE>]}
    [across <OBJECT> [as <'TITLE'>] {<OBJECT> as <'TITLE'>}]
    [<SYSTEM FUNCTIONS>]
  [where <SCREENING CONDITION>]
end report
```

**Figure 5. The syntax of the report generator command.**

form mm/dd/yy), and **text** (character string). The system can automatically extract the month, day, and year from attributes of type date. If, for example, the field CUSTADDR of the CUSTOMER table was used in a report, the corresponding column would automatically be assigned the heading CUSTOMER,ADDRESS (the comma specifies the word ADDRESS to be written below CUSTOMER). The user can define virtual fields, that is, pointers to fields of other tables. For example, in Figure 3 the fields CUSTNAME of the SALES and the CUSTOMER tables are identical for those records that have a matching CUST# field.

**Report generator.** Let us consider a few examples of report generation over the database just defined. In Figure 4(b), a tabular report is created by the AG program shown in Figure 4(a). The report lists all the customers together with the respective number of units that were sold to them in the years 1980 through 1982. First, the programmer has to specify the database on which the report is based, in this case the file SALES. Later on we will see an example of a program where two databases are combined in one report using the **join** operator, which is a standard relational database operator.[18] Furthermore, the programmer defines a title for the report. At the very end of the program he provides a screening condition, which, in this case, specifies the use of only those SALES records whose DATE field is between 1980 and 1982. Such a screening condition can be any arbitrarily complex Boolean expression over one or more fields of the database. In this example, we have used the built-in functions **sum**, **columntotal**, and **rowtotal**. These built-in functions constitute the report generator special-purpose commands that can be applied to any tabular report being generated.

Figure 5 outlines the basic syntax of the report generator command. The user has to specify the file name(s) on which the report is based. Optionally, a title can be specified. Possible verbs are **list**, **print**, **sort**, **sum**, etc. The objects listed after the **by** clause will appear in one column of the tabular report, those after the **across** clause create a new column for each different value, like YEAR in Figure 4(a). An object is either a field of the database or any function (or computation) applied to one or more fields, for instance, **sum** (UNITS) in Figure 4(a). The **where** clause provides for data screening in such a way that the only data records included in the report fulfill the screening condition, which can be any Boolean expression. The syntax of the screening condition is

```
where <field-id> <bool-op> <test-
   values> {and/or <field-id> <bool-
   op> <test-values> }
```

The possible system functions that are usually provided are too numerous to list here, but they include formatting control, like page break specifications, and numerical functions, such as computing averages, regression analysis, or simply the calculation of column and row totals.

We might argue that the basic report generator statement described in Figure 5 is not powerful enough when more complex calculations are asked

```
define
file <FILE NAME>
     {if <SCREENING CONDITION>then  <DEFINITION OF NEW FIELD(S)>
                                else  <DEFINITION OF NEW FIELD(S)>}
     [<DEFINITION OF ADDITIONAL FIELD(S)>]
end define

define
file SALES
     if UNITS gt 200 then do
          DPRICE=LSTPRICE
          NCOST=UCOST
     end
     else do
          DPRICE=LSTPRICE * 0.9
          NCOST=UCOST * 0.85
     end
   PROFIT=(LSTPRICE-UCOST)* UNITS
   DPROFIT=(DPRICE-NCOST) *UNITS
   DIFF=DPROFIT-PROFIT
end. define

report
file SALES
title'UNDISCOUNTED VERSUS DISCOUNTED PROFIT'
     list
       by YEAR
       sum(UNITS) as 'TOTAL,UNITS'
     PROFIT as 'UNDISCOUNTED,PROFIT'
     DPROFIT as 'DISCOUNTED,PROFIT'
     DIFF as 'DIFFERENCE'
   where YEAR in 1982 . . . 1983
end report
```

**(a)**

UNDISCOUNTED VERSUS DISCOUNTED PROFIT

| YEAR | TOTAL UNITS | UNDISCOUNTED PROFIT | DISCOUNTED PROFIT | DIFFERENCE |
|---|---|---|---|---|
| 1982 | 62412 | 2,255,587.52 | 2,907,591.64 | 652,004.12 |
| 1983 | 87098 | 2,824,039.17 | 3,634,877.83 | 810,838.66 |

**(b)**

**Figure 6. Report involving some more complex calculation: (a) define statement; (b) report generation.**

```
procedure SALES__OF__PROD
arguments YR:yy,PNAME: text
file SALES
title 'TOTAL UNITS SOLD OF &PNAME in 19&YR'
    list
          sum(UNITS) as 'TOTAL UNITS SOLD'
    where YEAR is &YR
              and PRODNAME is &PNAME
end procedure
```

This procedure can be invoked as follows:

```
exec SALES__OF__PROD (YR => 79,PNAME => WORKSTATION)
```

**Figure 7. Example of a parameterized procedure.**

for. For this reason, most AGs have some additional feature, such as the define feature shown in the program of Figure 6. This feature allows the user to temporarily define new fields (virtual fields) in the database, and make use of these fields in the generation of the report. Actually, we can view these fields as variables.

Thus, in Figure 6(a), for each SALES record, the new fields DPRICE, NCOST, PROFIT, DPROFIT, and DIFF are computed and temporarily stored (the value of these fields depends on the number of units sold; if more than 200 units, a special discount of 10 percent is granted). Note that the types of these fields are extracted from the type definition in the database; that is, the user is not concerned about this. For example, the system automatically determines the type of the new field DPRICE to be the same as for the field LSTPRICE, namely **money**. The basic syntax of the define statement is shown in Figure 6.

Note that the define program in Figure 6(a) contains an implicit loop since the calculation is performed for each record in the database. This is one of the main differences between this program and a program written in a conventional programming language. In the subsequent report generation phase, the newly defined fields can be used just like the fields physically stored in the database. In this case, the discounted profit (DPROFIT) is compared with the undiscounted profit (PROFIT) and the difference (DIFF) is listed for the years 1982 and 1983.

Earlier in this article we stated that report generators are nonprocedural. This, however, does not mean that they cannot have subroutines. In Figure 7, we see an example of a parameterized procedure. In this example, the last two digits of the year and the PNAME (for PRODNAME) are parameters. The program computes the total number of units sold of the product specified in the parameter PNAME during the year YR. Note that the syntax requires us to prefix the formal parameters by an ampersand whenever it is used in the program.

Now let us consider an example of a report generation that combines two databases. For this purpose, in Figure 8 two more database tables are defined: STUDENT and PROFESSOR. Let us assume the user wants to list all professors of the CSCI department and the average GPA of their advisees. This asks for a join of the two tables PROFESSOR and STUDENT. In Figure 9 these two tables are joined on the fields ADVISOR and PROF_NAME. Then the program generates a listing of all professors in the CSCI department together with the average GPA of their students. The syntax of the join operator is outlined as

join files (<FILE NAME>, <FILE NAME>) matching (<FIELD>, <FIELD>) {matching (<FIELD, > <FIELD>)}

Note that we can actually join two databases on more than one field. This means that the respective data records are only combined if they agree on all fields specified in the matching statement.

**Data manipulation language.** In this section we investigate another feature of application generators: the data manipulation language. This language is used to maintain the data stored in the database. It enables the user to perform the following transactions:

- insert data,
- update data,
- delete data, and
- perform integrity checks on the data.

The syntax of the data manipulation language follows closely the syntax of the report generator as far as this is possible, so that the user has to memorize as few concepts as possible. To modify a database, the user has to write a short program as illustrated in Figure 10. Then he has to provide the data for this program. In our example we want to modify the database SALES. The program will take as input the INVOICE# and the PROD#, and compare whether a record with these field values is already in the database. If so, it updates the other

```
schema

table STUDENT key(STUD_NAME)
        field STUD_NAME       text        heading 'STUDENT,NAME'
        field ADVISOR         text        heading 'ADVISOR'
        field GPA             number      heading 'GRADE POINT,AVERAGE'
end table definition

table PROFESSOR key(PROF_NAME)
        field PROF_NAME           text          heading 'PROFESSOR,NAME'
        field DEPT                text          heading 'DEPARTMENT'
end table definition

end schema definition
```

**Figure 8. Schema definition of tables STUDENT and PROFESSOR.**

```
report
file STUDENT
file PROFESSOR
join FILES (STUDENT,PROFESSOR) matching (ADVISOR,PROF_NAME)
        list
            by PROF_NAME
          AVE(GPA) as 'AVERAGE,GPA'
        where DEPT is 'CSCI'
end report
```

**(a)**

| PROFESSOR NAME | AVERAGE GPA OF HIS/HER STUDENTS |
|---|---|
| PROF. EASYGOING | 3.95 |
| PROF. SMITH | 3.25 |
| PROF. TOUGHMAN | 2.55 |

**(b)**

**Figure 9. Report generation using two tables (a), and final listing (b).**

```
modify
file SALES
  match INVOICE#,PROD#
  on match do
    update
      CUST#,UNITS,DATE
  on nomatch do
    include
end modify
```

Now the user has to provide the data, that is, the fields INVOICE#, PROD#, CUST#, UNITS, and DATE:

```
begin data
INVOICE# = 1023
PROD# = 132
CUST# = 12
UNITS = 200
DATE = 11/30/79

INVOICE# = 1024

end data
```

**Figure 10. Modification of the SALES database.**

```
modify
file <FILE NAME>
   match <FIELD> {<FIELD>}
   on match do
      <CODE FOR THE MATCHING CASE>
   on nomatch do
      <CODE FOR THE NONMATCHING CASE>
end modify

begin data

<DATA ENTRY SECTION>

end data
```

**Figure 11. Outline of the syntax of the modify statement.**

```
schema

table CARS key(CAR,COUNTRY)
        field CAR          text       heading'NAME OF,CAR'
        field COUNTRY      text       heading'COUNTRY'
        field PCOST        money      heading'PRODUCTION,COST'
        field SCOST        money      heading'SALES,OVERHEAD'
        field SALES        number     heading'NUMBER,SOLD'
        field PRICE        money      heading'PRICE'
        field MPG          number     heading'MILEAGE'
end table definition
end schema definition
```

**Figure 12. Schema definition of table CARS.**

fields according to the data provided in the data entry section (this is specified in the statements following **on match do**). If the record is not found in the database, it will be inserted, and the fields will get the values defined in the data entry section.

The basic syntax of the data manipulation language is outlined in Figure 11. As usual, the first thing the user has to specify is the file he wants to modify. Then he has to specify the fields of this database that he wants to match with the entered data in the data entry section. Then, should the entered data match some records in the database, the appropriate code is given. This code is placed after the key words **on match do**. This section can contain commands to **update**, **delete**, or **insert** data records. Following this, should none of the records in the database match the entry, then that code is defined. This is indicated by the key word **on nomatch do**.

**Graphics package.** Another way to generate reports in an application generator is in the form of graphs. In this section, "graphical report generation" refers to report generation using the graphics package distinct from the "tabular report generation" described in the previous section. We look at examples of graphical reports, the language for graphical report generation, issues involved in graphical report design, and reasons for graphical report effectiveness as a programming tool.

Graphical reports can be one of the following types:

- histograms,
- piecharts,
- barcharts,
- curve plots, and
- scatter diagrams.

All the features of the report generator, such as performing arithmetic and screening data, can be used in graphical report generation. Thus, the user is able to produce reports having a greater visual content with almost the same ease.

The following examples illustrate graphical report generation. The schema definition of the database used in the examples in this section is given in Figure 12.

The request in Figure 13 is a report in the form of a histogram of the total cost and price of the various cars. Note that the **over** feature enables us to split the total cost into its components and have them displayed one over the other in different shades; the **and** feature enables us to compare the cost and price of each car by producing adjacent bars.

The program in Figure 14 generates a barchart of the production cost and sales overhead of the different cars. The use of the **where** clause screens the data, such that only cars of the specified three types are included.

In Figure 15, a curve of the retail cost, dealer cost, and revolutions per minute of the cars is plotted against their fuel consumption. In Figure 16, a piechart of the fuel consumption of the various cars is shown.

Now let us take a closer look at the language of our programs. The basic syntax for graphical report generation is defined in Figure 17. <TYPE OF GRAPH> can be histogram, piechart, barchart, scatter diagram, or curve. <DEPENDENT OBJECT> refers to the attribute whose value is to be plotted in the graph. <INDEPENDENT OBJECT> is the one against which the other attributes are to be plotted. Note the similarity of this syntax and the syntax of tabular report generation. This similarity has been created deliberately to aid the users in learning and using the application generators.

In addition to what is described above, it is also possible to supply optional information to the graphics package in the form of specific titles and shades for the bars in the histograms (or barcharts), types of lines to be used in the curve plots, and the particular display area in which the report is to be generated.

Now let us consider three very important characteristics of application generators. First, as in the case of tabular report generators, the user need not concern himself with details of his data and its organization and retrieval. He only needs to specify the data that he wants to see plotted. Secondly, it suffices to specify the desired graph at a very high level. The user does not

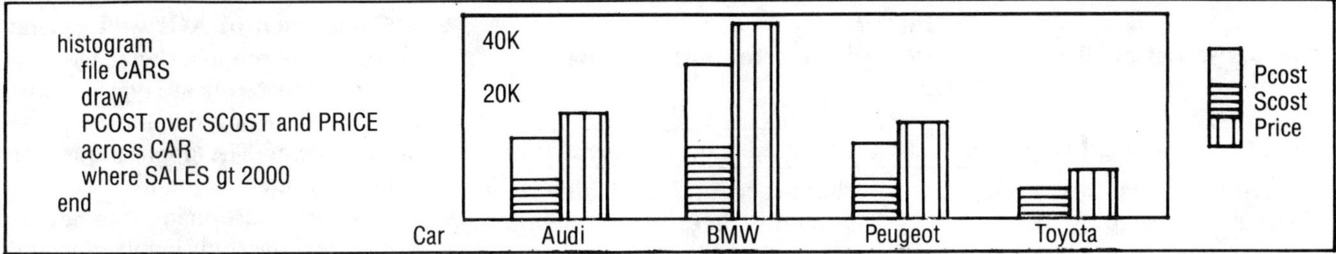


**Figure 13. Histogram.**

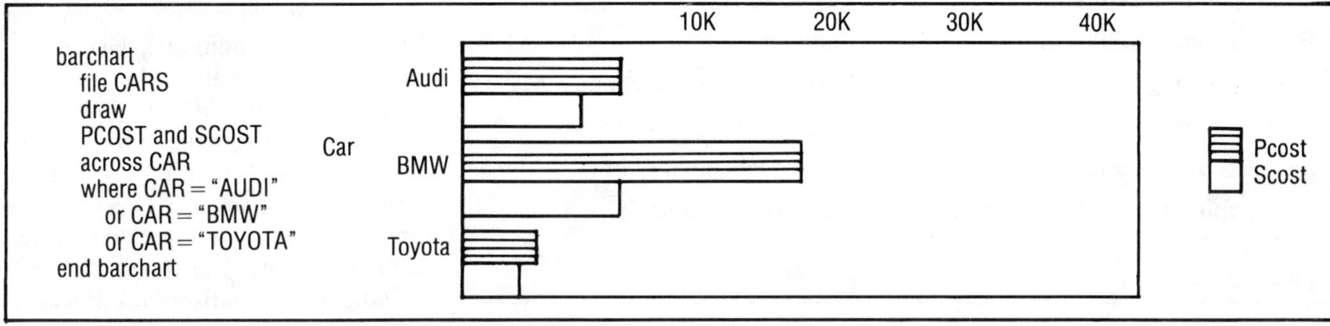


**Figure 14. Barchart.**

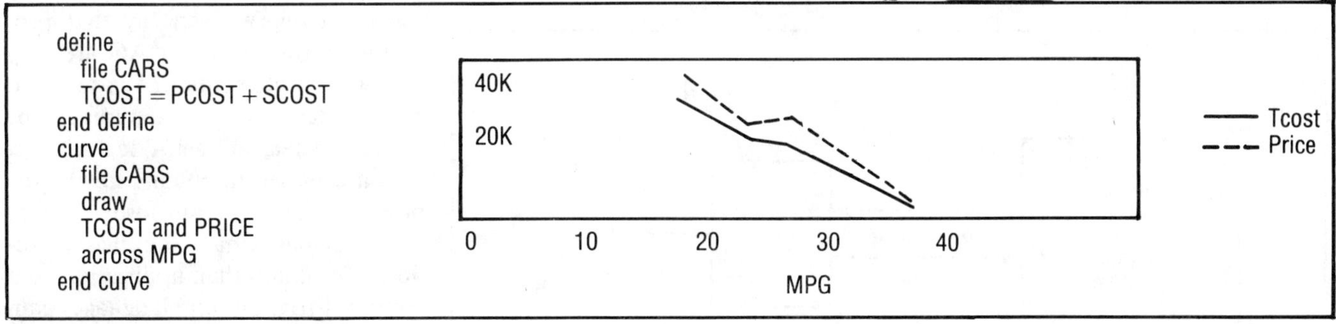


**Figure 15. Curve plot.**

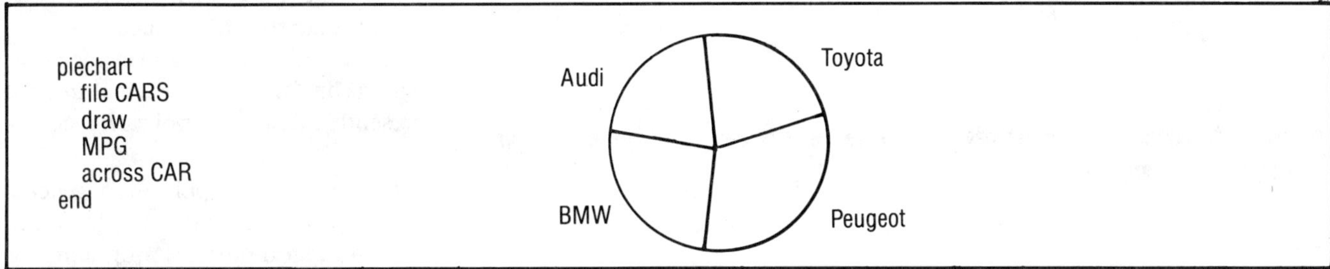


**Figure 16. Piechart.**

```
<definition part>
<TYPE OF GRAPH>
    file <FILENAME>
    [<options>]
    draw
    <DEPENDENT OBJECT> {over <DEPENDENT OBJECT>}
        {and <DEPENDENT OBJECT> {over <DEPENDENT OBJECT>}}
    across <INDEPENDENT OBJECT>
    where <SCREENING CONDITION>
end <TYPE OF GRAPH>
<DEPENDENT OBJECT>: : = <OBJ.NAME> [<OBJ.TITLE>] [<OBJ.SHADE>] [<OBJ.SCALE>]
<INDEPENDENT OBJECT>: : = <OBJ.NAME> [<TITLE>] [<OBJ.SCALE>]
```

**Figure 17. Syntax of programs using a graphics packaage.**

**Table 1.**
**Comparison of application generators with general-purpose programming languages.**

| Programming Languages | Application Generators |
|---|---|
| Procedural; programs define computations step by step | Non-procedural; very high level programs that mainly state the required results |
| Usually non-data-intensive | Data-intensive |
| Explicit iteration and loops | Implicit iteration |
| Explicit typing mechanisms | Implicit typing mechanisms |
| Very wide range of applications | Limited problem domains |
| Detailed documentation necessary | Mostly self-documenting |
| Prototyping is usually slow and error prone | Supports fast and correct prototyping |
| Difficult to maintain | Easier to maintain |

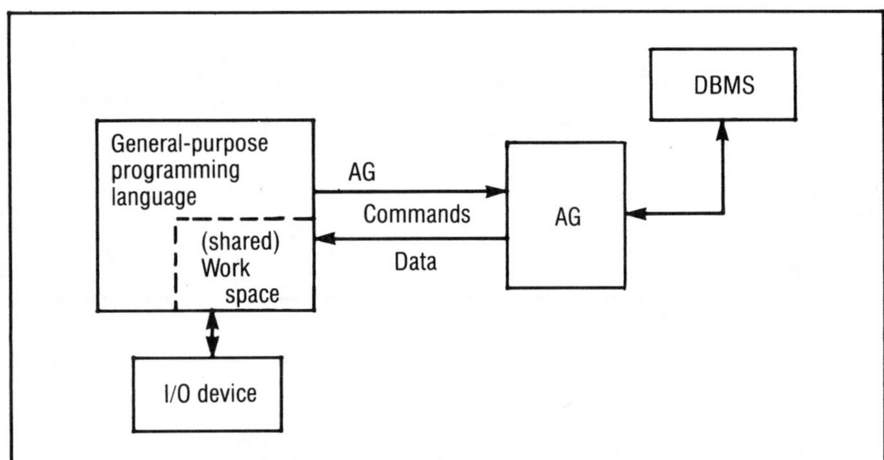


**Figure 18. Organization of a typical interface between a general-purpose programming language and an AG.**

have to "program" starting from graphical primitives. Finally, the application generators provide a smooth integration of report generation and graphics; without this integration it would be the responsibility of the user to combine the two aspects of the system in his programs explicitly.

These three characteristics give the graphics packages of report generators considerable power and create a simple and convenient medium, so the user can communicate his requirements to the computer. However, we should not fail to note the limitations of these packages. They are not general-purpose graphics packages; they derive their power precisely by not being general, by being limited to a certain domain.

## Can an AG be used for general-purpose programming?

In this section we examine the characteristics of application generators that distinguish them from programming languages. Then we analyze the possibility of combining the high-level features of application generators with general-purpose programming languages.

**Comparison of AGs with general-purpose programming languages.** Application generators are typically used in the context of a database management system. The applications normally do not entail the use of explicit iteration or recursion in the programs. Most often, they only involve applying the same operation on all records of a database (or all records that obey a set of screening conditions). Hence, the application generators do not offer looping constructs. For the same reason, application generators do not provide data structuring facilities or typing mechanisms. They only make use of the data types occurring in the database involved in the application. A tabular comparison of programming languages and application generators is provided in Table 1.

In general, we can say that programs written using an AG are very high level statements of the required results. Hence, those programs can be written faster, are self-documenting, and are easier to maintain. On the other hand, general-purpose programming languages have more computational flexibility than application generators. Programming languages gain this flexibility over application generators by having explicit iteration constructs; data structures, such as arrays, records, and pointers; and explicit typing mechanisms. All these features are presently missing in application generators.

Contemporary application generators typically provide an interface from a general-purpose programming language to the database management system and to some of the high-level AG commands. Graphically, this interface can be described as in Figure 18.

Figure 18 shows that in those systems the application generator and the general-purpose programming language can be viewed as two separate components. If the user wants to use some AG routine from within his program, he has to create a (shared) workspace in his program first, and then issue the AG command in the form of an external procedure call. Only the application generator has access to the DBMS. The AG will store the resulting data in the user-provided workspace, where it can then be accessed from within the general-purpose programming language program.

The problem with this organization is that using the application generator commands is very tedious. The user has to provide a workspace in the form of records, arrays, or the like before he can execute the application generator commands. The application generator returns data and stores it in the predefined workspace, from which the user can then retrieve it for processing. Since there is no real embedding of the application generator features in the general-purpose programming language, the user still has to explicitly iterate over the data stored in the workspace and retrieve each record individually from there. Also, the user has to know in advance the size of the resulting data in order to reserve a sufficiently large workspace.

```
type CUST_REL is
        relation (key CUST_NO) of
        CUST_NO:string(10);
        CUST_NAME:string(20);
        CUST_ADDR:string(20);
end relation;

type SALES_REL is
        relation (key INVOICE_NO,PROD_NO) of
        INVOICE_NO:string(10);
        CUST_NO:string(10);
        MoP,DoP,YoP:integer;        --Date of Purchase
        UNITS:integer;
        LSTPRICE:float;
        STATUS:(paid,unpaid);
end relation;
```

**Figure 19. Customer and sales relations in AdaRel.**

```
declare
  CUSTOMERS:CUST_REL:=EXTERNAL('CUSTOMERS');
  SALES:SALES_REL:=EXTERNAL('SALES');
  GOOD_CUSTOMERS:CUST_REL:
  TOTAL:float;

begin
for C in CUSTOMERS
     where C.Address='Los Angeles' loop
  TOTAL:=0.00;
  for S in SALES
       where S.CUSTOMER_NO=C.CUST_NO loop
     TOTAL:=TOTAL+S.LSTPRICE*S.UNITS;
  end loop
  if TOTAL>10_000.00 then
     GOOD_CUST:=GOOD_CUST union C;
end loop;
```

**Figure 20. AdaRel program to compute the good customer.**

**Embedding higher level data retrieval constructs in programming languages.** There appear to be two ways to correct the fact that AGs lack computational flexibility. One way is to incorporate a "full" programming language within an existing AG design. The second way is to extend a programming language so that it includes AG capabilities. We favor the second approach and in this section we outline such an attempt. Though in the last few years there have been other proposals for embedded programming languages, such as Pascal/R,[19] Theseus,[20] Plain,[21] Rigel,[22] and Adaplex,[23] no one has extended these efforts to include AG concepts.

To give the reader a better idea of embedded database programming languages, we briefly outline the design of AdaRel,[24] a relational extension of Ada that was designed by the first two authors of this article. AdaRel integrates high-level language constructs for database operations in Ada without modifying the base language. Thus, a valid Ada program is also a valid AdaRel program. Furthermore, the AdaRel language extensions to Ada are strongly typed to preserve one of the essential Ada design goals. AdaRel is based on the *relational* data model.[25] The relational model was chosen for its simplicity and user friendliness. Relations are a very natural extension of Ada records.

Besides the basic Ada types, therefore, AdaRel offers the new data type *relation*. Relations are sets of *tuples*, where each tuple consists of a certain number of fields of noncomposite type. An example definition of two relations is given in Figure 19. Each relation has one or more key fields that have to be unique for every tuple in the relation, for example, no two tuples in a relation of type SALES_REL could have the same INVOICE_NO and PROD_NO.

To demonstrate the basic retrieval constructs of AdaRel, let us look at the example program in Figure 20. This program is based on the relations defined in Figure 19. We first declare the relations CUSTOMERS of type CUST_REL and SALES of type SALES_REL. These relations are associated to the externally stored relations of the same name. It is necessary that the internal type definition matches the externally stored schema of the relations. This is checked by the system at compile time. Furthermore,

```
integrity OUTSTANDING (CUSTOMERS:CUST_REL:SALES:SALES_REL) is TOTAL:float;
. . .
begin
for C in CUSTOMERS loop
  TOTAL:=0.00;
  for S in SALES
        where S.CUST_NO=C.CUST_NO
        and S.STATUS=unpaid loop
      TOTAL:=TOTAL+S.LSTPRICE*S.UNITS;
  end loop;
  if TOTAL>5000.00 then
      raise INTEGRITY_VIOLATION;
end loop;
```

**Figure 21. Integrity definition in AdaRel.**

```
screen CHECK_INVOICE (S:recordtype SALES_REL) is
      format
            heading   (Enter the number of the invoice to be checked:);
            columns   (1;
            modify    S.INVOICE_NO:          --input by the
                                               --end user.
            display   S.CUST_NO;             --displayed by
                      S.UNITS;                 --the system.
                      S.LSTPRICE;
                      S.STATUS);
      end format;
      activate
        select
            when ENTERED(S.INVOICE_NO) =>
                      begin
                      S.CUST_NO:=SALES[INVOICE_NO=S.INVOICE_NO]
                        .CUST_NO;
                      S.UNITS:=SALES[INVOICE_NO=S.INVOICE_NO].UNITS:
                      . . .
                      end
            when TERMINATE =>
                      exit;
        end select
      end activate;
end screen;
```

```
            Enter the number of the invoice to be checked:

  INVOICE_NO: ____________________________

  CUST_NO:

  UNITS:

  LSTPRICE:

  STATUS:
```

**Figure 22. Example screen.**

we declare one more internal relation, GOOD_CUSTOMERS. This relation is used to store all those customers in Los Angeles that have bought goods for more than $10,000. These customers are determined in the program by looping through the SALES relation for each customer and summing up the total amount of purchase, that is, LSTPRICE*UNITS. Note that the **where** construct of the loop restricts the loop variable to only those tuples that fulfill the condition stated. If the TOTAL is larger than $10,000, the particular tuple is inserted into the relation GOOD_CUSTOMERS, from which it can then be retrieved for further processing, in the form of output, or whatever the user wants.

In addition to the basic data retrieval commands demonstrated in this program, AdaRel offers a number of high-level algebraic operators that transform existing relations. These include operators for projection, join, and selection.

One very important issue in database management is integrity control of the data stored in relations. To our knowledge, AdaRel is the only integrated database programming language that allows the programmer to define integrity constraints. An example of an integrity constraint would be: "No employee can earn more than his manager." The integrity control mechanism of AdaRel is tightly coupled to the existing Ada exception-handling feature. Integrity constraints are automatically checked each time the relation that they define is updated. If the update results in an integrity violation, the corresponding exception is raised.

An example of an integrity constraint definition is presented in Figure 21. This integrity constraint states that no customer is allowed to have more than $5000 outstanding. In case a customer tries to order more products beyond this limit the program rejects the order and raises the predefined exception.

The scope of this article does not allow us to present the semantics of AdaRel in more detail. We refer the interested reader to Horowitz and Kemper.[24]

Usually data in business applications is stored centrally so that many different users can access it. Examples are airline reservation and banking systems. This means that the database programming language has to have some mechanism to ensure mutually exclusive access to the database. In AdaRel this is done via the *atomic transaction* concept.[26] An atomic transaction is one *uninterruptable* processing unit, that is, no other process that accesses the same data segment can interrupt the execution. The locking of the data segment at the appropriate granularity can be achieved automatically.[27] Thus, all the programmer has to specify is the extent of the atomic transaction.

From the AG viewpoint, the deficiencies of the programs in Figures 20 and 21 are

- tedious explicit iteration over all the records in the relation,
- having to specify low-level computational details, for example, initializing the variable TOTAL to zero, and
- high overhead of type and variable declarations, which are actually implicit in the database definition.

These points are common to all existing embedded database programming languages, and therefore they contribute to making these systems hard to use, especially for nonprogrammers. None of these deficiencies would exist in an AG-based program. Therefore, the next step would be to extend AdaRel so that it includes the constructs defined above in the section on a generic application generator.

**Interactive screen management.** Application generators and embedded database programming languages offer language features that substantially enhance the expressive power to manipulate stored data. But, as industry surveys[28] indicate, around 50 percent of the coding effort in a typical database application is usually spent on the implementation of input and output routines. In the last few years there has been a major shift from batch to interactive applications, and hardware has become so cheap that many office employees have their own terminal. Therefore, the next generation of AGs must provide facilities for the creation of interactive dialogues. These dialogues involve frequent updates of the terminal screen and branching to different screens depending on the user input. The application generators that we investigated, with the exception of Dbase II, do not provide any language features that support the interactive screen management at a high level. Therefore, in this section we introduce a concept that substantially simplifies the creation of interactive man-computer dialogues.[29]

The language construct, called *screen,* is analogous to a subroutine; that is, it is invoked like a subroutine, can pass parameters, and has the same scoping rules as a subroutine. But in contrast to subroutines, a screen is a high-level abstraction for dealing with a computer terminal. Screens consist of two parts. One is the static part, in which the programmer specifies the format of the terminal screen and the syntactic structure of valid user entries. The screen format is specified in a high-level nonprocedural language analogous to report generator languages. The second part of a screen is the dynamic activation part, in which the system responses to user entries are specified.

In Figure 22 you see an example of a screen definition. This screen definition is based on the AdaRel database defined in Figure 19. In the format part the programmer can utilize system default functions to specify the layout on the terminal. Notice how the format part defines some data fields to be modifiable by the end user while others are only displayed by the system. Observe that the displayed data fields are extracted directly from the SALES relation, as specified in the activate part. These fields are displayed as soon as the end user inputs the field INVOICE_NO.

Though the scope of this article prevents a more complete elaboration of the facilities of the *screen* construct, the reader can see its utility.

The term "application generator" may well be a misnomer. It has come to us from the large mainframe community to describe a software system that integrates database management facilities with nonprocedural constructs for report generation, graphics, and screen handling. Recently, the personal computer software world has spawned several such systems with similar goals, but on a more modest scale. Our focus in this article has been to identify the salient components of such systems and to argue that their merger with conventional programming languages is both desirable and feasible. □

## Acknowledgment

This work has been supported by the Air Force Office of Scientific Research under Grant No. AFOSR 82-0232.

## References

1. J. B. Munson and R. T. Yeh, report by the IEEE Software Productivity Workshop, San Diego, Calif., Mar. 1981.
2. B. W. Boehm, "Software and its Impact: A Quantitative Assessment," *Datamation,* May 1973.
3. D. D. McCracken, *A Guide To Nomad For Application Development,* National CSS, 1980.
4. J. Martin, *Application Development Without Programmers,* Prentice Hall, Englewood Cliffs, N. J., 1982.
5. L. Druffel, *Strategy for a DoD Software Initiative,* US Department of Defense, Aug. 1982.
6. A. B. Tuçker, *Programming Languages,* McGraw-Hill, Computer Science Series, 1977.
7. M. Stonebraker et al., "The Design and Implementation of INGRES," *ACM-TODS,* Vol. 1, No. 3, 1976.
8. NOMAD 2: Reference Manual, National CSS, Wilton, Conn., 1982.
9. FOCUS Users Manual, Information Builders, Inc., New York, N.Y., 1982.
10. RAMIS 2: Users Manual, Mathematica Products Group, Inc., Princeton, N.J., 1982.
11. R. C. Johnson, "Automated Software Development Eliminates Application Programming," *Electronics,* June 1982.

12. Dbase II Users Manual, Ashton-Tate, Los Angeles, 1981.

13. IBM IMS Application Development Facility, IBM General Information Manual GB21-9869-2, IBM Corporation, East Irving, Tex., 1980.

14. B. M. Leavenworth and J. E. Sammet, "An Overview of Nonprocedural Languages. Proceedings of a Symposium on Very High Level Languages," *Sigplan Notices,* 1974.

15. B. M. Leavenworth, "Non-Procedural Data Processing," *The Computer Journal,* Jan. 1976.

16. M. M. Zloof, "QBE/OBE: A Language for Office and Business Automation," *IEEE Computer,* Vol. 14, No. 5, May 1981, pp. 13-23.

17. R. E. Williams and B. L. King, *The Power of VisiCalc,* Management Information Source, 1982.

18. C. J. Date, *An Introduction to Database Systems,* Addison-Wesley, 1977.

19. J. W. Schmidt, "Some High Level Language Constructs for Data of Type Relation," *ACM-TODS,* Vol. 2, No. 3, Sept. 1977.

20. J. E. Shopiro, "THESEUS-A Programming Language for Relational Databases," *ACM-TODS,* Vol. 4, No. 4, Dec. 1979, pp. 493-517.

21. A. I. Wasserman et al., "Revised Report on the Programming Language PLAIN," *ACM-SIGPLAN,* May 1981.

22. L. A. Rowe and K. A. Shoens, "Data Abstractions, Views and Updates in Rigel," *Proc. Int'l Conf. Management of Data,* ACM-SIGMOD, May 1979, pp. 71-81.

23. J. Smith, S. Fox, and T. Landers, *Reference Manual for ADAPLEX,* technical report, Computer Corporation of America, 1981.

24. E. Horowitz and A. Kemper, "Ada-Rel: A Relational Extension of Ada," technical report TR-83-218, University of Southern California, Nov. 1983.

25. E. F. Codd, "The 1981 Turing Award Lecture: Relational Database: A Practical Foundation for Productivity," *CACM,* Vol. 25, No. 2, Feb. 1982.

26. J. Ullman, *Principles of Database Systems,* Computer Science Press, Potomac, Md., 1980.

27. M. M. Astrahan et al., "System R: Relational Approach to Database Management, *ACM-TODS,* Vol. 1, No. 2, June 1976, pp. 97-137.

28. L. A. Rowe and K. A. Shoens, "Programming Language Constructs for Screen Definition," *IEEE Trans. Soft. Eng.,* Vol. 9, No. 1, Jan. 1983, pp. 31-39.

29. E. Horowitz and A. Kemper, "High-Level Input/Output Facilities in a Database Programming Language," technical report, University of Southern California, May 1984.

## Further reading

A. F. Cardenas and W. P. Grafton, "Challenges and Requirements for New Application Generators," *Proc. NCC,* Houston, Tex., June 1982.

A. Goodman "Application Generators at IBM," *Proc. NCC,* Houston, Tex., June 1982.

J. M. Grochow, "Application Generators: An Introduction," *Proc. NCC,* Houston, Tex., June 1982.

M. Hammer et al., "A Very High Level Programming Language for Data Processing Applications," *CACM,* Vol. 20, No. 11, Nov. 1977, pp. 832-840.

M. L. Kersten and A. I. Wasserman, "The Architecture of the PLAIN Data Base Handler," *Software-Practice and Experience,* Vol. 11, Feb. 1981.

N. S. Prywes, A. Pnueli, and S. Shastry, "Use of a Nonprocedural Specification Language and Associated Program Generator in Software Development," *ACM Trans. Progr. Lang. and Systems,* Vol. 1, No. 2, Oct. 1979, pp. 196-217.

J. W. Schmidt, "Type Concepts for Database Definition," *Proc. Int'l Conf. on Databases: Improving Usability and Responsiveness,* Academic Press, New York, 1978, pp. 215-244.

M. Stonebraker and L. Rowe, "Observations on Data Manipulation Languages and Their Embedding in General Purpose Programming Languages," *Proc. Third Int'l Conf. Very Large Data Bases,* 1977.

R. P. Van De Riet et al., "High Level Programming Features for Improving the Efficiency of a Relational Database System," *ACM-TODS,* Vol. 6, No. 3, Sept. 1981.

J. H. Waldrop, "Application Generators: A Case Study," *Proc. NCC,* Houston, Tex., June 1982.

A. I. Wasserman, "A Software Engineering View of Data Base Management," *Proc. Fourth Int'l Conf. Very Large Data Bases,* 1978.

M. Zloof and S. deJong, "The System for Business Automation (SBA): Programming Language," *CACM,* Vol. 20, No. 6, June 1977, pp. 385-395.

**Ellis Horowitz's** research interests have recently centered on the development of unusual personal computer programming environments. He received his BS degree from Brooklyn College and his PhD in computer science from the University of Wisconsin. He is now a professor of computer science and electrical engineering at the University of Southern California.

**Alfons Kemper** is now on the faculty of the Computer Science Department of the University of Karlsruhe, West Germany. His research interests include programming languages and database management systems. He received his German undergraduate degree, the Vordiplom, at the University of Dortmund in 1979. Kemper received an MS and a PhD degree in computer science from the University of Southern California in 1981 and 1984, respectively.

**Balaji Narasimhan** is currently a graduate student in computer science at the University of Southern California. His research interests are in user interfaces and artificial intelligence. He received his BTech degree in electrical engineering in 1979, and the MTech degree in computer science in 1981, both from the Indian Institute of Technology, Madras. He is a student member of IEEE, ACM, and ACL.

Questions about this article may be addressed to Ellis Horowitz, Computer Science Department, University of Southern California, Los Angeles, CA 90089.

# Chapter 2: User Interfaces to Database Management Systems

There has been much debate in the data management community over the relative merits of various data models. Only when the application environment is considered do these arguments make sense because the use of the data model must be known before an appropriate model can be chosen. The individual who advocates a single data model for all situations preempts the choice the user should rightfully make, based on her or his own experience and requirements.

The following criteria can be used to judge whether a data model meets the needs of the database user.

1. Do facilities exist in the data model to describe the information entities, their attributes, and their relationships that are of interest to the enterprise?
2. Do facilities exist to specify the semantic integrity constraints required on information needed by the enterprise? For example, can a database administrator specify allowable values that an attribute can have; consistency among values of attributes in the same entity (e.g., if SEX-CODE is male, then MAIDEN-NAME must be blank); consistency between new values of data and the old values of attributes already in the database (e.g., the new value of YEARS-OF-EXPERIENCE must be greater than or equal to the current value of YEARS-OF-EXPERIENCE. A technique to override this constraint is necessary to correct input errors); consistency among entities (e.g., if an employee enters "toy" as a value of DEPARTMENT-EMPLOYED-BY, there must be a DEPARTMENT entity for the toy department); and constraints among several entities (e.g., no more than twenty employees may work for the same department).
3. Enterprise personnel should find it easy to formulate and understand data description and data manipulation.

### 2.1: File Data Model

The following describes the major data models in use at this time. The file data model has been used almost as long as the FORTRAN and COBOL programming languages, to which it is closely related. The early designers of FORTRAN and COBOL recognized the need to provide a mechanism that allowed application programs to access data located on secondary storage devices. The file data model allowed the creation of data files that would exist after the creating program had terminated and that could be accessed by programs that would be executed in the future. The file data model and the file system were the forerunners of modern data models and database management systems. Although the file data model is primitive in scope, it is not facing extinction. Indeed, it is the most widely used data model today and will likely continue to be so in the foreseeable future.

The chief advantage of the file data description language is that most programmers understand it and find it easy to use. The chief disadvantage is that only a very limited form of relationship type can be represented, and very few validity and integrity constraints can be specified.

Although it is not universally recognized as a data model, the file data model deals with entities (called *records*), entity classes (*record types*), and attributes of entities (*fields* or *items* of a record) and attribute values (*item values*). The model even supports a primitive form of relationship type by the use of repeating segments, repeating items, and vectors. However, the general lack of support for relationship capabilities is one of the major differences between the file data model and more recent data models.

The data description language for the file data model has several dialects, one for each programming language that supports the model. Such languages include COBOL, FORTRAN, and PL/1. Basically, the description language supports the declaration of record types and attributes of record types. The term commonly used for the collection of data stored on secondary storage is *file.* A file may consist of records of one or more record types.

Each application program must contain declaration statements that describe the types of records in the file. Some programming language systems allow such declarations to be placed into a library. When programs are compiled, the compiler retrieves the file declaration statements from the library and inserts them into the declaration portion of the application program. For example, many COBOL compilers support the COPY command, which copies file descriptions from the COPY LIBRARY into the file description section of the application program. Many PL/1 compilers have a macro-preprocessor capability that supports a similar INCLUDE command. Such a library of data declarations is a forerunner to today's data dictionaries.

The basic data manipulation commands are used to access a single record. READ causes a single record to be transferred from the file to the program work space. WRITE causes a single record from the program work space to be placed into the file. Variations of these two basic commands include DELETE (remove a record from the file) and MODIFY or REWRITE (replace a record in the file with a record in the program work space). Other commands include OPEN (make the file available for use by the application program) and CLOSE (make the file available for use by other application programs).

## 2.2: CODASYL Network Data Model

In May 1959, a meeting was held in the Pentagon to consider establishing a common language for the programming of business-type applications. Computer users from the private sector and the federal government, as well as computer manufacturers, were present at this meeting, later known as the Conference on Data Systems Languages (CODASYL). CODASYL is dedicated to the development of data systems languages independent of any make or model of computer. Later, a subgroup of this committee was established to develop specifications for the languages used to access a database. In 1973, this subgroup, the CODASYL Data Base Language Task Group, published its final report, which subsequently had a dramatic influence on commercial database management systems. Since that report was issued, dozens of vendors have implemented database management systems that adhere in varying degrees to the Data Base Language Task Group specifications and later revisions. The report contained proposals for three distinct languages: schema data description language (schema DDL), subschema data description language (subschema DDL), and data manipulation language (DML). Later, the Data Description Language Committee was established to maintain the schema DDL. Because of their host language dependencies, the subschema DDL and DML maintenance was later taken over by COBOL and FORTRAN CODASYL subcommittees. The Data Base Language Task Group became inactive.

In the 1978 *CODASYL Data Description Language Journal of Development,* the data storage description language (DSDL) was separated from the schema DDL. The original DSDL specifications were developed by the Data Base Authority Working Group, a subcommittee of both the Data Description Language Committee and the British Computer Society.

Like the file data model, the CODASYL network DDL uses a record type to represent an entity class. A record type contains several data items, one for each attribute of the entity class. Each record in the database corresponds to an entity. Each record contains data values, one for each data item.

The CODASYL *set,* not to be confused with the mathematical concept of set, is used to specify relationship types

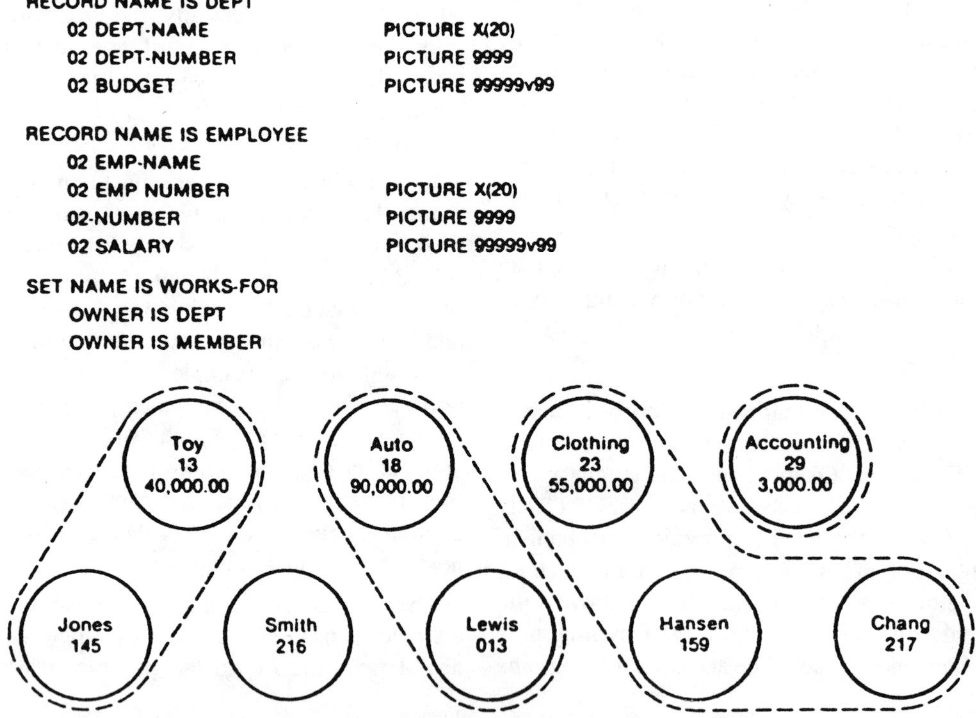


Figure 2.1. WORKS-FOR Set and Set Occurrences

between record types. One record type that participates in the relationship type is called the *owner record type.* Others are called *member record types.* For example, the two record types, the DEPT record type and the EMPLOYEE record type, make up the WORKS-FOR set illustrated in Figure 2.1. The DEPT record type is the owner record type, and the EMPLOYEE record type is the member record type.

A *set occurrence* in the database represents the actual relationships between an occurrence of the owner record type and one or more occurrences of the member record type. An occurrence of the owner record type that is not associated with any occurrences of the member is also considered to be a set occurrence. Such a set occurrence contains a single tenant, the owner record occurrence. Each set occurrence has one or more tenants. The owner record is always a tenant of a set occurrence. All member records associated with the owner record are also tenants.

Occurrences of the WORK-FOR set are illustrated by dashed ovals in Figure 2.1. Circles represent record occurrences in the database. Four set occurrences correspond to each of the four occurrences of the DEPT record type. The set occurrence owned by the toy DEPT record has two tenants: the toy DEPT record and the Jones EMPLOYEE record. The set occurrence owned by the clothing DEPT record has three tenants: the clothing DEPT record, the Hansen EMPLOYEE record, and the Chang EMPLOYEE record. The set occurrence owned by the accounting DEPT record has only one tenant, the accounting DEPT record. Each set occurrence has one owner record. One set occurrence that is owned by the accounting DEPT record has no members. The remaining set occurrences each have one member record, except for the set occurrence owned by the clothing DEPT record, which has two member records.

The Smith EMPLOYEE record does not participate in any set occurrence. However, there are data description language declarations that require that all record occurrences of the member types always be associated with some occurrence of the set. Smith can be associated with a set occurrence by data manipulation commands that will be discussed below. Occurrences of the member record type may also be disassociated from a set occurrence.

An important restriction enforced by all CODASYL database management systems is that no occurrence of the member record type may be a tenant in more than one occurrence of each set type; however, a record occurrence may be a tenant in occurrences of several different set types.

The CODASYL data description language is said to be *access path dependent* because it may be necessary for the programmer to specify a path in order to retrieve some records. For example, in Figure 2.1, a programmer can assess a specific employee record after accessing the record of the department for which the employee works. The relational data description language, on the other hand, is much more access path independent because a programmer seldom must access one table in order to access another.

Frequently sets are used to represent one-to-many relationships. The "many" of the one-to-many relationship corresponds to the member records of the set occurrence owned by the "one" owner record. Sets are used to represent multivalued dependencies.

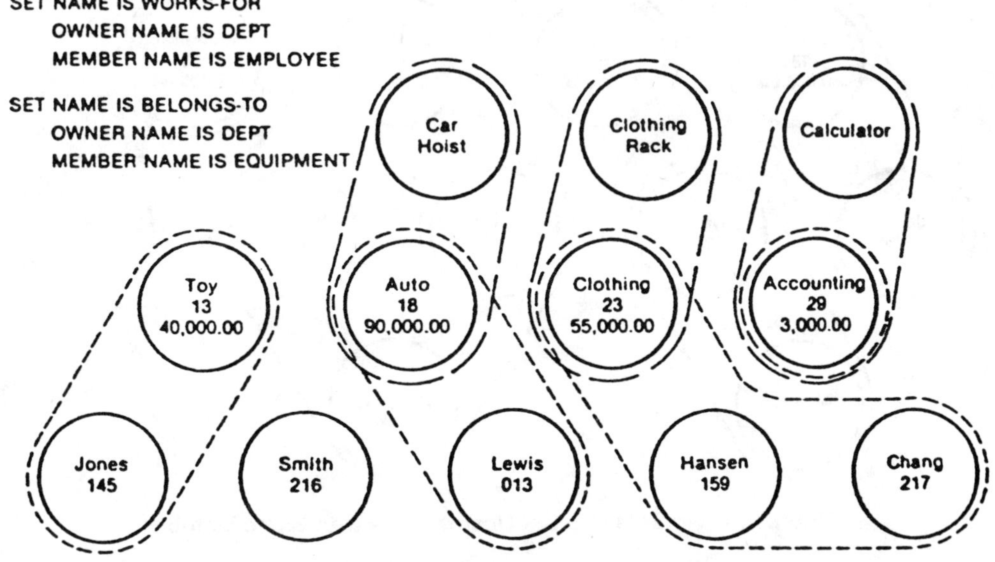


Figure 2.2. Two Sets with Same Owner and Occurrences

A record type can be the owner record type of more than one set type. For example, suppose we have three record types: DEPT, EMPLOYEE, and EQUIPMENT. There is also a WORKS-FOR association between EMPLOYEE and DEPT. There is also a BELONGS-TO association between EQUIPMENT and DEPT (Figure 2.2). Tenants of the WORK-FOR set occurrences are enclosed in short dashed ovals, while tenants of BELONGS-TO set occurrences are enclosed in long dashed ovals.

A record type can be a member record type of more than one set. Figure 2.3 illustrates an example of the record type EMPLOYEE as a member record type of two set types. There is a one-to-many relationship between INSURANCE-CO and EMPLOYEE. There is a one-to-many relationship between INSURANCE-CO and EMPLOYEE. As illustrated in Figures 2.2 and 2.3, two sets with the same member record type or the same owner record type can be used to represent many-to-many relationships.

Two different sets may have the same owner record type and the same member record type. For example, Figure 2.4 illustrates two records, DEPT and EMPLOYEE, and two set types, PERMANENT and ON-LOAN-TO. The PERMANENT set type associates EMPLOYEE record occurrences with the DEPT to which they are permanently assigned. If some employees are working temporarily for another DEPT to which they have been "loaned," this may be represented by the ON-LOAN-TO set type. Tenants of the PERMANENT SET occurrences are enclosed in short dashed ovals, and tenants of the ON-LOAN-TO set occurrences are enclosed in long dashed ovals.

A record type may be a member record type of one set and an owner record type of another set. Figure 2.5 illustrates three record types; DEPT, EMPLOYEE, and DEPENDENT; and two set types, WORKS-FOR and DEPENDENT-OF. The EMPLOYEE record type is the member record of the WORKS-FOR set and also the owner record of the DEPENDENT-OF set.

Figure 2.6 illustrates two record types, COMPANY and PERSON, and two sets, WORKS-FOR and OWNS-STOCK-IN. The COMPANY record type is the owner record type of the WORKS-FOR set and the member record type of the OWNS-STOCK-IN set. The PERSON is the member record type of the WORKS-FOR set type and the owner record type of the OWNS-STOCK-IN set type. Figure 2.6 illustrates a cycle of two sets.

Figure 2.7 illustrates a single record type, PART, and a single set type, PART-OF. The PART record type is both the owner record and the member record types of the PART-OF

```
SET NAME IS INSURED-BY
    OWNER NAME IS INSURANCE-CO
    MEMBER NAME IS EMPLOYEE

SET NAME IS WORKS-FOR
    OWNER NAME IS DEPT
    MEMBER NAME IS EMPLOYEE
```

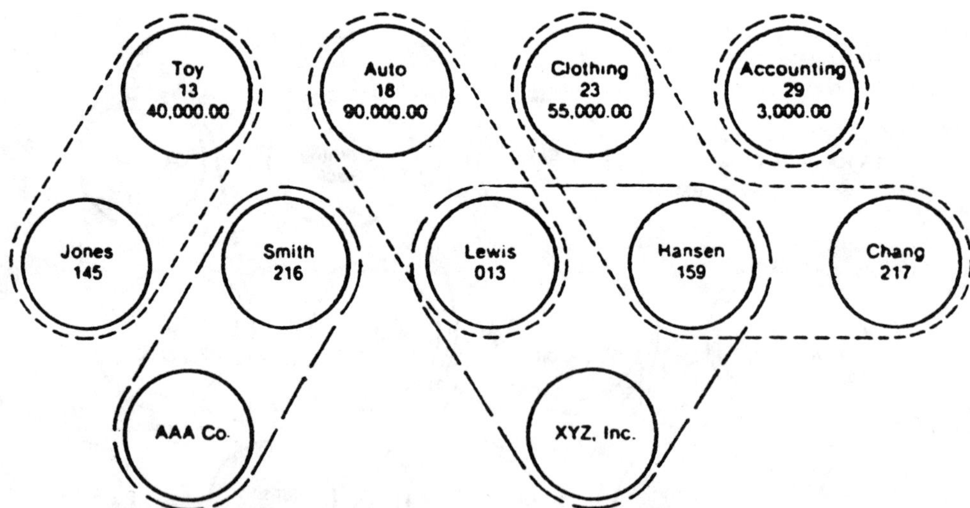


Figure 2.3 Two Sets and Set Occurrences with Same Member

```
SET NAME IS PERMANENT
    OWNER IS DEPT
    MEMBER IS EMPLOYEE

SET NAME IS ON-LOAN-TO
    OWNER IS DEPT
    MEMBER IS EMPLOYEE
```

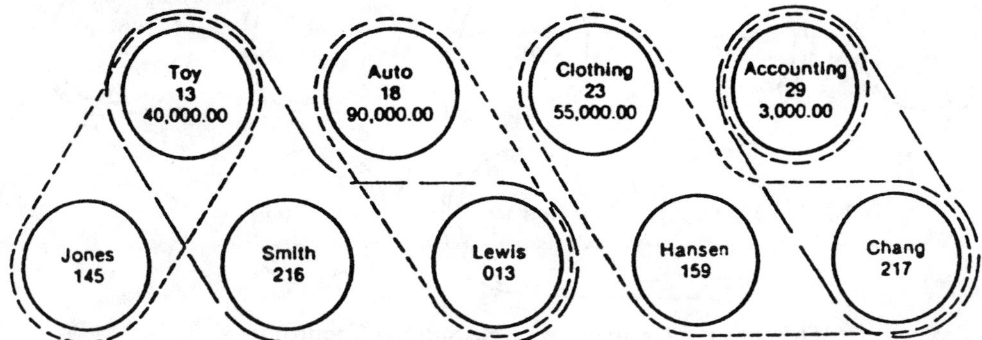


Figure 2.4. Two Sets and Set Occurrences with Same Owner and Member

```
SET NAME IS WORKS-FOR
    OWNER NAME IS DEPT
    MEMBER NAME IS EMPLOYEE

SET NAME IS DEPENDENT-OF
    OWNER NAME IS EMPLOYEE
    MEMBER NAME IS DEPENDENT
```

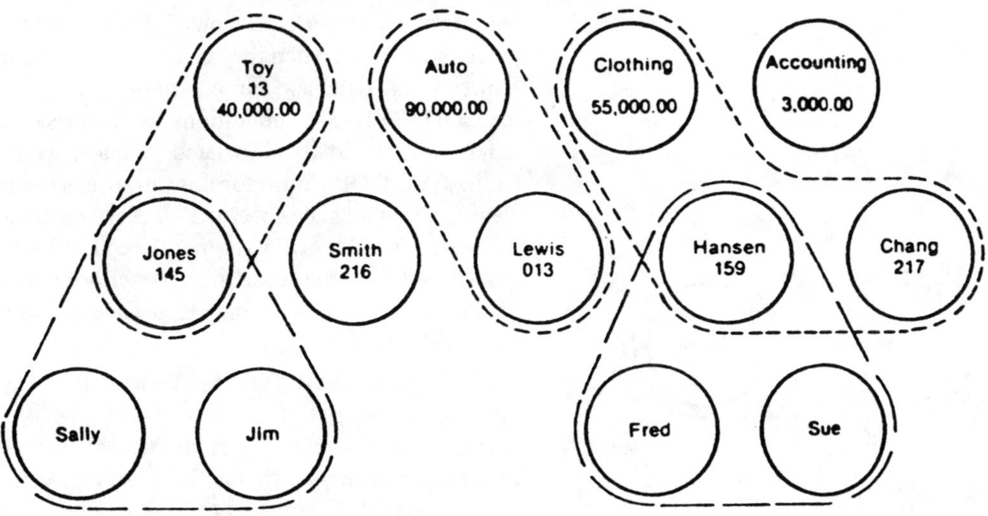


Figure 2.5. A Hierarchy of Two Sets and Set Occurrences

```
SET NAME IS WORKS-FOR
    OWNER NAME IS COMPANY
    MEMBER NAME IS PERSON

SET NAME IS OWNS-STOCK-IN
    OWNER NAME IS PERSON
    MEMBER NAME IS COMPANY
```

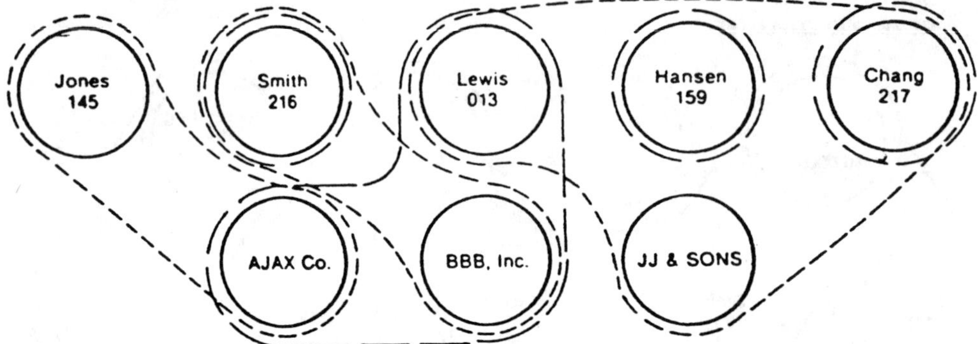


**Figure 2.6. A Cycle of Two Sets and Set Occurrences**

set type. The PART-OF set type is a cycle of one set. Another term for a set type with the same record type as both owner and member is a *recursive* set type.

A special kind of set type has no owner and only one set occurrence in the database. This special kind of set type is called a *SYSTEM owned set* type. Like other set types, member records in the SYSTEM owned set occurrence can be ordered. SYSTEM owned sets are used when it is desired to order some but not all record occurrences. For example, a SYSTEM owned set with member record type EMPLOYEE might have only EMPLOYEE records with age greater than 65 in the set occurrence. No EMPLOYEE record with age less than or equal to 65 may participate as a member of the set occurrence. Thus, an order can be specified on all EMPLOYEE records with age greater than 65, but this order is not maintained on EMPLOYEE records with age less than or equal to 65. Figure 2.8 illustrates a SYSTEM owned set type.

```
SET NAME IS PART-OF
    OWNER NAME IS PART
    MEMBER NAME IS PART
```

Bicycle
Frame
Wheel
Handle Bar
Hub
Tire

**Figure 2.7. A Recursive Set and Set Occurrences**

*Insertion Retention Options*

One might think that it is always the responsibility of the programmer who updates the database to specify when records of a member type should be associated with an occurrence of a set and when they can be disassociated (removed). However, the database administrator may specify, as part of the CODASYL DDL conditions, when a record occurrence may be automatically associated with a set occurrence. The CODASYL DDL clause for this purpose is the INSERTION clause, which must be specified for every member record type of each CODASYL set type. The INSERTION clause describes data in the sense that it describes what kind of data manipulation commands may be used to modify the tenancy of a CODASYL set.

INSERTION IS AUTOMATIC means that whenever a record occurrence of the member record type is stored in the database, it is automatically associated in the appropriate occurrence of the set by the database management system. The program does not need to issue an explicit data manipulation command that associates the new record with an occurrence of this set. The specification of INSERTION IS AUTOMATIC shifts the responsibility of association of a new record

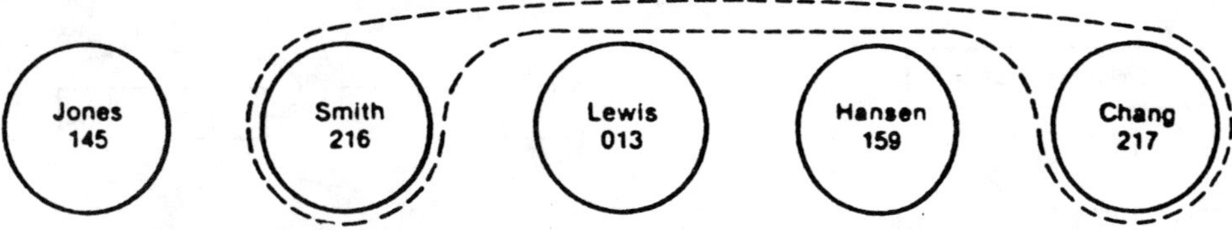


**Figure 2.8. System Owned Set and Set Occurrence**

with an occurrence of the set from the programmer who writes the program to the database management system itself.

INSERTION IS MANUAL means that whenever a member record occurrence is stored in the database, it is not automatically associated with an occurrence of the set. The program must issue a special data manipulation command if the new record occurrence is to be associated with an occurrence of the set.

The INSERTION specification deals with new records and whether they should be automatically associated with an occurrence of the set by the database management system. The RETENTION option of the INSERTION clause describes restrictions on how a member record may be disassociated from an occurrence of the set. RETENTION IS FIXED requires that a member record not be disassociated from a set occurrence unless the owner record occurrence is removed from a database. RETENTION IS MANDATORY requires that once a member record is associated with an occurrence of the set, it may be disassociated from that occurrence only if it is associated with some other occurrence of the set. RETENTION is OPTIONAL specifies that a member record may be disassociated from an occurrence of the set without associating it with another such occurrence.

The SET SELECTION clause is used to guide the database management system in selecting the appropriate set occurrence. When an occurrence of the member record must be automatically associated with a set occurrence, as is the case when INSERTION IS AUTOMATIC has been specified, the SET SELECTION clause specifies how the database management system can find the owner record of the appropriate set occurrence. Optionally, the set selection clause may specify that the most currently assessed owner record identifies the occurrence to which the new member record is to be attached.

*Set Order*

Every set must have an ORDER specified for its member record occurrences. The ORDER clause is used to specify the sequence of member record occurrences seen by the programmer when tenants of the set occurrence are accessed.

The sequence may be on the basis of the time the record is inserted into the set occurrence. ORDER IS LAST indicates that new records are inserted at the end of the set occurrence, and ORDER IS FIRST indicates that new records are inserted at the first of the set occurrence. ORDER IS NEXT places the new member record occurrence after the currently located set member record. ORDER IS PRIOR places the new member record occurrence before the currently located set member record.

The sequence may also be on the basis of one or more data items within member records. ORDER IS SORTED is used to specify that member records are retrieved in ascending sequence by value of the item named in the subsequent set key specification: ASCENDING KEY IS item-name. This specification itself may be followed by DUPLICATES ARE NOT ALLOWED, which guarantees that two or more records within a set occurrence may not have the same value for item name.

*Physical Representation of Sets*

The CODASYL Storage DDL describes index, pointer, and value-based data structures used as the physical representa-

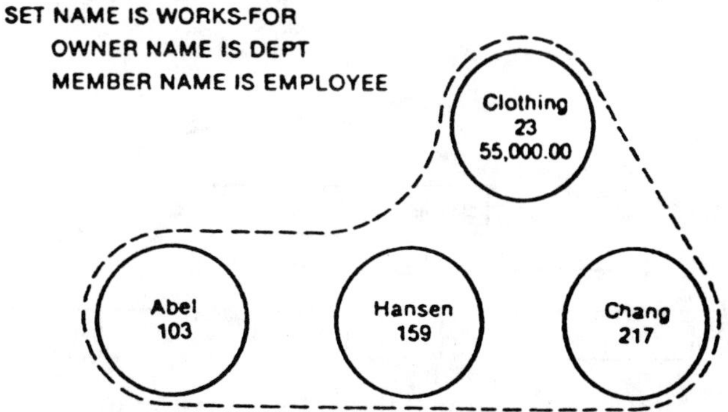


**Figure 2.9. WORKS-FOR Set and Set Occurrence**

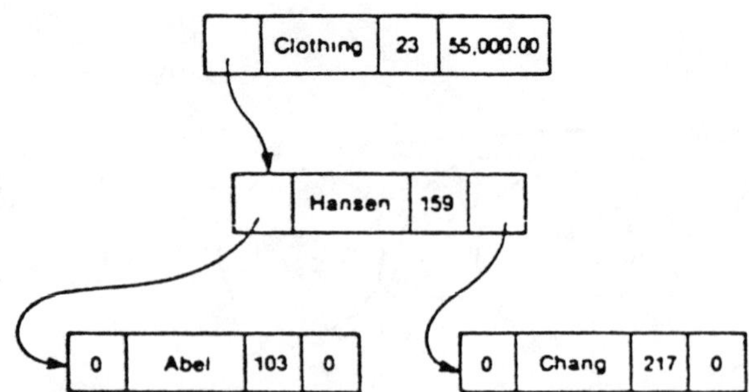


**Figure 2.10. Binary Tree Representation of a WORKS-FOR Occurrence**

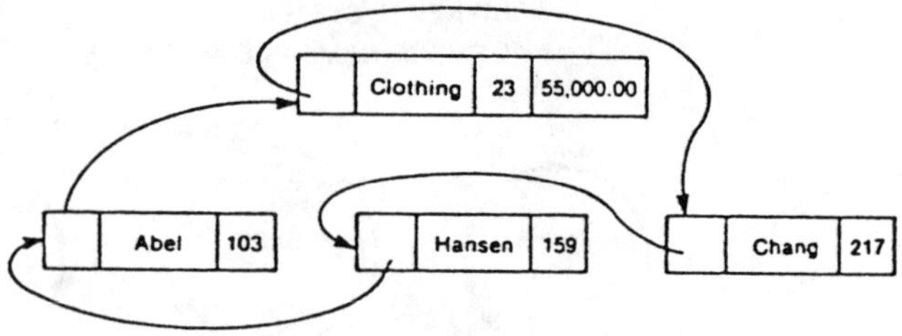

**Figure 2.11. Next Pointer Representation of a WORKS-FOR Set Occurrence**

tion of sets. Each set occurrence is represented using one of these types of data structures.

An index may be used to represent the association between a record occurrence corresponding to the single owner of a set and the several record occurrences of the member record type. The record that corresponds to the owner occurrence contains a pointer to an index, which contains pointers to each member record that is a tenant of that set occurrence. Figure 2.10 illustrates the use of a binary tree index to represent the set occurrence illustrated in Figure 2.9. Given the address of the record corresponding to the set owner, it is possible to use the binary tree to locate the addresses of all records that are member records of the set occurrence. Given the address of the record corresponding to any member record, it is also possible to locate the following member record of the set occurrence.

Another technique for representing associations between the owner and member record occurrences of a set occurrence is to chain together the records corresponding to the tenants of the set occurrence. Three such possible data structures are illustrated in Figures 2.11, 2.12, and 2.13. Figure 2.11 shows the use of next (forward) pointers. This representation supports the access of successive member record occurrences in ascending sequence. Figure 2.12 shows the use of prior pointers. This representation supports the access of successive member record occurrences in descending sequence. Figure 2.13 shows the use of owner pointers. This representative supports the access of an owner record occurrence given the address of any of its member record occurrences.

A set may be represented by a combination of pointer data structures. Because it is possible to change the storage schema and the physical representation of data structures without affecting the logic of application programs, it is possible to improve the performance of the application programs. A database can be fine tuned to support rapid access to set tenants by deleting, adding, or replacing pointers or indexes. The new pointers or indexes may provide a more appropriate path by which programs access set tenants.

## 2.3: Procedural Languages

Both the file data model and the CODASYL data model use the program work space as a communications area between the executing program and the database management system. The program work space consists of an area of computer memory that an application program directly references. All program valuables reside in the program work space. The program work space also contains buffers that hold data values delivered to the program work space from the database by the database management system. The database management

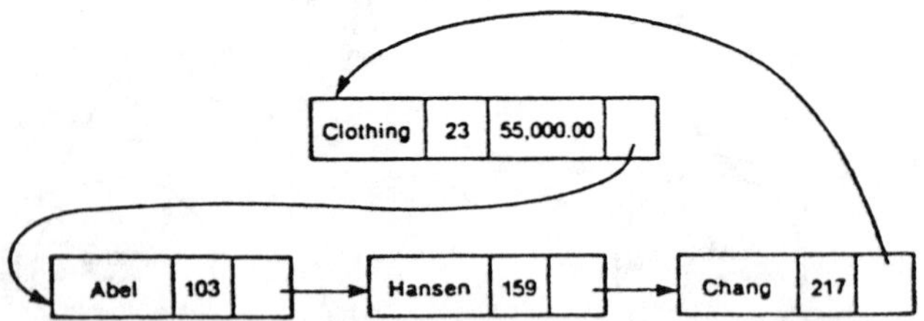


**Figure 2.12. Prior Pointer Representation of a WORKS-FOR Set**

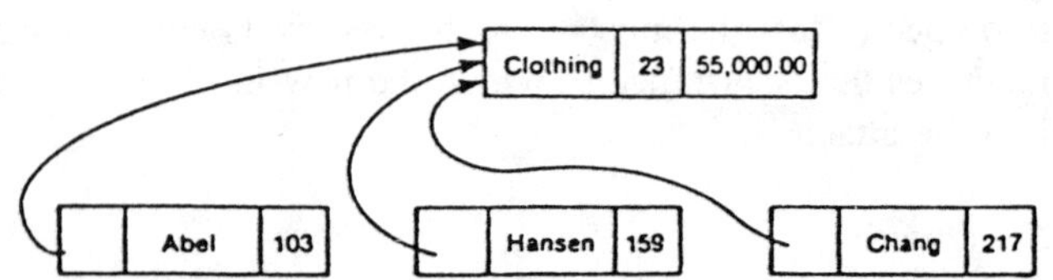


**Figure 2.13. Owner Pointers in a WORKS-FOR Set Occurrence**

system may also transfer data from the program work space to the database. The database management system is called upon to perform these and other data management functions during execution of data manipulation commands embedded into application programs.

The CODASYL data manipulation language consists of two classes of commands. One class, the basic class, consists of commands that locate data in the database and cause data to be transferred between the database and the program work space. The commands in this case are similar to the procedural commands of file systems. The other class of commands is bookkeeping commands, which give advice to the database management system to help it perform the processing of the basic class of commands.

The basic data manipulation commands of CODASYL are

FIND: Locates a specified record.

GET: Transfers a copy of the specific record from the database to the program work space.

MODIFY: Replaces the record in the database by the record in the program work space.

ERASE: Removes a record from the database.

STORE: Inserts a record into the database.

CONNECT: Associates a record of the set member type with a record of the set owner type.

DISCONNECT: Disassociates a record of the set member type from a record of the set owner type.

The class of bookkeeping commands includes:

READY: Makes available a collection of records for an application to use.

FINISH: Terminates the availability of a collection of records to an application program.

KEEP: Notifies the database management system that the record will be accessed again.

FREE: Cancels a KEEP command.

COMMIT: Guarantees that all previous database updates are permanent.

*FIND Command*

The FIND command causes the database management system to locate a specific record in the database. Other data manipulation commands may then be executed to transfer values of that record from the database to the program work space.

There are several options of the FIND command. "FIND FIRST record-name-1" causes the database management system to locate the first record of the named record type in the database. "FIND NEXT record-name-1" causes the database management system to locate the following record of the type record-name-1. A single FIND FIRST followed by repeated FIND NEXT commands is used for locating records sequentially. Sequential retrieval requires a GET command following each FIND command:

```
    FIND FIRST EMP-RECORD
    GET EMP-RECORD
    If <record not found> GO TO NEXT-P.
    <process record>.
LOOP.
    FIND NEXT EMP-RECORD
    If <record not found> GO TO NEXT-P.
    GET EMP-RECORD
    <process record>
    GO TO LOOP.
NEXT-P.
```

For direct access, move the value of the identifier of the record occurrence to be accessed to a variable (EMP-NUMBER in the following example) and issue the FIND ANY and GET commands:

```
    MOVE '95' to EMPL-NUMBER
    FIND ANY EMP-RECORD using EMP-NUMBER
    IF <record not found> GO TO NEXT-P.
    GET EMP-RECORD.
    NEXT-P.
```

The sequence of commands causes the first record with value of 95 for the EMP-NUMBER data item to be located in the database and then copied into the program work space. To find all records with value EMP-NUMBER equal to 95, use the FIND ANY followed by repeated FIND DUPLICATE commands:

```
    MOVE '95' TO EMP-NUMBER
    FIND AND EMP-RECORD USING EMP-NUMBER
    IF <record not found> GO TO NEXT-P.
    GET EMP-RECORD.
LOOP.
    FIND DUPLICATE EMP-RECORD USING EMP-
    NUMBER.
    IF <record not found> GO TO NEXT-P.
    GET EMP-RECORD.
    <process record>
    GO TO LOOP.
NEXT-P.
```

The success or failure of a FIND command can be determined by examining a special variable. After each FIND command has been executed, the database management system updates this variable with codes indicating the success or the reason for failure to execute the database command. The application program must check these variables after each FIND command to determine if the FIND command was completed successfully.

CODASYL sets are relationships that consist of a single owner and zero or more member entity occurrences. The following FIND commands locate the first member, the next member, the last member, the prior member, and the owner of the DEPT-SET set occurrence, respectively:

```
FIND FIRST EMP-RECORD WITHIN DEPT-SET
FIND NEXT EMP-RECORD WITHIN DEPT-SET
FIND LAST EMP-RECORD WITHIN DEPT-SET
FIND PRIOR EMP-RECORD WITHIN DEPT-SET
FIND OWNER WITHIN DEPT-SET.
```

*GET Command*

The GET command causes the database management system to transfer a copy of a record from the database to the program work space. The GET command is usually preceded by a FIND command:

```
FIND FIRST EMP-RECORD
GET EMP-RECORD.
```

*MODIFY Command*

The MODIFY command causes the program work space version of a record to be replaced into the database. For example,

```
FIND FIRST EMP-RECORD
GET EMP-RECORD
MOVE 45 to AGE of EMP-RECORD
MODIFY EMP-RECORD
```

causes the age of the first EMP-RECORD record to be changed to a value of 45 in the database. Note that the MODIFY command cannot be used to create a new record in the database. A STORE command accomplishes this.

*STORE Command*

The STORE command is used to place a new record from the program work space into the database. For example,

```
MOVE 95 to EMP-NUMBER OF EMP-RECORD
MOVE 45 TO AGE OF EMP-RECORD
MOVE "JONES" TO NAME OF EMP-RECORD
STORE EMP-RECORD
```

causes a new record with values of 95, 45, JONES for data items EMP-NUMBER, AGE, and NAME to be sorted into the database. The STORE command also involves an implicit locate so that if the following command is a GET, then the newly stored record would be copied back into the program work space.

If a record is declared to be a member of a set that is declared INSERTION IS AUTOMATIC, then when a record occurrence is STOREd into the database, the database management system also CONNECTs that record to the set occurrence identified by the SET SELECTION clause.

*ERASE Command*

The ERASE command causes a record to be erased from the database. For example,

```
LOCATE NEXT EMP-RECORD
IF <record found> ERASE EMP-RECORD
```

would cause the next EMP-RECORD record, if one exists, to be removed from the database.

*CONNECT and DISCONNECT Commands*

The CONNECT command causes a record to be placed into a set occurrence; that is, to establish a relationship between that record and the record that is the owner of a set occurrence. For example,

```
    MOVE 35 to DEPT-NUMBER
    FIND DEPT-RECORD USING DEPT-NUMBER
    IF <not found> GO TO NEXT-P.
    MOVE 77 to EMP-NUMBER
    FIND EMP-RECORD USING EMP-NUMBER
    IF <not found> GO TO NEXT-P.
    CONNECT EMP-RECORD to WORKS-FOR.
NEXT-P.
```

If the record types DEPT-RECORD and EMP-RECORD, are owner and member of the WORKS-FOR set, respectively, then the above statements cause the EMP-RECORD record with EMP-NUMBER = 77 to be inserted into the WORKS-FOR set occurrence owned by the DEPT-RECORD record with DEPT-NUMBER = 35, provided both records exist in the database.

A DISCONNECT command is used to disassociate a member from a set occurrence. For example,

```
DISCONNECT EMP-RECORD FROM WORKS-FOR.
```

## 2.4: Relational Data Model

The relational data model has received a great deal of interest since it was introduced by E.F. Codd in 1970. Many aspects of the relational data model will seem familiar to users of the file model, who often write programs that sort files, merge files, and select records from files. These operations correspond to data manipulation commands provided in many relational data manipulation languages. The conceptual simplicity of using a single unit, such as a record in a file, to represent a single entity is present in the data definition language of the relational data model.

In the relational data model, a data manipulation statement may consist of several data description phrases. Data description statements, in turn, may consist of several data manipulation phrases. The relational data description and data manipulation languages become so entwined that it is impractical (and not desirable) to try to keep them separated. The term *relational language* frequently is used to refer to both relational data manipulation and relational data description languages.

A *domain* is a collection of values that attributes of entities may assume. One of the purposes of the domain specification is to specify valid values of attributes. A domain may be specified by naming the domain and one of the following: specifying the type of values, listing the allowable values, or specifying a range of values.

In the relational data description language, a *table (relation)* is used to represent an entity class. A table is specified by naming the entity and listing its attributes. The term *column* is used in place of the term attribute. The domain of allowable values is specified for each column. No table may have more than one column with the same column name.

Consider the following example of domains and tables:

```
DOMAIN COURSE     FIXED
DOMAIN SUBJECT    CHAR 30
DOMAIN STUDENT    FIXED
DOMAIN PERSON     CHAR 30
DOMAIN ADDRESS    CHAR 50
DOMAIN GRADE      CHAR 1

TABLE COURSE
    COLUMN COURSE-ID UNIQUE OF DOMAIN
      COURSE
    COLUMN COURSE-NAME OF DOMAIN SUBJECT
    COLUMN COURSE-INSTRUCTOR OF DOMAIN
      PERSON

TABLE STUDENT
    COLUMN STUDENT-ID UNIQUE OF DOMAIN
      STUDENT
    COLUMN STUDENT-NAME OF DOMAIN PERSON
    COLUMN STUDENT-ADDRESS OF DOMAIN
      ADDRESS

TABLE GRADE
    COLUMN COURSE-# OF DOMAIN COURSE
    COLUMN STUDENT-# OF DOMAIN STUDENT
    COLUMN GRADE OF DOMAIN GRADE
```

The UNIQUE keyword indicates which columns are unique identifiers of rows (tuples) of each table. Each table must have at least one identifier.

A one-to-many relationship between COURSE and GRADE is indicated by the common domain of COURSE-ID and COURSE-#. The one-to-many relationship between STUDENT and GRADE is indicated by the common domain of STUDENT-ID and STUDENT-#. The column STUDENT-# is sometimes referred to as a *foreign key* of the GRADE table because it identifies a unique column (identifier) of a separate (foreign) table. COURSE-# is also a foreign key of the GRADE table because it identifies a unique column of the COURSE table.

Some relational languages support a trigger statement as part of the relational data description. The general format of a trigger statement is

TRIGGER action-1 WHEN action-2

where action-1 is a relational data manipulation statement that is executed when action-2 is executed. Triggers are very useful in specifying validity and integrity constraints on data in the database.

Data storage representation and index creation in a relational database may be determined automatically by the database management system. According to one school of thought, the database management system should be able to relieve programmers of such technical and time-consuming details, freeing them to spend more time to analyze and develop appropriate data manipulation commands. Another school of thought suggests that the use of such a system of defaults prohibits the programmer from fine tuning the database in order to optimize the performance of selected data manipulation commands. The author belongs to the first school because he feels that optimization should either be done by the database management system software or by DBMS experts, like the database administrator.

## 2.5: NonProcedural Languages

One of the advantages most frequently attributed to the relational data model is the ability to access multiple records using a single data manipulation command. The nonprocedural commands supported by the relational data model are indeed powerful. However, such commands are not unique to the relational data model. Most CODASYL database management systems now support nonprocedural languages.

A variety of relational data manipulation languages can be used to access data in a database. The relational calculus, the relational algebra, and SQL are examples of such languages that can be entered by database users at a terminal, as well as be embedded into programming languages such as FORTRAN, COBOL, PL/1, and PASCAL.

The relational data model may support several procedural commands. However, the true power of this model is in its nonprocedural commands. These multiple-record-at-a-time commands operate on either one or two tables and always produce a new table. Thus, a user can specify operations on the database at a very high level (at the level of entity types rather than at the level of individual entity instances as in the file or CODASYL data manipulation languages).

The basic functions that relational database management systems can perform include

RESTRICT create a new table containing some of the rows of an existing table.

PROJECT create a new table containing some of the columns of an existing table.

UNION create a new table containing all of the rows in either or both of two existing tables. The two existing tables must have the same domains for corresponding columns.

DIFFERENCE create a new table containing all of the rows in one existing table that do not appear in another existing table. The two existing tables must have the same domains for corresponding columns.

INTERSECT create a new table containing only the rows that appear in both of two existing tables. Again the two existing tables must have the same domains for corresponding columns.

CARTESIAN PRODUCT create a new table with a row containing the same values as each possible pair of rows from two existing tables.

EQUAL-JOIN create a new table containing a row that contains the same values as each pair of rows from two existing tables such that the two rows have the same values for two specified columns. The EQUAL-JOIN function can be accomplished by a CARTESIAN PRODUCT followed by a SELECTION function.

All of these functions are present in each of the three main relational languages: relational algebra, relational calculus, and SQL. Table 2.1 illustrates the syntax used in each of these three relational languages to specify these basic functions.

Because the result of any relational function is itself a table, relational functions can be applied to the results of other relational functions. To formulate database requests, the user formulates a sequence of relational functions on the tables in the database.

Because most relational data manipulation languages support nonprocedural access to a database, one relational data manipulation command will result in many more basic computer operations than a network, procedural data manipulation command. Thus, a computer takes longer to execute a relational data manipulation command than it takes to execute a typical network data manipulation command. This does not in itself imply that relational data manipulation commands are always inefficient. However, they may result in more basic computer operations than an equivalent sequence of network data manipulation commands. This can happen because a cleverly designed sequence of network data manipulation commands may take advantage of characteristics of data structures not visible to the programmer who writes a functionally equivalent relational data manipulation command. It is in this sense that relational data manipulation commands may be less efficient than network data manipulation commands. A similar statement is often made regarding FORTRAN and assembly languages. The machine code resulting from a FORTRAN statement may be less efficient than the equivalent machine code resulting from a cleverly written sequence of assembly language statements. On the other hand, fewer relational data manipulation commands than network data manipulation commands may be needed to specify the same function. Again, a similar statement is often made regarding FORTRAN and assembly languages. Fewer lines of FORTRAN source code than assembly source code are needed to specify the same function. The nonprocedural data manipulation languages have, compared to procedural languages, fewer lines of source code per program, which results in lower program-creation costs and lower program-maintenance costs. Whether these savings offset the potential inefficiencies is a critical systems-analysis decision that can be made only after examing the environment of the application.

Nonprocedural languages such as SQL have become very popular. They are much easier to learn and use than the CODASYL data manipulation language commands. The nonprocedural languages have enabled users with little computer training to access the information in databases. The next section describes how nonprocedural languages can be coupled with the traditional programming languages used for the majority of data processing applications.

## 2.6: Embedding DMLs into Host Programming Languages

The programming languages, into which the data manipulation commands are added, are called *host programming languages*. The data manipulation commands of data models with procedural data manipulation languages (the file and

**Table 2.1**

SELECT:

SQL:

```
SELECT STUDENT–ID, STUDENT–NAME, STUDENT–ADDRESS
FROM STUDENT
WHERE STUDENT–NAME = 'Jones'
```

Relational Algebra:

```
SELECT (STUDENT, STUDENT–NAME = 'Jones')
```

Relational Calculus:

```
RANGE OF X IS STUDENT
GET (X.STUDENT–ID, X.STUDENT–NAME, X.STUDENT–ADDRESS)
WHERE X.STUDENT = 'Name'
```

PROJECT:

SQL:

```
SELECT STUDENT–NAME
FROM STUDENT
```

Relational Algebra:

```
PROJECT (STUDENT, STUDENT–NAME)
```

Relational Calculus:

```
RANGE OF X IS STUDENT
GET (X.STUDENT–ID)
```

Equi-Join:

SQL:

```
SELECT STUDENT–ID, STUDENT–NAME, STUDENT–ADDRESS
        COURSE–#, STUDENT–#, GRADE
FROM STUDENT, COURSE
WHERE STUDENT–ID = STUDENT–#
```

Relational Algebra:

```
JOIN (STUDENT, COURSE, STUDENT–ID, STUDENT–#)
```

Relational Calculus:

```
RANGE OF X IS STUDENT
RANGE OF Y IS COURSE
GET X.STUDENT–ID, X.STUDENT–NAME, X.STUDENT–ADDRESS
    Y.COURSE–#, Y.STUDENT–#, Y.GRADE
WHERE X.STUDENT–ID = Y.STUDENT–#
```

CODASYL data models) were designed to be embedded into programming languages. However, most nonprocedural languages were designed to be *stand-alone* data manipulation languages in that requests could be formulated without using programming language constructs. However, it is often desirable for application programs to be written by using one of the major programming languages to access a database using the nonprocedural data manipulation languages. Reasons for this include the following points:

- Users only have to learn one data manipulation language if it can be used both stand-alone for ad hoc requests and also embedded into each of the host programming languages.
- The same software can be used to process the nonprocedural data manipulation language, irrespectively of whether it is embedded into a host programming language or used as a stand-alone language. This decreases the amount of software that vendors must design, implement, and support.
- Nonprocedural data manipulation languages are easier to learn and use than single-record-per-command data manipulation languages.

To embed a relational data manipulation language into a host programming language, the host language must deal with the concept of a relation. Three commonly suggested approaches for dealing with tables in a host language are (1) model the table by an array, (2) model the table by a file, and (3) introduce a new data type for the table.

*Model the relation by an array:* A two dimensional array is often suggested for representing a table. This is especially tempting because some programming languages even use the term "table" to mean an array. However, there are some subtle differences between an array and a database table. In an array, the rows are ordered (i.e., there is a first row, a second row, and an n-th row), while theoretically, the rows of a database table are not ordered. In an array, two rows of a table may have exactly the same values. However, this is prohibited in a database table. Finally, the number of rows of a table is bounded by the dimension of the table. At the same time, the number of rows in a database table should not be iimited by some prespecified upper bounds.

*Model the table by a file:* A file containing a single record type is another option for representing a table. Unlike arrays that have a fixed number of rows, a file can be dynamically extended. The programmer can use traditional file I/O commands to access the table.

*Introduce a New Data Type:* The host programming language can be extended by introducing a new type of data, which we will call a database table. For example,

```
EMP  TABLE KEY EMP-NO
     EMP-NO INTEGER
     EMP-NAME CHAR(20)
     DEPT-NAME CHAR(20)
```

could be used to define a database table with the name of EMP. There are three columns of the EMP table, EMP-NO, EMP-NAME, and DEPT-NAME. EMP-NO is a unique identifier of the EMP table.

Associated with each data type in a programming language is a set of operations that can be applied to that data type. First we describe row and column designators that are used to reference parts of tables in traditional programming language operations. Next we describe how the relational calculus can be embedded into traditional programming languages by using the range variable as an iteration variable. Finally we describe how relational algebra operations can be embedded into traditional programming languages.

A *row designator* is used to access a single row of the table. For example, the row designator

```
EMP[25]
```

could be used to refer to the row of the EMP table with value 25 as the unique identifier. Row designators can be used in arithmetic assignment statements, such as

```
TEMP := EMP[15]
```

which copies the row of the EMP database table to the TEMP program variable.

A *column designator* is used to access the value of a single column of a single row. For example, the column identifier

```
EMP[25].DEPT-NAME
```

is used to access the value of the DEPT-NAME column of the EMP table whose row has value 25 for the EMP-NUMBER column. Row and column designators can be in assignment statements, I/O statements, and where ever variables can be used in traditional programming languages.

Additional operations can be added to the programming language to delete and insert rows to and from a database table. For example

```
EMP :+ TEMP
```

inserts the values in the programming variable TEMP into the EMP database table.

```
EMP :- EMP[18]
```

causes the row of EMP with value 18 for the EMP-NUMBER column to be deleted from the EMP database table.

A *row variable* is a variable that ranges over the individual rows of a database table. It is frequently used in relational calculus requests. Suppose we have a database table declared as follows:

```
EMP  TABLE KEY NAME
     NAME CHAR (20)
     SALARY INTEGER
     MANAGER CHAR(20)
```

which gives the name of employees, their salaries, and the names of their managers. The classic request to display the names of employees and their managers, where the salary of the employee is greater than the salary of the employee's manager, can be formulated using the relational calculus language as follows:

```
RANGE OF E IS EMPLOYEE
RANGE OF M IS EMPLOYEE
RETRIEVE (E.NAME, M.NAME) WHERE
         E.MANAGER = M.NAME AND
         E.SALARY > M.SALARY
```

In this request, E and M are row variables. They take on values of the rows of EMPLOYEE.

An *iteration variable* is used in programming languages to range over specified values. For example,

```
FOR I FROM 1 TO 10 DO
     SUM := SUM + A[I]
     END-FOR
```

the I is an iteration variable that ranges over the values 1 to 10. When embedding the relational calculus into a host programming language, the range variable can be used as an iteration variable. Our example above about employees whose salary is greater than their manager's salary can be embedded into a host programming language as follows:

```
FOR E IN EMP DO
     FOR M IN EMP DO
          IF E.MANAGER = M.NAME AND
             E.SALARY > M.SALARY
        THEN PRINT E.NAME, M.NAME
        END-FOR
     END-FOR
```

In this manner, the relational calculus nonprocedural language can be embedded into traditional programming languages.

Many of the relational algebra commands can be directly embedded into the host programming language. For example,

```
EMP WHERE DEPT-NAME = 'TOY'
```

can be converted into a valid programming language command by assigning the results of the command to another database table:

```
ANS1 := EMP WHERE DEPT-NAME = 'TOY'
```

*Loosely Coupling a Data Manipulation Language with a Host Programming Language*

The easiest way for a vendor to embed a data manipulation language into a host programming language is to use CALL statements. Then a programmer can carefully code parameters of a CALL statement into his application program, which in turn, invokes the database management system, which then interprets the parameters, accesses the database, and places the results into a temporary file, and returns completion codes to the invoking program. The programmer then uses traditional file data manipulation commands to access data in the temporary file. By using this approach, the vendors do not have to modify (and maintain) programming language compilers.

However, this approach is more difficult for the programmer for the following reasons:

- Programmers must code the CALL statements carefully. There is no semantic checking by the host programming language compiler to verify that the parameters are semantically correct.
- Programmers must deal with two sets of error messages, one from the host programming language compiler and one from the database management system.

IBM has embedded SQL into PL/1. However, they modified the PL/1 compiler so that the programmer does not have to use CALL statements. IBM uses the concept of a *cursor* which both defines the request and iterates over individual rows of the resulting table. In the following example, the cursor is X.

```
LET X BE
     SELECT S#, SNAME, STATUS
     INTO S#, SNAME, STATUS
     FROM S
     WHERE CITY = 3; /* The cursor is defined using
                        the SQL multiple-record-
                        per-command language */

OPEN X; /* The SQL command is invoked */

DO WHILE more-to-come;
     FETCH X; /* obtain rows one at a time */
     . . .
END;

CLOSE X; /* delete temporary results of SQL command */
```

In the above approach, the table generated by executing the SQL request is basically treated as a file. The OPEN, FETCH, and CLOSE commands are used to access this file.

## 2.7: Nonlinear Two-Dimensional Languages

The nonprocedural languages described in the previous section are very popular because they are easy to learn and to

| ACCOUNT | ACCOUNT-NO | NAME | AMOUNT-OUTSTANDING |
|---|---|---|---|
| | | | |

Figure 2.14 Table Skeleton

| ACCOUNT | ACCOUNT-NO | NAME | AMOUNT-OUTSTANDING |
|---|---|---|---|
| | P. _ 341 | P. _ Joe | P. _ 1000.00 |

Figure 2.15: Print all of the columns of the ACCOUNT table

| ACCOUNT | ACCOUNT-NO | NAME | AMOUNT-OUTSTANDING |
|---|---|---|---|
| | | P. _ Joe | P. _ 1000.00 |

Figure 2.16: Print the NAME and AMOUNT-OUTSTANDING columns of the ACCOUNT table.

use. However, these languages suffer two drawbacks: (1) users must learn and remember the exact syntax and (2) users must learn and remember the names and relationships of the object types in the database. Nonlinear two-dimensional languages discussed below overcome these problems.

Graphical devices triggered the development of a new dimension for interfacing with a database management system. These devices allowed users to access the database using a two-dimensional screen rather than a linear string of symbols. Some high-level, nonprocedural database management languages provide database users with the ability to query, update, define, and control the database by the use of a two-dimensional screen.

*Query-by-Example*

The Query-by-Example user first selects from a menu the tables to be accessed. A *table skeleton* appears on the screen for each selected table. The table name is displayed to the left of the table skeleton. Following the table name are the names of each of the columns of the table. For example, the table skeleton for the ACCOUNT table is shown in Figure 2.14.

If the screen is too small to hold all of the table skeleton, then the user may scroll individual table skeletons onto the screen. To produce a report of all of the account numbers, names, and amounts outstanding, a user merely enters "P." and an example of a value (example values are always preceded by an underscore) under each column. For example, Figure 2.15 illustrates a request to print all of the columns of the ACCOUNT table.

If the report is to list only the names and amounts outstanding, nothing is placed in the ACCOUNT-NO column, as shown in Figure 2.16.

Figure 2.17 illustrates how to print the names and amounts outstanding for accounts having amounts outstanding equal to 1000.00. The value 1000.00 is not preceded by an underscore because it is constant and not an example.

Figure 2.18 illustrates how to print only the names of individuals with amounts outstanding greater than 1000.00.

To print the names of individuals with amounts greater than 1000.00 and account numbers less than 300, the values shown in Figure 2.19 would be entered on the screen:

Figure 2.19 illustrates how to specify a selection involving the Boolean AND operator (WHERE ACCOUNT-NO < 300 AND AMOUNT-OUTSTANDING > 1000.00). To print a report involving the Boolean OR operator, two rows of examples are needed. Conditions specified within a single row are "ANDed" while conditions specified in two rows are "ORed." For example, the Boolean OR operation ACCOUNT-NO < 300 OR AMOUNT-OUTSTANDING > 1000.00 would be specified as shown in Figure 2.20.

| ACCOUNT | ACCOUNT-NO | NAME | AMOUNT-OUTSTANDING |
|---|---|---|---|
| | | P. _ Joe | P. = 1000.00 |

**Figure 2.17 Print the NAME and AMOUNT-OUTSTANDING columns of the ACCOUNT table where the AMOUNT-OUTSTANDING is 1000.00**

| ACCOUNT | ACCOUNT-NO | NAME | AMOUNT-OUTSTANDING |
|---|---|---|---|
| | | P. _ Joe | < 1000.00 |

**Figure 2.18 Print the Name column of the ACCOUNT table where the AMOUNT-OUTSTANDING is greater than 1000.00**

| ACCOUNT | ACCOUNT-NO | NAME | AMOUNT-OUTSTANDING |
|---|---|---|---|
| | _ 300 | P. _ Joe | > 1000.00 |

**Figure 2.19: Print the Name column of the ACCOUNT table where the AMOUNT-OUTSTANDING is greater than 1000.00 and the ACCOUNT-NO is less than 300**

| ACCOUNT | ACCOUNT-NO | NAME | AMOUNT-OUTSTANDING |
|---|---|---|---|
| | < 300 | P. _ Joe | > 1000.00 |

**Figure 2.20 Print the NAME column of the ACCOUNT table where either the ACCOUNT-NO is less than 300 or the AMOUNT-OUTSTANDING is greater than 1000.00**

| ACCOUNT | ACCOUNT-NO | NAME | AMOUNT-OUTSTANDING |
|---|---|---|---|
| | < 300 | P. _ Joe<br>P. _ Joe | >1000.00 |

| PAYMENT | ACCOUNT-NO | AMOUNT-OF-PAYMENT |
|---|---|---|
| | _ 300 | P. 55.30 |

**Figure 2.21: Print the NAME column of the ACCOUNT table and the AMOUNT-OF-PAYMENT of the PAYMENT where the AMOUNT-OUTSTANDING is greater than 1000.00 and the two rows of the tables have the same value for ACCOUNT-NO.**

In Figure 2.20, the example value "Joe" is used to link the rows to be "ORed" together. Example values can also be used to link together values selected from two "forms" for different tables. Figure 2.21 illustrates the printing of names and payments for individuals with amount outstanding greater than 1000.00.

It is also possible to insert, delete, and modify tables by using the Query-by-Example language. The Query-by-Example syntax is simple and does not use keywords, parentheses, colons, commas, ANDs, or ORs. The user can formulate the query in any sequence desired and is not forced to think in a manner conforming to some predefined order of query specification. The use of linking value examples permits users to break complex queries into several simpler queries. It appears that Query-by-Example is easier to learn than most data manipulation languages, although it does require special terminals that support the display of forms and nonlinear formulation of requests.

### *Graphic Menus for Constructing Database Requests*

The reprinted paper titled "A Graphical Query Facility for ER Databases," by Elmasri and Larson, describes an interface where a graph representing the schema of the database is displayed to the user. The user uses this as a menu to formulate requests for processing by an underlying DBMS. The reprinted paper entitled "An Interface for Novice and Infrequent Database Management System Users" by Larson and Wallick, describes the use of graphics to display a menu of valid syntax options to the user learning a DBMS query language. By using this interface, the user can formulate only syntactically valid requests. Larson and Wallick's paper, "Tools for Forms Administrators," describes how to use the same graph representing the schema of the database to format a template that can be used to both formulate DBMS requests and display results from the database.

*Browsing in a DBMS*

Several approaches for browsing in a DBMS are summarized on page 130 in the reprinted paper entitled "Browsing in a DBMS," by Larson. This paper also describes an approach to browsing based on the form templates generated by the approach described in the reprinted paper, "Tools for Forms Administrators."

## 2.8: Query Language Evaluation

The reprinted paper entitled "Query Language Evaluation" contains another taxonomy of database languages and it also contains a taxonomy of database users. It presents a methodology for evaluating various database languages with respect to the needs of the database users. The authors recommendations for which query language is appropriate for each user class is summarized in Table 7. This figure should be used as a guideline in choosing database management systems as follows: First, determine what types of user classes exist in your enterprise. Second, determine from Table 7 which languages are useful for these classes of users. Finally, verify that the candidate database management system under consideration supports these interfaces.

## Additional Readings


Chamberlin, D.D., et al., "SEQUAL 2: A Unified Approach to Data Definition, Manipulation and Control," *IBM J Research and Development*, Vol. 20, No. 6, November 1976, pp. 560-565. This describes the language supported by IBM products DB2, SQL/DS, and QMF, as well as similiar products from other vendors.

Chamberlin, D.D., "A Summary of User Experience with the SQL Data Sublanguage." *Proc. International Conference on Databases, Aberdeen, Scotland,* 1980, pp. 181-203.

Codd, E.F., "A Relational Model of Data for Large Shared Data Banks," *CACM,* Vol. 13, No. 6, June 1970, pp. 377-387. Republished in *Milestones of Research—Selected Papers 1958-1982: CACM 25th Anniversary Issue, CACM,* Vol. 26, No. 1, January 1983, pp. 64-69. This famous paper layed the framework for the relational data model.

Date, C.J., "A Critique of the SQL Database Language," *ACM SIGMOD Record,* Vol. 14, No. 3, November 1984, pp. 8-54. Critical analysis of SQL's shortcomings.

Fogel, Marc H., "Natural Language Database Interfaces: The User View," *Proceedings, Micro-Delcon '80,* IEEE Computer Society, Washington, D.C., 1980, pp. 1-8. Describes sample dialogues with three natural language systems: LIFER, RENDEZVOUS, and ROBOT.

Herot, Christopher F., "Spatial Management of Data," *ACM TODS,* Vol. 5, No. 4, December 1980, pp. 493-513. Spatial data management is a technique for organizing and retrieving information by positioning it in a graphical data space viewed through a color raster-scan display that enables users to traverse the space surface or zoom into the image to obtain greater detail.

Reisner, P., R.F. Boyce, and D.D. Chamberlin, "Human Factors Evaluation of Two Data Base Query Languages: SQUARE and SEQUEL," *Proc. NCC,* Vol. 44, AFIPS Press, Reston, Virginia, May 1975, pp. 447-452. Describes experiments carried out on the usability of SEQUEL and an earlier language called SQUARE.

Shneiderman, Ben, "Improving the Human Factors Aspect of Database Interactions," *ACM TODS,* Vol. 3, No, 4, December 1978, pp. 417-439. Provides background for controlled psychological experimentation in exploring the person/machine interface.

Zloof, M.M. "Query By Example," *Proc. NCC,* Vol. 44 AFIPS Press, Reston, Virginia, May 1975. The first of several papers on Query By Example.

# A Graphical Query Facility for ER Databases

Ramez A. Elmasri

University of Houston

James A. Larson

Honeywell Inc.

A user-friendly interface to a database management system is presented. The interface is based on entities and relationships, and can be used with database systems where the user view is described using the Entity-Relationship model. The interface is based on the GORDAS query language and requires a graphics terminal which gives the user the ability to point at the screen with a movable cursor, light pen, or some other pointing device. A hierarchical view is presented to the user, with the entity-set of primary interest at the root of the hierarchy. Attributes and relationships of interest are then identified by the user, and the user is guided through formulation of the query. The query is rephrased using natural language and is presented to the user for verification.

Keywords: Entity-Relationship model, interactive query formulation, graphics, user-friendly

## 1. INTRODUCTION

The user interface to a computer system is that part of the system which is most visible to the users. As the use of computers increases, many non-technical persons will need to interact with the different computer systems, such as database systems. Therefore, the need for interfaces that are easy to understand and use by persons without a strong technical background becomes more important.

For a database management system, there are several different classes of users. These include the database designers and administrators that specify the data contents and authorize the use of the database, the transaction programmers that specify frequently used queries and transactions, and the "ad hoc" users that query the database, usually with different requests. Ad hoc users are usually not completely familiar with the database structure and contents, or with the languages used to access the database, and so need interfaces that assist them in accessing the database. The interface we present here is targeted to this class of users.

One popular user-friendly interface is Query-by-Example (QBE) [ZLOO75]. QBE presents the user with a tabular view of the database. The user specifies the data to be selected "by example". The user first selects the tables of interest from the set of all tables in the database. Then, as many of these tables as can fit on the terminal screen are displayed. The expressions needed to select the required rows of data and the columns (attributes) to be displayed are specified with respect to that table.

While the tabular representation of data is simple, some of the "semantics" of the data are not explicitly represented, such as (1) the precise meaning of the column headers, and (2) the relationships between the different tables. The user must relate the name of the column header to the meaning of the data which the column represents. When the user query requires data from more than one table, the user must know which column headers in the two tables represent the relationship, and then enter the same example value under both columns to materialize the relationship.

The interface presented here is based on a user view described in terms of the Entity-Relationship (ER) model [CHEN76]. Although an ER view is more complex than a simple tabular view, the additional complexity makes explicit some of the semantics that are only implicit in the tabular view, and so relieves the user of the burden of remembering these semantics when formulating a request. Hence, it is easier for users who use the database infrequently or may not be immediately familiar with its semantics, to be presented with an ER view in which the semantics are more explicit. Also, the ER model is frequently used in logical database design [CHAN79]; the ER graph may already exist as a product of the logical database design process.

The ER model represents sets of entities and the relationships among these sets. Both entity sets and relationship sets have attributes whose values describe properties of the individual entities and relationship instances. Relationship representation is symmetric with respect to each entity set which participates in the relationship. While this may be necessary for correct representation of the semantics of the data, it is often simpler for the user to consider a hierarchical view of the data when formulating a query, because of the reduced complexity and smaller number of choices. By hierarchical view, we do not mean hiearchical database system; we mean a view of the data that is hierarchical (or tree-structured). In the remainder of the paper, the terms hierarchy and

Reprinted from *The Proceedings of the 4th International Conference on Entity-Relationship Approach*, 1985, pages 236-245. Copyright © 1985 by The Institute of Electrical and Electronics Engineers, Inc.

tree structure are interchangeable.

In a hierarchical view, the entity set at the root of the hierarchy is the one that the user considers most important in formulating a particular query. The root may be different for different queries, or for different users when formulating the same query.

The main contribution of this work is the examination of the issues involved in presenting the user with a hierarchical view based on an underlying graphical (ER) view, and in presenting the framework for a user-friendly interface which guides the user through specification of complex queries on the hierarchical view. This contrasts with the proposals for user-friendly interfaces specified on tabular (relational) views of the data, such as QBE.

The interface we present is based on an underlying query language, GORDAS [ELMA80, ELMA81, ELMA85]. This interface has been implemented using PASCAL on a VAX 11/78 and the GIGI graphics display processor.

The organization of this paper is as follows. In the next section, the requirements for a user friendly interface, and components of a hierarchical query are discussed. Section 3 describes the interface. Section 4 discusses formulation of complex queries, and Section 5 illustrates how the language meets its requirements.

## 2. HIERARCHICAL FORMULATION OF HIGH-LEVEL QUERIES

In this section, we present the requirements for a user-friendly interface. Then, we define the components of a high-level hierarchical query and some problems associated with hierarchical query formulation. In order to illustrate our discussion, we first present an example database schema, which will be used throughout the paper.

### 2.1 An Example ER Schema

Figure 1 shows an Entity-Relationship schema for a university database. The entity sets are DEPARTMENTs, STUDENTs, INSTRUCTORs, COURSEs, and SECTIONs. Each student has attributes Name, Ssn (Social Security Number), and Class (such as Freshman, Senior, Graduate), and is related to one major department. Each student is also related to the sections of courses completed, and the Grade in that course is an attribute of the relationship. Each SECTION has attributes Number (the section number of a course), Year and Qtr (the year and quarter in which the section was given). A section is related to the course of which it is a·section, to the students that took that section, and to the instructor who taught the section. An INSTRUCTOR has attributes Name, Ssn, Rank (such as assistant professor) and Salary, and each instructor is related to a department and to the sections of a course that he or she taught. A DEPARTMENT has the attribute Name, and is related to the instructors in that department, the courses registered under the department, and the students who major in that department. Finally, each course has a Name (such as Introduction to Computing) and number (such as CS105), and is related to the sections given of that course, and the department under which the course is registered.

The cardinalities of the relationships are shown in Figure 1. For example, the S-S relationship is of cardinality M:N. Also shown are connection names for each participation of an entity set in a relationship. These connection names are not part of the standard ER model, and are used for functional reference to the entity or entities related to a given entity by a given relationship. For example, given a particular student, we refer to the set of sections that the student has completed by: sections_completed of STUDENT. To refer to the students who have completed a given section of a course, we write students_attended of SECTION.

Technically, connection names are not necessary for query formulation. However, they are important since they reflect the semantics of the relationship better than a single relationship name. Hence, in the user friendly interface, they are displayed to help the user understand the database semantics. Connection names also reflect the cardinality of the relationship in the direction of reference. Plural connection names (for example sections_completed, students_attended) are used to refer to a 1:N cardinality, while singular connection names (for example instructor, major-dept) are used to refer to 1:1 cardinalities.

We use the convention that entity set names such as STUDENT and SECTION are in uppercase. Attribute names such as Number and Year of a SECTION are capitalized, and connection names such as sections and students are lowercase.

### 2.2 Requirements for the User Friendly Interface

We have identified the following requirements for our interface:

Ease of use: The interface should not assume that the user knows the detailed contents of the database or the exact procedure to formulate a query. However, the procedure which guides the user through query formulation should not have an inordinate number of steps that it becomes cumbersome to use.

User tailorability: Different users approach query formulation from different perspectives. The interface should allow the user to view the database in the way the user is most comfortable with when formulating a particular query, and to proceed through query formulation differently.

Stability: Formulation of queries that only differ slightly should be possible without having to perform all major reformulation steps.

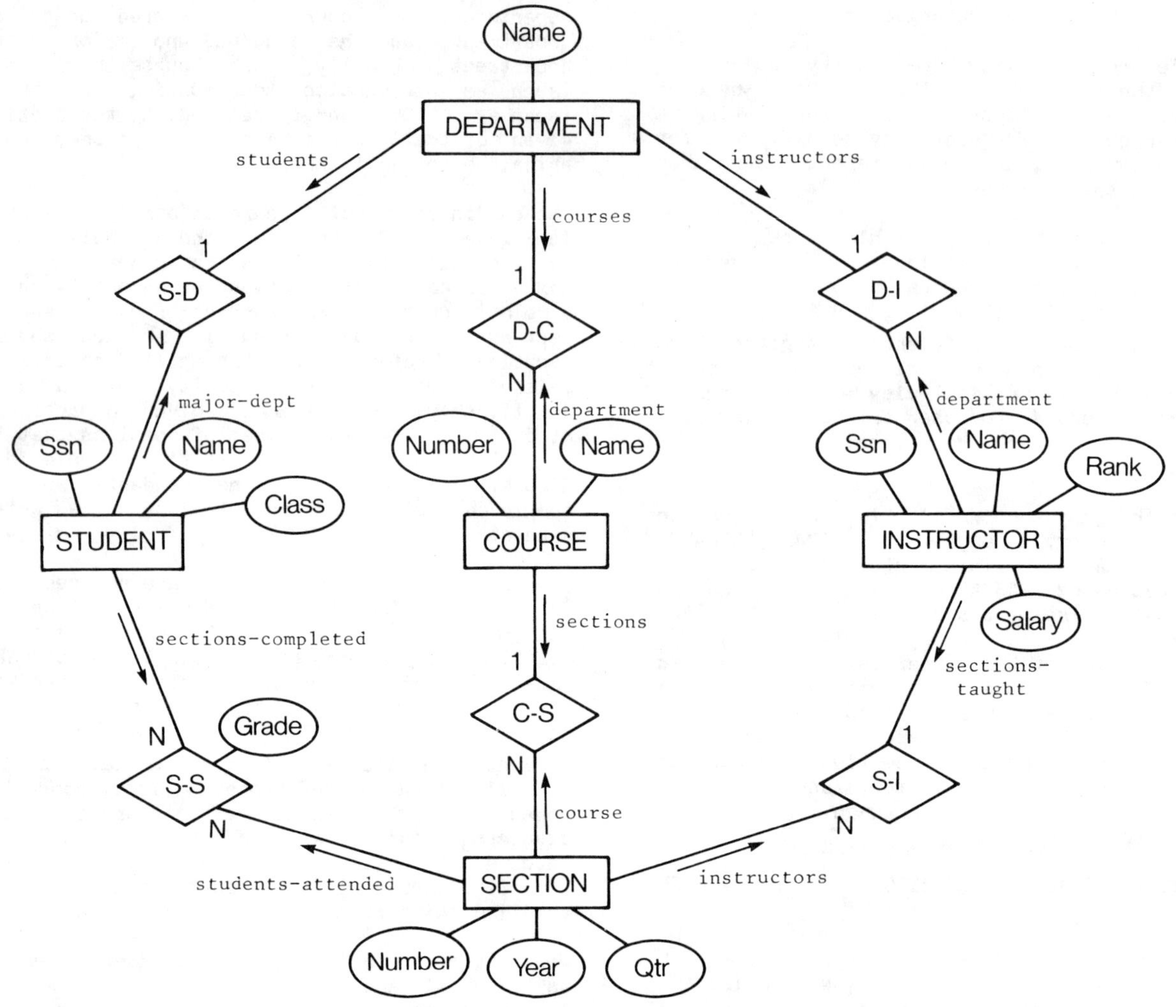


**Figure 1. Graphical Representation of Schema**

Expressive power: The query formulation mechanisms should be powerful enough to allow formulation of complex queries.

These are the four basic requirements which we see as important for formulating a query using a user-friendly interface. They do not include specification of the display format. Within our framework, the underlying system can analyse the query and the schema and automatically produce a satisfactory default display format. Techniques to override the default display format can be provided, but are outside the scope of this paper.

2.3 Components of a High-Level Hierarchical Query

The specification of a query can be broken down quite naturally into three components:

(a) Specifying the entity set of primary interest, the root (or primary) entity set.
(b) Specifying a selection expression that identifies specific entities from the set(s) which the user desires information about.
(c) Specifying the attributes whose values are to be displayed for each selected entity.

To utilize the above framework, we need a uniform mechanism to refer to both (1) the attributes of (a root) entity set E, and (2) the attributes of any entity set E1 related to entity set E by one or more relationship sets. We use the well known functional reference mechanism. This is used in both specifying conditions on attributes to select entities, and in specifying attributes to be displayed.

We encounter two problems when we attempt to formulate complex queries within this framework. Both problems arise from the fact that in a hierarchy, an entity e from entity set E can be related to a set of entities in some related entity set E1. The problems are:

(1) We may want to specify conditions to select entities from E based on attribute values of related entities in E1, and

(2) We may want to restrict the set of E1 entities related to an entity e in E based on conditions on E1.

We discuss these problems more fully and present the solutions to them in section 4.

We note that other frameworks for specifying hierarchical queries have been proposed. For example Hardgrave [HARD80] specifies selection conditions to select instances from any entity set node in the hiererchy, which leads to ambiguity in the meaning of the query. Because our approach only selects entities from the root entity set, there is no ambiguity. The flexibility to change the root node allows all four cases discussed in Hardgrave's paper to be specified unambiguously.

## 3. THE USER FRIENDLY INTERFACE

We now present our user-friendly interface. First, we outline the five main steps used to guide the user in formulating a query; then we present an example. We assume that the interface is implemented on a graphics terminal which gives the user the ability to point at the screen with a movable cursor or a light pen.

### 3.1 Query Formulation Steps

The user must perform five steps when formulating a query. A mode is associated with each step so that the system may interpret the actions taken at each step.

STEP 1: The ER schema is displayed to the user. If facilities for external schema (or view) definitions exist, then the external schema of the particular user is displayed. This step relieves the user from the burden of remembering the exact database structure.

STEP 2: The user identifies the entity and relationship sets of interest for the particular query. The user examines his or her query and points at each entity set and relationship set involved in the query. When all entity sets and relationship sets are identitied, the user exits this mode.

Those entity sets and relationship sets that have been identified are displayed on the screen, and the remainder of the user schema is erased. The selected entity sets and relationships constitute a subgraph which contains all of the information needed for formulating the query.

STEP 3: The user identifies the root entity set by pointing at it, and then exits this mode. The interface then converts the ER diagram previously on the screen into a hierarchy, with the specified entity set at the root (top).

In the displayed hierarchy, only the connection names that lead from the root (top) to the leaves (bottom) of the hierarchy are displayed. Also, attributes of binary relationships are migrated from the binary relationship downward to the entity set below the relationship in the hierarchy, and all binary relationship nodes are erased. This is because in the hierarchical view, M:N and 1:N relationships are both viewed as 1:N, while N:1 and 1:1 relationships are both viewed as 1:1. Any two entity sets in the hierarchical view with a 1:1 relationship between them are merged to form a single entity set with the attributes of both entity sets.

Note that it is still possible to have a hierarchy even if the graph selected in step 2 has a cycle. In this case, two leaf entity sets are different. For example, if we choose DEPARTMENT, COURSE, SELECTION, D-C, C-S, S-S, and S-D, we could have a hierarchy as shown in figure 2. Here, the STUDENT related to DEPARTMENT directly shows the students who majors in that department. The STUDENT related by COURSE and shows students who completed some section of some course offered by the department.

STEP 4: The user specifies the selection of entities. The user is prompted to specify each condition that should hold for an entity to be selected. First, conditions on the attributes of the primary entity set itself are specified. Then, conditions involving related entities are specified. These latter conditions may involve substeps when complex conditions are formulated. When all conditions are specified, the user exits this mode.

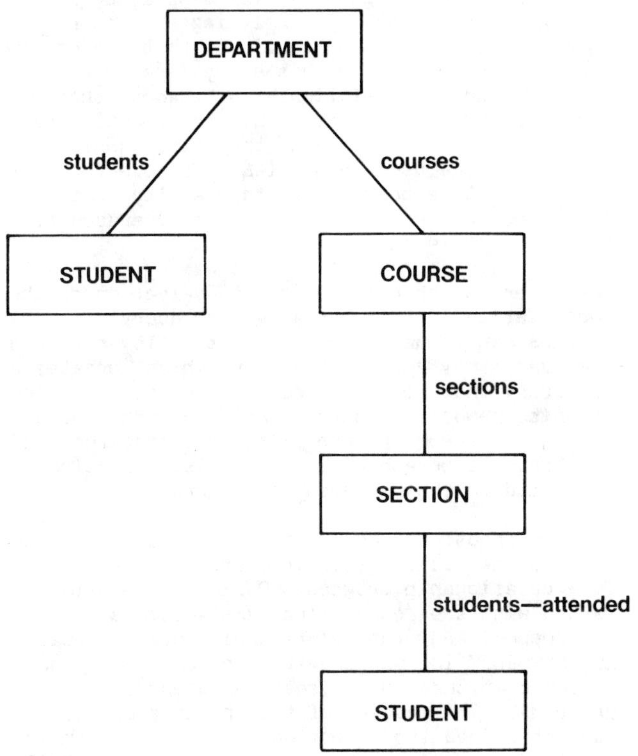


**Figure 2: Converting a cycle to a hierarchy**

After all the simple conditions have been specified, they are numbered and displayed on the screen. The user then combines them until they form a single, complex condition. Two conditions can be combined by an AND or OR while a single condition can be augmented by the NOT operator. After each interaction, the conditions are renumbered and redisplayed until only one complex condition remains. This allows for arbitrary nesting of conditions.

STEP 5: The user specifies the attributes which are to be displayed for each selected entity. Those attributes from the primary entity set are specified directly by pointing to them. Specifying attributes of related entity sets may require substeps. When all attributes to be displayed are specified, the user exits this mode and the query is formulated.

The order of STEP 4 and STEP 5 may be reversed or interleaved. For the remainder of the paper, we specify STEP 4 followed by STEP 5.

### 3.2 An Example:

We now illustrate the above steps with an example. Consider the query Q1:

Q1: Display the names of all students who took the course CS144.

The schema of Figure 1 is displayed on the screen. The user, by analyzing the query and looking at the screen realizes that the entity sets of interest for this query are COURSE and STUDENT, and the relationships between them via the SECTION entity set. The three entity sets are then selected, as are the relationships S-S and C-S. The user then exits the mode for STEP 2, and at this point all other entity sets and relationship sets are automatically erased from the screen (Figure 3a).

The user is then prompted for selection of the root entity set. For a given query, several choices can be made for the root entity set, and the user may choose the root which creates a hierarchy that best matches the conceptualization of his request. Assume that the user chooses COURSE as the root then exits the mode for STEP 3. The ER subgraph of Figure 3a is automatically converted to the hierarchy of Figure 3b.

Only connection names which flow down from the root to the leaves of the hierarchy are retained. The relationship between COURSE and SECTION is marked with the connection name sections (course is dropped) and the relationship between SECTION and STUDENT is marked with the connection name students_attended (sections_completed is dropped). The choice of the primary entity set has determined the direction of reference for the involved relationships: sections of a COURSE, and students_attended of a SECTION.

Relationship attributes are migrated to the entity sets at the lower end of the relationship in the hierarchy. Thus, the Grade attribute is migrated from the S-S relationship to the STUDENT entity set, and gives the grade value of each student who took the section of a course. Since our hierarchy refers to the set of students who attended a section, the user can refer to the Grade of each particular student who attended the section.

The user is then prompted for the condition to select entities from the primary entity set (STEP 4). The user points to each attribute upon which a condition is specified directly. In our example, the user points to the Number attribute of the COURSE entity set, selects the = comparison operator from those displayed in a menu on the screen, and then types: CS144. Since this is the only condition for the query, the user now exits from the mode for STEP 4.

Finally, the user enters the mode for specifying the attributes to be displayed (STEP 5). The user specifies attributes to be displayed of the root entity set, if any, by pointing at each attribute. In our example, no attributes of the root set are to be displayed.

Then, the user specifies the attributes to be displayed from other entity sets related to the root entity set, if any. This is accomplished by pointing at the entity set and then at each attribute from that entity set which is to be displayed. In our example, the user points at the Name attribute of the STUDENT entity set, then exits the mode for STEP 5. This completes formulation of Q1.

Query formulation is achieved by three activities: pointing at the screen, changing modes, and typing constant values. The system automatically takes care of all other display transformations.

## 4. SPECIFICATION OF COMPLEX QUERIES

In this section, we present solutions to the two problems given earlier. We first discuss the formulation of conditions based on set comparisons, and then discuss the restriction of a set of entities related to a given entity. Next, we give criteria for choosing a root entity set, and finally, we briefly discuss query rephrasing, which is a technique to have the user verify that the query formulated is the intended query.

### 4.1 Conditions Based on Set Comparisons

Selection conditions are based on a hierarchical view and entities selected from the root entity set E of a hierarchy. When we have a selection condition based on attributes of an entity set E1 related to the root entity set, we encounter the problem that, in general, several entities of E1 may be related to each entity in E. We illustrate this problem with an example by reconsidering the query Q1.

Earlier, we gave one formulation of Q1 with COURSE as the root entity set. A different user

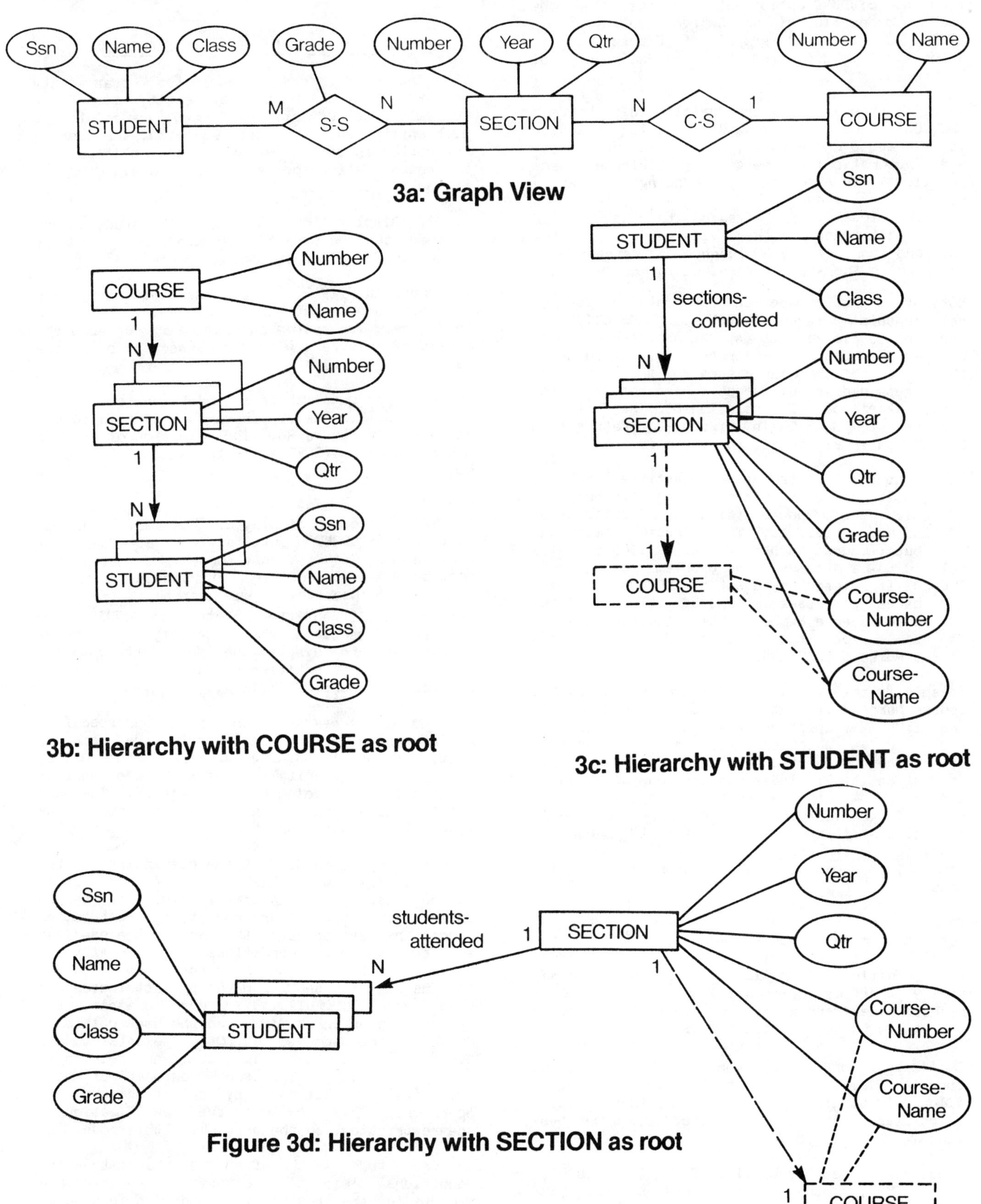


3a: Graph View

3b: Hierarchy with COURSE as root

3c: Hierarchy with STUDENT as root

Figure 3d: Hierarchy with SECTION as root

Figure 3: User Views for Query Q1

may prefer the view that he is selecting entities from the STUDENT entity set. In this view, the user chooses STUDENT as the root entity set in STEP 3. The ER graph of Figure 3a is automatically converted to the hierarchy of Figure 3c.

In this hierarchy, the relationship between SECTION and COURSE is viewed as 1:1 (each section is related to one course), so the two entity sets are automatically merged. Attribute name conflicts are resolved by appending the entity set name as shown. The Grade attribute of the S-S relationship is migrated to the SECTION entity set since in this view we refer to the sections_completed by a student and hence to the Grade which the student received in each section.

Note that the connection name retained for the relationship between STUDENT and SECTION is sections_completed (students_attended is dropped). Because the hierarchy of Figure 3c is the reverse of that in Figure 3b, the connection names retained are different. Also note that the Grade attribute of relationship set S-S is migrated to SECTION in Figure 3c, rather than STUDENT as in Figure 3b, for the same reason.

To select the desired student entities (STEP 4) the conditions do not involve any attributes of STUDENT. Hence, no conditions on attributes of STUDENT are specified. The selection is on the attribute Course_Number of the SECTION entities related to a student. The problem is that each STUDENT is related to a set of SECTION entities, and hence possesses a set of values for the attribute Course_Number. The condition desired is to select the student if any of his Course_Numbers is CS144.

To specify this condition, the user points to the Course_Number attribute of SECTION, then selects the INCLUDES operator from the menu, and then types: CS144, which specifies the condition that if the set of sections related to a particular student entity includes the section with course number CS144, that student is selected. Note that, if the user selects the = operator, he is selecting a different set of students; those who completed only the course CS144, since the equality comparison is interpreted as set equality.

This is a fine point which an unsophisticated user may miss. Hence, whenever a condition involves a set comparison, the system rephrases the condition in English so that the user may verify what is being specified. If the user rejects the rephrasing, the interface presents the user with the different options.

Set comparisons, when combined with a COUNT function (which is available in this interface) allow formulation of queries that involve quantifiers in a predicate calculus type language [PIRR78].

Concluding the formulation of Q1 in this view with STEP 5, the user points to the Name attribute of STUDENT and then exits from this mode.

### 4.2 Restriction of Sets of Related Entities

When the user refers to attributes of an entity set E1 related to a root entity set E, in general, a set of entities from E1 are related to each entity in E. In many queries, the user is interested in only a subset of the entities from E1 which satisfy certain conditions. Consider the query Q2:

> Q2; Display the names of all students who completed the COURSE CS144 in some SECTION of the COURSE given in Spring quarter 1981.

The user, in STEP 2, selects the same entity sets and relationship sets as for query Q1, then exits this mode. The system automatically replaces the schema of Figure 1 with the subschema of Figure 3a.

Suppose the user chooses COURSE as root entity set in STEP 3. The subschema is converted to the hierarchy in Figure 3b. The selection of desired COURSE entities (STEP 4) is the same as for query Q1.

For STEP 5, the same attribute as in Q1, Name of STUDENT, is to be displayed. However, we do not want the STUDENT entities who attended any section of CS144: only those who attended a section whose Qtr and Year attributes are Spring and 1981, respectively. We have to restrict the set of SECTION entities related to COURSE CS144 to those sections which satisfy the above condition, and display the Name attribute for only the STUDENT entities who attended one of the restricted subset of SECTIONS.

For the above reason, whenever a user specifies an attribute of some entity set other than the root, whether in STEP 4 or STEP 5, he must be given the opportunity to restrict the entities related to each selected root entity. The user automatically enters a mode for specifying restriction conditions.

In our example, in STEP 5 the user points to the attribute Name of STUDENT to specify that it is to be displayed. Automatically, the system enters the mode for specifying restriction conditions and prompts the user. The user can specify restriction conditions on any entity set along the path from the root entity set (COURSE) to the entity set from which attributes are specified (STUDENT). In our example, the restriction is on SECTION, so the user points to SECTION, then points at Qtr, selects =, and types: Spring, then points at Year, selects =, and types: 1981. The user then combines these two simple conditions by selecting the AND operator. This completes the specification of the restriction, so the user exits this mode.

In order to make the effect of the restricting conditions clear to the user, the interface prompts for the restricting condition in natural language: "Do you want all STUDENTS related to a COURSE?". If the user responds Yes, no restricting conditions are needed. If the user answers No, the system enters the mode for specifying the conditions, and prompts with: "Specify the conditions you desire on SECTIONS and STUDENTS.".

Specifying restricting conditions is as general as specifying conditions on the root entity set, except that they are applied to the subtrees specified by the user. In our example, when the user points at SECTION to specify restricting conditions, SECTION is considered the root node for these conditions. As in the general case, the conditions may involve related entity sets.

### 4.3 Criteria for Choosing the Root Entity Set

For a simple query where only one or two entity sets are involved, the choice of the root entity set should be the one the user is most comfortable with, since the query will be easy to formulate in any case. For more complex queries, certain criteria can be applied to help the user choose a root. The user should first analyze the query and examine the two main components: the attributes upon which conditions are specified, and the attributes desired for display. In each case, the attributes are grouped according to the entity set to which they belong. The root entity set is chosen based upon one or more of the following criteria:

(1) The entity set with the most attributes upon which conditions are specified.

(2) The entity set with the most attributes to be displayed.

(3) The entity set around which the attributes to be displayed are grouped.

Whenever attributes from several entity sets are to be displayed, criterion (3) is particularly valuable. For example, consider the query: Display the name of each course from which a section was given in Spring 1981, the Number of each section given in that course during Spring 1981, and for each section the Name and Grade of each student who attended that section. Clearly, the displayed attributes are grouped by each COURSE Number, within COURSE Number by SECTION Number, and within SECTION Number by STUDENT Name and Grade. Hence, the natural root entity set is COURSE. On the other hand, if the query was "Display the name of each student, and the course number, section number, instructor name and grade of each section that the student completed in the year 1981", the natural root node is STUDENT.

### 4.4 Query Rephrasing

Whenever complex conditions are specified, the system will rephrase the condition in natural language by using the names of entity sets, attributes and connections from the schema, and using the relationship cardinality information in the schema. The user can then understand how the system interpreted his condition, and match it with what he expected the condition to mean. Because of the limited structures of a hierarchical subschema, the rephrasing can be constructed using limited language constructs.

## 5. HOW THE USER INTERFACE MEETS ITS REQUIREMENTS

In this section, we discuss how the user interface meets the requirements specified above.

Ease of Use: The interface consists of only five main steps used to formulate a query. For simple queries, the only user activities are pointing, typing constant values and existing modes. For more complex queries, the user is guided through the more complex steps, and conditions are rephrased to ensure that he specified the correct condition.

User Tailorability: The user formulates a query by viewing the data in the manner in which he is most comfortable. The choice of a root entity set establishes the view. For example consider query Q1: Give the names of all students who completed the course CS144. It is equally valid to view the query in three ways:

(a) Select the COURSE entity whose Number attribute has value CS144; and display the Name attribute of all STUDENT entities who completed some SECTION of the selected COURSE.

(b) Select each STUDENT entity who completed some SECTION of the COURSE with Number CS144; and display the Name attribute of each selected STUDENT entity.

(c) Select each SECTION entity of the COURSE whose Number is CS144; and display the Name attribute of each STUDENT entity who attended one of the selected SECTION entities.

Figure 3b corresponds to (a) above, while Figure 3c corresponds to (b). We can also easily formulate the query to correspond to (c) if we choose SECTION as root entity set (Figure 3d). Clearly, the interface will allow the user to formulate the query with his own preferred view.

User tailorability is also possible in the order in which substeps of STEP 4 and STEP 5 are specified.

Stability: The system will store the user query, and display back the selection conditions and the attributes to be displayed on request. The user can then modify individual conditions, or add or delete conditions or attributes to be displayed. Thus, only minor changes to the formulation are needed to make a minor change in the query.

Expressive Power: Complex queries which involve quantifiers, groupings, and common functions can be expressed using this interface.

PROTOTYPE IMPLEMENTATION

A prototype implementation of this interface has been implemented at the Department of Computer Science, University of Houston. This prototype is being used to demonstrate the usefulness of this type of graphical interface. Research is being conducted regarding the ease with which users can learn the interface and formulate queries. Early results are promising, but carefully designed experiments need to be carried out. Query rephrasing has not yet been implemented.

At least two other systems, developed independently, bear a close resemblance to ours. GUIDE [WONG82] is a graphical interface that uses an E-R schema and the STRAND query language [JOHN81] which is implemented on top of INGRESS [HELD75]. In GUIDE, the user may formulate several local queries and link them together forming more complex queries. In our system, the user takes a more "top down" approach by choosing the root entity set (which effectively links together the branches of the hierarchy) before specifying the local queries along the branches.

GQL/ER [ZHAN83] is another graphics-based system for querying E-R databases. It maps E-R queries into relational queries against the MISTRESS relational database system. GQL/ER uses Query-by-Example-like skeletons to aid users in specifying selection conditions on entity sets. Our system uses a more hierarchical approach to specifying Boolean conditions. GQL/ER has a mechanism that specifies a default path among selected entity sets. Our system uses prompts to aid users in choosing paths and presents English-like descriptions of selected paths as feedback for user verification. The specific advantages and disadvantages of the various graphical approaches to querying ER databases will become apparent only after running carefully designed experiments involving the intended users of the graphical interfaces. We anticipate that various classes of users will find different features from all three systems desirable.

CONCLUSIONS

We have presented a user-friendly interface to guide the user in query formulation on a schema presented as an ER graph. Entity sets and relationship sets of interest are first identified, to isolate a subschema of interest. The subschema is then converted into a hierarchy based on the user's choice of root entity set.

The hierarchical view gives the user a structure which allows a clear distinction between the two main components of a query: conditions to select entities, and attributes to be displayed. Complex queries can be specified within the given framework.

The framework is based on the GORDAS query language [ELMA80, ELMA81, ELMA85,]. For a discussion of the power of the GORDAS language and hour it is used to express grouping functions and unusual quantification, see [ELMA81, ELMA85] Since forms are inherently hierarchical, the framework presented can also be easily used to support a forms-type interface such as that proposed in [Larson 84].

ACKNOWLEGEMENT

The authors would like to thank Jim Richardson, Jim Weeldreyer, and Gio Wiederhold for their comments. The implementation was done by Han-Kan Tan.

REFERENCES

[BUNE79] Buneman, P., and Frankel, R. E., "FQL: A Functional Query Language," Proceedings of the SIGMOD International Conference on Management of Data, ACM, May 1979, pp. 52-57.

[CHAN79] Chan, P., and Lochovsky, F., "A Graphical Database Design Aid Using the Entity-Relationship Model," Proceedings of the International Conference on Entity-Relationship Approach, Los Angeles, California, December 1979, (North-Holland), pp. 303-318.

[CHEN76] Chen, P. P-S., "The Entity-Relationship Model: Towards a Unified View of Data," ACM Transactions on Database Systems, Volume 1, Number 1, March 1976, pp. 9-36.

[ELMA80] El-Masri, R., "On the Design, Use, and Integration of Data Models," Reprdort STAN-CS-80-801 (Ph.D thesis), Computer Science Department, Stanford University, May 1980.

[ELMA81] Elmasri, R., and Wiederhold, G., "GORDAS: A Formal, High-Level Query Language for the Entity-Relationship Model," Proceedings of the Second International Conference on Entity-Relationship Approach, Washington, D.C., October 1981, (ER Institute), pp. 49-72.

[ELMA85] Elmasri, R., Wheeldreyer, J., and Hevner, A., "The Category Concept: An Extension to the Entity Relationship Model," Journal of Knowledge and Data Engineering Journal Vol 1, No. 1 1985, pp. 75-116.

[HARD79] Hardgrave, W., "Ambiguity in Processing Boolean Queries on TDMS Tree Structures: A Study of Four Different Philosophies," IEEE

Transactions on Software Engineering, Volume SE-6, Number 4, July 1980, pp. 357-372.

[HELD75] G. Held, M. Stonebrecker, and E. Wong "Ingress: A Relational Data Base Management System," Proc. NCC, Anaheim, CA, 1975.

[JOHN81] R. Johnson, "Modelling Summary Data," 1981 SIGMOD CONFERENCE .

[LARS84] Larson, J.A., "The Forms Pattern Language," Proceedings IEEE Data Engineering Conference, April 24-27, 1984, Los Angeles.

[PIRR78] Pirrotte, A., "High Level Data Base Query Languages," in Gaillaire, H., and Minker, J., (editors), Logic and Database Design, Plenum Press, New York, 1978.

[RHOD81] Rhodnius, Inc., Mistress: Principles of Operation, Versum 1.0, 1981.

[TAN83] Tan, H.-K. A User Friendly Query Interface Using Graphics, MS Thesis, Computer Science Dept., University of Houston, Dec. 1983.

[WONG82] H.K.T, Wong and I. Kuo, "GUIDE: Graphical User Interface for Database Exploration," Proceedings, Very Large Database Conference, Mexico City, Sept., 1983, pp. 22-31.

[ZHAN83] Zhang, Zhi-Qian, Alberto, O., Mendelzon, "A Graphical Query Language for Entity-Relationship Databases," Entity Relationship Approach to Software Engineering, (C.G. Daves, S. Jajodia, P.A. Ng, and R.T. Yeh (eds.) Elsevier Science Publishers B.V., 1983, pp. 441-448.

[ZLOO75] Zloof, M., "Query by Example," Proceedings of the National Computer Conference, Volume 44, AFIPS, 1975.

# An interface for novice and infrequent database management system users

*by* JAMES A. LARSON and JENNIFER B. WALLICK
*Honeywell, Inc.*
Bloomington, Minnesota

## ABSTRACT

Special interfaces are needed for novice and infrequent users of database management systems. Such interfaces must remind users of the structure and names of database objects as they guide users in formulating syntactically valid database commands. A prototype system developed at the Honeywell Corporate Technology Center provides such an interface by integrating schema displays depicting the contents and structure of the database and syntax diagrams representing the valid syntactic options of a database query language. By traversing these graphs, novice and infrequent database management system users can easily formulate syntactically valid database management system commands while learning the formal syntax of the database management system command language.

"An Interface for Novice and Infrequent Database Management System Users" by J.A. Larson and J.B. Wallick from *AFIPS Conference Proceedings, Volume 53, 1984 National Computer Conference*, 1984, pages 523-529.

## INTRODUCTION

The database management system (DBMS) presents formidable problems to users. New users of a DBMS must be trained to formulate commands acceptable to the DBMS. New users must also learn the structure of the database, the names and relationships of database objects, and which commands to use to access the various objects. Infrequent DBMS users may need to refresh their memories about both what data are in the database and how to formulate commands to access those data objects. An interface to the DBMS is needed for these users that will aid them in learning and relearning how to use the DBMS.

At the Honeywell Corporate Computer Sciences Center we have been investigating approaches to make DBMSs more friendly to novice users. The remainder of this paper describes one such interface under investigation. We first describe the requirements of an interface for novice and infrequent DBMS users and then give an overview of our system.

## INTERFACE REQUIREMENTS FOR NOVICE AND INFREQUENT DBMS USERS

Novice and infrequent DBMS users need an interface to a DBMS that guides them in formulating database requests. Requirements of such an interface include the following:

1. Display valid options. When formulating database requests, users should not be required to know or remember the contents of the database, the structure of the database, or the formal syntax of a query language. A system for novice and infrequent users should be designed so that users formulate requests by choosing from a set of syntactically and semantically valid options.
2. Break the problem into subproblems. Novice and infrequent users need assistance in knowing how in tell the computer what information they want from the database. A system for these users should allow piecemeal formulation of database requests so that a user may concentrate on one subproblem at a time.
3. Display current status. Novice and infrequent users should be reminded of what they have accomplished. The system should display what portions of a database request the user has formulated so that the user can decide what options to choose next.
4. Allow users to change their minds. Users should be able to back up to any previous state of command formulation and resume entering options from the state to which they backed up.
5. Permit only syntactically valid commands. A system should be designed so that it minimizes command input errors and permits the user to enter only syntactically valid commands.
6. Provide online help facilities. The system should aid users with additional instructions when users are not sure about a particular option of the system. These instructions should be designed to communicate the meaning of an option with respect to what users have previously accomplished, thereby aiding them in deciding what option to choose next.
7. Move novice users to more advanced interfaces. A system for novice users should provide mechanisms to move users to more advanced and expedient interfaces. In particular, the system should help users learn the syntax of a database language as well as the contents and structure of the database.
8. Control access to a database. Database interfaces should have a mechanism whereby the database administrator can prohibit classes of users from performing various types of operations on selected database objects.

Forms and menus are two database interfaces often used for novice and infrequent users. Unlike forms and menus, the interface developed at Honeywell is an easy-to-use graphical facility for building database commands that trains users to learn the linear keyword form of the language.

## SYSTEM OVERVIEW

Syntax diagrams have been used successfully in programming language manuals to illustrate visually the structure of programming languages. A syntax diagram (Figure 1) is a directed graph representing the syntactic structure of a formal language. Any path from the start node to a finish node constitutes a valid statement in the language. Our system uses syntax diagrams to guide users through DBMS commands as well as to teach the more frequent user the syntax of the DBMS language.

A syntax diagram of a query language is a directed graph that contains six types of nodes: (1) start nodes, (2) literal nodes, (3) value nodes, (4) database item nodes, (5) subgraph nodes, and (6) finish nodes.

For implementation purposes these nodes can be distinguished by color and shape; but novice users need not visually distinguish the nodes, because they will be prompted with appropriate instructions and information as each node is selected. Visual distinction of the nodes might be useful for helping users learn the command language.

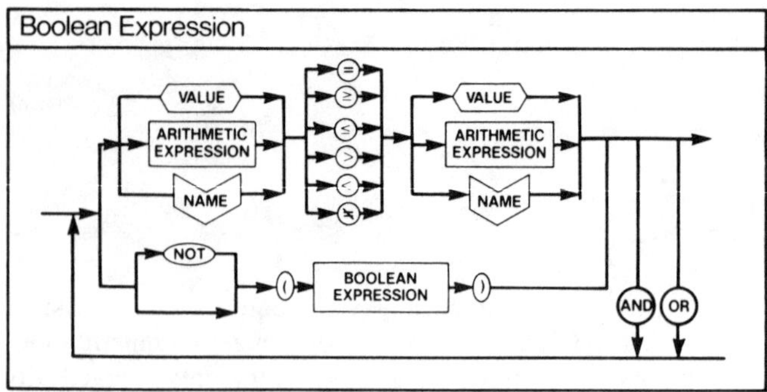


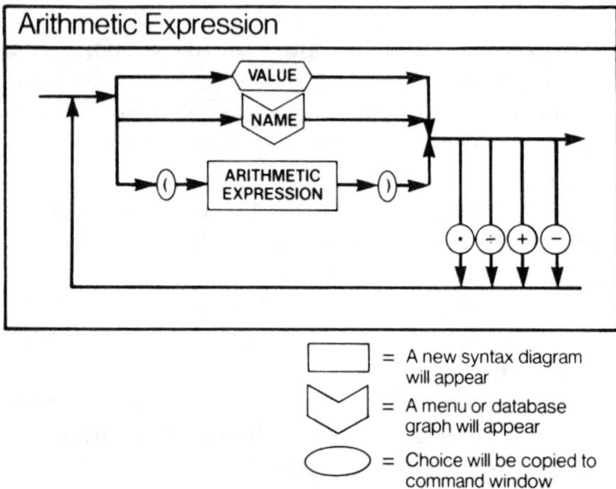


Figure 1—Syntax diagrams

### *Start Nodes*

Beginning with this node, the user selects nodes, one at a time, along a path in the graph. A complete path specifies a valid request.

### *Literal Nodes*

The names of these nodes correspond to the keywords of the query language. Each time the user selects a literal node, its name is appended to the request being formulated.

### *Value Nodes*

When the user selects a value node, the user is prompted to enter an integer or character string from the keyboard. Value nodes in a query language are used for specifying conditions on attributes of records to be retrieved. The value specified is appended to the request being formulated.

### *Database Item Nodes*

When the user selects a database item node from the syntax graph, the database schema is displayed and the user is asked to select a database object name from the schema. The selected database object name is appended to the request being formulated.

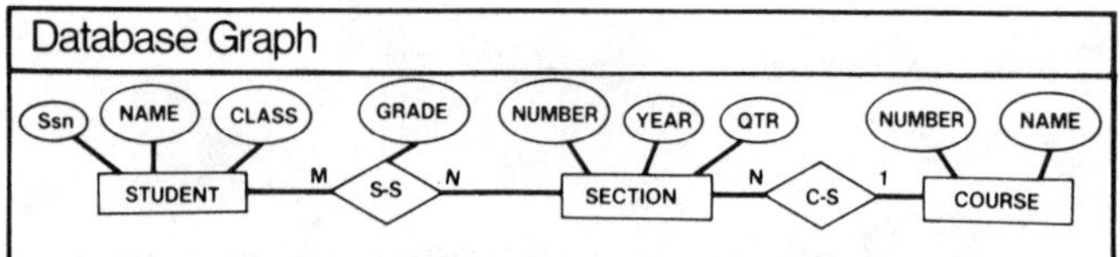


Figure 2—E-R graph representation of a database schema

### *Subgraph Nodes*

When the user selects this node, the current syntax graph is placed on a stack, and a syntax graph corresponding to the name of the subgraph node is displayed. This is useful for languages with complex syntax graphs, because it allows syntax graphs to be broken down into a series of subgraph displays.

### *Finish Nodes*

This node indicates that the user has completely specified a path through the currently displayed graph. If the graph is a subgraph, then the parent graph is redisplayed and the user may continue to select nodes from that graph. If the graph was the original starting graph, then the command has been completely specified and is passed to a DBMS for processing.

When a database item node is selected from the syntax graph, a schema describing the classes of objects in the database is displayed on the screen. The schema objects may be displayed as a menu or alternatively as a graph of data objects such as that illustrated in Figure 2. The rectangles in the graph represent classes of entities, and the diamonds represent classes of relationships between entity classes. The ovals represent attributes of entity or relationship classes. This is a graphical representation of Peter Chen's Entity Relationship (ER) data model,[1] a popular style for modeling data to be maintained by a DBMS. The user selects a class of objects from the database schema by positioning the cursor in the appropriate position on the screen or by typing in the name of the desired object at the keyboard.

As the user selects nodes from the syntax diagrams, a linear-keyword-oriented version of the command is constructed in a command window at the bottom of the screen. The user is able to view partially constructed commands as they are being formulated. The user may append keywords, database objects, or values to partially constructed commands either by typing in the keyword, database object name, or value at the keyboard or by positioning the cursor to the desired node on the syntax diagram or database schema display. It is expected that some users will prefer using the cursor and others will prefer entering options at the keyboard. More advanced users will eventually abandon this interface in favor of the more traditional keyboard-only interface.

Novice and infrequent users can be expected to make mistakes. At any point the user may position the cursor to a

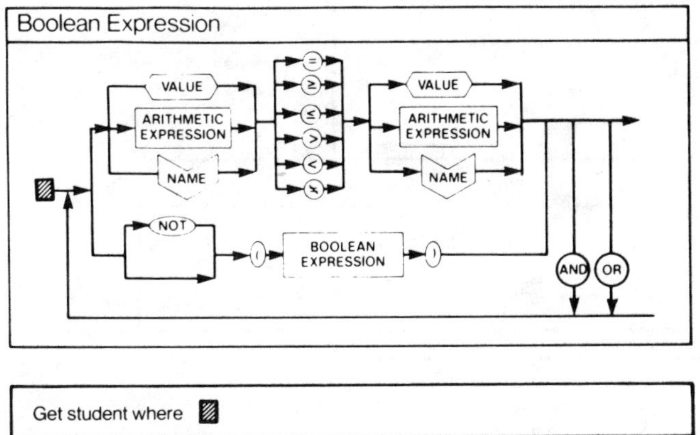


Figure 3—Terminal screen showing a partially formulated command; the user is about to formulate a Boolean expression

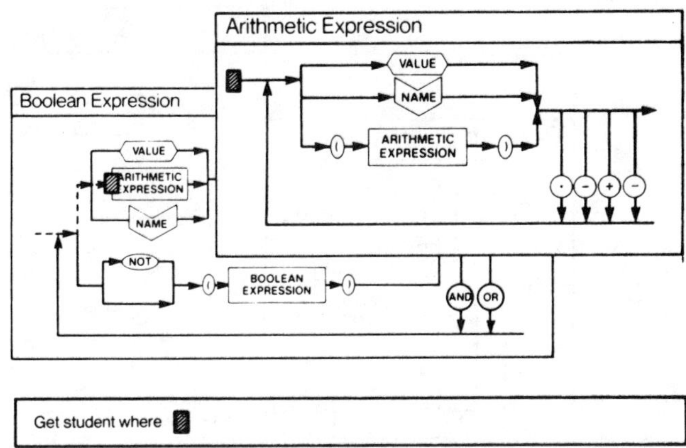


Figure 4—User selects "arithmetic expression" option, and the arithmetic expression syntax diagram is displayed

previously selected node in the syntax diagram (or backspace to a database object name, keyword, or value in the partially formulated command in the command window) and all database object names, keywords, or values following it will be erased from the command window. Thus a user can undo decisions and back up to any previous state, including the start state. The user may then continue formulating the command, possibly choosing options different from the ones previously entered.

If the user does not understand the meaning of any node or cannot decide which path to take on the graph, the user may move the cursor to the node or edge and press the HELP button. Additional information and messages to help the user will be displayed on the screen.

## EXAMPLE

Suppose that the user wishes to formulate the database command "GET STUDENT WHERE SECTION.NUMBER 1 = 2 's 3 AND COURSE.Number 1 = 2 's 177". Further suppose that the user has already formulated the first part of the request, "GET STUDENT WHERE." The syntax diagrams of Figure 1 and the ER graph of Figure 2 are used to aid the user to complete the query formulation. This is illustrated in Figures 3–11. The user may move the cursor only in the "top" (most recently displayed) syntax diagram or database schema. Alternatively, the user may move the cursor in the command window and enter database object names, keywords, and values via the keyboard.

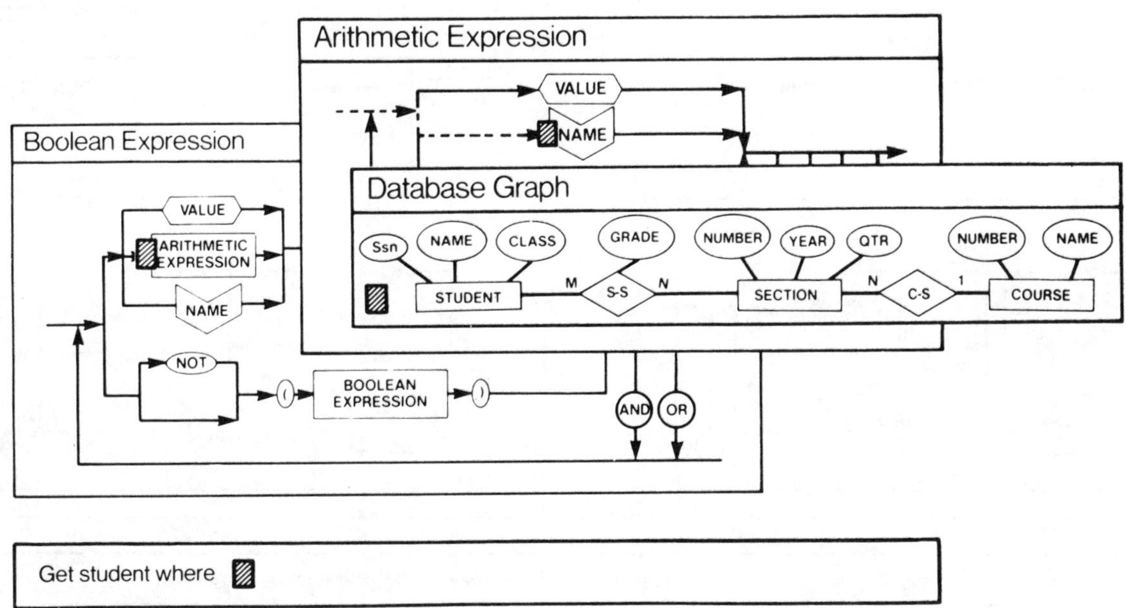


Figure 5—User selects "name" option, and the E-R graph is displayed

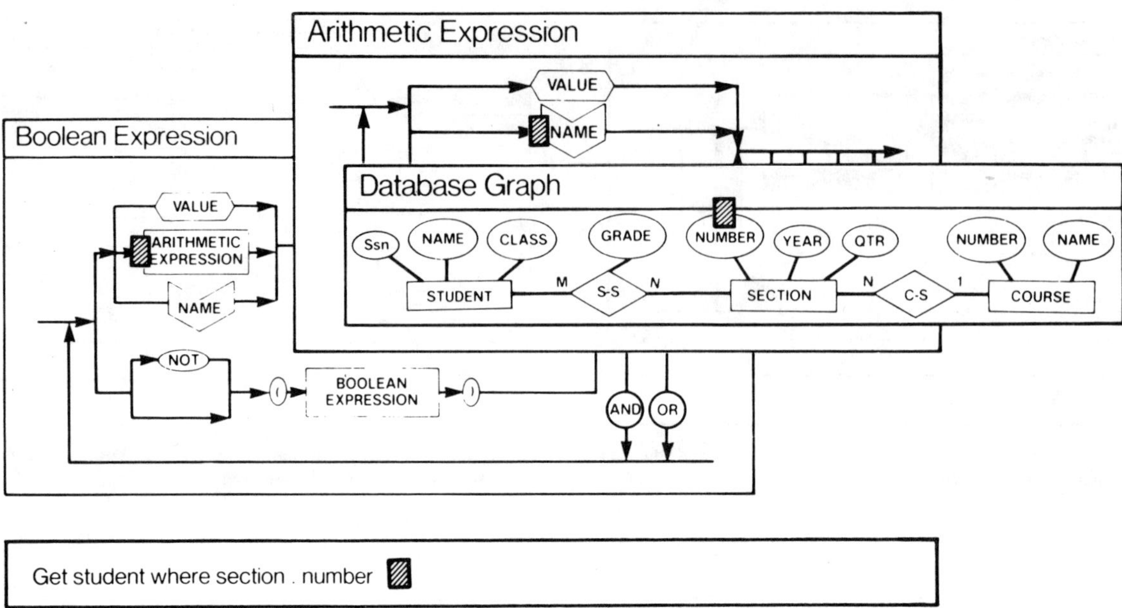


Figure 6—User selects "section.number" option from database graph

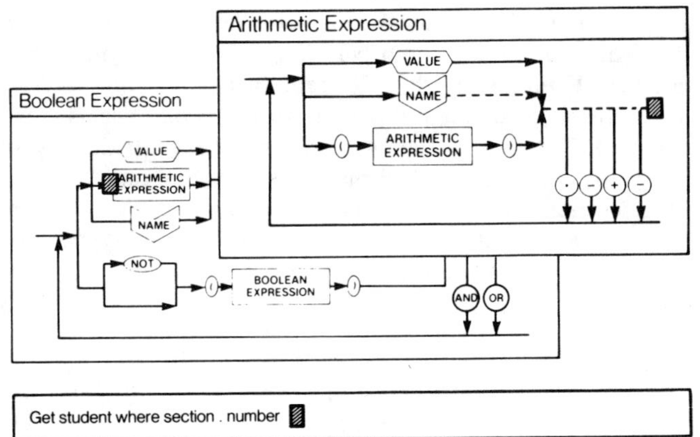


Figure 7—User selects no more options from arithmetic expression syntax diagram

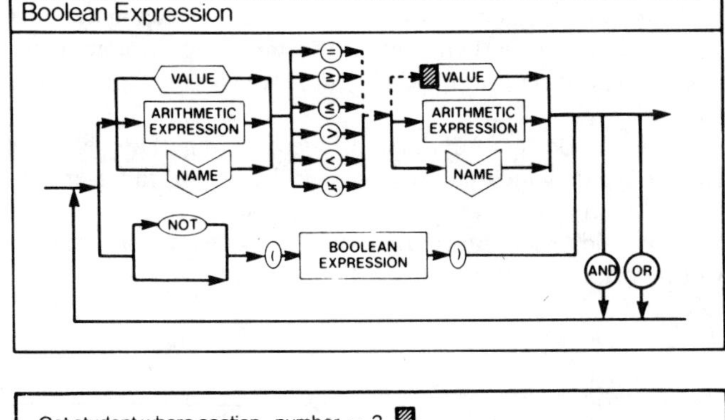


Figure 9—User selects "value" option and types "3"

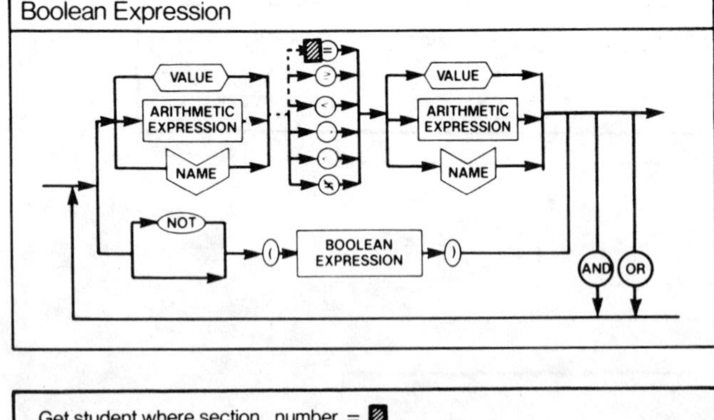


Figure 8—User selects " = " option

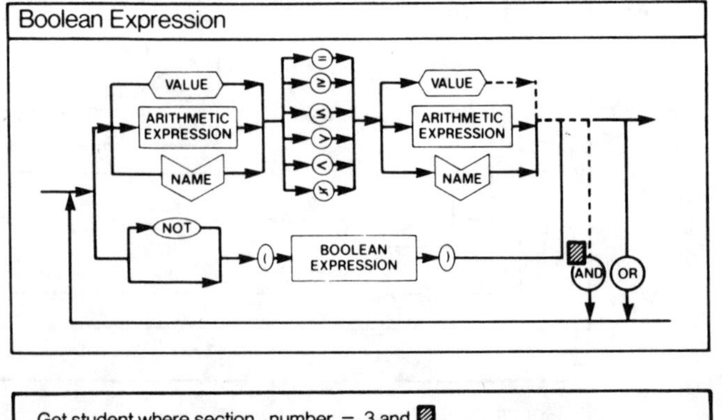


Figure 10—User selects "and" option

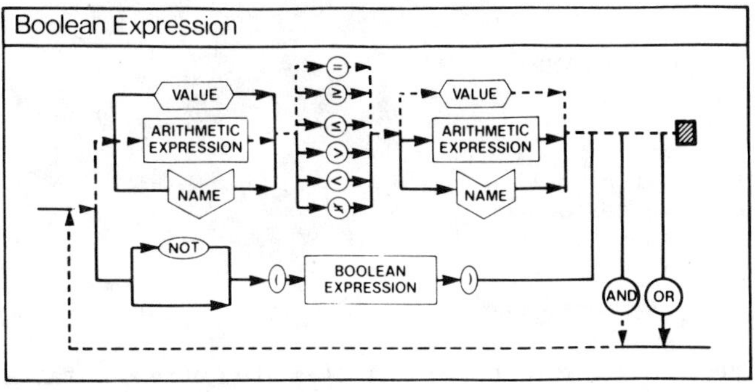


Get student where section . number = 3 and course . number = 177

Figure 11—After repeating steps similar to those of Figures 3 through 10, user selects no more options

## IMPLEMENTATION

A prototype of this system has been implemented at the Honeywell Corporate Computer Sciences Center in FORTRAN on a Honeywell Level 6 minicomputer interfaced with a Megatek Graphics Terminal. The system supports an interactive mode for building and storing arbitrary syntax diagrams as well as a mode for traversing syntax diagrams with a joystick to construct commands. Nodes can be varying sizes, with a separate color for each type of node.

## FURTHER RESEARCH

In this section we investigate ways this system could be used to control access, issues in displaying ER graphs of database schemas, and the automatic creation of syntax diagrams.

### *Controlling Access*

This system could be used to control access to a database by (1) displaying only the part of the schema that describes data the user is allowed to access and (2) modifying the syntax diagrams so that the user is prohibited from executing certain operations (such as delete or modify). We have not investigated a *dynamic syntax graph,* which would prohibit users from specifying certain selected operations on one part of the schema and other selected operations on another part of the schema.

### *Displaying ER Graphs*

Scrolling both up-down and left-right can partially solve the problem of displaying a schema with a large number of entities in the form of an ER graph. Several other approaches to displaying portions of an ER graph should be evaluated:

1. Optionally turning off the visibility of attributes so that the entity sets and relationships sets can be displayed more densely.
2. Positioning the ER graph nodes so that the graph can be displayed in little space while minimizing the number of arcs that cross each other.[2]
3. Partitioning the ER graph into subgraphs such that the objects in each subgraph are related. This clustering can be based on semantics[3] or on statistical clustering methods.

### *Automatic Creation of Syntax Diagrams*

The syntax diagrams and the Bachus-Naur form (BNF) of the command language are closely related. We feel that it is possible to build software that would convert BNF into equivalent syntax diagrams. However, we feel that such software needs human guidance so that (1) the resulting syntax diagrams are not too large to fit on a screen and not as small as a three-choice menu, (2) each syntax diagram corresponds to a single language concept, and (3) the nodes of the syntax diagram are positioned in an aesthetically pleasing layout.

## REFERENCES

1. Chen, P. "The Entity Relationship Model: Toward a Unified View of Data." *ACM Transactions on Data Base Systems,* 1 (1976), pp. 9–36.
2. Tamissia, R., C. Batini, and M. Talamo. "An Algorithm for Automatic Layout of Entity Relationship Diagrams." In C. Davis, S. Jajodia, P. Ng, and R. Yeh (eds.), *Entity-Relationship Approach to Software Engineering.* Amsterdam: Elsevier Science Publishers B.V., pp. 421–439.
3. Vermier, Dirk. "Semantic Hierarchies and Abstractions in Conceptual Schema." *Information Systems,* 8 (1983), pp. 117–124.

# TOOLS FOR FORMS ADMINISTRATORS

James A. Larson & Jennifer Wallick
Honeywell Computer Sciences Center
Bloomington, Minnesota

ABSTRACT

Two types of users of the electronic forms system are identified: Forms Administrators and Forms Users. The requirements of a Forms Administrator are specified. A description of part of the Electronic Forms System Prototype, under development at the Honeywell Computer Sciences Center, is presented. The features of this system includes facilities for semi-automatic generation of electronic templates from existing data description stored in a data dictionary and an interactive facility for directly modifying form templates. A scenario is described that illustrates how this system meets the requirements of the Forms Administrators.

## 1. Introduction

The Electronic Forms System prototype currently under development at the Honeywell Corporate Computer Sciences Center bridges the gap between the office worker and database management systems. Using a visual language, the office worker manipulates electronic forms displayed on a terminal screen to file, modify, and retrieve information from a database. The system provides all the capabilities of traditional database query languages in a way that is easy to learn and use.

There are two types of Electronic Forms System users. There are those who use the system to input, manipulate and view information in the database. We will refer to these people as office workers. In addition, there are people who define the electronic forms that office workers use. We will refer to these people as the forms administrators. The Electronic Forms system prototype satisfies both the office worker's needs and the forms administrator's needs.

This paper defines the requirements of a forms administrator and gives an overview of tools in the Electronic Forms System prototype that support these requirements. The main contribution of this paper is a description of an interactive interface for forms administrators to build and modify form templates which map to a database. This paper describes the Electronic Forms System prototype only from the form administrator's point of view. For the office worker, the Electronic Forms System prototype provides facilities to enter data, a pictorial language to formulate queries and updates, and methods to browse a database. For a more detailed description of the office worker requirements and tools, see [2,3].

Two visual representations are used in our prototype. An entity-relationship diagram is used to display the contents of the database to the forms administrator. A form template representation is used to display the contents of the database to the forms user. Figure 1 illustrates a visual representation of an Entity Relationship (ER) schema [1]. Rectangles represent entity sets, diamonds represent relationship sets between entity sets, and ovals represent attributes of entity sets and relationship sets. The cardinalities of a relationship set are indicated by numbers at the points of the diamond representing the relationship.

The form administrator manipulates the ER diagram to build a visual view or representation suitable to the office worker. The visual representation used to display this view of the database to the office worker is a form template. Figure 2 illustrates a form template. A form template is the office user's view of part of the database. It is a two dimensional layout of one or more database entities. When displayed on a video screen, all database entities conform to the layout of the form template. A form template contains background information that always appears on each occurrence of a form. Background information includes the form template name, the names of attributes and instructions that always appear on each form occurrence. A form template also contains variable information whose values may vary from form occurrence to form occurrence. In all of the figures in this paper, variable information will be denoted by example values and will be underlined. Form templates also contain format information which is indicated by the position and font type of information on the form template. As illustrated in Figure 2, form templates may be nested. The remainder of this paper describes how a forms administrator may create a form template corresponding to a subgraph of an ER graph schema.

## 2. Forms Administrator Requirements

A forms administrator defines the format and layout of an electronic form, called a form template, to be used by office workers. There may be several

Reprinted from *The Proceedings of the 1984 IEEE Workshop on Languages for Automation*, 1984, pages 221-226. 

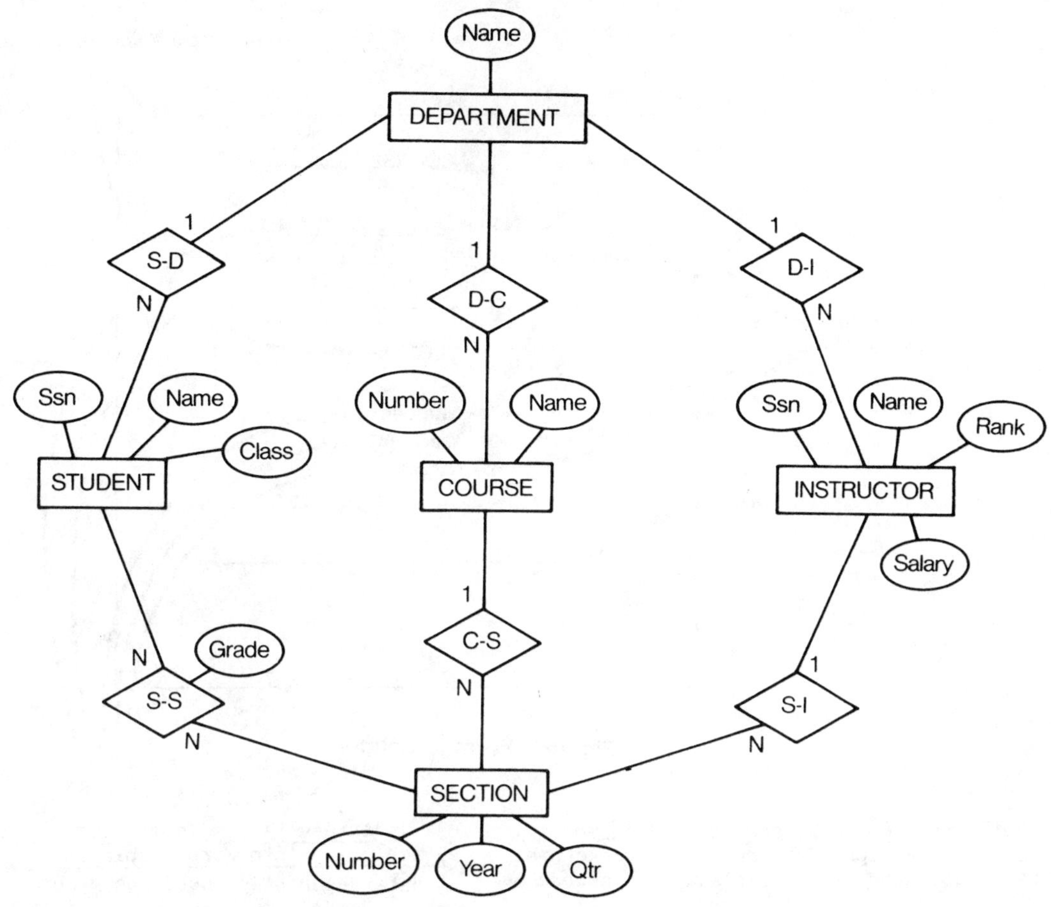


**Figure 1. Graphical Representation of Schema**

forms administrators in an enterprise. An experienced office worker may act as his/her own forms administrator if permitted by the policies set by the enterprise. A forms administrator must consider the office worker's needs, the requirements of the application, and database security constraints when designing form templates. A form template is the office worker's window to the database. It can be considered to be a view or subschema of a database and contains descriptions of data of interest to an office worker. When designing form templates the forms administrator must be aware of the types of information an office worker is going to need from the database when designing form templates. Through these form templates, a forms administrator controls who can access data in the database and how they can access it.

The Electronic Forms System Prototype will provide automated, flexible, and easy-to-use tools for building and modifying form templates so that the forms administrator can concentrate his/her efforts on designing form templates which meet the office worker's needs. The Electronic Forms System Prototype will provide two sets of functions for the forms administrator. The first set guides the forms administrator through a semi-automatic generation of form templates from data descriptions in a data dictionary. The second set allows the forms administrator to interactively modify existing form templates. The functional requirements of these tools are outlined as follows:

1. Interactive Facility for Translating Data Descriptions into Form Templates. The Electronic Forms System Prototype will provide semi-automated methods to access a data dictionary and design form templates using the data descriptions in the dictionary. The method should present information about the structure and contents of the database from the data dictionary and allow the forms administrator to interactively select which information belongs on the form template. The system should automatically generate a form template using the selected information.

2. Interactive Facility for Modifying Form Templates. Tools are needed that allow the forms administrator to view and interactively redesign any form template by editing background information, and modifying the layout of the form template, adding and deleting variable information in

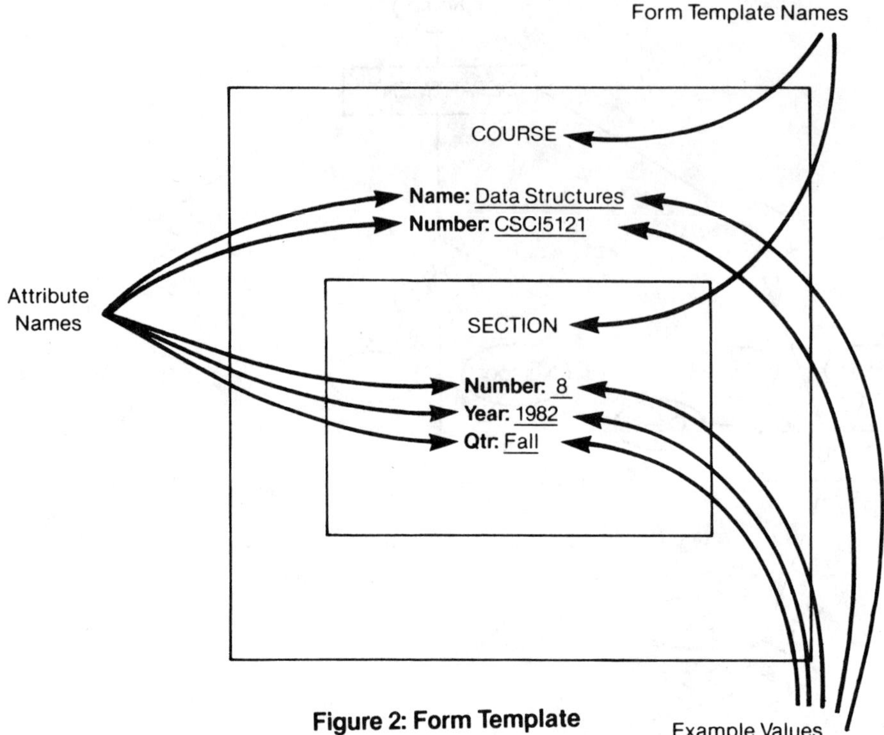


**Figure 2: Form Template**

the form template, and providing special help instructions for the office worker who will use the form template to access a database.

To facilitate the forms administrator, tools to build and design form templates should be designed to meet the following additional criteria:

- o The interface should be visually oriented so that forms administrators can see the results of each action.
- o The interface should be interactive so that forms administrators can quickly analyze the results of each action.
- o The interface should be as automated as possible so that the forms administrator can concentrate on making decisions and leave the bookkeeping details to the tool.
- o Information about the existing database should be provided to the forms administrator so the forms administrator does not need to be intimately familiar with the database contents and structure.
- o Forms administrators should be guided through the forms design choices so that the forms administrator needs little training and can easily use the system after long periods of non-use.

The remainder of this paper presents a more detailed description and scenarios of the form template building and modifying tools in the Electronic Forms System Prototype.

## 3. Interactive Tool for Translating Data Description into Form Templates

A data description used to generate form templates may reside in a data dictionary, in the file description section of an application program, or it may be supplied by a user. Data descriptions of almost any database management system can theoretically be used to generate form templates. The particular environment we have used includes a data description based on the ER data model. The data description resides in a data dictionary. The ER model is a graphical model which lends itself nicely to a pictorial interface. We now present a scenario of a graphical interface which guides the forms administrator through six steps to generate Form Templates that correspond to portions of a database described using the ER data model. First we describe the approach and then present an example.

1. An ER graph is automatically generated on the form administrator's video screen from information in a data dictionary. To generate this graph, the system reads adjacency information about entities, relationship sets, and attributes that reside in the database and then automatically displays the layout of the associated ER graph on a graphics terminal screen. This step relieves the forms administrator of the burden of remembering the exact contents of the database.

2. The forms administrator examines the ER graph, viewing the contents and structure of the database. The system supports various levels of visibility. For example, the system allows attribute visibility to

be turned off so that the forms administrator can view only the entity sets and relationship sets without being distracted by their attributes.

3. The forms administrator now trims off irrelevant information from the ER graph. The system supports two modes for doing this. The forms administrator can either specify the relevant information or specify the irrelevant information. In the first mode the forms administrator examines the graph and points to entity sets, attributes, and relationship sets that are relevant for the form template, i.e., that are to appear on the form template. The forms administrator would probably want to use this mode if the graph contained a lot of irrelevant information. In the second mode, the forms administrator examines the graph and points to entity sets, attributes and relationship sets and attributes which are irrelevant to the form template, i.e., which are not to appear on the form template. The forms administrator probably wants to use this mode if there is not much trimming to be done on the graph. When all relevant and irrelevant information has been identified, the system erases irrelevant information from the displayed graph. When the forms administrator has completed this stage, the displayed graph contains only entity sets, relationship sets and attributes to be contained on the form template.

4. The ER graph must now be converted from a graph structure to a tree-structured or form-view of the database. To aid in the conversion, the forms administrator identifies an entity set of primary interest on the screen. The designated entity set will become the root entity of the tree structure and the top-level or outermost template in the nested form template.

5. The system automatically translates the ER graph with the designated entity into a nested form template. There are two stages necessary for this translation. The first stage uses an approach suggested by Elmasri and Larson [4] to convert the ER graph into an tree structure of entities. The second stage converts the entity tree into a form template. To convert the ER graph into an entity tree the attributes of relationships are migrated from the relationship downward (from the root) to the entity set below the relationship in the tree, and all relationships nodes are eliminated. In the hierarchical view, M:N and 1:N relationships are viewed as 1:N, while N:1 and 1:1 relationships are viewed as 1:1. Any two entity sets in the hierarchical view with a 1:1 relationship between them are merged to form a single entity set with the attributes of both entity sets.

   The entity tree is then automatically converted into a collection of nested form templates as follows:

   a. The root of the entity tree becomes the top-level or outermost form template.

   b. While traversing the tree, all children nodes are translated into a form template nested inside the form template corresponding to the parent.

   c. Attribute names are positioned on the form template. Each attribute name appears on a separate line.

   d. An example value is a value from the domain of an attribute that is displayed on the form template as an example of a valid value that may be entered for that attribute. An example value for each attribute is selected from a default list of example values for the attribute. Example values are placed on the same line as and to the right of its attribute on the form template.

   e. Appropriate information is stored in the forms data dictionary. This includes information about entities that were merged during the hierarchical conversion and information about relationships connecting entities on the form. This information is used by the Electronic Forms System Prototype when translating queries formulated by office workers using the form template into equivalent queries suitable for processing by the underlying database management system.

   f. A form template name corresponding to the entity name is placed at the top of each form template.

The resulting form template may be used by the office worker to enter data, to formulate queries and updates to the database, or to browse through the database contents[2,3].

The above approach can also be applied to databases described by the CODASYL data model. If the database is described by a hierarchical data model, then the displayed graph is already a tree which the forms administrator trims. The description of a relational database can also be displayed as a graph structure by defining a node of the graph for each relation and an edge of a graph for each corresponding foreign key and primary key pair.

## An Example

As an example, suppose the schema of Figure 1 is displayed on the screen. Suppose that the forms administrator wants a form consisting of entity sets COURSE, STUDENT and SECTION entity sets. The forms administrator points to those three entities

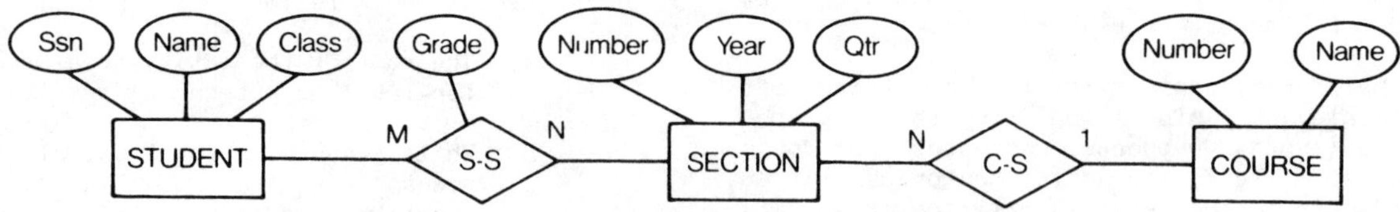


**Figure 3. Schema Subgraph**

and their relationships, S-S,C-S on the screen. The system then erases the remaining entities and relationships from the screen. The resulting subgraph is illustrated in Figure 3.

Now the forms administrator must choose a root entity set. Several choices can be made. We have extended the suggestions of Elmasri and Larson [4] to include the follow criteria for choosing a root entity set:

1. The entity set with the most attributes upon which conditions will be specified by office workers.

2. The entity set with the most attributes to be included on the form template.

3. The entity set which seems most natural for the types of information retrieved or paper-form look-a-likes. For example, suppose that the office worker would be most likely to ask "Get me all of the courses taken by a particular student," then the STUDENT should be the root entity set. On the other hand, if the office worker is more likely to ask "Get me all of the students who have taken a particular course," then COURSE should be the root entity.

Suppose the forms administrator chooses COURSE as the root. The ER subgraph of Figure 3 is converted into the hierarchy of Figure 4 and the corresponding form template for Figure 5.

Relationship attributes are migrated to the entity sets at the lower end (towards the leaves of the tree) of the relationship in the hierarchy. Thus the Grade attribute is migrated from the S-S relationship to the STUDENT entity set, and gives the grade value of each student who took the section of a course.

## 4. Interactive Tools for Modifying Existing Form Templates

The forms administrator might want to modify the format and layout of the form template created above in order to:

- o Make the form template more closely resemble paper forms used in the office.
- o Rearrange the order that attributes appear on the form template to make data entry easier.

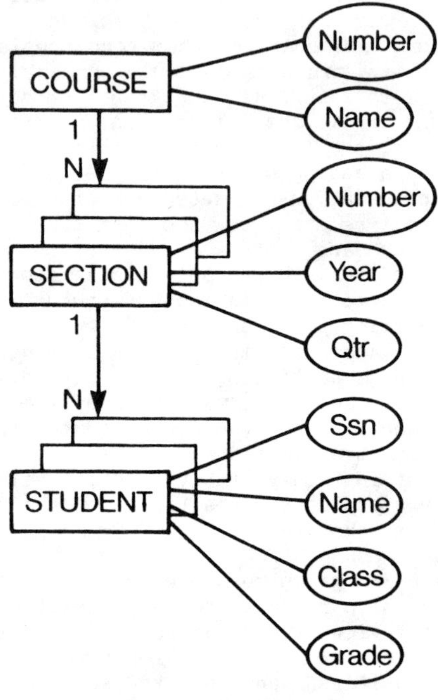


**Figure 4. Schema Hierarchy**

- o Hide certain information in the database from the office worker.
- o Change information on a form when the structure of a database is changed.
- o Create help messages and special instructions for office workers entering data.
- o Improve the aesthetics of the form template's appearance.

A rich set of interactive tools for modifying a form template to conform to the styles and needs of office workers are provided by the Electronic Forms System Prototype.

1. Modify Tool - This tool allows the forms administrator to interactively edit and reposition all background information on a form template.

2. Delete Tool - The forms administrator can delete attributes or sub-form templates from a form template. The forms administrator must alsc supply a default

**COURSE**

**Number:** 5121
**Name:** Data Structures

**SECTION**

**Number:** 8
**Year:** 1982
**Qtr.:** Fall

**STUDENT**

**SSN:** 578-64-6244
**Name:** Tom Smith
**Class:** Grad
**Grade:** B

**Figure 5. Form Template**

value for a deleted attribute used when the office worker uses the revised form template for data entry.

3. Undelete Tool - The forms administrator can bring back attributes, example values and subtemplates that have been deleted from a form template.

4. Move Tool - The forms administrator can interactively reposition information on the form template. Entire templates, background information, individual attributes, and individual example values cn be relocated on the form template.

5. Enlarge/Shrink Tool - The forms administrator can insert or delete lines in the form template.

6. Help Instruction Tool - The forms administrator can define help instructions corresponding to an attribute name on the form template. This provides additional information to the office worker who is unclear about the type of information associated with an item on a form. An office worker entering information into a database who encounters an attribute on the form template about which they are confused can press a help key and the predefined instruction or message is displayed.

7. Special editing and validation requirements - the forms administrator can specify a wide variety of validation constraints to be enforced during data entry and a wide variety of editing and formatting specifications to be used when data is displayed on a form template.

8. Add Derived Item Tool - The forms administrator can define attributes on the form template which are derived from other attributes on the form template.

The forms administrator may invoke any of these tools, which appear on a menu displayed in a window separate from the window displaying the form template. In effect, the user "repaints" the form template until he/she is satisfied with the resulting layout. Using these tools, the forms administrator is able to formulate a wide variety of form templates for office workers. The forms administrator can create a form template similar to the spread sheet of Visicalc; the added (derived) attributes being automatically calculated from non-added attributes in the form template. The retrieval and storage features of a database management system and the capabilities of a spread sheet are combined in Electronic Forms System Prototype.

## 5. Implementation

The requirements of a forms administrator have been identified and tools that can be used to meet those requirements have been specified. The Electronic Forms System Prototype, currently being implemented at the Honeywell Computer Sciences Center, will support these tools. Of the five steps for translating data descriptions into form templates, tools for steps 1 and 3 have been implemented. With the exception of the derived-item tool, all of the tools for modifying a form template have been implemented. After implementation is complete, the system will be evaluated and refined to make the tasks of a forms administrator as easy and flexible as possible.

## REFERENCES


[1] Chen, P. P-S., "The Entity-Relationship Model: Towards a Unified View of Data," ACM Transactions on Database Systems, Volume 1, Number 1, March 1976, pp. 9-36.

[2] Larson, J.A., "The Forms Pattern Language," Proc. IEEE Conference on Data Engineering, Los Angeles, Apr. 24-27, 1984, pp. 183-192.

[3] Larson, James A., "A Data Manipulation Language for Electronic Forms," Proceedings IEEE Computer Society International Conference on Software and Applications (COMPSAC81), Chicago, Illinois, Oct. 1981, pp 348-354.

[4] Elmasri, R.A., Larson, J.A., "A User Friendly Interface for Specifying Hierarchical Queries on an ER Graph Database," Honeywell Tech Report, Corporate Technology Center, HR-82-252: 17-38, March 1982.

Special Feature

# A Visual Approach to Browsing in a Database Environment

James A. Larson, Honeywell Computer Sciences Center

The operations of structuring, filtering, panning, and zooming can be used to browse the contents of a database.

A visual approach to browsing in a database environment is one way for users to access database contents easily and conveniently. People relate better to visual representations of the logical database than to other representations.

Users perform four basic operations when browsing a database: *structuring,* choosing a structure of the objects to be examined; *filtering,* selecting instances of the objects to be examined; *panning,* examining neighboring object instances; and *zooming,* determining the level of detail for examining object instances. My approach consists of four very flexible steps corresponding to each of the four basic operations. Each step uses visual representations to present information to the users. By manipulating these visual representations, users can structure, filter, pan, and zoom. Users may revise decisions and choices made during any of the four steps.

Most database management systems require users to formulate a complex specification describing the data that they wish to access. In order to do this, they must be familiar with the logical structure of the database; they must know the names of the types of objects to be accessed and how these objects are related. They must also be able to specify which occurrences of the objects are to be accessed by describing the criteria accessed occurrences must satisfy. This is difficult for many users because of their unfamiliarity with the syntax used to formulate requests, or because they have only a vague notion of what data they desire to access.

Users who have only a vague notion of the data to be accessed need to browse through the database. By browsing through the bookshelves of a library, it may be possible to locate one or more books of interest. By browsing through the pages of these books (perhaps making use of indices and tables of contents) readers may be able to locate the desired information that they could not previously characterize or describe. Database users have a similar need to browse through information in a database. A technique is needed for users of database management systems to locate information without having to specify an exact description of the information or where it is stored in the database. Such a technique is useful when users initially have only a vague idea of what they desire, but feel confident that they will recognize the desired information when they see it.

## Browsing operations

To understand the four basic browsing operations, consider a paradigm of a hardware store customer desiring to purchase

EH0252-7/87/0000/0124$01.00 © 1986 IEEE

some lightbulbs. The floor plan of the hardware store is arranged so that customers can locate desired merchandise by themselves. The customer quickly proceeds to the lightbulb counter, bypassing other merchandise not of interest. The customer scans the several brands and styles of lightbulbs on the counter and closely examines individual lightbulbs as he or she selects the desired lightbulbs for purchase. This paradigm illustrates the four browsing operations of structuring, filtering, panning, and zooming.

**Structuring.** Choose a structure for the objects to be examined. Often this is done by someone other than the person doing the browsing. For example, the hardware store manager would arrange the floor plan of the store in such a fashion that customers can easily browse through the items for sale. A few database management systems interfaces permit the user to structure objects to be examined. For example, GUIDE[1] permits the user to identify an object type to examine from a schema. The user may also examine object types that are related to the identified object type. The user may examine object types that are indirectly related to the identified object type via a chain of related object types. The result is a subschema that the user may use to formulate queries. Many database management systems permit only the database administrator to structure subschemas or views of the database.

**Filtering.** Select the instances of the objects to be examined. For example, if a customer is interested in purchasing lightbulbs, he or she will select one or more lightbulbs from the lightbulb counter containing lightbulbs of various wattages and brands. Some researchers[2] refer to this operation as *probing.*

Many degrees of filtering are possible:

*No filtering.* The user may not restrict the object instances to be displayed by specifying a query. SDMS [3] falls into this category.

*Manual query specification.* Most systems permit this option.

*Manual query modification.* Some systems save a user's query and permit the user to perform surgery on the query, modifying it in various ways.

*Assisted query modification.* System utilities allow the user to combine two queries into a single query, or to use the results of one query as part of the formulation of another query.

*Automatic query modification based on user feedback.* A revised query is automatically generated based on the user's determination of the relevance and nonrelevance of instances displayed as a result of the original query.

*Retraction.* This is a process of expanding a query to retrieve possibly relevant object instances when the original query fails to return any object instance. [2]

**Panning.** Examine the object instances adjacent to an object instance. In my example, the customer may examine several lightbulbs at the same counter. Motro[2] calls this operation *navigation.* Most interfaces to database management systems permit the scrolling or paging[4] of object instances onto a video screen permitting the user to pan.

**Zooming.** Determine the level of detail for examining object instances. For example, the customer may examine the guarantee in fine print on the lightbulb container, or may examine the lightbulb for flaws. Zooming permits the user to see (or hide) a level of detail that previously was (was not) visible. The user can zoom in or out to view object instances at the level of detail desired. SDMS,[3] VIEW,[5] PDB,[6] LID,[7] and the interactive language of Lochovsky and Tsichritzis[8] all permit zooming. However, the above systems place different restrictions on the number of levels of detail the user can view. For example, PDB and LID permit the user to view at most two levels at a time; the Lochovsky and Tsichritzis's language permits the user to view three levels, while SDMS and VIEW permit the user to view an arbitrary number of levels.

The MPS[9] is a system that could be used as an interface to a wide variety of computerized systems, including a database management system. MPS includes components that support these four operations. The MPS "presentation surface builder" is used for structuring and filtering a two-dimensional presentation surface containing the representation of instances of objects to be examined. The "presentation surface effector" is used for panning and zooming much like SDMS. [3]

## A visual approach to browsing

Users often have difficulty visualizing the logical structure of a database. One reason is that databases often have many instances of entities that may be related in many ways. A visual approach to browsing is desirable because many people tend to relate better to visual representations. In addition, users can understand entity relationships quickly and manipulate them easily.

To simplify the browsing of a database, a schema graph is used. A schema graph illustrates the logical structure of a database and hides the differences in syntax and data models of various database management systems. A *schema graph,* $S = (V, E)$ is a graph consisting of $V$, the set of vertices that represent entity types in the database, and $E$, the set of edges that represent relationships between entity types. In a CODASYL network database, $V$ represents CODASYL record types and $E$ represents CODASYL set types. In a relational database, $V$ represents the set of tables and $E$ represents relationships between tables as identified by common key column(s) of one table and the foreign key column(s) of another table.

In my approach to browsing, the user first chooses a portion of the schema that contains entity types in which the user has interest. The user then specifies restrictions to the instances of these entity types and finally examines the entity instances selected from the database. My approach to database browsing can be summarized by the following four steps, which correspond to the browsing operations outlined above.

*Step 1. Structuring.* Choose a subgraph of the schema graph that specifies a hierarchy of entity types in $V$. This subgraph defines a forest of trees, each tree consisting of several related entity instances from the database.

*Step 2. Filtering.* Thin the forest of trees defined by the subgraph. A query language is used to specify the desired tree instances from the database to be examined

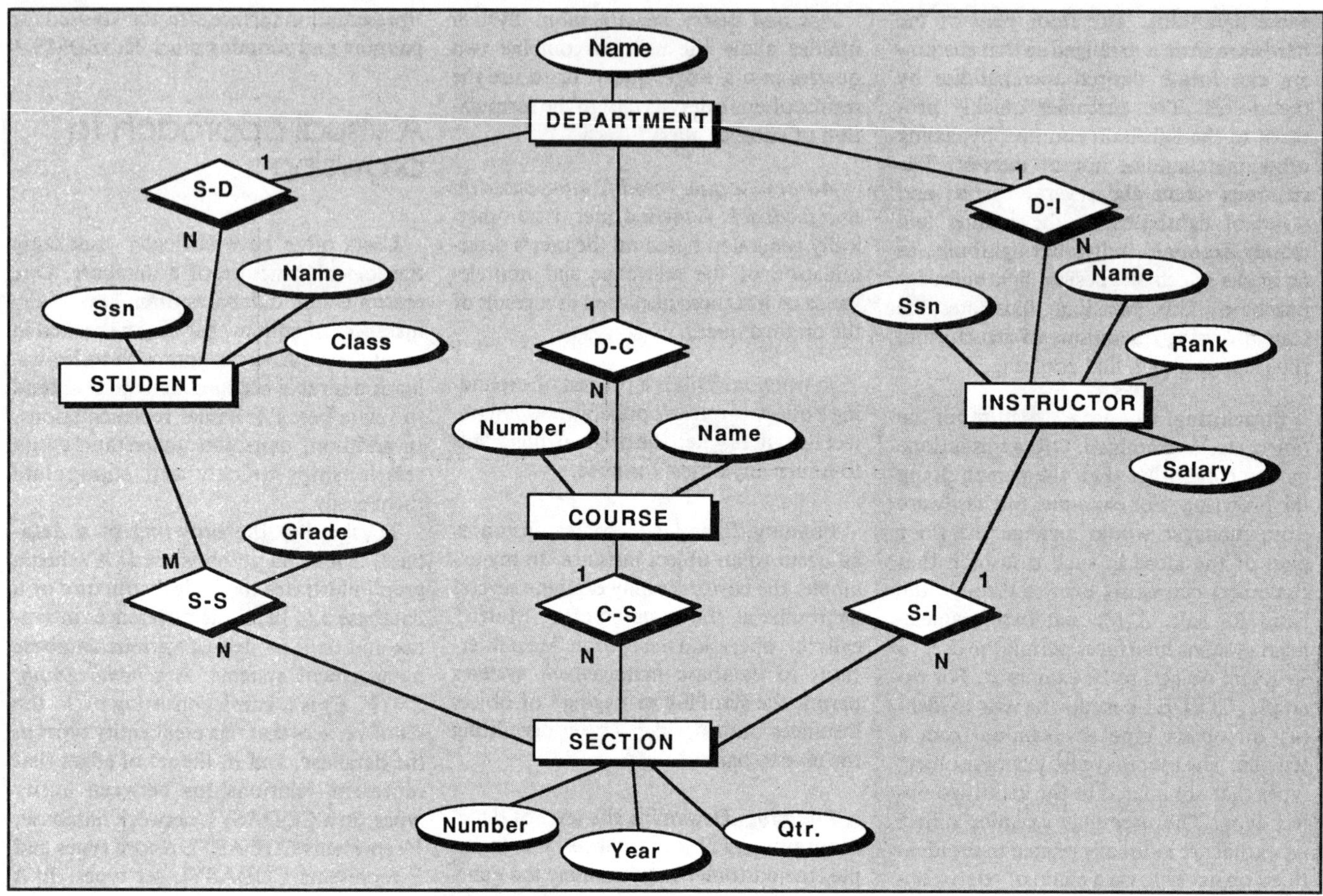


**Figure 1.** Graphical representation of schema.

in detail. The query language is a visual interface similar to Query-by- Example.[10]

*Step 3. Panning.* Display the selected entities in the trees of the thinned forest. The user views each tree as a series of nested documents on a video screen. Each document displays the attribute values of an entity instance from the database. The user may page and scroll through the documents.

*Step 4. Zooming.* Choose the entity types whose instances are to be displayed. The user may elect to display only the roots of the trees, only the leaves of the trees, only the entities at a specific level in the trees, or a combination of these.

Each of these steps makes use of visual representations to present information to the user. The user chooses options and specifies parameters by manipulating these visual representations. To better understand these steps I will describe the mechanisms that allow them to work.

**Step 1: Structuring.** In a graphical representation of a schema graph (Figure 1) based on Chen's Entity-Relationship data model,[11] rectangles represent entity types, diamonds represent relationships between entity types, and ovals represent attributes of entity types and relationships. The cardinalities of a relationship are indicated by numbers at the points of the diamond representing the relationship.

A form template (Figure 2) describes a hierarchical subgraph of the schema graph of Figure 1. The user chooses a subtree represented by a form template by following the six steps described later in this section.

A form template is a two-dimensional layout of one or more entity types. Each entity type is represented as a window on the screen. The nesting of windows corresponds to the hierarchical relationship of the entity types. When displayed on a video screen, a database entity is displayed in each window. Each window also contains "background" information that includes the window name and the names of attributes of the corresponding entity type. In Figure 2, the background information is that which is not underlined. Each window also contains example values. Example values are underlined in Figure 2. Attribute values from an entity instance replace these example values when entity instances are displayed. (Because attribute values are not underlined, they are not confused with example values.)

A visual interface[12] can guide the user through five steps to generate a form template that describes a subgraph of a schema graph.

*Step 1a.* A schema graph is automatically generated on the screen from information in a data dictionary. To generate this graph, the system reads adjacency information about entity types, relationships, and attributes that reside in the database and automatically derives the layout of the associated schema graph. This step relieves the user of the burden of remembering the exact contents and structure of the schema.[13,14]

*Step 1b.* The user examines the schema graph to view the structure of the database.

*Step 1c.* The user now trims off irrelevant entity types from the schema graph. The system supports two modes for doing this. The user can either specify the relevant entity types or specify the irrelevant entity types. When all relevant or irrelevant entity types have been identified, the system erases irrelevant entity types from the displayed graph. When the user has completed this stage, the displayed graph contains only entity types, relationships, and attributes that are to appear on the form template.

*Step 1d.* The schema graph must now be converted from a graph structure to a tree-structured, form-template view of the database. To aid in the conversion, the user identifies an entity type of primary interest. The designated entity type will become the root entity of the tree structure and will correspond to the top-level or outermost window in the form template.

*Step 1e.* The system automatically translates the schema graph into a nested form template. There are two stages necessary for this translation. The first stage[13] converts the schema graph into a tree of entity types. The second stage converts the entity tree into a form template. To convert the schema graph into a tree, the attributes of relationship type are migrated from the relationship downward (from the root) to the entity type below the relationship in the tree, and all relationship nodes are eliminated. In the hierarchical view, M:N and 1:N relationship types are viewed as 1:N, while N:1 and 1:1 relationship types are viewed as 1:1. Any two entity types in the hierarchical view with a 1:1 relationship type between them are merged to form a single entity type with the attributes of both entity types.

The tree is then automatically converted into a nested form template as follows:

1. The root of the tree becomes the top-level or outermost window of the nested form template.
2. The nesting structure of the form template windows is made to correspond to the tree of entity types.
3. Attribute names are positioned in the window corresponding to the appropriate entity type. Each attribute name appears on a separate line as background text.
4. An example value is a value from the domain of an attribute. It is displayed in the window as an example of a valid value for that attribute. An example value for each attribute is selected from a default list of example values for the attribute. Example values are placed on the same line as and to the right of the attribute name.
5. A name corresponding to the entity type name is placed as background text at the top of each window in the nested form template.
6. Appropriate information is stored in the data dictionary. This includes information about entities that were merged during the hierarchical conversion. This information is used when translating queries formulated using the form template into equivalent queries suitable for processing by the underlying database management system.

Users may manually change the layout of a window by repositioning the attribute names, example values, or entity type name within the window. Users may modify background information (attribute names and entity type name). The resulting form template describes a forest of trees embedded in the database graph. The form template may be used to thin this forest of trees.

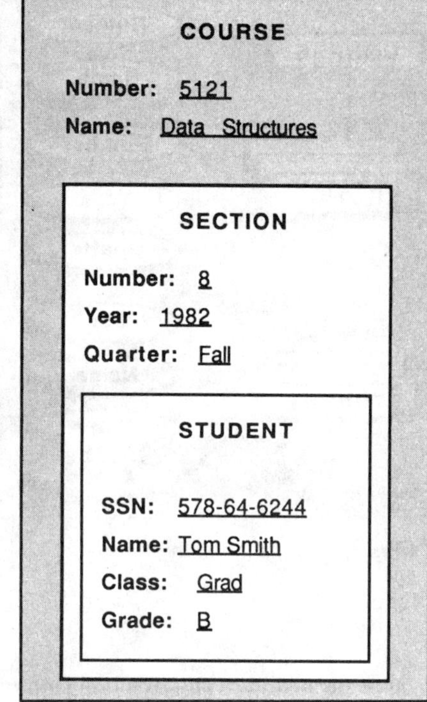


**Figure 2.** Form template.

*An example.* As an example, suppose the graph schema of Figure 1 is displayed on the screen. Suppose that the user wants a nested form template consisting of entity types COURSE, STUDENT, and SECTION. The user points to those three entity types and their relationships, S-S, C-S, on the screen. The system then erases the remaining entity types and relationships from the screen. The resulting subgraph is illustrated in Figure 3.

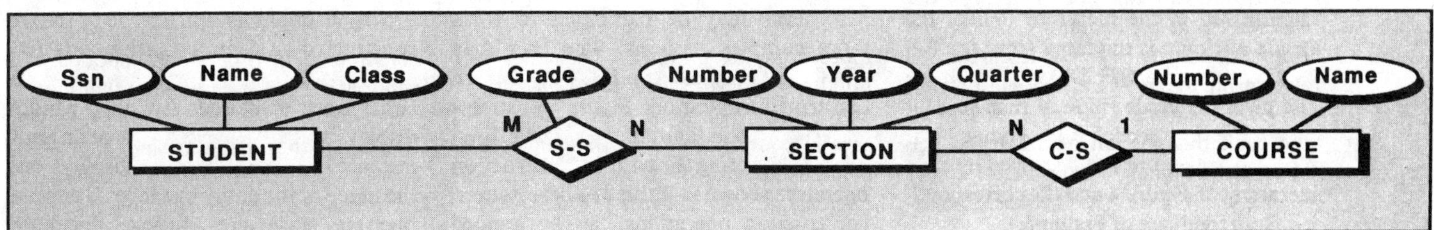


**Figure 3.** Schema subgraph.

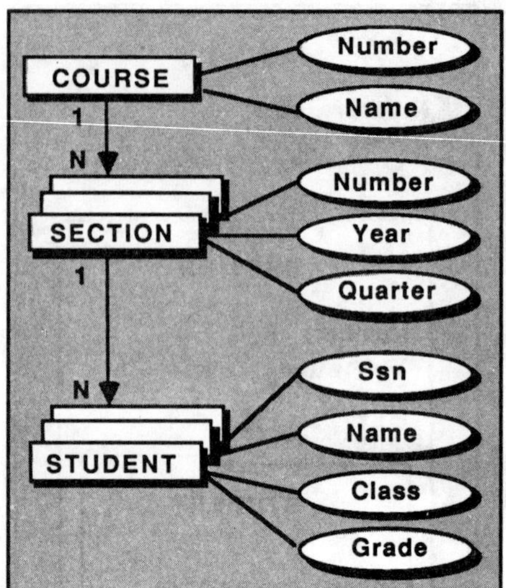


**Figure 4.** Schema hierarchy.

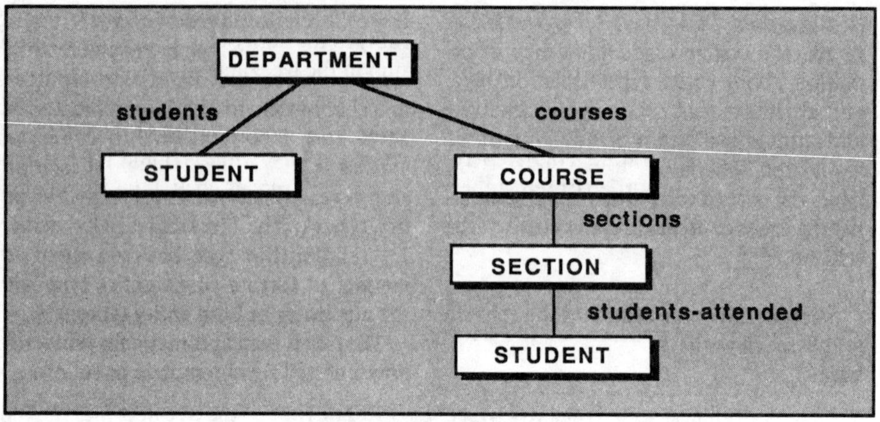

**Figure 5.** Converting a cycle to a hierarchy.

Now the user must choose a root entity type. Several choices can be made. Criteria[13] for choosing a root entity type include:

1. The entity type with the most attributes upon which conditions will be specified by users.
2. The entity type with the most attributes to be displayed in the nested form template.
3. The entity type that seems most natural for the types of information to be accessed. For example, if the user is most likely to browse between instances of STUDENT and only occasionally examine instances of SECTION or COURSE, then STUDENT should be selected as the root. On the other hand, if the user is more likely to browse between instances of COURSE, then COURSE should be selected as the root entity type.

Suppose the user chooses COURSE as the root. Relationship attributes are migrated to the entity types at the lower end (toward the leaves of the tree) of the relationship in the hierarchy. Thus, the Grade attribute is migrated from the S-S relationship to the STUDENT entity type, and gives the grade value of each student who took that section of a course. The subgraph of Figure 3 is converted into the hierarchy of Figure 4 and the corresponding form template of Figure 2.

Note that it is still possible to have a hierarchy even if the graph selected in step 4 has a cycle. In this case, two leaf entity sets are different. For example, if the user chooses DEPARTMENT, D-C, COURSE, C-S, SECTION, S-S, and STUDENT, S-D, then the user sees the hierarchy as shown in Figure 5. Here, the STUDENT related to DEPARTMENT directly shows the students who major in that department. The STUDENT related to COURSE shows students who completed some section of some course offered by the department.

**Step 2: Filtering.** The user thins the forest of trees to be viewed by specifying a pattern.[15] A *pattern* is a form template with zero, one, or more conditions. Figure 6 illustrates a pattern consisting of two conditions: (1) the attribute value for COURSE Name must be 'Databases' and (2) the attribute value for COURSE Number must be less than 5000. An instance of an entity must satisfy all conditions in the window if it is to be displayed to the user.

Patterns may be combined to form more complex patterns. The user may build a complex pattern by using pattern construction operators. Figure 7 illustrates several complex patterns that have been constructed using the pattern construction operators shown in Table 1. These pattern construction operations can be applied recursively to build patterns of arbitrary complexity.

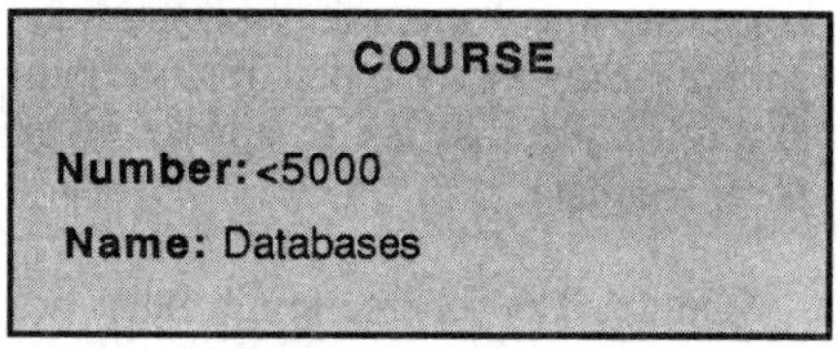

**Figure 6.** Example pattern.

**Step 3: Panning.** The user views the entity instances of each tree of the thinned forest as a series of nested documents. The entity instances of a tree are displayed in order sequence as a nested document (Figure 8). The user may page forward and backward between documents. By choosing a paging increment, the user may jump forward or backward a specified number of documents. The user may also display the first or last document and scroll within documents.

**Step 4: Zooming.** Each node of the tree constructed in Step 1 corresponds to a window in the form template that may be either open or closed. An *open* window displays all the attribute values of an entity instance. A *closed* window displays only the name of the entity instance. Users may open or close any window, depending upon if they wish the attribute values of entity instances of that entity type to be

NOT

COURSE
Number:<5000
Name:______

Pattern for accessing COURSES with numbers not less than 5000

ALL

COURSE
Number: <5000
Name:______

COURSE
Number: >3000
Name:______

Pattern for accessing COURSES with numbers between 3000 and 5000

ANY

COURSE
Number: <5000
Name:______

COURSE
Number: >8000
Name:______

Pattern for accessing COURSES with numbers less than 5000 or greater than 8000

COURSE
Number:______
Name:______
Includes

SECTION
Number:______
Year:=1982
Quarter:______

Pattern for accessing COURSES which were taught in 1982

COURSE
Number:______
Name:______
Includes only

SECTION
Number:______
Year: = 1982
Quarter:______

Pattern for accessing COURSES which were taught only in 1982

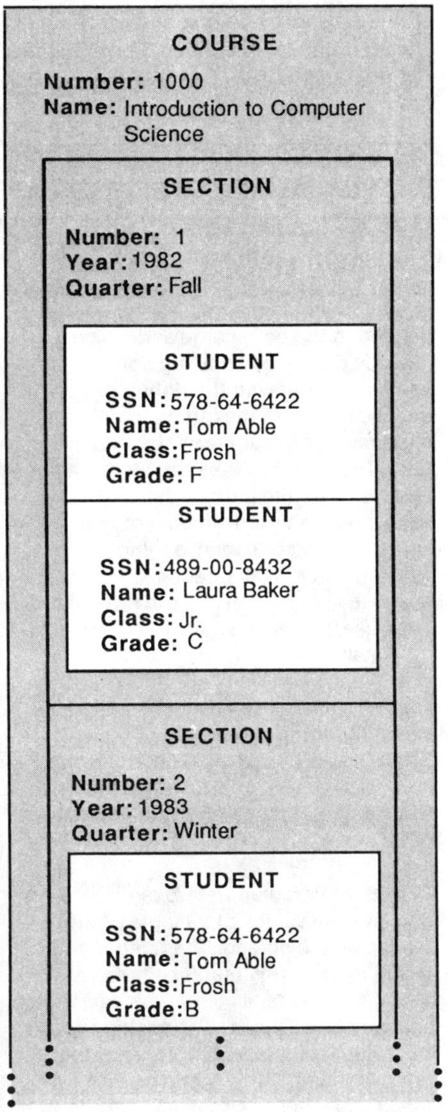

**Table 1.** Pattern construction operators.

| Pattern construction operator | Meaning | Restriction on use of this operator |
|---|---|---|
| Zero or more conditions | Select entity instances satisfying all conditions | Applies to exactly one window |
| NOT | Select entity instances NOT matching the pattern | Applies to exactly one pattern |
| ALL | Select entity instances matching ALL of the patterns | Applies to two or more patterns |
| ANY | Select entity instances matching ANY of the patterns | Applies to two or more patterns |
| INCLUDES | Select entity instances that have related entity instances that INCLUDE an instance matching these patterns | Applies to one window nested within another window |
| INCLUDES ONLY | Select entity instances that have ONLY related entity instances matching these patterns | Applies to one window nested within another window |

COURSE
Number: 1000
Name: Introduction to Computer Science

SECTION
Number: 1
Year: 1982
Quarter: Fall

STUDENT
SSN: 578-64-6422
Name: Tom Able
Class: Frosh
Grade: F

STUDENT
SSN: 489-00-8432
Name: Laura Baker
Class: Jr.
Grade: C

SECTION
Number: 2
Year: 1983
Quarter: Winter

STUDENT
SSN: 578-64-6422
Name: Tom Able
Class: Frosh
Grade: B

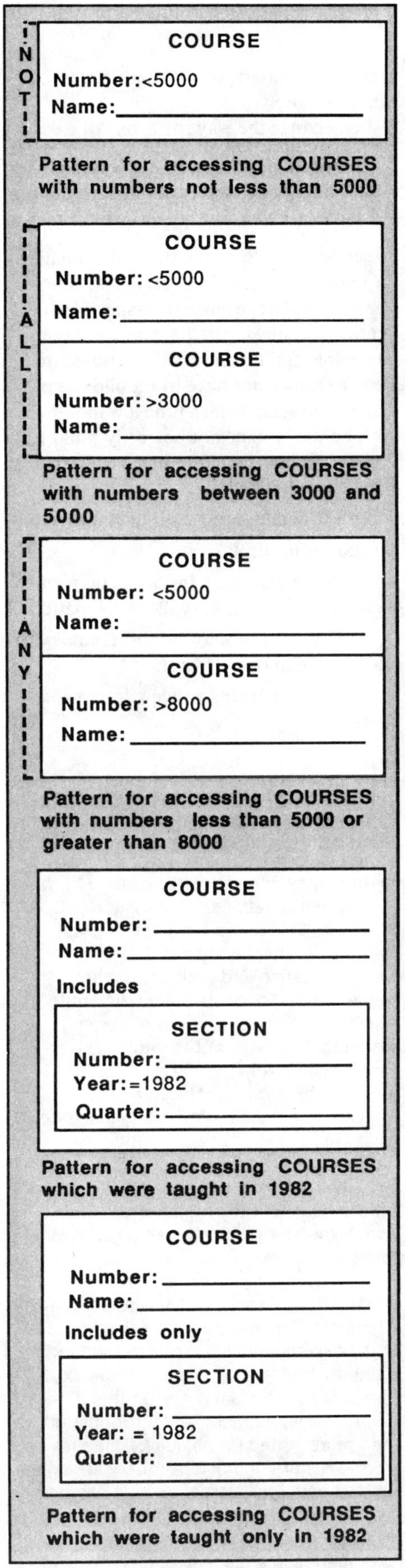

**Figure 7.** (Left) Example patterns.

**Figure 8.** Nested document.

COURSE

**Number:** 5133
**Name:** Compilers

SECTION

**a. Window for COURSE open**

COURSE

**Number:** 5133
**Name:** Compilers

SECTION

**Number:** 1
**Year:** 1984
**Quarter:** Fall

STUDENT

SECTION

**Number:** 2
**Year:** 1984
**Quarter:** Fall

STUDENT

**b. Windows for COURSE and SECTION open**

**Figure 9.** Opening and closing windows.

visible when the selected entities are displayed. Opening and closing windows allow the user to control the level of detail in which the results are viewed. Figure 9a illustrates the Figure 2 form template with the windows for SECTION closed. Figure 9b illustrates the result of opening the SECTION.

## Revising choices

A user may revise decisions and choices made during any of the four steps allowing for a great deal of flexibility. The user may always go back to step 1 and choose a new tree structure. The user may return to step 4 at any time to open (or close) any closed (or opened) windows. This changes the entity types that may be viewed. Within step 3, the user may view any of the selected entity instances by paging and scrolling between instances of entities. The remainder of this section discusses how the user can revise the pattern formulated in step 2 to thin the forest.

To change the way the forest of trees is thinned, the user may return to step 2. This capability is important because it encourages the user to thin the forest in an experimental fashion. In this way, the user does not have to worry about formulating a pattern correctly the very first time; a pattern that has been used to specify which entity instances can be viewed remains available for further modifications; and, the user does not have to rebuild the pattern from scratch each time it is modified.

The user might not correctly build the pattern in the first attempt for reasons including the following:

- The user is unclear about which entity instances to display.
- Particular entity instances may motivate the user to modify the initial pattern.
- The pattern may be too complex to formulate in one attempt.
- The user wants to view intermediate results.

## Some existing approaches to browsing using graphics

FORAL LP,[1] Query By Example,[2] CUPID,[3] and GOING[4] are examples of pictorial graphical interfaces for database management systems. With these systems the user formulates a request using the pictorial interface, and then scrolls through the results. As with keyword-oriented query languages, the user can browse through only the results. The user must formulate a new request if the original request does not produce the desired results. Several efforts at providing more natural approaches to browsing through a database make use of graphics.

**Lochovsky and Tsichritzis's interactive query language.**[5] This language is designed for accessing several databases using a videotex system. The user sees a video screen divided into three basic windows. One window specifies the path taken by the user to arrive at the collection of named information that can be examined. A second window of the screen is used for system feedback to the user. Finally, the third window is used for the specification and display of data. This window may display a menu consisting of two columns of named information. When the user selects a name in the left-hand column, that name is appended to the path name and a new menu is displayed showing some of the names previously in the right-hand column as names in the left-hand column. New names appear in the right-hand column. The user can thus browse as he or she specifies the path to the desired information. The third window of the screen may also display a template into which the user may directly enter names rather than select them from the menu. Thus users familiar with the structure of the databases may enter path information directly. The third window of the screen may also display a template into which users may enter one or more values to select specific pieces of information, to be displayed. However, the selectiveness of this facility is not as great as other query languages.

**PDB, or Personal Data Base.**[6] This displays the values of a single entity instance on the screen. The relationships in which the entity instance takes part is also displayed as a menu. The user selects one of these relationships and the system displays the values of the corresponding entity instance and a new menu. The user can thus navigate from entity instance to instance of different entity types in any desired order. LID, or Living In a Database,[7] is similar to PDB; however, LID uses a bit-mapped graphics terminal to display the attributes of an entity instance and entities that are related to it. To locate a specific entity instance, the user may either scroll through instances of the entity type or use a search function by filling values in a template. A graph structure is displayed that shows other entity instances that are related to the current entity instance. When the user moves the cursor to a related entity instance, the attributes of the related entity instance are displayed and a new relationship graph is drawn.

**GUIDE, or Graphical User Interface for Database Exploration.**[8] This displays a database schema in graphical form as relationship types. Queries can be expressed as traversal paths on this network. Partial queries can be formulated and represented graphically. Database retrieval results of any local query are available at any time. Partial queries can be linked together to form more complex queries and provide the bases for building queries in a piecemeal fashion. Parts

• The user makes a mistake when constructing the original pattern.

• Three approaches for pattern modification are explicit pattern modification, relevance feedback, and approximate matching.

**Explicit pattern modification.** The user can modify a pattern by explicitly modifying the conditions in any simple pattern, by creating or deleting patterns, and by changing the pattern construction operators of a complex pattern. The user may also move one or more entity instances into a pattern and use the pattern operators to combine the entity instances as patterns into more complex patterns.[16] This is especially useful because a particular database tree may motivate the user to modify the original pattern.

**Relevance feedback.** This is a technique for reformulating a pattern based on the initial retrieval. The aim is to use the revised pattern for a second retrieval that improves on the first. While explicit pattern modification permits the user to "perform surgery" directly on the pattern, relevance feedback performs this surgery automatically as follows:

1. The user formulates the initial (seed) pattern that is applied to the database.
2. The user examines some of the selected trees and determines if they are relevant or not relevant for his or her needs. Based on these relevance decisions, the original pattern is replaced by the conjunction of two patterns: the first describes the relevant documents and the second is the NOT of the pattern describing the nonrelevant trees. The revised pattern is applied to the remaining unexamined trees. This step is repeated until the user either examines all of the trees or determines that a sufficient number of relevant trees are examined for his or her needs.

**Approximate matching.** It may be desirable to access a database tree that "almost matches" a pattern (or a document being used as a pattern) for reasons including the following:

• The user wishes to view trees that could be viewed with only minor changes to a pattern without actually changing the pattern.

• The user is viewing a tree and is unable to formulate a pattern that will cause similar trees to be viewed.

• The user formulates a pattern that results in no trees and wishes to generalize the pattern by relaxing the conditions that the trees must satisfy so that more trees will be selected.

• The standard rules of a Boolean logic-based system may not be an ideal method of retrieving relevant trees. The operators "ALL," "ANY," and "NOT" (Boolean operators *and, or,* and *not*) have a strict interpretation. This may produce less than desirable results in certain cases. For example, in a pattern containing many subpatterns connected by an "ANY" operator, a tree satisfying all of the subpatterns would be treated the same as one satisfying only one of the subpatterns. Also, in a pat-

of the schema can be selectively made visible or invisible; this provides the basis of representing multiple levels of details of the schema.

**SDMS, or Spatial Data Management System.**[9] This is a human-machine interface that uses computer graphics to aid a user in interrogating a database. Objects in the system are represented graphically as icons positioned in a spatial framework consisting of a set of flat surfaces that can be viewed using a set of color, raster-scan displays. The user can create and examine data surfaces larger than the display screen, zooming in and out to control the level of detail displayed. The system allows the user to browse through a wide range of data by using a joystick. VIEW[10] extends the SDMS technique by enabling a variety of presentations of the data to be generated, without the need for painstakingly explicit instructions from the database administrator. Changes in the presentation of data include rearranging, adding, and deleting entities on the display; adding or deleting displayed attributes of entities; and altering the means of presentation of an entity or attribute. A further extension, MPS, or Multipurpose Presentation System,[11] combines database, graphics, and AI technologies. Both the user and the application system may operate on the data, describe image layouts, manipulate viewing windows, and build display images.

## References


1. Michael E. Senko, "FORAL LP: Design and Implementation," *Proc. Fourth VLDB,* 1978, pp. 225-267.
2. M. Zloof, "Query By Example: A Data Base Language," *Proc. 1975 Nat'l Computer Conf.,* Anaheim, Calif., June 1975.
3. N. McDonald and M. Stonebeaker, "CUPID: A User Friendly Graphics Query Language," *Proc. 1975 ACM-PACIFIC,* San Francisco, Calif., April 1975.
4. Yosihisa Udagawa and Setsuo Ohsuga, "Novel Technique to Interact with Relational Databases by Using a Graphics Display," *J. Information Processing,* Vol. 5, No. 4, 1982, pp. 256-264.
5. F. H. Lochovsky and D. C. Tsichritzis, "An Interactive Query Language for External Data Bases," *Proc. Eighth VLDB,* Mexico City, Sept. 1982, pp. 11-21.
6. R. G. Cattell, "An Entity-Based Database User Interface," *Proc. ACM SIGMOD Conf. Management of Data,* May 1980, pp. 144-150.
7. Dennis Fogg, "Lessons from a 'Living in a Database' Graphical Query Interface," *Proc. ACM SIGMOD Conf. Management of Data,* 1984, pp. 100-106.
8. Harry K. T. Wong and Ivy Kuo, "GUIDE: Graphical User Interface for Database Exploration," *Proc. Eighth VLDB,* Mexico City, Sept. 1982, pp. 22-32.
9. C. F. Herot, "Spatial Management of Data," *ACM TODS,* Vol. 5, No. 4, pp. 493-513.
10. Gerald A. Wilson and Christopher F. Herot, "Semantics vs. Graphics—To Show or Not to Show," *Proc. Sixth VLDB,* Montreal, October 1-3, 1980, pp. 183-197.
11. Gerald A. Wilson et al., "The Multipurpose Presentation System," *Proc. Ninth VLDB,* Florence, Italy, Oct. 30-Nov. 2, 1983, pp. 56-69.

It is possible to retrieve trees by relaxing the interpretation of the Boolean operators.

tern containing "ALL'ed" subpatterns, a tree satisfying all but one of the subpatterns would be just the same as a tree satisfying none of the subpatterns.

It is possible to retrieve trees by relaxing the strict interpretation of the Boolean operators. One approach is to replace the ALL and ANY operators by a more general operator that requires an entity occurrence to satisfy a certain percentage (or a minimum number) of subpatterns. I have not pursued this approach because I feel it would be difficult for users to apply such a general operator. Unlike the next approach, this approach cannot rank the selected documents by the expected degree of relevance to the user's request.

Another approach to selecting trees that are "close" but don't quite match a pattern is to use a metric that has been specified for calculating the distance between a pattern and a tree. Using this metric, trees that are "close" to a pattern can be ranked according to their closeness to the pattern and presented to the user. Using relevant feedback, the initial query can be made more general. This has an effect similar to automatic retraction.[2]

## Future work

Future work includes conceptual extension of the four browsing operations to support an interface to expert systems, application libraries, and graphical information.

**Expert system interface.** The browsing system is an easy-to-use interface to a database management system. A similar interface can also be used to access the capabilities of an expert system. Briefly, the schema graph would represent the capabilities of the expert system. Structuring corresponds to organizing the display of capabilities and selecting the desired functions. Filtering consists of specifying parameters values required to perform the selected functions. Panning corresponds to examining the results of similar problems. Zooming displays clarification about how the expert system derived the result.

**Application library interface.** Form templates can also be used to application software in a library. By filling in the input parameters for a form template, the user invokes the corresponding application program. Results of executing the application are displayed as output parameters on the same form template and may also be automatically entered as input parameters on other form templates. Browsing through form templates would be equivalent to viewing the results of automatically invoked applications, each application using information entered by the user or derived by previously invoked applications.

**Graphical information.** The current implementation of the browsing system will permit only alphanumeric text to be displayed on the screen. Techniques to support the following functions are needed to fully integrate graphics into a browsing system: create, modify, and save graphical images as part of the background information of a form template; store and access graphical images within a database and display and modify those images within a form template; translate information represented alphanumerically in the database into graphical images and icons for display within form templates; and modify the database information when the user manipulates the corresponding graphical image in the form template.

We have seen that browsing in a database environment consists of the four basic operations of structuring, filtering, panning, and zooming. An interactive, visual interface to database management systems that supports these four operations has been designed and is being implemented. In my approach, it is always possible to revise choices made in earlier operations. Future work includes extending the interface to support expert systems, application libraries, and graphical data. An experimental evaluation is needed to analyze the strengths and weaknesses of this approach to browsing.

New technology such as video text that allows individuals to access databases from their television sets at home can make many databases available to everyone. A visual approach to browsing will be needed by individuals with little training in traditional command languages so that they can quickly and easily access desired information.

Information that cannot be accessed by a user is useless. Browsing is a natural way for people to access information in a database. Laboratory systems incorporating the four main features of browsing (structuring, filtering, panning, and zooming) already exist. These features will find their way into existing and new database management systems, making accessing data easier for a wider range of database management system users. □

## Acknowledgments

Tim Giebelhaus, Jennifer Wallick, John Nomura, and Jim vanDruten each designed and implemented portions of a prototype system for browsing. Many of the ideas for structuring are due to Ramez Elmasri.

## References

1. Harry K. T. Wong and Ivy Kuo, "GUIDE: Graphical User Interface for Database Exploration," *Proc. Eighth VLDB,* Mexico City, Sept. 1982, pp. 22-32.
2. Amihai Motro, "Browsing in a Loosely Structured Database," *Proc. ACM-SIGMOD Conf. Management of Data,* June 18-21, 1984, pp. 197-207.
3. C. F. Herot, "Spatial Management of Data," *ACM TODS,* Vol. 5, No. 4, pp. 493-513.
4. Michael Stonebraker and Joseph Kalash, "Timber: A Sophisticated Relation Browser," *Proc. Eighth VLDB,* Mexico City, Sept. 1982, pp. 1-10.
5. Gerald A. Wilson and Christopher F. Herot, "Semantics vs. Graphics—To Show or Not to Show," *Proc. Sixth VLDB,* Montreal, October 1-3, 1980, pp. 183-197.

6. R. G. Cattell, "An Entity-Based Database User Interface," *Proc. ACM SIGMOD Conf. Management of Data,* May 1980, pp. 144-150.

7. Dennis Fogg, "Lessons from a 'Living in a Database' Graphical Query Interface," *Proc. ACM SIGMOD Conf. Management of Data,* 1984, pp. 100-106.

8. F. H. Lochovsky and D. C. Tsichritzis, "An Interactive Query Language for External Data Bases," *Proc. Eighth VLDB,* Mexico City, Sept. 1982, pp. 11-21.

9. Gerald A. Wilson et al., "The Multipurpose Presentation System," *Proc. Ninth VLDB,* Florence, Italy, Oct. 30-Nov. 2, 1983, pp. 56-69.

10. M. Zloof, "Query By Example: A Data Base Language," *Proc. 1975 Nat'l Computer Conf.,* Anaheim, Calif. June 1975.

11. P. P-S Chen, "The Entity-Relationship Model: Toward a Unified View of Data," *ACM TODS,* Vol. 1, No. 1, March 1976, pp. 9-36.

12. James A. Larson and Jennifer Wallick, "Tools for Forms Administrators," *IEEE Workshop on Languages for Automation,* New Orleans, Nov. 1984; also, *Languages for Automation,* Shi-Kuo Chang (ed.), Plenum Publ. Corp., New York, 1985.

13. R. A. Elmasri and J. A. Larson, "A User Friendly Interface for Specifying Hierarchical Queries on a ER Graph Database," *Fourth Int'l Conf. Entity-Relationship Approach,* Chicago, Oct. 28-30, 1985.

14. Kazuo Sugihara et al., "A Semantic Approach to Usability in Relational Database Systems," *Proc. IEEE Conf. Data Engineering,* Los Angeles, April 24-27, 1984, pp. 203-210.

15. James A. Larson, "The Forms Pattern Language," *Proc. IEEE Conf. Data Engineering,* Los Angeles, April 24-27, 1984, pp. 183-192.

16. Jim VanDruten, *Incremental Refinement of Queries in an Electronic Forms System,* Honeywell Computer Sciences Center Technical Report, Aug. 1984.

**James A. Larson** is a Senior Research Fellow at the Honeywell Computer Sciences Center in Minnesota, where he is involved in research in distributed databases. Previously he has been involved in the design of integrated automated office systems for Olivetti, Italy, and research in database computers for Sperry Univac. He has participated on the CODASYL Data Description Language Committee and the ANSI/SPARC Relational Database Task Group.

Readers may write to the author at Honeywell Computer Sciences Center, 1000 Boone Ave., North, Golden Valley, MN 55427.

# A Framework for Choosing a Database Query Language

MATTHIAS JARKE and YANNIS VASSILIOU

*Computer Applications and Information Systems Area, Graduate School of Business Administration, New York University, New York, N.Y. 10006*

This paper presents a systematic approach to matching categories of query language interfaces with the requirements of certain user types. The method is based on a trend model of query language development on the dimensions of functional capabilities and usability. From the trend model the following are derived: a classification scheme for query languages, a criterion hierarchy for query language evaluation, a comprehensive classification scheme of query language users and their requirements, and preliminary recommendations for allocating language classes to user types.

The method integrates the results of existing human factors studies and provides a structured framework for future research in this area. Current and expected developments are exemplified by the description of "new generation" database query languages. In a practical query language selection problem, the results of this paper can be used for preselecting suitable query language types; the final selection decision will also depend on organization-specific factors, such as the available database management system, hardware and software strategies, and financial system costs.

Categories and Subject Descriptors: D.3.2 [**Programming Languages**]: Language Classifications—*very high-level languages*; H.1.2 [**Models and Principles**]: User/Machine Systems—*human factors*; H.2.3 [**Database Management**]: Languages; H.3.3 [**Information Storage and Retrieval**]: Information Search and Retrieval—*query formulation*

General Terms: Human Factors, Languages

Additional Key Words and Phrases: Databases, language evaluation, query language, user classification

## INTRODUCTION

A *query language* (QL) is defined as a high-level computer language for the retrieval and modification of data held in databases or files [Samet 1981]. It is usually interactive, on line, and able to support queries that are ad hoc (not predefined). It is often assumed that the main users of QLs have limited technical expertise, so user interaction tends to be of limited complexity and the displayed answer is usually relatively short.

Many different query language interfaces can be built on top of the standard languages offered by a database management system (DBMS) manufacturer. In fact, the number and variety of query language interfaces available or under development have grown so rapidly that a framework for evaluating query languages in terms of their functionality and usability by different types of users is needed. The goal of this paper is to propose a methodology for selecting a type of query language interface on the basis of its functionality and "user

CONTENTS



friendliness" characteristics, a goal that has not been attempted in previous surveys and categorizations of QLs [Brodie and Schmidt 1982; Lacroix and Pirotte 1977, 1980; Lehmann and Blaser 1979; Leavenworth and Sammet 1974; Lochovsky and Tsichritzis 1984; McDonald and McNally 1982; Samet 1981; Stonebraker and Rowe 1977]. In order to avoid becoming outdated before its publication, the paper concentrates on general query interface types rather than on specific language systems currently on the market.

In order to reach this goal, well-structured taxonomies of query languages and language users are developed. The proposed methodology for selecting a type of query language provides a framework for contrasting both taxonomies and combining them with existing technical and human factors research to recommend the types of language best suited for a known user class. However, as the existing human factors research—traditionally focused on specific systems—does not suffice for generalized conclusions, the main contribution of this paper is the proposed framework that can be seen as a structured set of hypotheses for future studies. The usefulness of our methodology has been demonstrated by its application in the development of evaluation schemes for a set of major empirical studies comparing natural versus formal query languages [Jarke et al. 1986a; Turner et al. 1984].

The next section is an overview of the proposed methodology; subsequently, each of its steps will be considered in more detail.

## 1. QUERY LANGUAGE SELECTION PROCEDURE

Our approach to query language evaluation can be understood as a specialized *cost–benefit analysis* method. It is a cost–benefit analysis in the sense that multiple evaluation criteria are based on a simple economic model of query language usage and the trade-off between costs and benefits depends on the user type. The method is specialized toward the specific task of evaluating query languages from the viewpoint of a single user.

This approach has the advantage of permitting specific recommendations with available data from technical and human factors research. On the other hand, most of the cost and benefit criteria are nonquantifiable, or at least very difficult to measure precisely. Consequently, one can only expect a preselection of "usable" language types from such a method. When confronted with the actual language selection problem, the user community must still consider costs, available hardware, compatibility with existing software systems, the type of "host" programming languages, and common use by different user types. In other words, the user may not always have a choice of what query language to use, or his or her choice may be limited to a few prespecified alternatives. It may often be possible, however, to construct more suitable specialized query language interfaces on top of existing ones via application programs in order to accommodate different user classes simultaneously. The proposed methodology is geared toward selecting those end-user query interfaces rather than the underlying programming languages.

However, the fact that the query language is only a part, although a central one, of the *total interface* between the user and the computer system should not be overlooked. For instance, one problem arises for programming users whose QL may be embedded in a host programming language. Such users require compatibility and smooth data transfer between the two languages. Lacroix and Pirotte [1980] differentiate among four types of embedding, which are listed here in ascending order of integration between host and query language: (1) subroutine calls, for example, DL/I [IBM 1975] and TOTAL-IQ [CINCOM Systems 1978]; (2) simple extension, for example, COBOL/DML [CODASYL 1971]; (3) procedural operators, for example, C/QUEL [Stonebraker et al. 1976] and APL/EDBS [Lochovsky and Tsichritzis 1977]; and (4) full integration, for example, PASCAL/R [Schmidt 1977] and ADAPLEX [Smith et al. 1981].

Having stated these limitations of the approach, we now present an overview of the method of selecting query languages. An outline of the proposed method is given in Figure 1.

The general problem of query language selection is characterized by a large and rapidly growing number of alternatives (query languages) and an even larger number of decision makers (potential users). The first step in the evaluation scheme is to develop an abstraction mechanism that generates a limited number of classes. To achieve this, well-structured taxonomies of both query languages and users are developed in Sections 2 and 3. A summary of recent human factors research in the area of query languages using these taxonomies is given in Section 4.

The next step in the evaluation scheme is the development of a hierarchy of evaluation criteria. The goals for developing good evaluation criteria are

- measuring all important costs and benefits of QL usage,
- discriminating clearly among both user and language types, and
- yielding simple criteria at the lowest level of the criteria hierarchy.

These goals are achieved by relating the evaluation criteria hierarchy to the dimensions of functional capabilities (benefit) and usability (cost) of the QL taxonomy (Section 5). The costs and benefits of a particular QL are not usually quantifiable. Roughly speaking, the "costs" are determined by the initial training effort (the user's investment) and the effort of continuing work with the language (the production costs). The "benefits" derive from language functions, such as result selection and composition, output presentation, and flexibility of interaction.

After establishing evaluation criteria, the method proceeds in Section 6 to apply them to both users (determine requirement profiles for each user type) and languages (characterize usability and functional capabilities of each language class). By matching user profiles with language profiles, the final step derives recommendations for the selection of query languages (Section 7). Note that it may be appropriate from a practical viewpoint to select several query language interfaces for several classes of users, because, on the one hand, many users with different needs will access the same DBMS and, on the other, many current DBMSs offer multiple query and/or programming languages that allow easy construction of a variety of interfaces. Therefore, the above analysis can be conducted for each major user group. The results of the final "optimization step" as presented in Section 7 are supported by results of human factors studies and by knowledge of technical restrictions, but can be only preliminary because of insufficient empirical research in the area.

In summary, the proposed preselection methodology includes three major processes, corresponding to the levels shown in Figure 1: (a) classification of users and languages, and establishment of evaluation criteria (the *technical* process, shown in the upper two levels of Figure 1); (b) evaluation of language types and determination of user

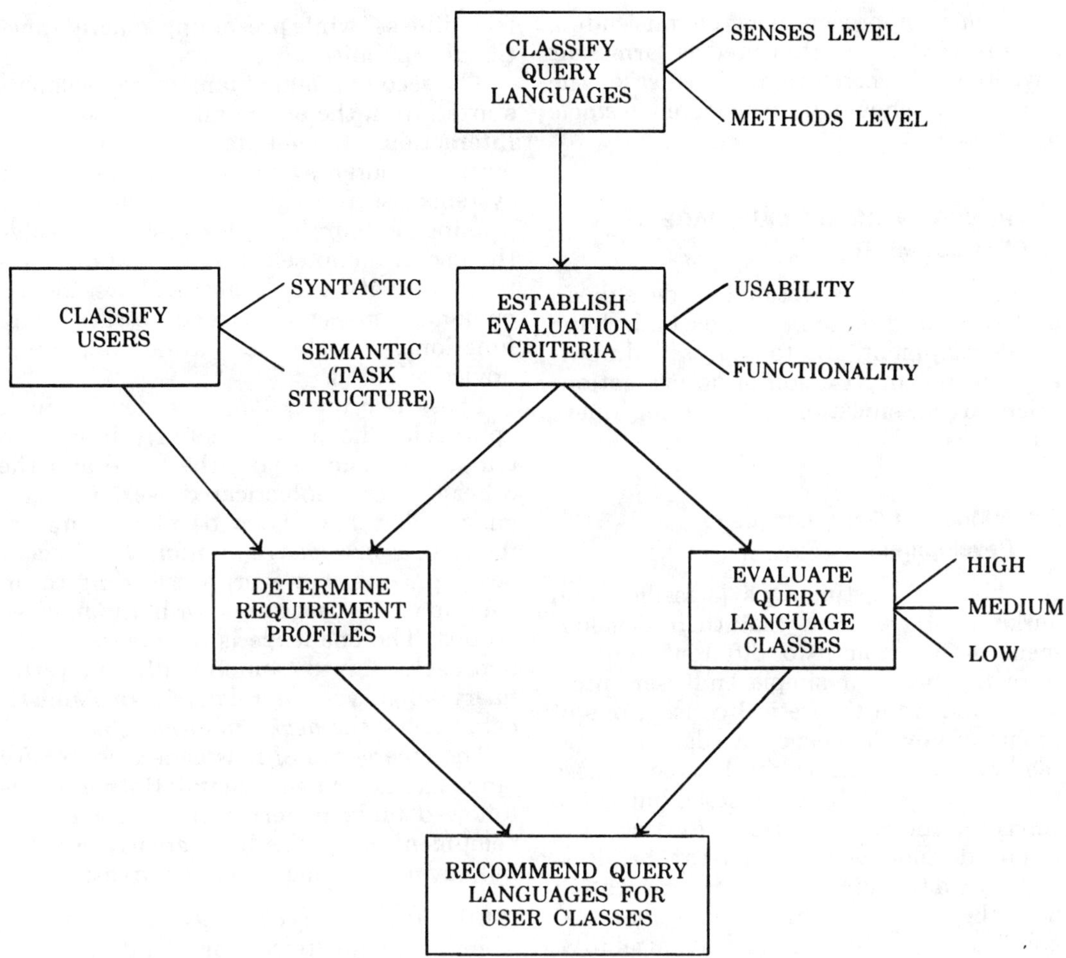


**Figure 1.** Evaluation methodology for query languages.

requirements (the *evaluation* process in the third level); (c) matching user requirements with query language evaluations (the final *choice* process).

In a practical decision situation, additional studies must follow this preselection of language types. In particular, the hardware and software strategies of the organization (e.g., choice of manufacturer, hardware, programming languages, and software packages) must be taken into account. Furthermore, sunk costs of existing investments, or high financial costs of the "optimal" language may reduce the choices. These further steps are not specific to query languages and are therefore omitted here (see, e.g., King and Schrems [1978] for an overview of the uses of cost–benefit analysis in information systems).

The evaluation of language types centers around several tables. For generating and filling these tables a simple Delphi-like method was used, which also served as a validity check. The evaluation parameters in the tables (the column headings) were agreed upon after surveying the literature, extracting and generalizing important contributions, and reconciling differences for precise definitions. The tables were filled independently with the direct or indirect application of available human factors research results. In cases in which empirical data were not available, experience and common sense were relied upon. The common sense approach may be misleading [Moran 1981]; it is often cited as "armchair psychology." Therefore, in these cases the evaluations should be considered *testable hypotheses*.

## 2. TRENDS IN QUERY LANGUAGE DEVELOPMENT

The purpose of this section is to develop an understanding of some trends underlying QL development, and to apply this knowledge to the construction of an evaluation-oriented classification scheme for query languages.

### 2.1 A Model of Query Language Development

A review of existing QLs [Vassiliou and Jarke 1984] revealed that their development stems from two different sources: from the need for simple end user interfaces, and from theoretical conceptions of programming language or database research. The relationship between these areas is not yet fully understood but is the subject of increasing current research.

The development of QLs can be illustrated by a two-dimensional representation with the axes denoting the functional capabilities of a system and its usability. Roughly speaking, functional capabilities refer to what one can do with the system, whereas usability refers to the effort of actually doing it. Clearly, usability can only be valued with a specific user group in mind.

Figure 2 summarizes our QL development trend analysis. One group of QL developers, originating from the disciplines of programming languages and database theory, concentrates on the syntactic form and semantic meaning of database interactions. Languages developed by these disciplines are characterized by the full specification of an operation by a command or a sequence of commands. Starting from formal, mathematically oriented language concepts, this group of developers has moved to "English-like" keyword languages and finally restricted natural languages. The overall trend has been toward more "user friendliness" while preserving general functional capabilities.

The second group of language developers started from the ergonomic analysis of the interaction of computer-naive end users with computer systems. Whereas simple systems use function keys or line-by-line prompting, more complex systems involve the use of menu selection or graphical interaction with the database. These developments represent a trend toward more functional capabilities while remaining novice oriented.

These two query language development approaches have evolved fairly independently, with one serving the more and the other the less sophisticated user. The languages that have been developed are referred to as *previous generation QLs*. Recent developments, however, are leading to an overlap of the usage area for both language groups. The challenge is to integrate both approaches into functionally powerful query languages for relatively unsophisticated users, the *new generation QLs*.

The emergence of new generation query languages is not coincidental. Rather, it has followed (and, in terms of decreasing development costs, has been greatly assisted by) advances in many related areas:

(a) *Hardware Technology Developments*. Microprocessor technology and new devices, such as video disks, content addressable memories, holographic memories, and optical storage devices, allow for increased capabilities in storing and accessing data in several forms. Additionally, voice recognizers and synthesizers and eye-tracking and pointing devices lead to increased use of multimedia interactions.

(b) *Developments in Graphics and Artificial Intelligence*. The ability to display information in the most natural and dense form, that of an image, coupled with high-resolution display devices and the use of color, greatly contributes to the immediate comprehension of query output and the direct representation and manipulation of objects of interest [Foley and Van Dam 1982; Moorhead 1976; Newman and Sproull 1979]. Research in artificial intelligence—particularly in natural language processing, expert systems, and robotics—assists

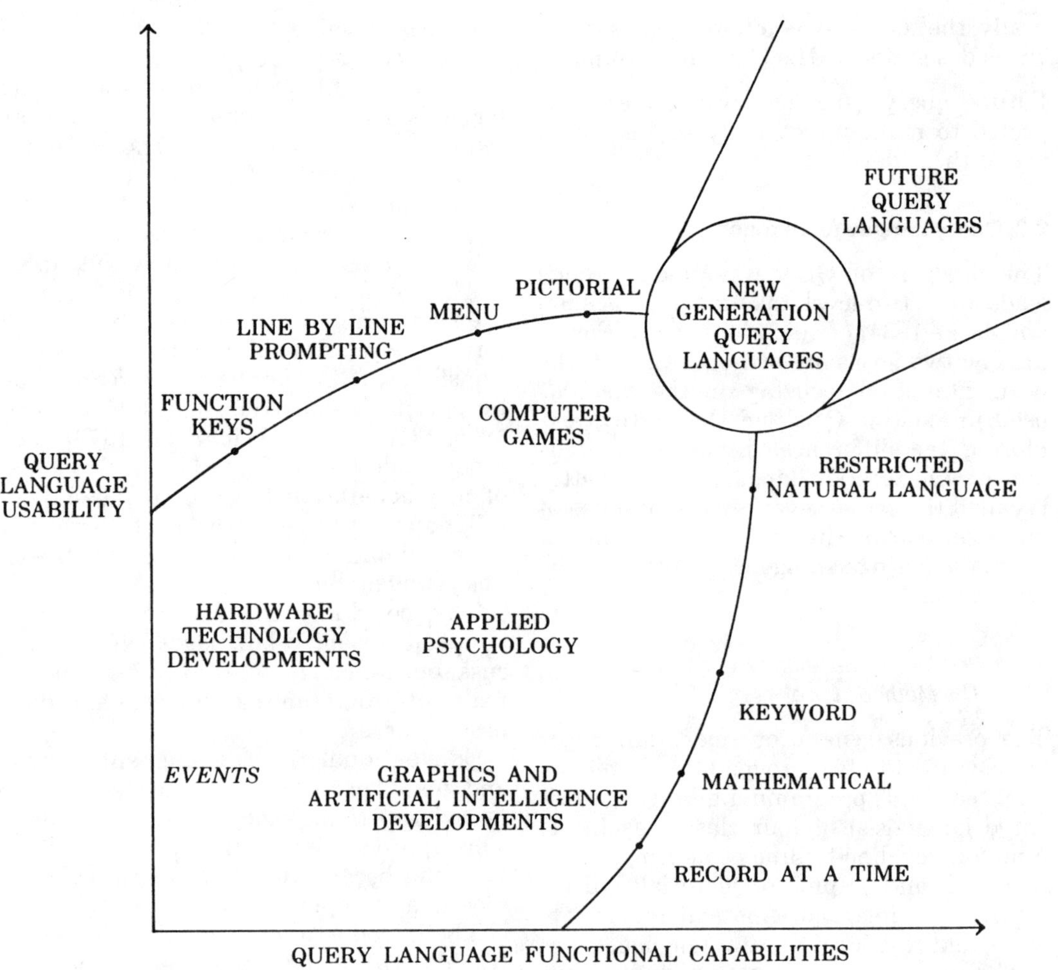


**Figure 2.** Query language development trends.

in query formulation and user feedback [Gable and Page 1980].

(c) *Developments in Applied Psychology and Related Sciences.* There is a new interest in "bridging the gap" between researchers concerned with the human factors aspects of query languages and their colleagues who are primarily concerned with the technology of query language design. Because of the tremendous possibilities for interaction with new generation query languages, the need for scientific methods to deal with the complex considerations of "convenience," "friendliness," and "effectiveness" of QLs becomes apparent. Several psychological studies of QLs have recently been reported [Brosey and Shneiderman 1978; Jarke et al. 1985; Reisner 1975, 1981; Shneiderman 1978; Small and Weldon 1983; Vassiliou et al. 1983; Welty and Stemple 1981], and considerable interest is evidenced by new professional meetings and special issues of publications focusing on human factors in computer systems [Moran 1981; Vassiliou 1984].

(d) *Success of Computer Games.* The pleasant and simple interaction of computer games has revolutionized the way in which people perceive interfaces to computer systems and helped remove many psychological barriers that people have when faced with a computer system. Naturally, the success of computer games influences designers of QLs [Malone 1982].

Future query language systems are expected to make increasingly sophisticated use of these developments.

### 2.2 Query Language Taxonomy

The analysis of QL development trends leads to a two-level taxonomy [Vassiliou and Jarke 1984] of query languages (Figure 3). The two levels are orthogonal, with the horizontal level focusing on the *methods* used in existing QLs and the vertical exploring the differences between previous and new generation languages. The latter is called the *senses* level because the use of more senses for the interaction is one of the main distinguishing factors between the two classes.[1]

#### *2.2.1 Previous Generation Query Languages: The Methods Level*

The previous generation query languages are classified in two groups (ergonomically oriented and programming-language-oriented languages) of four classes each: (1) function key, line-by-line prompting, menu selection, and graphic or pictorial and (2) record-at-a-time, mathematical, linear keyword, and restricted natural languages.

The first three language classes are typically exemplified by custom-made languages for specific applications.

The use of *function keys* is a limited but effective method of interaction for inexperienced users. By pressing a special key on the keyboard, a previously prepared transaction or report is processed.

*Line-by-line prompting*, also called parameterized interaction [Lehmann and Blaser 1979], is a simple system-driven dialogue. In the typical case, the user will be prompted to enter (line at a time) the name of the object of interest, a field name, a comparison value, etc. The query is built up from the user's responses.

A more sophisticated system-driven dialogue is *menu selection*. Here, users are required to point to their choice from a menu of options offered by the system. Menus are structured hierarchically; the choice of an option may cause the presentation of a new menu [Ellis and Nutt 1980].

In *graphic* or *pictorial* query languages the user can manipulate visual symbols to formulate queries. The entities and relationships in the database are represented by specific geometric shapes [McDonald 1975; Senko 1978; Tsichritzis 1976]. This group could be considered an early version of new generation languages that did not fully succeed because the necessary hardware and understanding of user needs were not yet available.

This concludes the discussion of ergonomically oriented languages. Next we discuss four language types evolving from the realm of programming language and database theory.

Conventional file management systems and many early database systems use a *record-at-a-time* logic for data retrieval. This approach is mentioned for completeness and because most QLs still use it for modification operations.

The introduction of the relational model [Codd 1970] led to set-oriented data retrieval. Some query languages use the precise notation of *mathematical* formalism for short and succinct expression of powerful operations. Examples include ALPHA [Codd 1971], PASCAL/R [Schmidt 1977], and ISBL [Todd 1976]. These languages are especially suited as target languages for very high-level user interfaces. Languages that use the position of the command operators and operands to convey meaning [Boyce et al. 1975] are also included in this group.

The majority of query languages available today fall into the category of *linear keyword*. These languages use statements that are similar to a programming language like COBOL but more English-like. The commands have a definite syntax, and only words from a specific reserved list can be used. Some typical examples of linear key-

[1] It is noted that the choice of communication media used for the interaction (keyboard, audio, etc.) is somewhat independent of the choice of methods (menu, function key, etc.). The taxonomy is designed to reflect this independence by placing the two levels orthogonally.

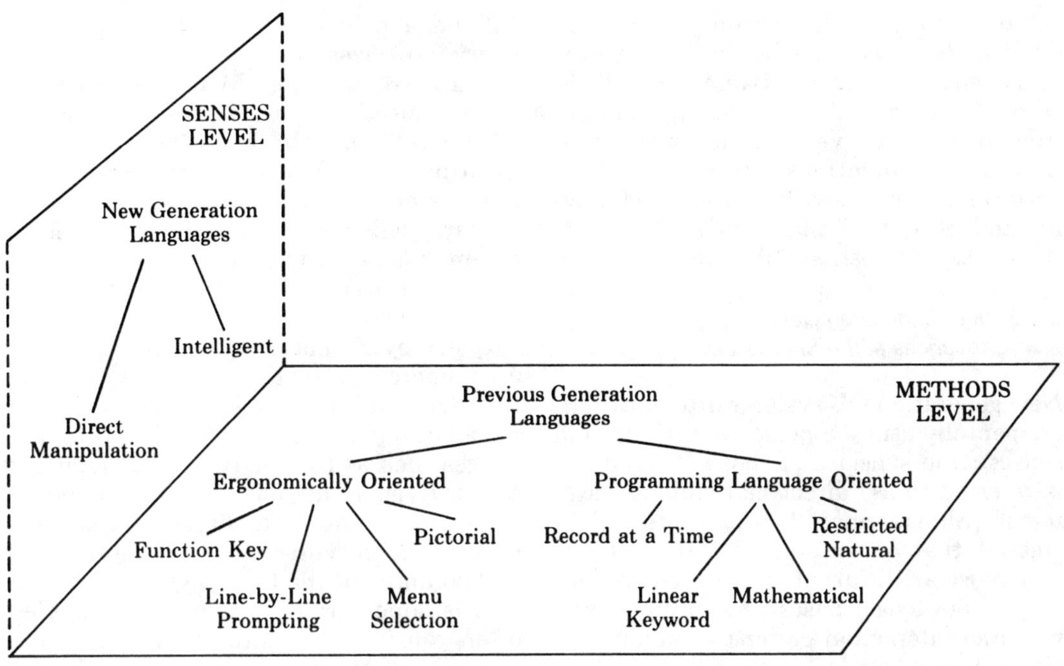


**Figure 3.** Query language taxonomy levels.

word languages are SQL [Astrahan et al. 1976] and QUEL [Stonebraker et al. 1976].

The *restricted natural language* mode has attracted interest in recent years. The intention is that the user can employ native natural language (e.g., English, German, French) for the interaction with the database. At least one such QL system is commercially available [Artificial Intelligence Corporation 1982; Harris 1977], and several others are under development in research laboratories [Bates and Bobrow 1983; Codd 1974; Hendrix et al. 1978; Hoeppner et al. 1983; Lehmann et al. 1978; Plath 1976; Thompson et al. 1983; Waltz 1978; Woods et al. 1972].

Some natural language systems will engage in a dialogue with the user to resolve any ambiguity in requests [Codd 1978]. Nevertheless, the natural language communication in all such state-of-the art QL systems is still far from close to person-to-person communication; this is the reason for using the prefix "restricted." Restrictions of current natural language query systems are at least twofold [Woods 1984]. On the one hand, most systems do not understand a sufficient range of complex grammatical constructs. On the other hand, all successful natural language systems thus far have been restricted to very narrow semantic domains of discourse and frequently do not degrade gracefully if the user exceeds their capabilities.

In summary, previous generation QLs provide only a restricted interactive environment. The user has a limited hardware interface (terminal, keyboard), and a relatively artificial conceptual model of formatted data and their organization. The user also has a formal query language syntax (the rules of the game), and uses experience and mastery of the system to accomplish a task (how to play and win the game).

The user's visual ability while interacting with the database is limited; the objects of interest are rarely displayed directly. Rather, they are represented by formatted text, thereby not giving the user any iconic clues (what the data look like) or spatial clues (where the data are) to help the querying process. Furthermore, the user does not fully employ his or her senses and cognition; for instance, query formulation does not use voice, touch, hearing, or gesture. Finally, the interaction is "static." A previous generation query system shows little or no "intelligence" in deducing answers from incomplete, yet obvious representations of user intentions. The user may still perform a task but with limited productivity and at the possible expense of more stress, less interest, and less pleasure.

#### 2.2.2 New Generation Query Languages: Advances at the Senses Level

New generation QL systems attempt to incrementally utilize a person's instincts and senses. One subclass of these QL systems is referred to as "direct manipulation systems" [Shneiderman 1984]. Another subclass is that of "intelligent" QL systems, which use artificial intelligence techniques (e.g., knowledge bases) to bring man–machine interaction closer to communication between people.

Shneiderman [1984] identifies the basic features of *direct manipulation* QL systems: (a) object of interest visibility, (b) rapid reversible actions, and (c) replacement of command language syntax by direct manipulation of objects. The following examples indicate the directions taken in direct manipulation language development.

A prototype system based on the principle of spatial database management, called SDMS, has been developed and implemented at Computer Corporation of America [Herot 1981, 1984]. The advantages of this query system include the ability to locate objects of interest by browsing and zooming, and the use of icons, color, highlighting, and a natural arrangement of objects in the database.

The environment of Cedar [Brown et al. 1981] offers another example of a new generation QL. The language was developed at Xerox Palo Alto Research Center as a derivative of the Smalltalk [Goldberg and Robson 1981] family. It is object oriented and views data primarily through an entity-based browser with the help of dynamic windows. Window managers, in particular, are becoming standard in powerful small computer systems (often called workstations), and it is projected that windows will be a principal component in future query languages.

The Architecture Machine group at Massachusetts Institute of Technology [Schmandt and Hulteen 1982] is experimenting with a voice and gesture interactive system called "Put-That-There." The scenario calls for the database user to issue commands by intermixing voice, gesture (e.g., pointing), and eye positioning at the desirable object.

Query-by-Example (QBE) [Zloof 1977] is a commercially available direct manipulation QL that is based on the relational model of data. In contrast to keyword languages such as SQL, QBE makes relations directly visible as objects (table schemas) to be manipulated on the screen, and the user moves the cursor freely along the rows and columns of the tables. Query formulation is done through the use of examples, often considered a natural education process [Thomas and Gould 1975]. Several extensions of QBE have been proposed, for example, query by pictorial example (QBPE [Chang and Fu 1979]), and QBE-like systems have been developed in related areas such as office systems.

The other major class of new generation QLs is that of *intelligent* QL systems. Most of these QL systems address important aspects of the human–computer interactions such as (a) the (semi-) automatic refinement of queries based on feedback [Codd 1978], (b) the ability of the user to ask questions about the logical structure of the database and about the use of the language, (c) the ability of the system to explain query failures and understand (to some degree) the context of the interaction [Woods 1984], and (d) the automatic modification of queries to obtain meaningful results [Motro 1984]. The examples that follow illustrate these aspects.

Advisory Systems [Schank and Slade 1984] support a natural language user interface by the application of stored knowledge that is acquired by experience. For example, the story-understanding system IPP [Lebowitz 1980] acquires its experience by reading stories in its domain of knowledge. Additionally, such systems also try to infer the user's intentions [Carbonell

1979]. In these respects, advisory systems go beyond conventional natural language front ends and can therefore be called new generation. Learning by experience rather than relying on a given set of stored rules also distinguishes these systems from simpler deductive front ends to databases [Jarke and Vassiliou 1984] in which the knowledge has to be programmed.

RABBIT [Tou et al. 1982] is a QL system developed at Xerox Palo Alto Research Center that assists the user in formulating a query. The basic principle underlying RABBIT's design philosophy is "retrieval by reformulation," a paradigm derived from a psychological theory of long-term memory. Roughly speaking, RABBIT initially provides the partial description of an example instance from the database. The user manipulates this instance and its associated descriptors to incrementally construct the next iteration of the query. The mechanism used in RABBIT is termed "perspective" for the query and is a way of viewing objects while highlighting only certain attributes. In formulating the next query iteration, the user works on a perspective for the query and a database instance. The user may modify the query descriptors by specifying "required" attributes, "prohibited" attributes, specializations of the given descriptors, etc. At any time during the interaction, the user may ask for descriptions of descriptors (metadata).

Although slightly outside the boundaries of query language interfaces, languages for the conceptual design of data-intensive information systems should also be briefly mentioned as examples of intelligent database languages using knowledge representation mechanisms. Users of such languages are programmers rather than novice end users. An early language of this type is TAXIS [Mylopoulos et al. 1980], which, in order to support a paradigm of database software development by specialization of data and procedures (as opposed to stepwise decomposition used in structured programming), relies heavily on the inheritance mechanisms provided by generalization hierarchies of data and transaction structures.

A more recent design language, Galileo [Albano et al. 1985], also offers type inheritance but, in addition, provides an interactive prototyping environment for database applications, which is integrated with a generator for application-dependent form-based query language interfaces. In contrast, the language CML [Borgida et al. 1986] consciously avoids being close to a system implementation but instead extends the TAXIS ideas by modeling real-world concepts such as objects, time, or precision of knowledge representation. This approach recognizes the need for multiple interfaces for requirements modeling, database design, and database usage, and tries to control the interaction among these languages via a knowledge-based system [Jarke et al. 1986b].

In Table 1 some features of the new generation languages described in the above examples are compared with those of the previous generation languages discussed in the preceding section. The table demonstrates that the sparse set of input and output media available in previous generation QLs is substantially expanded in the new interface types and that these expanded media also result in a few new method types (e.g., browsing) that are not meaningful without the additional media. The other major difference between the two generations of QLs, the intelligence acquired from an underlying deduction system, is less visible from the external interface features presented in the table, but no less important. A more detailed comparison and evaluation of both language types is given by Vassiliou and Jarke [1984].

A word of caution is needed. New generation QLs provide a new burden of responsibility for the application developer. For instance, the appropriate icons to represent objects, the use of color and highlighting, and the "natural" arrangements of the objects in the database greatly influence the success of the system. Application designers may need additional skills, which are not found in the traditional systems analysis education.

## 3. USER CLASSIFICATION

Many criteria for classifying users have been proposed [Codd 1974; Cuff 1980; Lehmann and Blaser 1979; Shneiderman

**Table 1.** Characteristics of Previous and New Generation Languages

| Query formulation | | Output presentation | |
|---|---|---|---|
| Medium | Method | Medium | Method |
| *Previous generation query languages* | | | |
| Keyboard | Function key use | Screen | Lists |
| Function keys | Line-by-line prompting | Printer | Tables |
| | | | Forms |
| | | | Text |
| | Menu selection | | |
| | Graphic | | |
| | Keyword command | | |
| | Restricted natural language | | |
| *New generation query languages* | | | |
| Keyboard | Keyword command | Screen | Lists |
| Function keys | Menus | Voice synthesizer | Tables |
| Picking devices | Windows | Color graphics | Forms |
| Touch screens | Gesture | Video display | Templates |
| Voice recognizers | Eye positioning | Printer | Icons |
| Gesture tracking devices | Zooming | Plotter | Color |
| Eye-positioning tracking | Voice | | Highlighting |
| | Browsing | | Images |
| | By example | | Sounds (voice) |
| | Touch | | Arrangement |
| | Deduction | | Text |

1980; Yormark 1977; Zloof 1978]. Even though the classifications have several common points, their relationships have hardly been studied. Shneiderman [1980] uses a two-dimensional scheme classified by syntactic and semantic knowledge. The analysis in this section is related to this idea but includes other criteria that have been proposed elsewhere. The criteria fall into four classifications: familiarity with programming concepts, frequency of query language usage, knowledge about the application, and range of operations required.

*Familiarity with programming concepts* is a more general concept than the often-cited distinction between programmers and nonprogrammers, which may lead to different and at times inconsistent interpretations [Cuff 1980; Greenblatt and Waxman 1978; Moran 1981]. "High" familiarity with programming concepts characterizes a user who is not afraid of computers and has acquired logical or algorithmic problem-solving abilities.

The dimension *frequency of system usage* [Lehmann and Blaser 1979] is one of the most important dimensions in that many of the other dimensions appearing in the literature are derived from it. Frequency of use directly determines the acceptable amount of training; the more one wants to use the system, the greater an initial investment is justified. The amount of training in turn determines the typical skill level after the training period.

In the authors' opinion the transient skill levels during the QL training phase are of interest only if the frequency of use is so low that each use of the system requires relearning or if the turnover of users is extremely high. Thus the distinction between "novice" user (task: learning) and "expert" (task: routine skill) made in Moran [1981] and Schneider [1984] can be reduced to the frequency of usage dimension. We therefore use the term "novice" not only for new users but also for other infrequent users with little programming knowledge.

In combination, these two dimensions determine the user's ability to technically interact with the system, or "syntactic knowledge" [Shneiderman 1980]. The relationship between the two basic dimensions and the level of *interaction skill* is shown in Table 2a. Three user types are

**Table 2a.** User Types: Interaction Capability (Syntactic Knowledge) as a Function of Familiarity with Programming Concepts and Frequency of System Usage

| Frequency of system usage | Familiarity with programming concepts: Low | High |
|---|---|---|
| Low | Low (novice user) | Medium (skilled user) |
| High | Medium (skilled user) | High (professional user) |

**Table 2b.** User Types: Task Structure (Semantic Knowledge) as a Function of Application Knowledge and Range of Operations

| Range of operations | Application knowledge: General | Detailed |
|---|---|---|
| Narrow | Casual user | Clerical user |
| Broad | Managerial user | Application specialist user |

derived. Note that the "skilled" user is one who has a "high" score for either of the two dimensions and a "low" score for the other.

The semantic dimensions are concerned with application knowledge and range of operations of the user. In the database context, *application knowledge* refers to the precision of the user's conceptual model about the structure and contents of the database. The other dimension, *range of operations*, describes how many different types of queries the user requires. Together, these two dimensions give a picture of the *task structure* (semantic knowledge) of the user (Table 2b). By combining high or low scores on the two underlying dimenions, four user types are derived from this classification: (1) casual users who approach the system without real interest to achieve a narrowly defined set of functions, (2) clerical users who perform a narrowly defined set of tasks but have detailed knowledge of their application, (3) managerial users who have little interest in details but require broad functionality, and (4) application specialists who have excellent application knowledge and need to fulfill a fairly broad range of tasks. In Section 7, the requirements of these user types are outlined in more detail.

## 4. HUMAN FACTORS RESEARCH IN QUERY LANGUAGES

One of the most important sources of information for determining the users' QL requirements are human factors experiments. Below, recent human factors research relevant in this context is briefly reviewed. The major results are displayed in Table 3. It is not the intention of this paper to critique these experiments (see, e.g., Reisner [1981] and Shneiderman [1980]). The reader should note, however, that many studies have not been "controlled" experiments that deliver statistically sound and generalizable results.

Since the now classic experiments of Reisner et al. [1975] and Thomas and Gould [1975], a number of laboratory studies and field experiments of human factors in use of query languages have been reported. For the purposes of this paper, these studies are classified either as comparisons between languages that use different methods (as defined in Section 2.2) or as studies of usability of certain features within a language type.

The first group of experiments consists of comparisons of keyword versus new generation languages [Greenblatt and Waxman 1978; Thomas and Gould 1975], keyword versus positional languages [Reisner et al. 1975], and keyword versus restricted natural languages [Jarke et al. 1985; Shneiderman 1978; Small and Weldon 1983; Vassiliou et al. 1983]. The reader is cautioned, however, that the majority of these experiments were not directed toward a general comparison of methods but rather toward specific comparisons of languages.

The second group of experiments concentrates on the usability of certain languages or language features within a given method. One focal point of laboratory experiments has been the keyword language SQL [Reisner 1977; Thomas 1976; Welty 1979; Welty and Stemple 1981], and another has been the influence of conceptual data models [Brosey and Shneiderman 1978; Lochovsky 1976; Lochovsky and Tsichritzis 1977]. In addition, there have been a number of field studies concerned with the usability of restricted natural languages in various settings [Damerau 1979; Harris 1977; Jarke et al. 1985; Krause 1982; Lehmann et al. 1978; Woods et al. 1972].

As concerns user types, most studies in the syntactic knowledge (interaction capability) dimension focus on the novice user. Virtually all laboratory experiments are learning and retention tests and therefore apply mainly to infrequent users. In addition, most experimenters explicitly chose subjects with little knowledge of programming concepts, often contrasting them with another group having more programming background. All experiments of this design show better performance for users with programming background [Reisner et al. 1975; Lochovsky and Tsichritzis 1977; Turner et al. 1984; Welty and Stemple 1981]. Some of the results of these experiments indicate that novices

- have difficulties with explicit quantification [Thomas 1976],
- perform better with a relational model of data than with a network or hierarchy when using a keyword language embedded in APL [Lochovsky and Tsichritzis 1977],
- learn a new generation language (QBE) faster than a keyword language (SQL) of similar power [Greenblatt and Waxman 1978; Thomas and Gould 1975],
- perform better on hard queries with a more procedural approach (TABLET versus SQL) for problem solving than a keyword language [Welty and Stemple 1981],
- can be offered a (closed) subset in a layered language [Reisner 1977].

The semantic classification of experimental subjects is less clear. Although the subjects of most laboratory experiments are students, whose semantic knowledge is difficult to establish, the thrust of the field experiments is more often toward the application specialist than the managerial user [Damerau 1979; Harris 1979; Jarke et al. 1985; Krause 1980].

The goal of this paper is to suggest classes of languages for known user types. The above survey demonstrates that the existing human factors research in query languages is insufficient for the solution of the pressing problem of language selection. Experiments have been criticized for sloppiness, very few repetitions, and limited coverage of issues. Most important for the purposes of this paper, little emphasis has been given to the consideration of language methods (classes) in connection with user types.

## 5. EVALUATION CRITERIA FOR QUERY LANGUAGES

The proposed methodology for QL selection (depicted in Figure 1; see Section 1) proceeds with the development of evaluation criteria for QLs. Like the QL taxonomy, the evaluation scheme is related to the trend analysis of QL development in that it relies on the same two dimensions: usability and functional capabilities. These basic dimenions must be refined further, however, in order to yield practical evaluation criteria.

The *functional capabilities* determine to a large degree the value of the information ("benefit") that one can get from the system. In a QL context, this can be described by the language power and the alternatives that the user has for output presentation. On the other hand, the *usability* of a system (the effort or "cost" to work with it) is mainly related to the process of query formulation.

Figure 4 is an overview of a criterion hierarchy derived from these considerations. All criteria are described below.

### 5.1 Usability Criteria

*Query formulation effort* describes the overall effort of the user to work with the system. The total effort is the sum of the initial training effort to learn the QL system and the repeated efforts to perform productive tasks on it. The relative importance of these two parts is determined by the frequency of system usage, in the sense that both repeated training may be necessary for infrequent users and training time accounts for a large percentage of overall effort for that group.

**Table 3.** Human Factors Experiments with Query Languages and Features

| Reference | Type of experiment | User classes | Research question | Tasks and tests | Major results |
|---|---|---|---|---|---|
| Greenblatt and Waxman [1978] | Laboratory | Novices | Learnability of QBE vs. SQL | Composition | Formulation in QBE is faster |
| Jarke et al. [1985] | Field | Novice application specialists (advisors) | Productivity of natural language vs. SQL | Problem-solving<br>Query acceptance | SQL has higher success rate; natural language less effort to use |
| Reisner et al. [1975] | Laboratory | Programmers<br>Nonprogrammers | Learnability of SQL vs. SQUARE | Composition | Programmers are superior; SQL is better than SQUARE for beginners |
| Shneiderman [1978] | Laboratory | Novices | Productivity of natural vs. SQL subset | Query generation | Natural language user generated more invalid queries |
| Small and Weldon [1983] | Laboratory with simulated processor | Novices | Productivity of natural vs. SQL subset | Interactive problem solving | Formulation in SQL is faster |
| Turner et al. [1984] | Laboratory | Novice application specialists (advisors) | Learnability of natural language vs. SQL | Composition | Natural language and SQL about equal in error rates |
| Vassilliou et al. [1983] | Laboratory | Novices | Learnability of natural language vs. SQL | Composition | Natural language less verbose; manageable language subset used |
| Brosey and Shneiderman [1978] | Laboratory | Programmers<br>Nonprogrammers | Relational vs. hierarchical model | Comprehension<br>Memorization<br>Problem solving | Programmers are better on relations than nonprogrammers; hierarchies are good for natural tree applications |
| Gould and Ascher [1975] | Laboratory | Novices | Query formulation process (IQF) | Composition | Influence of task complexity and ambiguity |
| Lochovsky and Tsichritzis [1977] | Laboratory | Programmers<br>Nonprogrammers | Comparison of three data models embedded in APL | Composition<br>Debugging | Programmers are superior; relational model best for nonprogrammers |
| Reisner [1977] | Laboratory | Programmers<br>Nonprogrammers | Feature analysis of SQL | Composition | Recommended layered structure for novice and skilled user |
| Thomas [1976] | Laboratory | Novices | Use of quantifiers | Various noncomputerized tasks | Universal quantification is difficult for novices |
| Thomas and Gould [1975] | Laboratory | Novices | Learnability of QBE | Composition | 67 percent successful after short training |
| Welty and Stemple [1981] | Laboratory | Programmers<br>Nonprogrammers | Learnability of TABLET vs. SQL (procedurality) | Composition<br>Retention | Programmers are superior; TABLET is better for hard queries |
| Damerau [1979] | Field | Novice application specialists | Productivity of TQA/REQUEST | Problem solving | 65 percent accepted queries |
| Harris [1977] | Field | Application specialists | Productivity of ROBOT | Problem solving | 80–90 percent accepted queries |
| Krause [1982] | Field | Skilled application specialists | Productivity of USL | Problem solving | More than 90 percent successful after adaptation |
| Lehmann et al. [1978] | Field | Skilled application specialists | Functions of USL | Problem solving | Statistics on use of various functions |
| Woods et al. [1972] | Field | Novice application specialists | Usability of LSNLIS (LUNAR) | Problem solving | Good success rate for application-specific system |

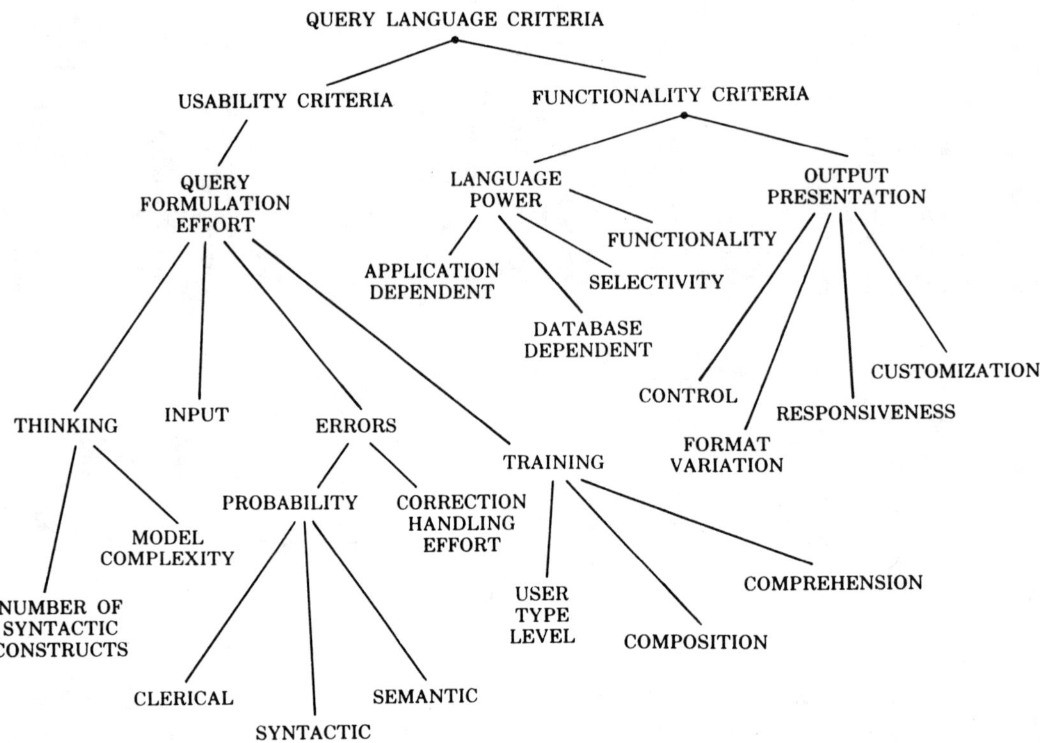


**Figure 4.** Query language evaluation parameters.

The analysis of a language's suitability for performing tasks is based on the simple query language interaction model presented in Figure 5 [Stohr et al. 1982]. It can be seen that productivity is determined by think time, input effort, and error handling time. Although this model captures the effort of query formulation fairly well, it does not completely reflect the overall productivity in performing a task; productivity also improves through increased functional capabilities that reduce the number of queries necessary for solving a problem.

*Thinking effort* includes the requirement that users remember *syntactic constructs.* Issues that influence this factor are command names and abbreviations, the number of different constructs, and the syntax for the composition of complex commands [Schneider 1984]. In addition to these static properties of a query language interface, the dynamics of how it allows a user to formulate a query also influences thinking effort. Reisner [1981] introduces the notion of a "model of the process of query writing" that users develop. This refers to the strategy that the user adopts to express the request. The *complexity* of this model is also part of the thinking effort.

*Input* refers to the amount of clerical effort required to express the request. When the interaction is via a keyboard, this may be measured by the number of keystrokes. When pointing devices are used, a good measure of input is the number of pointed objects [Lochovsky and Tsichritzis 1984].

Major system usage costs are induced by the efforts to detect and handle *errors.* The overall effort can be described as a combination of the error *probability* and the *correction handling effort* required for detecting and correcting an error that has occurred. As can be seen from Figure 5, three main types of error may occur during query formulation: *clerical* (e.g., typos), *syntactic* (not following the correct syntax of the language), and *semantic* (formulation of a syntactically correct query that does not solve the task at hand).

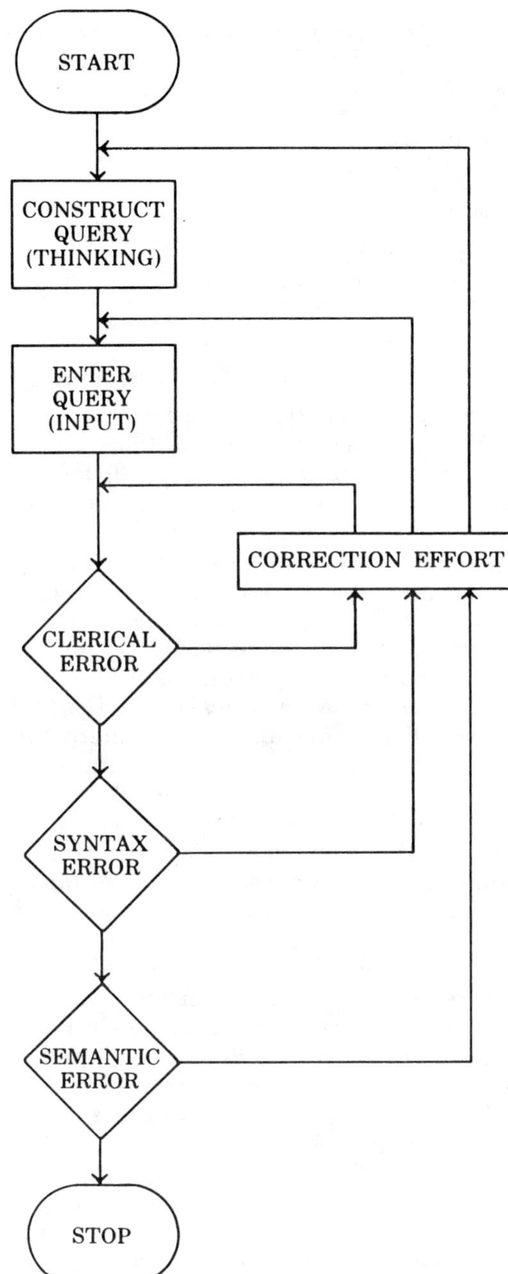


**Figure 5.** Query language interaction model.

The amount of *training* necessary for the user to perform useful tasks is a very important consideration in language selection. Training depends upon who learns (*user type level*) and what has to be learned (*composition* and *comprehension* of queries). The *user type level* refers to the degree of expertise required before the user can utilize the language. Low level corresponds to novice user, medium level to skilled user, and high level corresponds to professional user. *Composition* describes the degree of difficulty in learning how to formulate queries. A facility that is easy to learn (composition) is not necessarily easy to use (thinking effort). A comparable example in programming is the language BASIC; it takes only a short time to learn, but writing a complex program in BASIC is not an easy task. Finally, *comprehension* refers to the amount of training required to understand a query formulated by another user.

### 5.2 Functional Capabilities Criteria

Besides usability, there are two other criteria groups for query language evaluation: language power (how much a user can do with the language) and the alternatives that the user has for output presentation. These criteria are concerned with input to and output from the system. The first functional capability parameter for query language evaluation is *language power*, which can be described in terms of four parameters: application dependency, database dependency, selectivity, and functionality.

*Application dependency* is the sensitivity of a QL to the application domain: the degree to which the language has to change when it is used in a different application. Application dependency is common in many of the ergonomically oriented QLs, which optimize the user interface for specific narrow tasks. For instance, the keywords or labels on function keys of a query language interface may depend on the application, as may the sequencing and structural composition of menus.

Similarly, *database dependency* refers to the degree of language dependence on the underlying database model (e.g., network, relational). In early discussions [Codd 1970], network models were associated with navigational query languages, whereas the relational model offered nonprocedural access descriptions. Today, database dependency is a question of specific DBMS products, rather than one of principal limitations of the underlying database model.

In principle, the user interface design decision can be largely decoupled from the choice of a database model. For example, Codd [1972] and Pirotte [1978] have shown that the various forms of relational query languages (mapping, tuple and domain relational calculus, relational algebra) are essentially equivalent in expressive power. There are also optimizing translation algorithms that allow the installation of efficient navigational interfaces on relational systems [Katz and Wong 1982], and of relational query languages on network databases [Rosenthal and Reiner 1985]; see Larson [1983] for an overview. However, a specific DBMS product may not offer these facilities and thus introduce database dependency for the user.

For the other two criteria (functionality and selectivity), database theory has developed more formal methods of evaluation based on complexity theory. *Functionality* broadly refers to the range of different tasks for which the language can be used (e.g., queries, browsing, zooming, report generation, inserts, deletes, updates).

*Selectivity* is the availability of operators that allow the user to specify as precisely as possible what data he or she wishes to retrieve. Codd [1972] introduced the notion of relational completeness that has long served as a yardstick of selectivity. A QL is called relationally complete if it allows the expression of any query that is expressible in a single predicate of the so-called relational calculus, a query language based on first-order logic.

Zloof [1977] and Aho and Ullman [1979] were among the first to point out simple queries that were not expressible in relationally complete languages, and to propose language extensions. For exampie, the "transitive closure" of a relation cannot be expressed in relational calculus; among other things, this prevents answering queries such as "Is there a train connection between two cities?" from a database that contains the direct train connections. Chandra and Harel [1982] developed a complete hierarchy of QL expressiveness (Table 4). The levels below (appearing "before" in the table) relational completeness have been used to identify special cases in query optimization [Jarke and Koch 1984] or to offer simple query interfaces, for example, in microcomputer DBMSs.

**Table 4.** Query Language Expressiveness Hierarchy

| |
|---|
| Propositional calculus |
| Tableau queries |
| Conjunctive queries |
| Existential queries |
| FIRST-ORDER QUERIES (RELATIONALLY COMPLETE) |
| Fixpoint queries (Horn clause queries) |
| Full first-order logic and disjunction/negation |
| Second-order queries |
| Computable queries (full programming capabilities) |

Queries at the level of *propositional calculus* only allow access to a single file. Connections among different files have to be implemented in a programming language environment, or established manually by the user. *Tableau queries* are those that can be represented in a special tabular representation called tableaus [Aho et al. 1979]; owing to their mathematical properties (see below), they have caused much interest in the database theory community and have laid the foundation for "universal relation databases," which are characterized by the property that users need not know the partitioning of a database into its different relations. Instead, the user interface of a universal relation database is a single large table from which query results are constructed by projection on certain columns.

*Conjunctive queries* inherit their name from the fact that no "or's" are allowed in their specification. For example, the query "Give me the managers of age less than 35 and salary above $80,000" is conjunctive, whereas "List the students older than 30 and the Ph.D. students" is disjunctive; it is equivalent to the query "List all students whose age is greater than 30 or whose status is Ph.D. student." *Existential queries* allow disjunctive query conditions but require that the query be at least decomposable into a set of conjunctive queries. First-order (or, equivalently, relationally complete) queries that are not existential include those that contain universal quantification in their query condition, for example, "List the students who have taken *all* the courses in the database area."

The levels beyond relational completeness in Table 4 only recently have received the attention of language designers. For example, the *fixpoint* query level is exactly the level of queries available in Horn clause-based deductive query languages, such as Prolog [Clocksin and Mellish 1982]. Beyond this level, *full first-order logic* allows the representation of incomplete knowledge [Levesque 1984]; this permits the statement and querying of disjunctive information, such as "John is in New York or in Toronto" (but it is unknown in which of the two). *Second-order logic* allows queries about the relations, such as "Which tables contain information about John?" Although no QL offers this capability in general, many systems allow access to stored metadata that help to answer certain queries of this type.

Finally, the set of *computable queries* would provide full programming language capabilities *in the QL* and thus constitute the upper bound on selectivity. For complexity reasons, existing database systems can offer these capabilities at best in their host programming environment. Only a small set of efficiently computable functions has traditionally been built into QLs (e.g., count, sum, average). Broader capabilities (in which much of the responsibility for efficiency rests with the user) are provided by the so-called fourth generation languages, in which high-level programming language operators are offered the opportunity to execute more general functions on database data.

The other major functionality criterion for QL comparison is the quality of *output presentation.* This is subdivided into *control* (ability of the user to control the pace at which the output is presented), *format variation* (flexibility in selecting an output presentation format and/or redirecting output to alternative devices), *responsiveness* (how rapid and consistent the system's response is), and *customization* (the ability to have the best suited output for the application).

Again, these parameters tend to depend on the system rather than the language type. For example, a query compilation approach will usually lead to faster response times and better customization than a purely interpretive approach, especially in the case of repetitive query patterns, where query processing can be supported by access paths. However, the philosophy behind certain language types leads to a more natural adaptation of an appropriate output feature than others.

Moreover, it turns out that the expressiveness hierarchy in Table 4 is closely related to a hierarchy of query complexity [Chandra and Harel 1982]. Query complexity imposes a worst-case lower bound on responsiveness. It can be measured as data complexity (a function of operand size) or as expression complexity (a function of query length). Vardi [1982] found that expression complexity in query languages tends to be one exponential higher than data complexity.

Immerman [1982] has provided a theoretical underpinning to the use of Horn clause query languages (such as Prolog) by proving that the fixpoint queries can be computed with polynomial data complexity. Similarly, a subclass of tableau queries called simple queries can be optimally simplified in polynomial time [Aho et al. 1979], and a subclass of conjunctive queries called tree queries [Goodman and Shmueli 1982] can be processed with polynomial expression complexity.

Beyond these boundaries, execution times—in the worst case—may grow exponentially with the size of the expression or even of the database. Moreover, the higher levels of queries and data/knowledge representation (e.g., full first-order logic), which use theorem proving rather than finite search for question answering, run into decidability problems that may prevent the construction of a complete answer altogether [Brachman and Levesque 1984].

## 6. EVALUATION OF LANGUAGE CLASSES AND USER REQUIREMENTS

The results of applying the 18 evaluation criteria at the leaves of the hierarchy to the 9 language classes defined in Section 1 are shown in Table 5. In addition, the 12 user classes that result by combining interaction

**Table 5.** Evaluation of Query

| QL types | QL parameters: Query formulation: Thinking: No. of syntactic constructs | Model complexity | Input | Errors: Probability of error: Clerical | Syntactic | Semantic | Correction handling effort | Training: User type level | Composition | Comprehension |
|---|---|---|---|---|---|---|---|---|---|---|
| Function-key use | Low | Low | Low | Low | Low | Low | Low | Low | Low | Medium |
| Menu selection | Low | Low | Low | Low | Low | Low-medium | Low-medium | Low-medium | Low | Low-medium |
| Line-by-line prompting | Medium | Low | Medium | Medium | Low | Low-medium | High | Medium | Medium | Medium |
| Graphic or pictorial | Medium | Medium | Low-medium | Low-medium | Medium | Low-medium | Medium | Medium | Medium-high | Medium |
| Restricted natural | Low-high | Low | High | High | Low-medium | High | High | Low-medium | Low-medium | Low |
| Linear keyword | High | Medium-high | High | High | Medium-high | Medium-high | High | Medium | Medium-high | Low-medium |
| Positional keyword | High | High | Medium-high | High | High | High | High | Medium-high | High | Medium-high |
| Mathematical | High | High | Medium | High | High | Medium-high | High | High | Medium-high | Medium-high |
| New generation | Medium | Low | Medium | Low-medium | Low-medium | Medium-high | Medium-high | Low-medium | Low | N/A |
| Optimal | Low | Low | Low | Low | Low | Low | Low | N/A | Low | Low |

capability and task structure are related to the evaluation criteria in Table 6 (see Section 6.2). In filling the table entries for usability criteria, empirical data (if available) from the human factors area were used. Functionality criteria evaluations were based on technical restrictions of language classes.

As can be seen, the tables use a simple three-point scale (low, medium, high) for all criteria. A few finer distinctions are made by using intermediate values (low-medium, medium-high). There are several reasons to restrict oneself to such a simple structure. On the one hand, a finer scale would be problematic for several usability criteria in which empirical data for supporting the entries are missing or can only be applied indirectly.

On the other hand, any scoring method like this requires a uniform representation of criterion values. Therefore, it seemed wise to choose a simple, uniform range of values for all criteria, even though more detailed information from empirical data or formal analysis was available for some of them.

### 6.1 Query Language Evaluation

Technical language specifications determine the values in Table 5 that relate to functional capabilities. In that table, the row labeled "optimal" indicates which values of a criterion are considered "good" and which are considered "bad" from the user's viewpoint. For the usability criteria, an effort was made to apply results from human factors research. The application of such results was mostly indirect. For instance, Thomas and Gould [1975] indicate short training requirements for the composition of correct QBE queries. A generalization of this result places a "low" score for composition in new generation QLs (the class in which QBE belongs).

There are inherent dangers of misinterpretation, overgeneralization, and reliance on experiments of dubious validity. Reiterating, these values should be taken

Languages at the Methods Level

| QL Parameters | | | | | | | | |
|---|---|---|---|---|---|---|---|---|
| Language power | | | | Output presentation | | | | |
| Application dependence | Database dependence | Selectivity | Functionality | Control | Format variation | Responsiveness | Customization | Examples |
| High | Low | Low | Low | Low | Low | Low-medium | High | Application dependent |
| High | Low | Low-medium | Low-medium | Low-medium | Low | High | High | Application dependent |
| High | Low | Low-medium | Low-high | Low | Low | Medium-high | Medium-high | Application dependent |
| Low | Medium-high | Medium-high | Low-medium | Low-high | Low-medium | High | Medium | LSL, CUPID |
| Medium-high | Low | Medium | Medium | Low | Low | Low | Medium | INTELLECT, USL, RENDEZVOUS |
| Low | High | High | High | Medium | Medium | Low | Low-medium | SQL, DL/I, NOMAD |
| Low | High | High | High | Medium | Medium | Low | Low | SQUARE |
| Low | High | High | High | Medium | Medium | Low | Low | ISBL, PASCAL/R |
| Medium | Low | Medium-high | Low-medium | High | High | High | High | SDMS, VGQF, QBE |
| Low | Low | High | High | High | High | High | High | |

as testable hypotheses in a homogeneous framework where the evaluation variables have been set out carefully.

The entries in Table 5 give a more structured and precise description of the language classes introduced in Section 2. For example, it can be seen that the main advantages of new generation query languages are in the areas of output presentation, training, and query formulation. On the other hand, mathematical languages are strong in language power but awkward in query formulation and often awkward in output presentation. Thus these two language groups can be envisioned as complementary tools for different tasks.

### 6.2 Determining User Requirement Profiles

An abstraction of the evaluation criteria to the basic categories of usability and functionality is made in Table 6. At this level of abstraction, the user requirements are mostly inherent in the definition of a user class as given in this paper. For example, the range of operations determines the necessary selectivity and functionality. Similarly, the criterion "user type level" determines the prerequisites for working with a language directly in terms of interaction capability.

In other cases, the relationship is more indirect but still fairly obvious. For instance, users with only a general application knowledge will require a high quality of output presentation to understand the answers they get from the database.

A third possibility is that the user classification only determines the relative importance of evaluation criteria. The previously cited trade-off between training effort and day-to-day productivity is such a case.

## 7. RECOMMENDATIONS OF QUERY LANGUAGES FOR USER TYPES

In this section, languages are related to user types, and preliminary recommendations for allocating language classes to user types

**Table 6.** Minimal Requirements by User Type

| User type | | Evaluation criteria | | |
|---|---|---|---|---|
| Interaction capability | Task structure | Query formulation effort | Language power | Output presentation |
| Novice (low) | Casual | Low-medium | Low | Low-medium |
| | Managerial | Low | Medium | Medium-high |
| | Clerical | Low-medium | Low-medium | Low-medium |
| | Application specialist | Medium | Medium | Medium-high |
| Skilled (medium) | Casual | Low-medium | Low-medium | Low-medium |
| | Managerial | Low | Medium-high | High |
| | Clerical | Low-medium | Low-medium | Medium |
| | Application specialist | Low-medium | High | Medium-high |
| Professional (high) | Casual | Medium | Low-medium | Low-medium |
| | Managerial | Low-medium | Medium-high | High |
| | Clerical | Medium-high | High | Medium |
| | Application specialist | Medium-high | High | High |

are offered. In order to improve readability, highlights of the users' minimal requirement profiles are discussed together with recommendations. A summary of these recommendations is given in Table 7, which is a combination of Tables 5 and 6. As an illustration of its development, consider the entries of Table 7 corresponding to the novice–casual user. From Table 6, the minimal requirements of this user class are determined. A consultation of Table 5 shows that these requirements are met in varying degrees, by menu selection, line-by-line prompting, new generation QLs, and function keys; these constitute the entries in Table 7.

The results are discussed for each user type and then summarized by language class.

The *casual user* is characterized as having only a general idea about structure and content of the database; the range of needed operations is also limited so that he or she may not require the full power of a query language [Reisner 1977]. Typical examples are the users of external databases like videotex [Lochovsky and Tsichritzis 1984] or electronic funds transfer systems. Most casual users are not familiar with programming concepts (which is why the lower left field of Table 7 is nearly empty), but their frequency of system usage may vary. The system must guide the infrequent casual user (novice) by offering simple menu choices or line-by-line prompts, whereas the more frequent user (skilled) may wish to adopt a more active role (new generation languages) or at least a faster sequence of actions (use of function keys).

The *managerial user* is probably the most demanding user type. Unwilling to "waste" time to acquire detailed knowledge of the database, he or she still wants to perform quite complicated and varied tasks, for example, generating summary information. Today, menu systems can be used for simple tasks, and intermediaries must handle complex ones unless the manager has programming background and uses the database routinely (professional managerial user).

A more direct path to the database is the great promise of advanced language concepts such as new generation QLs or restricted natural language. Studies of the use of natural language show, however, that novice users may have problems with the syntactic restrictions of the language [Jarke et al. 1985] or the semantic restrictions of the database [Brosey and Shneiderman 1978]. For this reason, restricted natural language is positioned in third place

**Table 7.** Relating Language Methods to User Types

| Interaction capability (syntactic knowledge) | Task structure (semantic knowledge) | | | |
|---|---|---|---|---|
| | Casual user | Managerial user | Clerical user | Application specialist user |
| Novice user | Menu selection<br>Line-by-line prompting<br>New generation<br>Function keys | New generation<br>Menu selection<br>Restricted natural | Function keys<br>Menu selection<br>Line-by-line prompting | New generation<br>Restricted natural<br>Menu selection<br>Keyword |
| Skilled user | Menu selection<br>New generation<br>Function keys<br>Line-by-line prompting | New generation<br>Restricted natural<br>Menu selection | Menu selection<br>Keyword<br>Function keys<br>Graphic/pictorial | Keyword<br>Restricted natural<br>Graphic/pictorial |
| Professional user | (New generation) | Keyword<br>Graphic/pictorial<br>New generation<br>Restricted natural | Mathematical<br>Keyword<br>Function keys | Mathematical<br>New generation<br>Keyword<br>Positional |

for novice managerial users. Some field studies indicate that more frequent users of this type can adapt to the limitations [Krause 1980].

Similar to the casual user, the *clerical user* (or parametric user) has to perform only a limited number of operations on the database, but may have detailed knowledge about the available data. The use of function keys or menus with little system guidance improves productivity for day-to-day tasks.

For the more computer-oriented or more frequent clerical user, keyword languages or even the more concise mathematical languages allow for powerful operations. Many studies exist for this user type in general (e.g., Embley and Nagy [1981]), but little has been published on tailoring query languages to clerical users.

As the range of operations becomes broader, the clerical user turns into an *application specialist user* (the synonymous "professional user" is assigned to another category). This type of user may have detailed knowledge of the database and requires multiple operations (data analysis, decision support) but often lacks programming background.

Whereas conventional programming and query languages mainly support the professional application specialist (frequent user with programming background), much of the recent research focuses on novice and skilled application specialists, who are expected to become a dominant group of computer users [Shneiderman 1984].

Studies of the use of natural language interfaces thus far have been inconclusive. The authors hypothesize that natural language is competitive if restricted to a narrow domain [Woods et al. 1972], relatively simple or tailored database structures [Damerau 1979; Harris 1977], or frequent users who adapt to the limitations [Krause 1982; Lehmann et al. 1978]. It appears that more novice users have trouble if their knowledge of the data is limited and if the quality of the overall interface (e.g., operating system command language) does not match that of the query language itself [Jarke et al. 1985]. As systems are improved, the somewhat optimistic preference for restricted natural language over keyword languages in the upper right field will become more realistic. For skilled users, natural language offers concise formulation of some queries, but in general a keyword language or a mathematical language with its more powerful operators is preferable. The inclusion of new generation languages at the lower right results from their rapid reversible actions, which support exploratory use of the database [Shneiderman

1984]. A promising research direction for natural language systems is their combined use with other media, such as menus [Thompson et al. 1983] or direct manipulation, for those tasks where natural language is too ambiguous. Essentially, this enhancement moves natural language interfaces to new generation QLs.

This section concludes with a summary of recommendations by language class. Interestingly, the pattern of query language development outlined in Section 2 repeats in the usage distribution of methods.

Formal query languages (keyword and mathematical) center around the lower right of Table 7, that is, around skilled or professional users with detailed database knowledge. Keyword languages have a more general scope than mathematical languages, which in turn may be more efficient for specialized task structures such as application programming. Natural language can be thought of as an extension of this kind of previous generation language intended for less sophisticated users.

Another line of development starts with choosing from a limited set of functions prompted by the system and then gradually enriching this set to accommodate more skilled or ambitious users.

From Table 7, it can be seen that the higher levels of both developments, new generation languages, restricted natural language, and, to a lesser degree, keyword languages and sophisticated menu selection, overlap in their usage. Currently, there is competition rather than cooperation, but the long-term trend should be toward integration.

## 8. SUMMARY AND CONCLUSIONS

A methodology for choosing a database query language category for particular user classes has been developed and its application indicated. The proposed framework is based on a new interpretation model of the development of database query languages as evolving along two lines, one influenced by the areas of programming language and database theory, the other by human factors engineering.

This observation immediately leads to a two-level classification of query languages: by the senses employed by the user and by the language methods. It was demonstrated that this classification can serve as a tool for evaluating query languages in a structured manner. The model can also be related to a comprehensive classification scheme of query language users from which most existing user categorizations can be derived. Finally, the query language development model forms the base for a hierarchy of criteria to be used for evaluating language types and determining user requirements.

The language and user evaluations taken together lead to recommendations for assigning suitable language methods to user types and applications. However, the recommendations cannot be fully general at this time, since—as the paper demonstrates—there are substantial gaps in empirical query language evaluation research. Scientifically sound human factors experiments are sparse. Furthermore, conclusive research to support the user profiles and language selection recommendations is not presently available. Until more empirical data are collected, however, it is the authors' opinion that this work is a useful tool for query language developers and users.

For the practitioner interested in fast solutions, the preliminary recommendations may serve as a preselection of possible query language types for which the software selection process can proceed. The actual selection of a query language must also include (and may be dominated by) financial and organizational considerations. A practitioner planning a major investment based on QL technology may want to follow the methodology outlined in this paper to do an analysis, possibly with specialized usability and functionality criteria and more refined user classes.

Finally, researchers may use the framework proposed here for defining empirical or theoretical studies to clarify issues that had to be left open in this paper owing to a lack of data or precise metrics. There is much need for such work. Perhaps the most important contribution of this paper, therefore, is the identification of a well-structured framework for testing the recommendations presented in Section 7 as research hypotheses.

A few examples of important hypotheses that need further study follow. As noted, few experiments in the field have been directed toward comparison at the general methods level, and experiments with natural language systems have not been conclusive. Thus the conclusions in Section 7, based on existing experiments with specific languages, may be overgeneralized. Similarly, development of "deep psychological models" of query formulation is only in the initial stage. There seems to be little research on database usage for clerical users and the long-term performance of skilled users. Finally, new generation languages are in too early a stage of development for the differentiation of methods within this group to be clearly understandable. It is hoped that the framework developed in this paper contributes to a refinement of research questions in this field.

Each single language type will have problems accommodating the variety of user types discussed in this paper. The authors envision that future query languages will employ multiple interaction modes in order to have a broader coverage and usability. For data consistency and system efficiency, such user interfaces must be integrated with well-understood formal query or database programming languages, and provide facilities allowing users to customize the interaction to their own needs and preferences.

## ACKNOWLEDGMENTS

The authors are indebted to Margi Olson, Ron Weber, Associate Editor Sal March, and the anonymous referees for a large number of useful comments on earlier versions of this paper.

## REFERENCES

AHO, A. V., AND ULLMAN, J. D. 1979. Universality of data retrieval languages. In *Proceedings of the 6th ACM Symposium on Principles of Programming Languages* (Jan. 29–31, San Antonio, Tex.). ACM, New York, pp. 110–120.

AHO, A. V., SAGIV, Y., AND ULLMAN, J. D. 1979. Efficient optimization of a class of relational expressions. *ACM Trans. Database Syst. 4*, 4 (Dec.), 435–454.

ALBANO, A., CARDELLI, L., AND ORSINI, R. 1985. Galileo: A strongly-typed, interactive conceptual language. *ACM Trans. Database Syst. 10*, 2 (June), 230–260.

ARTIFICIAL INTELLIGENCE CORPORATION, 1982. Intellect Query System, Reference Manual.

ASTRAHAN, M. M., BLASGEN, M. W., CHAMBERLIN, D. D., ESWARAN, K. P., GRAY, J. N., GRIFFITHS, P. P., KING, W. F., LORIE, R. A., MCJONES, P. R., MEHL, J. W., PUTZOLU, G. R., TRAIGER, I. L., WADE, B. W., AND WATSON, V. 1976. System-R: Relational approach to database management. *ACM Trans. Database Syst. 1*, 2 (June), 97–137.

BATES, M., AND BOBROW, R. J. 1983. A transportable natural language interface for information retrieval. In *Proceedings of the 6th Annual International ACM-SIGIR Conference on Research and Development in Information Retrieval* (Bethesda, Md., June 6–8). ACM, New York, pp. 81–86.

BORGIDA, A., GREENSPAN, S., MYLOPOULOS, J., AND VASSILIOU, Y. 1986. Towards a knowledge description language. In *On Knowledge Base Management Systems*, J. Mylopoulos and M. L. Brodie, Eds. Springer-Verlag, New York (in press).

BRACHMAN, R., AND LEVESQUE, H. J. 1984. What makes a knowledge base knowledgeable? A view of databases from the knowledge level. In *Proceedings of the 1st International Workshop on Expert Database Systems* (Kiawah Island, S.C., Oct. 24–27), L. Kershberg, Ed., pp. 30–39.

BOYCE, R. E., CHAMBERLIN, D. D., KING, W. F., AND HAMMER, M. M. 1975. Specifying queries as relational expressions: The SQUARE data sublanguage. *Commun. ACM 18*, 11 (Nov.), 621–628.

BRODIE, M., AND SCHMIDT, J. W., Eds. 1982. Final report of the ANSI/X3/SPARC DBS-SG relational database task group. *ACM SIGMOD Record 12*, 4.

BROSEY, M., AND SHNEIDERMAN, B. 1978. Two experimental comparisons of relational and hierarchical database models. *Int. J. Man-Mach. Stud. 10*.

BROWN, R. M., CATTELL, R. G. G., AND SUZUKI, N. 1981. The Cedar DBMS: A preliminary report. In *Proceedings of the International Conference on Management of Data* (Ann Arbor, Mich., Apr. 29–May 1). ACM, New York, pp. 205–211.

CARBONELL, J. 1979. Subjective understanding: Computer models of belief systems. Unpublished Ph.D. dissertation, Computer Science Dept., Yale Univ., New Haven, Conn.

CHANDRA, A., AND HAREL, D. 1982. Structure and complexity of relational queries. *J. Comput. Syst. Sci. 25*, 2, 99–128.

CHANG, N. S., AND FU, K. S. 1979. Query-by-pictorial example. In *IEEE Proceedings of the 3rd International Computer Software and Application Conference*. IEEE, New York.

CINCOM SYSTEMS, INC. 1978. Total Information System, The Next Generation of Software.

CLOCKSIN, W. F., AND MELLISH, C. S. 1982. *Programming in PROLOG*. Springer-Verlag, New York.

CODASYL DATA BASE TASK GROUP, 1971. Final report. In *Conference on Data System Languages* (Apr.). ACM, New York.

CODD, E. F. 1970. A relational model of data for large shared data banks. *Commun. ACM 13*, 6 (June), 377–387.

CODD, E. F. 1971. A data base sublanguage founded on the relational calculus. In *Proceedings of the ACM SIGFIDET Workshop on Data Description, Access and Control* (San Diego, Calif.). ACM, New York, pp. 35–68.

CODD, E. F. 1972. Relational completeness of data base sublanguages. In *Data Base Systems*, R. Rustin, Ed. Prentice-Hall, Englewood Cliffs, N.J., pp. 65–98.

CODD, E. F. 1974. Seven steps to Rendezvous with the casual user. In *Data Base Management*, J. W. Klimbie and K. L. Koffeman, Eds. North-Holland, New York, pp. 179–199.

CODD, E. F. 1978. How about recently? In *Databases: Improving Usability and Responsiveness*, B. Shneiderman, Ed. Academic Press, Orlando, Fla., pp. 3–29.

CUFF, R. N. 1980. On casual users. *Int. J. Man-Mach. Commun. 12*, 2, 163–187.

DAMERAU, F. J. 1979. The transformational question answering (TQA) system operating statistics. IBM Res. Rep., RC 7739, IBM Thomas J. Watson Research Laboratory, Yorktown Heights, N.Y.

ELLIS, C. A., AND NUTT, G. J. 1980. Office information systems and computer science. *ACM Comput. Surv. 12*, 1 (Mar.), 27–60.

EMBLEY, D. W., AND NAGY, G. 1981. Behavioral aspects of text editors. *ACM Comput. Surv. 13*, 1 (Mar.), 33–70.

FIELDS, C., AND NEGROPONTE, N. 1976. Using new clues to find data. In *Proceedings of the 2nd International Conference on Very Large Data Bases.*

FOLEY, J. D., AND VAN DAM, A. 1982. *Fundamentals of Interactive Computer Graphics.* Addison-Wesley, Reading, Mass.

GABLE, A., AND PAGE, C. V. 1980. The use of artificial intelligence techniques in computer-assisted instruction. *Int. J. Man-Mach. Stud. 12*, 3, 259–282.

GOLDBERG, A., AND ROBSON, 1981. Special issue on Smalltalk. *BYTE* (Aug.).

GOODMAN, N., AND SHMUELI, O. 1982. Tree queries: A simple class of relational queries. *ACM Trans. Database Syst. 7*, 4 (Dec.), 653–677.

GOULD, J. D., AND ASCHER, R. 1975. Use of an IQF-like query language by nonprogrammers. Tech. Rep. RC5279, IBM Thomas J. Watson Research Center, Yorktown Heights, N.Y.

GREENBLATT, D., AND WAXMAN, J. 1978. A study of three database query languages. In *Databases: Improving Usability and Responsiveness*, B. Shneiderman, Ed. Academic Press, Orlando, Fla., pp. 77–97.

HARRIS, L. R. 1977. User oriented database query with the ROBOT natural language query system. *Int. J. Man-Mach. Stud. 9*, 6, 697–713.

HENDRIX, G. G., SACERDOTI, E. D., SAGALOWICZ, D., AND SLOCUM, J. 1978. Developing a natural language interface to complex data. *ACM Trans. Database Syst. 3*, 2 (June), 105–147.

HEROT, C. F. 1980. Spatial management of data. *ACM Trans. Database Syst. 5*, 4 (Dec.), 493–513.

HEROT, C. F. 1984. Graphical user interfaces. In *Human Factors and Interactive Computer Systems*, Y. Vassiliou, Ed. Ablex, Norwood, N.J., pp. 83–103.

HOEPPNER, W., CHRISTALLER T., MARBURGER, H., MORIK, K., NEBEL, B., O'LEARY, M., AND WAHLSTER, W. 1983. Beyond domain-independence: Experience with the development of a German language access system to highly diverse background systems. In *Proceedings of the 8th International Joint Conference on Artificial Intelligence* (Karlsruhe, West Germany), pp. 588–594.

IBM, 1975. IBM Information Management System/Virtual Storage (IMS/VS). General Information Manual, G 20-1260-3, IBM Corp.

IMMERMAN, N. 1982. Relational queries computable in polynomial time. In *Proceedings of the 14th ACM Symposium on Theory of Computing* (San Francisco, Calif., May 5–7). ACM, New York, pp. 147–152.

JARKE, M., AND KOCH, J. 1984. Query optimization in database systems. *ACM Comput. Surv. 16*, 2 (June), 111–152.

JARKE, M., AND VASSILIOU, Y. 1984. Coupling expert systems with database management systems. In *Artificial Intelligence Applications for Business*, W. Reitman, Ed. Ablex, Norwood, N.J., p. 65–85.

JARKE, M., TURNER, J. A., STOHR, E. A., VASSILIOU, Y., WHITE, N. H., AND MICHIELSEN, K. 1985. A field evaluation of natural language for data retrieval. *IEEE Trans. Softw. Eng. SE-11*, 1, 97–114.

JARKE, M., KRAUSE, J., AND VASSILIOU, Y. 1986a. Studies in the evaluation of a domain-independent natural language system. In *Cooperative Interfaces to Information Systems*, L. Bolc and M. Jarke, Eds. Springer-Verlag, New York, (in press).

JARKE, M., MYLOPOULOS, J., SCHMIDT, J. W., AND VASSILIOU, Y. 1986b. KBMS for software development. In *Logic and Knowledge Base Management Systems*, C. Thanos and J. W. Schmidt, Eds. Springer-Verlag, New York (in press).

KATZ, R. H., AND WONG, E. 1982. Decompiling CODASYL DML into relational queries. *ACM Trans. Database Syst. 7*, 1 (Mar.), 1–23.

KING, J. L., AND SCHREMS, E. L. 1978. Cost–benefit analysis of information systems development and operation. *ACM Comput. Surv. 10*, 1 (Mar.), 19–34.

KRAUSE, J. 1980. Natural language access to information systems: An evaluation study of its acceptance by end users. *Inf. Syst. 4*, 297–318.

KRAUSE, J. 1982. *Mensch-Maschine-Kommunika-*

*tion in natuerlicher Sprache*. Niemeyer, Tübingen, West Germany.

LACROIX, M., AND PIROTTE, A. 1977. Domain-oriented relational languages. In *Proceedings of the 3rd International Conference on Very Large Data Bases* (Tokyo, Oct. 6–8). IEEE, New York, pp. 370–378.

LACROIX, M., AND PIROTTE, A. 1980. User interfaces for database application programming. Tech. Rep., Phillips MBLE Research Laboratory, Brussels, Belgium.

LARSON, J. A. 1983. Bridging the gap between relational and network databases. *IEEE Comput. 16*, 9, 82–92.

LEAVENWORTH, B. M., AND SAMMET, J. 1974. An overview of nonprocedural languages. In *Proceedings of a Symposium on Very High Level Languages. SIGPLAN Not. 9*, 4 (Apr.), 1–12.

LEBOWITZ, M. 1980. Generalization and memory in an integrated understanding system. Unpublished Ph.D. dissertation, Computer Science Dept., Yale Univ., New Haven, Conn.

LEHMANN, H., AND BLASER, A. 1979. Query languages in data base systems. TR 79.07.004, IBM Heidelberg Scientific Center, Heidelberg, West Germany.

LEHMANN, H., OTT, N., AND ZOEPPRITZ, M. 1978. User experiments with natural language for data base access. In *Proceedings of the 7th International Conference on Computational Linguistics* (Bergen, Norway).

LEVESQUE, H. J. 1984. The logic of incomplete knowledge bases. In *On Conceptual Modeling*, M. L. Brodie, J. Mylopoulos, and J. W. Schmidt, Eds. Springer-Verlag, New York, pp. 165–186.

LOCHOVSKY, F. H. 1976. Data base management system user performance variables. Ph.D. dissertation, Computer Science Dept., Univ. of Toronto, Toronto, Ontario, Canada.

LOCHOVSKY, F. H., AND TSICHRITZIS, D. C. 1977. User performance considerations in DBMS selection. In *Proceedings of the International Conference on Management of Data* (Toronto, Ontario, Aug. 3–5). ACM, New York, pp. 128–134.

LOCHOVSKY, F. H., AND TSICHRITZIS, D. C. 1984. Querying external databases. In *Human Factors and Interactive Computer Systems*, Y. Vassiliou, Ed. Ablex, Norwood, N.J., pp. 117–140.

MALONE, T. 1982. Heuristics for designing enjoyable user interfaces: Lessons from computer games. In *Proceedings of the Conference on Human Factors in Computer Systems* (Gaithersburg, Md.), pp. 63–68.

MCDONALD, N. H. 1975. CUPID: A graphic oriented facility for support of nonprogrammer interactions with a database. Ph.D. dissertation, Computer Science Dept., Univ. of California, Berkeley.

MCDONALD, N. H., AND MCNALLY, L. P. 1982. Query language feature analysis by usability. Unpublished paper, Computer Science Dept., University of South Florida.

MOORHEAD, W. G. 1976. GXRAM—A relational data base interface for graphics. Tech. Rep. RJ1735, IBM Research Laboratory, San Jose, Calif.

MORAN, T. P. 1981. Guest editor's introduction: An applied psychology of the user. *ACM Comput. Surv. 13*, 1 (Mar.), 1–11.

MOTRO, A. 1984. Query generalization: A technique for handling query failure. In *Proceedings of the 1st International Workshop on Expert Database Systems* (Kiawah Island, S.C., Oct. 24–27), L. Kershberg, Ed., pp. 314–326.

MYLOPOULOS, J., BERNSTEIN, P. A., AND WONG, H. K. T. 1980. A language facility for designing interactive database-intensive applications. *ACM Trans. Database Syst. 5*, 2 (June), 185–207.

NEWMAN, W. S., AND SPROULL, R. F. 1979. *Principles of Interactive Computer Graphics*. McGraw-Hill, New York.

PIROTTE, A. 1978. High-level database query languages. In *Logic and Databases*, H. Gallaire and J. Minker, Eds. Plenum, New York, pp. 409–436.

PLATH, W. J. 1976. REQUEST: A natural language question answering system. *IBM J. Res. Dev. 20*.

REISNER, P. 1977. Use of psychological experimentation as an aid to development of query languages. *IEEE Trans. Softw. Eng. SE-3*, 3, 218–229.

REISNER, P. 1981. Human factors studies of database query languages: A survey and assessment. *ACM Comput. Surv. 13*, 1 (Mar.), pp. 13–31.

REISNER, P., BOYCE, R. F., AND CHAMBERLIN, D. D. 1975. Human factors evaluation of two data base query languages—Square and Sequel. In *Proceedings of the National Computer Conference* (Anaheim, Calif., May 19–22), vol. 44. AFIPS Press, Reston, Va., pp. 447–452.

ROSENTHAL, A., AND REINER, D. 1985. Querying relational views of networks. In *Query Processing in Database Systems*, W. Kim, D. Reiner, and D. Batory, Eds. Springer-Verlag, New York, pp. 109–126.

SAMET, J., Ed. 1981. Query languages—A unified approach. Report of the British Computer Society Query Languages Group. Heyden University Press, Cambridge, England.

SCHANK, R. C., AND SLADE, S. 1984. Advisory systems. In *Artificial Intelligence Applications for Business*, W. Reitman, Ed. Ablex, Norwood, N.J., pp. 249–265.

SCHMANDT, C., AND HULTEEN, E. A. 1982. The intelligent voice-interactive interface. In *Proceedings of the Conference on Human Factors in Computer Systems* (Gaithersburg, Md.).

SCHMIDT, J. W. 1977. Some high-level language constructs for data of type relation. *ACM Trans. Database Syst. 2*, 3 (Sept.), 247–261.

SCHNEIDER, M. 1984. Ergonomic considerations in the design of control languages. In *Human Factors and Interactive Computer Systems*, Y. Vassiliou, Ed. Ablex, Norwood, N.J., pp. 141–161.

SENKO, M. E. 1977. DIAM II with FORAL LP: Making pointed queries with a light pen. In *Proceedings of the International Federation of Information Processing* (Toronto, Ontario). North-Holland, Amsterdam, pp. 635–640.

SHIPMAN, D. W. 1981. The functional data model and the data language DAPLEX. *ACM Trans. Database Syst. 6*, 1 (Mar.), 140–173.

SHNEIDERMAN, B. 1978. Improving the human factors aspect of database interactions. *ACM Trans. Database Syst. 3*, 4 (Dec.), 417–439.

SHNEIDERMAN, B. 1980. *Software Psychology*. Winthrop, Cambridge, Mass.

SHNEIDERMAN, B. 1984. The future of interactive systems and the emergence of direct manipulation. In *Human Factors and Interactive Computer Systems*, Y. Vassiliou, Ed. Ablex, Norwood, N.J., pp. 1–27.

SMALL, D. W., AND WELDON, L. J. 1983. An experimental comparison of natural and structured query languages. *Human Factors 25*, 3, 253–263.

SMITH, J. M., FOX, S., AND LANDERS, T. 1981. Reference manual for ADAPLEX. Tech. Rep. CCA-81-02, Computer Corporation of America, Cambridge, Mass.

STOHR, E. A., TURNER, J. A., VASSILIOU, Y., AND WHITE, N. H. 1982. Research in natural language retrieval systems. In *Proceedings of the 15th International Conference on System Sciences* (Honolulu, Hawaii).

STONEBRAKER, M. R., AND ROWE, L. A. 1977. Observations on data manipulation languages and their embedding in general purpose programming languages. In *Proceedings of the 3rd International Conference on Very Large Data Bases* (Tokyo, Oct. 6–8). IEEE, New York, pp. 128–143.

STONEBRAKER, M., WONG, E., KREPS, P., AND HELD, G. 1976. The design and implementation of INGRES. *ACM Trans. Database Syst. 1*, 3 (Sept.), 189–222.

THOMAS, J. C. 1976. Quantifiers and question-asking. IBM Res. Rep. RC 5866, T. J. Watson Research Laboratory, Yorktown Heights, N. Y.

THOMAS, J. C., AND GOULD, J. D. 1975. A psychological study of Query by Example. In *Proceedings of the National Computer Conference* (Anaheim, Calif., May 19–22), vol. 44. AFIPS Press, Reston, Va., pp. 439–445.

THOMPSON, C. W., ROSS, K. M., TENNANT, H. R., AND SAENZ, R. M. 1983. Building usable menu-based natural language interfaces to databases. In *Proceedings of the 9th International Conference on Very Large Data Bases* (Florence, Italy, Oct.). VLDB Endowment, Saratoga, Calif., pp. 43–55.

TODD, S. J. P. 1976. The Peterlee Relational Test Vehicle—A system overview. *IBM Syst. J. 15*, 4, 285–308.

TOU, F. N., WILLIAMS, M. D., FIKES, R. E., HENDERSON, D. A., AND MALONE, T. W. 1982. Rabbit: An intelligent database assistant. In *Proceedings of the National Conference on Artificial Intelligence* (Menlo Park, Calif.). AAAI, Menlo Park, Calif., pp. 314–318.

TSICHRITZIS, D. C. 1976. LSL: A link and selector language. In *Proceedings of the International Conference on Management of Data* (Washington, D.C., June 2–4). ACM, New York, pp. 123–134.

TURNER, J. A., JARKE, M., STOHR, E. A., VASSILIOU, Y., AND WHITE, N. H. 1984. Using restricted natural language for data retrieval—A plan for field evaluation. In *Human Factors and Interactive Computer Systems*, Y. Vassiliou, Ed. Ablex, Norwood, N.J., pp. 163–190.

VARDI, M. 1982. The complexity of relational query languages. In *Proceedings of the 14th Annual ACM Symposium on Theory of Computing* (San Francisco, Calif., May 5–7). ACM, New York, pp. 137–146.

VASSILIOU, Y., Ed. 1984. *Human Factors and Interactive Computer Systems*. Ablex, Norwood, N.J.

VASSILIOU, Y., AND JARKE, M. 1984. Query languages—A taxonomy. In *Human Factors and Interactive Computer Systems*, Y. Vassiliou, Ed. Ablex, Norwood, N.J., pp. 47–81.

VASSILIOU, Y., JARKE, M., STOHR, E. A., TURNER, J. A., AND WHITE, N. H. 1983. Natural language for database queries: A laboratory study. *Manage. Inf. Syst. Q. 7*, 4 (Dec.), 47–61.

WALTZ, D. L. 1978. An English language question answering system for a large relational database. *Commun. ACM 21*, 7 (July), 526–539.

WELTY, C. 1979. A comparison of a procedural and a non-procedural query language: Syntactic metrics and human factors. Ph.D. dissertation, Computer Science Dept., Univ. of Massachusetts, Amherst, Mass.

WELTY, C., AND STEMPLE, D. W. 1981. Human factors comparison of a procedural and a nonprocedural query language. *ACM Trans. Database Syst. 6*, 4 (Dec.), 626–649.

WOODS, W. A. 1984. Natural language communication with machines: an ongoing goal. In *Artificial Intelligence Applications for Business*, W. Reitman, Ed. Ablex, Norwood, N.J., pp. 195–209.

WOODS, W. A., KAPLAN, R. M., AND NASH-WEBBER, B. 1972. The lunar sciences natural language information system. Tech. Rep., Bolt Beranek and Newman, Cambridge, Mass.

YORMARK, B. 1977. The ANSI/X3/SPARC/SGDBMS architecture. In *The ANISI/SPARC DBMS Model*, Jardine, Ed. North-Holland Publ., Amsterdam, p. 521.

ZLOOF, M. 1977. Query By Example: A data base language. *IBM Syst. J. 16*, 4, 324–343.

ZLOOF, M. 1978. Design aspects of the Query-by-Example data base management language. In *Databases: Improving Usability and Responsiveness*, B. Shneiderman, Ed. Academic Press, Orlando, Fla.


Received May 1984; revised May 1985; final revision accepted February 1986.

# Chapter 3: Database Design

Designing databases is a four step process consisting of (1) view design, designing separate views for each of several classes of users; (2) view integration, merging the views to form a global schema; (3) accommodation, converting the schemas to a data model that can be supported by the database management system; and (4) physical data design, designing the physical data structures and access paths to provide efficiency.

This chapter addresses each of these four steps.

A more extensive methodology for database design is described in the paper, "An Adaptable Methodology for Database Design," by Roussopoulos and Yeh. In this approach, designers begin by defining the application environment and then work inward until they reach a level that can be handled by available DBMSs. Roussopoulos and Yeh propose four phases: (1) environment and requirements analysis, (2) systems analysis and specification, (3) conceptual data modeling (corresponding to steps 1, 2, and 3 above), and (4) derivation of a logical access path schema (corresponding to step 4 above). The design specification techniques used in this methodology are valuable for system maintenance, as well.

### 3.1: View Design

When I design a database, I first design several database views (also called external schemas), one for each major class of database users. A *view* is like a window to the database that hides data not needed by the class of users and allows them to see data that they need in a convenient format.

My favorite data model for view design is the Entity-Category-Relationship (E-C-R) data model.

- It is easy to learn. (Initially, I do not tell users about categories or structural constraints.) Most people can readily grasp the concepts of entity types, relationship sets, and attributes.
- It is easy to draw an evolving view using the E-C-R data model on a blackboard or large pad of paper.
- It is easy to convert from E-C-R to the data models used by most existing database management systems.

Let us first review the important aspects of the E-C-R data model and then summarize how it can be used in view design.

*The E-C-R Data Model* is an extension of the popular Entity-Relationship Model (E-R) proposed originally by Chen. These models and several others, which are sometimes classified as "semantic" data models, tend to describe the semantics of data by classifying the application domain into entities (which may be objects, events, things, or concepts) and relationships among the entities.

The E-C-R model, like the E-R model, views the world as consisting of entities and relationships among entities. Entities and relationships have attributes that describe them. Entities that have similar basic attributes are classified into *entity types*. For example, the particular vehicle with registration number XXY-123 is an entity, whereas a set of vehicles can be considered an entity type. Entity types are disjoint, in that a given entity can be a member of only one entity type. In Figure 3.1, the VEHICLE and OWNER entity types are represented by rectangles. Figure 3.2 illustrates some entities that conform to the E-C-R model of Figure 3.1. Individual entities are represented by ovals in Figure 3.2.

An *attribute* of an entity type is an interesting characteristic of the entity class. An *attribute value* is a number or symbol associated with the attribute that describes a particular entity. For example, the entity type CAR has an attribute REGISTRATION-NUMBER. The attribute value of REGISTRATION-NUMBER may be XXY-123 for one car entity while the value of the REGISTRATION-NUMBER may be FBN-707 for another CAR entity. In Figure 3.1, black dots denote the attributes of each entity type.

A *category* is a subset of entities from an entity type. Categories allow the representation of generalization hierarchies. In Figure 3.1, the categories CAR and TRUCK are subsets of the VEHICLE entity type. All entities in the CAR and TRUCK categories are also entities of the VEHICLE entity type and although they share most of their attributes, they have a few attributes that are not shared. TONNAGE applies only to TRUCK, while CAR-TYPE applies only to CAR. Note that both entity types and categories are sets of entities. In Figure 3.1, the contains sign indicates that CAR and TRUCK are subsets of VEHICLE.

A relationship associates entities from two or more entity types. A collection of relationships involving the same entity types is called a *relationship set*. In Figure 3.1, a diamond shaped box represents the set of relationships between VEHICLE and OWNER. The actual relationships between the VEHICLE and OWNER entities are represented by arcs between ovals in Figure 3.2.

For semantic integrity, rules exist in the real world situation that govern the possible ways in which entities can par-

EH0252-7/87/0000/0161$01.00 

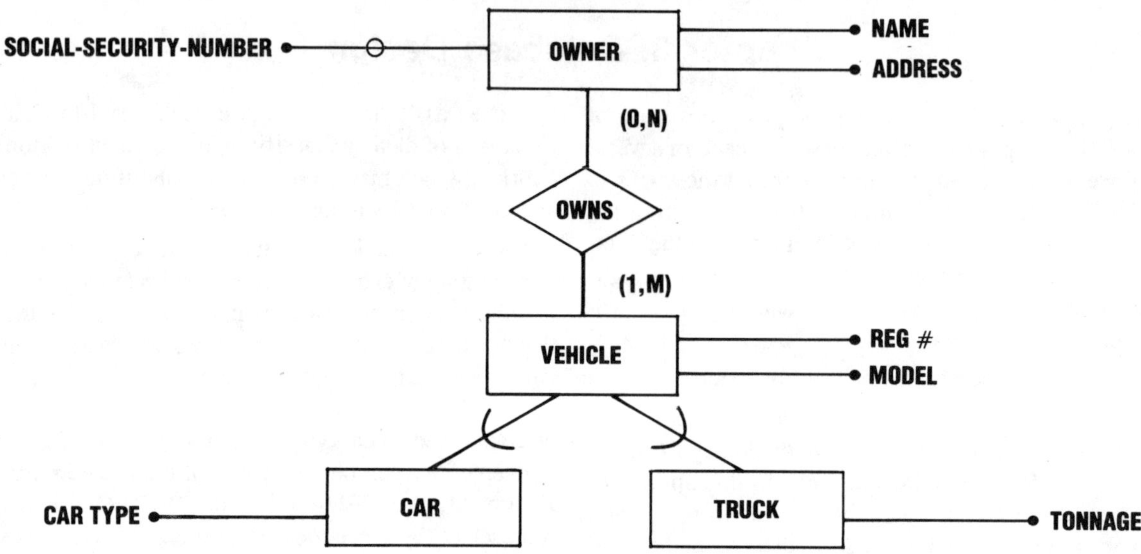


**Figure 3.1. Example Entity-Category-Relationship Schema**

ticipate in a relationship. We call these rules the *structural constraints* of the relationship. We can specify a type of structural constraint called a *cardinality constraint* on the participation of an entity type in a relationship by two numbers (i1, i2) where $0 \leq i1 \leq \overset{8}{2}$ and $i2 > 0$. The numbers mean that each entity that is a member of the entity type must participate in at least i1, and in at most i2 relationship instances in the relationship set. The cardinality constraint numbers are very useful for describing constraints of the relationship. If i1 is zero, then the entity may or may not participate in the relationship. For example, some OWNER may not actually own a vehicle and thus does not participate in any OWNER relationship. This is the case for Lewis in the database illustrated in Figure 3.2. This type of semantic constraint corresponds to the CODASYL set specification

INSERTION MANUAL
RETENTION OPTIONAL

If i1 is one, then the entity must participate in exactly one relationship. For example, each vehicle must be owned by an owner and thus must participate in an OWNER relationship.

This type of constraint corresponds to the CODASYL set specification

INSERTION AUTOMATIC
RETENTION MANDATORY

If i2 is one, then the entity may participate in at most one relationship. For example, each vehicle can be owned by at most one OWNER. This type of constraint always applies to the member record type of a CODASYL set. If i2 is greater than one, then the entity may participate in several relationships. For example, each VEHICLE can be owned by several OWNERS. This is the case for the vehicle with registration number XXY-123 in Figure 3.2. This type of constraint is always possible for the owner record type of a CODASYL set but is not possible for the member record type of a CODASYL set.

Each entity type must have at least one unique identifier such that no two entities have the same values for the identifier. Some entities can be identified by the value of one of their attributes. For example, in Figure 3.2 an OWNER entity can be uniquely identified by the attribute SOCIAL-SECURITY-NUMBER. We indicate the SOCIAL-SECURITY-NUMBER is a unique identifier of OWNER by the small oval on the arc between SOCIAL-SECURITY-NUMBER and OWNER.

Some entities are identified by a combination of attributes. For example, it may be possible to uniquely identify a PERSON entity by the two attributes, PERSON-NAME and PERSON-BIRTH-DATE. We indicate such a composite identifier by using the same type of oval for each attribute of the composite key. In Figure 3.3, both PERSON-NAME and

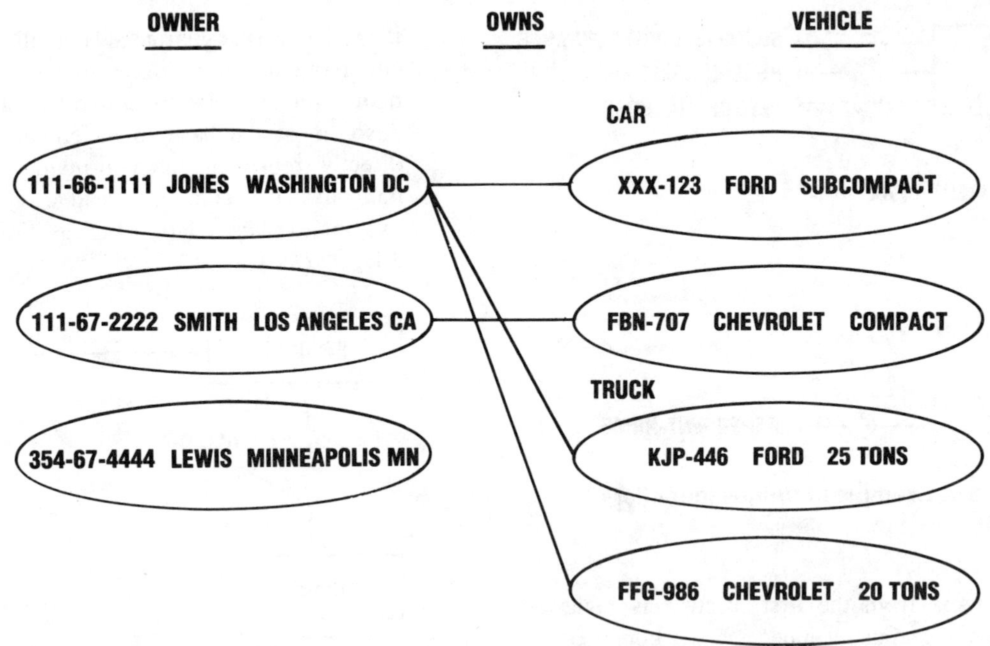


**Figure 3.2. Example Entity-Category-Relationship Database**

PERSON-BIRTH-DATE form a composite identifier of the PERSON entity type.

If an entity has more than one unique identifier, we use different types of ovals to distinguish them. In Figure 3.3, for example, a single oval is used for the SOCIAL-SECURITY-NUMBER identifier, and a double oval is used for the composite identifier of PERSON-NAME and PERSON-BIRTHDATE.

Some entities can be uniquely identified by a combination of attributes of that entity and a unique identifier of a related entity. In Figure 3.3, for example, each DEPENDENT is DEPENDENT-UPON at most one PERSON (the set participation of DEPENDENT in the DEPENDENT-UPON relationship is constrained to the range (il, i2) where i2 is 1). The DEPENDENT can be identified by the combination of the identifier of the PERSON and the DEPENDENT-NAME. This composite key is identified by a triple oval in two places: (1) by DEPENDENT-NAME, and (2) between the DEPENDENT entity type and the DEPENDENT-UPON relationship.

The E-C-R data model can be used to describe data needed by a class of users. The following two sections give some guidelines for constructing an E-C-R view and for making these E-C-R views useful for latter stages of the database design process.

*Constructing the E-C-R Data Model*

Usually, a class of users is in a single department or departments that work closely together. I make a special effort to invite the clerks and support staff to the initial view design meeting. Frequently, the clerks and support staff understand database needs better than high-level administrators.

At the view design meeting, I begin by briefly explaining entity types, attributes, and relationship sets and the notation for these concepts by using examples that will likely be part of the view to be designed. Then I encourage each attendee to participate by asking him/her either to name another entity type or to name an attribute that is associated with an entity type already written on the blackboard. As each attribute name or entity type name is suggested, I write it on the blackboard by using E-C-R diagrams. To clarify what the entity type is, I often ask users to name attributes associated with the entity type.

After an entity type has about a dozen attributes, I sometimes ask if all of these attributes really belong to the entity type, or should the entity type be broken into two entity types, each with some of the attributes. This usually results in some discussion among the users, who generally come to a conclusion in five to ten minutes. This type of discussion is important, because during such discussions, the users develop a common terminology and, more importantly, a common understanding of the meaning of each entity type and its attributes.

After either a dozen entity types have been identified (or the allotted time for the design meeting has passed), the first meeting is adjourned.

I hold a second meeting within a day or two so that the results of the first meeting are still fresh in everyone's mind.

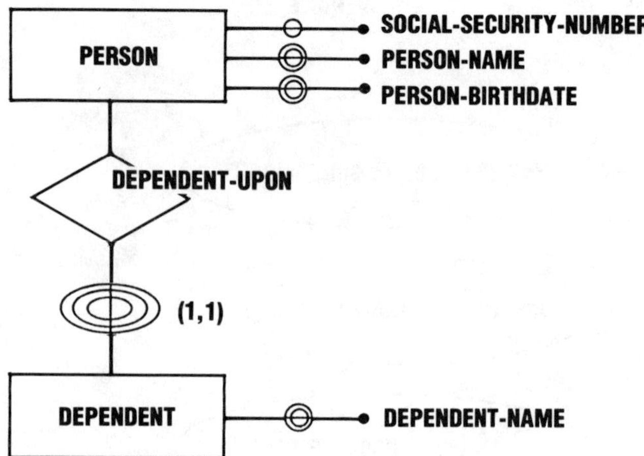


**Figure 3.3. Example of Unique Identifiers**

The E-C-R schema from the first meeting is reviewed. Usually there is some adjustment necessary (a couple of new entity types are inserted and some names of existing entity types and attributes are modified). During the second meeting I usually introduce categories, but only if they are necessary to model a subset of an existing entity type. I also introduce the relationship cardinality constraints and ask the users to help specify the cardinality constraint bounds for each object participating in a relationship set.

In most cases, two meetings are all that are necessary. However, occasionally, users cannot reach agreement on an E-C-R schema at the end of two meetings. This may be because there are more than one class of users trying to define a common view, in which case I try to hold separate meetings for each class. Sometimes the users are not clear on the use of the database, in which case the goals of the database and associated applications needed to be re-examined.

*Well-defined E-C-R Views*

I find the following guidelines* helpful when drawing E-C-R diagrams:

1. Every entity must have at least one identifier. The value of an attribute of an identifier can never be null. (This prohibits two entities with null for identifier attributes. There is no way to uniquely identify such entities.)
2. Attribute names should be singular rather than plural. (This is not a strict rule, but is useful if it helps avoid repeating attributes or multi-valued attributes.)
3. When two entity types form a relationship, the cardinality constraints of the participation of one entity type must be (i1, i2) where i2 = 1 and either i1 = 0 or i1 = 1. This rule guarantees that all relationships are either one-to-one or one-to-many. Many users find many-to-many relationships difficult to understand. Also, most database management systems cannot directly represent many-to-many relationships. A many-to-many relationship can always be replaced by two one-to-many relationships as illustrated in Figure 3.4.

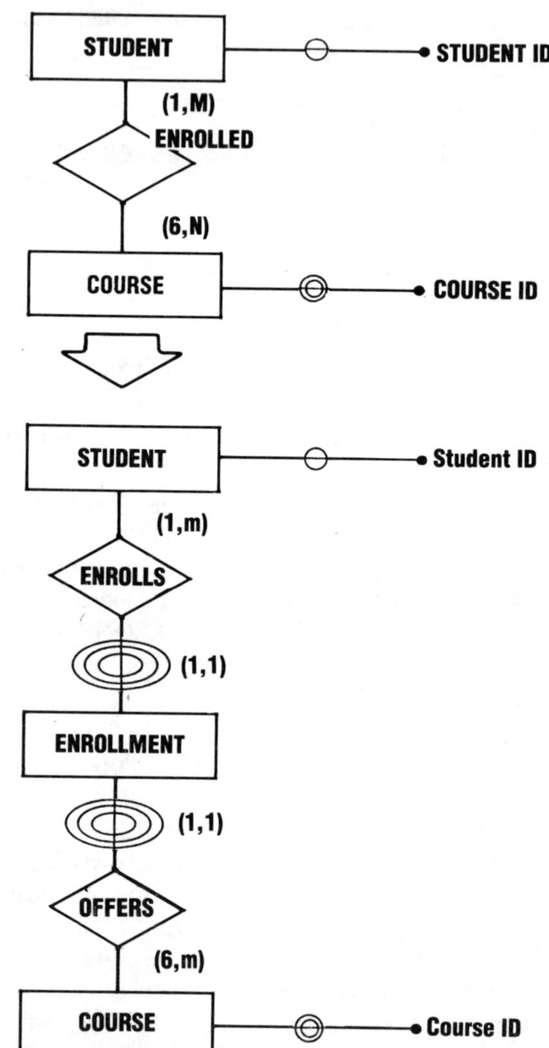


**Figure 3.4. Replacing a Many-to-Many Relationship by Two One-to-Many Relationships.**

4. If the values of several attributes of an entity type have the same values for several subsets of entities in the entity type, evolve the attributes to a new entity type and a relationship set between the new entity type and old entity type, as illustrated in Figure 3.5.
5. If an attribute can have several values for a single entity, evolve that attribute to a new entity type and a rela-

*These guidelines are a variation of guidelines developed by John Carlis, University of Minnesota.

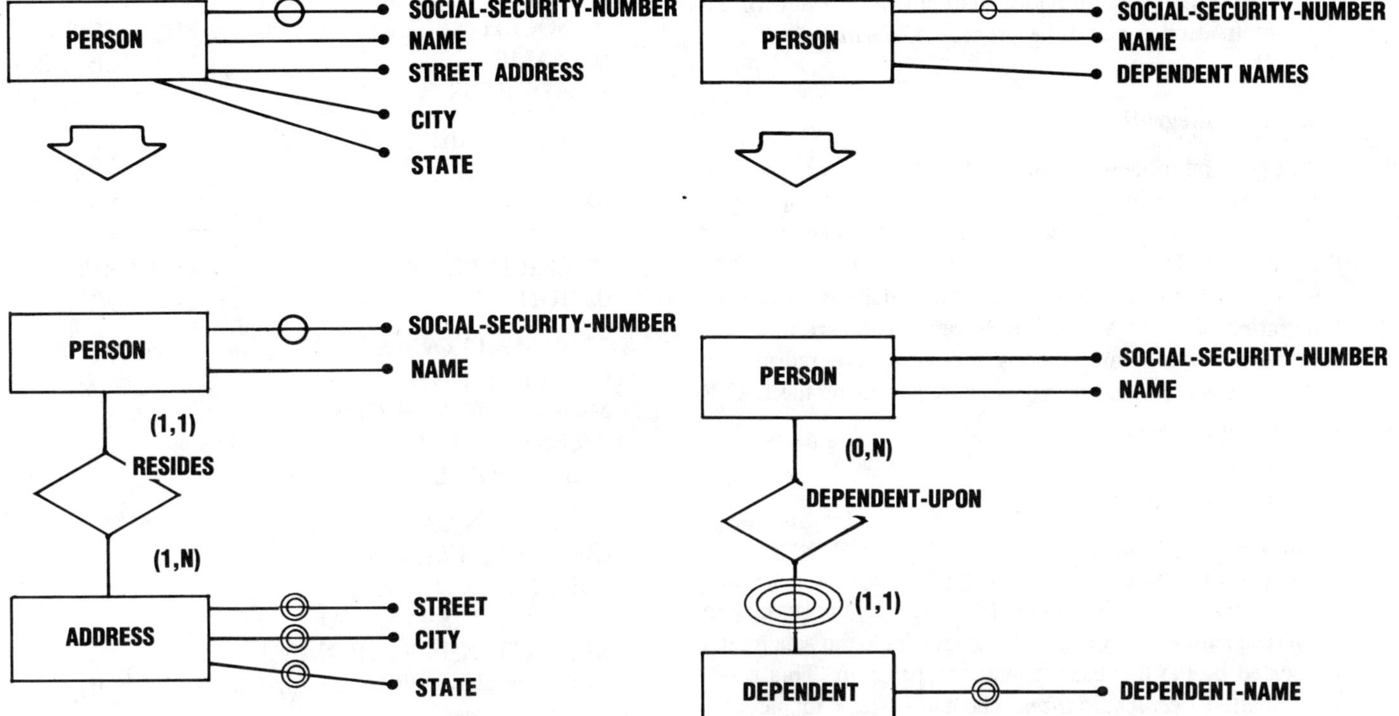


**Figure 3.5. Evolving Several Attributes to an Entity Type**

**Figure 3.6 Evolving an Attribute into an Entity Type**

tionship set between the new entity type and old entity type, as illustrated in Figure 3.6.

6. If several attributes represent the same type of characteristic of the entity, then merge those attributes to a single attribute with several values as illustrated in Figure 3.7.

7. The entity types should be normalized. *Normalization* is a process of examining each entity type to verify that it represents exactly one concept, event, idea, object, or thing. If an entity type represents more than one concept, event, idea, object, or thing, then update anomolies may occur. An *update anomaly* is an undesirable side effect of an update operation. Of

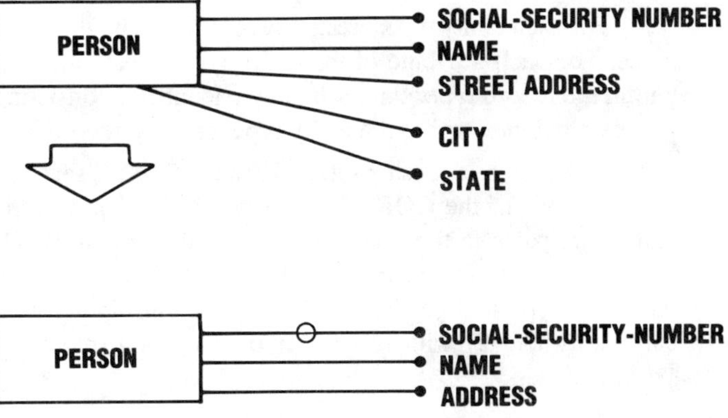


**Figure 3.7. Merging Attributes**

course, if very little updating is to be done, normalization is not necessary. Entity types can be normalized by using the exact same rules used to normalize relational tables. The reprinted paper, "A Simple Guide to Five Normal Forms in Relational Database Theory," by William Kent provides an excellent overview of the motivation for and the process of normalizing.

### 3.2: View Integration

After several models of individual views have been created, it is necessary to merge the individual views into a single, global schema that represents all of the data to be stored in the database. This process is called *view integration*. The reprinted paper, "A Methodology for Database Design by Integration of Users Views," by Navathe, Elmasri, and Larson describes the motivations for view integration and describes how to integrate views expressed using the E-C-R data model.

### 3.3: Accommodation

The E-C-R data model is very useful in designing views and integrating views, but few database management systems can support the E-C-R data model. Thus, it is necessary to convert schemas from the E-C-R data model to the data model supported by the database management system. This process is called *accommodation*. The basic steps for accommodating E-C-R schemas to the widely supported CODASYL Network and relational data models are summarized below.

*CODASYL Network Data Model*

To convert an E-C-R schema to a CODASYL Network schema, the designer needs to perform the following steps:

1. For each entity type, create a record type with the same name. For each attribute of the entity type, create an item within the record type. For each unique identifier consisting of only attributes within the entity type, create a record key.

2. For each relationship set, create a CODASYL set. The owner record of the CODASYL set will be the entity type that participates in the relationship set with cardinality (i1, i2) with i2 > 1. The member of the CODASYL set will be the entity type that participates in the relationship set with cardinality (i1, i2) with i2 = 1. If i1 = 0, then specify

```
INSERTION IS MANUAL
RETENTION IS OPTIONAL
```

If i1 = 1 then specify

```
INSERTION IS AUTOMATIC
RETENTION IS MANDATORY.
```

3. For each category, create a SYSTEM-owned set.

For example, the following represents the CODASYL data description for the E-C-R schema of Figure 3.1:

```
RECORD NAME IS OWNER
  KEY IS SOCIAL-SECURITY-NUMBER
  02 SOCIAL-SECURITY-NUMBER PICTURE 9(10)
  02 NAME                   PICTURE X(20)
  02 ADDRESS                PICTURE X(20)
RECORD NAME IS VEHICLE
  KEY IS REG
  02 REG#                   PICTURE XXX999
  02 MODEL                  PICTURE X(10)
  02 CAR-TYPE               PICTURE X(10)
  02 TONAGE                 PICTURE 9(7)
SET NAME IS OWNS
  OWNER IS OWNER
  MEMBER IS VEHICLE
  INSERTION IS MANUAL
  RETENTION IS OPTIONAL
SET NAME IS CAR
  OWNER IS SYSTEM
  MEMBER IS VEHICLE
  INSERTION IS MANUAL
  RETENTION IS OPTIONAL
  (Only vehicles with values for CAR-TYPE will
belong to this set.)
SET NAME IS TRUCK
  OWNER IS SYSTEM
  MEMBER IS VEHICLE
  INSERTION IN MANUAL
  RETENTION IS OPTIONAL
  (Only vehicles with values for Tonnage will belong
to this set.)
```

*Relational Data Model*

To convert an E-C-R schema to relational schema, perform the following steps:

1. For each entity type, create a relational table. For each attribute of the entity type, create a column in the relational table. For each unique identifier of the entity type, create a key of relational table.
2. For each relationship in the E-C-R schema, create one or more new columns in the relational table corresponding to the entity with the cardinality constraint (i1, i2) where i2=1. These new columns will have the same names as the attributes forming a unique identifier of the other entity type participating in the E-C-R relationship. These new columns consititute a *foreign key* because they will contain values from the key of another (foreign) table.

3. For each category, create a table. The unique identifier of entities in the category should be included as columns of the table. Any attributes associated with the category that are not also associated with the entity type on which the category is based should also be included as columns of the table. (The database user can obtain all of the columns of the category by joining the table corresponding to the category with the table corresponding to the entity type on which the category is based.)

For example, the following represents the relational data description for the E-C-R schema of Figure 3.1:

TABLE OWNER
  KEY IS SOCIAL-SECURITY-NUMBER
  COLUMN SOCIAL-SECURITY-NUMBER
  COLUMN NAME
  COLUMN ADDRESS

TABLE VEHICLE
  KEY IS REG#
  COLUMN REG#
  COLUMN MODEL
  COLUMN SOCIAL-SECURITY-NUMBER
  (SOCIAL-SECURITY-NUMBER is a foreign key.)

TABLE CAR
  KEY IS REG#
  COLUMN REG#
  COLUMN CAR-TYPE
  (REG# is a foreign key.)

TABLE TRUCK
  KEY IS REG#
  COLUMN REG#
  COLUMN TONAGE
  (REG# is a foreign key.)

## 3.4: Physical Data Design

A physical representation of the database objects must be selected that provides good performance for the anticipated mix of retrievals and updates. Structuring database records by considering data item usage can yield substantial efficiencies in the operating cost of the database management system. The reprinted paper, "Physical Database Design Techniques for Improved Database Performance," by March and Carlis describes techniques that can be used to determine efficient record structures quickly for large, shared databases.

### Additional Reading


Aho, A.V., C. Berri, and J.D. Ullman, "The Theory of Joins in Relational Databases," *ACM TODS* Vol. 4, No. 3 September 1979, pp. 297-314. First published in *Proc. 19th IEEE Symp. on Foundations of Computer Science,* IEEE Computer Society, Washington, D.C., October 1977. Introduces the concept of join dependencies.

Beeri, C., R. Fagin and J.H. Howard, "A Complete Axiomatization for Functional and Multivalued Dependencies," *Proc. 1977 ACM SIGMOD International Conference on Management of Data,* ACM, New York, 1977.

Bernstein, P.A., "Synthesizing Third Normal Form Relations from Functional Dependencies," *ACM TODS,* Vol. 1, No. 4 December 1976, pp. 277-298. Presents an algorithm to generate a collection of relations in their normal form given a complete set of functional dependencies.

Fagin, R., "Multivalued Dependencies and a New Normal Form for Relational Databases," *ACM TODS,* Vol. 2, No. 3, September 1977, pp. 289-298. Introduces fourth normal form.

Fagin, R. and M. Y. Vardi, "The Theory of Data Dependencies—A Survey," *IBM Research Report RJ4321,* June 1984.

Schkolnick, M., "A Survey of Physical Database Design Methodology and Techniques," *Proc. 4th International Conference on Very Large Data Bases,* IEEE Computer Society, Washington, D.C., September 1978, pp. 474-487. Surveys a large number of techniques for physical database design.

*In this truly adaptable approach, designers begin by defining the application environment and then work inward until they reach a level that can be handled by available DBMSs.*

# An Adaptable Methodology for Database Design

Nicholas Roussopoulos and Raymond T. Yeh, University of Maryland

Database design has changed considerably since its inception. A large part of the design used to deal with physical data allocation, load factors, and access methods of secondary storage. These aspects are no longer part of the database design process because they are part of all commercial database management systems and cannot be modified. Most current database designs, and possibly all future ones, will stop at logical access path optimization and use existing database systems with fixed physical designs. Consequently, the emphasis will be on design at the information system level.

The design method presented here is based on this very philosophy—that database design must be done "from the outside in." We must analyze the proposed system's environment and proceed progressively inward toward the computer implementation of the application. In most cases the analyst is then directly exposed to the requirements, which is really the key to a successful system design, if the system is to operate effectively within a particular environment. Take, for example, a project that automates existing manual procedures; the computer system is a direct reflection of the current operations, that is, of the environment.

The parts of the database design of most concern to us here are analyzing information processing requirements, constructing a conceptual model that specifies these requirements, and developing and optimizing a logical access path schema. The underlying assumption in our approach to database design is that conceptual modeling can be based on how information flows between an enterprise and its environment and among its components. [One may argue that some kind of model (possibly not precise) has already been conceived, and therefore that conceptual modeling has already begun before the information flow is conceived. Regardless of how true this supposition may be, our purpose here is to model the database, not to deal with how the human brain handles "chicken-or-the-egg" problems!] We consider conceptual modeling as a technique for specifying, in a formal language, concepts and ideas that can be interpreted by other humans familiar with the context of the enterprise and its environment.

For this reason, we start with the environment of the enterprise rather than the environment of the data processing system. In many cases, the requirements of the data processing system may be distorted by established practices, existing hardware and/or software, or personnel resistance to system upgrading. Starting conceptual modeling at the information system level rather than the data processing level helps avoid these low-level distortions. Furthermore, the goals and requirements of this level are more understandable to management. Hence, managers are more apt to make correct decisions.*

In our methodology, we also analyze the operational behavior of the enterprise, which we call system analysis, the word "system" referring to operational behavior, not to the data processing system. Without a complete understanding of how the enterprise operates, no effective design can be developed either for current operations or for future improvements.

*Several other design methodologies start from the environment and proceed inward. Jefferson et al.'s[1] database design departs from the requirement analysis at the corporate level where many of the interactions are between the organization and its environment. Kahn[2] also proceeds from corporate level requirements to information analysis where again interactions include the information flow between the environment and the organization. BIAITI[3] has also incorporated these kinds of interactions into its questionnaires.





Reprinted from *Computer*, May 1984, pages 64-80. Copyright © 1984 by The Institute of Electrical and Electronics Engineers, Inc.

Another main objective of the outside-in methodology is to provide a framework for the use of well-understood and proven techniques for both the analysis and the specification of the enterprise's objectives, requirements, and design. We have incorporated established data flow techniques,[4,5] control flow specification techniques,[6-8] structured interviewing and questionnaire techniques,[9] well-understood data modeling techniques,[10-16] and logical optimization techniques.[17-20] Emphasis has been placed on the understandability and the completeness of the requirements specification. All referenced approaches deal with *either* database design or program design. This methodology integrates techniques from *both* approaches because a database system is neither just a schema (structural component) nor just a set of transactions (procedural component). It is a schema with transactions running against this schema; consequently, the schema and the transactions must be designed hand in hand.

A major advantage of this framework is that significant design decisions are made explicit at the appropriate design phase. For example, obtaining optimal physical parameters, makes no sense if the logical design is ineffective. Similarly, obtaining optimal logical organization and indexing makes no sense if the corresponding conceptual schema is incorrect and violates the integrity of the data. Again, a good conceptual schema is useful only if it corresponds to the right operational behavior of the enterprise within its environment. This framework and the design decisions along with their specification are the important concepts of this proposal. The individual models and techniques to obtain, specify, and document these decisions can be chosen from the wide variety found in literature.

## Methodology overview

Our proposed modular methodology consists of four phases: (1) environment and requirements analysis, (2) system analysis and specification, (3) conceptual data modeling, and (4) derivation of a logical access path schema. A schematic diagram of the methodology is given in Figure 1.

The objectives of the first phase are to understand the actual state of the enterprise and to collect all the information needed by the subsequent steps, including information and data processing requirements. Information requirements will be used in the conceptual data modeling phase to generate the conceptual schema of the target system. The data processing requirements will be passed to the logical access path schema derivation phase in which the logical optimization and the application programs are designed.

The objective of the second phase is to identify the applications that will use the database. Using input from the environment analysis phase, we obtain a good understanding of the target system. The output is a set of "tasks" to be performed during the database operation.

The objective of the third phase—conceptual data modeling—is to translate the knowledge about the target system collected in phases 1 and 2 into a formal representation—a conceptual data model. In this phase, designers are concerned only with the characteristics of the "entities" in the application environment and the relationships among them. They should not be concerned with the way they are represented in the computer.

In the last phase, we have several objectives: (1) to map the conceptual schema into the organization's data model structure, (2) to generate logical access paths of the tasks, (3) to integrate all paths into another schema that models their relationships and their cumulative usage weights, (4) to optimize this access schema, and (5) to realize the tasks' logical access paths against the optimized schema.

Numerous related papers have influenced our work. Phases 1 and 2 have been influenced by the works of Burnstine,[3] Bubenko,[21] Chen,[22] Lum et al.,[23] Tsichritzis and Lochovsley,[24,25] Sheppard-Rund,[9] and Kahn.[2] Phase 3 is based mainly on our work on the semantic models of databases that started with the semantic network model of databases[12,26,27] and its continuation in providing a language to support the design of conceptual schemata.[13] Approaches by Mylopoulos et al.,[14] Weber,[28] Hammer and McLeod,[29] Chen,[10] Sowa,[30] Falkenberg,[31] Smith and Smith,[32] and Brodie[33] can also be used in phase 3 as can other semantic models. Phase 4 has been influenced by Chang and Cheng,[34] Chang and Ke,[35] and Schkolnick.[18]

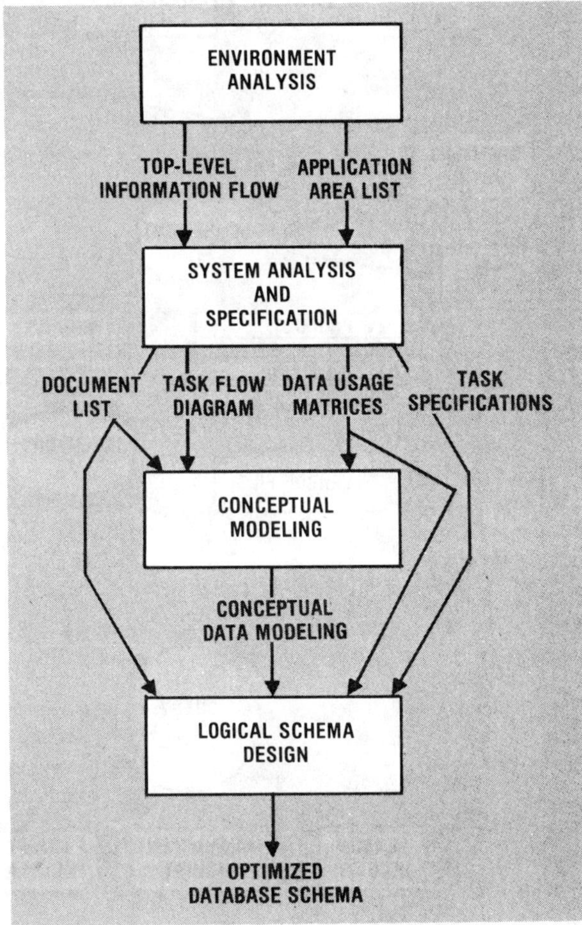


**Figure 1. Schematic diagram of the phases of the database design methodology.**

## Phase 1: Environment and requirements analysis

In this phase, we investigate the information needs of and activities within the enterprise and determine the boundary of the design problem. Much of this phase involves information collection. An overall model of the enterprise as an information processing system is constructed. Since we are not attempting to model or discipline the way humans conceive "understanding," we provide only a list of information sources on which this understanding must be based and a list of things to be generated. In other words, we specify the input and the desired output of this phase, thus leaving the processing to human ingenuity.

**Information sources: phase 1 input.** The basic technique for collecting information consists of reviewing documents, interviewing people, and analyzing questionnaires to determine facts, policies, objectives, and constraints. These information sources describe the current status of the enterprise, possible inefficiencies, plans for the future, and constraints that have to be satisfied in conducting business.

Other sources of information include organization charts, reports, forms, files, and software documentation (if such documentation exists).

**Functional specification: phase 1 output.** In this step, we establish a functional model of the enterprise by identifying its major activities or functions and their relationships. This functional model will take the form of an information flow diagram.

Usually, the function associated with each operational activity is too complex to comprehend and model using a flat, single-level presentation. Therefore, we must usually divide the functions into smaller units called *tasks.*

Identification of activities and tasks is important in the design of the database system. If the system under design is to support the activities of an established enterprise, an organization chart can be used for identifying functions and tasks. However, this process becomes more difficult if (1) a new organization is to be established and its components have not yet been identified or (2) a system is designed to change part or certain aspects of an

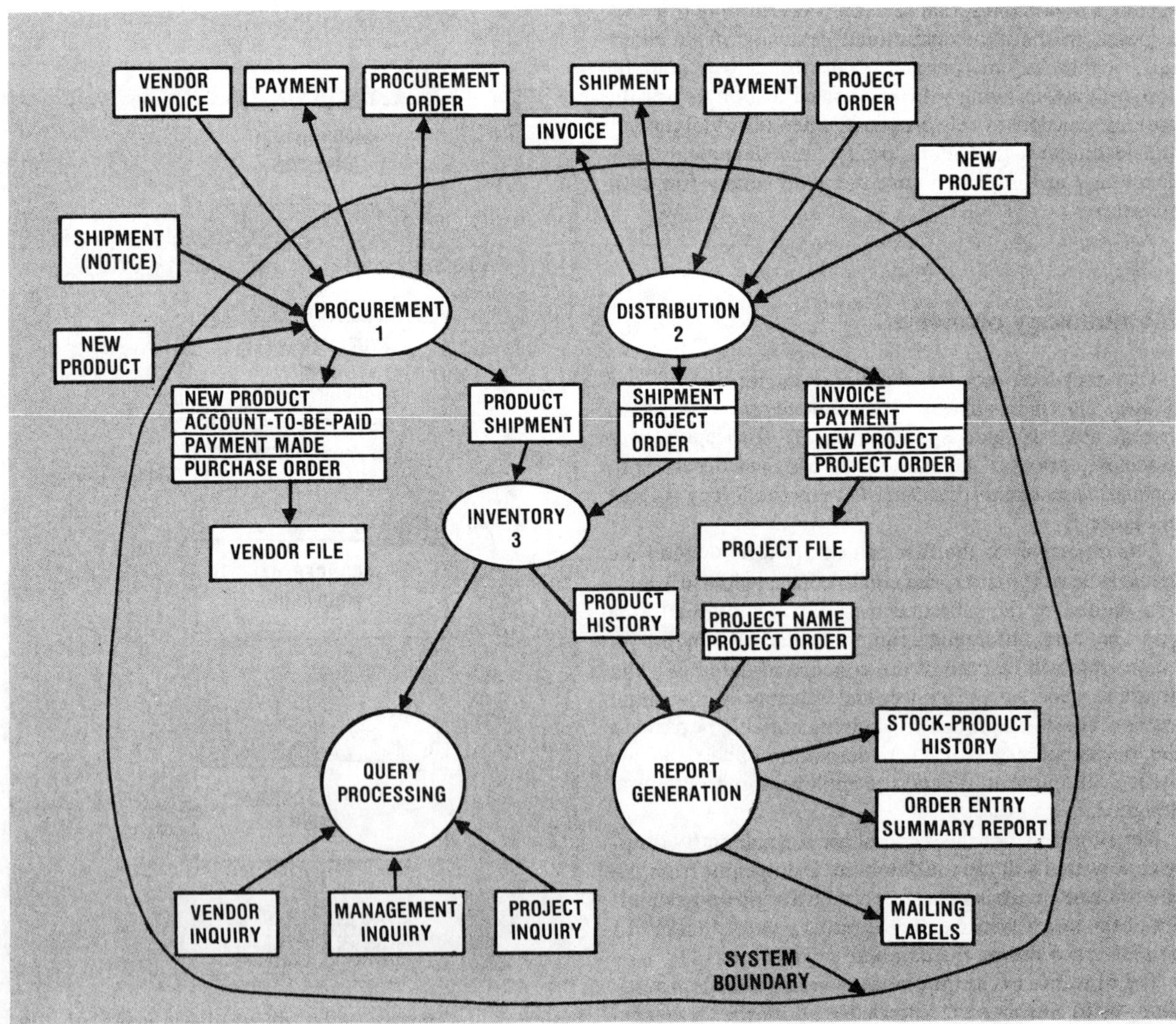


Figure 2. Top-level information flow diagram.

enterprise's activities. In these cases, we must use information collected from the previously described information sources to derive tasks.

The main activities of the enterprise, the interactions of the external entities and the enterprise, and the interactions of the main components can be described by a *system flow diagram* like the one shown in Figure 2.* This flow diagram, which is the goal of the first phase, contains (1) the main activities of the system (PROCUREMENT, INVENTORY, DISTRIBUTION), shown in the ellipses; (2) the data processing functions (QUERY-PROCESSING, REPORT-GENERATION), shown in circles; and (3) the documents that carry the data between components of the organization, shown in rectangles. (A document here is merely a general information-recording medium for information transfer. All messages, forms, files, inquiries, and reports will be referred to as documents.) The boundary of the system shows the interactions of the environment and the enterprise. Clearly, Figure 2 describes not only data flow but also control flow because many of these documents could be simple control messages that trigger tasks in the organization.

## Phase 2: System analysis and specification

In this phase, we start with the overall information-flow diagram like that in Figure 2. Each activity is divided hierarchically into more and more detailed tasks and subtasks. The tasks should be reasonably independent so that we will have a small number of task-task interfaces. During the division process, the (data) documents used by each activity are also broken down into their component data elements or subsets of data elements. The tasks are further divided into subtasks until they become small enough to be clearly understood, and the I/O data documents can be conveniently expressed in terms of data elements that cannot be further divided. A new data- and control-flow diagram is developed using the tasks established through this breakdown. The following tasks were obtained for the Distribution activity through this process.

ENTER-NEW-PROJECT
ENTER-GRANT-ORDER
ORDER-PICKING
SELECT-SHIP-ROUTE
MAINTAIN-PROJ-TRANSACTION-RECORD
PROJECT-BILLING

**Specifying tasks.** For each task, the following attributes need to be specified:

- the person in charge (task performer),
- documents used and/or generated (I/O documents),
- procedure for carrying out the task,
- frequency of the task,
- conditions that specify the prerequisites for the task's activation and the effects after its termination,
- events triggered during the task's performance, and
- error (anomaly) conditions of the task.

Among these attributes, the I/O specifications, task frequency, and the operations performed are the ingredients needed to emulate the task and construct the logical access path schema for its optimization. The pre- and post conditions, events triggered, and error conditions specify the control and each task's interactions with the rest of the system.

A standardized task form has been designed to assist the responsible designer in extracting the important characteristics, features, and attributes of each task. A sample of this standardized form, which task performers and designers can cooperate in filling out, is shown for the Distribution activity (Figure 3).

This task allows the designer to analyze both existing activities and those considered for implementation that have not been divided into tasks and subtasks. Thus, starting with the main activities of the enterprise, the designer can specify all functional requirements in terms of this task form.

The following rules of thumb can be used to decide when a given task should be divided into subtasks:

| | | |
|---|---|---|
| Task-number: | S-1 | |
| Task-name: | DISTRIBUTION | |
| Performer: | Distribution Department | |
| Authorization: | Various authorizations to be specified in the subtasks | |
| Purpose: | Distributes products to the projects and handles accounts | |
| Enabling-conditions: | Permanently executing | |
| Description: | Order Forms (D3) are used to determine which products are to be shipped to which customers. | |
| Frequency: | N/A | |
| Duration: | N/A | |
| Importance: | Very important | |
| Maximum-delay: | N/A | |
| Input: | Documents: | D2 (NEW-PROJ-FORM)<br>D3 (ORDER-FORM)<br>D5 (DAILY-ORDER-BATCH)<br>D6 (PROJECT-BALANCE)<br>D11(PAYMENT)<br>D12(ADJUSTMENT) |
| Output: | Documents: | D4 (WEEKLY-ORDER-HISTORY)<br>D5 (DAILY-ORDER-BATCH)<br>D6 (PROJECT-BALANCE)<br>D7 (PROJECT-INVOICE)<br>D8 (PRODUCT-QUANTITY-ON-HAND)<br>D9 (PRODUCT-TO-BE-SHIPPED)<br>D10(SHIPPING-ROUTE)<br>D13(MONTHLY-STATEMENT)<br>D14(EXCEEDING-LIMIT-PROJ-LIST) |
| Use of documents: | All columns of D2, D3, D6, D11, D12 | |
| Operations-performed: | The detailed operations are described in the subtasks. | |
| Subtasks: | ENTER-NEW-PROJECT (S-1-1)<br>ENTER-GRANT-ORDER (S-1-2)<br>ORDER-PICKING (S-1-3)<br>SELECT-SHIP-ROUTE (S-1-4)<br>MAINTAIN-PROJ-TRANSACTION-RECORD (S-1-5)<br>PROJECT-BILLING (S-1-6) | |
| Error-conditions: | N/A | |

**Figure 3. Task form filled for the Distribution activity.**

*To facilitate an understanding of our methodology, we have chosen a model organization called the ABC Agency. The ABC Agency procures products from vendors and retails them to government projects. Each vendor can furnish several products, and products can exist in several versions or models. Similarly, each product model can be furnished by several vendors. A project may be located in several places. An order may be shipped to any location, but the invoice is always sent to the project's home office.

Naturally, the ABC Agency is only one type of a wide variety of organizations. The steps in our methodology, however, can be broadly applied.

- Many performers are required to carry out the task and each performer has different skills, or each can carry out a part independently.
- Different levels of authorization exist for carrying out different parts of the task.
- Different enabling conditions activate parts of the task.
- Different frequencies and durations apply to different parts of the task.
- Input documents are not used uniformly within the task.
- Different documents are used for different parts of the task.
- Many diversified operations are carried out within the task.
- Many subtasks are controlled by the task.

There are basically two ways of subdividing a task. In the first, the new task is a subtask of the original task. In this case, a "parent-child" relationship is established and part of the responsibilities are transferred to the subtask. However, control stays with the original task, which has to wait for the subtask to terminate before it can terminate. In the second type of subdivision, the new task is a "sibling" of the original task. In this situation, the "parent" of the original task assumes control, but the "sibling" tasks are carried out independently.

During the "parent-child" task division, the input documents of the original task are separated and split among the subtasks. If parts of one or more documents are needed for a subtask, then a new document is defined. The new document will include all the necessary data elements.

During the "sibling-sibling" task division, the original task's input documents may need to be further divided, as in the "parent-child" case, to account for splitting responsibilities between the two. Some additional control documents may have to be introduced for communication among the tasks if they are required to pass data and/or synchronize some activities.

Figure 3 shows a list of subtasks obtained for the Distribution activity. By examining the input documents of the Distribution activity, new tasks such as ENTER-NEW PROJECT, ENTER-GRANT-ORDER, and ORDER-PICKING are identified. Further division may then be necessary as the forms for tasks ENTER-GRANT-ORDER and ORDER-PICKING show. (Figures 4 and 5).

| | |
|---|---|
| Task-number: | S-1-2 |
| Task-name: | ENTER-GRANT-ORDER |
| Performer: | Tom Keener, Distribution Coordinator |
| Authorization: | Scott Farley |
| Purpose: | Enters orders in the database and grants orders |
| Enabling-conditions: | Arrival of ORDER-FORM (D3) |
| Description: | ORDER-FORMS (D3) are distributed and recorded. Balance of ordering project is checked to determine whether order should be granted. Order history is generated every week. |
| Frequency: | 300 per day |
| Duration: | N/A |
| Importance: | Very important |
| Maximum delay: | 2 days |
| Input: | Documents: D3 (ORDER-FORM)<br>D6 (PROJECT-BALANCE)<br>D5 (DAILY-ORDER-BATCH) |
| Output: | Documents: D6 (PROJECT-BALANCE)<br>D5 (DAILY-ORDER-BATCH)<br>D4 (WEEKLY-ORDER-HISTORY) |
| Use of documents: | All columns of D3, D6, D5 |
| Operations-performed: | Upon receipt of D3, it is numbered and distributed. Information on D3 is then entered into the database. The balance of the ordering project (D6) is updated and checked. If the project balance does not exceed its limit, the order is granted. Every morning all granted orders of the previous day are batched in (D5) together for a pickup. Every Friday D4 is generated. |
| Subtasks: | ORDER-FORMS-RECEIVE-DISTRIBUTE<br>ENTER-ORDER-INFO<br>UPDATE-PROF-BALANCE<br>INSUFFICIENT-BUDGET-HANDLING<br>ORDER-HISTORY-GENERATION |
| Error-conditions: | Operation of this task halts if the information of the projects and products does not match with the data in the database. |

**Figure 4. Task form filled for subtask ENTER-GRANT-ORDER.**

**Specification of documents.** From the I/O specifications of the activities and tasks, we can obtain a list of the documents (reports, files, data elements, inquiries to files, forms, etc.). The list includes documents used within the enterprise or documents discovered by the requirements analysis. Messages received by the task performer during task execution are also considered data documents. Below is a partial document list for our sample enterprise:

D1 - PROJECT-RECORD
D2 - NEW-PROJ-RECORD
D3 - ORDER-FORM
D4 - WEEKLY-ORDER-HISTORY
D5 - DAILY-ORDER-HISTORY
D6 - PROJ-BALANCE
D7 - PROJ-INVOICE
D8 - PRODUCTION-QUANT-ON-HAND
D9 - PRODUCTS-TO-BE-SHIPPED
D10 - SHIPPING-ROUTE
D11 - PAYMENT
D12 - ADJUSTMENT
D13 - MONTHLY-STATEMENT
D14 - EXCEEDING-LIMIT-PROJECT-LIST
etc.

Each document is then expressed in terms of data elements. If a document is already being used, the data elements constituting it are readily available. The newly introduced documents must be divided into new or already established data elements. Documents D1 through D4 and their data elements are shown below

```
Document D1: PROJECT-RECORD
  PROJ-NO
  PROJ-NAME
  CRDT-CODE
  CRDT-LIMIT
  PROJ-MAIN-LOC-NO (zip code)
  PROJ-MAIN-LOC-ADDR
    PROJ-BRANCH-LOC-NO
    PROJ-BRANCH-LOC-ADDR
Document D2: NEW-PROJ-FORM
  PROJ-NAME
  PROJ-MAIN-LOC-NO
```

PROJ-MAIN-LOC-ADDR
PROJ-BRANCH-LOC-NO
PROJ-BRANCH-LOC-ADDR

Document D3: ORDER-FORM
ORD-NO
DATE-ENTERED
DATE-POSTED
PROJ-NO
PROJ-MAIN-LOC-NO
PROJ-BRANCH-LOC-NO
ITEM-LINE-NO
PROD-NO
PROD-MOD-NO
QUANT-ORDERED

Document D4: WEEKLY-ORDER-HISTORY
ORD-NO
DATE-POSTED
PROJ-NO
ITEM-LINE-NO
PROD-NO
PROD-MOD-NO
QUANT-ORDERED
PRICE

**Specification of data usage.** From the I/O specification of tasks, and the document specifications, we can construct two usage matrices. The first is the task-document usage matrix, which specifies the task I/O in terms of documents (Figure 6). The second usage matrix is called the task-data element usage matrix and specifies task I/O in terms of data elements (Figure 7). Note that the task-data matrix is constructed from the task-document matrix and the document specifications.

Both data usage matrices can be easily obtained from the task forms and the document specifications. They can also be automatically generated as a report, as PSL/PSA does.[5]

**Specification of task flow diagrams.** The task-document usage matrix is now used to construct the task flow diagram, a chart that shows the control and data flow among the tasks in the system. Figure 8 shows the TFD of the Distribution function.

## Phase 3: Conceptual modeling

The goal of this phase is to translate the knowledge about each activity, collected in the previous phases, into a formal representation called a *conceptual schema.* This data modeling refers only to the structural specification. (The general term of conceptual modeling used in phases 1 and 2 included the procedural specification as well.)

During the conceptual data modeling phase, we are concerned only with the conceptual entities used in each activity, their properties, and the conceptual relationships among them. The physical or computerized representation of the entities and their instances is irrelevant at this point.

To represent conceptual objects, then, we need a computer-independent semantic model that

- can capture the meaning of the conceptual objects;
- has well-defined interpretation rules so that people other than those in the design group (other designers or users of the system) understand the intended meaning; and
- has a friendly human interface with multiple representations (text and graphical) and high-level operators that manipulate the conceptual schema.

A modeling language like the conceptual schema definition language, or CSDL,[13] is best suited for expressing conceptual entities, their properties, and the relationships among them. The language has been slightly extended to offer two levels of syntax. The first is high-level syntax

| | |
|---|---|
| Task-number: | S-1-3 |
| Task-name: | ORDER-PICKING |
| Performer: | Bruce Smith, Inventory Controller |
| Authorization: | Howard Daniel |
| Purpose: | Pick up products of granted orders from the inventory. |
| Enabling-condition: | The arrival of the DAILY-ORDER-BATCH (D5) |
| Description: | The inventory is checked against the products specified in D5. Available products are then picked up for shipment. |
| Frequency: | 5000 picked products per day |
| Duration: | One day |
| Importance: | Very important |
| Maximum delay: | 4 hours |
| Input: | Documents: D5 (DAILY-ORDER-BATCH)<br>D8 (PRODUCT-QUANT-ON-HAND) |
| Output: | Documents: D7 (PROJECT-INVOICE)<br>D8 (PRODUCT-QUANT-ON-HAND)<br>D9 (PRODUCT-TO-BE-SHIPPED)<br>D17(STOCK-UP-REQUEST)<br>D18(UNFULFILLED-ORDERS) |
| Use of documents: | Parts of D5 and D8, all columns of D7, D9 (as shown in Figure 7). |
| Operations-performed: | Upon arrival of D5 (DAILY-ORDER-BATCH), the inventory is checked to determine whether the quantity on hand for each ordered product in D8 is sufficient to satisfy all orders. If so, shipping tickets (D9) and invoices (D7) are issued. |
| Subtasks: | CHECK-INVENTORY<br>ISSUING-SHIPPING-TICKETS<br>PRODUCT-PICK-UP<br>PROJECT-INVOICE-GENERATION |
| Error-conditions: | When the quantity on hand is not sufficient to satisfy all orders, a request for stocking up is issued (D17) and the order is queued (D18) for future fulfillment. |

**Figure 5. Task form filled for subtask ORDER-PICKING.**

| DOCUMENT \ TASK | ENTER-NEW-PROJ | ENTER-GRANT-ORDER | ORDER-PICKING | . . . | . . . |
|---|---|---|---|---|---|
| D1 - PROJECT-RECORD | O | | | | |
| D2 - NEW-PROJ-RECORD | I | | | | |
| D3 - ORDER-FORM | | I | | | |
| D4 - WEEKLY-ORDER-HISTORY | | O | | | |
| D5 - DAILY-ORDER-BATCH | | O | I | | |
| D6 - PROJ-BALANCE | | I | | | |
| | | | | | |

**Figure 6. Task-document usage matrix. *I* and *O* represent input and output, respectively.**

very similar to Chen's entity-relationship (E-R) model.[10] The second level of syntax is more detailed and is needed for formal data definition. Both levels have a graphical representation that helps designers to visualize the underlying semantic connections among conceptual objects. In addition, the language's computer implementation provides a number of support facilities, such as data dictionary facilities, display facilities, and zoom-in/zoom-out facilities, which allow the designer to display the conceptual schema at different levels of detail. Such facilities are important in modeling large and complex systems, where unassisted manual modeling is tedious and error prone. A detailed description of CSDL is given elsewhere.[13]

Other modeling languages and/or modeling methodologies are suitable for this phase. The most notable are Taxis,[14] D-graphs,[28] semantic database model (SDM),[29] E-R model,[10] aggregation-generalization,[32] conceptual graphs,[29] and object-role model.[31] This list is by no means exhaustive; many other models can also be used.

**Discovering entities, properties, and relationships.** Conceptual data modeling consists of identifying the *entities,* the *properties,* and the *relationships* (called EPRs hereafter) in the application. In general, we have no algorithmic methods for identifying EPRs, but we can use some rules of thumb.

In the technique described here, we discover EPRs merely by examining nouns, adjectives, and verbs in the system's requirements. Nouns usually correspond to entities, verbs to relations, and adjectives to properties. The advantage of this technique is that the entities and relationships discovered in this way have meaning for the user because they draw on concepts from the application world. The disadvantage is that the naming process is very subjective, and different designers may come up with different names for the same entities or relationships. Other difficulties are the well-known dilemma of whether we should use a relationship "ship," the entity "shipment," or both to model the concept of shipping. The same difficulties are encountered in all similar techniques. A somewhat structured way for discovering EPRs is to use the document/data element specification as input (see Figures 6 and 7). The method can be used to discover the following:

| DATA ELEMENT \ TASK | ENTER-NEW-PROJ | ENTER-GRANT-ORDER | ORDER-PICKING | ... | ... |
|---|---|---|---|---|---|
| PROJ-NO | O | IO | O | | |
| PROJ-NAME | IO | I | | | |
| CRDT-CODE | O | | | | |
| CRDT-LIMIT | O | | | | |
| PROJ-MAIN-LOC-NO | IO | I | | | |
| PROJ-BRANCH-LOC-NO | IO | I | | | |
| PROJ-BRANCH-LOC-ADDR | IO | | | | |
| ⋮ | | | | | |

**Figure 7. Task-data element usage matrix. *I* and *O* represent input and output, respectively.**

- *Unique code identifiers* are usually introduced when organizations refer repeatedly to instances of entities (physical or abstract objects). In most cases, these identifiers uniquely identify the objects even though their names are not unique. For example, PROJ-NO and ORDER-NO denote entities PROJECT and ORDER.
- *Properties* can be discovered by asking the question: "Does element *A* characterize *B*?" If so, then *B* is usually an entity, and *A* is a property of *B*. For example, ADDRESS characterizes PROJECT; NAME characterizes PROJECT, etc.
- *Structural relationships* (*part-of relationships*) are discovered by asking the question: "Is element *D* a component of *C*?" If so, *C* is usually an entity, and an is-part-of relationship is identified. For example, LINE is-part-of ORDER. *D* can be either an entity by itself or a property of *C*. MODEL-NO, PRODUCT-NO, and QTY-ORD are all related to LINE by is-part-of relationships.
- *Is-a* (*-kind*) *relationships* are discovered by classifying data elements into generic types of entities; SHIP-LOCATION is-a LOCATION, DATE-ORDERED is-a DATE, etc. Both partners in these relationships are entities.
- *Events and actions* that involve data elements indicate general relationships among entities. For example, the event ORDER-PLACEMENT indicates a relationship between PROJECT and ORDER; similarly, the event FULFILLED-ORDERS indicates a relationship among the entities PROJECT, ORDER, SHIP-LOCATION, and DATE.
- *Numerical dependencies* of the entities in relationships are important; we must discover whether a relationship is one-one, one-many, or many-many. For example, an ORDER may have multiple LINES but each LINE has one PROD-NO and one QTY-ORD.

If we apply the preceding rules to our sample enterprise, we get the following EPRs.

```
entities
  PROJECT
  ORDER
  LOCATION
  SHIP-LOCATION
  PRODUCT
  DATE
properties
  LOCATION           characterizes  PROJECT
  ADDRESS            characterizes  PROJECT
  PROJ-BALANCE       characterizes  PROJECT
  SHIP-LOCATION      characterizes  ORDER
  DATE-ENTERED       characterizes  ORDER
  DATE-ORD           characterizes  ORDER
part-of-relationships
  LINE               is-part-of     ORDER
  PROD-NO            is-part-of     LINE
  QTY-ORD            is-part-of     LINE
is-a-kind relationships
  SHIP-LOCATION      is-a           LOCATION
  DATE-ORD           is-a           DATE
general relationships
  ORDER-PLACEMENT relates           ORDER, PROJECT, and
                                    SHIP-LOCATION
```

| | |
|---|---|
| FULFILLED-ORDERS relates | PROJECT, ORDER, SHIP-LOCATION, and DATE |

Note that after we discover the EPRs, we need to define the dependencies between the data values. These could be one-many or many-many. We especially need to define data dependencies of relationships requiring numerical quantification and arbitrary constraints, for example, "Every agency must procure every product from at least two suppliers."

**Expressing EPRs in a multiple-level language.** EPRs can be graphically represented as shown in Figure 9. The numerical quantifiers, can take the form[*m*} = at least *m*, [*m*] = exactly *m*, {m] = at most *m*, and [all] = all instances.

These quantifiers are used to express *m-n* relationships among entities and to define their constraints. For example, in Figure 9, the quantifiers on the line between ORDER-LINE and LINE show that each ORDER has at least one LINE. Further, each LINE is in one-one correspondence with PROD-NO and QTY-ORD through the LINE-PROD-NO-QTY-ORD relationship.

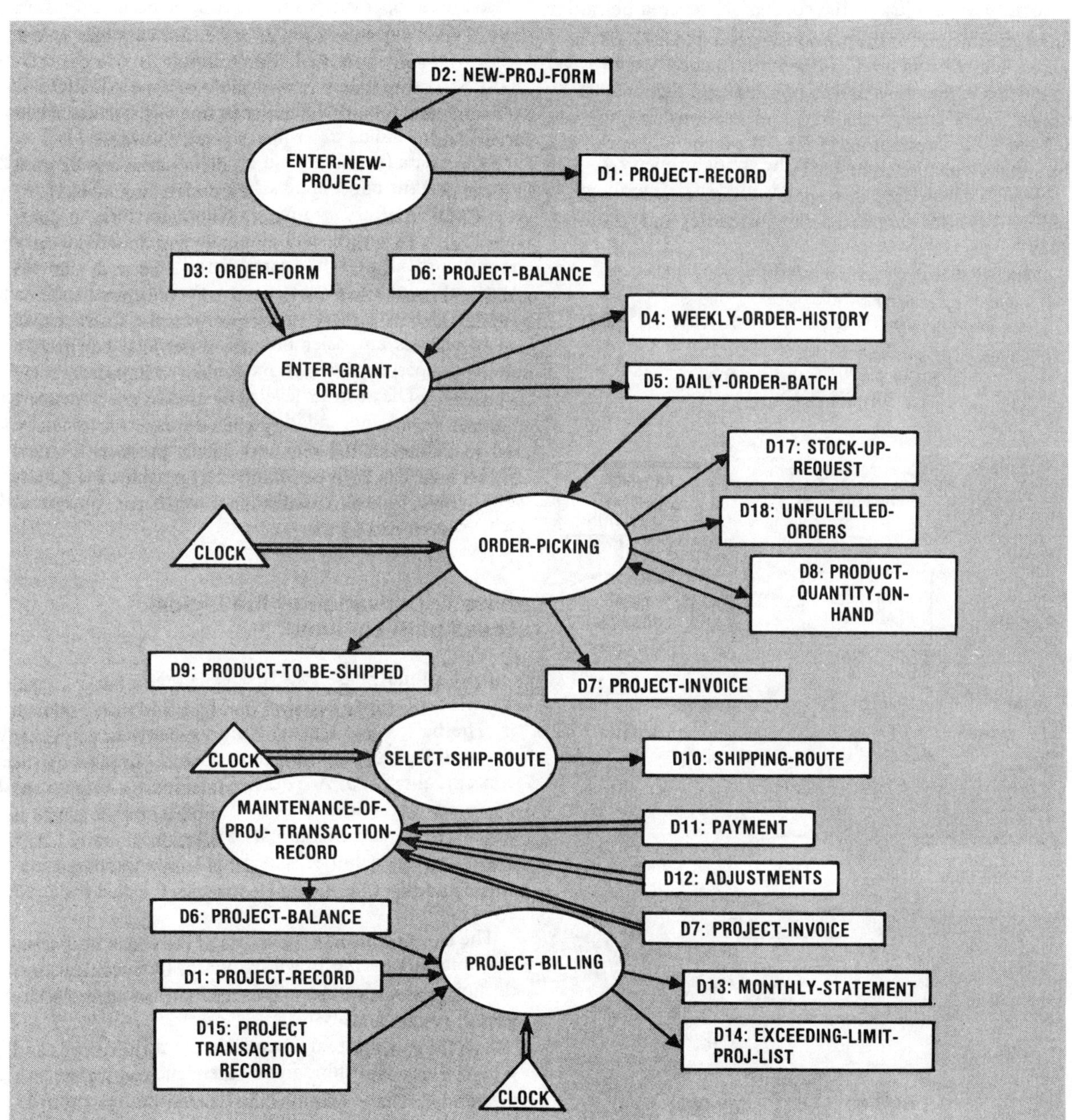


**Figure 8. A task flow diagram for the Distribution activity. A triangle represents the clock, and any connected task is activated at a specific time and not by data passed to it by another task. Single-line arrows denote data flow, while double-line arrows denote control flow. For example, the single arrow between D5: DAILY-ORDER-BATCH and ORDER-PICKING means that D5 is used to carry information to the task, but does not activate it. The task, when activated by some other means, uses D5 to carry out its job. The task MAINTENANCE-OF-PROJ-TRANSACTION-RECORD, however, is activated whenever D7, D11, or D12 is passed to it.**

This level of syntax is an extended version of Chen's E-R model,[10] the difference being the addition of numerical quantifiers. The implication of no numerical quantifier is that any *m-n* relationship $m \geq 1$ and $n \geq 1$, can be satisfied between the related values. However, the first level of syntax cannot express arbitrary quantified expressions because the scope of the quantifiers is not represented. For these types of relationships, we must use a language equivalent to first-order logic. Nevertheless, the preceding notation can express most common data relationships.

The second level of syntax specifies the details of the rectangles (relationships) and ellipses (entities). The second-level syntax of the conceptual schema definition language for some of the previously described EPRs is presented below. This level can be used to specify arbitrary quantified expressions and to provide data dictionary facilities. Every entity, property, and relationship must be defined by a "definitional frame," which fully specifies the system's understanding of the entity, property, or relationship. The keyword *concept* is used to define an entity, and the keyword *frame* to define properties and relationships.

```
Concept PROJECT (x) primary denoted-by PROJ-NO
   frame   PROJ-DEFINITION
        [x   of-type INTEGER is-defined-by 10000 ≤x≤99999]
   frame   PROJECT-PROPERTIES
           [x of-type PROJECT has-property:
              [1] y of-type NAME
              [1] z of-type LOCATION-NO
              [1] w of-type ADDRESS
              [1] u of-type PROJ-BUDGET-CODE
              [1] v of-type PROJ-BUDGET-LIM
              [1] r of-type PROJ-BALANCE
              [1} s of-type SHIP-LOCATION-NO
              [1} t of-type SHIP-ADDRESS]
   frame   ORDER-PLACEMENT
              [all] x of-type PROJ-NO
              [all] y of-type ORDER-NO
              [1]   z of-type SHIP-LOCATION;
            order (agent:x, object:y, destination:z)]
```

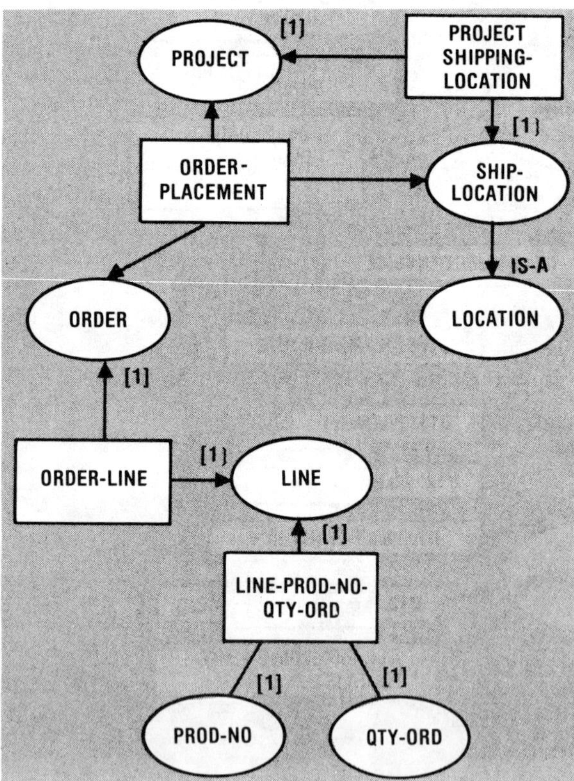


**Figure 9. Graphical representation of entities, properties, and relationships, or EPRs, where circles represent entities and rectangles represent relationships and where [1} means at least one and and [1] means exactly one EPR.**

A *simple frame* provides scoping rules for the qualified expressions. *Composite frames* are built by applying standard logical operations such as conjunctions and disjunctions. Typed variables such as *x,y,z,* are variables whose type is explicitly specified. For example, *y* of-type ADDRESS denotes that *y* is a variable of type ADDRESS. The numerical quantifiers are the same as those described earlier. (A detailed description is given elsewhere.[13])

Other data languages and data dictionaries can be used in place of the conceptual schema design language. However, CSDL offers two major advantages. First, it combines both a data modeling language and data dictionary report capabilities in the same notation. Second, the two levels of syntax allow us to view the conceptual schema specification from different perspectives: the abstract level that provides an easier but more superficial perspective and the expert level, which is equivalent to first-order logic languages. The abstract level can be used by the nonexpert to express concepts and ideas, while the expert level can be used to define all the required details precisely. A new abstract level can then be obtained by masking the details of the second level and used again to verify the conceptual schema developed by the experts.

## Phase 4: Derivation of the logical access path schema

In the final phase, we first generate the basic logical schema for the target system's database and then optimize it. The basic logical schema must explicitly or implicitly cover all logical relationships expressed or implied by the conceptual schema. A sequence of database accesses used to generate all (either explicit or implicit) relationships is called a *logical access path.* The collection of many LAPs integrated into a unified schema that combines shared subpaths by adding their usage frequencies is called the *LAP schema.*[20]

The input for this phase consists of the conceptual schema obtained by the previous phase, task specifications, document specifications, and usage matrices generated by phase 2, system analysis.

From the conceptual schema, we extract the records and the logical relationships among them and express them in a data model. These relationships correspond to the relations of the basic logical schema, which we call the *enterprise logical base schema.* Next, we generate the I/O data requirements of each task by writing queries against the ELBS. The data input requirements of a task are the queries; the data output requirements are either reports or updates to the database. The LAPs of these queries are collected and integrated into a schema, which is then optimized for maximum efficiency on both retrieval and updates.[19]

The output of this phase consists of the LAP schema to be maintained; the task emulations, which are at this point the application programs of the database; and the constraints that must be considered to maintain data integrity.

**Mapping to the enterprise logical base schema.** Our objective here is to map the conceptual model onto other data models, such as the relational or Codasyl models supported by commercial database management systems. We can then use the resultant ELBS to define the logical access paths of each task by emulating the tasks against the ELBS.

The input to this step is the conceptual schema, expressed in the graphical notation described previously or in equivalent notation. The mapping to the relational data model is given below. A similar one has been done for the Codasyl data model.[36] During this mapping, we need not be concerned with issues of efficiency or redundancy. The efficiency and the amount of redundancy allowed in the obtained logical schema will be taken into account later during optimization.

*Entities.* For every entity, a one-column table (unary relation) is constructed. The name given to the relation is the same as the name of the entity. The attribute name is either the same as the entity name or the same as its database denotation (such as PROJ-NO and SUPPLIER-NO, if such denotation is available). In Figure 10, for example, the entity PROJECT (10a), is mapped onto the unary relation PROJECT (10b). INTEGER is the domain over which attribute PROJ-NO of relation PROJECT ranges. Thus, we have an explicit representation of the domain.

*Properties and relationships.* Most relationships expressed in the conceptual schema are mapped onto other relations. Property relationships are mapped onto two-column (binary) relations. The name of such a relation is the concatenation of the concept and property names. The attribute names used are PROPERTY-OF and VALUE. Take for example, the mapping of PROJECT-PROPERTIES in the CDSL second-level syntax.

Two things should be noted here. First is that the dependencies (one-one, one-many, or many-many) are constraints, so they are explicitly written in the attribute box of the relations. The quantifier [1] denotes that there is exactly one value of attribute VALUE for every value of attribute PROPERTY-OF. PROPERTY-OF and VALUE range over the domains PROJ-NO and NAME (or LOCATION-NO, ADDRESS), respectively. Second, whenever a concept is used to define a property and this concept has some denotation, this system denotation is used in the domain box of the relations; in Figure 11, LOCATION-NO is used in the domains of PROJECT-LOCATION rather than LOCATION.

For some property relationships, we are interested only in the *intension* and not the *extension*. The intension of a relationship is expressed using symbols and/or properties that define the elements of the relationship. The extension, on the other hand, is given in terms of the actual values satisfying it. A relationship defined by intension can be found in the frame PROJECT-DEFINITION

$10001 \leq$ PROJ-NO
PROJ-NO $\leq 99999$.

One of its extensions is

$10001 \leq$ PROJ-NO $= 10001 \leq 99999$
$10001 \leq$ PROJ-NO $= 10002 \leq 99999$
$10001 \leq$ PROJ-NO $= 10003 \leq 99999$.

Clearly, for most applications we would not be interested in storing such extensions. Instead we would like to include the intensions only and use them as the logical schema integrity constraints, which are activated to validate every new instance of PROJ-NO that enters the system.

Another type of relationship in the conceptual schema is expressed in the form of *procedural attachments* of frames. For example, the "assign" procedural attachment in the PROJECT-DEFINITION frame represents a procedure followed by the DISTRIBUTION-MANAGER in assigning a PROJ-NO to a new project. In this case, the manager examines the characteristics of the new project so

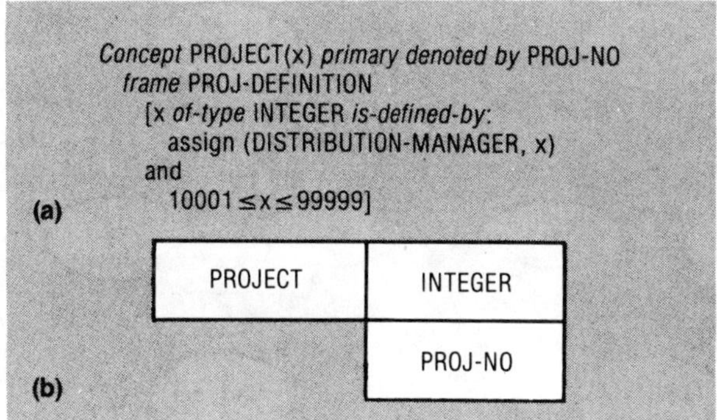


**Figure 10. Mapping an entity.**

| PROJECT-NAME | PROJ-NO | NAME |
|---|---|---|
| | PROPERTY-OF | [1] VALUE |
| | 10001 | watergate |
| | 10002 | eggplant |
| | • | • |
| | • | • |
| | • | • |

| PROJECT-LOCATION | PROJ-NO | LOCATION-NO |
|---|---|---|
| | PROPERTY-OF | [1] VALUE |
| | 10001 | 21742 |
| | 10002 | 95193 |
| | • | • |
| | • | • |
| | • | • |

| PROJECT-ADDRESS | PROJ-NO | ADDRESS |
|---|---|---|
| | PROPERTY-OF | [1] VALUE |
| | 10001 | white house |
| | 10002 | monterey |
| | • | • |
| | • | • |
| | • | • |

**Figure 11. Mapping a property relationship.**

```
frame ORDER-PLACEMENT (x,y,z)
      [[all] x of-type PROJ-NO
       [all] y of-type ORDER-NO
       [1]  z of-type SHIP-LOCATION :
        order(agent:x, object:y, destination:z) ]
```

| ORDER-PLACEMENT | PROJ-NO | ORDER-NO | SHIP-LOCATION-NO |
|---|---|---|---|
| | {all} AGENT | {all} OBJECT | [1] DESTINATION |
| | 10001 | OM-336 | 21742 |
| | 10001 | OS-112 | 21742 |
| | 10002 | OM-348 | 95193 |
| | • | • | • |
| | • | • | • |
| | • | • | • |

**Figure 12. Mapping an event relationship.**

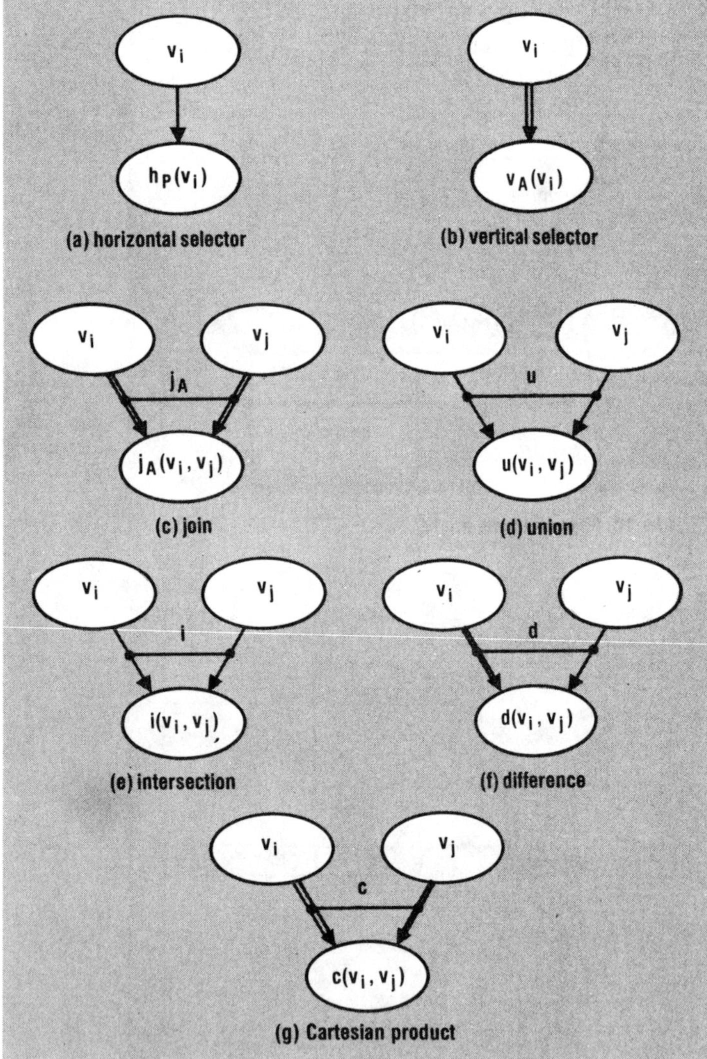


**Figure 13. Graphical notation for the relational operators: (a) horizontal selector, (b) vertical selector, (c) join, (d) union, (e) intersection, (f) difference, and (g) Cartesian product. Single-line arrows (arcs) denote "subset" relations; that is, the head node has tuples that are included in the tail node. Double-line arrows denote "project" relations; that is, the head node has as attributes a subset of the attributes of the tail node. Links between arrows represent the derivations of views (dots).**

that he can assign the PROJ-NO. Because these characteristics are of no interest to the system or to the system's users, they are hidden. Such assignments may be done, for example, on the basis of the information about project location, priority, and budget limits—notions that will not be needed again by system users.

The preceding discussion has focused on property relationships. Another kind of relationship expressed in the conceptual schema is the *event relationship*. These relations are mapped onto *n*-column relations. The name of the event is used as the relation name. The domains of the relation are the entities that participate in the relationship. Attribute names are chosen from a relatively small set of "roles" such as agent, recipient, object, source, destination, and time, which define the part each entity plays in the relationship. Figure 12a is an example of the event relationship ORDER-PLACEMENT which is mapped onto a synonymous relation (12b).

**Emulating tasks.** In this step, we obtain a query and an update model, which respectively reflect the data input and output requirements of each task. The result of the task emulation step is a collection of logical local subschemata, each of which is tailored to the data I/O requirements of a task.

Each task is emulated using the ELBS generated by the previous step. In this emulation, the data input required by each task (see the "input" line in the task form in Figure 3) is expressed by queries against the ELBS. For example, if information is needed about a project's location, a query is made against the PROJECT-LOCATION relation.

The term "query" implies a well-formed expression in a relational query language. However, since every query in a relational query language can be expressed by a relational algebraic expression, we assume that a query is a valid relational expression. Some queries are *generic;* that is, they produce a set of values, each of which may be the answer to a simple query. For example, a query that specifies the retrieval of projects located in New York generates as an answer a set of projects (possibly empty). This result may, in turn, be accessed by another application program to process each of the New York projects individually.

The answers to generic queries, called *views,* are, in general, virtual relations that have a form similar to a base relation except that they may be stored differently. The collection of these virtual relations, which corresponds to the data input of a task, is nothing but a local logical subschema tailored to the needs of this task.

Updates are generated from the output specifications of the task and are expressed in a data manipulation language. Only updates to the *base relations* of the enterprise logical base schema are allowed. Base relations are those that cannot be derived by queries made against other relations. Updates to views are in general problematic because some of these updates may not reflect valid updates to the base relations.[37-39] Since the only view updates that can be handled correctly are those that can be translated into sets of updates to base relations, we consider only base relation updates. The queries and the updates obtained during each task's emulation and their usage frequencies are used to construct the query and update model, which is then used to optimize the collection of logical access paths. In other words, the query and the update models are the composition of the data input and output requirements of all the tasks. The task emulation step is divided into the following substeps: (1) generate the data input requirements of each task, (2) compute the probabilities of all queries, and (3) compute the update probabilities for the base relations.

*Generate the data input requirements of each task.* Each query made to generate data input requirements of a task is represented by a *query graph* composed of view nodes. A view node (or simply a view) is a representation of the answer that corresponds to a relation derived by a query. For example, the virtual relation EXCEEDING-BUDGET-PROJECT is a view node that corresponds to the answer of the query "Give me the projects whose balance exceeds their budget limit."

A graphical representation for query graphs is introduced (Figure 13) in which each relational operator is represented by one or two linked arcs (depending on whether the operator is unary or binary). Any relational query can be represented by such a query graph because this set includes all relational operators. Figure 14 is a query graph for local projects. Here, LOCAL-PROJECT is a view obtained from PROJECT of ELBS by selecting projects that are local (LOCAL ≡ LOCATION ≡ Washington, DC).

*Compute the probabilities of query graphs.* The global probability of a query graph is the probability of executing the corresponding query against the database from within any task. These computed probabilities are then used during optimization, a step required by any optimization algorithm.[18,19,40]

The technique for computing global capabilities uses the frequency of each task found in the task forms and the number of times each query graph is executed from within each task. Weights indicating the importance of each task or application can also be used as an alternative or in addition.

Assume that there is a total of $n$ tasks and $m$ query graphs. We use a simple computation matrix for obtaining the global probabilities of all queries. Figure 15 is the task-query frequency matrix, where the upper $m \times n$ portion contains the frequencies of the query graphs within the tasks. For example, $a_{ji}$ (where $1 \leq j \leq m$ and $1 \leq i \leq n$) is the number of times the query graph $q_j$ is executed from within task $t_i$. If $q_j$ is never made from within $t_i$, then the orresponding entry is zero. The $(m+1)$ row, shown in the matrix as

$$\sum_{j=1}^{m} a_{ji}$$

is used to store the total number of query graphs made by task $t_i$. The $(m+2)$ row (labeled $F_{t_i}$) contains the frequencies of the task's activations. The $(n+1)$ column with label $p_j$ stores the computed global probabilities of each query graph. The following algorithm[20] computes the query graph probabilities by filling out the matrix in Figure 15.

```
BEGIN
  FOR i=1 UNTIL n DO
     BEGIN
       qnum=0
       FOR j=1 UNTIL m DO qnum=qnum+a_ji
       a_m+1,i =qnum
     END
  ftot=0
  FOR j=1 UNTIL n DO ftot=ftot+a_m+2,i
  FOR j=1 UNTIL m DO
     BEGIN
     psum=0
       BEGIN
         FOR i=1 UNTIL n DO
                psum=psum+(a_ji ÷a_m+1,i)*(a_m+2.i, ÷ftot)
       END
     a_j,n+1 =psum
    END
END
```

The first double loop in the algorithm fills out the $(m+1)$ row. The second simple loop computes the total number of tasks $f_{tot}$. The last double loop computes the global probability $p_{sum}$ of each query $q_j$.

Figure 16 is the result of applying the algorithm to the matrix in Figure 15. Note that the probabilities were computed as if there were no updates against the database. In real life, of course, queries and updates are intermixed activities of each database system. Thus, the global probabilities should be computed so that the updates are also taken into account. To account for the influence of the updates onto the probabilities of the queries, we can add to the $(m+1)$ row the number of updates done from

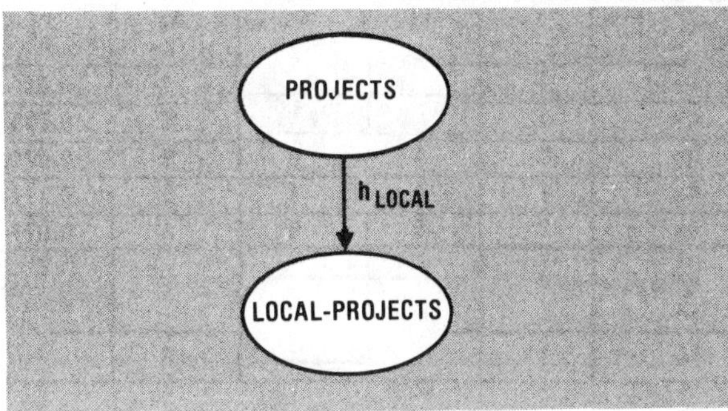


**Figure 14. A query graph for local projects.**

| $q_i$ \ $t_i$ | $t_1$ | $t_2$ | $t_3$ | $t_4$ | $p_j$ |
|---|---|---|---|---|---|
| $q_1$ | 0 | 2 | 1 | 1 | |
| $q_2$ | 1 | 0 | 0 | 0 | |
| $q_3$ | 0 | 1 | 0 | 0 | |
| $q_4$ | 1 | 1 | 1 | 0 | |
| $q_5$ | 2 | 0 | 0 | 0 | |
| $\sum_{j-1}^{m} a_{ji}$ | | | | | |
| $F_{t_i}$ | 1 | 2 | 1 | 3 | 7 |

**Figure 15. A task-query frequency matrix in which $(q_1 \ldots q_5) \times (t_1 \ldots t_5)$ contains the frequencies of query graphs within the tasks. The remainder of the matrix is used to store the total number of graphs made by task $t_i$ and how often the task is activated.**

within each task, assuming that the cost of retrievals and updates is about the same. Or, before we add anything to the $(m+1)$ row, we may want to multiply the number of updates by a weight, depending on the cost of the updates when they are compared with the retrieval queries.

*Generate update probabilities.* We can get the probabilities of updates on base relations from task output. We are not considering updates against views because studies show that only a few view updates can be reflected into valid sequences of valid updates on the base relations used to derive the updated views.[37-39] We assume here that all updates considered correspond to valid updates on base relations and that they have been translated onto base relation updates. The update probabilities $u_j$ (where $j=1,2,\ldots,k$) of base relations are computed in a manner similar to that for queries. Figure 17 is an example of a probability computation matrix for updates. It differs from the query matrix in that the first column of this matrix corresponds to base relations $r_j$ rather than to views. For example, in Figure 17, task $t_1$ makes two updates: one on the base relation $r_1$ and one on $r_3$. Task $t_3$ makes two updates on $r_2$. Note that the task frequencies for this example are the same as the ones on the query computation matrix. The same algorithm described previously is used to fill out the rest of the computation matrix as shown in Figure 18.

| $q_i$ \ $t_i$ | $t_1$ | $t_2$ | $t_3$ | $t_4$ | $p_j$ |
|---|---|---|---|---|---|
| $q_1$ | 0 | 2 | 1 | 1 | 0.641 |
| $q_2$ | 1 | 0 | 0 | 0 | 0.035 |
| $q_3$ | 0 | 1 | 0 | 0 | 0.071 |
| $q_4$ | 1 | 1 | 1 | 0 | 0.177 |
| $q_5$ | 2 | 0 | 0 | 0 | 0.071 |
| $\sum_{j-1}^{m} a_{ji}$ | 4 | 4 | 2 | 1 | |
| $F_{t_i}$ | 1 | 2 | 1 | 3 | 7 |

**Figure 16. Figure 15 matrix after applying an algorithm to compute query graph probability.**

| BASE REL. \ TASKS | $t_1$ | $t_2$ | $t_3$ | $t_4$ | $q_j$ |
|---|---|---|---|---|---|
| $r_1$ | 1 | 0 | 0 | 1 | 0.21 |
| $r_2$ | 0 | 0 | 2 | 0 | 0.14 |
| $r_3$ | 1 | 0 | 0 | 1 | 0.21 |
| $r_4$ | 0 | 0 | 0 | 0 | 0 |
| $r_5$ | 0 | 1 | 0 | 1 | 0.42 |
| $\sum_{j-1}^{m} a_{ij}$ | 2 | 1 | 2 | 3 | |
| $F_{t_i}$ | 1 | 2 | 1 | 3 | 7 |

**Figure 17. Probability computation matrix for updates in which the base relations are the first column rather than views (Figures 15 and 16).**

**Integrating query graphs into a LAP schema.** In this integration step, we use the query graphs generated by the task emulation, the global probabilities, and the update probabilities to generate a logical access path schema that models the use of LAPs in the database. This schema is based on database activities, (retrievals and updates) found in the tasks, and integrates their logical access paths by recognizing common subpaths and increasing the weight of the shared subpaths. The schema provides a comprehensive picture of LAPs and the cumulative use of the shared subpaths and/or intermediate results. It is both a model of the access requirements during database design and a model for optimization during database operation.

Integration is achieved when two query graphs are merged to form a single one. During this merging, a simple algebra is defined that adds the probabilities of the common views on the obtained LAP schema. When the first two graphs have been merged, a third one is merged with the first two, and so on until eventually all query graphs have been merged into the final LAP schema. (More rigorous descriptions of merging algorithms are given elsewhere.[20,41]) Figure 18 shows query graphs for (a) EXCEEDING-BUDGET-PROJECTS, (b) SHIPPED-ORDERS, and (c) ORDERS-IN-PROCESS. Since 18a and 18b have no common views, they remain disconnected after merging. Figure 19 shows the merging of Figures 18a, b, and c. Note that the query probabilities of the common view ORDERS have been added. In Figure 20, the query graph for "Orders in process for projects exceeding their budgets" is shown.[1] The graph is obtained by making (1) two horizontal selections on PROJECTS and ORDERS to obtain EXCEEDING-BUDGET-PROJECTS and ORDERS-IN-PROCESS and (2) a join on the last two views on the attribute PROJ-NO. When we merge this query graph with Figure 19, we get the graph in Figure 21. As the figure shows, the probabilities of accessing PROJECTS and EXCEEDING-BUDGET-PROJECTS have been increased because they appear in a number of query graphs. The more each view appears in query graphs, the higher its probability of being supported in the optimal schema becomes.

A view (which does not correspond to a base relation) may be affected by an update to any of the base relations used in the derivation of the view. Since we assume that the updates on base relations are independent, the update probability $u$ that a view may be affected by any update is the sum of the update probabilities of all base relations used in the derivation of the view. In Figure 21 we show the update probabilities $u_n$ as they propagate from the base relations to the views. The view ORDERS-IN-PROCESS-FOR-PROJECTS-EXCEEDING-BUDGET is affected by both updates in PROJECT and ORDERS and thus its $u$ probability is $u_1+u_2$. The graph obtained by this step along with the retrieval and update probabilities is the LAP schema of the database.

**Optimizing the LAP schema.** The goal of this step is to enhance the execution efficiency of the frequently used (or important) tasks by explicitly indexing the subschemata they operate on. Clearly, not all of the subschemata should be indexed because a great deal of redundancy is generated, costing both storage and update time.

A view in the LAP schema can either be supported by an index to the base relation tuples that make up the view's tuples or constructed on demand from the base relations it is derived from. The construction is associated with I/O and CPU cost—to be called the "cons" cost. On the other hand, if an index is kept for the view, the cons cost is avoided. In this case, however, storage is required for the index, and updates become more time consuming because the index needs maintenance.

A useful indexing policy is to retain all indexes until an update is required. Consequently, an index is updated if it corresponds to a frequently accessed view but dropped if the view is infrequently accessed. In this manner, existing indexes are used as cache memory aids. These aids do not cost much overhead because they are created to answer queries. The only overhead is for the recognition of such cache indexes. The payoff can be significant because we trade CPU time (required for the recognition/matching algorithm) with extra I/O (required by the construction cost of a view). Given that (1) certain logical access paths among data expressed in some subschemata are used more often than others, and (2) in general not all paths should be indexed, we clearly need an optimization process that decides which paths must be supported.

The optimization is based on the following elements:

- the set of the derived views;
- the sizes of the indexes for those views, when the views are explicitly supported (cardinality times the size of the pointer);
- the construction cost of the derived views assuming that their index is not available;
- the probabilities of making queries against those derived views;
- the update cost of the indexes; and
- the probabilities of the updates.

Estimates of these elements could be easily obtained during the design in terms of upper bounds and complexity order of the algorithms. They are even more easily obtained when the database is operational. In the latter case, the index size and the construction cost of the index can be measured by monitoring the execution of the views. The same is true for the update cost, which can be measured by executing the updates. Optimization would then be based on actual costs of the index mechanism's implementation, the operating system, the database system, the buffering facilities, and all the other influencing parameters of the execution environment.

A cost model is needed to give us the cost of querying views and updating indexes. First we define index allocation and the construction cost based on this allocation. An index allocation $A$ over a set of views $V$ is a mapping

$$A : V \rightarrow \{0, 1\}$$

where $A(v) = 1$ means that view $v$ has been indexed, whereas $A_v = 0$ means the opposite. For simplicity, we treat base relations as views (even though they are explicitly stored) and assume that $A(r) = 1$ for all base relations $r$. A construction cost function *cons* over a set of views $V$ is a mapping

$$cons: (f, v) \rightarrow \{0, \infty\}$$

where $v \epsilon V$ is a derived view and $f$ is the set of views or base relations from which $v$ can be constructed. Clearly, more than one set $f$ can be used to construct a given view. Note also that a base relation has no $f$ set because by definition base relations cannot be constructed from others.

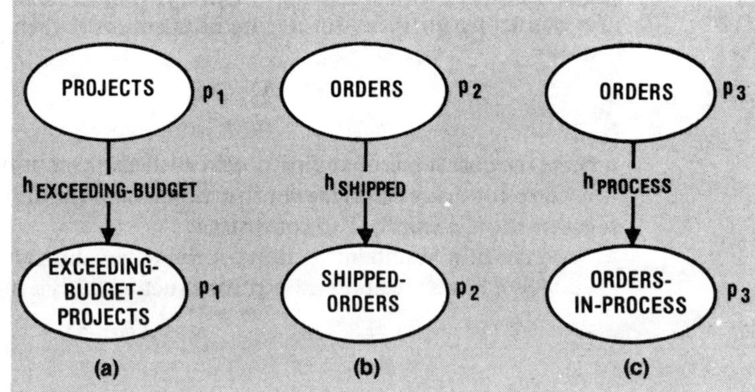


**Figure 18. Query graphs for (a) EXCEEDING-BUDGET-PROJECTS, (b) SHIPPED ORDERS, and (c) ORDERS-IN-PROCESS.**

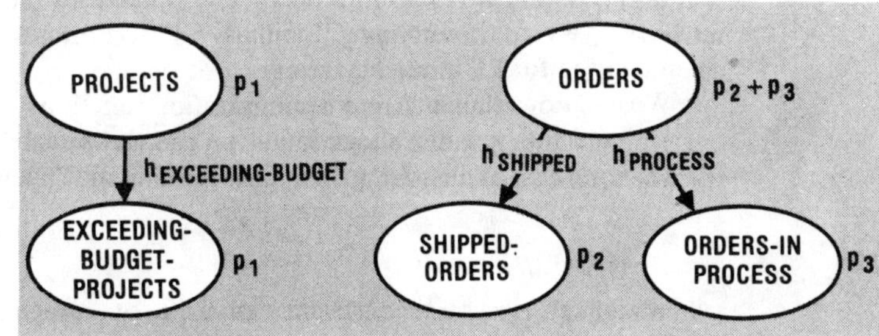


**Figure 19. Merging of the three graphs in Figure 18. Note that 18a remains disconnected from the others because it has no views in common with 18b and c.**

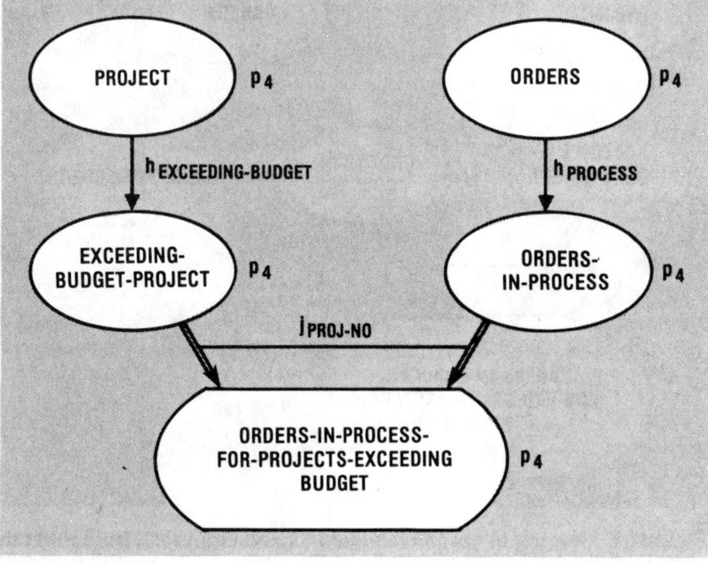


**Figure 20. Query graph for "orders in process for projects exceeding their budgets."**

The cost of answering a query that uses view $v$, given index allocation $A$, is

$$C(v) = c_r(v) \qquad \text{if } A(v) = 1$$

or

$$C(v) = \min_f [cons(f,v) + \sum_{x \in f} C(x)] \qquad \text{if } A(v) = 0$$

where $C_r(v)$ is the cost of retrieving the view from its index and is linear with size $|v|$. If $cons(f,v)$ is the cost of constructing the index for $v$ from its ancestors $f$, then quantity

$$cons(f,v) + \sum_{x \in f} C(x)$$

reflects the cost required to first obtain all elements $x$ in $f$ needed to construct $v$ plus the construction cost of putting together the elements of $f$ to construct $v$.

The cost of maintaining an index for view $v$ during an update of a base relation used in constructing this view is

$$UC(v) = c(v) \qquad \text{if } A(v) = 1$$

or

$$UC(v) = 0 \qquad \text{if } A(v) = 0$$

This cost reflects the cost $c_r$ of retrieving and updating the view's index, if one is maintained for it; otherwise, it is zero.

Both costs reflect results in term of I/O operations of retrieving a view or modifying it. Similarly CPU time costs can be used for CPU-bound systems.

We can now define different optimization functions:

(1) Find the best index allocation $A$ on the views such that the total cost of answering all queries is minimal. That is

$$\sum \{C(v)p_v + UC(v)u_v\}$$

is minimal subject to the constraint that the total storage used for indexing does not exceed SLIMIT. That is

$$\sum |v| A(v) \leq \text{SLIMIT}$$

In the previous formula, $p_v$ is the probability of accessing $v$, and $u_v$ the probability that $v$ needs to be maintained because of an update for a base relation.

(2) Find the best index allocation $A$ such that for weights $w_1$ and $w_2$

$$\sum \{w_1 C(v)p_v + w_2 UC(v)u_v\}$$

is minimal

(3) Find the best index allocation $A$ such that

$$\sum A(v) \; |v|$$

is minimal subject to the constraint that no query takes more than TLIMIT time to answer; that is

$$\sum C(v) \leq \text{TLIMIT}$$

If I/O operation cost is used, TLIMIT can be estimated by multiplying the cost by the time in milliseconds to do one I/O operation.

(4) Find the best allocation $A$ such that

$$\sum C(v)p_v$$

is minimal,

$$\sum UC(v)u_v$$

is minimal, and

$$\sum A(v) \; |v| \leq \text{SLIMIT}$$

Algorithms for obtaining the best index allocation for any of these optimization functions are computationally very difficult (NP-complete[42]). However, heuristics and knowledge on the accessing provided by the logical access path schema can help optimization. A heuristically directed algorithm, which guarantees that whenever a solution is reached, it is the optimal allocation for the LAP schema, is described elsewhere.[19]

We have now completed the last phase of the database design methodology. At this point, we have obtained the optimized logical access path schema and the application programs (task emulations). Now the operational phase of the database can begin.

We have presented a comprehensive step-by-step methodology for an adaptable database design—adaptable because each phase can be facilitated by a number of models and representation primitives.

Many of the tools and analysis techniques in the methodology can be and have been automated. Others, such as tools that help us to analyze objectives, constraints, policies, etc., or formal verifiers for consistency, are more difficult to automate. To help solve these problems, we must rely on user-directed instead of system-directed walkthroughs and/or specialized presentation techniques and reports.

The design specification techniques used in this methodology are valuable for system maintenance, as well. Changes in the environment and/or requirements can be traced back to the specification (output) of each phase to see the effects of these changes. Efficiency improvement from statistical observations and/or changes in access usage can be handled when deriving and optimizing a logical access path schema.

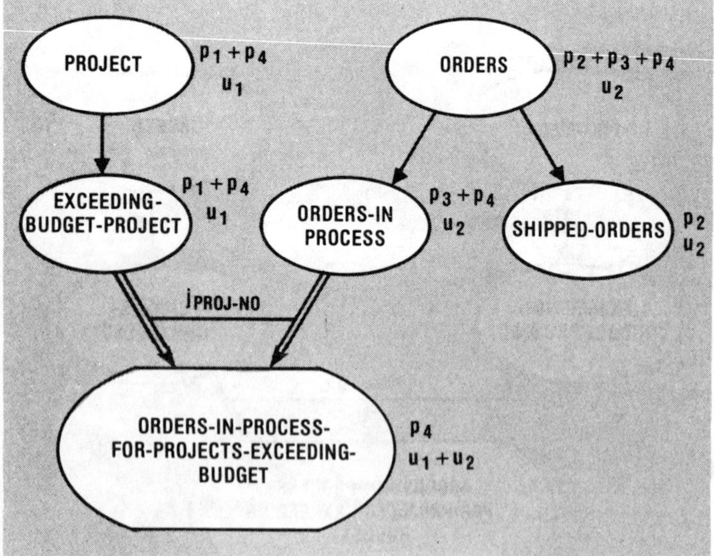


**Figure 21. Merging of graphs in Figure 19 and Figure 20. Note that the probability of accessing PROJECTS and EXCEEDING-BUDGET-PROJECTS has increased because each appears in a number of query graphs.**

We have successfully used our methodology in a number of applications including the ABC Agency inventory database, Naval Printing Office database, a Telephone Answering Service Processing System, a Happy-Boozer Bar database and a database to support an IFIP conference. We found that the method is easy to teach to people because the designer has the freedom to use familiar models.

We have also been using the methodology in a class of approximately 50 students taking their first undergraduate database course. The students receive one to two lectures for each phase (squeezed between regular lectures.) For the course term project, the students teamed up in groups of two to find the information requirements of an organization, designed the database system, and implemented it on an available database management system. The only step of the methodology not required in completing this project was the optimization of the LAP schema. From the approximately 20 designs and implementations on each application, about five were excellent. Ten were good designs with complete requirements and design specifications.

One of our initial hypotheses was that task emulation would speed up implementation. The experiment with the students verified this assumption. Task emulation helps to ensure that the logical schema is complete, because if some parts of the schema are not covered, some tasks cannot be emulated. Also, each emulated task forms the skeleton of the application program (transaction) that is to carry out the task—the part that deals with the necessary I/O interactions with the database. Therefore, very little work is left to complete the implementation of the application program. ✱

## Acknowledgments

This work was supported in part by the Air Force Office of Scientific Research contract F49620-83-K0018-AFOSR to the University of Maryland. Computer support was provided in part by the Computer Science Center at the University of Maryland.

## References

1. D. Jefferson, V. Lum, and D. Sheppard-Rund, "Corporate Requirements Analysis," *New Orleans Workshop Data Base Design,* 1978.
2. B. K. Kahn, "A Structured Logical Database Design Methodology," *Proc. NYU Symp. Database Design,* 1978, pp. 15-24.
3. D. C. Burnstine, "The Theory Behind BIAITI Business Information Analysis and Integration Technique," BIAIT International, 1979.
4. T. De Marco, *Structured Analysis and System Specification,* Prentice-Hall, Englewood Cliffs, N.J., 1979.
5. D. Teichroew and A. Hershey, III, "PSL/PSA, A Computer-Aided Technique for Structured Documentation and Analysis of Information Processing Systems," *IEEE Trans. Software Engineering,* Vol. SE-3, No. 1, Jan. 1977, pp. 71-79.
6. G. Myers, *Structured/Composite Design,* John Wiley & Sons, New York, 1979.
7. E. Yourdon and L. Constantin, *Structured Design,* Prentice-Hall, Englewood Cliffs, N.J., 1979.
8. M. W. Alford, "A Requirements Engineering Methodology for Real-Time Processing Requirements," *IEEE Trans. Software Engineering,* Vol. SE-3, No. 1, Jan. 1977, pp. 60-69.
9. D. Sheppard-Rund, *Database Design Methodology—Parts I and II,* Auerbach Data Base Management Series, portfolios 23-01-01 and 02, 1977.
10. P. P. Chen, "The Entity-Relationship Model—Toward a Unified View of Data," *ACM Trans, Database Systems,* Vol. 1, No. 1, Mar. 1976, pp. 9-36.
11. J. R. Abrial, "Data Semantics," in *Database Management,* North-Holland, Amsterdam, 1974, pp. 1-59.
12. N. Roussopoulos, "A Semantic Network Model of Databases," Dept, of Computer Science, University of Toronto, TR-104, PhD dissertation, 1976.
13. N. Roussopoulos, "CSDL: A Conceptual Schema Definition Language for the Design of Data Base Applications," *IEEE Trans. Software Engineering,* Vol. SE-5, No. 5, Sept. 1979, pp. 481-496.
14. J. Mylopoulos, P. A. Bernstein, and H. K. T. Wong, "A Language Facility for Designing Database-Intensive Applications," *ACM Trans. Database Systems,* Vol. 5, 1980, pp. 185-207.
15. M. R. Gustafsson, T. Karlsson, and J. A. Bubenko, "A Declarative Approach to Conceptual Information Modeling," Dept. of Information Processing & Computer Science, The University of Stockholm, Syslab report 8, 1982.
16. J. Sowa, *Conceptual Structures: Information Processing in Mind and Machine,* Addison-Wesley, Reading, Mass., 1984.
17. M. Schkolnick, "Secondary Index Optimization," *Proc. ACM Sigmod,* 1975, pp. 186-192.
18. M. Schkolnick, "Physical Database Techniques," *NYU Symp. Database Design,* 1978.
19. N. Roussopoulos, "View Indexing in Relational Databases," *ACM Trans. Database Systems,* Vol. 7, No. 2, June 1982, pp. 258-290.
20. N. Roussopoulos, "The Logical Access Path Schema of a Database," *IEEE Trans. Software Engineering,* Vol. SE-8, No. 6, Nov. 1982, pp. 563-573.
21. J. A. Bubenko, Jr., "Information Modeling in the Context of System Development," *Proc. IFIP,* 1980, pp. 395-411.
22. *Entity-Relationship Approach to Systems Analysis and Design,* P. P. Chen, ed., North-Holland, Amsterdam, 1980.
23. V. Y. Lum et al., "The 1978 New Orleans Data Base Design Workshop Report," *Proc. Fifth Int'l Conf. Very Large Data Bases,* ACM Press, New York, 1979, pp. 328-350.
24. D. C. Tsichritzis and F. H. Lockovsky, "Designing the Data Base," *Datamation,* Vol. 24, No. 28, 1978, pp. 147-151.
25. D. C. Tshichritzis and F. H. Lockovsky, *Data Models,* Prentice Hall, Englewood Cliffs, N.J., 1982.
26. N. Roussopoulos and J. Mylopoulos, "Using Semantic Networks for Database Management," *Proc., First Int'l Conf. Very Large Databases,* ACM Press, New York, 1975.
27. N. Roussopoulos "ADD: Algebraic Data Definition," *Sixth Texas Conf. Computing Systems,* University Press, Austin, Tex., 1977.
28. H. Weber, The D-Graph Model of Large Shared Data Bases: A Representation of Integrity Constraints and Views as Abstract Data Types, IBM Research Report RJ1875, IBM Corp. San Jose, Calif., Nov. 1976.
29. M. Hammer and D. McLeod, "Database Description With SDM: A Semantic Database Model," *ACM Trans. Database Systems,* Vol. 6, No. 3, Sept. 1981.
30. J. Sowa, "Conceptual Graphs for a Database Interface," *IBM J. Research and Development,* Vol. 20, No. 4, July 1976.

31. E. Falkenberg, "Concepts for Modeling Information," in *Modeling in Data Base Management Systems,* G. M. Nijssen, ed., North-Holland, Amsterdam, 1976.
32. J. M. Smith and D. C. P. Smith, "Database Abstractions: Aggregation and Generalization," *ACM Trans. Database Systems,* Vol. 2, No. 2, 1977.
33. M. L. Brodie, "The Application of Data Types to Database Semantic Integrity," *Information Systems,* Vol. 5, 1980, pp. 287-296.
34. S. K. Chang and W. H. Cheng, "Database Skeleton and Its Application to Logical Database Synthesis," *IEEE Trans. Software Engineering,* Vol. SE-4, No. 1, Jan. 1978, pp. 18-30.
35. S. K. Chang, and J. S. Ke, "Translation of Fuzzy Queries," *IEEE Trans. Pattern Analysis and Machine Intelligence,* Vol. PAMI-1, No. 3, July 1979.
36. N. Roussopoulos and R. T. Yeh, *Logical Database Design,* NBS final report, National Bureau of Standards, Washington, DC, Feb. 1982.
37. U. Dayal and P. A. Bernstein, "On the Updatability of Relational Views," *Proc. Fourth Int'l. Conf. Very Large Databases,* ACM Press, New York, 1978.
38. F. M. Bancilhon and N. Spyratos, "Update Semantics of Relational Views," *ACM Trans. Database Systems,* Vol. 6, No. 4, Dec. 1981, pp. 557-575.
39. A. M. Keller, "Updates to Relational Databases Through Views Involving Joins," *Second Int'l Conf. Databases,* Academic Press, New York, 1982, pp. 363-384.
40. K. Y. Whang, G. Wiederhold, and D. Sagalowicz, "Separability: An Approach to Physical Database Design," *Proc. Seventh Int'l Conf. Very Large Databases,* ACM Press, New York, 1981, pp. 320-332.
41. R. Masri and G. Wiederhold "Data Model Integration Using the Stuctural Model," *Proc. ACM-Sigmod Conf.* Bernstein, ed., 1979, pp. 191-202.
42. K. M. Chandy, "Models of Distributed Systems," *Proc. Third Int'l Conf. Very Large Databases,* ACM Press, New York, 1977, pp. 105-120.

**Nicholas Roussopoulos** is an assistant professor of computer science at the University of Maryland. His research interests include database design and conceptual modeling of information systems, distributed databases, software engineering, and artificial intelligence. He has held positions at the IBM Research Lab and the University of Texas at Austin. Roussopoulos received a BA in mathematics from the University of Athens, and an MS and PhD in computer science from the University of Toronto.

**Raymond T. Yeh** is professor of computer sciences at the University of Maryland. He has served as chairman of the Computer Science Departments at the Universities of Maryland and Texas at Austin. He was also director of the Center for Information Sciences Research at Maryland. Yeh received a BS in electrical engineering, an MA in mathematics, and a PhD in mathematics from the University of Illinois. He is the founding editor-in-chief of IEEE *Transactions on Software Engineering*.

Questions about this article can be addressed to either author, Dept. of Computer Sciences, University of Maryland, College Park, MD 20742.

# Integrating User Views in Database Design

Shamkant Navathe, University of Florida
Ramez Elmasri, University of Houston
James Larson, Honeywell Computer Sciences Center

**View integration is key to the design of databases that must be accessed by several classes of users—all with different requirements.**

Designing a database is an important data engineering activity, and view integration is one of the important phases in logical database design. During this phase, the individual views designed by separate user groups are integrated into a conceptual schema for the entire organization.

Views of data may originate from two sources:[1]

- *User views*—The perception of users about what a proposed database (or an ideal database) should contain.
- *Existing database schemas*—The description of data in an existing information system, either manual or automated.

User view integration is applicable to initial design, while existing schema integration applies to existing databases. Here, view integration refers to the activity of designing a global structure (integrated schema) starting from individual component structures (views).

We feel that view integration can be accomplished only with interactive design tools and a continuous dialog with the designer. Integration is thus somewhat subjective, with the designer helping to resolve semantic conflicts. The main goal in view integration is to aid the designer in identifying possible ways of integration and to help him resolve inconsistencies while working with large, real-life problems. The best mode of operation is an interactive design tool environment in which the system is strictly an aid. The Incod system[2] is an example of such an environment.

## The Entity-Category-Relationship data model

Any design methodology similar to that illustrated by the figure in the box at right must be based on some underlying data model. A data model is the basis for describing the structure of data and operations on that structure. The data model also provides notation that allows concise data descriptions and statements about interrelationships. A methodology that is general in scope ought to use a model general enough to describe a large variety of situations.

We have adopted a model called the Entity-Category-Relationship (E-C-R) model,[3,4] which is an extension of the popular Entity-Relationship (E-R) model proposed by Chen.[5] These models and several others, which are sometimes classified as conceptual data models, tend to describe the semantics of data by classifying the application domain into entities (which may be objects, events, things, con-

EH0252-7/87/0000/0185$01.00 © 1986 IEEE

Reprinted from *Computer*, January 1986, pages 50-62. Copyright © 1986 by The Institute of Electrical and Electronics Engineers, Inc.

cepts) and relationships among the entities.

The E-C-R model includes the following extensions to the E-R model:

(1) The concept of a category is introduced to represent generalization hierarchies[6] and subclasses.[7]

(2) Structural constraints on relationships are used to specify how entities may participate in relationships.

The E-C-R model, like the E-R model, views the world as consisting of entities and relationships among entities. Entities and relationships have attributes that provide information. Entities with similar basic attributes are classified into *entity types*. For example, the particular car with registration number XXY-123 is an entity; whereas a set of cars defines an entity type. Entity types are disjoint in that a given entity can be a member of only one entity type.

A *category* is a subset of entities from an entity type. (This definition serves our purposes here. A more precise definition is available elsewhere.[3]) Categories allow the representation of generalization hierarchies. In Figure 1, the categories Car and Truck are subsets of Vehicle. Each entity in the Car and Truck categories is also an entity of Vehicle, and although the categories share most attributes, a few are not shared. Tonnage applies only to Truck while Car Type applies only to Car. Note that both entity types and categories are sets of entities. A set of entities is called an *object class*, whether the set is an entity type or a category.

A *relationship* associates entities from two or more object classes. A collection of relationships involving the same object classes is called a relationship set. For semantic integrity, rules exist in the real-world situation that govern the possible ways in which entities of an object class can participate in a relationship. We call these rules the *structural constraints* of the relationship. We can specify a type of

## Database design

Designing a large database for a commercial, industrial, or government enterprise is a difficult task. A frequently suggested approach,* illustrated at right, consists of the following steps:

**1. Design views of data.** Each group of anticipated users analyze their requirements and specify their view of the data as a schema. Each view describes some of the database entities, attributes, and relationships between entities in a format convenient for a specific class of users. Various types of data dependencies and normalization rules may be used in designing each view.

**2. Combine individual views into an integrated conceptual schema.** The integrated schema describes all data to be contained in the database and is usually specified in the same data model as the views in step 1. This step is frequently difficult because the entities in different views do not always align easily. The reason is that different user classes have different requirements that result in different perceptions about the data structure.

**3. Map the integrated conceptual schema to a logical schema.** The logical schema is expressed in terms of the data model supported by the enterprise's database management system. This step bridges the conceptual modeling of steps 1 and 2 to the style of modeling specific to the enterprise's database management system.

**4. Design the physical data structures and access paths and implement the database.** Implementation is based on the options available in the enterprise's database management system. This step is frequently performed by system specialists using sophisticated software tools to derive the physical representation and structure of the database that minimizes the storage costs and response times of frequently executed requests.

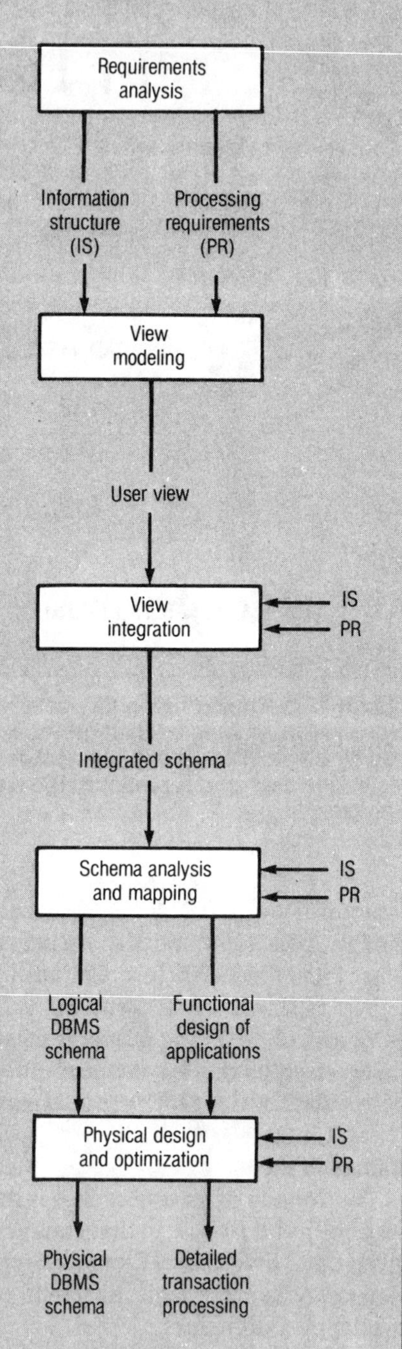


**Overall database design methodology.**

*S. Navathe and S. Gadgil, "A Methodology for View Integration in Logical Database Design," *Proc. Eighth Very Large Data Base Conf.*, Sept. 1982, pp. 142-152.

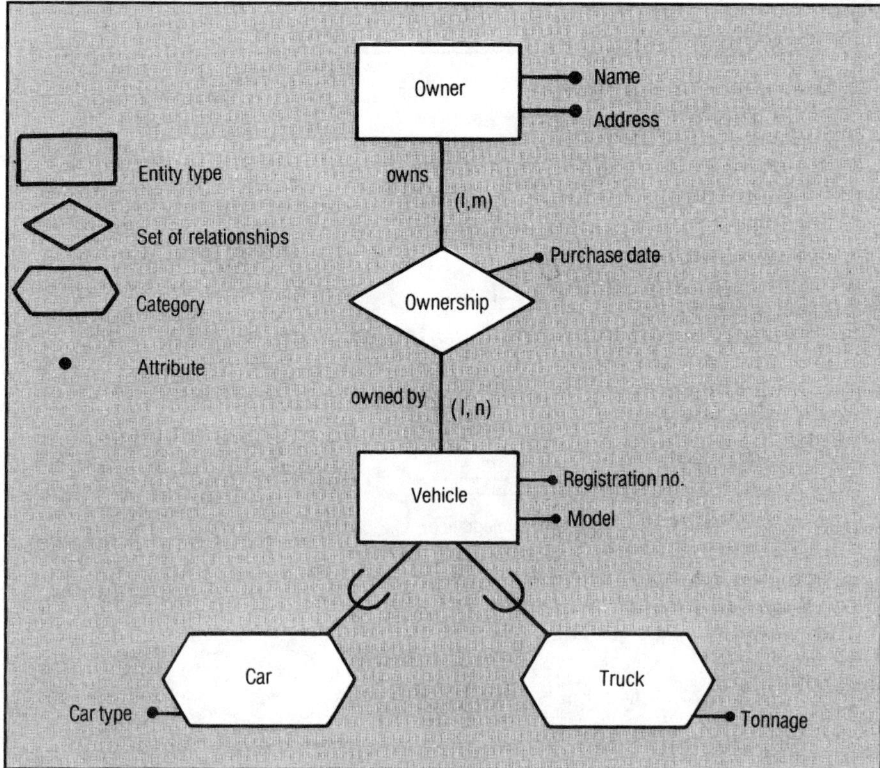


**Figure 1.** Example of an entity-category-relationship (E-C-R) schema. Entity types are in rectangles, categories are in hexagons, and attributes are identified by black dots. The ⊂ symbol means that car and truck are subsets of Vehicle. The diamond represents the set of relationships between Owner and Vehicle.

structural constraint, called a cardinality constraint, on the participation of an object class in a relationship by two numbers ($i1$, $i2$), where $0 \leq i1 \leq i2$ and $i2 > 0$. The numbers mean that each entity that is a member of the object class must participate in at least $i1$, and in at most $i2$ relationship instances in the relationship set.

The *domain* of an object class is the set of object instances in that class at a given time. Two classes from different views may have the same, different, or overlapping domains.

## The view integration framework

Figure 2 shows the overall framework for a view integration environment. This framework can be interpreted both in a manual and semiautomated context, but we are interested in automating as much of the process as possible. A semiautomated view integration environment requires an interactive system with continuous designer interaction in addition to the following input: views, intra- and inter-view assertions, and an integration policy or a priority ranking of views.

Output of the view integration includes the integrated schema and mappings between each view and the integrated schema and statements of conflicts among views. A data dictionary system may be used to manage both input and output.

The view integration system drives the integration process by repeatedly calling on the object class integration module and the relationship integration module (Figure 2). We have designed such a system and are currently implementing it.

The problem of integrating relationship sets is closely tied to that of integrating object classes. These two types of integrations can be invoked repeatedly one after another. However, for ease of presentation, we apply object class integration first as much as possible and then deal with relationship integration.

## The view integration process

**Preintegration.** The preintegration phase establishes a number of assertions and correspondences among individual views. The first is to establish naming correspondences for object classes and attributes. The problems encountered here are that synonyms occur when classes with different names represent the same concept, and homonyms occur when the names are the same but different concepts are represented. An automated tool could be developed to assist designers in establishing class correspondences by comparing the strings for class names. This solution works well for homonyms. However, because different views can have different synonyms that are not easily detected by inspection, the synonym information must be specified to the schema integration system in the form of assertions by the designer. The ultimate responsibility for establishing similar classes falls on the database designers.

Another purpose of the preintegration phase of view integration is to define the candidate keys and domains for each object class. By candidate key, we mean a set of attributes whose values can potentially serve to uniquely identify each entity. The domain refers to all instances of the class at some given time. For example, if one view uses the term Domestic-Customer to mean all customers in the US, while another view uses the term Buyer to refer to exactly the same set of customers, then the domains of these two object classes are identical. That is,

Dom(Domestic-Customer) = Dom(Buyer).

The domain equality essentially guarantees that two object classes refer to the same real-world concept. In our methodology, the designer is asked to supply this information for pairs of object classes from different views.

Also, in the preintegration phase, precise relationships between the domains of pairs of classes from different views are specified as one of the following possibilities:

Case 1: Identical domains:
Dom(A) = Dom(B)
Case 2: Contained domains:
Either Dom(A) ⊆ Dom(B) or
Dom(B) ⊆ Dom(A)
Case 3: Overlapping domains: No constraints are known to hold on the domains.
Case 4: Disjoint domains:
Dom(A) ∩ Dom(B) = ∅

These domain assertions are specified when they hold on the domains of the object classes at every moment in time. Again, it is the database designer's responsibility to specify the exact correspondence between pairs of object classes.

Finally, the preintegration phase involves specifying mappings between equivalent attributes of corresponding object classes. If two corresponding object classes contain similar attributes, but the attributes are expressed in different units, then a mapping must be specified between the two attributes. For example, if the distance attribute of object class Travel is expressed in kilometers, and the distance attribute of object class Trip is expressed in miles, then a mapping function converting kilometers to miles (or miles to kilometers) must be specified.

As another example, suppose the Student object class has candidate key student-number and the Graduate-Student object class has composite candidate key department and student-name. The correspondences between values of the two candidate keys may be stored in a lexicon (a type of cross reference) as suggested by Wiederhold and Elmasri.[8,9]

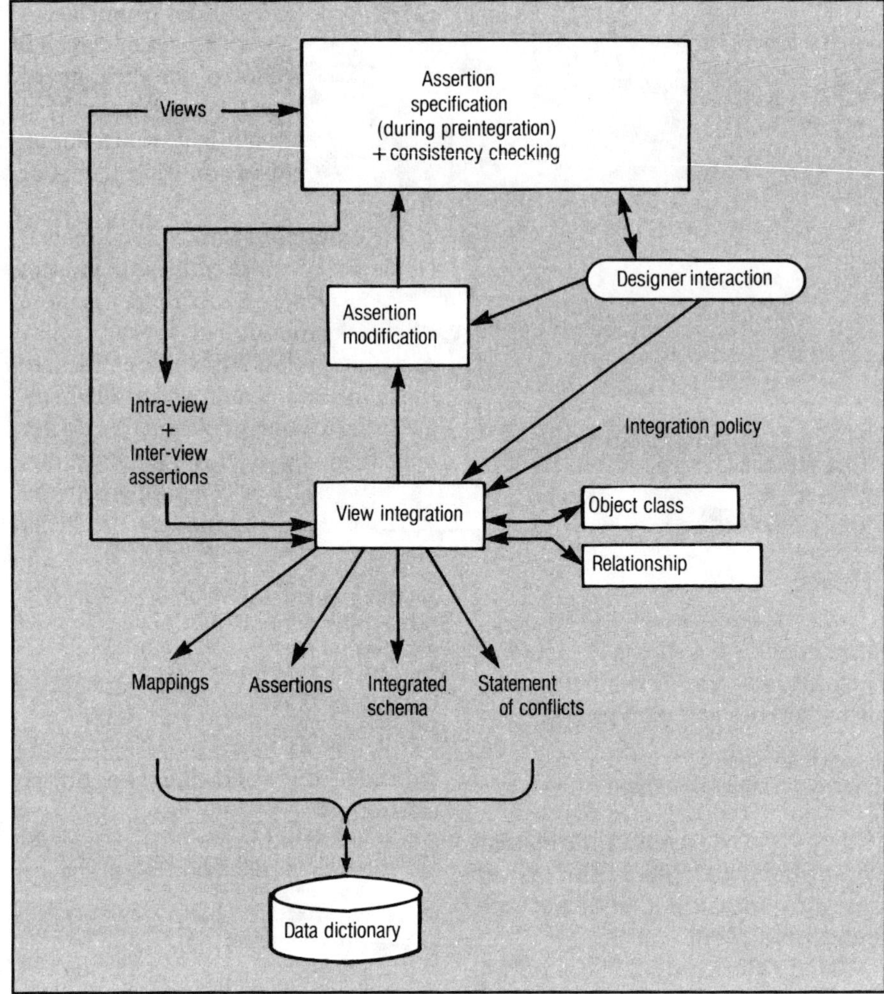


**Figure 2.** General framework for a view integration system.

Once the equivalence of attributes and the domain assertions that describe the correspondences of object classes have been specified, we can integrate object classes that represent similar concepts.

**Integration of similar object classes.** We shall first consider the integration of two object classes, $A$ and $B$, and then generalize to the case in which $n$ similar classes from several views are integrated. Let Attrs($A$) be the set of attributes of class $A$. We assume that equivalent attributes in different views have been identified and are given the same name.

Below are the different possibilities of each of the four cases identified earlier. In each case, the integrated schema is designed to represent both views correctly and to limit redundancy in the integrated schema. By limiting redundancy, fewer problems arise with update anomalies.

*Identical domains.* We are guaranteed that object classes in both views are the same at all times. A single class $C$ is created in the integrated schema. Its attributes are the union of the attributes of class $A$ and class $B$.

*Contained domains.* If Dom ($A$) ⊂ Dom($B$), then the integrated schema will have two classes: class $A1$ and class $B1$, where class $A1$ is a subset of class $B1$. This relationship—$A1$ is a

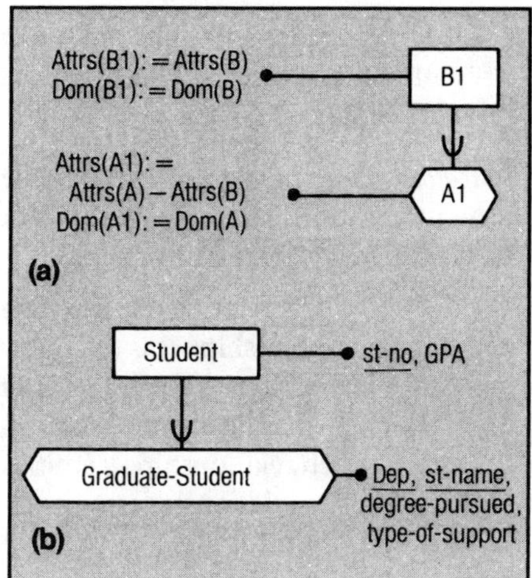


**Figure 3.** Object integration with contained domains.

category of $B1$—is shown in Figure 3a. The attributes are distributed among the two classes as follows:

Attrs(B1) : = Attrs(B)
Attrs(A1) : = Attrs(A) – Attrs(B)

where – (set difference) means that the attributes of object class $A1$ are those attributes of $A$ that do not have equivalent attributes in $B$.

All individual entities in class $B$ will exist in class $B1$ in the integrated schema. Entities in class $A$ will exist in category $A1$. More formally,

Dom(A1) : = Dom(A)
Dom(B1) : = Dom(B)

Consider the following two object classes:

Graduate-Student (dep, st-name, degree-pursued, GPA, type-of-support)
Student (st-no, GPA)

The attributes of each object class are shown in parentheses, and the key attributes are underlined. Obviously, Dom(Graduate-Student) $\subset$ Dom(Student). The result of integrating these two object classes is shown in Figure 3b.

*Overlapping domains.* In the integrated schema, we create three object classes. The first, class $AB$, includes the union of the entities from class $A$ and class $B$. The attributes of class $AB$ are the intersection of the attributes of class $A$ and class $B$ because an entity in class $AB$ might not have values for an attribute that exists only in either $A$ or $B$.

Two subsets of class $AB$ are created: (1) class $A1$, whose entities are those in class $A$ and whose attributes are those of class A that do not appear in class $AB$, and (2) class $B1$, whose entities are those in class $B$ and whose attributes are the attributes of class $B$ that do not appear in class $AB$. Figure 4a shows this case. The relationships between the views and the integrated schema are

Attrs(AB) : = Attrs(A) $\cap$ Attrs(B)
Attrs(A1) : = Attrs(A) – Attrs(AB)
Attrs(B1) : = Attrs(B) – Attrs(AB)
Dom(AB) : = Dom(A) $\cup$ Dom(B)
Dom(A1) : = Dom(A)
Dom(B1) : = Dom(B)

Consider the following two object classes:

Graduate-Student (dep, name, age, degree-pursued)
Instructor (dep, name, SSN, age, salary, experience)

Assume that some but not all graduate students may be instructors (and not all instructors are graduate students). The result of integrating these two object classes is shown in Figure 4b.

*Disjoint domains.* In this case, even though the object classes are specified similar by the designer, they never have entities in common. The designer must then decide whether to attempt to merge the two classes or to keep them as separate classes in the integrated schema. One decision criterion is whether the object classes have any attributes in common. Even when they have common attributes, the designer may not want to integrate them. For example, suppose we have the following two classes:

Full-Professor (dep, name, salary)
Graduate-Student (dep, name, salary, yrs-service)

Even though object classes Full-Professor and Graduate-Student share most of their attributes, the designer will probably not wish to integrate them because these classes represent different real-world concepts. On the other hand, the object classes

Secretary ( empno, sal, name, grade)
Engineer ( empno, sal, name, engineer-type)

may be integrated as Employee even though their domains are always disjoint.

When two object classes share some attributes, and the designer decides that they should be integrated, then they may be integrated in the same way as overlapping domains. The only difference is that class $A1$ and class $B1$ are disjoint in the integrated schema.

**Integration of different object classes.** The integration rules just described can be generalized to the integration of $n$ object classes in a similar

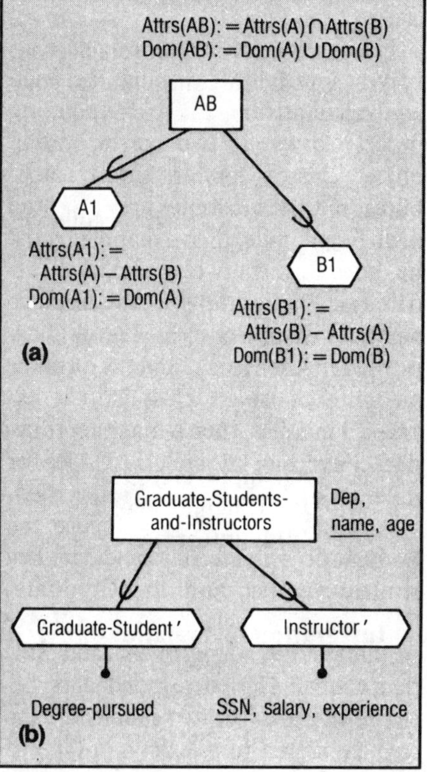


**Figure 4.** Object integration with intersecting domains.

way. Consider the integration of *n* object classes (*A*1,...,*An*) from *n* different views. Binary integration can be done repeatedly, but some domain relationships may allow simultaneous *n*ary integration. To give a flavor for what sort of strategy may be developed for *n*ary integration, we present the simple case of contained domains. (A detailed discussion of all four cases is presented elsewhere.[10])

Here we have a total ordering on the object classes. The integrated schema will have *n* object classes (*A'*1,...,*A'n*), where *A'*1 is a subset of *A'*2, *A'*2 is a subset of *A'*3,..., and *A'n* − 1 is a subset of *A'n*. This ordering is shown in Figure 5a.

Attributes are distributed among the *n* classes as follows:

Attrs(A'n) := Attrs(An)
Attrs(A'n−1) := Attrs(An−1) −Attrs(An)
Attrs(A'n−2) := Attrs(An−2)
  −{(Attrs(An−1) ∪ Attrs(An)}
.
.
.
Attrs(A'1) := Attrs(A1) − {Attrs(A2) ∪
  Attrs(A3) ∪ . . . ∪ Attrs(An)}

For entities, the relationship between the views and the conceptual schema is described by

Dom(Ai') := Dom(Ai); i=(1, . . . ,n)

For example, consider the following object classes in three different views:

Employees (SSN, empname, sal, bdate)
Engineers (SSN, empname, sal, bdate,
  degree, engtype)
Engineering-Managers (SSN, empname,
  sal, bdate,

Here, Dom(Employees) ⊃ Dom(Engineers) ⊃ Dom(Engineering-Managers). The resulting integrated schema is shown in Figure 5b.

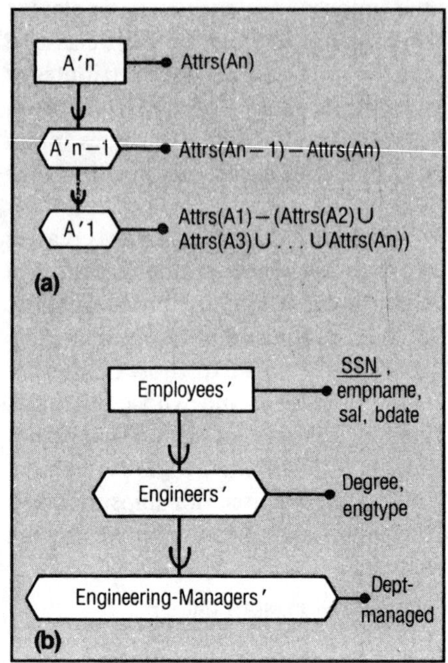


**Figure 5.** Integration of multiple objects with contained domains.

**Integration of relationships.** In Figure 2, we indicated that the view integration module repeatedly calls on both the object class integration module and the relationship integration module. Relationship integration involves integrating the relationship sets that were associated with the object classes integrated during object integration.

*The relationship integration problem.* Previous approaches concentrate on aligning or accommodating the structures from different views.[11,12] We consider both semantic as well as structural information in analyzing the integration of relationship sets. Designer input is necessary to supply this semantic information.

Given an object class *A*1 in view *V*1, whenever a similar or compatible object class *A*2 is in view *V*2, all relationship sets in which *A*1 participates become potentially subject to integration with all relationship sets in which *A*2 participates. The actual merging of the relationship sets, however, is subject to the semantics, which are determined by the roles of the object classes and the degree and cardinality constraints of the relationship sets. Only after semantic scrutiny of these relationships can some be integrated.

We integrate two relationship sets at a time. Simultaneous integration of *n* relationship sets is an extension of our present methodology, which we are now investigating.

*Relationship set classification.* For view integration, relationship sets can be classified by three characteristics:

(1) Degree of a relationship set. The degree of a relationship set is the number of object classes (not necessarily distinct) participating in the relationship set. In each relationship, *n* entities participate in a relationship set of degree *n*. Relationship sets of degree greater than two may be desirable when more than two entities participate in a single event.

(2) Roles in a relationship set. A role name signifies the role played by an object class in a relationship set. Every object class participating in a relationship set is given a distinct role name prior to integration. As discussed earlier, the preintegration phase establishes correspondences among role names. Two relationship sets from different views having the same degree are equivalent if both role names and the relationship instances correspond. (Some database query languages directly support role names in their selection expressions.[14] Both view modeling and data retrieval are facilitated for the end user if role names are used.)

(3) Structural constraints. A relationship set between two object classes is a mapping that associates the instances from one object class with instances from other object classes. Any specification rules supported by the data model to express the constraints are called structural constraints. Cardinality constraints are one type of structural constraint used in the integration process.

*Merging relationship sets of the same degree and same role.* The three aspects just described provide the framework (Figure 6) for classifying pairs of relationship sets for possible integration. The terminal nodes of this hierarchical structure represent possible outcomes when relationship sets from different views are compared.

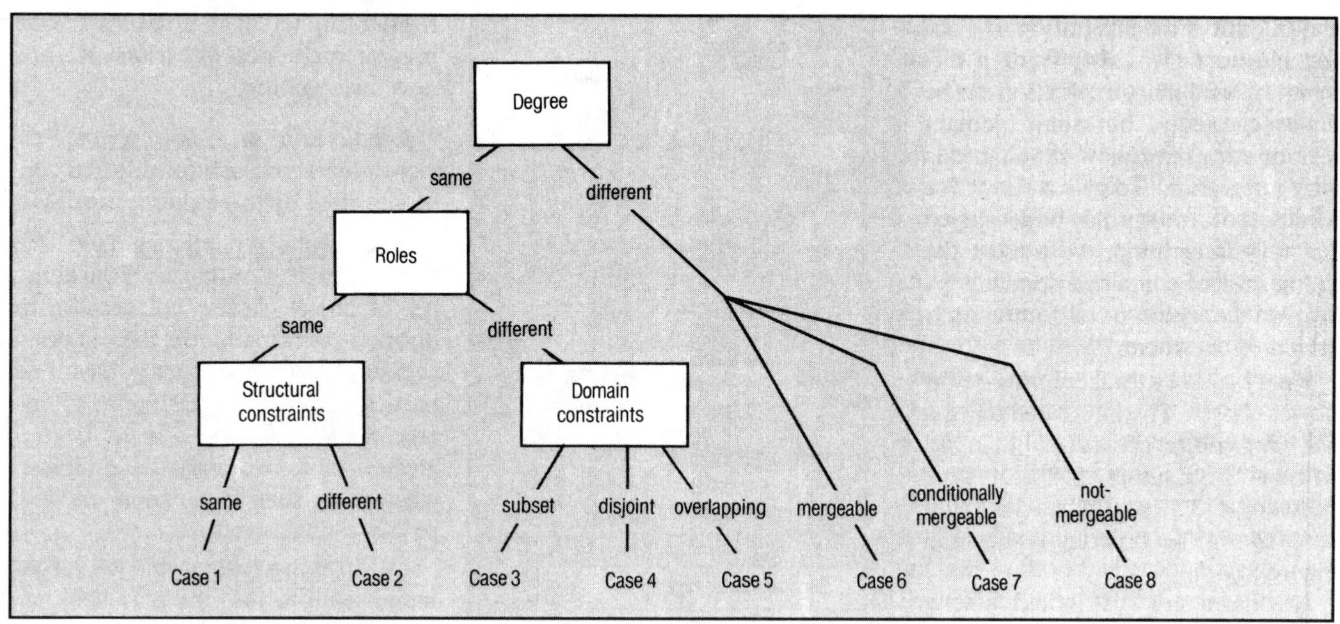


**Figure 6.** Classification of cases for relationship integration.

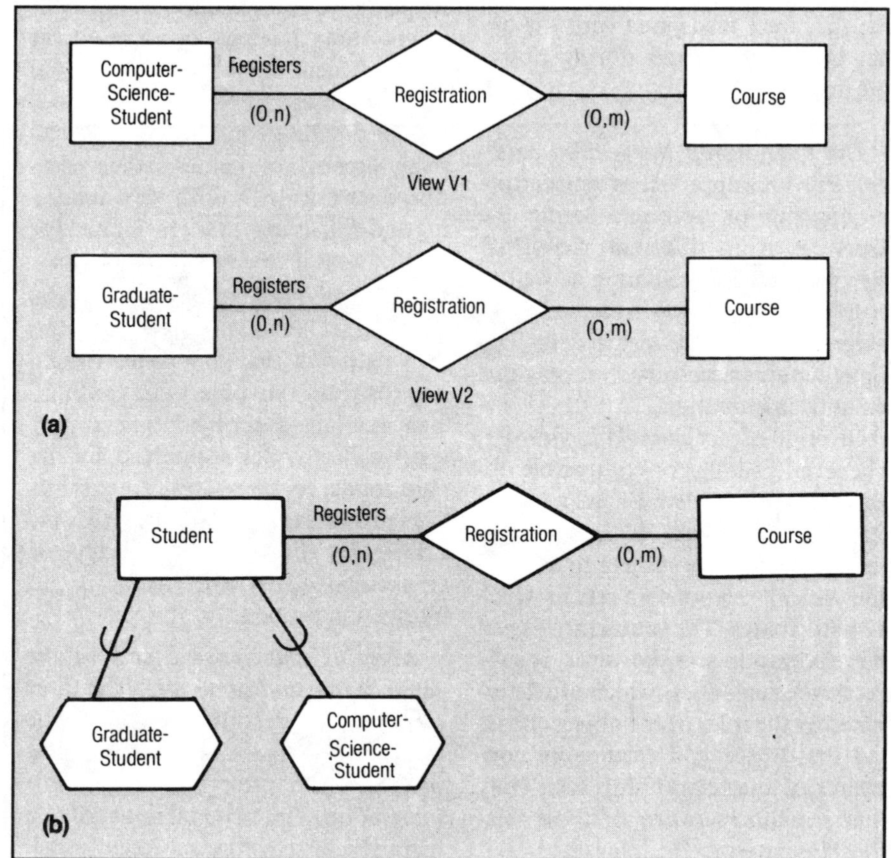


**Figure 7.** Relationship set integration—Case 1: Same role, same structural constraints.

Case 1: Same structural constraints. This case is the simplest form of relationship set integration. Only one relationship set is placed in the integrated schema. Figure 7a shows the two input views, where the domains of the entity types Graduate-Student and Computer-Science-Student overlap. The integrated schema (Figure 7b) uses two categories called Graduate-Student and Computer-Science-Student and a single relationship set, Registration.

Case 2: Different structural constraints. In this case, one view is more constrained than the other. Consider Figure 8, where the relationship sets being integrated have different cardinality constraints. In the first view, some students are included who are possibly not currently enrolled in any courses. This view is held by the Registrar's Office. The second view is held by the Accounting Office. In this view, only currently enrolled students are included. In the integrated schema, a category Registered-Student is created to contain all the students participating in the Enrollment relationship set. Any Student entity participating in the Enrollment relationship set is automatically made a member of the Registered-Student category.

*Merging relationship sets with different roles.* Different roles in relationship sets typically convey different semantics. However, in many cases, the relationship sets may still be considered mergeable. Relationship sets that occur among the same participating object classes in two views are definite candidates for integration. As shown in Figure 6, depending on the domains of the relationship sets, we consider three possibilities: *subset* (occurrences of one relationship set are always contained in the other), *disjoint* (occurrences of two relationship sets are always disjoint), and *overlapping* (occurrences of two relationships sets can overlap).

Case 3: Subset relationship. In Figure 9a, the relationship set Advisor in view *V1* is a subset of the relationship set Committee in view *V2* in the sense that all pairs of instances <student, faculty> in the Advisor relationship set are included in the pairs of instances <student, faculty> in the Committee relationship set. The integrated schema in Figure 9b contains a new subrelationship notation with double lines between the relationship sets Committee and Advisor. This set-subset association should be interpreted as an integrity constraint: that is, inserting a new pair in Advisor implies that it must be inserted into Committee; deleting the committee member who is also an advisor implies deleting Advisor.

Case 4: Disjoint relationships. Two relationships among the same pair of entity classes in two views may be completely disjoint as illustrated by the Major-Dept, Minor-Dept relationship sets in Figure 10a. When the relationship sets in the views convey different semantics and are unrelated, then both relationship sets are included in the integrated schema without any modifications, as shown in the integrated schema of Figure 10b.

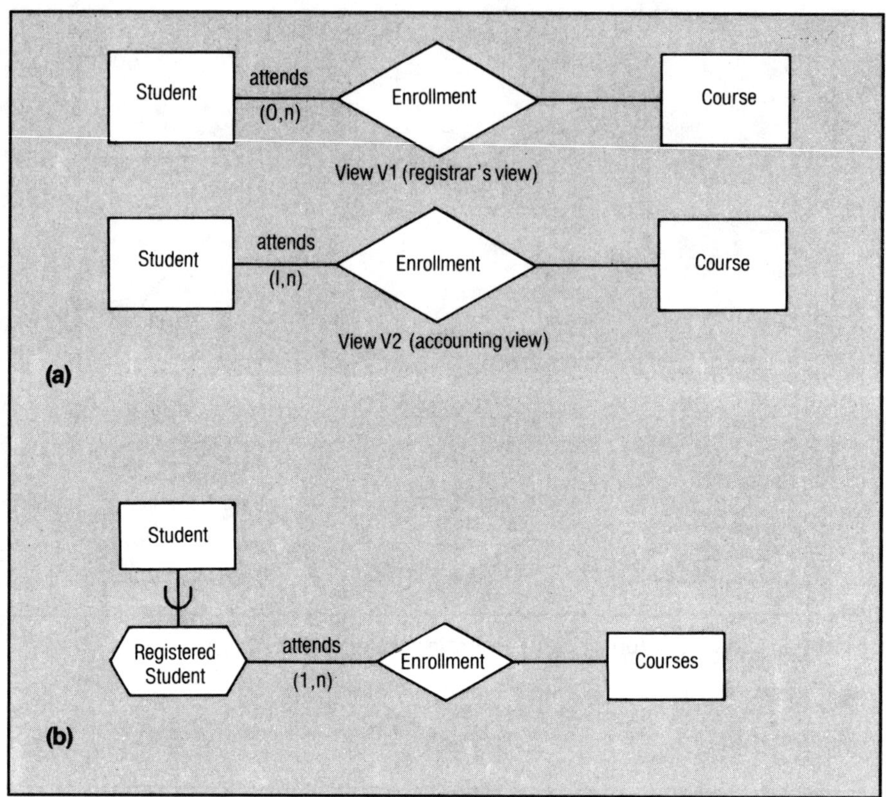


**Figure 8.** Relationship set integration—Case 2: Same role, different structural constraints.

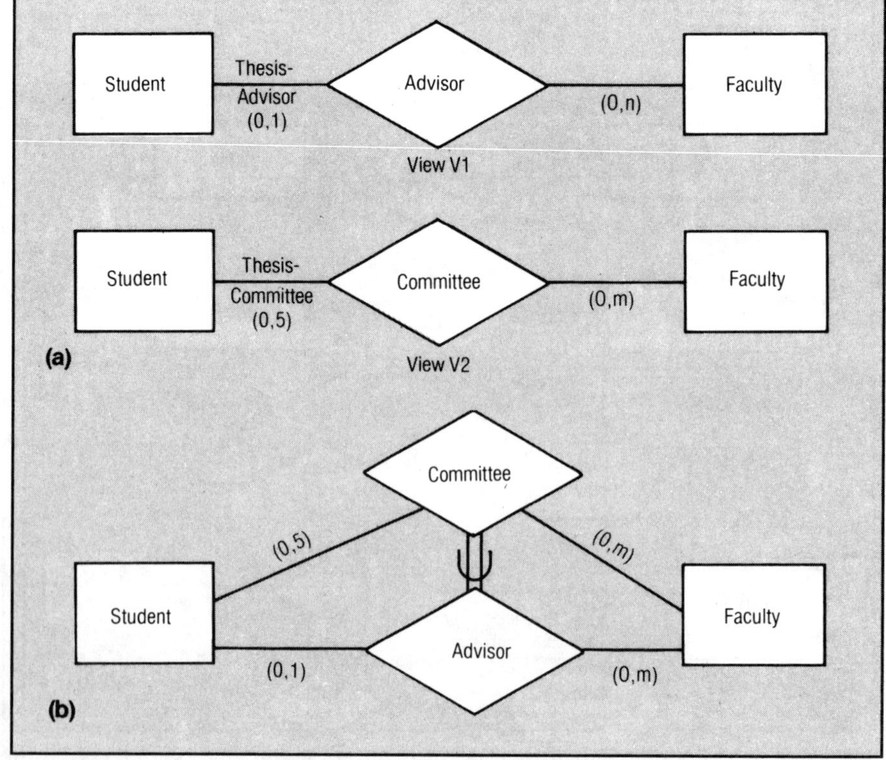


**Figure 9.** Relationship set integration—Case 3: Subset relationship sets.

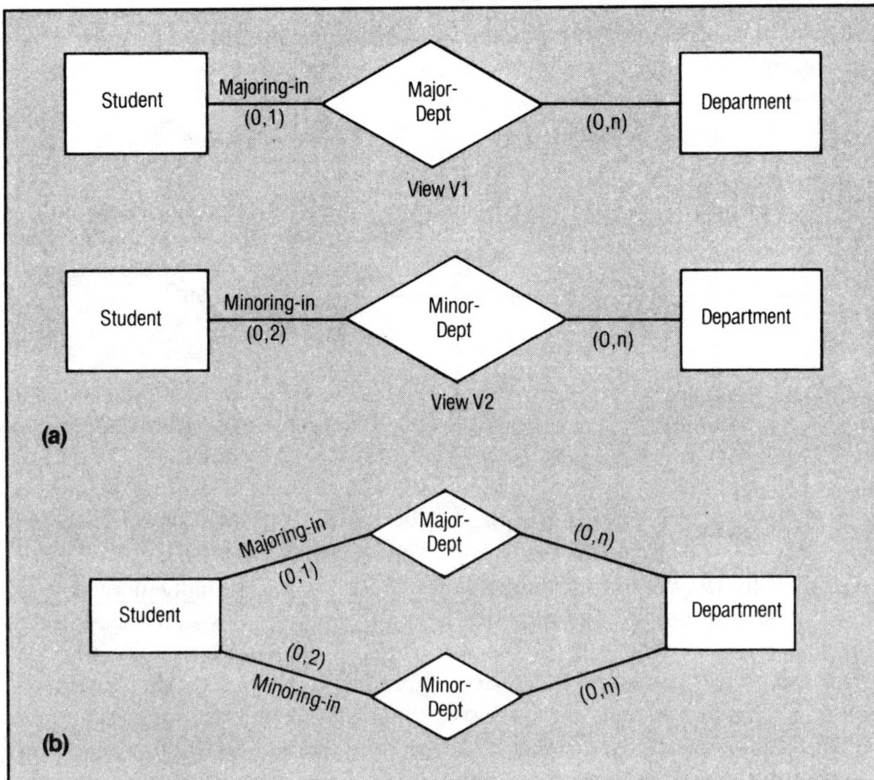


**Figure 10.** Relationship set integration—Case 4: Disjoint relationship sets.

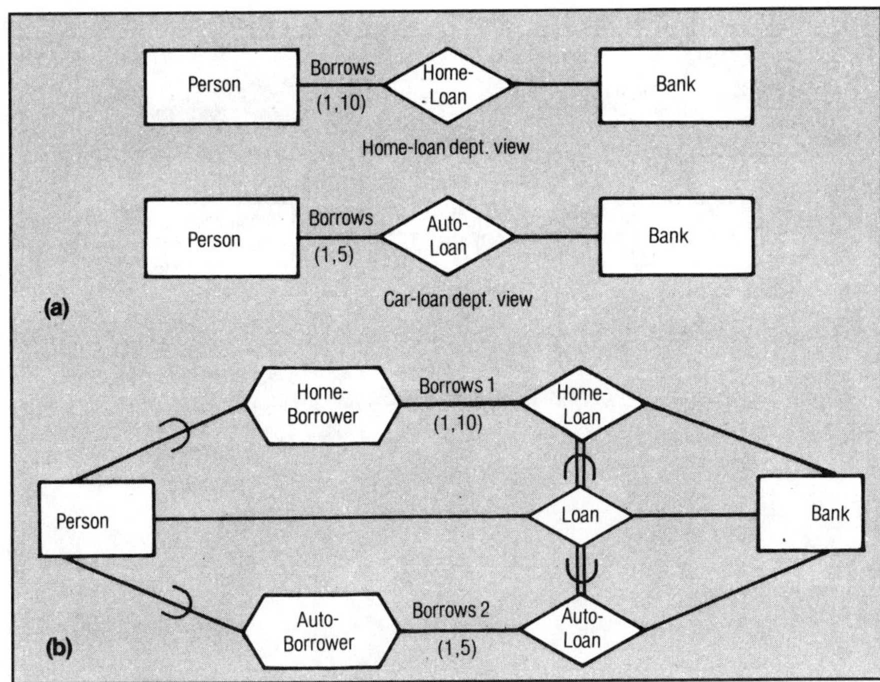


**Figure 11.** Relationship set integration—Case 5: Overlapping relationship sets.

Case 5: Overlapping relationships. Relationship sets described between the same pairs of object classes in two views could have some common instances, but neither of the relationship sets in the views may be a subrelationship of the other. Consider the views shown in Figure 11a. The relationship sets Home-Loan and Auto-Loan are potentially overlapping in that they may relate some common pairs of <person, bank>. Moreover, the domains of the Person entity class in the two views themselves are overlapping. The entities Person in the two views would be categorized (during object class integration) into Home-Borrower and Auto-Borrower, depending on the distinct borrow role they perform. The result of relationship integration after this object class integration is shown in Figure 11b.

*Merging relationship sets of different degree.* The degree of a relationship set refers to the number of object classes participating in it. A number of possibilities must be considered during the integration of relationship sets of different degree. The first is derivable relationships. The relationship set $R2$ of lower degree may be derivable from one of a higher degree, $R1$, in the following sense: Instances of $R2$ can be projected (as in Codd's relational model[15]) from $R1$, or instances of $R2$ can be generated from instances of $R1$ by some high-level language specification such as SQL[13] or GORDAS.[14]

The second possibility is that different relationship sets can be made compatible by enforcing additional semantic constraints. These constraints are of the following types:

- Cardinality constraints among three or more entity classes. Lenzerini and Santucci[16] provide some good examples of different cardinality constraints.
- Set-subset constraints among entity classes.
- Derivability constraints to make one view derivable from the other under certain conditions. These

constraints would take the form of more complex specifications that can be given using higher level languages.

The last possibility that must be considered during relationship integration is that if the different relationship sets cannot be dealt with in either of the first two possibilities, then they coexist separately in the integrated schema.

On the basis of these possibilities, Figure 6 classifies relationships of different degree into three classes: *mergeable* (when they exactly correspond or are derivable), *conditionally mergeable* (when they are derivable subject to constraints), or *not mergeable*.

When integrating relationship sets of different degree, we propose that the higher degree relationship set always appear in the integrated schema. Any attempt to derive the higher degree relationship sets by combining lower degree relationship sets using operators from high-level languges has to be carefully evaluated case-by-case by the designer. If the full semantics of the relationship is not understood, spurious results are possible.

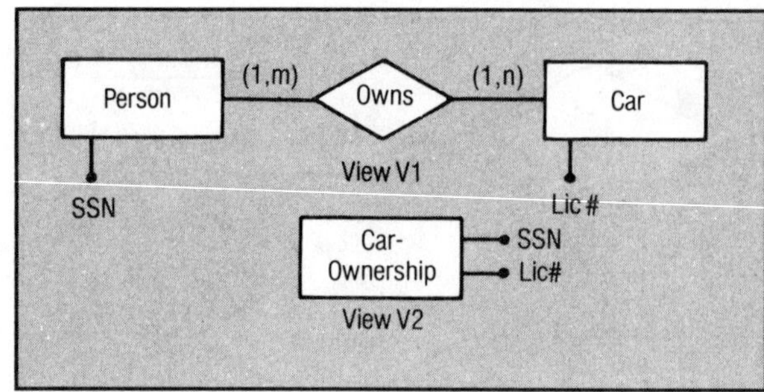


**Figure 12.** Relationship set integration—Case 6: Mergeable relationship sets.

Case 6: Mergeable relationship sets of different degree. In this category, we include pairs of relationship sets of different degree that represent essentially the same information. The equivalency of two representations has to be confirmed by the designer. Figure 12 shows such a situation. The relationship set Owns is of degree 2; the other relationship set is of degree 1. (By degree 1, we mean that the relationship set is an entity class itself.) In view *V*2, the entity Car-Ownership does not have any implicit cardinality constraints as far as the relationship between Person (as identified by Lic#) and Car (as identified by SSN) is concerned; that is, it may be considered to be many-to-many. Therefore, views *V*2 and *V*1 are equivalent. The result of integration in this case is the same as the relationship set in view *V*1, and *V*2 can be derived from *V*1.

Case 7: Conditionally mergeable relationship sets. Two relationship sets can be integrated because the lower degree relationship set is derivable from the higher degree relationship set, and some additional derivability conditions hold. In a view integration system, such an integration has to be initiated by the designer with the knowledge that the derivability holds and that the conditions under which it holds are ac-

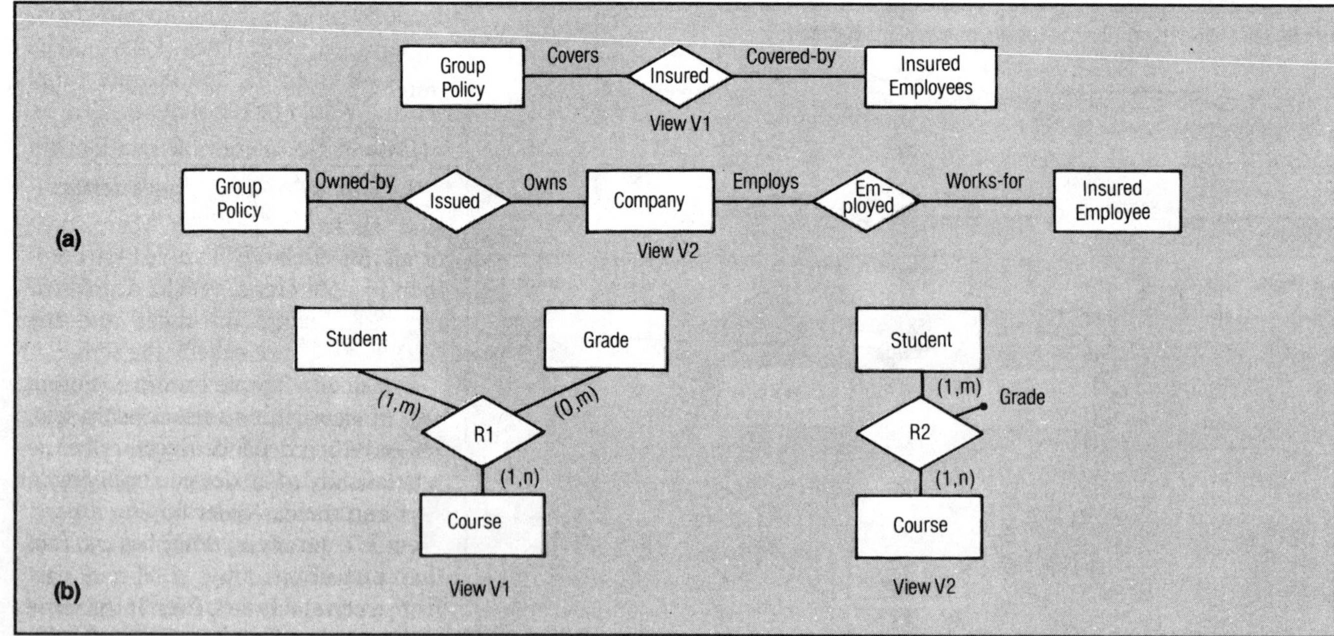


**Figure 13.** Relationship set integration—Case 7: Conditionally mergeable relationship sets.

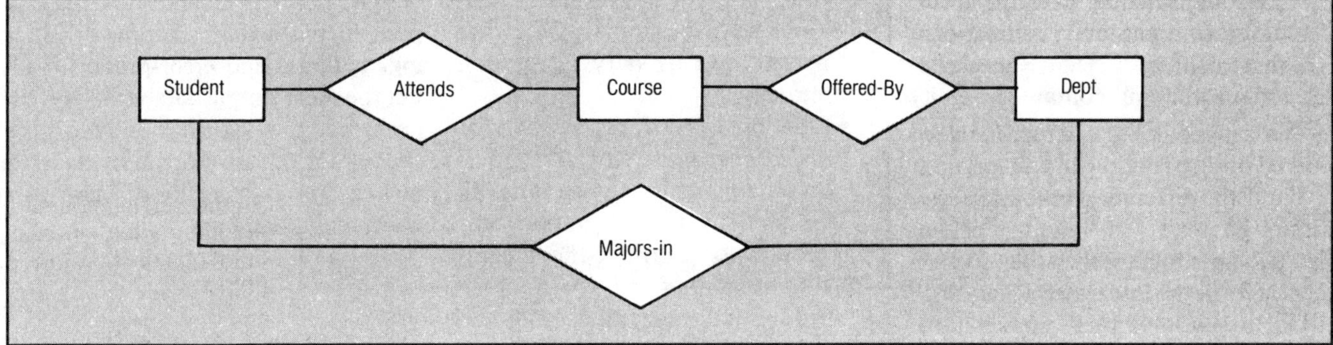

Figure 14. Relationship set integration—Case 8: Not-mergeable relationship sets.

ceptable to users. For example, view $V1$ is derivable from view $V2$ in Figure 13a if all attributes of Insured in $V1$ are also attributes of Issued, Company, or Employed in $V2$. Here, view $V2$ is retained in the integrated schema. Similarly, given the (1;1) cardinality constraints of (student, course): (grade) entity classes in Figure 13b, the relationship sets $R1$ and $R2$ can be integrated—provided all grade attributes are absorbed in $R2$. Here, view $V1$ is retained as the integrated schema. [Note the implied functional dependency (student, course) → Grade.]

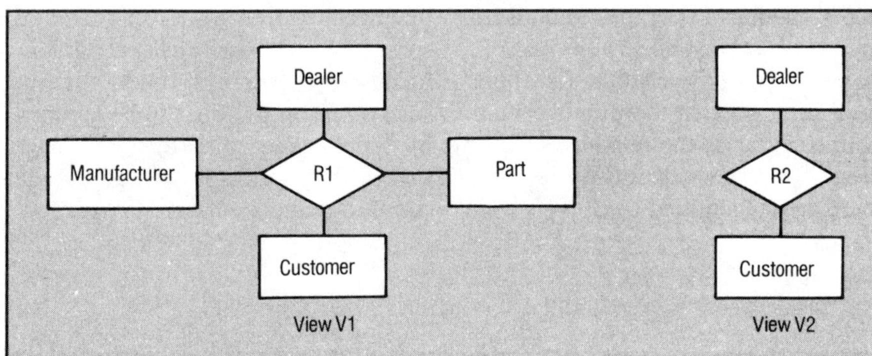

Figure 15. Conditionally mergeable relationship sets.

In Figure 14, however, the Majors-In relationship set is not derivable from (nor is a composition of ) the Attends and Offered-By relationship sets. Hence, all relationships are retained in the integrated schema. (This example belongs in Case 8.)

Figure 15 shows a relationship set of degree 4 in $V1$ and a relationship set of degree 2 in $V2$. Suppose "Dealer $d$ and Customer $c$ are associated in $V2$" implies that "c bought some $p$ (part) made by some $m$ (manufacturer) from $d$," and vice versa. Then, $V2$ would be derivable from $V1$, and the integrated schema would be the same as $V1$.

Case 8: Not-mergeable relationship sets. This category includes relationship sets from two views where some or all object classes involved are common to both views, yet the degrees of relationships are dissimilar and the semantics are not exactly the same.

Consider a simple example (Figure 16). In view $V1$, two relationship sets, $R1$ and $R2$, independently describe the relationship of a dealer supplying a part and the customer buying a part. View $V2$, however, describes the fact that a customer buys a certain part from a certain dealer. Even if the same entity classes are involved in both views, relationship sets $R1$ and $R2$ can-

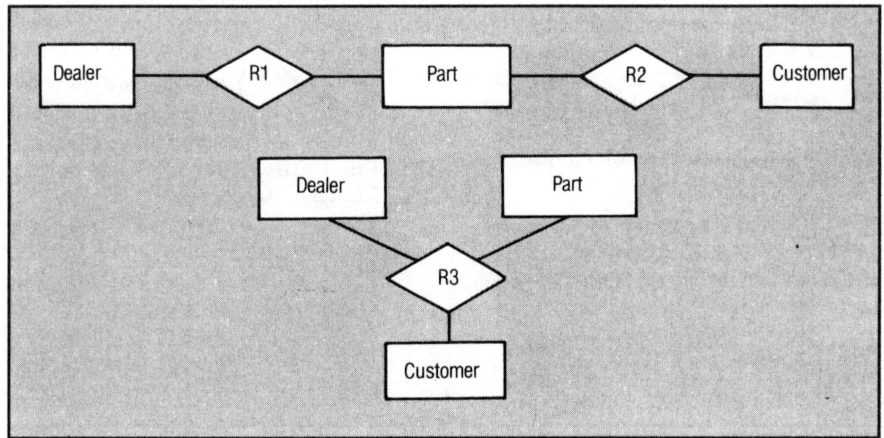

Figure 16. Not-mergeable relationship sets.

not be considered derivable from *R*3. This case is a classical example of a connection trap.[15] Hence, the integrated schema will contain the entity classes Dealer, Part, Customer, and all the relationship sets *R*1, *R*2, and *R*3.

View integration is but a small part of the complex problem of database design. Object classes in two or more views can be integrated by comparing the domains of the entities that will exist in these object classes. The integrated view for each of four cases—identical domains, contained domains, intersecting domains, and disjoint domains—can be constructed along with the distribution of attributes among the entities in the integrated schema. Relationship sets can be classified by degree, role, and structural constraints.[17] It is possible to give definitive rules of integration when the relationship sets have the same degree. The problem becomes harder when relationship sets of different degree are integrated.

Although our discussion was in the context of the Entity-Category-Relationship model, we believe that, with minor modification, the results can be easily applied to other data models.

Much work remains to be done, however, to develop comprehensive and usable tools to aid view integration. The following have yet to be solved:

- Develop rules to match and integrate object classes in two views with more complex interrelationships among object classes and relationship sets. These rules will complement the rules for matching and integrating object classes and matching and integrating relationship sets.
- Define operations that enable a designer to align views appropriately for comparison and integration.
- Study the order in which matching, integration, and modification may be applied.
- Study the advantages and disadvantages of a binary (two views at a time) versus *n*ary integration strategy.
- Develop a practical approach for specifying intraview and interviews constraints. Constraints will be used by the integration procedures to determine the integration rules that may be applied. Additional constraints may be generated during integration.
- Develop techniques for mapping operations on the original views to operations on the integrated view and vice versa.

Work underway at the Honeywell Computer Sciences Center and the University of Florida is addressing these problems in the design of a comprehensive methodology and tools for view integration and distributed database schema integration. Database design, in general, and view integration, in particular, are time-consuming, tedious, and error-prone for all but the most simple databases. A well-developed methodology and tools are needed for one or more individuals to manage the complexity of view integration and database design. □

## Acknowledgments

This work was supported by both the National Science Foundation, grant DMC-84-12085, for Navathe, by grant INT-84-00216, and the Honeywell Computer Sciences Center, Golden Valley, Minnesota. Research contributions of T. Sashidhar of the University of Florida are appreciated. We also thank Sharon Grant for her assistance in preparing the manuscript.

## References

1. C. Batini, M. Lenzerini, and S. Navathe, "A Comparative Analysis of Methodologies for Database Schema Integration," CIS tech. report TR-84-2, University of Florida, Dec. 1984.
2. P. Atzeni et al., "INCOD: A System for Conceptual Design of Data and Transactions in the Entity-Relationship Model," *Proc. Second Int'l Conf. Entity-Relationship Approach,* Oct. 1981, pp. 375-410.
3. R. Elmasri, A. Hevner, and J. Weeldreyer, "The Category Concept; An Extension to the Entity-Relationship Model," *Data and Knowledge Engineering*, Vol. 1, No. 1, June 1985, pp. 75-116.
4. J. Weeldreyer, "Structural Aspects of the Entity-Category-Relationship Model," tech. report HR-80-250, Honeywell Computer Sciences Center, 1980, pp. 17-38.
5. P. Chen, "The Entity-Relationship Model: Towards a Unified View of Data," *ACM Trans. Database Systems,* Vol. 1, No. 1, Mar. 1976, pp. 9-36.
6. J. Smith and D. Smith, "Database Abstractions: Aggregation and Gener-

alization," *ACM Trans. Database Systems,* Vol. 2, No. 2, June 1977, pp. 105-133.

7. M. Hammer and D. McLeod, "Database Description with SDM: A Semantic Database Model," *ACM Trans. Database Systems,* Vol. 6, No. 3, Sept. 1981, pp. 351-386.

8. G. Wiederhold, *Database Design,* 2nd ed., McGraw-Hill, New York, 1983.

9. G. Wiederhold and R. Elmasri, "The Structural Model for Database Design," *Proc. Int'l Conf. Entity-Relationship Approach,* Dec. 1979, pp. 247-267.

10. R. Elmasri and S. Navathe, "Object Integration in Logical Database Design," *Proc. Int'l Conf. Data Engineering,* Apr. 1984, pp. 426-433.

11. C. Batini, M. Lenzerini, and G. Santucci, "A Computer-Aided Methodology for Conceptual Database Design," *Information Systems,* Vol. 7, No. 3, 1982, pp. 265-280.

12. R. Elmasri and G. Wiederhold, "Data Model Integration Using the Structural Model," *Proc. ACM Sigmod Conf.,* May 1979, pp. 319-326.

13. D. Chamberlin et al., "SEQUEL 2: A Unified Approach to Data Definition, Manipulation, and Control," *IBM J. R&D,* Vol. 20, No. 6, Nov. 1976, pp. 560-575.

14. R. Elmasri, "GORDAS: A Data Definition, Query and Update Language for the Entity-Category Relationship Model of Data," tech. report HR-81-250, Honeywell Corporate Technology Center, Jan. 1981, pp. 17-38.

15. E. Codd, "Relational Model of Data for Large Shared Data Banks," *Comm. ACM,* Vol. 13, No. 6, June 1970, pp. 377-387.

16. M. Lenzerini and G. Santucci, "Cardinality Constraints in the Entity Relationship Model," *Proc. Third Int'l Conf. Entity Relationship Approach,* Oct. 1983, pp. 529-549.

17. S. Navathe, T. Sashidhar, and R. Elmasri, "Relationship Merging in Schema Integration," *Proc. 10th Int'l Conf. Very Large Data Bases,* Aug. 1984, pp. 78-90.

**Shamkant Navathe** has been with the Database Systems Research and Development Center and the Department of Computer and Information Sciences at the University of Florida. Gainesville, since 1979. Internationally known for his research in database modeling, conversion, logical design, and distributed database design, he has been active in CAD/CAM, expert systems, and the OBE project in Office Systems at IBM Research. He is now principal investigator on a Honeywell-NSF project to develop a database schema integration methodology.

Prior to his current position, Navathe was on the faculty of New York University's Graduate School of Business Administration and a system engineer for IBM World Trade Corporation and Electronic Data Systems. Navathe received a BE in electrical communications engineering at the Indian Institute of Science, Bangalore, India, an MS from Ohio State University, and a PhD from the University of Michigan.

**Ramez Elmasri** is assistant professor in the Department of Computer Science, University of Houston, where his research interests include semantic integrity of databases, distributed databases, database design and integration, and query languages and user interfaces. He designed the high-level query language GORDAS for the E-R model and designed and implemented an experimental DBMS based on the E-C-R model and GORDAS.

From 1980 to 1982, Elmasri was a principal research scientist with Honeywell Computer Sciences Center where he worked on the design of the Distributed Database Testbed System.

Elmasri received a PhD in computer science from Stanford University in 1980 for his work in the design, use, and integration of data models.

**James Larson** is a senior research fellow working on distributed databases and end-user facilities at the Honeywell Computer Sciences Center in Minnesota. Previously, he was involved in the design of integrated automated office systems for Olivetti, Italy, and research in database computers at Sperry Univac. Larson has been active on the Codasyl Data Description Language Committee and has taught courses in database management for the University of Minnesota. He is editor of three IEEE tutorials: *Data Base Management in the 1980's, End User Facilities in the 1980's, and Distributed Database Management* and is the author of numerious technical papers and articles.

He received a PhD in computer science from Washington State University, Pullman, in 1977.

Questions about this article can be directed to James Larson, Honeywell Computer Sciences Center, 1000 Boone Ave. N., Golden Valley, MN 55427, Mail Station MN 63-C060.

COMPUTING PRACTICES

# A SIMPLE GUIDE TO FIVE NORMAL FORMS IN RELATIONAL DATABASE THEORY

**WILLIAM KENT** *International Business Machines Corporation*

*SUMMARY: The concepts behind the five principal normal forms in relational database theory are presented in simple terms.*

## 1. INTRODUCTION

The normal forms defined in relational database theory represent guidelines for record design. The guidelines corresponding to first through fifth normal forms are presented, in terms that do not require an understanding of relational theory. The design guidelines are meaningful even if a relational database system is not used. We present the guidelines without referring to the concepts of the relational model in order to emphasize their generality and to make them easier to understand. Our presentation conveys an intuitive sense of the intended constraints on record design, although in its informality it may be imprecise in some technical details. A comprehensive treatment of the subject is provided by Date [4].

The normalization rules are designed to prevent update anomalies and data inconsistencies. With respect to performance trade-offs, these guidelines are biased toward the assumption that all nonkey fields will be updated frequently. They tend to penalize retrieval, since data which may have been retrievable from one record in an unnormalized design may have to be retrieved from several records in the normalized form. There is no obligation to fully normalize all records when actual performance requirements are taken into account.

Author's Present Address: William Kent, International Business Machines Corporation, General Products Division, Santa Teresa Laboratory, San Jose, CA



## 2. FIRST NORMAL FORM

First normal form [1] deals with the "shape" of a record type. Under first normal form, *all occurrences of a record type must contain the same number of fields.* First normal form excludes variable repeating fields and groups. This is not so much a design guideline as a matter of definition. Relational database theory does not deal with records having a variable number of fields.

## 3. SECOND AND THIRD NORMAL FORMS

Second and third normal forms [2, 3, 7] deal with the relationship between nonkey and key fields. Under second and third normal forms, *a nonkey field must provide a fact about the key, the whole key, and nothing but the* key. In addition, the record must satisfy first normal form.

We deal now only with "single-valued" facts. A single-valued fact could be a one-to-many relationship such as the department of an employee or a one-to-one relationship such as the spouse of an employee. Thus, the phrase "Y is a *fact* about X" signifies a one-to-one or one-to-many relationship between Y and X. In the general case, Y might consist of one or more fields and so might X. In the following example, QUANTITY is a fact about the combination of PART and WAREHOUSE.

### 3.1 Second Normal Form

Second normal form is violated when a nonkey field is a fact about a subset of a key. It is only relevant when the key is composite, i.e., consists of several fields. Consider the following inventory record.

| PART | WAREHOUSE | QUANTITY | WAREHOUSE-ADDRESS |
|---|---|---|---|

..... key ..............

The key here consists of the PART and WAREHOUSE fields together, but WAREHOUSE-ADDRESS is a fact about the WAREHOUSE alone. The basic problems with this design are:

- The warehouse address is repeated in every record that refers to a part stored in that warehouse.
- If the address of the warehouse changes, every record referring to a part stored in that warehouse must be updated.
- Because of the redundancy, the data might become inconsistent, with different records showing different addresses for the same warehouse.
- If at some point in time there are no parts stored in the warehouse, there may be no record in which to keep the warehouse's address.

To satisfy second normal form, the record shown above should be decomposed into (replaced by) the two records:

| PART | WAREHOUSE | QUANTITY |
|---|---|---|

.... key ...................

| WAREHOUSE | WAREHOUSE-ADDRESS |
|---|---|

..... key .....

When a data design is changed in this way, i.e., replacing unnormalized records with normalized records, the process is referred to as *normalization*. The term "normalization" is sometimes used relative to a particular normal form. Thus, a set of records may be normalized with respect to second normal form but not with respect to third.

The normalized design enhances the integrity of the data by minimizing redundancy and inconsistency, but at some possible performance cost for certain retrieval applications. Consider an application that wants the addresses of all warehouses stocking a certain part. In the unnormalized form, the application searches one record type. With the normalized design, the application has to search two record types and connect the appropriate pairs.

### 3.2 Third Normal Form

Third normal form is violated when a nonkey field is a fact about another nonkey field, as in

| EMPLOYEE | DEPARTMENT | LOCATION |
|---|---|---|

..... key ......

The EMPLOYEE field is the key. If each department is located in one place, then the LOCATION field is a fact about the DEPARTMENT—in addition to being a fact about the EMPLOYEE. The problems with this design are the same as those caused by violations of second normal form.

- The department's location is repeated in the record of every employee assigned to that department.
- If the location of the department changes, every such record must be updated.
- Because of the redundancy, the data might become inconsistent, e.g., different records showing different locations for the same department.
- If a department has no employees, there may be no record in which to keep the department's location.

To satisfy third normal form, the record shown above should be decomposed into the two records:

| EMPLOYEE | DEPARTMENT |
|---|---|

.... key ....

| DEPARTMENT | LOCATION |
|---|---|

...... key ......

To summarize, a record is in second and third normal forms if every field is either part of the key or provides a (single-valued) fact about exactly the whole key and nothing else.

### 3.3 Functional Dependencies

In relational database theory, second and third normal forms are defined in terms of *functional dependencies*, which correspond approximately to our single-valued facts. A field Y is "functionally dependent" on a field (or fields) X if it is invalid to have two records with the same X value but different Y values. That is, a given X value must always occur with the same Y value. When X is a key, then all fields are by definition functionally dependent on X in a trivial way, since there cannot be two records having the same X value.

There is a slight technical difference between functional dependencies and single-valued facts as we have presented them. Functional dependencies only exist when the things involved have unique and singular identifiers (representations). For example, suppose a person's address is a single-valued fact, i.e., a person has only one address. If we do not provide unique identifiers for people, then there will not be a functional dependency in the data.

| PERSON | ADDRESS |
|---|---|
| John Smith | 123 Main St., New York |
| John Smith | 321 Center St., San Francisco |

Although each *person* has a unique address, a given *name* can appear with several different addresses. Hence, we do not have a functional dependency corresponding to our single-valued fact. Similarly, the address has to be spelled identically in each occurrence in order to have a functional dependency. In the following case, the same person appears to be living at two different addresses, again precluding a functional dependency.

| PERSON | ADDRESS |
|---|---|
| John Smith | 123 Main St., New York |
| John Smith | 123 Main Street, NYC |

We are not defending the use of nonunique or nonsingular representations. Such practices often lead to data maintenance problems of their own. We do wish to point out, however, that functional dependencies and the various normal forms are really only defined for situations in which there are unique and singular identifiers. Thus, the design guidelines as we present them are a bit stronger than those implied by the formal definitions of the normal forms.

For instance, we as designers know that in the following example there is a single-valued fact about a nonkey field, and hence the design is susceptible to all the update anomalies mentioned earlier.

| EMPLOYEE | FATHER | FATHER'S-ADDRESS |
|---|---|---|
| Art Smith | John Smith | 123 Main St., New York |
| Bob Smith | John Smith | 123 Main Street, NYC |
| Cal Smith | John Smith | 321 Center St., San Francisco |

However, in formal terms, there is no functional dependency here between FATHER'S-ADDRESS and FATHER, and hence, no violation of third normal form.

## 4. FOURTH AND FIFTH NORMAL FORMS

Fourth [5] and fifth [6] normal forms deal with multivalued facts. A multivalued fact may correspond to a many-to-many relationship, as with employees and skills, or to a many-to-one relationship, as with the children of an employee (assuming only one parent is an employee). By "many-to-many" we mean that an employee may have several skills and/or a skill may belong to several employees. Note that we look at the many-to-one relationship between children and fathers as a single-valued fact about a child but a multivalued fact about a father.

In a sense, fourth and fifth normal forms are also about composite keys. These normal forms attempt to minimize the number of fields involved in a composite key, as suggested by the examples that follow.

### 4.1 Fourth Normal Form

Under fourth normal form, *a record type should not contain two or more independent multivalued facts about an entity*. In addition, the record must satisfy third normal form. The term "independent" will be discussed after considering an example.

Consider employees, skills, and languages, where an employee may have several skills and several languages. We have here two many-to-many relationships, one between employees and skills, and one between employees and languages. Under fourth normal form, these two relationships should not be represented in a single record such as

| EMPLOYEE | SKILL | LANGUAGE |
|---|---|---|

...............key...............

Instead, they should be represented in the two records

| EMPLOYEE | SKILL |
|---|---|

..........key.......

| EMPLOYEE | LANGUAGE |
|---|---|

...........key..........

Note that other fields, not involving multivalued facts, are permitted to occur in the record, as in the case of the QUANTITY field in the earlier PART/WAREHOUSE example.

The main problem with violating fourth normal form is that it leads to uncertainties in the maintenance policies. Several policies are possible for maintaining two independent multivalued facts in one record.

(1) A disjoint format, in which a record contains either a skill or a language, but not both.

| EMPLOYEE | SKILL | LANGUAGE |
|---|---|---|
| Smith | cook | |
| Smith | type | |
| Smith | | French |
| Smith | | German |
| Smith | | Greek |

This is not much different from maintaining two separate record types. We note in passing that such a format also leads to ambiguities regarding the meanings of blank fields. A blank SKILL could mean the person has no skill, that the field is not applicable to this employee, that the data is unknown, or, as in this case, that the data may be found in another record.

(2) A random mix, with three variations

(a) Minimal number of records with repetitions.

| EMPLOYEE | SKILL | LANGUAGE |
|---|---|---|
| Smith | cook | French |
| Smith | type | German |
| Smith | type | Greek |

(b) Minimal number of records, with null values.

| EMPLOYEE | SKILL | LANGUAGE |
|---|---|---|
| Smith | cook | French |
| Smith | type | German |
| Smith | | Greek |

(c) Unrestricted.

| EMPLOYEE | SKILL | LANGUAGE |
|---|---|---|
| Smith | cook | French |
| Smith | type | |
| Smith | | German |
| Smith | type | Greek |

(3) A "cross-product" form where, for each employee, there must be a record for every possible pairing of one of his skills with one of his languages.

| EMPLOYEE | SKILL | LANGUAGE |
|---|---|---|
| Smith | cook | French |
| Smith | cook | German |
| Smith | cook | Greek |
| Smith | type | French |
| Smith | type | German |
| Smith | type | Greek |

Other problems caused by violating fourth normal form are similar in spirit to those mentioned earlier for violations of second or third normal form. They take different variations depending on the chosen maintenance policy.

- If there are repetitions, then updates have to be done in multiple records, and the records could become inconsistent.
- Insertion of a new skill may involve looking for a record with a blank skill, inserting a new record with a possibly blank language, or inserting multiple records pairing the new skill with some or all of the languages.
- Deletion of a skill may involve blanking out the skill field in one or more records (perhaps with a check that this does not leave two records with the same language and a blank skill) or deleting one or more records, coupled with a check that the last mention of some language has not been deleted also.

Fourth normal form minimizes such update problems.

***4.1.1 Independence*** We mentioned *independent* multivalued facts earlier, and we now illustrate what we mean by that term. The two many-to-many relationships, employee:skill and employee:language, are independent in that there is no direct connection between skills and languages. There is only an indirect connection because they belong to some common employee. That is, it does not matter which skill is paired with which language in a record; the pairing does not convey any information. That is precisely why all the maintenance policies mentioned earlier can be allowed.

In contrast, suppose that an employee can only exercise certain skills in certain languages. Perhaps Smith can cook French cuisine only, but can type French, German, and Greek. Then the pairing of skills and languages becomes meaningful, and there is no longer an ambiguity of maintenance policies. In the present case, only the following form is correct.

| EMPLOYEE | SKILL | LANGUAGE |
|---|---|---|
| Smith | cook | French |
| Smith | type | French |
| Smith | type | German |
| Smith | type | Greek |

Thus, the employee:skill and employee:language relationships are no longer independent. These records do not violate fourth normal form. When there is an interdependence among the relationships, it is acceptable to represent them in a single record.

***4.1.2. Multivalued Dependencies*** For readers interested in pursuing the technical background of fourth normal form a bit further, we mention that fourth normal form is defined in terms of *multivalued dependencies* that correspond to our independent multivalued facts. Multivalued dependencies, in turn, are defined essentially as relationships that accept the "cross-product" maintenance policy mentioned above. For our example, every one of an employee's skills must appear paired with every one of his languages. It may or may not be obvious to the reader that this is equivalent to our notion of independence; since every possible pairing must be present, there is no "information" in the pairings. Such pairings convey information only if some of them can be absent, i.e., only if it is possible that some employee cannot perform some skill in some language. If all pairings are always present, then the relationships are really independent.

We should also point out that multivalued dependencies and fourth normal form also apply to relationships involving more than two fields. For example, suppose we extend the earlier example to include projects, in the following sense:

- An employee uses certain skills on certain projects.
- An employee uses certain languages on certain projects.

If there is no direct connection between the skills and languages that an employee uses on a project, then we could treat this as two independent many-to-many relationships of the form EP:S and EP:L, where EP represents a combination of an employee with a project. A record including employee, project, skill, and language would violate fourth normal form. Two records, containing fields E, P, S and E, P, L, respectively, would satisfy fourth normal form.

**4.2. Fifth Normal Form**

Fifth normal form deals with cases where information can be reconstructed from smaller pieces of information which can be maintained with less redundancy. Second, third, and fourth normal forms also serve this purpose, but fifth normal form generalizes to cases not covered by the others.

We will not attempt a comprehensive exposition of fifth normal form, but will illustrate the central concept with a commonly used example, namely, one involving agents, companies, and products. If agents represent companies, companies make products, and agents sell products, then we might want to keep a record of which agent sells which product for which company. This information could be kept in one record type with three fields:

| AGENT | COMPANY | PRODUCT |
|---|---|---|
| Smith | Ford | car |
| Smith | GM | truck |

This form is necessary in the general case. For example, although agent Smith sells cars made by Ford and trucks made by GM, he does not sell Ford trucks or GM cars. Thus, we need the combination of all three fields to know which combinations are valid and which are not.

But suppose that a certain rule is in effect: if an agent sells a certain product and he represents the company making that product, then he sells that product for that company.

| AGENT | COMPANY | PRODUCT |
|---|---|---|
| Smith | Ford | car |
| Smith | Ford | truck |
| Smith | GM | car |
| Smith | GM | truck |
| Jones | Ford | car |

In this case, it turns out that we can reconstruct all the true facts from a normalized form consisting of three separate record types, each containing two fields.

| AGENT | COMPANY |
|---|---|
| Smith | Ford |
| Smith | GM |
| Jones | Ford |

| AGENT | PRODUCT |
|---|---|
| Smith | car |
| Smith | truck |
| Jones | car |

| COMPANY | PRODUCT |
|---|---|
| Ford | car |
| Ford | truck |
| GM | car |
| GM | truck |

These three record types are in fifth normal form, whereas the corresponding three-field record shown previously is not.

Roughly speaking, we may say that a record type is in fifth normal form when its information content cannot be reconstructed from several smaller record types, i.e., from record types each having fewer fields than the original record. The case where all the smaller records have the same key is excluded. If a record type can only be decomposed into smaller records which all have the same key, then the record type is considered to be in fifth normal form without decomposition. A record type in fifth normal form is also in fourth, third, second, and first normal forms.

Fifth normal form does not differ from fourth normal form unless there exists a symmetric constraint such as the rule about agents, companies, and products. In the absence of such a constraint, a record type in fourth normal form is always in fifth normal form.

One advantage of fifth normal form is that certain redundancies can be eliminated. In the normalized form, the fact that Smith sells cars is recorded only once; in the unnormalized form, it may be repeated many times.

It should be observed that although the normalized form involves more record types, there may be fewer total record occurrences. This is not apparent when there are only a few facts to record, as in the example shown above. The advantage is realized as more facts are recorded, since the size of the normalized files increases in an additive fashion, while the size of the unnormalized file increases in a multiplicative fashion. For example, if we add a new agent who sells $x$ products for $y$ companies, where each of these companies makes each of these products, we have to add $x + y$ new records to the normalized form, but $x \cdot y$ new records to the unnormalized form.

It should also be noted that all three record types are required in the normalized form in order to reconstruct the same information. From the first two record types shown above we learn that Jones represents Ford and that Ford makes trucks. But we cannot determine whether Jones sells Ford trucks until we look at the third record type to determine whether Jones sells trucks at all.

The following example illustrates a case in which the rule about agents, companies, and products is satisfied, and which clearly requires all three record types in the normalized form. Any two of the record types taken alone will imply something untrue.

| AGENT | COMPANY | PRODUCT |
|---|---|---|
| Smith | Ford | car |
| Smith | Ford | truck |
| Smith | GM | car |
| Smith | GM | truck |
| Jones | Ford | car |
| Jones | Ford | truck |
| Brown | Ford | car |
| Brown | GM | car |
| Brown | Toyota | car |
| Brown | Toyota | bus |

| AGENT | COMPANY |
|---|---|
| Smith | Ford |
| Smith | GM |
| Jones | Ford |
| Brown | Ford |
| Brown | GM |
| Brown | Toyota |

Fifth Normal Form

| COMPANY | PRODUCT |
|---|---|
| Ford | car |
| Ford | truck |
| GM | car |
| GM | truck |
| Toyota | car |
| Toyota | bus |

Fifth Normal Form

| AGENT | PRODUCT |
|---|---|
| Smith | car |
| Smith | truck |
| Jones | car |
| Jones | truck |
| Brown | car |
| Brown | bus |

Fifth Normal Form

Observe that:

- Jones sells cars and GM makes cars, but Jones does not represent GM.
- Brown represents Ford and Ford makes trucks, but Brown does not sell trucks.
- Brown represents Ford and Brown sells buses, but Ford does not make buses.

Fourth and fifth normal forms both deal with combinations of multivalued facts. One difference is that the facts dealt with under fifth normal form are not independent, in the sense discussed earlier. Another difference is that, although fourth normal form can deal with more than two multivalued facts, it only recognizes them in pairwise groups. We can best explain this in terms of the normalization process implied by fourth normal form. If a record violates fourth normal form, the associated normalization process decomposes it into two records, each containing fewer fields than the original record. Any of these violating fourth normal form is again decomposed into two records, and so on until the resulting records are all in fourth normal form. At each stage, the set of records after decomposition contains exactly the same information as the set of records before decomposition.

In the present example, no pairwise decomposition is possible. There is no combination of two smaller records which contains the same total information as the original record. All three of the smaller records are needed. Hence, an information-preserving pairwise decomposition is not possible, and the original record is not in violation of fourth normal form. Fifth normal form is needed in order to deal with the redundancies in this case.

## 5. UNAVOIDABLE REDUNDANCIES

Normalization certainly does not remove all redundancies. Certain redundancies seem to be unavoidable, particularly when several multivalued facts are dependent rather than independent. In the example shown in Sec. 4.1.1, it seems unavoidable that we record the fact that "Smith can type" several times. Also, when the rule about agents, companies, and products is not in effect, it seems unavoidable that we record the fact that "Smith sells cars" several times.

## 6. INTERRECORD REDUNDANCY

The normal forms discussed here deal only with redundancies occurring within a single record type. Fifth normal form is considered to be the ultimate normal form with respect to such redundancies [6].

Other redundancies can occur across multiple record types. For the example concerning employees, departments, and locations, the following records are in third normal form in spite of the obvious redundancy.

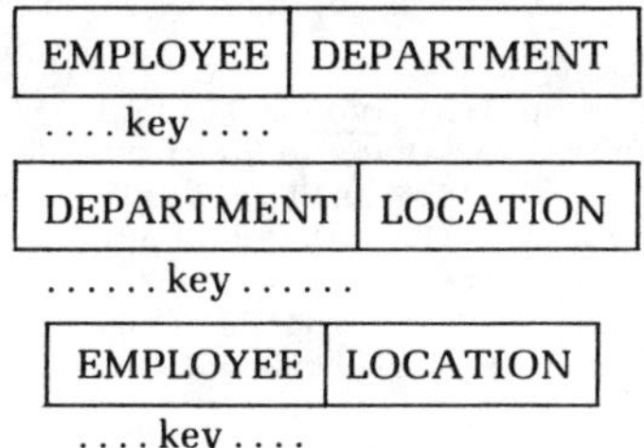


In fact, two copies of the same record type would constitute the ultimate in this kind of undetected redundancy. Interrecord redundancy has been recognized for some time [1], and has recently been addressed in terms of normal forms and normalization [8].

## 7. CONCLUSION

While we have tried to present the normal forms in a simple and understandable way, we are by no means suggesting that the data design process is correspondingly simple. The design process involves many complexities that are quite beyond the scope of this paper. In the first place, an initial set of data elements and records has to be developed as candidates for normalization. Then the factors affecting normalization have to be assessed:

- Single-valued vs. multivalued facts.
- Dependency on the entire key.
- Independent vs. dependent facts.
- The presence of mutual constraints.
- The presence of nonunique or nonsingular representations.

Finally, the desirability of normalization has to be assessed in terms of its performance impact on retrieval applications.

***Acknowledgments.*** I am very grateful to Ted Codd and Ron Fagin for reading earlier drafts and making valuable comments, and especially to Chris Date for helping to clarify some key points.

**References**

1. Codd, E.F. A relational model of data for large shared data banks. *Comm. ACM 13* 6, (June 1970) 377–387.
2. Codd, E.F. Normalized data base structure: A brief tutorial. *ACM SIGFIDET Workshop on Data Description, Access, and Control.* Nov. 11–12, 1971, San Diego, California. E.F. Codd and A.L. Dean (Eds.)
3. Codd, E.F. Further normalization of the data base relational model. R. Rustin (Ed.), *Data Base Systems* (Courant Computer Science Symposia 6). Prentice-Hall, Englewood Cliffs, NJ, 1972. Also IBM Research Report RJ909.
4. Date, C.J. *An Introduction to Database Systems.* 3rd Ed. Addison-Wesley, Reading, MA, 1981.
5. Fagin, R. Multivalued dependencies and a new normal form for relational databases. *ACM Transactions on Database Systems 2* 3, (Sept. 1977). Also IBM Research Report RJ1812.
6. Fagin, R. Normal forms and relational database operators. *ACM SIGMOD International Conference on Management of Data.* May 31–June 1, 1979, Boston, Mass. Also IBM Research Report RJ2471, Feb. 1979.
7. Kent, W. A primer of normal forms. *IBM Technical Report TR02.600,* Dec. 1973.
8. Ling, T.-W., Tompa, F.W., and Kameda, T. An improved third normal form for relational databases. *ACM Transactions on Database Systems 6* 2, (June 1981) 329–346.

**CR Categories and Subjects:** H.2.1 [**Database Management**]: Logical Design—*normal forms*
**General Term:** Design

*Received 3/82; revised 8/82; accepted 9/82*

# Physical Database Design: Techniques for Improved Database Performance

Salvatore T. March and John V. Carlis

ABSTRACT

In recent years, the information processing requirements of business organizations have expanded tremendously. With this expansion, the design of databases to efficiently manage this information has become critical. This paper addresses two areas of physical database design: record structuring (the grouping of data items into records that are physically stored and accessed together) and access path design (the design of algorithms and system structures used to determine the physical location of records and to support content dependent retrieval). The performance of a database system is largely dependent on the design choices made in these two areas. Techniques to support a database designer in making these choices are discussed.

## 1. INTRODUCTION

Databases exist to meet the information and processing requirements of some community of users. To be effective, a database must not only contain the right information, but it must also provide timely and efficient access to that information [Edel81]. Modern databases are typically large and service user communities with widely divergent information and processing needs.

Database design is commonly viewed at two levels: logical and physical [Nava78]. While the dividing line between logical and physical design is not precise [Lum79], the distinction may be thought of in terms of WHAT versus HOW. Logical database design addresses the WHAT of the database: what is the data content, what are the retrieval and update activities, what are the response time requirements. Physical database design addresses the HOW of the database: how is the data physically organized in secondary memory, how is it accessed, how is it maintained.

This paper addresses techniques for physical database design given a logical database design. The criterion for selecting among alternative database designs is the minimization of total system operating cost. This is typically approximated by the sum of storage, retrieval, and update costs. The data storage cost for a physical database is estimated by multiplying the size of the database by the storage cost per character for the media on which the data is maintained. Retrieval and update costs depend on the retrieval and update activities of the user community as well as the physical database design.

Physical database design is difficult. A myriad of physical design alternatives can support a given logical database. The performance of a particular physical design depends on many factors, such as the database management system (DBMS) software, the retrieval and update patterns of the user community, and the operating costs and accessing characteristics of the computer system. Typically the accessing characteristics of different users are in conflict. Data organizations that are efficient for one user may be inefficient for others. Tradeoffs must be evaluated and a compromise design selected which most efficiently meets all information requirements. Despite much work in the area, physical database design is still an art that relies heavily on human intuition and experience. Consequently, its practice is becoming more difficult as the applications that databases must support become more sophisticated.

Physical database design may be viewed as two interrelated tasks [Wied83, Marc83a]:

(1) record structuring and
(2) access path design.

The record structures of a database define the grouping of data items into records that are physically stored and accessed. The access paths of a database determine how those records are physically organized in secondary memory and they define retrieval criteria that are efficiently supported. Both tasks are discussed in the following sections.

## 2. LOGICAL AND PHYSICAL DATABASE CONCEPTS

At the logical level a database contains and provides controlled access to descriptions of instances of entities as required by its community of users. An entity is a category or grouping of things [Chen76, Kent78]; entity instances are



Reprinted with permission from *Query Processing in Database Systems*, Topics in Information Systems Series, edited by W. Kim, D.S. Reiner and D.S. Batory, 1985, pages 279-296. 

members of that category. The description of an entity instance is a set of values for selected characteristics or descriptors of the entity instance. Two types of descriptors are distinguished: (1) attribute descriptors (or attributes), which are single valued characteristics of a single entity, and (2) relationship descriptors, which characterize an association between the entity described and some other (describing) entity. A relationship between two entities has two relationship descriptors, one for each direction of the relationship. The degree of a relationship descriptor is the (average) number of instances of the describing entity that exist for each instance of the described entity.

Each entity has some (subset of) data items(s) termed the identifier schema, whose value(s) is(are) used to identify unique entity instances. Each entity also has a cardinality or number of instances. Each attribute descriptor has an (encoded) length. Relationship descriptors may be thought of as "logical connectors" from one entity to another. How they are represented in the database is a physical design decision.

Figure 1 shows a graphical representation of a logical database containing four entities, DEPARTMENT, EMPLOYEE, PROJECT and ASSIGNMENT. The entity PROJECT has three attribute descriptors, proj-no, proj-budget and proj-due-date. It also has two relationship descriptors, MANAGER-OF-PROJECT (associating each project with the EMPLOYEE who manages the PROJECT) and ASSIGNMENT-OF-PROJECT (associating ASSIGNMENTs to PROJECTs). The degree of MANAGER-OF-PROJECT is one; the degree of ASSIGNMENT-OF-PROJECT is M (indicated by "chicken feet" on the ASSIGNMENT side of the relationship). Proj-no is the identifier schema for PROJECT (denoted by the dot on the proj-no arc). Entity cardinality and attribute length are not shown in the figure.

The logical retrieval and update activities of a user community are defined in terms of the logical data content. A retrieval is described by selection (of entity instances), projection (of descriptors pertaining to those instances) and sorting (descriptors used to order the output) criteria, and by a frequency of execution. An update activity is described by selection (of entity instances) and projection (descriptors to be updated for those instances) criteria, and again, by frequency of execution. Insertions and deletions project all descriptors for the selected entities. Retrieval and update activities may be quite complex and involve multiple entities (e.g., joins in a relational algebra).

At the physical level, data items (or fields) corresponding to logical level descriptors are grouped to define database records (or records). Records may be quite complex, containing repeating groups, termed aggregations, of data items describing one or more entities. Conversely, records may contain data items corresponding to only a subset of an entity's descriptors. These are termed record segments and are connected either explicitly by pointers or implicitly by physical positioning. Hence a record may describe all or a part of one or more entities.

Many different physical record structures can support the same logical database. To assure that the physical database accurately reflects the entire logical database, each attribute descriptor must have a corresponding data item in some record. Relationship descriptors, on the other hand, may or may not have corresponding data items. Relationship descriptors with corresponding data items

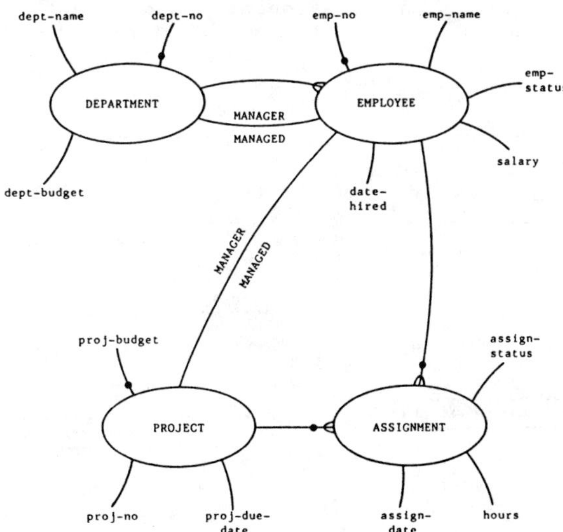


FIGURE 1. AN EXAMPLE LOGICAL DATABASE

are linksets [Bato82] connecting the records describing the appropriate entities. Relationship descriptors may also be represented implicitly by physical proximity, i.e., an aggregation. Finally, since each relationship has two descriptors, no information is lost if only one of them is phyically represented in the database - the other can be derived.

A record instance contains a part of the description of one or more entity instances at the logical level (i.e., strings of bits that represent the values of the appropriate descriptors). A set of record instances for a particular record is called a file. Similarly, a set of all segment instances for a particular record segment is termed a subfile. Files and subfiles reside permanently in secondary memory in groups called datasets; that is, a dataset is a physical allocation of secondary memory in which some number of files and subfiles are maintained.

One of literally millions of record structures that represent the logical database of Figure 1 is shown in Figure 2. The entity EMPLOYEE is represented in two record segments (denoted RS1 and RS2 in Figure 2). These two segments are connected by a symbolic pointer (the identifier item emp-no is contained in both). RS1 also represents part of the entity ASSIGNMENT. The relationship descriptor ASSIGNMENT-OF-EMPLOYEE is implicitly represented by the placement of ASSIGNMENT data. The relationship descriptor DEPARTMENT-OF-EMPLOYEE is represented by a symbolic pointer (dept-no) in RS1. EMPLOYEE-OF-DEPARTMENT is not explicitly represented.

The aggregation (hierarchic arrangement) of ASSIGNMENT data with EMPLOYEE data is an efficient physical arrangement for database activities directed through EMPLOYEE to ASSIGNMENT. Since EMPLOYEEs and their ASSIGNMENTs are physically clustered, this information can be retrieved in the minimum time. If EMPLOYEEs and their ASSIGNMENTs were stored in different files and ASSIGNMENTs were not clustered by EMPLOYEE-OF-ASSIGNMENT, then each ASSIGNMENT for an EMPLOYEE could require a secondary memory access, thus substantially increasing the retrieval time.

The aggregation RS1 does not contain all of the EMPLOYEE data or all of the ASSIGNMENT data - both EMPLOYEE and ASSIGNMENT are segmented. For activities that require EMPLOYEE and ASSIGNMENT data, the retrieval costs depend on the projection criteria of the activity. If only data in RS1 is required, then the retrieval cost is reduced over the aggregation of all EMPLOYEE and ASSIGNMENT data since the subfiles of aggregated segments are smaller than the aggregated files would be. If the data items required by an activity are distributed over multiple segments, then evaluating the cost is more complex. If subfiles are independent and may be processed "in parallel," then cost may still be reduced. However, this is not common in practice; usually access to multiple subfiles proceeds serially and thus at greater cost than access to a single subfile.

While record segmentation may significantly reduce retrieval costs, it can also increase database maintenance costs. In particular, inserting or deleting an instance of a record typically requires access to each of the record's segments. The more segments a record has, the more expensive insertions and deletions become.

The logical retrieval and update activities must be supported by access paths at the physical level. Access paths determine how records are physically organized in secondary memory and they define retrieval criteria that are efficiently supported. A dataset with its associated access paths is termed a file organization. A physical database is a set of interconnected file organizations.

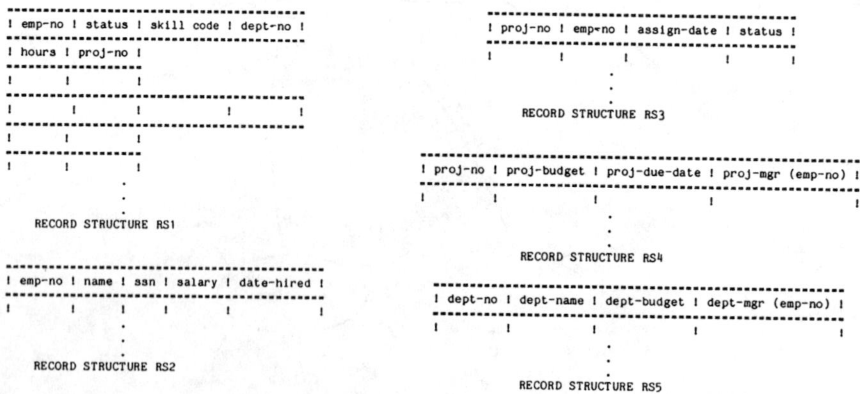


FIGURE 2. A POSSIBLE SET OF RECORD STRUCTURES FOR THE EXAMPLE LOGICAL DATABASE

Each access path of a file organization is defined by a record selection criterion which it efficiently supports. A record selection criterion consists of a set of data items, termed the key data items or the database key of the access path, and possibly a set of values for each key data item. Each file organization of a database has exactly one primary access path which dictates the physical positioning of records in secondary memory and some number of secondary or auxiliary access paths, that are used to retrieve subsets of records (segments) which have been stored via the primary access path.

Three types of primary access paths are differentiated: hashed, sequential and indexed sequential [Mart77]. A hashed access path uses an algorithm to transform its database key into the secondary memory location where the record should be stored. A sequential access path provides access only to the next record physically stored in the dataset. An indexed sequential access path (e.g., ISAM or VSAM [IBM74]) logically maintains an ordered sequential file based on its database key and maintains a hierarchic block index to support rapid access to individual records by key value.

Retrievals requiring individual records are most efficiently satisfied by a hashed primary access path. In practice, a hashing algorithm only supports one database key, and hence one selection criterion. If different individual record retrievals have different selection criteria then one may be selected as the key of the primary access path, others must be supported by secondary access paths.

Retrievals requiring a large proportion of the data records are most efficiently met by sequential access paths which retrieve the entire file. In order to eliminate sorting costs, each retrieval would prefer to have the sequential access path ordered by its ordering criterion. Clearly, only one ordering is possible for the sequential access path.

Finally, retrievals which require a small subset of the data records are most efficiently met by an indexed sequential access path. In this way, records are clustered according to the key of the access path and direct access is supplied to clusters by the index. Again, each retrieval would prefer to have its selection criterion define the key of the primary access path.

Since a file organization can only have one primary access path (i.e., a record can only be physically stored in one location), secondary access paths support retrieval activities that are not efficiently supported by the primary access path. Secondary access paths are grouped into two categories: list (or chained) and inverted [Seve77]. A list connects a subset of data records by maintaining a pointer in each data record which is used to locate "the next" record in the list. Membership in a list is determined by the list key; all records with a given (set of) value(s) for a (set of) data item(s) are members. A multilist is a set of mutually exclusive lists each having a different (set of) value(s) for the same key data item(s). Lists and multilists have list headers which denote the (data item, value) pair for the list (or for each list in a multilist) and a pointer to the first record in the list. If there are a large number of lists in a multilist, the list header may be a separate file with its own primary access path (hashing, sequential or indexed sequential).

An inverted access path similarly connects a subset of data records. Rather than maintaining a pointer in each data record, however, the pointers are maintained as a separate file (which has a primary access path). An inverted list is analogous to a list and an inverted file is analogous to a multilist.

If the key for a secondary access path is an identifier, then there is only one record in each subset and the access path is commonly called a full index. The full index has a primary access path, typically hashing or indexed sequential. The terms hashing via a full index and hierarchic full index are used, respectively, for these types of access paths. As a final step, the values of the key data item(s) may be implicitly maintained by position in an inverted file; the resulting structure is commonly termed a scatter table or trie [Come79]. Hashing is typically used as the primary access path for a scatter table. The term hashing via a scatter table is used for this type of access path.

The result of processing multiple inverted access paths prior to data record retrieval is called a virtual access path. This type of processing is extremely important in a class of database management systems called "inverted file" DBMSs [Hoff80]. In such systems the number of records which must be accessed to satisfy a user retrieval request can be reduced, and hence the cost of satisfying that request reduced, by intersecting existing inverted access paths. Consider, for example, a retrieval request that selects records based on two data items, say EMPLOYEE Status and Skill Code. Suppose that 40 percent of the records satisfy the Employee Status criterion and 20 percent satisfy the Skill Code criterion. If an inverted access path with Employee Status as its key was used to satisfy this request, then 40 percent of the records would be accessed; if an inverted access path based upon Skill Code was maintained then only 20 percent of the records would be accessed. If, however, inverted access paths were maintained for both Employee Status and Skill Code, then then these access paths could be intersected and, assuming that values of these data items are independent, only 8 percent of the records would be accessed. This reduction in required records could significantly reduce the cost of satisfying this request. Inverted access paths are preferred over list access paths for the above reasons and because they can be dynamically created and deleted without altering any data records.

Secondary access paths can reduce data retreival time (and hence cost) when the proportion of records required is "small". Otherwise, if the proportion of required records is "large", simply scanning all records may be more efficient [Seve77]. The problem is to determine "how big is small?". This value is a function of dataset, storage device, and computer environment characteristics as well as detailed database design decisions.

The dominant secondary storage device is the moving head disk. Access time on a disk has three components: seek time (to move the head to the proper cylinder), rotational delay or latency time (waiting for the data to move under the appropriate read/write head), and data transfer time (to move data across a channel). The unit of transfer is a block, typically containing several data records. These components of access and the fact that blocks contain multiple records makes the calculation of "how big is small" complicated. In a computer environment where there is no contention for the disk, scanning all records can be done with a minimum amount of disk arm movement and virtually no rotational delay. If there is contention for the disk, then each block accessed could require an average arm movement and an average rotational delay. Secondary access paths, on the other hand, almost always require arm movement and rotational delay for each block accessed.

Consider the disk, dataset, and design decisions shown in Figure 3. What is the dividing line between "large" and "small"? This question is significant for physical database design since the choice of access paths depends on the answer. Figure 4 shows the answer. Assuming no contention and unsegmented records, the dividing line is approximately 2.1 percent. That is, if a retrieval request requires more than 21,000 records, then scanning the million records is as efficient as using a secondary access path. If there is contention for the disk, then the dividing line goes up by a factor of four. If records are segmented, then these proportions are reduced for retrievals requiring only one segment. The amount of the reduction depends on the segment length.

To summarize, just these factors make physical database design difficult:

1. there are millions of different possible record structures to choose from for a given logical database,
2. records can be physically organized in secondary memory according to only one database key,
3. access path, segmentation, and maintenance choices are interdependent,
4. the times for random and sequential disk accesses can vary by an order of magnitude, and
5. the unit of disk access is a block, not a record

## 3. REPRESENTING PHYSICAL DESIGNS IN COMMERCIAL DATABASE MANAGEMENT SYSTEMS

Commercially available database management systems (DBMSs) are differentiated by their underlying data models. The three most common data models are: hierarchic, network (CODASYL) and relational [Date82]. Each type of DBMS requires both record structuring and access path design.

**DISK PARAMETERS**

| | |
|---|---|
| Characters per track | 13030 characters |
| Tracks per cylinder | 20 |
| Data transfer rate | 1 M chars/sec |
| Rotation time | 24 milliseconds |
| Average rotational delay | 12 milliseconds |
| Minimal arm access time | 10 milliseconds |
| Average arm access time | 25 milliseconds |

**Dataset Parameters**

| | |
|---|---|
| Number of records | 1 million |
| Record size | 500 characters |

**Implementation Parameters (Detailed Design Decisions)**

| | |
|---|---|
| Records per block | 12 |
| Blocksize | 6000 characters |
| Blocks per track | 2 |
| Blocks for the dataset | 83,334 |
| Cylinders for the dataset | 2,084 |

FIGURE 3. DISK, DATASET, AND IMPLEMENTATION PARAMETERS

Record structures are termed hierarchic segments in IMS, record types with owner member sets in CODASYL DBMSs and relations in Relational DBMSs. Record structuring may be viewed as the aggregating and segmenting of logically defined data, within the context of a database management system. IMS [McGee77] supports aggregation by permitting multiple hierarchic segments to be stored in the same dataset (termed "dataset group"in IMS). In this case, children segments are physically stored immediately following their parent segments. CODASYL DMBSs [CODA78] support aggregation by allowing repeating groups in the definition of a record type and by permitting the storage of a MEMBER record type in the same dataset (termed "area" in CODASYL) as its OWNER, i.e., "NEAR OWNER". In CODASYL, a SET defines a relationship by connecting OWNER and MEMBER record types (e.g., if EMPLOYEE and ASSIGNMENT are record types, then ASSIGNMENT-OF-EMPLOYEE could be implemented as a SET with EMPLOYEE as the OWNER and ASSIGNMENT as the MEMBER). Storing a MEMBER record type "NEAR OWNER" directs the DBMS to place all MEMBER records physically near (presumably on the same block as) their respective OWNER records and indicates that access to the MEMBER records occurs primarily from the OWNER record via the SET relationship. Most relational DBMSs do not support aggregation per se (i.e., "normalizing" relations requires, among other things, the removal of repeating groups [Date82]); however, substantial efficiencies can be achieved through the use of aggregation. In System R [Cham81], aggregation can be approximated by initially loading several tables into the same dataset (termed "segment" in System R) in hierarchic order and supplying "tentative record identifiers" during INSERT operations to maintain the physical clustering. Several relational DBMSs (e.g., RIM [RIM83]) allow arrays within a relation thus supporting a single level of aggregation.

All three types of DBMSs support record segmentation. In IMS, segmentation is accomplished simply by removing data items from one segment to form new segments, which become that segment's children. Similarly, in a CODASYL DBMS, segmentation is accomplished by removing data items from one record type to form new record types and defining SETs with these new record types as MEMBERS and OWNED BY the original record type. The new (MEMBER) record types are stored VIA SET to maintain the connection but not NEAR OWNER for efficient processing of the OWNER. In addition, a proposed CODASYL physical level specification [CODA78] suggests that record segmentation be supported at the physical level by allowing the definition of multiple record segments, termed storage records, for a single record type. In a relational DBMS, record segmentation is accomplished by breaking up a "base relation" [Date82] into multiple relations, each of which contains the identifier (key) of the original; these then become "base relations".

Given a set of record structures which define a set of interrelated file organizations, the access paths of each file organization must be designed. Commercial DBMSs restrict the types of primary and secondary access paths supported. IMS, for example, supports sequential, indexed sequential (ISAM and VSAM [IBM74]) and hashing as primary access paths and hierarchic full indexes as secondary access paths [Date82]. CODASYL Network DBMSs [CODA78] typically support sequential and hashed (CALC) as primary access paths (at least one CODASYL based system, DMS 1100 [SPER81] also supports indexed sequential as a primary access path). Secondary access paths are created by defining an OWNER record type that only contains pointers to the MEMBER record type to be accessed. This OWNER record type may be sequential (full index scan) or CALC (hashed full index). System R stores records directly in chronological sequence. Again, record clustering may be maintained by supplying tentative TIDs during insert operations. System R also supports hierarchic full indexes as secondary access paths.

## 4. TECHNIQUES FOR SUPPORTING DATABASE DESIGN DECISIONS

A database designer may understandably be overwhelmed by the many and varied design decisions which must be made; inappropriate database designs often result [Mart77]. This section briefly describes techniques which support physical database design. Techniques for record structuring are presented first, followed by techniques for access path design. Finally, an approach to solving the combined record structuring and access path selection problem is discussed.

### 4.1 Record Structuring

Record structuring is accomplished by aggregating and segmenting logically defined data within the context of a database management system. March [Marc83a] surveys techniques for solving this database design subproblem. These are briefly described below.

| Disk Environment | Sequential Scan Time (dataset) | Random Retrieval Time (per record) | Dividing Line Between "large" and "small" |
|---|---|---|---|
| no contention | 17.5 min. | 49 millisec | 2.1% |
| high contention | 68 min. | 49 millisec | 8.3% |

FIGURE 4. THE DIVIDING LINE BETWEEN "LARGE" AND "SMALL"

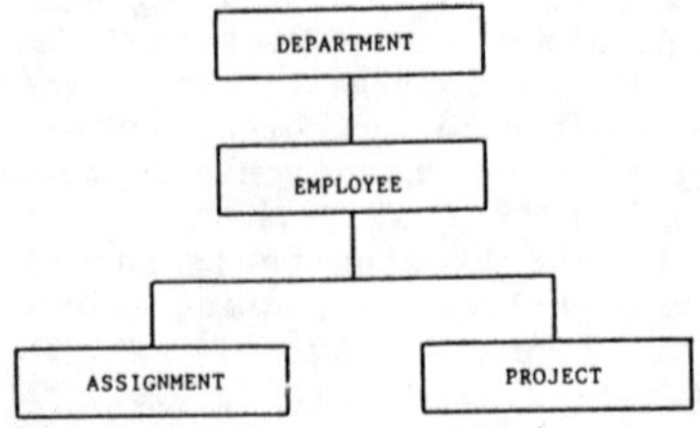


FIGURE 5. A HIERARCHY FORMED FROM THE LOGICAL DATABASE OF FIGURE 1

#### 4.1.1 Aggregation

Aggregation is a type of record structuring that physically arranges groups of data items that have been defined by some data model. This section discusses a technique termed hierarchic aggregation. As its name implies, hierarchic aggregation assumes that the logical data structure is expressed in the hierarchic data model. Thus the set of aggregations from which a record structure is selected is restricted to "child" segments being aggregated iteratively into "parent" segments. Such an approach is also possible for the network and relational data models; however, its efficiency is highly dependent on the single parent restriction of the hierarchic model, and this restriction does not apply to the network or relational models.

Schkolnick [Schk77] developed hierarchic aggregation for use in designing IMS databases. The scope of the problem addressed by Schkolnick is restricted to hierarchic organizations of data stored without redundancy in a paged secondary memory environment, and sequentially processed via hierarchic scans. A hierarchic organization of data is simply one which can be represented by a tree structure. The basic element considered is termed a segment. Each segment is described by length (the number of characters required to store the segment) and type (an identifier for the items stored within the segment). Segments are organized into trees by means of a type tree. A type tree is an (m + 1)-tuple $T = (S, T_1, T_2, \ldots, T_m)$, where S is the root segment of the type tree, $T_1, T_2, \ldots T_m$ are children type trees of S, and m is termed the root fanout of T; if m = 0, then T is called a root tree. The number of instances of a type tree $T_j$ associated with a root segment S, is denoted $Z_j$ and is called the Z-fanout of segment j.

Figure 5 shows a graphical representation of a hierarchy formed from the logical database of Figure 1. To create a hierarchy from a logical database, some relationship representations must be prespecified. Representing DEPARTMENT-OF-MANAGER and PROJECT-OF-ASSIGNMENT by symbolic pointers yields the hierarchy of Figure 5. Many other hierarchies can be created for this logical database, however, to apply the Schkolnick procedure, one hierarchy must be selected.

The hierarchy shown in Figure 5 can be represented by the type tree T = (DEPARTMENT, $T_1$), where $T_1$ = (EMPLOYEE, $T_2$, $T_3$). $T_2$ = (ASSIGNMENT) and $T_3$ = (PROJECT) are root trees. Given such a type tree, a physical storage scheme must be devised which efficiently supports the activity upon that structure. Two storage schemes are immediately obvious. First, one may use the hierarchic preorder [Knut73] to linearize the structure and then simply store segments sequentially, according to that ordering, in a single file organization. Alternatively, one may store each segment in a separate file organization. The first structure has advantages for the retrieval of all information for a particular instance of the main type tree (e.g., all information describing a single department), while the second has advantages for the retrieval of all instances of a single segment tree (e.g., assignment information for all employees).

Schkolnick developed sets of equations to evaluate the cost of retrieval activities based on transitions from one segment to another in retrieval activities (e.g., a retrieval requiring assignment information for an employee requires a transition from the employee segment to the assignment segment). Specifically he developed cost equations for. parent-child transition, twin transition, and child-parent transition (hierarchic uncle). He characterized the activities on the hierarchy by the number of each type of transition for each segment in the tree. He then developed a branch and bound procedure to efficiently search the space of all possible aggregations. He concludes that the procedure produces record structures which are at least as efficient as those produced by experienced database designers - in some cases they are much more efficient.

This approach was developed only for the restricted case of the hierarchic data model; however, it is also applicable to other data models. Teorey and Fry [Teor82] suggest a two-step approach to aggregating network structures which was later extended by Chiang and Teorey [Chia82]. In the first step, the network structure is broken down into a set of overlapping hierarchies and the Schkolnick algorithm directly applied to each hierarchy. Forming a set of hierarchies from a network structure is relatively straightforward: when a record type is a MEMBER of only one SET, then the OWNER and MEMBER record types are already hierarchically related and no further work need be done; however, when a record type is a MEMBER of more than one SET, then a distinct hierarchy must be formed for each OWNER record type, with the MEMBER record type appearing as a child. Since a record type may appear in more than one hierarchy, it may also appear in more than one aggregation. Assuming that data are stored nonredundantly, then record types appearing in more than one aggregation conflict with the method of implementation. Such conflicts are resolved in the second step of the procedure by simply evaluating all possible combinations of conflicting aggregations. A similar procedure is applicable to any logical database. To insure optimality, the Schkolnick algorithm would have to be applied to all possible hierarchies. The difficulty lies in the number of possible hierarchies that could be created for a given logical database.

4.1.2 Record Segmentation

The aggregation approach discussed above assumes that logical entities will not be decomposed. It is possible that database performance may be improved by <u>segmenting</u> these logical structures.

The record segmentation problem is to determine an assignment of data items to segments (recall that each segment defines a subfile) that will optimize performance for all users of the database. The problem may be formally stated as

$$\min_{A \in R} \sum_{u_r \in U} v_r \sum_{s \in A} X_{rs} RC(r,s) + \sum_{s \in A} SC(s),$$

where R is the set of all possible segmentations (i.e., assignments of data items to segments), A is one particular segmentation, s is a segment of the segmentation A, $v_r$ is the frequency of retrieval request $u_r$, and $X_{rs}$ is a boolean variable defined as follows:

$$X_{rs} = \begin{cases} 1, & \text{if segment s is required by user request } u_r; \\ 0, & \text{otherwise} \end{cases}$$

RC(r,s) is the cost of retrieval for the subfile defined by segment s for the retrieval request $u_r$ and SC(s) is the cost of storage for segment s, including overhead space required for its access paths (if any).

Three major techniques have been suggested for the determination of efficient record segmentations: <u>clustering</u>, <u>iterative grouping refinement</u>, and <u>bicriterion programming</u>. Each technique varies in the assumptions it makes about access paths and the secondary memory environment it considers. These variations yield significantly different problem formulations. Each, however, is restricted to a single flat file representation, and none permit the replication of data.

Mathematically, <u>clustering</u> is simply the grouping together of things which are in some sense similar. The general idea behind clustering in record segmentation is to organize the data items physically so that those data items that are often required together are stored in the same segment; in a processing sense, such data items are "similar". Conversely, data items that are not often required together are stored in different segments; they are "dissimilar". In this way user retrieval requirements can be met with a minimal amount of extraneous data being transferred between main and secondary memory. Unfortunately, user retrieval requirements are typically diverse, and a method of evaluating tradeoffs among user requirements must be determined.

Hoffer and Severance [Hoff75a,Hoff75b] developed a heuristic procedure for the record segmentation problem that uses a mathematical clustering algorithm and a branch-and-bound optimization algorithm. Their procedure is restricted to sequential access paths but includes a detailed costing model of secondary memory (in a moving-head disk environment). The solution to this problem is an assignment of data items to segments such that the sum of retrieval, storage, and maintenance costs is minimized.

Their approach first establishes a measure of similarity between each pair of data items. This measure reflects the performance benefits of storing those data items in a common segment. It then forms initial segments by using a mathematical clustering algorithm [McCo72] to group data items with high similarity measures. Finally, a branch-and-bound algorithm selects an efficient merging of these initial segments to define a record segmentation.

Hammer and Niamir [Hamm79] developed an heuristic procedure for the record segmentation problem which iteratively forms and refines record segments based on a stepwise minimization ("hill climbing") approach. Their procedure considers the number of page accesses for multiple record segments that have been stored nonredundantly. Access may be either sequential or random via any combination of predefined secondary indexes (i.e., direct access paths), each of which is associated with exactly one data item. In order to evaluate random retrieval, they define the selectivity $S_i$ of a data item as the expected proportion of records that contains a given value for $S_i$. The selectivity of a data item is estimated by the inverse of the number of distinct values the data item may assume. If an index exists for a data item, then the selectivity of the index is equal to the selectivity of the data item.

The performance of a segmentation is evaluated by the number of pages that must be accessed in order to satisfy all user requests. Several expressions exist to estimate the number of pages that must be accessed to satisfy a retrieval request [Yao77]. An exact expression is given by:

$$\frac{N}{b}\left(1 - \frac{C_s^{N-b}}{C_s^N}\right)$$

where $C_j^k$ is the number of combinations of k objects taken j at a time, N is the number of records in the file organization, b is the blocking factor (i.e., segments per page) for the subfile, and s is the number of segments required from the subfile.

The record structuring proceeds as follows. An initial segmentation is formed, with each data item stored in a separate segment. This is termed the <u>trivial segmentation</u>. The procedure iteratively defines new segments by selecting the pair of existing segments that, when combined, yields greatest performance improvement. When no pairwise combination of existing segments yields improved performance, all single data item variations of the current segmentation are evaluated. A single data item variation moves one data item from its current segment to another segment. If any variation is found that improves the performance, then the procedure is repeated, using that variation as the initial segmentation; otherwise, the procedure terminates. While it is possible for the procedure to cycle a large number of times, experimental evidence suggests that for reasonable design problems it is not expected to cycle more than once before terminating with an efficient, if not optimal, record structuring.

Eisner and Severance [Eisn76] proposed a mathematical programming approach to the record segmentation problem, which was extended by March and Severance [Marc77,Marc78]. This approach views record segmentation as a constrained optimization problem in which the objective is to minimize the sum of retrieval and storage costs.

Based on a behavioral model of database usage that predicts subsets of "high"-use and "low"-use data items, the procedure is restricted to considering at most two segments: "primary" and "secondary." Data items with high usefulness, relative to their storage and transfer costs, are isolated and stored in a primary segment; the remaining data items are stored in a secondary segment. All activity must first access the primary subfile, and may access the secondary subfile (at additional cost) only if the request cannot be satisfied by the primary subfile. The possibility of retrieving data items by accessing only the secondary subfile is not considered.

Eisner and Severance [Eisn76] analyze this design problem by assuming that activity to the primary subfile is either all random (with both subfiles unblocked) or all sequential (with a blocked primary subfile and an unblocked secondary subfile). In addition, they assume that pointers stored in the primary segments link the corresponding secondary segments. They formulate the program as a bicriterion mathematical program and develop a parametric solution procedure based on a network flow model.

Consider a database with N records and assume that primary and secondary subfiles are both unblocked. Let $a_1$ be the cost of a single access to the primary subfile, $t_1$ be the unit cost of data transfer from the primary subfile, and $s_1$ be the unit cost of primary subfile storage over the time interval T. Similarly define $a_1$, $t_2$, and $s_2$ for the secondary subfile. Given a specific segmentation A and assuming that the primary and secondary subfiles are both sequentially processed, then

$$\begin{aligned} \mathrm{Cost}_A = N((a_1 + t_1 W_A)V \\ + (a_2 + t_2\overline{W}_A)\overline{V}_A \\ + s_1 W_A + s_2\overline{W}_A) \end{aligned}$$

where $W_A$ is the length of the primary segment, $\overline{W}_A$ is the length of the secondary segment, V is the total retrieval frequency and $\overline{V}_A$ is the retrieval frequency for the secondary subfile.

Defining R to be the set of all possible record segmentations, the design problem becomes:

$$\min_{A \epsilon R} N((a_1 + t_1 W_A)V + (a_2 + t_2 \overline{W}_A)\overline{V}_A + s_1 W_A + s_2 \overline{W}_A).$$

This expression can be reduced to one in $W_A$ and $\overline{V}_A$ to yield

$$\min_{A \epsilon R} K3 - K4(K1 - W_A)(K2 - \overline{V}_A),$$

where

$$K1 = W + a_2/t_2,$$
$$K2 = (t_1 V + s_1 - s_2)/t_2,$$
$$K3 = N(a_1 V + s_2 + t_2 K1 K2),$$
$$K4 = Nt_2.$$

For reasonable values of $a_i$, $t_i$, and $s_i$, K1, K2, K3, and K4 are nonnegative constants and the objective function is minimized by that segementation which solves:

$$\max_{A \epsilon R}(K1 - W_A)(K2 - \overline{V}_A).$$

This expression is termed a bicriterion mathematical program because its objective function is the product of two expressions (i.e., $(K1 - W_A)$ and $(K2 - \overline{V}_A)$).

Geoffrion [Geof67] has shown that if $K1 \geq W_A \geq 0$, $K2 \geq \overline{V}_A \geq 0$ and R is a continuous convex set, then a solution A* with a maximum value for the objective:

$$\max_{A \epsilon R} c(K1 - W_A) + (1 - c)(K2 - \overline{V}_A)$$

all $c \in [0,1]$ also solves the above bicriterion program.

By using standard network theory, Eisner and Severance developed a procedure that produces a family of "parametric" solutions for the parameter c. On the basis of conditions established by Eisner and Severance [Eisn76] the procedure terminates either with a parametric solution, which is known to be optimal, or with the best parametric solution and a lower bound on the optimal solution. If the best parametric solution is not "sufficiently close" to the lower bound, a branch-and-bound procedure is used to find the optimal solution.

March and Severance [Marc77] extended this work in the area of blocked sequential retrieval. They generalized the analysis to a situation in which primary and secondary subfiles are arbitrarily blocked, subject to the constraint of a limited buffer area; they then presented an algorithm that determines an optimal combination of record segmentation and block size, given a fixed main memory buffer allocation.

### 4.2 Access Path Design

The problem of access path selection has been addressed by many authors. Cardenas [Card75,Card77], Hulten and Soderlund [Hult77], and Anderson and Berra [Ande77] all address the problem of secondary index selection by providing models with which to evaluate the costs of alternative choices of key data items to be indexed. They do not provide algorithms which optimally or nearly optimally select which data items to index nor do they evaluate alternative types of access paths.

Gerritsen [Gerr75] and Gambino and Gerritsen [Gamb77] provide an evaluator for alternative access paths; however, it is restricted to CODASYL based [CODA78] database management systems (DBMSs). Hoffer [Hoff80] characterizes the process of key selection for inverted file DBMSs, but like others provides no support for selecting among the numerous alternatives.

Duhne and Severance [Duhn78] proposed a branch-and-bound approach to this problem which was utilized by March and Severance in a computer aided file organization design system [Marc78]. The class of access paths considered, however, is limited; individual record retrieval is not supported and inverted files and multilist structures are not considered. In addition, the algorithm is lengthy and complex.

As an example of access path selection techniques, the procedure developed by March [Marc83b] is briefly discussed. The procedure has three major components. First, a set of "potentially useful" access paths is automatically generated based on the set of selection data items required by each retrieval and on a set of file generation constraints imposed by the designer. Multiple types of both primary (sequential, ISAM, hashed) and secondary (inverted files, inverted lists, lists, multilists, hashing via scatter tables, and hashed and hierarchic full indexes) access paths are generated as required. Next, a file organization costing model is used to evaluate the fixed cost of storage and maintenence and the variable cost of retrieval for each access path generated. Finally, these evaluations are used in a mathematical program which selects a set of access paths that minimizes total operating cost.

The access path selection problem is formulated using the network representation illustrated in Figure 6. AP is the set of potentially useful access paths to be considered and EX is the set of user retrieval requests or extracts to be supported. Access paths and extracts are each represented by nodes in the network. In Figure 6 there are 8 access paths and 4 extracts. Access paths and extracts are connected via a set, G of generated access paths. A generated access path is either a real or a virtual access path. The concept is used in the costing model to represent the cost of record retrieval required to satisfy an extract. Each generated access path, g, is connected to a set of access paths $APG(g) \subset AP$, each of which must be implemented in order to use that generated access path. In Figure 6 there are 11 generated access paths. Generated access paths 1 through 8 require one access path each (access paths 1 through 8 respectively); they are real access paths. Generated access paths 9 and 11 require two access paths each and generated access path 10 requires three access paths; they are virtual access paths. Virtual access paths are used to model the processing of multiple inverted access paths to satisfy a single extract. Each extract, ex, is connected to a set of generated access paths, $GEX(ex) \subset G$, any of which can be used to satisfy the extract. In Figure 6, extract 3 can be satisfied by generated access paths 6, 8, or 10. If it is satisfied by generated access path 10, then access paths 6, 7, and 8 must be implemented (presumably they are inverted access paths which are processed together).

Associated with each access path, $ap \in AP$, is a cost $AC_{ap}$ required to store and maintain that access path for one period. Associated with each (generated access path, extract) pair, $(g,ex)(ex \in EX,\ g \in GEX(ex))$, is cost, $GC_{g,ex}$, incurred when extract ex is retrieved via generated access path g; both record retrieval and extract sorting costs are included. The problem of access path selection is to assign each extract to a generated access path so that the sum of fixed and variable cost is minimized.

Equations for calculating the fixed and variable costs for various types of access paths were briefly discussed earlier and have been presented in detail elsewhere (see, e.g., [Hoff75b,Ande77,Marc78]). Given such costs, the task of access path selection may be formulated as a constrained, integer, linear program [Marc83b]. The objective may be stated as:

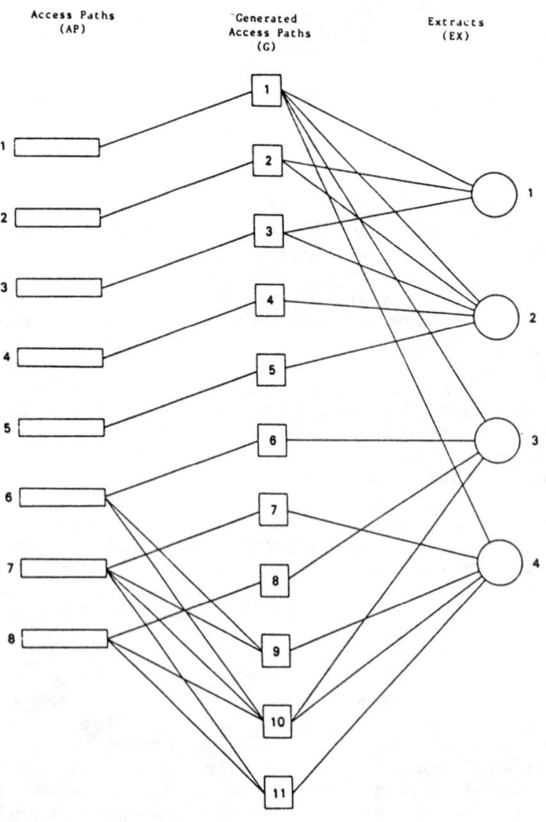


FIGURE 6. A NETWORK REPRESENTATION OF THE ACCESS PATH SELECTION PROBLEM

$$\text{Min} \sum_{ap \in AP} AC_{ap} X_{ap} + \sum_{ex \in EX} \sum_{g \in GEX(ex)} GC_{g,ex} Y_{g,ex}$$

where
$$X_{ap} = \begin{cases} 1 & \text{if access path ap is implemented} \\ 0 & \text{otherwise;} \end{cases}$$

and
$$Y_{g,ex} = \begin{cases} 1 & \text{if extract ex is obtained via generated file g,} \\ 0 & \text{otherwise} \end{cases}$$

Two sets of constraints are also required. First, each extract must be retrieved from some generated access path, that is, one member of each set GEX(ex) must have a value of 1. Given that all $Y_{g,ex}$ are binary, these constraints may be stated

$$\sum_{g \in GEX(ex)} Y_{g,ex} = 1 \text{ for all ex} \in \text{EX}.$$

Second, all access paths required by a generated access path from which any extract is retrieved must be implemented; that is, if g is used for any extract then all members of the set APF(g) must have a value of 1. Again, given that all $X_{ap}$ are binary, and that the $Y_{g,ex}$ variables are 1 if and only if g is used for ex, these constraints must be stated:

$$X_{ap} \geq Y_{g,ex} \quad \begin{array}{l} \text{for all ex} \in \text{EX} \\ \text{and g} \in \text{GEX(ex)} \\ \text{ap} \in \text{APG(g)}. \end{array}$$

A file organization must have one primary access path which accounts for the cost of data record storage and maintenance. To assure the inclusion of a primary access path, the set of extracts is augmented by an extract which may be retrieved from any primary access path, but NOT from any secondary access path. Its frequency of execution is zero times per month; hence it does not impact the total cost.

This integer program does not explicitly limit the number of primary access paths to one. An additional constraint could, of course, enforce this requirement. We do not include such a constraint because the selection of more than one primary access path indicates that data duplication is cost justified and should be considered. That is, each primary access path includes the cost of data record storage and maintenance. If more than one is selected then the retrieval cost reduction exceeds the storage and maintenance cost increase associated with the data duplication. Hence the designer should consider multiple duplicate file organizations. If this is not acceptable, then the designer may simply eliminate one of the selected primary access paths and resolve the integer program.

This integer program may be solved by evaluating all possible combinations of access paths and selecting that combination with minimal cost. Unfortunately there are $2^{NA}$ possible combinations of access paths, where NA is the number of access paths under consideration. While not all of these combinations will be feasible (i.e., meet all user information requirements) this approach is clearly inadequate for reasonably sized problems.

As an alternative approach, the program can be relaxed by removing the integer constraints; it can then be solved using classical linear programming techniques (see, e.g., [Baza77]). If the solution is integer, then the solution to the relaxed problem also solves the integer program. Otherwise, the solution to the relaxed problem provides a lower bound on the optimal solution. An upper bound may be obtained by simply rounding up all non-zero $X_{ap}$ variables, then assigning each extract to the least cost generated file available, and finally eliminating any access paths which are not used.

If the upper and lower bounds are "sufficiently close" then use the current solution (the objective in database design is to select an "efficient" not necessarily optimal solution); otherwise apply a branch and bound procedure which alternately forces access paths into and out of the solution (by adding constraints of the form $X_{ap} = 1$ and $X_{ap} = 0$ respectively) and again solves the relaxed problem. If at any branch, the solution to the relaxed problem is either integer or not "significantly" less than a known upper bound then that branch may be pruned.

Theoretically the procedure discussed above may become rather time consuming due to the potential for branch and bound. However, in a series of 40 experiments using the procedure (discussed in [Marc83b]) the linear program produced an optimal solution 24 times. In the remaining 16 experiments the maximum difference between the lower bound obtained from the linear program and upper bound obtained by the rounding heuristic described above was less than 1 percent. While this does not guarantee that branch and bound will never be required, it does suggest that this approach is of practical significance for real world design problems.

## 4.3. The Combined Record Structuring and Access Path Selection Problem

As discussed above, record structuring and access path selection are interrelated problems. Record structuring techniques assume a given set of access paths; the cost evaluations associated with access path selection techniques depend on the record (segment) lengths.

An approach to the combined problem has been presented by March and Severance [Marc78] as part of a more global file organization design procedure. They first heuristically generate a set of access paths and use the Eisner-Severance procedure to determine an optimal record segmentation for the assumed set of access paths. Using that segmentation; an efficient set of access paths is selected using a branch and bound procedure developed by Duhne [Duhn78]. Using this set of access paths, the record segmentation algorithm is applied again. If the segmentation has not changed, then the procedure stops, otherwise, if the segmentation has changed, the access path selection algorithm is repeated with the new segmentation.

Theoretically this procedure could cycle many times and never converge. March and Severance limit the number of cycles to a maximum of 2 and select the record segmentation and set of access paths which minimize cost. The procedure is heuristic and cannot guarantee optimality; however, the physical design selected in a series of experiments have been intuitively reasonable and considerably more efficient than the simplistic designs to which they were compared (see [Marc78]).

Carlis and March [Carl83b] took a similar approach to this problem; however, the branch and bound algorithm was replaced by the linear programming approach discussed above. In addition, they suggest a heuristic procedure to generate potentially useful record aggregations prior to applying the segmentation and access path selection techniques.

# 5. SUMMARY AND DIRECTIONS FOR FURTHER RESEARCH

This paper has discussed techniques for physical database design. Specifically the subproblems of record structuring and access path selection were addressed. Techniques for record structuring include hierarchic aggregation, which seeks to group logically defined records and three segmentation techniques (clustering iterative grouping - refinement and bicriterion programming), which seek to partition logically defined records. Techniques for access path selection include evaluation procedures and optimization procedures utilizing branch and bound and linear programming. Finally, an approach to the combined record structuring-access path selection problem was presented.

We believe that the integration of record structuring with the selection of data access paths is a major area for future research. What is needed is a comprehensive model that will include both aggregation and segmentation and explicitly incorporate the effects of alternative data access paths. Such a model would serve as the basis for a more integrated approach to database design optimization than has previously been possible.

A second area for future research is integrating the database design and the software design activities. The activities on the physical database depend in part on the procedures used to access data. Alternate implementations for various queries could significantly impact the selection of record structures and access paths. This type of analysis is the subject of query optimization; however such techniques have not as yet been applied to the database design problem.

A third area for research is that of determining the effects of update operations. The costs associated with doing update operations are significantly different from those of retrieval operations and therefore affect the selection of record structures and access paths in different ways. In addition, alternative record structures and access paths vary greatly in their requirements for backup and recovery procedures. A record structure that isolates all data items that are subject to update may reduce backup and recovery costs; however, it may increase retrieval costs.

Finally, in any database serving a diversified user community, the question of data security must also be considered. Although in certain cases segmented record structures may be more expensive to implement, for security reasons it may be desirable to isolate sensitive data items in a high-security segment, perhaps stored on a separate disk device and requiring specific access authority. Similarily, some efficient access paths may not be implemented due to data security considerations.

References

(ANDE77) (BATO82, see BATO82b) (BAZA77) (CARD75) (CARD77) (CARL83a) (CARL83b) (CHAM81) (CHEN76) (CHIA82) (CODA78) (COME79) (DATE82) (DUHN78) (EDEL81) (EISN76) (GAMB77) (GEOF67) (GERR75) (HAMM79) (HOFF75a) (HOFF75b) (HOFF80) (HULT77) (IBM74) (KENT78) (KNUT73) (LUM79) (MARC77) (MARC78) (MARC83a, see MARC83) (MARC83b) (MART77) (MCCO72) (MCGE77) (NAVA78) (RIM83) (SCHK77) (SCHK79) (SEVE77) (SPER81) (TEOR82) (WIED77, see WIED83) (YAO77, see YAO77a)

# Chapter 4: DBMS Design

This chapter deals with the nuts and bolts issues of how a database management system works. In Section 4.1, we discuss how to translate commands into the canonical command language. Such a command translator is needed for each type of user interface supported by the database management system.

Section 4.2 describes approaches for query optimization, the process of choosing the optimal or near optimal access paths to access the desired data.

Section 4.3 introduces the concept of transaction and describes the requirements of transaction processing.

Backup and recovery is an important feature of database management systems. Section 4.4 describes what types of redundant data are needed if database recovery is to occur. Also described are techniques for recovering all or part of the database by using this redundant data.

To increase database usage, it is desirable that several users (both human and software) can access the database at the same time. Techniques for controlling concurrent access to the data is described in Section 4.5.

### 4.1: Command Translation

The commands entered via each user interface must be translated to a single canonical command language for processing by the rest of the database management system. In effect, the command translators hide the user interface specific formats from the other processors in the database management system.

If the user interface is fairly similar to the canonical commands, then the translation is fairly simple, perhaps making only minor changes in syntax. If the user interface is menu oriented, the menu subsystem could be used to generate the canonical command language.

If, however, the user interface is quite different from the canonical command language, then more complex transformations are necessary. This may be the case if the user interface uses one data model while the canonical command language uses another data model. The paper, "Bridging the Gap between Network and Relational Database Management Systems," by Larson reprinted in this chapter, discusses the translations between data structures and the translations between commands of two of the most widely used data models.

### 4.2: Query Optimization

Efficient methods of processing queries are necessary for the success of a database management system. A large body of knowledge has been developed to solve this problem. The paper, "Query Optimization in Database Systems," by Jarke and Koch presents a framework for query optimization. In addition to describing the optimization problem, this paper discusses query transformation, query evaluation, and the development of access plans.

### 4.3: Transaction Processing in a DBMS

A *transaction* consists of program code that may contain several database commands. A transaction preserves database *consistency* by transforming the database from one consistent state to another. When executed, there are two possible outcomes. First, the transaction *commits* if no errors are detected. After the transaction commits, all of the changes made by the database update commands are made permanent in the database. Second, if an error is detected during the processing of the transaction, the transaction is *aborted.* When this happens, any changes made to the database are undone. If the transaction aborts, none of the changes by the transaction are made permanent in the database.

A transaction is said to be *atomic* because either all of its updates are made permanent in the database or no updates are made to the database. This is convenient because it provides a way to write software modules (which are often called transactions) that either perform several database update commands or none at all.

A transaction is said to have *durability,* which means that once committed, the results of a transaction will never be lost. Backup and recovery mechanisms, described in Section 4.4, are used for this purpose.

The following is an example transaction that transfers an amount between two accounts.

```
TRANSFER: BEGIN TRANSACTION;
  GET (SOURCE-ACCOUNT-NUMBER, TARGET-
                    ACCOUNT-NUMBER, AMOUNT);
  FIND UNIQUE (ACCOUNT WHERE ACCOUNT-
        NUMBER = SOURCE-ACCOUNT-NUMBER);
  IF <FIND NOT SUCCESSFUL> THEN DO;
    PUT ('TRANSACTION FAILS: SOURCE
                    ACCOUNT NOT FOUND');
    ABORT;
    END;
  ACCOUNT.BALANCE = ACCOUNT.BALANCE -
                                AMOUNT;
  IF SOURCE-ACCOUNT.BALANCE < O THEN DO;
    PUT ('TRANSACTION FAILS: INSUFFICIENT
                FUNDS IN SOURCE ACCOUNT);
```

```
    ABORT;
    END;
  UPDATE (ACCOUNT WHERE ACCOUNT-
          NUMBER= SOURCE-ACCOUNT-NUMBER);
  FIND UNIQUE (ACCOUNT WHERE ACCOUNT-
          NUMBER = TARGET-ACCOUNT-NUMBER);
  IF <FIND NOT SUCCESSFUL> THEN DO;
    PUT ('TRANSACTION FAILS: TARGET
                       ACCOUNT NOT FOUND');
    ABORT;
    END;
  ACCOUNT.BALANCE = ACCOUNT.BALANCE -
                                   AMOUNT;
  UPDATE (ACCOUNT WHERE ACCOUNT-
          NUMBER = TARGET-ACCOUNT-NUMBER);
  PUT ('TRANSACTION SUCCESSFUL, FUNDS
                             TRANSFERED');
  COMMIT;
  END TRANSFER;
```

When the above transaction is executed, either the specified amount is transferred from the source account to the target account and the database is updated permanently or an error message is displayed and no change is made permanently to the database.

Two transactions are said to be *serial* if they do not overlap in time. Two transactions are said to be *concurrent* if they overlap in time. It is often desirable to process transactions concurrently because processing transactions decreases the average response time. However, sometimes the concurrent processing of transactions results in a *conflict* when one transaction needs to modify the data that another transaction needs to reference. For example, suppose two programs attempt to credit the same account. Program A is to record a $10 payment and program B is to record a $12 payment. The following sequence of events could take place:

1. The unmodified account record is copied from the database into A's work space.
2. The unmodified account record is copied from the database into B's work space.
3. The outstanding-balance field in the account record in A's work space is decreased by $10, and the revised record is copied from A's work space back into the database.
4. The outstanding-balance attribute value in B's work space is decreased by $12, and the revised record is copied from B's work space back into the database.

The revised record from step 4 replaces the revised record from step 3; the credit of $10 is lost. This occurs because both A and B updated identical copies of the record from the database. To prevent two programs or interactive users from updating identical copies of a record, steps 2 and 3 must be interchanged so that A copies the revised record back to the database before B copies the database. Serial transactions preserve the database *consistency*, each transaction changing the database from one consistent state to another. No lost updates of the type illustrated above can occur to make the database inconsistent.

To understand database consistency better, we introduce the concept of a transaction history. If the histories of several transactions satisfy certain requirements, then the database is consistent.

A *transaction history* is a partial or total order on the READs and WRITEs of a set of transactions. An example history is

H = R1[X] W2[X] W1[X] W2[Y]

which is interpreted as

T1 reads X
T2 writes X
T1 writes X
T2 writes Y

A *serial history* is a history of two transactions that execute serially. For example,

H = R1[X] W1[X] R2[X] R3[Y] W3[Y]

is a serial history of transaction T1 (which reads X and writes X), followed by transaction T2 (which reads X), finally followed by transaction T3 (which reads Y and then writes Y). Any serial history preserves the database consistency.

Two histories are *equivalent* if they produce the same output and leave the database in the same state after execution. Consider the following histories:

H1 = R1[X] W1[X] R2[X] W2[X]
H2 = R2[X] W2[X] R1[X] W1[X]
H3 = R1[X] R2[X] W1[X] W2[X]
H4 = R1[X] R2[X] W2[X] W1[X]

Histories H1 and H2 are equivalent while histories H1 and H3 are not. Histories H1 and H4 are not equivalent.

A history is *serializable* if there exists an equivalent serial history for it. Serializable histories preserve the database consistency. A serializable history does not imply that the history is serial (although serial histories are by definition serializable). For example,

H5 = R1[X] R1[Y] R2[X] W1[Y] R2[Z]

is equivalent to the serial history

H6 = R1[X] R1[Y] W1[Y] R2[Z] R2[Z]

Serializable histories allow some overlapping of transactions, but not enough overlapping to lose database consistency. Section 4.5 describes approaches to guarantee that overlapping transactions have serial histories.

The results made by a transaction must be hidden from other transactions until the transaction itself has committed. Otherwise, intermediate results of a transaction that might eventually abort could be used by another transaction.

In summary, there are five important properties of transactions:

- *Atomicity:* Transactions are atomic, either all or none of the transactions database operations are recorded permanently in the database.
- *Durability:* The results of a transaction are durable. Once committed, the results will never be lost.
- *Serializability:* The execution of several overlapping transactions is serializable; the result is the same as if they were executed serially.
- *Isolation:* An incomplete transaction cannot reveal results to other transactions before the transaction itself is committed.
- *Consistency:* A transaction transforms the database from one consistent state to another.

Transactions keep the database consistent. However, other factors can affect the database contents. Making the database available when the data are needed is discussed in the next section.

### 4.4: Data Availability

Data must be available when they are needed by an enterprise; however, data can be destroyed or lost due to a variety of hardware or software problems. Natural causes such as flood, fire, or prolonged humidity can destroy magnetic storage media. Human factors can also result in loss of valuable data. Loss of data could occur, for example, if a machine room manager dropped a disk pack or if a Boy Scout was touring the tape vault with a magnet in his pocket. Mechanical factors such as a disk head's scrapping the surface of a disk or a tape drive's stretching a magnetic tape can also cause data to be lost. Update programs may be terminated abnormally, leaving the database in a partially updated, inconsistent state. Correct data can be replaced by incorrect data because of a bug in either the program or the system software. Hardware may also fail to perform accurately and result in the storing of incorrect data.

Since no one can predict when a partial or total loss of the data might occur, it is wise to take precautionary steps so that the database can be recovered or reconstructed easily if data are lost. Such precautionary steps usually consist of storing redundant data at a separate location. Database backup procedures differ depending on the type and the form of the redundant data. Below is an overview of techniques that ensure data availability.

*Duplicate database*

Maintaining a duplicate copy of the database is one technique to guarantee data availability. All updates are made to both databases. Data lost from one of the databases can be copied from the duplicate. However, the cost of maintaining duplicate databases can be expensive. In practice, such databases are used only when data must always be available and when the expense of lost data is greater than the cost of maintaining a duplicate database.

*Database Backup*

A less expensive technique than maintaining a complete database duplicate is to make a complete copy of the database, called a *database backup.* Usually, a database is backed-up (copied) to a magnetic tape by a special unload procedure. If the database is lost, a reload procedure is used to restore it from the backup. All database processing that occurred after creation of the database backup must be reprocessed.

If updates are being reprocessed against a database that is also being backed-up, care must be taken to record the new values of any updated data that have already been backed-up. The reload procedure must first copy the backed-up database and then update any data modified after being backed-up.

If the database is very large, creating the backup may require a long period to complete. Creating the backup is usually done during slack time when few or no updates are being processed and when the full computer resources can be allocated to the backup procedure.

Another form of data redundancy is the log. There are several types of logs. Each type is used to record redundant data that can be used to reconstruct a lost database.

To process a transaction, a database management system must perform the following steps:

1. Receive the transaction from a terminal or calling program.
2. Retrieve one or more entities to be updated from the database or verify that the entity to be added to the database does not already exist.
3. Construct revised entities to be replaced in the database or construct new entities to be added to the database.
4. Write constructed entities into the database and create an update-completed message.

*Transaction Log*

One popular backup technique is to copy each update entered into the database management system. The database management system makes a copy of each update after step 1 and prior to step 2. The transaction is copied to a transaction log, which is not part of the database and usually resides on a magnetic tape. If the database is lost, it can be reconstructed by copying the most recent database backup and reprocessing all transactions recorded on the transaction log since the backup was created. All BEGIN transaction, COMMIT transaction, and ABORT transaction commands are also recorded on the transaction log.

A transaction log may be used for other purposes. Special programs can be written that examine the transaction log to determine the frequency of various types of updates or the frequency of updating various parts of the databases. Often the identification of the person or program that initiates the update is also recorded on the transaction log, which can then serve as a complete history of all updates against the database. This information is very useful for auditing purposes and for identifying which individuals or programs are responsible for changing various portions of the database.

*After-Image Log*

Between steps 3 and 4 above, a copy of the updated entity is written to an after-image log. Each entry on the after-image log contains such information as time the update was processed, update type (such as insert, modify, or delete), identification of the program or user that entered the update, address of new or revised entities, and values of new or revised entities.

If the database is lost, the most recent database backup is copied back to the database. All MODIFY and INSERT entries on the after-image log are then placed into the database. With DELETE transactions the record is removed from the database. The process of restoring a database by using an after-image log is similar to restoring a database by using the update log. However, with the after-image log, updates are not reprocessed because the revised entities rather than the updates themselves are recorded.

*Before-Image Log*

Between steps 2 and 3 of the processing of a database update, a copy of the entity or entities to be updated are written to a *before-image log*. Each entry on this log contains information such as time the update was processed, update type, program or user identification, address of the old entity, and values of the old entity.

If the database becomes invalid due to a program bug or because incorrect data were added to it, the before-image log can be used to back out or remove the erroneous entities from the database. A special process reads the before-image log backward, beginning with the most recent update, and replaces all revised entities by unrevised entities and inserts all entities that had been deleted. The processing is stopped when all erroneous updates have been removed. The database is now restored to a point in time prior to the processing of the erroneous updates.

All updates occurring after this point in time, however, have been lost. The nonerroneous updates can be restored by either of the following techniques: (1) reprocess all programs and on-line updates not responsible for the erroneous data or (2) reprocess all transactions from the update log, excluding updates from programs or online updates responsible for the erroneous data.

Having made preparations for data loss by storing redundant data, let us investigate when and how to use this redundant data to reconstruct a data loss in the database.

*Reconstructing Databases*

An error that has been introduced into a database can be propagated to other data in the database as a result of updates dependent on the erroneous data. The results of programs reading the erroneous data may also be affected. Suppose program A erroneously updates Jones' record by indicating that Jones has received an educational degree. Later, program B causes the salary of all employees with that degree to receive a 10 percent salary increase. The result is that Jones would have an undeserved salary recorded in the database. Because a single invalid piece of datum can contaminate other data, the sooner an error is discovered and corrected, the less damage will be done to the database.

The basic approach for recovery consists of the following steps:

1. Search transaction log from the beginning to identify transactions with BEGIN TRANSACTION but no COMMIT or ABORT.
2. Undo any changes made to the database by these transactions (by replacing the after images in the database by the before images from the before-image log), then restart them.

This approach suffers from one problem. The transaction log may be very large. To overcome this, the concept of a quiet point is introduced. A *quiet point* is when the database management system accepts no new transactions until all of the current transactions have committed and the quiet point record is written to the transaction log. Now step 1 above is modified by searching the transaction log from the most recent quiet point record to identify transactions with BEGIN TRANSACTION but no COMMIT or ABORT.

However, some applications cannot tolerate disruption in service even to create a quiet point. For these applications, a checkpoint is created. A *checkpoint* is a special entry on the transaction log that contains all of the transactions active at the time of the checkpoint. All log information is also forced to the log file during a checkpoint. The checkpoint is used in the following recovery procedure:

1. Locate the most recent checkpoint in the transaction log. Let UNDO be a list of all transactions that were active when the checkpoint record was created. Let REDO be empty.
2. Search the log beginning with the most recent checkpoint record. For each begin transaction found, place the transaction on the UNDO list. For each commit found, move the transaction from the UNDO list to the REDO list.
3. For each transaction on the UNDO list, undo the transaction (by replacing after images in the database with before images from the before-image log) and restart the transactions.
4. For each transaction on the REDO list, redo the changes in the database (by applying the after images from the after-image log).

The next section describes a technique for processing transactions that does not use logs. It uses a different form of redundant data called a differential file.

*Differential Files*

Updating a database in place means data are changed by removing their old value from the database and replacing it with a new value; thus the old value is no longer availabale. In differental files, data in the database are marked as updated, but no change is actually made to the data. The revised data are stored in a separate location called a *differential file.* The database is static; no changes or modifications are made to it. Associated with each record in the database is a single bit in a bit table separate from the database. If the bit has value 0, then the corresponding entity in the database is accurate. If the bit has value 1, the corresponding entity has been modified. The revised entity is found in the differential file. After the user approves the results, the modified data recorded in the differential file are moved to the appropriate positions in the database, and the corresponding positions in the bit table are set to 0.

Differential files provide for deferred updates, which are reported as having been made but actually have been deferred until it is certain that the updates are valid.

The use of differential files allows changes to be made in the differential file of a database while a separate process is unloading the database to a backup. It lends itself to *incremental dumping*, the unloading of a portion of the database followed by some modifications of the database followed by unloading another portion of the database, and so on.

The paper, "Principles of Transaction-Oriented Database Recovery," reprinted here, by Haerder and Reuter describes a framework for describing and relating different transaction-oriented recovery schemes.

## 4.5: Concurrency Control

There are three principle methods for providing concurrency control: (1) locks, (2) timestamps, and (3) optimistic methods.

*Locks*: A *lock* is a mechanism that can be set (or locked) by a user who wants to update data in the database. As long as a lock is set, no other user may access that data. After a user completes all modifications to the data, the lock is opened and other users may again access the data. A transaction is *well formed* if it locks data before using it and releases the lock after using the data. To prevent data loss due to a concurrent update, the execution of transactions A and B of Section 4.1 can be revised to

1. A sets the lock. The unmodified record is copied from the database into A's work space.
2. B attempts to set the lock but finds it already locked. B must wait until the lock is opened before updating the data.
3. The outstanding-balance value in A's work space is decreased by $10. The revised data are copied from A's work space back into the database. The lock is opened.
4. B again attempts to set the lock. Finding the lock open, B sets the lock and copies the entity from the database into B's work space.
5. The outstanding-balance value in B's work space is decreased by $12. The revised data are copied from B's work space back into the database. The lock is opened.

The auditors are happy because no payments are lost. The individual making the payments is happy because the outstanding-balance attribute value was decreased by $22 instead of just $12.

A lock can be implemented by using a one-bit variable. When the lock bit is set to 1 by a program that wishes to update the database, no other program may have access to the data. When the updating program has completed its modification of the data and the data are copied back into the database, the lock is opened by setting the lock bit to 0. Now other programs again may access the data in the database.

Two types of locks are possible:

- *Shared locks*: Any number of transactions can hold a read-lock on an item at the same time. This means that several transactions can read the same data.

- Exclusive locks: Only one transaction can hold a write-lock on an item. No other transaction can have a lock (either read or write) on the item.

Locking the entire database for one program to perform updates may deny many other programs and interactive users access to the database. Only that portion of the database being updated needs to be locked. Locking more of the database only prohibits other programs from accessing data not affected by the updating program. The database can be partitioned with a lock bit associated with each partition. When a program is to update data in a partition, it sets the lock associated with the partition of the database. No program may access a database partition whose lock is set.

The database must be divided into partitions that do not overlap. There are several disjoint partitionings of a database, including (1) the entire database is a single partition, (2) each record type in the database is a partition, and (3) each physical page of data is a partition (a page is a unit of physical storage such as a disk track).

Another technique that may be used to keep track of locked partitions of the database is a *lock list.* The name or address of each partition to be locked is placed on the list of locked partitions when a program is to update that partition. The entry is removed from the list after updates to that partition are completed. A partition can appear only once in the locked list; thus, concurrent updating against the same partition is prohibited.

*Two-phase Locking:* In Section 4.3 we defined the concept of transaction serializability. Serializability is necessary to prohibit transactions from being interweaved to such an extent that conflicts occur. The following protocol, called *two-phase locking,* guarantees that if all transactions adhere to the protocol, then the transaction histories are serializable.

1. There is a growing phase in which each transaction obtains all of its locks.
2. Then, there is a shrinking phase when each transaction releases all of its locks.

Once a transaction releases a lock, it should not obtain another lock. To ensure isolation, a transaction should release all of its locks after the COMMIT is executed.

*Deadlocks:* A corollary of Murphy's law states that a correct solution to one problem generates another problem. That is the case when locks are used to solve the loss of integrity caused by concurrent updating. Suppose the following happened:

1. Program A locks record 1.
2. Program B locks record 2.
3. Program A attempts to lock record 2 and finds it already locked. Program A waits for entity 2 to become unlocked.
4. Program B attempts to lock record 1 and finds it already locked. Program B waits for record 1 to become unlocked.
5. Both A and B wait on each other.

Programs A and B are deadlocked. Neither program can spring to life and continue processing; neither can die and be removed from the system. There are three ways of dealing with deadlocks: (1) detection, (2) prevention, and (3) timeout.

*Deadlock Detection:* A deadlock exists if there is a circular chain of requests to set locks. For example:

A waits on a lock set by B.
B waits on a lock set by A.

The circular chain may involve more than two programs:

A waits on a lock set by B.
B waits on a lock set by C.
.
.
.
Y waits on a lock set by Z.
Z waits on a lock set by A.

Deadlocks can be detected by checking continuously for cycles every time a transaction blocks. In periodic detection, cycles are searched for periodically.

A deadlock can be abolished only by breaking the circular chain of locks. A transaction in the chain is chosen and aborted. (Recall that when a transaction is aborted, all of its database changes are not permanently recorded in the database.) The aborted transaction releases all of its locks. The deadlock cycle is broken, and the remainder of the deadlocked transactions may be completed. Then, the aborted transaction is restarted.

Which transaction should be aborted? There are several criteria:

1. *Current blocker* Transaction that most recently blocked.
2. *Random blocker* Choose a transaction at random.
3. *Min locks* Transaction that holds the fewest locks.
4. *Youngest* Transaction with the most recent initial start-up time.
5. *Min work* Transaction that has performed the least amount of work.

*Deadlock Prevention:* In *deadlock prevention* strategies, a deadlock never occurs. Any potential conflicts are detected before a lock is granted.

In one deadlock prevention strategy, a transaction starts only if all locks needed for the completion of the transaction are granted. This implies that the transaction must request all locks at the beginning of the transaction. This approach may preclude some possible and harmless transaction concurrency. Other approaches to deadlock prevention vary in how potential conflicts are resolved:

- *Wound-wait:* If Ti requests a lock that conflicts with a lock held by Tj and Ti is older than Tj, then restart Tj (Ti wounds Tj). Otherwise, lock Ti (Ti waits for Tj).
- *Wait-die:* If Ti requests a lock that conflicts with a lock held by Tj and Ti is older than Tj, then block Ti (Ti waits for Tj). Otherwise, restart Tj (Ti dies).
- *Immediate-restart:* If Ti requests a lock that conflicts with a lock held by Tj, then restart Ti.
- *Running-priority:* If Ti requests a lock that conflicts with a lock held by Tj and if Tj is waiting for some Tk, then restart Tj.

*Timeout:* Probably the most common method of dealing with deadlocks is aborting a transaction that has been in a wait state for a certain amount of time. A critical parameter is the *timeout interval,* the amount of time to wait before aborting the waiting transactions. If the timeout interval is too large, then resources are held unnecessarily long by the waiting transaction. If the timeout interval is too small, then nondeadlocked transactions are aborted. Agrawal, Carey and McVoy in "The Performance of Alternative Strategies for Dealing with Deadlocks in Database Management Systems," reprinted here, suggest that best results are obtained when the timeout interval is

average(W) + Standard deviation(W)

where W is the request waiting time.

The reprinted paper by Agrawal, Carey, and McVoy describes a simulation involving these choices. It concludes that the best deadlock resolution strategy is dependent upon the system's operating region. In a low conflict situation, the performance of all deadlock resolution strategies is basically identical. In a situation where resources are heavily utilized, continuous deadlock detection is the deadlock resolution strategy of choice. The min locks strategy is best for selecting the transaction to abort. For interactive transactions, wound-wait deadlock prevention appears to be the best alternative.

*Timestamps:* An entirely different approach for dealing with concurrency control is the use of timestamps. Each transaction is assigned a timestamp when the transaction begins execution. Normally, the timestamp is nothing more than a counter that increments after each new transaction has started. Each item in the database has two timestamps:

- *READ Timestamp:* Timestamp of the transaction that last read the item in the database, and
- *WRITE Timestamp:* Timestamp of the transaction that last updated the item in the database.

To determine if a transaction should be aborted, the following protocol is used:

- Transaction T1 wants to read a database item with timestamp T2 as a WRITE timestamp, and Timestamp(T1) < Timestamp(T2), then T1 must abort.
- Transaction T1 wants to update database item with Timestamp(T2) as a READ timestamp, and Timestamp(T1) < Timestamp(T2), then T1 must abort.
- Ti wants to update database item with Timestamp(T2) as a WRITE timestamp and Timestamp(T1) < Timestamp(T2), then T1 does not write the database item.

The following sequence of actions is an example of the use of timestamps. Initially, the READ and WRITE timestamps of database item A are both zero.

1. Transaction T1 reads A. The READ timestamp of A is set to 200 (the timestamp of transaction T1).
2. Transaction T2 reads A. The READ timestamp of A is set to 210 (the timestamp of transaction T2).
3. Transaction T1 increments the value of A by 5.
4. Transaction T2 increments the value of A by 6.
5. Transaction T2 writes A back into the database. The WRITE timestamp of A is set to 210 (the timestamp of transaction T2).
6. Transaction T1 attempts to write A back into the database. However, because the timestamp of transaction T1 (which is 200) is less than the WRITE timestamp of database item A (which is 210), transaction T1 must be aborted and restarted.

When using timestamps as a concurrency control method, deadlocks cannot occur. Thus, no deadlock detection is necessary. However, there is potential for a high number of restarts. There is also a potential for *live locks*, which occurs when a transaction is restarted over and over again, but aborts each time.

*Optimistic Approaches to Concurrency Control:* In this approach to concurrency control, each transaction is run uninterrupted to completion. All database updates are temporarily stored in a differential file. When the transaction commits, the transaction is validated by checking to see if its history is serializable. If validation is successful and the history is serializable, then the transaction is committed (and the updates are copied to the real database). Otherwise, the transaction is aborted (and the updates in the differential file thrown away).

Generally, two-phase locking is used in commercial database systems. It appears to perform best under low or no conflict conditions. Timestamps appears to be best when there is a high number of conflicts. The optimistic approach is seldom used.

### Additional Readings

Gray, James, "Notes on Data Base Operating Systems." In Operating Systems: An Advanced Course edited by R Bayer, R.M. Graham, and G. Seegmuller, Springer-Verlag, New York, 1978. Excellent reference for material on transaction management.

Kim, Won, "On Optimizing an SQL-Like Nested Query," *ACM TODS*, Vol. 7, No. 3, September 1982, pp. 443–469. Describes some of the optimizing strategies used in System R.

Rosenthal, A. and D. Reiner, "An Architecture for Query Optimization," *Proc. 1982 ACM SIGMOD International Conference on Management of Data,* ACM, New York, June 1982.

Wong, E. and K. Youssefi, "Decomposition—A Strategy for Query Processing," *ACM TODS*, Vol. 1, No. 3 , September 1976, pp. 223–241.

*A single database management system can support both the network and relational styles of describing and manipulating data.*

# Special Feature

# Bridging the Gap Between Network and Relational Database Management Systems

**James A. Larson,**
**Honeywell Corporate Computer Sciences Center**

The advantages and disadvantages of network and relational database management systems have been debated extensively. Supporters of the relational model claim it is simpler, more uniform, and provides more data independence. Supporters of the network data model claim it provides a more natural structure for modeling the world, that the semantics are built into the structure, and that data repetition is reduced, resulting in a more consistent database. Moreover, relational data manipulation languages appear easier to use, while network data manipulation languages can lead to more computer efficiency. Recently researchers and practitioners have recognized that, while both data models are useful for different applications, neither is best for all applications.

This article surveys strategies whereby one database management system can support both facilities. These strategies must be understood by those who design and implement database management systems that support multiple data models. Designers and implementors of applications using database management systems, database administrators, and others interested in database management should also be familiar with these strategies so they can evaluate alternative approaches for supporting multiple data models within a single database management system.

A data model is a style of describing and manipulating data stored in the database. Several data models have become prominent, including the network and relational data models, but most database management systems support only one data model. Thus, a relational database management system supports the relational style of describing and manipulating data, while a network database management system supports the network style of describing and manipulating data. *Network database* and *relational database* are sometimes used to refer to databases accessed by, respectively, network and relational database management systems. We shall see, however, that a single database management system may support both relational and network data description and manipulation facilities.

A database management system that supports only one data model presents several difficulties:

- The data model may not lend itself to the application at hand.
- A massive conversion may be necessary if a database management system using a different data model is installed. (A change in vendor hardware may require a new database management system.)
- It is usually difficult for one database management system to access data maintained by another system using a different data model.

A database management system supporting more than one data model eases these problems:

- The programmer can choose the data model that best suits the application at hand, is most familiar to him, and allows him to be the most productive.
- Moving applications and databases to a multi-model database management system is easier than converting applications and databases from one data model to another.
- Communications between two different database management sytems is eased because of the common style of data description and manipulation.





Reprinted from *Computer*, September 1983, pages 82-92. Copyright © 1983 by The Institute of Electrical and Electronics Engineers, Inc.

The network and relational data models differ in two important aspects: they use different languages to describe data stored in a database and different languages to manipulate data in the database.

**Network data description.** Several revisions have been published of the network data model first specified by the Codasyl Database Task Group in 1971.[1] Briefly, a network database contains *records* consisting of *data items.* Associations among records are called *sets.* In the network database shown in Figure 1a, records are illustrated by rectangles. All records participating in a set are within an oval shaped by a broken line.

The network data description language describes homogeneous records called *record types* and homogeneous sets called *set types.*

Figure 1b uses a Z-diagram[2] to represent the description of the network database shown in Figure 1a. This type of representation graphically illustrates certain features of a database relevant to our discussion. In Z-diagrams, rectangles represent record types while arrows indicate set types. Figure 1b shows two record types, Company and Product, and one set type, Produces. The record type at the tail of the arrow is called the *set owner.* Each set in the database must contain exactly one record of this type. The record type at the head of the arrow is called the *set member.* The Company record type consists of two item types, Company Name and City. The Company Name item type is underlined to indicate that no two Company records may have the same value for a Company Name item. In this discussion, *record key* refers to the collection of items which must have unique values across all occurrences of the record type.

Each record in the database can belong to, at most, one set of a set type. In some circumstances, records of the set member type will not belong to any set of the set type. Sets may exist without records of the member type. Member records within a set are sequenced. They may be logically sequenced according to the values in one or more item types. In Figure 1b, Product records within a Company set are sequenced by the value of the Product Name item. Alternative criteria may determine where a new member record is to be positioned within the set. For example, the Codasyl specification ORDER IS PRIOR requires that a new member record must be inserted prior to the most recently accessed member record. It is also possible to specify that no two member records in the same set occurrence may have the same value for an item or collection of items. Other specifications include constraints on inserting and retaining member records within a set. The description of all data in a network database is called a *network schema.*

**Relational data description.** The relational data model was first introduced by E. F. Codd[3] in 1970. A relational database consists of tables (also called *relations*) made up of rows and columns. No ordering is implied among the rows of a table. Each column is atomic, and repeating items within a column are not allowed. A column or collection of columns for which different rows must have distinct values is called a *table key.* Figures 2a and 3a illustrate two relational databases, each containing the same information as the database in Figure 1a. Because there is no standard relational description language, Z-diagrams are used in Figures 2b and 3b to illustrate the descriptions of the relational databases in Figures 2a and 3a. Rectangles represent tables; table keys are underlined. (Later, under "The Mapping Approach," we will discuss the relative merits of these two alternative relational databases for the network database of Figure 1.) The description of all data in a relational database is called a *relational schema.*

To support both data models, a multi-model database management system must support both the network and the relational styles of describing and manipulating data.

**Since existing programming languages are inherently procedural, constructs must be added to support nonprocedural database manipulation commands.**

**Network and relational data manipulation.** The Codasyl network data manipulation language permits the programmer to navigate through the database by accessing a single record for each command. He may access either another record within the same record type or a record of a different type within the same set as the current record. He may also write efficient applications by carefully coding sequences of database commands to take advantage of the structure of the network database by specifying how the database management system is to access the data. This style of data manipulation language is often called *procedural* because the programmer must specify how the database management system is to access the database by describing a sequence of data manipulation commands to access the desired records.

Most relational data manipulation languages, on the other hand, are *nonprocedural.* They permit the programmer to specify what results are desired from the database management system without specifying how that system is to access the database. The database management system, rather than the programmer, chooses the appropriate access paths. Nonprocedural languages allow users to access several records for each data manipulation command. Nonprocedural database manipulation languages are useful as stand-alone query languages.

Graphical languages, such as Query by Example,[4] have been developed as nonprocedural, end-user-oriented interfaces to relational databases. Several nonprocedural data manipulation languages also have been implemented to directly access network databases. Because existing programming languages such as Fortran and Cobol are inherently procedural, additional constructs must be added to them to support nonprocedural database manipulation commands. This has been done for many programming languages.

Besides being nonprocedural, one relational data manipulation command can be constructed by combining two other commands. For example, the two relational commands GET COMPANY NAME WHERE

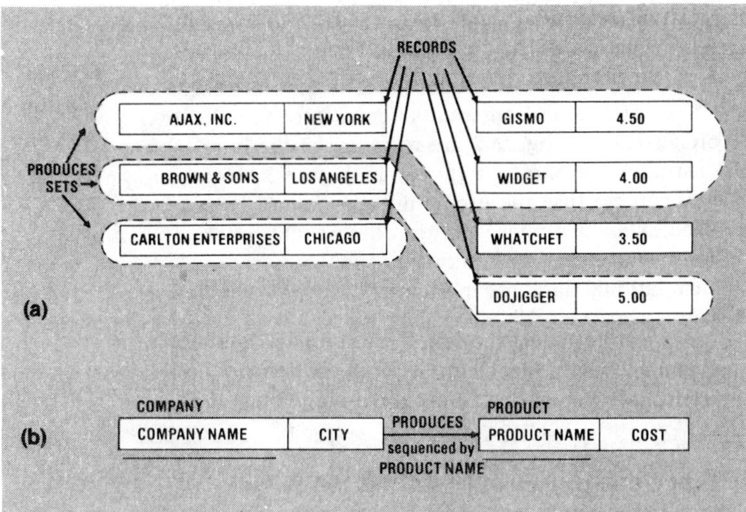


Figure 1. A network database (a) and schema (b).

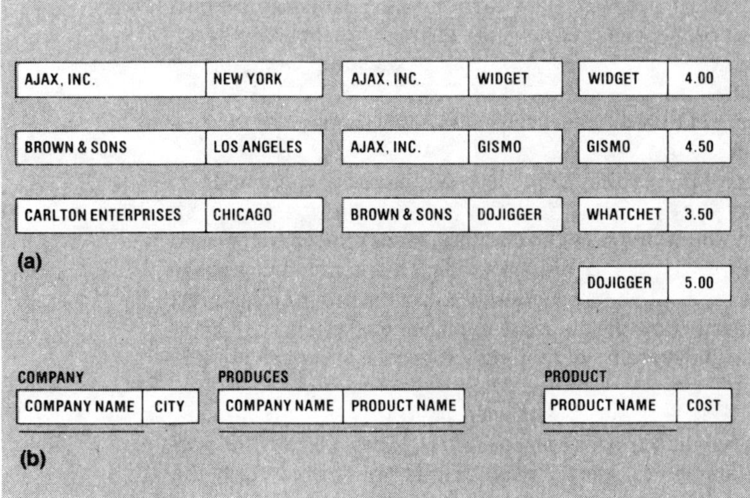


Figure 2. A relational database (a) and schema (b).

| | |
|---|---|
| AJAX, INC. | NEW YORK |
| BROWN & SONS | LOS ANGELES |
| CARLTON ENTERPRISES | CHICAGO |

| | | |
|---|---|---|
| AJAX, INC. | WIDGET | 4.00 |
| AJAX, INC. | GISMO | 4.50 |
| BROWN & SONS | DOJIGGER | 5.00 |
| (NULL) | WHATCHET | 3.50 |

(a)

COMPANY

| COMPANY NAME | CITY |
|---|---|

PRODUCT

| COMPANY NAME | PRODUCT NAME | COST |
|---|---|---|

(b)

Figure 3. A relational database (a) and schema (b).

CITY = "Chicago" and GET COMPANY NAME WHERE CITY = "Los Angeles" may be combined into one command: GET COMPANY NAME WHERE CITY = "Chicago" OR CITY = "Los Angeles." Relational commands also may be used to define views of the database where a view is a table that can be derived from other tables in the database.

Both nonprocedural and procedural styles of data manipulation are useful. Because high-level languages may be easier to learn and write, they are more suitable for the casual database user. Procedural languages, on the other hand, are more suitable for the technical programmer because these languages may provide greater efficiency. A multi-model database management system should support both styles.

**Requirements for a multi-model database management system.** A multi-model database management system must meet two main requirements: it must support both nonprocedural and procedural languages, and it must support both relational and network schemas. Figure 4 illustrates two main approaches to a multi-model database management system, which we call *mapping* and *composite*. The mapping approach suggests that a schema for one data model be generated from a schema of the other data model. Data manipulation commands against the generated schema are translated to equivalent commands, which can be processed against the original schema. A database management system in which a relational schema can be mapped to an underlying network schema exemplifies the mapping approach.

The composite approach suggests that a schema for one data model be embedded into a schema of the other data model. The resulting *common schema* contains objects which can be viewed as both relational and network objects. Relational and network data manipulation commands use the common schema.

From the user's perspective, there is one significant difference between the two approaches; in the mapping approach, a program is restricted to one or the other type of command; in the composite approach, however, a program can mix network and relational commands.

## The mapping approach

Because more network than relational databases exist, we will first examine how to generate a relational schema from an existing network schema, then illustrate how nonprocedural relational commands can be translated to sequences of procedural network commands.

**Building a relational schema from a network schema.** Two schemas are equivalent if (1) they describe the same database, (2) any command expressed in terms of the objects of one schema can be translated into commands expressed in terms of the objects of the other schema, and (3) the same changes are made to the database if either source command or the target commands are executed. Biller[5] provides a more formal definition for the equivalence of two schemas. In Chapter 14 of *Data Models*, Tsichritzes and Lochovsky[6] provide an excellent summary of data model mappings.

For the information in a network database to be available in a relational database management system, the network schema must be mapped to an equivalent relational schema. In general, a network record type is mapped to a table. Each data item of the network record is mapped to a column of the table. Each record key is mapped to a table key. For example, the network database in Figure 1 maps to both of the relational databases in Figures 2 and 3. Network structures deserving careful examination to determine their relational equivalents include set participation, set ordering, repeating groups, system-owned sets, and areas.

*Set participation.* A table may be used to represent each network record type. A table also may be used to represent each set type. When this transformation is applied to the network database in Figure 1, the result is the relational database in Figure 2. A table column is a *foreign key* if it may take on only the values of a key of a separate table. In the database in Figure 2, both Company Name and Product Name of the Produces table are foreign keys. Foreign keys represent a special type of *inter-table constraint.* Each value of Product Name in the Produces table must also appear as a Product Name in the Product table. Likewise, each Company Name of the Produces table must also appear as a Company Name in the Company table. These constraints can be enforced either by prohibiting certain relational operations (such as deleting a row of the Products table before deleting the corresponding row of the Produces table) or by permitting side effects (such as the automatic removal of the corresponding row of the Produces table whenever a row of the Product table is removed).

McGee[7] suggests the replication of table columns among tables and adopts the reasonable convention that the two rows are related whenever the values of their common columns are the same. Zaniolo[2,8] has developed techniques for generating relational schemas of this type from network schemas. In 1979, J. Goldman developed a translator based on these techniques that requires limited user interaction. When applied to the network database in Figure 1, Zaniolo's technique produces the relational database in Figure 3. In effect, the record key Company Name of the owner record Company has been propagated through the set into the member record Product. Company Name becomes a foreign key in the Product table. A null symbol is used in the Company Name column of the Product table to indicate that a Product is not produced by any Company. De, Hoaseman, and Kriebel[9] suggest another method for building up a network schema from a relational schema. The network schema generated is optimal in the number of items and record types.

Biller[5] shows how to construct a relational schema from a network schema by using an intermediate semantic data model and data definition language. An intermediate data definition language facilitates the translation of consistency constraints and is useful in proving the equivalence of source and target schema. When applied to the network schema in Figure 1, Biller's approach results in the schema of Figure 3 plus the explicit integrity constraint: each value of the Company Name column of the Product table must exist as a value of some Company Name column of the Company table. This inter-table constraint is implicit in the foreign-key declaration suggested by Johnson, Larson, and Lawrence.[10]

The inter-table constraints represented by the two foreign keys in Figure 2 are replaced by the inter-table constraints of one foreign key in Figure 3. However, users can confuse the use of null to indicate "not produced by any Company" with other possible interpretations of null, such as "unknown" or "does not apply." The relational database in Figure 3 views the association

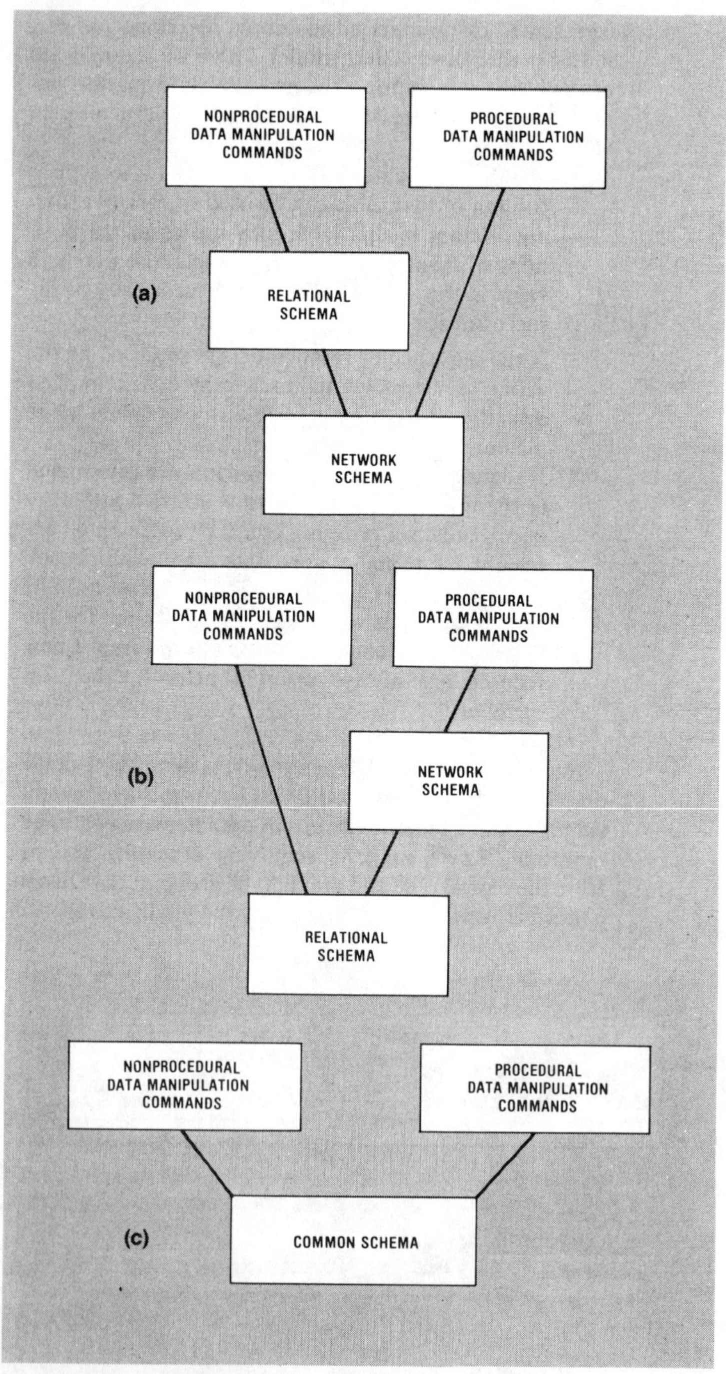


**Figure 4. Two main approaches to a multi-model database management system—mapping (a), (b) and composite (c).**

of Company rows and Product rows as the column Company Name of the Product table. In Figure 2, the association of Company rows and Product rows is viewed as a separate table, the Produces table. This approach requires that whenever a Company record is deleted, the associated rows of the Produces table also must be deleted.

*Set ordering.* A construct is *essential* if it carries information that would be lost if the construct were removed. In the relational style of describing data, all essential information stored in the database must be explicitly visible as values in tables. No implicit information can be represented by pointers or positional placement, as permitted in the network data model. There are several ways of explicitly representing the essential information implied by the sequence of member records within a set:

(1) If a separate table is used to represent a set type, a column of that table can be used to specify ordering. Values in this table may represent the positions of member records in the set. Alternately, a value in this column may be the record key of the successor (or predecessor) record.
(2) If the sequence of set members is specified by the values of items within each record, the implied essential information is visible as item values in the member records.
(3) If sequences of set member records are determined at the time a member record is inserted into a set occurrence, set ordering could be represented explicitly by using a new data item within each member record to indicate the relative position of member records within the set. The value for the new data item could be a date-time stamp if new records are always inserted after the last set member.

*Repeating groups.* A repeating data item has a single description within a record type, but may have several values within a record. Groups of data items may also be repeating. Kay[11] suggests removing repeating groups from the record type and making the group of data items a member record of a set owned by the modified record.

| AJAX, INC. | NEW YORK | WIDGET | 4.00 |
|---|---|---|---|
| AJAX, INC. | NEW YORK | GISMO | 4.50 |
| BROWN & SONS | LOS ANGELES | DOJIGGER | 5.00 |

(a)

COMPANY-JOIN-PRODUCT

| COMPANY NAME | CITY | PRODUCT NAME | COST |
|---|---|---|---|

(b)

**Figure 5. Relational database (a) and schema (b) that result from joining Figure 3's Company and Product tables.**

Other researchers have suggested that repeating groups be mapped to repeating values within a single column. For individual occurrences of repeating values to be accessed individually, the relational data manipulation language must be extended, becoming more complicated.

*System-owned sets.* All member records in a system-owned set—a special set type with a single set occurrence—are considered to be owned by the database management system. A new column is added to the table that corresponds to the record type that is the member of the system-owned set. This new column indicates whether the record belongs to the system-owned set. It may also indicate positional ordering within the system-owned set.

*Areas.* Many network database management systems still support the concept of areas, although Codasyl removed the concept of an area as a logical container for records of different types from the Codasyl Data Description Language in 1978. For these systems, a new column in each table can store the area name in which the corresponding network record belongs. Because a record cannot be moved from one area to another, the relational user is not allowed to change the value of this new column.

**Transforming commands.** Having described how a relational schema can be generated from a network schema, we will now describe how nonprocedural relational data manipulation commands can be mapped onto sequences of procedural network commands.

*Select.* The nonprocedural select command causes several rows of one table to be moved to another table. Those rows satisfying a Boolean condition for columns of the source table are moved to the target table. This nonprocedural operation corresponds to a looping statement in a procedural database manipulation language in which each record is retrieved and examined. Records satisfying the Boolean condition are moved to a separate buffer which corresponds to the target table.

*Project.* A project command causes the specified columns of all rows of a table to be copied to another table. This nonprocedural operation corresponds to a looping statement in which each record is retrieved and the specified items are copied to a separate buffer. Some relational languages require that the rows of the target table of a project operation be unique. In this case, the resulting records are sorted so that duplicate records can be removed.

*Join.* A join command causes two tables to be combined, forming a third table. Two rows, one from each table, are joined if their values satisfy a Boolean condition. For example, joining the Company and Product tables in Figure 3—where the Company Name of the Company row equals the Company Name of the Product row —results in the table in Figure 5. This operation corresponds to two nested loops in a procedural language. The outer loop reads successive Company records. The inner loop reads successive Product records in the Produces set owned by the current Company record. When the Company and the Product records satisfy the Boolean condition, these records are combined and written to a separate buffer. If there are $n$ owner records and $m$ member records, this operation has the complexity of $m+n$.

Any two records may be joined if they have equal values in two selected columns, one column from each record. If the compatible columns do not reflect the association of a member record with an owner record, an operation with the complexity of $mn$ is required to compare each occurrence of one record type with each occurrence of the other record type.

Sequences of joins, selects, and projects can be optimized. For example, a select followed by a project can be combined into a single loop that selects records satisfying the Boolean condition and copies the projected items. Onuegbe, Rahimi, and Hevner[12] suggest an optimization strategy which examines sequences of nonprocedural relational commands and produces sequences of procedural network commands embedded in loops nested to several levels. Dayal and Goodman[13] show how to synthesize a program containing procedural commands that is equivalent to any command from a class of nonprocedural queries.

Two problems must be overcome if a multi-model database management system is to support dynamic creation of tables. First, most current network database management systems do not support dynamic updates to the network schema. If the network database management system is extended to support the relational data model, it may also be necessary to extend it to permit dynamic schema updates in order to support dynamic creation of tables. Second, programming languages such as Fortran and Cobol do not permit dynamic allocations of program variables. If these languages are extended to include nonprocedural database commands, extending them to permit dynamic allocation of tables may be necessary as well.

**Command binding.** The process of translating a data manipulation command expressed in a nonprocedural language into one or more procedural commands is called *command binding*. There are several stages in a program's life when addresses referenced by an application program may be transformed or bound to physical hardware addresses; similarly, there are several stages when nonprocedural data manipulation commands may be command bound to procedural commands. This transformation may be performed when the program is written or as late as the first execution of a data manipulation command. In general, the earlier the command binding takes place, the fewer number of times the command-binding process takes place. However, the earlier the command binding takes place, the more stages of a program's life there are that must be reprocessed whenever the database is restructured.

Command binding can be performed after the program has been written but before the source code is compiled. The command binding could be accomplished by a "preprocessor" or "precompiler," which replaces nonprocedural data manipulation commands by sequences of statements containing procedural commands. The source code from the preprocessor then may be compiled by a traditional compiler. New user-oriented data manipulation commands can easily be made available to the user by modifying the preprocessor to produce compilable statements equivalent to new nonprocedural commands. If the database is restructured, different procedural data manipulation commands may be needed to access the same data because the command produced by the preprocessor may no longer be valid. Whenever the database is restructured, the preprocessor and the compiler must be reinvoked to reprocess each program accessing the database.

The preprocessor performs many of the same functions as the compiler. This duplicated processing could be avoided if the compiler were used to perform the command binding. The compiler itself may perform the translation from nonprocedural data manipulation commands into sequences of procedural commands. A traditional compiler modified to perform this function, although it would be somewhat more complex and time-consuming than the unmodified compiler, would be less time-consuming than the combination preprocessing-compiler strategy. The modified compiler can also deal with interactions between data manipulation commands and other programming language statements. For example, the compiler can verify that the target and source variables of data manipulation commands are of the same type; if they are not, the compiler can choose appropriate transformation algorithms to invoke during execution of those commands. Using the compiler to perform command binding, however, requires modification of the compiler for each user language into which data manipulation commands are to be embedded. Each program accessing a database may need to be recompiled whenever the database is restructured.

Alternatively, command binding can take place after compilation and prior to execution. This approach assumes that only minor changes are made to traditional compilers so that the nonprocedural data manipulation commands accepted by a compiler are changed only syntactically. No command binding is done by a compiler. Each compiler modifies the nonprocedural commands only to the extent that user-language dependencies are removed. The canonical nonprocedural data manipulation commands produced by one compiler are indistinguishable from those produced by other compilers. The process of command binding is factored out of compilers. There are two advantages to this approach: the command-binding process is isolated to one software module rather than replicated through several preprocessors or compilers; and if the database is restructured, programs accessing the database need not be recompiled (a fairly expensive process). The command-binding process may be a stand-alone process invoked prior to execution but after compilation, or it may be invoked by the linkage-editor software module. Upon database restructuring, all programs accessing the database must be command bound again.

The process that loads a link-edited program into main storage and prepares it for execution may also invoke the command-binding process. No programs are made invalid when the database is restructured because each program is command bound at the time it is loaded. The expense of command binding a program each time it is loaded for execution may be excessive for frequently run programs.

To minimize the expense of binding at load time while retaining the flexibility of restructuring the database without causing programs to become invalid, command binding can be invoked dynamically during program execution. Command binding may be carried out for each data manipulation command when it is first executed, or it may be carried out for all commands associated with a portion of the database when that portion is opened. Savings may occur only if several data manipulation commands are not performed during program execution.

Command binding may be performed at several stages, binding only selected data manipulation commands at each stage. Optionally, data manipulation commands may be partially bound at one stage and completely bound at a later stage.

**Implementation.** A network database management system can be extended to suppport the relational data model by providing a relational schema and mapping nonprocedural relational data manipulation commands to sequences of procedural network commands. These commands are then executed by the underlying network database management system. This approach allows existing network database users to continue viewing the database as a network database, while allowing users to develop new applications using either data model. As more and more applications are implemented using nonprocedural languages, special hardware becomes more cost-justifiable. After the critical break-even point is surpassed, hardware assists such as associative memory, logic in memory, and parallel processing support very rapid execution of nonprocedural commands. To realize the benefits of special hardware, the underlying database management system should be relational with a network interface for existing applications using procedural interfaces (see Figure 4b).

The mappings between the network and relational schemas remain the same when switching from the approach shown in Figure 4a to that in Figure 4b; however, the roles of the network and relational schemas are interchanged. The procedural network data manipulation commands must now be mapped to nonprocedural relational commands. If each procedural command is translated to one or more nonprocedural commands that access at most a single record, the potential efficiency of special hardware assists will not be realized. Applications using procedural data manipulation commands should be gradually replaced by ones using nonprocedural commands.

Katz and Wong[14] observe that mapping procedural commands into nonprocedural commands is analogous to decompiling in programming languages. Progam code must be examined for patterns consisting of loops and procedural network commands. Program code matching a pattern can be replaced by the equivalent nonprocedural relational command. Katz and Wong present an algorithm that maps many programs written using the Codasyl Data Manipulation Language into programs that access data via a relational interface.

## The composite approach

The mapping approach suggests that the schema of one data model be generated from the schema of the other. Two sets of commands are available to the user, one set for use against each of the schemas. On the other hand, the composite approach suggests that a single schema be used to support data manipulation commands of both models. Such a composite schema must support both procedural and nonprocedural data manipulation commands, as well as provide the user with both a network and relational perception of the database. The value-based set construct accomplishes these goals.

**Value-based schemas.** A value-based set[10] is a construct in which the essential information of set participation and set ordering is explicit as values in member records. A set is value-based if a copy of the owner's record key appears in each member. Each of the following applies:

- a record of the member type belongs to a set *if and only if* the member's copy of the owner's record key is non-null;
- when the member's copy of the owner's record key is non-null, its value is the same as the record key in the owner record of the set; and
- the sequence of member records within a set is based on the values of items within the member records.

For a value-based set, the owner and member records of a set can be completely determined by examining the values of a record key of the owner records and values of a copy of the record key in member records. Value-based sets are similar to the relations obtained by using the Zaniolo mapping technique cited earlier in this discussion.

A network schema is value-based if all sets in the schema are value-based. Value-based schemas support the relational perception of data; all information conveyed by data structure in the schema is explicitly visible as values. A member record can be moved to a different set by changing the value of the record key copied from the owner record and letting the database management system switch the record to the new set. Value-based schemas also support the network preception of data. A member record can be moved to a different set by explicit command. The database management system changes the value of the record key copied from the owner record.

Suppose that Carlton Enterprises begins to produce Whatchets. Using the value-based schemas in Figure 6a, a programmer can insert the Whatchet record into the Produces set with owner Carlton Enterprises by either of two techniques:

(1) The programmer supplies the value of "Carlton Enterprises" for Company Name of the Product

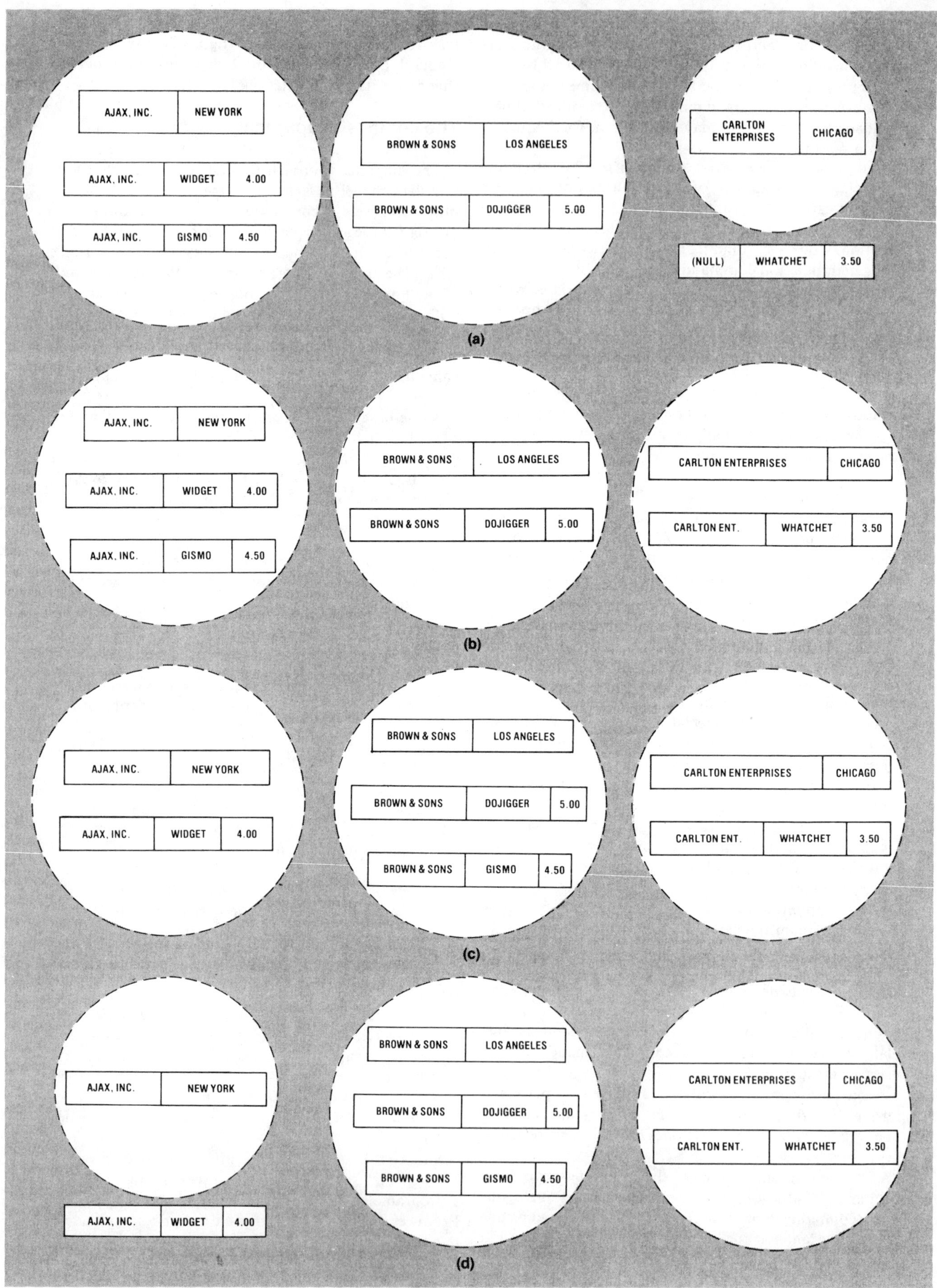


**Figure 6. Value-based schemas.**

record and performs the relational data manipulation command MODIFY. The database management system uses this value to identify the appropriate owner and connects the Product record to that set.

(2) The programmer performs the network data manipulation command INSERT, which associates the Product record with the appropriate owner. The database management system gets the Company Name of "Carlton Enterprises" from the owner record and appropriately modifies the copy of that key in the member Product record.

The result is illustrated in Figure 6b.

Suppose Gismo now is made only by Brown & Sons. The programmer may explicitly remove the Gismo Product record from the set owned by Ajax, Inc., and insert the Gismo Product record into the Produces set owned by Brown & Sons. Or the programmer may change the Company Name item in the Gismo Product record from "Ajax, Inc.," to "Brown & Sons." The revised database is shown in Figure 6c.

Finally, suppose Ajax, Inc., no longer makes Widgets. The desired database is illustrated in Figure 6d. The programmer may accomplish this by removing the Widget Product record from the Produces set owned by Ajax, Inc., or by changing the Company Name of the Product item to the null state by a modify command.

Using value-based schemas, a programmer does not need to modify the values of data items in member records when an insert or remove command is issued. The database management system performs this task for the programmer. Explicit insert and remove commands may be performed on sets of value-based schemas. An insert will change the state of the appropriate item of the member record from null to non-null. A remove will change the state of the appropriate item of the record that participated as a member of a value-based set from non-null to null.

On the other hand, a programmer never needs to issue an insert or remove command when using value-based schemas. Changing the value of the appropriate member's copy of an owner's key of a value-based set causes an implicit insert and remove. Changing the member's copy of an owner's key to null causes an implicit remove. Changing the appropriate member's copy of an owner's key in a record of the member type of a value-based set from the null state causes an implicit insert.

**Table 1.**
**Relationships between declarations and constraints on member's copy of owner's record key.**

| DECLARATION | CONSTRAINTS |
|---|---|
| Insertion is automatic | Null is not allowed on store of member record |
| Insertion is manual | Null is allowed on store of member record |
| Retention is mandatory | Value may not be changed to null on modify of member record |
| Retention is optional | Value may be changed to null on modify of member record |
| Retention is fixed | Value may not be changed on modify of member record |

Like all network set types, value-based set types must be declared with either the *automatic* or *manual* insertion option and with the *mandatory, fixed,* or *optional* retention options. These options specify constraints on commands affecting set membership. Although the insert and remove commands may be avoided, the constraints affecting set membership still apply. These constraints may be expressed in terms of permissible null and non-null states and permissible transitions between states of the member's copy of the owner's key.[10]

If the Produces set is declared *automatic*, then whenever Product record is initially stored, it is automatically inserted into a set; the Company Name of the Product record is set equal to Company Name of a Company record. Thus, the null state is not allowed for Company Name of Product if the record is being stored in the database and the Produces set is *automatic*.

A Product record may be stored in the database without connecting it to an occurrence if the set is declared to be *manual*. In this case, Company Name may be null in a Product record when it is stored into the database. *Mandatory* prohibits a member record from existing in the database without belonging to a set once the record has been connected to some set; Company Name of Product may change values, but it may not be set to the null state by a modify command.

*Fixed* prohibits a member from being removed from a set; Company Name of Product may not be modified once it has a non-null value. *Optional* allows a member record to be removed from a set occurrence; Company Name of Product may be changed to the null state. Table 1 summarizes the relationships between the insertion/retention options and the constraints on items in the member's copy of the owner's key.

As with Codasyl sets, constraints are also needed on the record types which are owners. For example, such constraints may prohibit the removal of owner records, require that any record members of a set owned by the owner record be removed when the owner record is removed, or change the member's copy of the owner's record key to null for all members in the set owned by a member record. Details may be found in Vassiliou and Lochovsky.[15]

Value-based sets provide users with a network schema (users ignore the migrated keys) and a relational schema (users ignore the set construct) of the same database. They may use procedural or nonprocedural commands or a combination of both to access the database.

While a value-based set supports relational and network schemas, it presents a redundant description of essential information: set membership is represented by both owner record keys being copied to each member record and the owner-member set construct. Such redundancy may add to the perceived complexity of a schema.

**The Unified Database Language.** C. J. Date[16] has proposed the Unified Database Language which supports data description and data manipulation of several data models. This language has an "onion-layer' structure, as

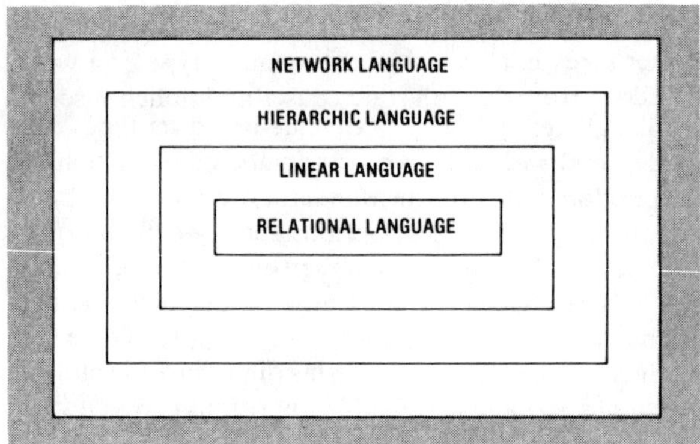


**Figure 7. Structure of the Unified Database Language.**

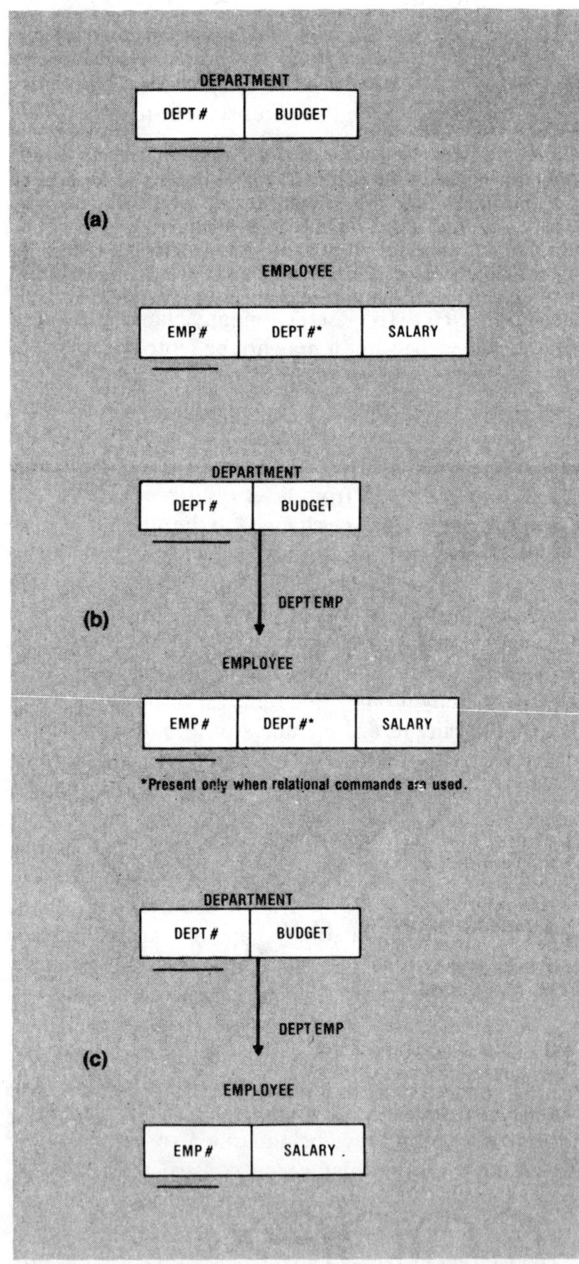


**Figure 8. Z-diagrams for a relational schema (a), a Unified Data Language schema (b), and a non-value-based network schema (c).**

illustrated in Figure 7. The commands needed to manipulate data defined at an inner level are a subset of those needed to manipulate data defined at an outer level. The data description language needed to declare data structures at an inner level is a subset of the data description language needed to declare data structures at the next outer level.

Figure 8 illustrates Z-diagrams for a relational schema, a Unified Data Language schema, and a non-value-based network schema. In the Unified Data Language schema, the member's copy of the owner's key is marked with an asterisk. Marked items are returned to the user in records accessed using relational commands, but they are not present when the records are accessed using network commands. The redundancy of set membership and the member's copy of the owner's record keys is minimized by marking the member's copy. To be a truly embedded approach, the member's copy of the owner's key must always be present in the member record. This is the case in value-based schemas because the member's copy of the owner record key is always present. This is not the case with Unified Data Language schemas because the marked items are sometimes omitted. The perceived complexity present in value-based schemas is decreased in the Unified Data Language. Like the composite approach, the Unified Data Language uses a common schema.

Neither the relational nor the network data model is best for all applications. A database management system is needed which supports not only the network and the relational styles of describing data but also several styles of manipulating data. The two basic approaches to supporting multi-model data management described in this article—the mapping and the composite approaches—resolve the differences between network and relational data models. ■

## References

1. Database Task Group of Codasyl Programming Language Committee, *Report*, Apr. 1971.
2. Carlo Zaniolo, "Design of Relational Views Over Network Schemas," *Proc. ACM Sigmod Int'l Conf.*, 1979, pp. 179-190.
3. E. F. Codd, "A Relational Model of Data for Large Shared Data Banks," *Comm. ACM*, Vol. 13, No. 6, June 1970, pp. 377-387.
4. M. M. Zloof, "Query by Example," *AFIPS Conf. Proc.*, Vol. 44, 1975, NCC, AFIPS Press, Arlington, Va., pp. 431-438.
5. Horst Biller, "On the Equivalence of Data Base Schemas —A Semantic Approach to Data Translation," *Information Systems*, Vol. 4, No.1, 1979, pp. 35-47.
6. Dionysios Tsichritzis and Frederick Lochovsky, *Data Models*, Prentice-Hall, Englewood Cliffs, N.J., 1982.

7. W. C. McGee, "A Contribution to the Study of Data Equivalence," *Database Management,* J. W. Klimbie and K. L. Koffeman, eds., North-Holland, Amsterdam, 1974, pp. 123-146.

8. Carlo Zaniolo, "Multimodel External Schemas for Codasyl Database Management Systems," *Proc. IFIP TC-2 Working Conf. Data Base Architecture*, G. Bracchi and G. M. Nijssen, eds., 1979, North-Holland, Amsterdam, pp. 157-176.

9. P. De, W. D. Hoaseman, and C. H. Kriebel, "Towards an Optimal Design of a Network Database from Relational Descriptions," *Operations Research*, Vol. 26, No. 5, Sept.-Oct. 1978, pp. 805-823.

10. H. R. Johnson, J. A. Larson, and J. D. Lawrence, "Network and Relational Modeling in a Common Data Base Architecture Environment," Sperry Univac Research Report #TMA00720, Mar. 1979.

11. M. H. Kay, "Data Independence in Database Management Systems," PhD thesis, University of Cambridge, Jan. 1976.

12. Emmanual Onuegbe, Said Rahimi, and Alan Hevner, "Local Query Translation and Optimization," *AFIPS Conf. Proc.*, Vol. 52, 1983 NCC, AFIPS Press, Arlington, Va., May 1983, pp. 229-239.

13. Umeshware Dayal and Nathan Goodman, "Query Optimization for Codasyl Database Systems," *Proc. Int'l Conf. Management of Data*, 1982, pp. 138-150.

14. R. H. Katz and E. Wong, "Decompiling Codasyl DML into Relational Queries," *TODS*, Vol. 7, No. 1, Mar. 1982, pp. 1-23.

15. Y. Vassiliou and F. H. Lochovsky, "DBMS Transaction Translation," *Proc. Compsac 80*, pp. 89-96.

16. C. J. Date, "An Architecture for High-Level Language Database Extensions," *Proc. ACM-Sigmod Int'l Conf. Management of Data*, J. B. Rothnull, ed., 1976, pp. 101-122.

**James A. Larson,** currently doing research in distributed databases at the Honeywell Corporate Technology Center, was involved previously in the design of integrated automatic office systems for Olivetti, Italy, and research in database computers at Sperry Univac. He has been a member of the Codasyl Data Description Language Committee and has taught courses in databases for the University of Minnesota. Larson is author of *Database Management System Anatomy*, editor of the IEEE Computer Society *Tutorial: End User Facilities in the 1980s*, co-editor of the IEEE Computer Society *Tutorial: Data Base Management in the 1980s*, and author of numerous technical papers and articles. He holds a BS degree in mathematics from Utah State University and MS and PhD degrees in computer science from Washington State University.

# Query Optimization in Database Systems

MATTHIAS JARKE

*Graduate School of Business Administration, New York University, New York, New York 10006*

JÜRGEN KOCH

*Fachbereich Informatik, Johann Wolfgang Goethe-Universität, 6000 Frankfurt 1, West Germany*

Efficient methods of processing unanticipated queries are a crucial prerequisite for the success of generalized database management systems. A wide variety of approaches to improve the performance of query evaluation algorithms have been proposed: logic-based and semantic transformations, fast implementations of basic operations, and combinatorial or heuristic algorithms for generating alternative access plans and choosing among them.

These methods are presented in the framework of a general query evaluation procedure using the relational calculus representation of queries. In addition, nonstandard query optimization issues such as higher level query evaluation, query optimization in distributed databases, and use of database machines are addressed. The focus, however, is on query optimization in centralized database systems.

Categories and Subject Descriptors: A.1 **[General Literature]**: Introductory and Survey; H.2.2 **[Database Management]**: Physical Design—*access methods*; H.2.3 **[Database Management]**: Languages—*query languages*; H.2.4 **[Database Management]**: Systems—*query processing*; H.2.6 **[Database Management]**: Database Machines; I.1.1 **[Algebraic Manipulation]**: Expressions and Their Representation—*simplification of expressions*

General Terms: Algorithms, Performance

Additional Key Words and Phrases: Database implementation, query optimization, query simplification

## INTRODUCTION

Database management systems (DBMS) have become a standard tool for shielding the computer user from details of secondary storage management. They are designed to improve the productivity of application programmers and to facilitate data access by computer-naive end users.

There have been two major areas of research in database systems. One is the analysis of data models into which the real world can be mapped and on which interfaces for different user types can be built. Such conceptual models include the hierarchical, the network, the relational, and a number of semantics-oriented models that have been reviewed in a large number of books and surveys [Brodie et al. 1984].

A second area of interest is the safe and efficient implementation of the DBMS. Computerized data have become a central resource of most organizations. Each implementation meant for production use must take this into account by guaranteeing the safety of the data in the cases of concurrent access [Bernstein and Goodman 1981c], recovery [Verhofstad 1978],

CONTENTS



and reorganization [Sockut and Goldberg 1979]. One major criticism of many early DBMSs has been their lack of efficiency in handling the powerful operations they offer, particularly the content-based access to data by queries. *Query optimization* tries to solve this problem by integrating a large number of techniques and strategies, ranging from logical transformations of queries to the optimization of access paths and the storage of data on the file system level.

Traditionally, each of these approaches has used a different language. This is probably one of the reasons why no comprehensive survey of query optimization techniques has yet been presented. The goal of this paper is to review query optimization techniques in the common framework of relational calculus. This has been shown to be technically equivalent to a relational algebra representation [Codd 1972; Klug 1982a] and extendable to the implementation of network DBMSs [Dayal and Goodman 1982]. Moreover, many popular query languages, such as SQL [Astrahan and Chamberlin 1975] or QUEL [Stonebraker et al. 1976], map easily into relational calculus.

In the interest of space, the focus of the paper is primarily on the problem of optimizing queries in the centralized DBMS. Centralized query optimization is not only important in many mainframe databases—and more recently in microcomputer DBMSs—but also appears as a subproblem of query optimization in distributed systems. Distributed query optimization itself [Bayer et al. 1984; Sacco and Yao 1982; Ullman 1982] is only addressed briefly, and the following two related areas are not treated at all:

*User Optimization.* The overall cost of an information system is composed of the DBMS cost and the costs of user efforts to work with the system. The interface in the two areas consists of the functional capabilities and usability of the query language [Vassiliou and Jarke 1984], mainly in the response time of the system. If one assumes given functional capabilities of the query language and a response time minimization goal of the query evaluation system, query optimization can be handled as a separately tractable subproblem of user optimization.

*File Structures.* A query optimization algorithm has to choose among a variety of existing access paths to resolve a query. The internal details of implementing such access paths and the derivation of the related cost functions (see, e.g., Teorey and Fry [1982]) are beyond the scope of this paper.

The paper is organized into six sections, following a top-down approach. In Section 1 we present a global framework for query optimization. In Section 2 we compare four techniques for representing queries in terms of their suitability for optimization. In Section 3 we utilize one of these techniques, the relational calculus, for presenting logic-based transformations, including the emerging methods of semantic query optimization.

After being transformed, a query must be mapped into a sequence of operations that return the requested data. In Section 4 we analyze the implementation of such operations on a low-level system of stored data and access paths. In Section 5 we present optimization procedures for integrating these operations into a globally optimal access plan.

A number of query optimization problems require special treatment because of higher query complexity or certain characteristics of the underlying hardware. Three such problem areas—higher level queries, distributed queries, and queries using database machines—are summarized in Section 6.

## 1. THE QUERY OPTIMIZATION PROBLEM

Exact optimization of query evaluation procedures is in general computationally intractable and is hampered further by the lack of precise statistical information about the database. Query evaluation algorithms must rely heavily on heuristics. Nevertheless, the term "query optimization" will be used to refer to strategies intended to improve the efficiency of query evaluation procedures. In this section we state the objectives of query optimization and present a general procedure designed to structure the solution process.

### 1.1 Queries

A *query* is a language expression that describes data to be retrieved from a database. In the context of query optimization, it is often assumed that queries are expressed in a content-based (and mostly set-oriented) manner, giving the optimizer sufficient choices among alternative evaluation procedures.

Queries are used in several settings. The most obvious application is that of direct requests by end users who need information about the structure or content of the database. If the requests are limited to a set of standard queries, they can be optimized manually by programming the associated search procedures and restricting the user's input to a menu format. However, an automatic query optimization system becomes necessary if ad hoc queries are to be asked by use of a general-purpose query language.

A second application of queries occurs in transactions that change the stored data based on their current value (e.g., "give all assistant professors a 10 percent salary increase"). Finally, querylike expressions can be used internally in a DBMS, for example, to check access rights [Griffiths and Wade 1976], maintain integrity constraints [Stonebraker 1975], and synchronize concurrent accesses correctly [Reimer 1983].

### 1.2 Optimization Objectives

The economic principle requires that optimization procedures either attempt to maximize the output for a given number of resources or to minimize the resource usage for a given output. Query optimization tries to minimize the response time for a given query language and mix of query types in a given system environment. This general goal allows a number of different operational objective functions. The response time goal is reasonable only under the assumption that user time is the most important bottleneck resource. Otherwise, direct cost minimization of technical resource usage can be attempted. Fortunately, both objectives are largely complementary; when goal conflicts arise, they are typically resolved by assigning limits to the availability of technical resources (e.g., those of main memory buffer space).

In order to allow a fair comparison of efficiency, the functional capabilities of the query evaluation systems to be compared must be similar. The requirement of "relational completeness" coined by Codd [1972] (compare Section 2.1) has become a quasi-standard. The techniques surveyed in this paper are presented as contributions to the implementation of queries in a relationally complete language with minimal evaluation cost or response time. Queries of higher complexity [Chandra and Harel 1982a] are considered in Section 6.1. The total cost to be minimized is the sum of the following:

*Communication Cost:* The cost of transmitting data from the site where they are stored to the sites where computations are performed and results are presented. These costs are composed of costs for the communication line, which are usually related to the time the line is open, and costs for the delay in processing caused by transmission. The latter, which is more important for query optimization, is often assumed to be a linear function of the number of data transmitted.

*Secondary Storage Access Cost:* The cost of (or time for) loading data pages from secondary storage into main memory. This is influenced by the number of data to be retrieved (mainly by the size of intermediate results), the clustering of data on physical pages, the size of the available buffer space, and the speed of the devices used.

*Storage Cost:* The cost of occupying secondary storage and memory buffers over time. Storage costs are relevant only if storage becomes a system bottleneck and if it can be varied from query to query.

*Computation Cost:* The cost for (or time of) using the central processing unit (CPU).

The structure of query optimization algorithms is strongly influenced by the trade-off among these cost components. In long-range distributed DBMSs with relatively slow communication lines, communication delay dominates the costs, whereas the other factors are relevant only for local suboptimization. In centralized systems, the costs are dominated by the time for secondary storage accesses although the CPU costs may be quite high for complex queries [Gotlieb 1975]. In locally distributed DBMSs, all factors have similar weights, which results in very complex cost functions and optimization procedures.

Since the focus of this paper is on centralized databases, comuunication costs are not considered because in such systems communication requirements are independent of the evaluation strategy. For the optimization of single queries, storage costs are usually also assumed to be of secondary importance. They are considered only for the simultaneous optimization of multiple queries.

There remain the costs of secondary storage accesses (usually measured by the number of page accesses) and CPU usage (often measured by the number of comparisons to be performed). A number of common ideas underly most techniques developed to reduce these costs. They try to (1) avoid duplication of effort, (2) use standardized parts, (3) look ahead in order to avoid unnecessary operations, (4) choose the cheapest way to execute elementary operations, and (5) sequence them in an optimal fashion. The following simple example demonstrates what can be expected from query optimization.

Consider the relational schema of a database that describes employees offering computer lectures to departments of a geographically distributed organization:

employees (enr, ename, status, city)
papers (enr, title, year)
departments (dname, city, street address)
courses (cnr, cname, abstract)
lectures (cnr, dname, enr, daytime)

Key attributes are underlined; a given combination of key attribute values identifies a relation element uniquely. Assume that a user is interested in the

> "names of departments located in New York offering courses on database management."

There are many possible strategies to solve this query, three of which are compared with respect to the following assumptions on actual data values. Note that the detailed data used for the computations below are not usually available to the query optimizer, but have to be estimated.

There are 100 "departments", 5 of which are located in New York. A physical block can take 5 department records or 50 dname values.

There are 500 "courses", 20 of which are on database management. The physical block size is 10 records.

There are 2000 "lectures". Three hundred are on database management, 100 are held in New York departments, and 20 (from 3 departments) satisfy both conditions. The physical block size is 10 records.

Assume further that sorting time is $N * \log(2)N$, where $N$ is the file size in blocks, and that there is a buffer of one block for each relation. Finally, all relations are physically sorted by ascending key values.

The first strategy presented here follows a straightforward approach of translating a relational calculus expression into a sequence of algebra operations [Codd 1972]. Together with each step of the strategy, the numbers of secondary storage accesses required to read (r) or write (w) a physical block are given:

*Strategy 1*

1. Form the Cartesian product of the "courses", "lectures", and "departments" relations, and (r: 200000)
2. Retain the dname column of those "department" records, for which

   the cnr of "courses" and "lectures" match, and
   the dname of "lectures" and "departments" match,
   and cname = 'database management'
   and city = New York. (w: 1)

*total:* approximately 200000 accesses.

The extremely high cost of this strategy results from the fact that it generates an intermediate result, of which only a very small portion is actually relevant for further processing. Efficiency can be improved substantially by considering only those combinations of elements from different relations that have matching values in common attributes. By making use of existing sort orders, such combinations can be formed by "merging" the participating relations. This operation is called a "join":

*Strategy 2*

1. Merge "courses" and "lectures". (r: 50 + 200; w: 400)
2. Sort the result by dnames. (r + w: 400 log(2)400)
3. Merge the result with "departments". (r: 400 + 20; w: 400 + 400)
4. Select the combinations with city = 'New York' and cname = 'database management', and (r: 800)
5. keep only the dname column. (w: 1)

*total:* approximately 6000 accesses.

The cost for answering the query can be reduced further by performing value-based selections as early as possible and thereby reducing the cost for sorting and merging intermediate results:

*Strategy 3*

1. Merge "courses" with "lectures", and (r: 50 + 200)
2. keep only the dnames of combinations with cname = 'database management' (w: 2)
3. Sort the dname list generated. (r + w: 2)
4. Merge the result with the "departments" relation, and (r: 2 + 20)
5. keep only those dnames with city = 'New York'. (w: 1)

*total:* 277 accesses.

Thus a reduction by a factor of approximately 700 has been achieved. For larger databases and more complex queries, more sophisticated techniques may result in even higher reductions.

### 1.3 Top-Down Approach to Query Optimization

Query optimization research in the literature can be divided in two classes, which can be described as bottom up and top down. Researchers found the overall query optimization problem to be very complex. Theoretical work began with a bottom-up approach, studying special cases, such as the optimal implementation of important operations and evaluation strategies for certain simple subclasses of queries. Subsequently researchers attempted to compose larger building blocks from these early results.

A need for working systems triggered the development of full-scale query evaluation procedures, which stressed the generality of solutions and handled query optimization in a uniform and heuristic manner [Astrahan and Chamberlin 1975; Makinouchi et al. 1981; Niebuhr et al. 1976; Palermo 1972; Schenk and Pinkert 1977; Wong and Youssefi 1976]. As this often did not achieve competitive system efficiency, the current trend seems to be a top-down approach that incorporates more knowledge about special case optimization opportunities into the general procedures. At the same time, the general algorithms themselves have been augmented by combinatorial cost-minimization procedures for choosing among strategies.

This paper follows the top-down approach, utilizing the general evaluation procedure that follows as a framework for the specific techniques developed in query optimization research:

*Step 1.* Find an internal query representation into which user queries can easily be mapped that leaves the system all necessary degrees of freedom to optimize the evaluation.

*Step 2.* Apply logical transformations to the query representation that (1) standardize the query, (2) simplify the query to avoid duplication of effort, and (3) ameliorate the query to streamline the evaluation and to allow special case procedures to be applied.

*Step 3.* Map the transformed query into alternative sequences of elementary operations for which a good implementation and its associated cost are known. The result of this step is a set of candidate "access plans".

*Step 4.* Compute the overall cost for each access plan, choose the cheapest one, and execute it.

The first two steps of this procedure are to a large degree data independent and thus often can be handled at compile time. The quality of Steps 3 and 4, that is, the richness of the access plans generated and the optimality of the choice algorithm, heavily depends upon knowledge about the values in the database.

The consequences of data dependence are twofold. First, if the database is volatile, Steps 3 and 4 can be done only at run time. This means that the possible gain in efficiency must be traded off against the cost of the optimization itself. Second, a metadatabase (e.g., an augmented data dictionary) must maintain general information about the database structure as well as statistical information about the database contents. As in many similar operational research problems (e.g., inventory control), the costs of obtaining and maintaining this additional information must be compared to its value.

## 2. QUERY REPRESENTATION

Queries can be represented in a number of forms. In the context of query optimization, an appropriate query representation form must fulfill the following requirements: It should be powerful enough to express a large class of queries, and it should provide a well-defined basis for query transformation. In this section we present four different query representation forms, each of which has been used in a number of approaches to query optimization.

### 2.1 The Relational Calculus

The (tuple) relational calculus as introduced by Codd [1971, 1972] is a notation for defining the result of a query through the description of its properties. The representation of a query in relational calculus consists of two parts: the target list and the selection expression.

The *selection expression* specifies the contents of the relation resulting from the query by means of a first-order predicate (i.e., a generalized Boolean expression possibly containing existential and/or universal quantifiers). The *target list* defines the free variables occurring in the predicate and specifies the structure of the resulting relation. Example 2.1 demonstrates the relational calculus representation using the syntax of the database programming language Pascal/R [Schmidt 1977].

*Example 2.1.* Names of processors who published some paper in 1981.

```
[⟨e.ename⟩ OF
EACH e IN employees:
    e. status = professor
      AND
    SOME p IN papers
      (e.enr = p.enr AND p.year = 1981)]
```

In the target list, that is, the subexpression preceding the colon, the range of the (free) variable e is restricted to elements of the relation "employees". The relation "employees" is therefore called the *range relation* of e. The target attribute specification

"⟨e.ename⟩" indicates that only the names of employees are retained for the query result.

The selection expression—the predicate following the colon—defines constraints on the free variable. The first constraint is a restrictive or *monadic term*, restricting the free variable to those "employees" records that have the status value "professor". This constraint is AND-connected with a join or *dyadic term*, relating "employees" to "papers", and another monadic term, further restricting the result to those employees who published some paper in 1981. The comparison operators usually allowed in terms are $=, \neq, <, >, \leq$, and $\geq$.

In contrast to the one-sorted predicate calculus, the relational calculus allows variables to be bound to different sorts (range relations); for instance, variable e is bound to "employees" and variable p is bound to "papers". The consequences of the many sortedness of the relational calculus with respect to query transformation are discussed in Section 3.1.

In addition to the logical operator AND, the operators OR and NOT can also be used in predicates. Relational calculus predicates are completely defined by the following recursive rules:

1. Atomic predicates:

   (i) A (monadic or dyadic) term is an atomic predicate.
   (ii) TRUE is an atomic predicate.
   (iii) FALSE is an atomic predicate.

2. An atomic predicate is a predicate. Let $A$ be a predicate, $r$ an element variable, and rel a relation. Then

   (i) SOME $r$ IN rel($A$),
   (ii) ALL $r$ IN rel($A$)

   are also predicates.
3. Let $A$ and $B$ be predicates. Then

   (i) NOT ($A$) (negation),
   (ii) $A$ and $B$ (conjunction),
   (iii) $A$ OR $B$ (disjunction)

   are predicates.
4. No other formulas are predicates.

In Codd [1972] the relation calculus has been introduced as a yardstick of expressive power. A representation form is said to be *relationally complete* if it allows the definition of any query result definable by a relational calculus expression. Clearly, relational completeness has to be considered as a minimum requirement with respect to expressive power. An often cited example for a conceptually simple query that goes beyond relational completeness is "find the names of employees reporting to manager Smith at any level", provided that a hierarchy of employees is modeled in a single relation (e.g., via a name and manager attribute) [Pirotte 1979]. Furthermore, queries in today's applications often contain aggregations that cannot be expressed in pure relational calculus. However, the extension of relational calculus by aggregate functions is rather straightforward [Klug 1982b; Maier and Warren 1981].

### 2.2 The Relational Algebra

The relational algebra as defined by Codd [1972] is a collection of operators on relations. These operators fall into two classes, that is, traditional set operators, such as Cartesian product, union, intersection, and difference, and special relational algebra operators, such as restriction, projection, join, and division. The special operators are defined below by relating them to equivalent relational calculus expressions.

The *restriction* operator applied to a relation "rel" constructs a horizontal subset according to a quantifier-free predicate containing only monadic terms or intrarelational dyadic terms (comparisons between two attributes of the same relation element):

Rest(rel, pred) = [EACH $r$ IN rel: pred].

The *projection* operator serves to construct a vertical subset of a relation "rel" by selecting a set $A$ of specified attributes and eliminating duplicate tuples within these attributes:

Proj(rel, $A$) = [⟨$r.A$⟩ OF EACH $r$ IN rel: true].

The *join* operator permits two relations "$\text{rel}_1$" and "$\text{rel}_2$" to be combined into a single relation whose attributes are the union of the attributes of "$rel_1$" and "$rel_2$":

Join($rel_1$, $A$ op $B$, $rel_2$)
= [EACH $r_1$ IN $rel_1$, EACH $r_2$ IN $rel_2$: $r_1.A$ op $r_2.B$].

The comparison operators "op" allowed in joins are the same as those in dyadic terms of the relational calculus. If "op" is the equality operator '=', the "natural" join omits either $A$ or $B$ in the result.

The *division* operator provides an algebraic counterpart to the universal quantifier. It is defined as follows:

Divi($rel_1$, $A$ by $B$, $rel_2$)
= [⟨$r$.compl($A$)⟩ OF EACH $r_1$ IN $rel_1$:
ALL $r_2$ IN $rel_2$ SOME $r_3$ IN $rel_1$
($r_1$.compl($A$) = $r_2$.compl($A$) AND
$r_2.B = r_3.A$)].

where compl($A$) is the complement of $A$ in the attribute set of "$rel_1$". As the definition indicates, division is a rather complex operation, which can make the understanding of a query a difficult job.

Example 2.2 represents the query of Example 2.1 in relational algebra.

*Example 2.2.* Names of professors who published some paper in 1981.

```
Proj(Rest(Join(employees,
               enr = enr,
               Rest(papers, year = 1981)),
          status = professor),
     ename)
```

As opposed to a relational calculus expression, which describes the relation resulting from a query by means of its properties, a relational algebra expression defines an algorithm for the construction of the resulting relation. A calculus expression appears to be a better starting point for query optimization since it provides an optimizer only with the basic properties of the query; optimization opportunities may become hidden in a particular sequence of algebra operators. With respect to relational completeness, however, the relational algebra is at least as powerful as the relational calculus. In Codd [1972] it has been shown that any relational calculus expression can be translated into an equivalent algebra expression. An analogous result for algebra and calculus expressions extended by aggregate functions has been proven by Klug [1982a].

### 2.3 Query Graphs

Graphs have been used for the visual representation of structured objects in a number of areas. Two well-known examples are the use of syntax trees in compiler construction and the use of AND/OR graphs in artificial intelligence applications. Graphs are used in query optimization for the representation of queries or query evaluation strategies. Two classes of graphs can be distinguished: object graphs and operator graphs.

Nodes in *object graphs* represent objects such as (relation) variables and constants. Edges describe predicates that these objects are to fulfill [Bernstein and Chiu 1981; Palermo 1972; Youssefi and Wong 1979]. Object graphs contain the properties of the query result and are therefore closely related to the relational calculus. *Operator graphs* describe an operator-controlled data flow by representing operators as nodes that are connected by edges indicating the direction of data movement. In Smith and Chang [1975] and Yao [1979], operator graphs have been used for the representation of algebra expressions. Figures 1 and 2 give one example, respectively, for an object graph and an operator graph.

Query graphs have many attractive properties. The visual presentation of a query contributes to an easier understanding of its structural characteristics. In addition, graph theory offers a number of results useful for the automatic analysis of graphs, for example, discovery of cycles and tree property. Finally, an important advantage of query graphs is that they can be easily augmented with additional information. For example, the augmentation of graphs with details of the physical data organization of a database has been proposed by Rosenthal and Reiner [1982].

### 2.4 Tableaus

Tableaus as defined by Aho et al. [1979a, 1979b, 1979c] are tabular notations for a

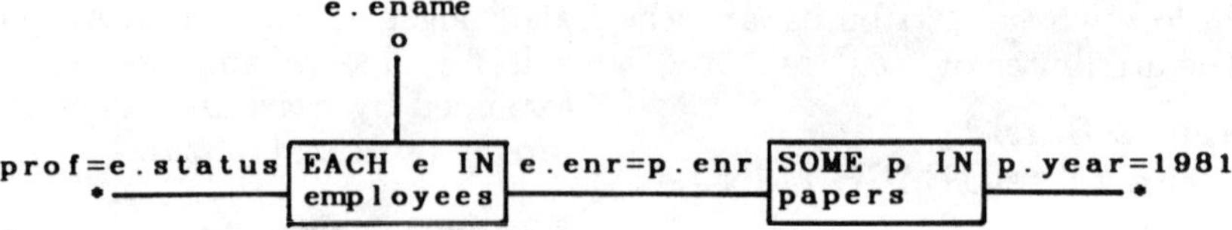


**Figure 1.** An object graph representing the example query.

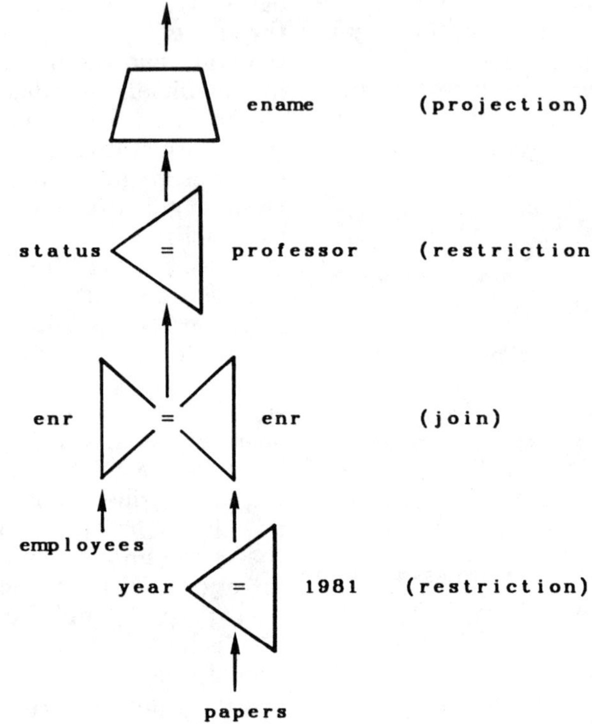


**Figure 2.** An operator graph representing the example query.

subset of relational calculus queries, characterized by containing only AND-connected terms and no universal quantifiers. Thus tableau queries are a particular kind of *conjunctive queries* [Chandra and Merlin 1977; Rosenkrantz and Hunt 1980].

Tableaus are specialized matrices, the columns of which correspond to the attributes of the underlying database schema. The first row of the matrix, the summary, serves the same purpose as the target list of a relational calculus expression. The other rows describe the predicate. The symbols appearing in a tableau are distinguished variables (corresponding to free variables), nondistinguished variables (corresponding to existentially quantified variables), constants, blanks, and tags (indicating the range relation).

Figure 3 illustrates the construction of a tableau representing the query of Example 2.1. It starts with tableaus for single relations and proceeds by combining these tableaus into new tableaus for larger and larger subexpressions. Distinguished variables are denoted by $a$'s; nondistinguished ones are denoted by $b$'s.

Expressions containing disjunction (set union) and negation (set difference) can be represented by sets of tableaus [Sagiv and Yannakakis 1980]. Klug [1983] and Johnson and Klug [1983] use sets of tableaus

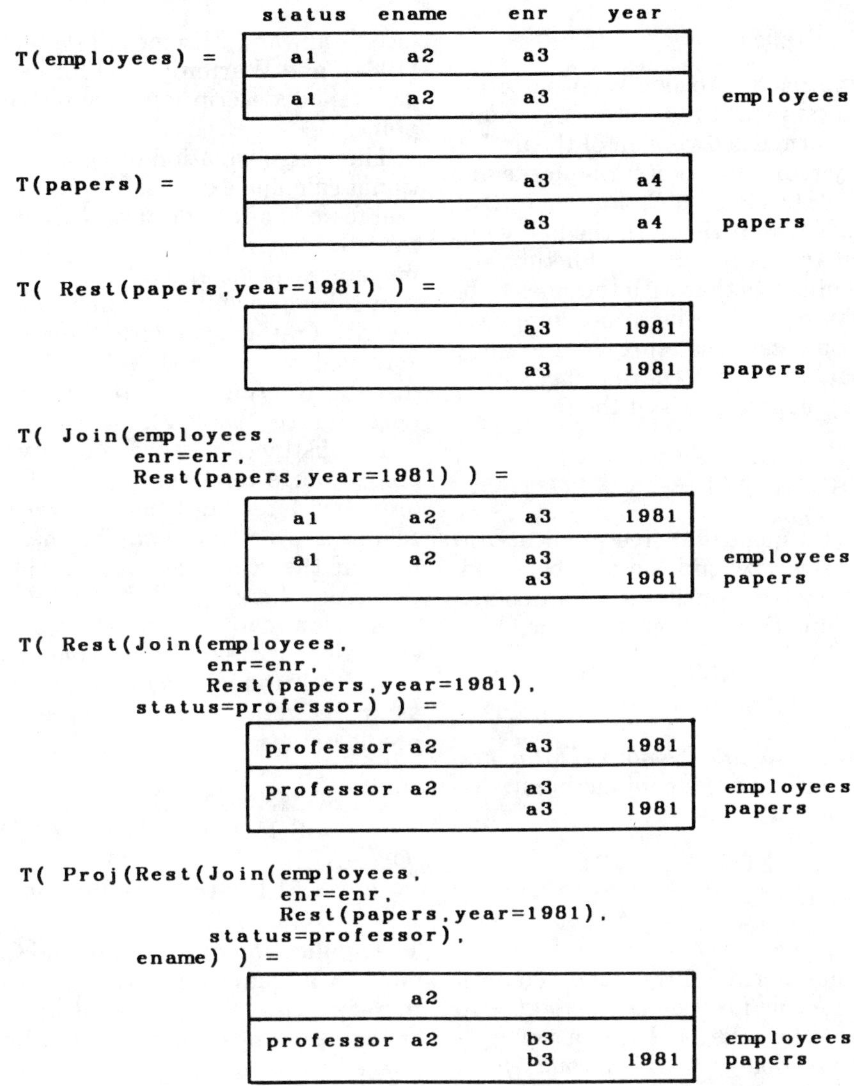

**Figure 3.** Stepwise construction of a tableau $T$ representing the query of Example 2.1.

for representing general conjunctive queries. The specific value of tableaus with respect to query optimization is discussed in Section 3.2.

## 3. QUERY TRANSFORMATION

We have seen that queries can be expressed in a number of different representation forms. Additionally, a number of semantically equivalent expressions may exist for each query, even within a given language. The transformation of a given expression into an equivalent one by means of well-defined rules is the subject of this section. The goals of query transformation are threefold: (1) the construction of a standardized starting point for query optimization (*standardization*), (2) the elimination of redundancy (*simplification*), and (3) the construction of expressions that are improved with respect to evaluation performance (*amelioration*).

### 3.1 Standardization

Several approaches to query optimization define a standardized starting point through a normalized version of the underlying query representation form [Jarke and Schmidt 1981; Kim 1982; Palermo 1972; Wong and Youssefi 1976]. In the following, we present two normal forms for the relational calculus together with the rules to be obeyed by a normalization procedure.

A relational calculus representation of a query is said to be in *prenex normal form* if its selection expression is of the form

$$\text{SOME/ALL } r_1 \text{ IN rel}_1 \cdots \text{ SOME/ALL } r_n \text{ IN rel}_n(M),$$

where $M$ is a quantifier-free predicate. $M$ is called the *matrix* and can also be standardized. A matrix consisting of a disjunction of conjunctions (of terms $A_{ij}$), such as

$$(A_{11} \text{ AND } \cdots \text{ AND } A_{1n}) \text{ OR } \cdots \text{ OR } (A_{m1} \text{ AND } \cdots \text{ AND } A_{mn}),$$

is said to be in *disjunctive normal form*, and a matrix consisting of a conjunction of disjunctions, such as

$$(A_{11} \text{ OR } \cdots \text{ OR } A_{1n}) \text{ AND } \cdots \text{ AND } (A_{m1} \text{ OR } \cdots \text{ OR } A_{mn}),$$

is in *conjunctive normal form.*

The prenex normal form combined with the normal forms for the matrix yields two normal forms for relational calculus expressions: *disjunctive prenex normal form* (DPNF) and *conjunctive prenex normal form* (CPNF). The use of DPNF is motivated by the goal to optimize and evaluate independent query components separately [Bernstein et al. 1981]. The CPNF has proved useful for the decomposition of queries [Wong and Youssefi 1976] and for data-dependent amelioration (e.g., testing the most restrictive disjunction first).

Queries in CPNF can be transformed further into a quantifier-free form popular in artificial intelligence theorem-proving applications, the so-called *clausal form* [Nilsson 1982]. Logic-based database languages such as Prolog [Kowalski 1981] are based on clausal form. Since clausal form has been rarely used in query optimization (see Grant and Minker [1981], Jarke et al. [1984], and Warren [1981] for exceptions), a detailed description is omitted at this point.

The transformation of an arbitrary relational calculus expression into prenex normal form is a matter of moving quantifiers over terms (from right to left). Quantifier movement is governed by the transformation rules of Table 1. Normalization of the matrix is rather straightforward and can be achieved by using DeMorgan's rules, the distributive rules, and the rule of double negation (see Table 2).

The distinction between empty and nonempty range relations in rules Q2 and Q3 of Table 1 results from the variability of relations over time and the many sortedness of the relational calculus [Jarke and Schmidt 1982]. A relational calculus expression can be transformed into an equivalent expression of a one-sorted calculus by introducing a range definition such as ($r$ IN rel) as another type of atomic predicate:

O1: SOME $r$ IN rel(pred) $\Leftrightarrow$ SOME $r$(($r$ IN rel) AND pred),
O2: ALL $r$ IN rel(pred) $\Leftrightarrow$ ALL $r$(($r$ IN rel) $\Rightarrow$ pred).

The application of rules Q2a and Q3a when moving a quantifier over a term would therefore yield a wrong result in the case of an empty range relation. It follows that normalization of an arbitrary relational calculus expression at compile time must preserve information about the original range definition of variables so that run-time modifications according to rules Q2b and Q3b can be performed when necessary.

### 3.2 Simplification

We have already seen that there might be several semantically equivalent expressions representing one and the same query. One source of differences between any two equivalent expressions is their degree of redundancy [Hall 1976; Stroet and Engmann 1979]. A straightforward evaluation of a redundant expression would lead to

**Table 1.** Transformation Rules for Quantified Expressions

```
Q1: A AND SOME r IN rel (B(r))
         <==>
    SOME r IN rel (A AND B(r))

Q2: A OR SOME r IN rel (B(r))
         <==>
 a) SOME r IN rel (A OR B(r))   rel ≠ []
 b) A                           rel = []

Q3: A AND ALL r IN rel (B(r))
         <==>
 a) ALL r in rel (A AND B(r))   rel ≠ []
 b) A                           rel = []

Q4: A OR ALL r IN rel (B(r))
         <==>
    ALL r IN rel (A OR B(r))

Q5: SOME r1 IN rel1 SOME r2 IN rel2 (A(r1,r2))
         <==>
    SOME r2 IN rel2 SOME r1 IN rel1 (A(r1,r2))

Q6: ALL r1 IN rel1 ALL r2 IN rel2 (A(r1,r2))
         <==>
    ALL r2 IN rel2 ALL r1 IN rel1 (A(r1,r2))

Q7: SOME r IN rel (A(r) OR B(r))
         <==>
    SOME r IN rel (A(r)) OR SOME r IN rel (B(r))

Q8: ALL r IN rel (A(r) AND B(r))
         <==>
    ALL r IN rel (A(r)) AND ALL r in rel (B(r))

Q9: NOT ALL r IN rel (A(r))
         <==>
    SOME r IN rel (NOT(A(r)))

Q10:NOT SOME r IN rel (A(r))
         <==>
    ALL r IN rel (NOT(A(r)))
```

the execution of a set of operations, some of which are superfluous. Therefore query optimization aims at the elimination of redundancy by means of transforming a redundant expression into an equivalent nonredundant one.

A redundant expression can be simplified by applying the transformation rules M4a to M4j, which consider *idempotency* (see Table 2). The application of these rules is complicated by the fact that idempotency can occur at any level in the expression, owing to the presence of *common subexpressions*, that is, subexpressions that occur more than once in the expression representing the query. Thus, in order to simplify an expression such as

```
[EACH e IN employees:
        e.ename = 'Smith'
          OR
        (e.status = assistant
            OR e.status = professor)
          AND
        NOT(e.status = professor
                OR e.status = assistant)]
```

to

[EACH e IN employees: e.ename = 'Smith']

by means of rules M4d and M4g, the subexpressions

(e.status = assistant OR e.status = professor)

and

(e.status = professor OR e.status = assistant)

**Table 2.** Transformation Rules for General Expressions

```
M1: Commutative rules
 a) A OR B              <==> B OR A
 b) A AND B             <==> B AND A
M2: Associative rules
 a) (A OR B) OR C       <==> A OR (B OR C)
 b) (A AND B) AND C     <==> A AND (B AND C)
M3: Distributive rules
 a) A OR (B AND C)      <==> (A OR B) AND (A OR C)
 b) A AND (B OR C)      <==> (A AND B) OR (A AND C)
M4: Idempotency rules
 a) A OR A              <==> A
 b) A AND A             <==> A
 c) A OR NOT(A)         <==> TRUE
 d) A AND NOT(A)        <==> FALSE
 e) A AND (A OR B)      <==> A
 f) A OR (A AND B)      <==> A
 g) A OR FALSE          <==> A
 h) A AND TRUE          <==> A
 i) A OR TRUE           <==> TRUE
 j) A AND FALSE         <==> FALSE
M5: De Morgan's rules
 a) NOT (A AND B)       <==> NOT (A) OR NOT (B)
 b) NOT (A OR B)        <==> NOT (A) AND NOT (B)
M6: Double negation rule
    NOT (NOT (A))       <==> A
```

must first be recognized as being equivalent. Algorithms are given by Downey et al. [1980] and Hall [1974, 1976]. The recognition of common subexpressions and the application of idempotency rules have to be performed concurrently rather than sequentially, since the simplification of an expression by means of idempotency rules may yield further common subexpressions, which, in turn, are subject to simplification. Expressions that are bound to *empty relations* can also be simplified. Transformation rules for their simplification are given in Table 3. (Note that these rules can be applied only at run time.)

Terms as defined in Section 2.1 serve as atomic predicates in the relational calculus. However, these terms can be simplified or removed if the semantics of the comparison operators are explicitly taken into account. An important application is the so-called *constant propagation*, which uses transitivity laws, such as

$$r.A \text{ op } s.B \text{ AND } s.B = \text{const} \Rightarrow r.A \text{ op const},$$

**Table 3.** Transformation Rules for Expressions with Empty Relations

```
E1: [EACH r in []: pred]                           <==> []
E2: [<r.A1,...,r.An> OF EACH r IN []: pred]        <==> []
E3: SOME r IN [] (pred)                            <==> FALSE
E4: ALL r IN [] (pred)                             <==> TRUE
```

to reduce the number of dyadic terms in a query. Algorithms that minimize the number of rows in tableaus as introduced in Section 2.4 systematically exploit such simplification rules for conjunctive queries [Aho et al. 1979a; Sagiv 1981, 1983]. Since the number of rows in a tableau is one more than the number of joins (dyadic join terms) in the expression, the minimization of the number of rows corresponds to the elimination of redundant joins.

Sagiv and Yannakakis [1980] extend the tableau techniques to cover the simplification of expressions containing disjunctions. The generalization to all expressions of a relationally complete language, however, is still an open problem.

Information about semantic integrity constraints can be exploited for "semantic" query simplification [Aho et al. 1979a, 1979b, 1979c; Jarke et al. 1984; Johnson and Klug 1982; Ott and Horlaender 1982; Rosenthal and Reiner 1984]. As a simple example, consider the case of key constraints. If $r$ and $r'$ are (free or existentially quantified) variables ranging over the same relation "rel", equijoin terms of the form "$r$.key = $r'$.key" are superfluous in the sense that the term and one of the variables, say $r'$, can be deleted, followed by the substitution of $r'$ by $r$ in any term referring to $r'$. This type of simplification is most relevant in the context of view processing, in which the reduction of user queries addressing views to system queries addressing stored relations may introduce substantial redundancy. Its application range can be extended by considering additional constraints implied by the query structure [Klug 1980; Koch et al. 1981].

A final opportunity for simplification occurs when one or more matrix conjunctions of the standardized query can be shown to be unsatisfiable [Eswaran et al. 1976; Klug 1983; Munz et al. 1979; Ozsoyoglu and Yu 1980]. For example, consider the expression

$$r.A \geq s.B \text{ AND } s.B > t.C \text{ AND } t.C \geq r.A,$$

which implies the contradiction, $r.a > r.a$, and can therefore be replaced by the Boolean value, false. Satisfiability can be efficiently decided at compile time for a conjunction of terms with comparison operators ($=, <, \leq, >, \geq$) [Rosenkrantz and Hunt 1980], but is computationally intractable when the nonequality comparison operator is allowed.

### 3.3 Amelioration

Query simplification does not necessarily produce a unique expression. Other nonredundant expressions may exist that are semantically equivalent to the one generated by some simplification technique. The evaluation of expressions corresponding to one and the same query may differ substantially with respect to performance parameters, for example, the size of intermediate results and the number of relation elements accessed. Below, a number of query transformation heuristics are presented that, when applied to expressions, yield ameliorated expressions with respect to evaluation performance.

The simplest transformations considered in this section are the *combination of a sequence of projections* into a single projection, and the *combination of a sequence of restrictions* into a single restriction [Hall

1976; Smith and Chang 1975]. The corresponding transformation rules are

A1: Proj(⋯ Proj(Proj(rel, $A_1$) $A_2$), ..., $A_n$)
$\Leftrightarrow$
Proj(rel, $A_n$),

A2: Rest(⋯ (Rest(Rest(rel, $\text{pred}_1$), $\text{pred}_2$), ..., $\text{pred}_n$)
$\Leftrightarrow$
Rest(rel, $\text{pred}_1$ AND $\text{pred}_2$ AND ⋯ AND $\text{pred}_n$).

The combination of intrarelational operations results in two advantages: First, repetitive reading of the same relation is avoided, and second, existing access paths may be used for the combined operation, and not only for the first operation in the sequence.

Minimization of the size of intermediate results to be constructed, stored, and retrieved is the goal of a number of ameliorating transformations. An important heuristic moves selective operations, such as restriction and projection, over constructive operations, such as join and Cartesian product, in order to perform the selective operations as early as possible [Smith and Chang 1975]. In the context of relational calculus, the consideration of a certain evaluation sequence can be represented by a nested expression. The evaluation of a nested expression starts with the evaluation of the innermost nesting, followed by its surrounding nesting, and so on until the outermost nesting is reached. A nested expression implying the early evaluation of monadic terms (restrictions) is given in Example 3.1.

*Example* 3.1. A nested expression equivalent to the expression in Example 2.1.

```
[⟨e.ename⟩ OF
 EACH e IN [EACH e IN employees:
              e.status = professor]:
   SOME p IN [EACH p IN papers:
                p.year = 1981]
     (e.enr = p.enr)]
```

The early evaluation of selective operations forms a special case of *query detachment* as introduced by Wong and Youssefi [1976]. A subexpression that overlaps with the rest of the expression on a single variable is detached and forms an inner nesting. Detachment is performed recursively at any nesting level until the expression cannot be reduced further. Experiments reported by Youssefi and Wong [1979] have shown this heuristic to be very strong. Example 3.2 demonstrates the detachment of a subexpression in a complex expression.

*Example* 3.2. Departments offering lectures that are held by professors who live in the same city where the department is located and who have published some paper in 1981.

The corresponding expression is

```
[EACH d IN departments:
   SOME l IN lectures
     SOME e IN employees
       (e.status = professor
         AND
         d.dname = l.dname
             AND l.enr = e.enr
             AND e.city = d.city
           AND
         SOME p IN papers
           (p.year = 1981
               AND p.enr = e.enr))]
```

An equivalent expression produced by query detachment is

```
[EACH d IN departments:
   SOME l IN lectures
     SOME e IN [EACH e IN
                 [EACH e IN employees:
                     e.status = professor]:
                 SOME p IN [EACH p IN
                     papers: p.year = 1981]
                   (e.enr = p.enr)]
       (d.dname = l.dname AND l.enr = e.enr
           AND e.city = d.city)]
```

An object graph representing the query is shown in Figure 4.

Note that the resulting nested expression is irreducible [Goodman and Shmueli 1980]; that is, it cannot be separated into two subexpressions overlapping on a single variable. In other words, the nested expression contains a cycle (see Figure 4).

The importance of the distinction between cyclic and acyclic (treelike) expressions for query processing is discussed further in Section 4.3. At this point, we mention only that there are cycles that can be transformed into equivalent acyclic

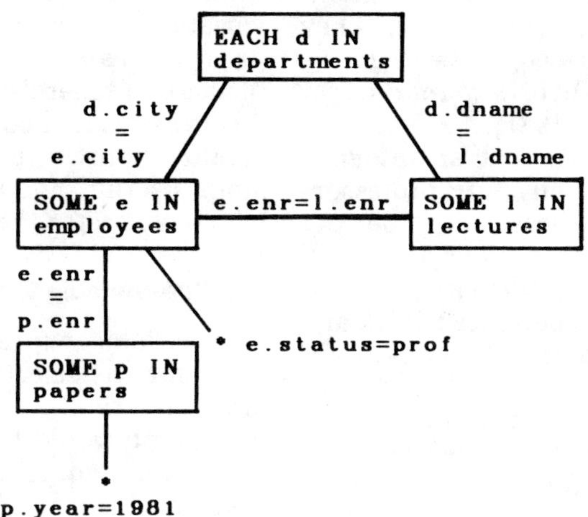


**Figure 4.** Object graph for Example 3.2.

query graphs. Such cycles include those that (1) are introduced by transitivity [Bernstein and Chiu 1981; Yu and Ozsoyoglu 1979], (2) contain certain combinations of inequality join term edges [Bernstein and Goodman 1981b; Ozsoyoglu and Yu 1980], (3) are "closed" by universally quantified variables [Jarke and Koch 1983], and (4) contain variables that can be decomposed by use of functional dependencies [Kambayashi and Yoshikawa 1983].

The concepts of *extended range expressions* [Jarke and Schmidt 1982] and *range nesting* [Jarke and Koch 1983] provide a generalization of query detachment in that they also consider expressions containing universal quantification. Database relations defining the range of a relation variable are replaced by calculus expressions according to the following transformation rules:

A3: [EACH $r$ IN rel: $\text{pred}_1$ AND $\text{pred}_2$]

$\Leftrightarrow$

[EACH $r$ IN [EACH $r$ IN rel: $\text{pred}_1$]: $\text{pred}_2$],

A4: SOME $r$ IN rel($\text{pred}_1$ AND $\text{pred}_2$)

$\Leftrightarrow$

SOME $r$ IN [EACH $r$ IN rel: $\text{pred}_1$] ($\text{pred}_2$),

A5: ALL $r$ IN rel: (NOT($\text{pred}_1$) OR ($\text{pred}_2$)

$\Leftrightarrow$

ALL $r$ IN [EACH $r$ IN rel: $\text{pred}_1$] ($\text{pred}_2$).

Note that transformation rule A5 for universally quantified variables is especially profitable since, through the reduction of the number of conjunctions in the outer nesting, the intermediate results can be expected to be considerably smaller in size.

The ameliorating transformations presented thus far use information from three sources: general transformation rules and heuristics guiding their usage, knowledge about the relational data structures, and the query itself. Two other knowledge bases that have not yet been considered are the integrity constraints that complement the structural schema definition in many database systems and the actual data stored in the database.

Integrity constraints are predicates that must be true for each element of a certain relation, or for each combination of elements of a certain group of relations. They therefore can be added to the selection expression of any query without changing its truth value. There are a few approaches exploiting this observation for amelioration rather than simplification (which was mentioned in the previous subsection). They have been called knowledge-based [Hammer and Zdonik 1980] or *semantic query processing* [King 1979, 1981].

Assume, for example, that an integrity constraint says: "We only hire professors who have published at least one paper per year." In this case, the evaluation of Example 2.1 (asking for professors with papers published in 1981) becomes trivial, and the evaluation of Example 3.2 is substantially simplified.

Adding an integrity constraint to a selection expression can also change the structure of the query in order to make it more tractable. Consider the constraint: "We only hire local professors." In this case, the term "d.city = e.city" in Example 3.2 can be omitted. The remaining query no longer contains a cycle in its object graph.

The success of semantic query processing depends largely on the development of efficient heuristics for choosing among the many transformations made possible by the addition of any combination of integrity constraints to the query. In King [1981] and Xu [1983], artificial intelligence type rules are used to make this decision for a special class of relational databases.

Yao [1979] points out that cases exist in which the optimal transformation is *data dependent*. The heuristics presented above may not always be optimal, especially when certain access paths are supported by physical data structures. One consequence of such data dependence is that, in addition to the query compiler, the run-time support must also be equipped with query transformation facilities. Furthermore, if heuristics do not yield satisfactory results, simultaneous optimization is required on the physical and the logical level. Before turning to such integrated approaches, however, the physical evaluation of query components must be described.

## 4. QUERY EVALUATION

In this section we present methods for the evaluation of query components of varying complexity, such as one-variable expressions, two-variable expressions, and multivariable expressions. The individual approaches can be viewed as the building blocks of a general query evaluation system. Their associated costs and ranges of applicability constitute the input to the last stage of the query optimization process, which generates the optimal access plan.

### 4.1 One-Variable Expressions

One-variable expressions describe conditions for the selection of elements from a single relation. A naive approach to their evaluation would be to read every element of the relation, and to test whether it satisfies each term of the expression. Since this approach is very costly in the presence of large relations and complex expressions, various techniques have been used to reduce the number of element accesses and the number of tests applied to an accessed element.

The number of element accesses can be reduced by employing data structures that provide access paths other than those of exhaustive sequential search. One possibility is to keep the relation *sorted* with respect to one or more attributes so that it can be accessed in ascending or descending order, or binary search can be performed. This has proved useful for the evaluation of range queries (i.e., expressions that define an interval of attribute values [Bolour 1981; Davis and Winslow 1982]). Another alternative, hashing, provides fast direct access without necessarily preserving order.

Direct and ordered access can be provided by *indexes*, possibly combined with multilist structures [Welch and Graham 1976; Yang 1977]. Conceptually speaking, an index is a binary relation that associates attribute values with references to relation elements, usually called tuple identifiers (TIDs). We distinguish *one-dimensional indexes*, which support access via a single relation attribute, from *multidimensional indexes*, which support access via a combination of attributes. One-dimensional indexes are usually implemented by ISAM [IBM 1966] or B-tree [Bayer and McCreight 1972] structures. An overview of multidimensional index structures is given by Bentley and Friedman [1979]. Some examples include the work by Shneiderman [1977] on combined indexes, Nievergelt et al. [1984] on grid files, and Gardarin et al. [1984] on predicate trees. Although access paths are usually invisible to the user, efforts have been reported to develop high-level language representations directly available to those database programmers who insist on extreme efficiency. Such language constructs range from TIDs [Jarke and Schmidt 1981; van de Riet et al. 1981] to abstract representations of complete access paths [Mall et al. 1984; Schmidt 1984; Tsichritzis 1976].

The number of tests applied to an accessed relation element during expression evaluation can be reduced by means of run-time transformations of the expression. The optimization of a special class of expressions, *Boolean expressions,* has been a research topic in compiler construction for a long time [Gries 1971]. Boolean expressions (i.e., quantifier-free AND/OR connected terms) are an integral part of a number of control structures in high-level programming languages. The purpose of code optimization for Boolean expressions is to generate code that skips over the evaluation of expression components no longer relevant to the value of the expression as a whole. For example, in the statement

```
IF A AND B THEN
   statement_1
  ELSE
   statement_2
  END
```

the evaluation of term $B$ is superfluous, and the ELSE-branch can be executed right away in case term $A$ has already been evaluated as "false". If the same idea is applied to the evaluation of one-variable expressions in query languages [Gudes and Reiter 1973; Liu 1976], queries can be simplified at run time.

Another approach designed to improve evaluation efficiency is that of changing the order in which individual expression components are evaluated. Several algorithms are known to lead to optimal evaluation sequences in certain situations; some assume a priori probabilities for attribute values [Hanani 1977], whereas others work without such assumptions [Breitbart and Reiter 1975]. Warren [1981] applies a similar technique for optimizing database programs expressed in logic.

### 4.2 Two-Variable Expressions

Two-variable expressions describe conditions for the combination of elements from two relations. In general, two-variable expressions are composed of monadic terms, which restrict single variables independently of each other, and dyadic terms, which establish the link between both variables. In this section we first describe the basic methods for the evaluation of a single dyadic term, corresponding to the join operator in Section 2.2, and then strategies for the evaluation of arbitrary two-variable expressions.

Approaches to the implementation of the join operation can be classified into order-dependent and order-independent strategies [Todd 1974]. A simple method that is independent of the order of element access is the so-called *nested iteration* method [Pecherer 1975, 1976; Selinger et al. 1979] in which every pair of relation elements is accessed, and concatenated if the join condition is satisfied. A sketch of the algorithm follows:

```
FOR i := 1 TO N1 DO
  read ith element of rel1;
  FOR j := 1 TO N2 DO
    read jth element of rel2;
    form the join according to the join condition;
  END;
END;
```

Let $N_1 (N_2)$ be the number of elements of the relation read in the outer (inner) loop. $N_1 + N_1 * N_2$ secondary storage accesses are required to evaluate the dyadic term, assuming that each element access needs one secondary storage access.

The nested iteration method can be augmented by the use of an index on the join attribute(s) of "$rel_2$." Instead of scanning "$rel_2$" sequentially for each element of "$rel_1$," the matching "$rel_2$" elements are retrieved directly [Griffeth 1978; Klug

1982b]. Thus only $N_1 + N_1 * N_2 * j_{12}$ accesses are required, where $j_{12}$ is a join selectivity factor describing the reduction of the Cartesian product of "$rel_1$" and "$rel_2$" by the join condition.

The *nested block method* [Kim 1980] adapts the nested iteration method to a paged-memory environment. It assumes that a main memory buffer will hold one or more pages of both relations, where each page contains a set of records.

The algorithm itself is basically identical to the one of the nested iteration method, except that memory pages are read instead of single relation elements. The number of secondary storage accesses needed to form the join is reduced bo $P_1 + (P_1/B_1) * P_2$, where $P_1(P_2)$ is the number of pages occupied by the outer (inner) relation and $B_1$ is the number of pages of the outer relation held in the main memory buffer. The formula demonstrates that it is always preferable to read the smaller relation in the outer loop (i.e., make $P_1 < P_2$). Note that only $P_1 + P_2$ accesses are necessary if one of the relations can be kept entirely in the main memory buffer.

The *merge method* [Blasgen and Eswaran 1977; Selinger et al. 1979] is based on the order in which relation elements are accessed. Both relations are scanned in ascending or descending order of join attribute values and merged according to the join condition. Approximately $N_1 + N_2 + S_1 + S_2$ secondary storage accesses are required, where $S_1$ and $S_2$ denote the number of secondary storage accesses necessary to sort the relations. If the two relations are already sorted by the same criterion, the merge method appears to be the most efficient one for evaluating a dyadic term [Merrett 1981; Merrett et al. 1981]. Exceptions occur when one of the two relations is small enough to fit in main memory (the nested block method is preferable) or one relation is much larger than the other and indexes are available (nested iteration with indexes is better).

Methods for the evaluation of *arbitrary two-variable expressions* are created on the basis of strategies for one-variable expressions and algorithms for the computation of dyadic terms. They differ in the way they make use of or even create access paths, such as indexes and sorting, and the order in which the terms are processed. One such method is illustrated in Figure 5. It makes extensive use of indexes. Tuple identifiers resulting from the processing of monadic terms and those that satisfy the join condition are intersected and then used to access the relation elements. These elements are projected onto attributes appearing in the dyadic term and in the target list. The projected elements are concatenated and finally projected on the target attribute.

Blasgen and Eswaran [1976], Niebuhr and Smith [1976], Yao and DeJong [1978], and Yao [1979] present various other algorithms and compare them systematically with respect to their efficiency. Their results demonstrate that often no a priori best algorithm exists. The optimizer must either rely on heuristics or perform an expensive cost comparison of many alternatives for each query.

An important case of two-variable expressions is a join in which one of the participating variables (the "inner" one) is existentially or universally quantified. The result of such an expression contains only elements of one relation. Furthermore, access to the other relation needs to establish only whether, for a given value of the "outer" variable, the join condition is satisfied with any (respectively all) elements of the range relation of the "inner" variable. These elements themselves are of no interest. This means that for the evaluation of quantified queries intermediate results can be represented in a compressed fashion [Dayal 1983a; Jarke and Schmidt 1981]. If the two-variable expression contains just one join term with a comparison operator of $<$, $\leq$, $>$, or $\geq$, only one attribute value (the minimum or maximum attribute value appearing in the inner relation) is required. That is, the quantified two-variable expression can be converted into a monadic term [Jarke and Koch 1983]. Incidentally, a similar use of aggregate functions (maximum or minimum) has also been proposed in the context of integrity maintenance [Bernstein et al. 1980].

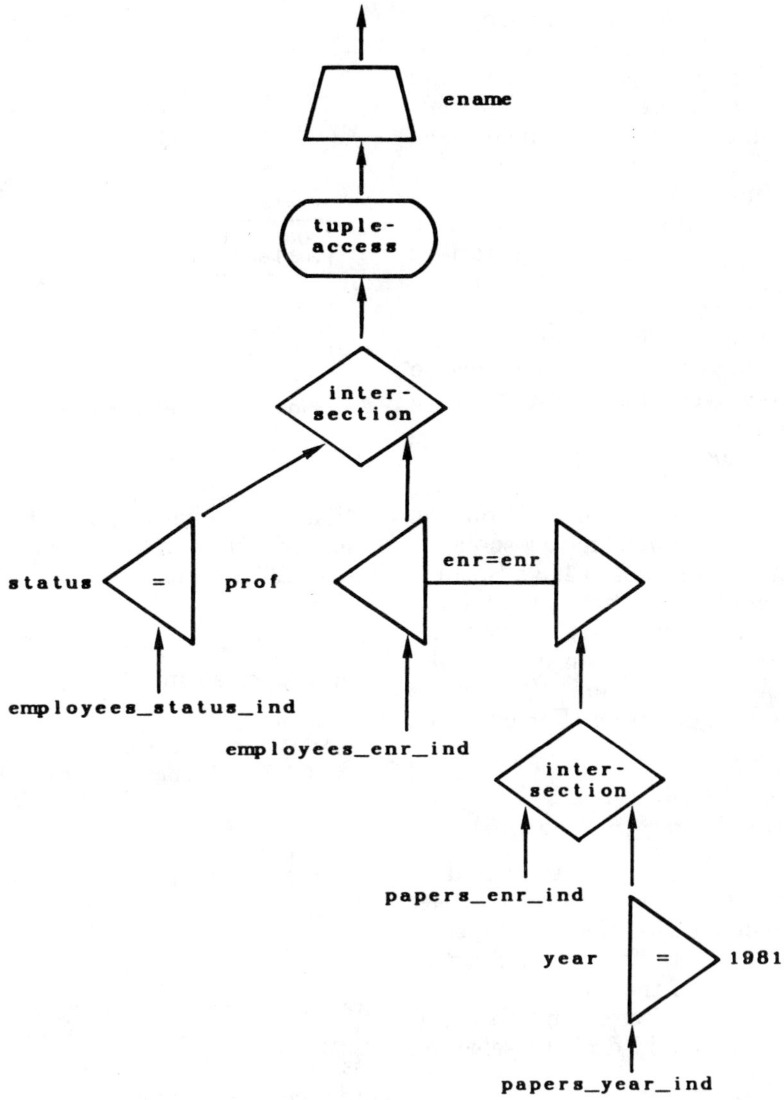


**Figure 5.** Operator graph illustrating the evaluation of the query of Example 2.1. The existence of various indexes is assumed.

### 4.3 Multivariable Expressions

Stategies for the evaluation of multivariable expressions are the largest building blocks for a general query-processing system. Two basic approaches exist, which are referred to as parallel processing and stepwise reduction.

The *parallel processing* of query components serves to avoid repeated access to the same data. Repeated access to the same data can be avoided by simultaneous evaluation of multiple-query components. In Palermo [1972], all monadic terms associated with a variable are completely evaluated and all dyadic terms in which the same variable appears are partially processed concurrently with scanning of the range relation of the variable. Even AND-connections existing among the terms can be evaluated in parallel, which further reduces the size of intermediate results [Jarke and

Schmidt 1982]. A similar approach on a higher level has been described by Klug [1982b] in which aggregate functions and complex subqueries are computed in parallel. Scheduling strategies for the parallel processing of query components are discussed by Schmidt [1979].

Pipelining operations that can work on the partial output of preceding operations is another technique that exploits parallel processing opportunities [Smith and Chang 1975; Yao 1979]. For example, restriction and projection can be pipelined so that only a relatively small buffer for data exchange is required rather than the creation and subsequent reading of a possibly large temporary relation.

Aspects of simultaneous evaluation and pipelining are combined in the so-called "feedback" method [Clausen 1980; Rothnie 1974, 1975], which uses partial results of a join operation in order to restrict its input. The degree to which this can be done depends on the quantification of variables occurring in the join term. For example, consider the expression

[EACH $r_1$ IN $\text{rel}_1$:
    ALL $r_2$ IN $\text{rel}_2$ ($r_1.A$ op $r_2.B$)].

Assume that the join term is evaluated by nested iteration. While testing some element, $r_1$, it is found that the term "$r_1.A$ op $r_2.B$" evaluates to false for a certain $r_2$ with $r_2.B = c_1$. Because of the universal quantification of $r_2$, $r_1$ is rejected, and an elimination filter can be added to the selection expression

[EACH $r_1$ IN $\text{rel}_1$:
    NOT ($r_1.A$ op $c_1$)
    AND ALL $r_2$ IN $\text{rel}_2$ ($r_1.A$ op $r_2.B$)]

because the same $r_2$ would cause the rejection of all elements $r_1$ of "$\text{rel}_1$" that do not satisfy the first term. On the other hand, if $r_1$ with $r_1.A = c_2$ passes the test, a true filter can be added to the selection predicate:

[EACH $r_1$ IN $\text{rel}_1$:
    $r_1.A$ op $c_2$ OR
        NOT ($r_1.A$ op $c_1$) AND $\cdots$].

Both filters can be updated subsequently to sharpen the constraints.

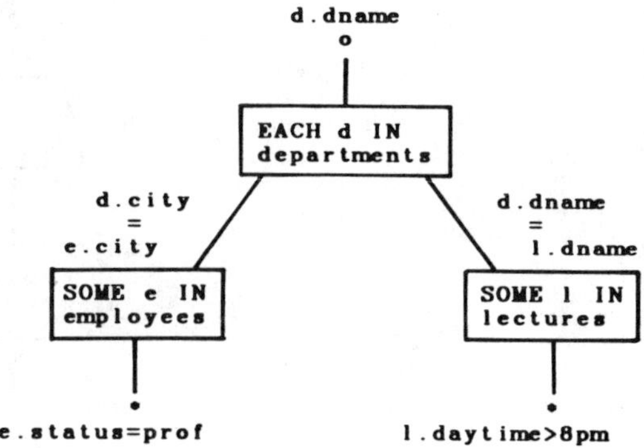


**Figure 6.** Object graph for Example 4.1.

The second basic approach to the evaluation of multivariable expressions will be motivated by means of the following example.

*Example 4.1.* Figure 6 shows an object graph representing the expression

[⟨d.dname⟩ OF
  EACH d IN departments:
    SOME e IN employees(e.status = professor
                    AND
                    e.city = d.city)
    AND
    SOME l IN lectures (l.daytime > 8 pm
                    AND
                    l.dname = d.dname)]

Expressions like the one in Example 4.1 are called *tree expressions* [Goodman and Shmueli 1982; Shmueli 1981], since their associated query graph is a tree. The standard approach for evaluating such an expression would be to form the join of the three relations, restrict the intermediate result according to monadic terms, and finally project it onto the attributes appearing in the target list. As has been shown in the introductory example (Section 1.2, Strategy 2), this method performs rather poorly. It is even more problematic in a distributed environment where each relation resides on a different site, as entire relations must be transmitted from site to site. Moreover, the relation at the target site is temporarily expanded through the formation of the join, although the final result is only a horizontal and vertical subset of it.

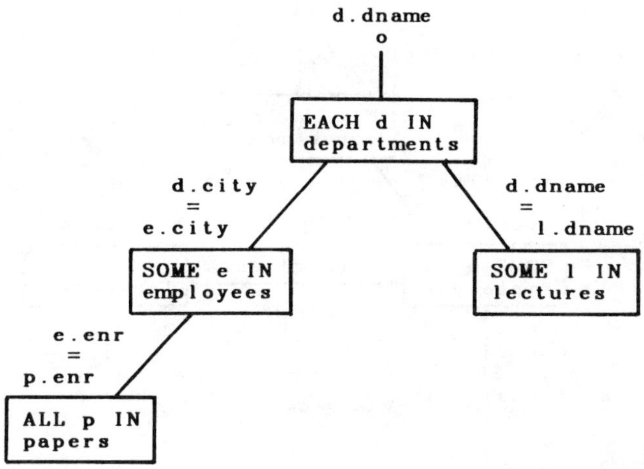

d.dname

EACH d IN departments

d.city = e.city

SOME e IN employees

d.dname = l.dname

SOME l IN lectures

e.enr = p.enr

ALL p IN papers

**Figure 7.** Object graph for Example 4.2.

In Bernstein and Chiu [1981], Bernstein et al. [1981], and Bernstein and Goodman [1981a, 1981b, 1981c], the *stepwise reduction* of tree expressions (with free and existentially quantified variables) has been introduced. This method often outperforms the simple approach above in a decentralized as well as in a centralized setting. It is based on a modified join operation, and uses the so-called semijoin operator.

The *semijoin* of a relation "$rel_1$" by a relation "$rel_2$" equals the join of these relations projected back onto the attributes of relation "$rel_1$":

$$\text{semijoin}(rel_1, A \text{ op } B, rel_2) = \text{proj}(\text{join}(rel_1, A \text{ op } B, rel_2), \text{attributes}(rel_1)).$$

The operation thus forms "half of a join." The main advantages of semijoin over join are as follows: (1) its evaluation only requires the transmission of value lists of the joining attributes instead of that of an entire relation, and (2) it has a "reductive" effect since the result of semijoin ($rel_1$, $A$ op $B$, $rel_2$) is always a subset of $rel_2$, whereas a join may produce a Cartesian product in the worst case. In terms of relational calculus, a semijoin corresponds to a two-variable expression, where one variable is existentially quantified, as discussed in Section 4.2.

The simplest evaluation of a tree expression by means of stepwise reduction can be described as follows. Starting from the leaves of the query tree representing the expression, one semijoin per edge is executed in breadth-first leaf-to-root order. Thus a tree expression containing one free and $n - 1$ existentially quantified variables can be completely processed by $n - 1$ semijoins.

If all variables are free, an additional semijoin sequence in reverse order must be performed. In a centralized setting, this kind of semijoin strategy is inferior to a merge join operation combined with parallel quantifier evaluation. Even in a distributed system, the simple bottom-up/top-down sequence is often less efficient than a middle-out sequence that begins with semijoins that achieve very strong reduction [Chiu and Ho 1980; Chiu et al. 1981].

Strategies for the evaluation of tree expressions containing both existential and universal quantifiers must take into account the order in which these quantifiers appear in the expression. Stepwise reduction is possible only when the processing of the edges of the query tree (breadth-first leaf-to-root) corresponds to the order of the quantifiers in the expression (right to left).

*Example 4.2.* Consider the query tree of Figure 7 representing the expression

```
[⟨d.dname⟩ OF
  EACH d IN departments:
    ALL p IN papers
      SOME e IN employees
        (p.enr = e.enr AND e.city = d.city)
      AND
    SOME l IN lectures (l.dname = d.dname)]
```

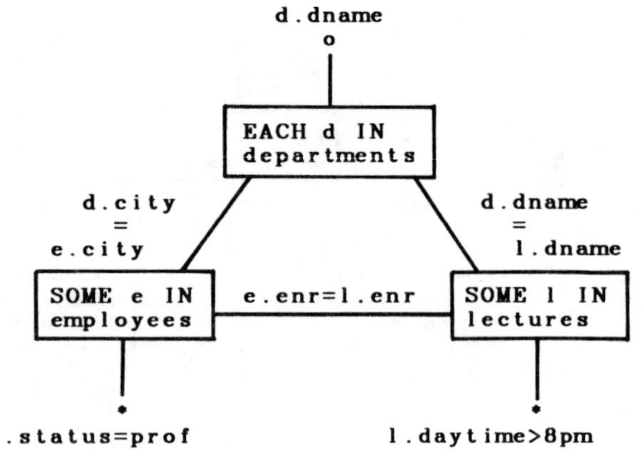


**Figure 8.** A cyclic calculus expression and its corresponding object graph.

departments

| dname | city | street address |
|---|---|---|
| d1 | ci1 | s1 |
| d2 | ci2 | s2 |

employees

| enr | ename | status | city |
|---|---|---|---|
| e1 | en1 | st1 | ci1 |
| e2 | en2 | st2 | ci2 |

lectures

| cnr | enr | dname | daytime |
|---|---|---|---|
| c1 | e1 | d2 | da1 |
| c2 | e2 | d1 | da2 |

**Figure 9.** Some possible database state.

Processing the tree in breadth-first leaf-to-root order would yield the value of the expression

```
[⟨d.dname⟩ OF
  EACH d IN departments:
    SOME e IN employees
      ALL p IN papers
        (p.enr = e.enr AND e.city = d.city)
      AND
    SOME l IN lectures (l.dname = d.dname)]
```

which is not equivalent to the original expression.

The position of an existential and a universal quantifier cannot be interchanged without changing the meaning of the expression, except in cases where rules Q1 through Q4 of Table 1 apply. Expressions containing only one type of quantifier allow the sequence of variables to be interchanged arbitrarily, according to transformation rules Q5 and Q6. Jarke and Koch [1983] describe a directed, so-called "quant graph" that supports the application of these rules.

*Cyclic expressions* are the complement of tree expressions with respect to the entire set of expressions. Although we quoted some benign exceptions in Section 3.3, cyclic expressions in general cannot be fully reduced by means of semijoins [Bernstein and Goodman 1981a, 1981b; Goodman and Shmueli 1982].

*Example 4.3.* Consider the query: "names of departments that offer lectures after 8 pm given by professors who live in the city where the department is located". The corresponding relational calculus expression and a query graph are shown in Figure 8.

If the database is in the state shown in Figure 9, no sequence of semijoins (corresponding to edges of the query graph of Figure 8) will produce the correct result (the empty relation). The reason is that the semijoin technique only considers one edge at a time, and thus loses restrictive conditions introduced through the feedback effect of the cycle:

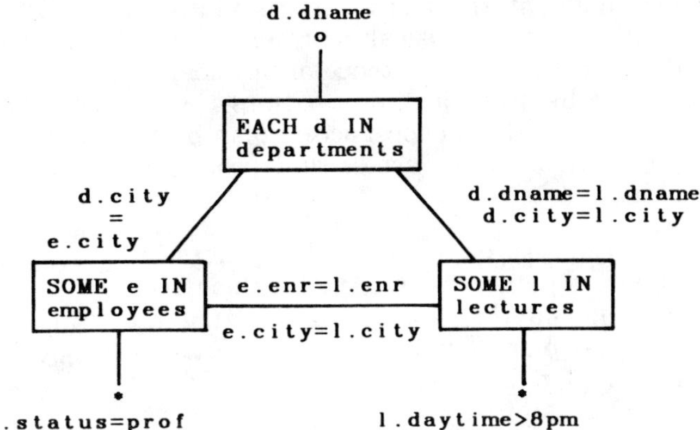


**Figure 10.** Augmented object graph for Example 4.3.

```
[⟨d.dname⟩ OF
  EACH d IN departments:
    SOME e IN employees
      (e.status = professor
        AND
      SOME l IN lectures
        (l.daytime > 8 pm
          AND
        d.dname = l.dname AND l.enr = e.enr
            AND e.city = d.city))]
```

In Kambayashi et al. [1982] a proposal is made that is intended to generalize the applicability of the semijoin technique to cyclic expressions. The overall idea is to transform the cyclic query graph into a tree by adding appropriate terms to edges of the graph. Figure 10 demonstrates the technique applied to the cyclic expression of Example 4.3.

The additional terms "d.city = l.city" and "l.city = e.city" imply the condition "d.city = e.city" by transitivity. Thus the resulting graph is equivalent to a chain query, a special form of tree query. Note that addition of the new terms corresponds basically to addition of the city attribute to the schema of the lectures relation (initialized with null values).

The query tree then is processed by stepwise reduction, executing a generalized semijoin for each edge while taking into account the newly introduced attributes. The number of data transfers are reduced by means of specialized compression techniques.

Methods for the efficient implementation of operations, such as the ones presented in this section, are candidates for hardware components in specialized database machines. However, such components often allow parallelism and therefore require somewhat different join and semijoin algorithms [Bitton et al. 1983; Maekawa 1982; Missikoff and Scholl 1983; Valduriez 1982; Valduriez and Gardarin 1984]. A brief survey of hardware approaches to query optimization is presented in Section 6.3.

## 5. ACCESS PLANS

In the previous section we dealt with techniques for the efficient evaluation of query components that can be used as building blocks of a general query evaluation algorithm. The final step of our query evaluation framework requires the combination of these blocks into an efficient evaluation procedure for an arbitrary standardized, simplified, and ameliorated expression. Unfortunately, work in this area is still incomplete.

The inputs of such a procedure are a logically preprocessed query (as described in Section 3), the existing storage structures and access paths, and a cost model. The output is an optimal (or at least heuristically "good") access plan. The procedure consists of the following steps.

(1) Generate all reasonable logical access plans for evaluating the query. A logical access plan describes a sequence of operations or of intermediate results leading from existing relations to the final result of a query.

(2) Augment the logical access plans by details of the physical representation of data (sort orders, existence of physical access paths, statistical information).
(3) Choose the cheapest access plan by applying a model of access and processing costs.

In this section we review the generation of access plans, cost models for their evaluation, and the problem of selecting the cheapest plan. The quality of the final solution plan is strongly influenced by the existing storage structures and access paths, which usually cannot be optimized for a single ad hoc query. In Section 5.4 we therefore briefly consider the simultaneous optimization of multiple queries.

### 5.1 Generation of Access Plans

Access plans describe sequences of operations (represented by operator graphs) or intermediate results (object graphs) leading from the existing data structures to a query result. The query optimizer should generate a set of plans rich enough to contain the optimal plan but small enough to keep the optimization effort acceptable.

Two extreme approaches are exemplified by Smith and Chang [1975] and Yao [1979]. Smith and Chang use a rigid set of "automatic programming" query transformation rules similar to the ones discussed in Section 3. Their procedure generates exactly one access plan, which need not be optimal. Yao's method generates all nondominated access plans possible in a given physical environment. While this may be feasible in the context of two-variable queries, it becomes prohibitively costly for very complex queries.

Other approaches seek a compromise between heuristic selection and detailed generation of alternative access plans. For example, System R [Chamberlin et al. 1981; Selinger et al. 1979] applies a hierarchical procedure based on the nested block concept of SQL. On the lower level, evaluation plans for each query block are generated and compared. On the upper level, the sequence in which the query blocks are evaluated is determined. Kim [1982] notes that this concept places too much emphasis on the user-specified block structure of the query and therefore introduces query standardization steps into SQL query processing.

A similar compromise was chosen in INGRES [Youssefi and Wong 1979]. The heuristic decomposition approach reduces a query to a set of subqueries containing at most two variables. For each of these subqueries a more detailed analysis of its optimal implementation is performed.

A comprehensive procedure for generating access plans to solve conjunctive queries without universal quantifiers and aggregates has been proposed by Rosenthal and Reiner [1982]. An expanded object graph representation is used for modeling evaluation strategies that exploit auxiliary direct access structures. To avoid the generation of an excessive number of strategies to be generated, the generation of access plans is interleaved with the selection step: Strategies known to be infeasible or dominated by other procedures are not created.

### 5.2 Cost Analysis of Access Plans

The selection of physical access plans is determined by heuristic rules or is based on a cost model of storage structures and access operations [Merrett 1977]. In this section, cost models and their integration into optimization procedures are reviewed.

Whereas a few researchers consider working storage requirements [Kim 1982; Lang et al. 1977; Sacco and Schkolnick 1982] or CPU costs [Gotlieb 1975; Selinger et al. 1979], most cost models are based on the number of secondary storage accesses. For a given operation, this figure is influenced by the size of its operands, the access structures used, and the size of main memory buffers.

At the beginning of the evaluation, the operands are existing data structures of known size, such as relations or indexes. In later stages, however, most operands are results of preceding operations, and the cost model must estimate their size by using information about the original data structures and the selectivity of the operations already performed on them. Although there is much ongoing work, no generally accepted formulas for *estimating the size of intermediate results* have evolved thus far. This results in part from the fact that the trade-off between the amount of information used and the accuracy of the result is not very well understood.

In general, the more restrictive the assumptions about the data, the fewer are the parameters needed to compute the size of the results of operations. For example, in Demolombe [1980] a recursive procedure for estimating the size of a quantifier-free calculus expression is described, for which five types of parameters must be known if fairly detailed database statistics are available. Under more restrictive assumptions, however, only three of them are needed. The size estimates given by Selinger et al. [1979] use only information already existing in the database but make many assumptions about data and queries [Astrahan et al. 1980]. At the other extreme, Yao [1979] assumes (implicitly) that detailed selectivity data are known; no statement is made as to how these data are obtained. (See, however, Yao [1977b] for an access cost model.)

More recently researchers recognized the need to carefully state and critically review all underlying assumptions about database characteristics to generate formally valid parameter systems that allow one to

(1) compute a size estimate for any feasible operation, and
(2) compute parameter values for intermediate results required for further operations.

Such techniques view the database state at run time as the result of a random process that generates relation elements from the Cartesian product of the attribute domains, governed by some probability distribution (usually assumed to be uniform) and by general laws (e.g., functional dependencies) of the database schema [Gelenbe and Gardy 1982; Richard 1981]. From these assumptions, parameters are derived whose values must be known in order to compute the size of any intermediate result of complex operations. For example, Richard [1981] demonstrates that it is sufficient to know the size of all projections in the database if the attribute value distributions are uniform and independent both within an attribute and between attributes of the same domain.

Christodoulakis [1981, 1983] and Montgomery et al. [1983] have critically reviewed such assumptions and have proved that they lead to a bias against direct-access structures in selection plans. However, no practical formulas with more general assumptions, but without excessive data requirements, have yet been published.

The final cost measure is the *number of secondary storage accesses*, not the sizes of intermediate results. A large number of researchers estimate the relationship between the two figures [Cardenas 1975; Chan and Niamir 1982; Cheung 1982b; Luk 1983; Whang et al. 1983; Yao 1977a; Yu et al. 1978]. In essence, it depends on the physical storage structures involved and the proportion of elements to be accessed.

Assume first that all elements of an operand of size $N$ have to be accessed. The optimal number of secondary storage accesses would then be $N/B$, where $B$ is the blocking factor of the operand. This can be achieved only if the elements are stored densely and it is clear from the beginning on which physical records the elements reside. As a counterexample, the so-called "segment scan" of System R requires access to a superset of the necessary pages to find all elements of a relation [Selinger et al. 1979]. If it is necessary to read the elements in some predetermined sequence, they must not only be stored densely but also sorted by the given reading order.

If direct access to a subset of the elements is used, the number of secondary storage accesses required to retrieve $n$ of the $N$ elements will depend on the clustering of elements in physical blocks. Most of the models cited above assume random placement of records on pages, which in some sense describes a worst case [Christodoulakis 1981]. Optimal clustering can reduce the number of pages to be accessed to $n/B$.

In conclusion, the traditional assumptions about value distributions and element placements tend to overestimate costs and thus to bias cost estimates against the use of direct-access structures. On the other hand, more sophisticated techniques require more statistical information about the database. The question of how to keep such information up-to-date is not yet fully resolved.

### 5.3 Selection of Access Plans

How are the cost estimates used in query optimization? As mentioned in Section 5.2, there are heuristic procedures that do not use them at all. Other approaches combine heuristic reduction of choices with enumerative cost minimization in the "end game" [Youssefi and Wong 1979]. Experiments indicate that combinatorial analysis can improve database performance considerably [Epstein and Stonebraker 1980].

There are two ways to utilize cost estimates in the selection process. First, the costs of each alternative access plan can be determined *completely* [Blasgen and Eswaran 1976; Yao 1979]. This approach has the advantage of covering techniques like parallelism or feedback in a realistic way. On the other hand, the optimization effort is high.

Second, the cost of strategies can be computed *incrementally* in parallel to their generation. This approach allows whole families of strategies with common parts to be evaluated in parallel, which considerably reduces the optimization costs. For example, the method proposed by Rosenthal and Reiner [1982] retains only the cost minimal way to obtain each intermediate result, and discards any other method as soon as its nonoptimality is detected.

An extension of this second approach is a *dynamic* query optimization procedure, which derives from the observation that, at each moment, only the next operation to be performed has to be decided. To guarantee overall optimality, only the consequences of this decision for the remainder of the evaluation must be evaluated. A dynamic procedure has actual information about all its operands, including intermediate results. This information can also be used to update the estimates of the remaining steps. The dynamic method has two drawbacks: its cost and the danger of getting stuck in local optima if no look ahead is applied. However, if used carefully, the method can reduce the evaluation costs for queries, in which the sizes of actual intermediate results differ from the expected sizes.

### 5.4 Support for Multiple Queries

All of the query evaluation procedures considered thus far concentrate on optimizing the evaluation of a single query. Chesnais et al. [1983] have also investigated the performance effect of multiple users accessing a database in parallel. However, query optimization strategies can even go beyond simple parallelism by *sharing* the execution costs of common operations among queries. Additionally, a strategy that optimizes the evaluation of multiple queries simultaneously can consider *investments* in additional access paths, the creation of which would not be cost effective for a single query. The few existing approaches to multiple-query optimization can be classified in three groups, according to the time scope for which decisions are made: (1) simultaneous optimization of batched queries, (2) index selection, and (3) physical database design.

A set of queries submitted by one or more users at approximately the same time can be *batched* for more efficient evaluation [Shneiderman and Goodman 1976]. The techniques for batched evaluation are similar to those described in Section 4.3 for multivariable expressions. First, results of common subexpressions can be shared among queries [Grant and Minker 1981; Jarke 1984], and subexpressions accessing the same physical data page can do so with one secondary storage access. Second, temporary physical access paths such as sorting, hashing, or indexes can be provided whose costs pay off for the batch as a whole. Finally, results of some queries can be retained for processing subsequent queries [Finkelstein 1982; Hevner and Yao 1981]. There seems to be no coherent theory in this area yet. Kim [1981, 1984] and Jarke [1984] present language constructs and preliminary architectures, and a number of ongoing research projects are described in IEEE [1982].

Many of the examples in this paper have demonstrated the importance of using *indexes* for the performance of query evaluation algorithms. From this viewpoint, indexes can hardly hurt anywhere but are most profitable if they are very selective and support access to attributes frequently referred to in queries [Gilles and Schuster 1975]. However, index selection must also take into account altering transactions because they must change the index in addition to the base data. The index selection problem has been described in several surveys [Batory 1982] and tutorial papers [March 1983; Putkonen 1979; Schkolnick 1975; Severance and Carlis 1977]. Selection and maintenance of more general indexes that support user views have been investigated by Roussopoulos [1982a, 1982b]. The use of high-level language constructs for extended view concepts has been discussed by Jarke [1984] and Schmidt [1984].

Finally, query optimization influences the *physical database design.* However, long-term query optimization is only one of many aspects of physical database design (see, e.g., Carlis et al. [1981], Carlson and Kaplan [1976], Schkolnick [1982], and Teorey and Fry [1982]). Important design strategies with an impact on query processing efficiency include the horizontal clustering of relation elements by attribute values [Salton 1978] and the vertical partitioning of attributes by frequency of combined access [Hammer and Niamir 1979].

## 6. NONSTANDARD QUERY OPTIMIZATION

We have described query optimization in the framework of relational calculus queries in centralized database systems. While this approach covers much of the work done in the area, some query-processing problems exceed the framework either because of a query complexity that goes beyond relational completeness or as a result of the structure of the underlying physical database. Without claiming completeness, in the following sections we briefly survey some important developments. The reader is referred to the cited literature for further details.

### 6.1 Higher Level Queries

Queries expressed in a relationally complete language retrieve such relation elements (or sets of elements) from a database that can be described by a predicate of the relational calculus. Whereas this method is sufficient for most transaction-oriented business applications, certain other applications may require more complex data objects or more powerful query predicates. These requirements can be characterized as language extensions that yield query languages more powerful than the relationally complete ones. Optimization techniques for such extensions are addressed in this section.

*Hierarchical and network database systems* support data objects that are more complex than flat records and thus contain information-bearing access paths [Astrahan and Ghosh 1974]. Relational interfaces to such systems therefore require efficient translation of relational queries to navigational access programs. (The reverse problem—program conversion from network code to relational queries—has also been studied [Katz and Wong 1982].) Several approaches have been described: interpretative, translational, and view processing.

Interpretative models (e.g., Zaniolo [1979]) directly interpret relational queries as sequences of tuple-at-a-time operations on a network database. Similarly, direct translation methods (e.g., Vassiliou and Lochovsky [1980]) frequently do not address optimization; such methods may yield quite inefficient code. Dayal and his co-workers [Dayal et al. 1981; Dayal and Goodman 1982] and Gray [1981, 1984] have developed query optimization strategies for network databases. Alternatively, one can represent network structures as relational views with particular integrity constraints [Rosenthal and Reiner 1984]. In this way, existing relational view optimization facilities can be used for compiling an efficient navigational program working on the network database.

Applications in *computer-aided design and manufacture* and *text processing* usually work on even more complex objects composed of related elements from different relations. On top of a traditional relational (or network) database, one can define structures that allow access to either the whole object or to part of it, using multiple views of the data [Johnston et al. 1983]. Another approach is an extension of the relational model by nonfirst normal form relations [Lamersdorf 1984; Schek and Pistor 1982]. Such extensions support access to substructures by specialized indexing schemes or use pattern-searching mechanisms similar to those used in information retrieval [Davis and Kunii 1982]. Dayal [1983b] investigates the related problem of answering queries in generalization hierarchies, which has to take into account the fact that data objects inherit properties of more general objects.

A relational calculus query retrieves a set of data as they come from the database, but does not support grouping and abstracting from the stored data to more complex data objects within the query language. The grouping of and summarizing over elements of the same relation by certain so-called category attributes lies in the domain of *statistical* query processing. Some query languages offer a limited set of built-in aggregate functions to support such applications. Aggregate functions can be defined as extensions to either the relational calculus [Klug 1982a] or the relational algebra [Ozsoyoglu and Ozsoyoglu 1983], and can be evaluated by using nested iteration with indexes as described in Section 4 [Klug 1982b]. However, many statistical databases are characterized by high redundancy and a large percentage of null values. Therefore the data must be compressed and stored in ways that differ from standard relational databases. An overview of these issues can be found in Shoshani [1982]. Special software [Eggers and Shoshani 1980] and hardware [Bancilhon et al. 1982; Hawthorn 1982] have been devised for processing queries on such databases. Walker [1980] discusses the use of small abstracted databases in decision support systems.

Database applications in *artificial intelligence*, especially expert systems [Nau 1983] and natural language user interfaces [Marburger and Nebel 1983; Sagalowicz 1977], require inferences to be performed over the raw data coming from the database [Buneman 1979; Chang 1979; Minker 1975, 1978]. Whereas parts of such an inference mechanism can be provided by traditional view mechanisms with some additional optimization [Jarke et al. 1984; Ott 1977; Ott and Horlaender 1982; Paige 1982], more complex requests—use of recursion, for example—must be treated in a different way.

A number of alternative architectures for coupling expert systems with DBMSs are presented by Jarke and Vassiliou [1984]. A request to the expert system usually translates to a sequence of related database calls. Optimization techniques include the combination of multiple tuple-oriented database calls into set-oriented operations [Kunifuji and Yokota 1982; Vassiliou et al. 1984], the simplification of such retrieval requests [Grishman 1978; Jarke et al. 1984; Reiter 1978], the reordering of conditions to be tested [Warren 1981], and the sharing of intermediate results [Grant and Minker 1981], which is particularly useful in executing recursive database calls [Chang 1978; Henschen and Naqvi 1984; Kellogg 1982; Minker and Nicolas 1983]. A tool often proposed in this context is the logic programming language Prolog [Kowalski 1981]. Parsaye [1983] proposes extensions to Prolog specifically designed for database and knowledge-base management.

The language extensions presented in this section can be characterized theoretically by their expressive power and by the difficulty of their evaluation. Chandra and Harel [1982a, 1982b] analyze several classes of higher level query languages, such as (in order of increasing language power and computational complexity) first-order relational calculus queries, Horn clause queries, fix-point queries, second-order queries, and general computable queries. The user of a traditional query language has to achieve the power of such high-level languages through the use of general programming language constructs in a database programming language [Schmidt 1984]. The disadvantage of this solution, besides the increased programming effort, is that the responsibility for efficient implementation shifts from the database management system to the user.

### 6.2 Distributed Databases

In a distributed database fragments of one logical database (the database as seen by the user) reside on several physical databases, each accessed by a separate computer. Databases can be distributed for higher availability of data (through data replication [Andler et al. 1982]), improved accessibility by the most frequent users (through local storage of data [Wong 1983]), and increased execution speed of queries (through parallel processing of fragments [Su and Mikkilineni 1982; Wong and Katz 1983]). Examples of distributed database systems include Distributed INGRES [Stonebraker and Neuhold 1977], POREL [Neuhold and Biller 1977], SIRIUS [Esculier and Clorieux 1979], VDN [Munz 1979], SDD-1 [Bernstein et al. 1981], and R* [Williams et al. 1982].

The fact that data are physically dispersed and may be replicated strongly influences database design [Chen and Akoka 1980], concurrency control [Bernstein and Goodman 1981c], and query processing. Rothnie and Goodman [1977] give an overview of the major research issues.

If data are distributed, the cost of data transfer becomes a decision variable rather than a constant in the query optimization problem. Since communication costs tend to dominate local processing costs, query optimization requires a completely different objective function: the minimization of communication delay, often represented by the amount of data transmitted from one site to another.

The primary decision influencing data transfer is the selection of the site(s) where computations are performed. The general strategy is to distribute the evaluation of the query rather than collect all the data and execute the query at one site (e.g., where the query was issued). The benefits of this approach have been impressively demonstrated by Tanenbaum [1981] and Gavish and Segev [1982]. Within this general strategy, the most important tactical objectives are the maximal reduction of data to be transmitted by local preprocessing [Forker 1982], and the selection of the site(s) where the global operations are performed (e.g., Bernstein et al. [1981] and Ceri and Pelagatti [1982]). If data are replicated, there is a choice of which copy to use in order to minimize data transfer [Ullman 1982; Williams et al. 1982].

A large number of distributed query processing strategies have been devised. The choice among such strategies is influenced by several factors.

#### 6.2.1 *Trade-Off between Communication and Local Processing Costs*

If the communication lines are relatively slow, communication costs usually dominate the costs of distributed evaluation to the extent that all other costs become negligible. Some of the more theoretical models (e.g., Apers et al. [1983], Hevner [1979], and Muthuswamy and Kerschberg [1983]) ignore local processing costs altogether. In practice [Bernstein et al. 1981; Smith et al. 1981] there will be a two-level optimization procedure that first plans the global strategy and then develops an optimal subquery evaluation plan for each local site.

As the communication speed increases, local processing costs have to be taken into account [Chu and Hurley 1982; Gouda and Dayal 1981]: No longer can an arbitrary amount of local preprocessing be justified to reduce data transfer between sites. Kerschberg et al. [1982] report experience with a two-computer network that demonstrates the relative importance of local processing. Of course, simultaneous minimization of data transfer and local processing increases the number of alternatives to be compared considerably since the problem no longer can be decomposed into a hierarchy of independent subproblems.

#### 6.2.2 *Network Structure*

The topology of the computer network on which the distributed database is implemented has an impact on the complexity of query optimization. In networks with arbitrary message routing, queuing delays at intermediate nodes play an important role [Muthuswamy and Kerschberg 1983; Tanenbaum 1981]. However, they can be considered only within a global optimization of all network traffic. To avoid this complication, many optimization algorithms (e.g., Hevner and Yao [1979]) assume a fully connected network with node-independent communication delays. Another simple structure is a star computer network [Kerschberg et al. 1982], in which a major central processor is connected to several (usually smaller) local processors.

The network structure can be homogeneous (i.e., it can consist of processors of the same type) or heterogeneous. For a homogeneous network (equal processor speed, processor-independent linear communication costs), Chu and Hurley [1982] have proved a number of theorems, the application of which restricts the search space for optimal solutions. For instance, the local preprocessing of monadic operations (restriction, projection) is shown to be globally optimal under these assumptions. Even within a homogeneous computer network, a heterogeneous distributed database may exist if the local databases work on different data models or DBMS [Chan et al. 1983; Smith et al. 1981].

#### 6.2.3 Data Distribution Strategy

A relation can be physically partitioned horizontally (the set of tuples is divided into subsets according to the pattern of local reference), vertically (the set of attributes is partitioned according to different applications at different locations), or into arbitrary fragments, with or without overlap among them [Mahmoud et al. 1979].

Gavish and Segev [1983] describe an algorithm for optimizing set operations in horizontally partitioned relational databases. The problem is proven to be computationally untractable, and heuristics for its solution are developed. Ullman [1982] describes the use of "guard conditions" for simplifying queries on horizontally distributed databases by identifying the relevant fragments. Work on general nondisjoint fragments has just begun [Maier and Ullman 1983].

The main focus of the existing literature is on vertically distributed databases. In this case, restriction and projection can be performed locally; research has therefore concentrated on the optimal implementation and scheduling of joins and other multirelation operations. The main tool used in this context is the semijohn operation described in Section 4.3. As discussed, tree queries can be completely solved by using semijoins. For the special case of chain queries, an efficient algorithm exists that computes the optimal semijoin schedule when the reduction factors of each semijoin are known [Chiu et al. 1981]. Similar algorithms for general tree queries are given by Chiu and Ho [1980] and Gouda and Dayal [1981]. However, owing to the computational complexity of exact methods, heuristic procedures are normally preferred [Bernstein et al. 1981; Chang 1982; Cheung 1982a; Yu and Chang 1983].

Some early algorithms do not use semijoins. Wong [1977] employs a hill-climbing procedure to improve incrementally on an initial solution that processes the complete query at one site. Epstein et al. [1978] present a model for minimizing processing time or network traffic separately for each operation in a query. No global optimality is guaranteed. The optimization algorithm for R* (a distributed extension of System R [Williams et al. 1982]) performs an exhaustive search over combinations of several alternative join strategies in multijoin queries. Within its search space and the limits of data estimation, an optimal solution is found [Daniels 1982; Daniels et al. 1982; Ng 1982; Selinger and Adiba 1970].

As in the centralized case, many distributed query evaluation algorithms have been criticized for either assuming too much statistical information to be practical or for making unrealistic simplifications. Muthuswamy and Kerschberg [1983] describe a procedure for obtaining detailed database statistics by observing database usage.

The computational complexity of the distributed query optimization problem has lead to the same phenomenon that we observed for centralized queries: One group of researchers is looking for optimal solutions in special cases, while another employs general heuristics in order to be able to answer all queries. If one plans to implement a distributed DBMS, the challenge is to combine both approaches in a homogeneous way. A good example of such a comprehensive strategy, which includes the efficient handling of fragments, data replication, and dynamic access plans (avoiding some of the aforementioned pitfalls of complicated statistical estimates), is given by Yu and Chang [1983].

### 6.3 Database Machines

The use of database machines is motivated primarily by the goal of relieving a general-purpose host computer from the burden of database processing so that overall system performance may be improved. Off-loading DBMS functionality from the host to a back-end database machine can be achieved with a software-oriented or hardware-oriented approach.

In the *software backend approach* (surveyed, e.g., by Maryanski [1980]), the database—together with DBMS software—is transferred to a standby general-purpose computer. The software back end completely processes each database request, thus enabling the host to execute nondatabase tasks in parallel. Another attractive property of the approach is the reasonable cost of conventional computers. For very database-intensive applications, however, the software back-end approach does not seem to be appropriate. In these situations, the back-end computer itself becomes the system bottleneck since it has the same limitations as a general-purpose host. Overall performance may be even worse than in a host-only configuration because of the additional interprocessor communication requirements.

In such a case, a *hardware backend approach* (surveyed, e.g., by Hsiao [1979] and Langdon [1979]) could be chosen. From the viewpoint of query optimization, hardware back ends can be used to support important optimization strategies, such as early evaluation of restrictive operations and parallel processing, by placing on-board logic as close as possible to the base data and dividing labor among existing hardware components.

In general, a hardware back end consists of a set of cooperating special-purpose processors. A wide bandwidth of architectural alternatives exists, ranging from the association of identical processors with disjoint fragments of the database to the assignment of specific processors to different DBMS functions; these assignments can be made either statically or dynamically.

The so-called "cellular logic" [Su 1979] is characterized by the fragmentation of the database (e.g., residing on a disk) into equal-sized cells (e.g., disk tracks), each of which is associated with a special-purpose processor. Usually, these processors have an identical repertoire and are connected with a master processor controlling the concurrent operations of its slaves. Various cellular logic prototypes, such as CASSM [Su and Lipkovsky 1975], RAP [Ozkarahan 1982], and RARES [Lin et al. 1976], have received wide attention.

Some designs of database machines have also experimented with associative arrays [Berra and Oliver 1979]. However, owing to their relatively high cost and limited capacity, they do not constitute a realistic solution for the permanent storage of entire databases. Associative arrays therefore are usually proposed to be used as staging devices for relatively inexpensive mass storage devices.

The specialization of processors to specific DBMS functions has been realized in a number of database machine architectures. Specific cost models [Bernadat 1983] and optimization algorithms [Valduriez and Gardarin 1984] have been developed. In the DBC [Banerjee and Hsiao 1979], access control, directory maintenance, and query processing are performed by different computers. The dynamic assignment of single processors to query-processing tasks, such as the evaluation of distinct subqueries, has been pursued in DIRECT [DeWitt 1979], as well as the search processor of the Technical University of Braunschweig [Leilich et al. 1978]. More recently, LSI and VLSI technology have been explored for the purposes of close integration of data storage and query-processing capabilities, as well as hardware implementations of language constructs usually available in high-level query languages [Kim et al. 1981; Menon and Hsiao 1981].

## 7. SUMMARY

An overview of logical transformation techniques and physical evaluation methods for database queries was given, using the framework of the relational calculus. It was shown that a large body of knowledge has been developed to solve the problem of processing queries efficiently in conventional centralized and distributed database systems.

Query optimization research is still an active field. Promising directions include the development of simple yet realistic cost estimates, the optimization of queries on databases with deductive or computational capabilities, and the simultaneous optimization of multiple queries and update transactions. Other interesting areas only briefly addressed in this survey are query optimization in database systems that utilize more advanced access paths, such as multiple-attribute indexes or database machines, and query optimization in systems that work on the complex data structures required for artificial intelligence, office, statistical, decision support, or computer-aided design and manufacture applications.

## ACKNOWLEDGMENTS

The work of Matthias Jarke was supported in part by a joint study with the IBM Corporation. The work of Jürgen Koch was supported in part by the Deutsche Forschungsgemeinschaft under Grant SCHM450/2-1 (principal investigator: J. W. Schmidt). The authors are grateful to Joachim Schmidt and Arnie Rosenthal for many discussions and suggestions, and to the referees and editors for helpful comments on the presentation of this material.

## REFERENCES

AHO, A. V., BEERI, C., AND ULLMAN, J. D. 1979a. The theory of joins in relational databases. *ACM Trans. Database Syst. 4,* 3 (Sept.), 297–314.

AHO, A. V., SAGIV, Y., AND ULLMAN, J. D. 1979b. Efficient optimization of a class of relational expressions. *ACM Trans. Database Syst. 4,* 4 (Dec.), 435–454.

AHO, A. V., SAGIV, Y., AND ULLMAN, J. D. 1979c. Equivalences among relational expressions. *SIAM J. Comput. 8,* 2, 218–246.

ANDLER, S., DING, I., ESWARAN, K., HAUSER, C., KIM, W., MEHL, J., AND WILLIAMS, R. 1982. System D: A distributed system for availability. In *Proceedings of the 8th International Conference on Very Large Data Bases* (Mexico City). VLDB Endowment, Saratoga, Calif., pp. 33–44.

APERS, P. M. G., HEVNER, A. R., AND YAO, S. B. 1983. Optimization algorithms for distributed queries. *IEEE Trans. Softw. Eng. SE-9,* 1, 57–68.

ASTRAHAN, M. M., AND CHAMBERLIN, D. D. 1975. Implementation of a structured English query language. *Commun. ACM 18,* 10 (Oct.), 580–588.

ASTRAHAN, M. M., AND GHOSH, S. P. 1974. A search path selection algorithm for the Data Independent Accessing Model (DIAM). In *Proceedings of the ACM–SIGMOD Workshop on Data Description, Access and Control* (Ann Arbor, Mich., May 1–3). ACM, New York, pp. 367–388.

ASTRAHAN, M. M., SCHKOLNICK, M., AND KIM, W. 1980. Performance of the System R access path selection algorithm. In *Information Processing 80.* Elsevier North-Holland, New York, pp. 487–491.

BANCILHON, F., RICHARD, P., AND SCHOLL, M. 1982. On line processing of compacted relations. In *Proceedings of the 8th International Conference on Very Large Data Bases* (Mexico City). VLDB Endowment, Saratoga, Calif., pp. 263–269.

BANERJEE, J., AND HSIAO, D. K. 1979. DBC—A database computer for very large databases. *IEEE Trans. Comput. C-28,* 6, 414–429.

BATORY, D. S. 1982. Index selection. In *Principles of Database Design*, S. B. Yao, Ed. Springer, New York.

BAYER, R., AND MCCREIGHT, E. 1972. Organization and maintenance of large ordered indexes. *Acta Inf. 1,* 173–189.

BAYER, R., ELHARDT, K., KIESSLING, W., AND KILLAR, D. 1984. Verteilte Datenbanksysteme. *Inf. Spektrum 7,* 1, 1–19.

BENTLEY, J. L., AND FRIEDMAN, J. H. 1979. Data structures for range searching. *ACM Comput. Surv. 11,* 4 (Dec.), 397–409.

BERNADAT, P. 1983. Decomposition et évaluation de questions dans une machine base de données relationnelles. Thèse IIIme cycle, Départment d'Informatique, Université de Paris VI, Paris, France.

BERNSTEIN, P. A., AND CHIU, D. M. W. 1981. Using semi-joins to solve relational queries. *J. ACM 28,* 1 (Jan.), 25–40.

BERNSTEIN, P. A., AND GOODMAN, N. 1981a. The power of natural semijoins. *SIAM J. Comput. 10,* 4, 751–771.

BERNSTEIN, P. A., AND GOODMAN, N. 1981b. The power of inequality semijoins. *Inf. Syst. 6,* 4, 255–265.

BERNSTEIN, P. A., AND GOODMAN, N. 1981c. Concurrency control in distributed database systems. *ACM Comput. Surv. 13*, 2 (June), 185–221.

BERNSTEIN, P. A., BLAUSTEIN, B. T., AND CLARKE, E. M. 1980. Fast maintenance of semantic integrity assertions using redundant aggregate data. In *Proceedings of the 6th International Conference on Very Large Data Bases* (Montreal, Oct. 1–3). IEEE, New York, pp. 126–136.

BERNSTEIN, P. A., GOODMAN, N., WONG, E., REEVE, C. L., AND ROTHNIE, J. B., JR. 1981. Query processing in a system for distributed databases (SDD-1). *ACM Trans. Database Syst. 6*, 4 (Dec.), 602–625.

BERRA, B., AND OLIVER, E. 1979. The role of associative array processors in database machine architectures. *IEEE Comput. 12*, 3, 53–61.

BITTON, D., BORAL, H., DEWITT, D., AND WILKINSON, W. K. 1983. Parallel algorithms for the execution of relational database operations. *ACM Trans. Database Syst. 8*, 3 (Sept.), 324–353.

BLASGEN, M. W., AND ESWARAN, K. P. 1976. On the evaluation of queries in a relational data base system. IBM Res. Rep. RJ 1745, IBM Research Laboratories, San Jose, Calif.

BLASGEN, M. W., AND ESWARAN, K. P. 1977. Storage and access in relational databases. *IBM Syst. J. 16*, 363–377.

BOLOUR, A. 1981. Optimal retrieval for small range queries. *SIAM J. Comput. 10*, 4, 721–741.

BREITBART, Y., AND REITER, A. 1975. Algorithms for fast evaluation of Boolean expressions. *Acta Inf. 4*, 107–116.

BRODIE, M., MYLOPOULOS, J., AND SCHMIDT, J. W., Eds. 1984. *On Conceptual Modelling. Perspectives from Artificial Intelligence, Databases, and Programming Languages.* Springer, New York.

BUNEMAN, P. 1979. The problem of multiple paths in a database schema. In *Proceedings of the 5th International Conference on Very Large Data Bases* (Rio de Janeiro, Oct. 3–5). IEEE, New York, pp. 368–372.

CARDENAS, A. F. 1975. Analysis and performance of inverted data base structures. *Commun. ACM 18*, 5 (May), 253–263.

CARLIS, J. V., MARCH, S. T., AND DICKSON, G. W. 1981. Physical database design: A DSS approach. In *Proceedings of the 2nd International Conference on Information Systems* (Boston, Mass.). ACM, New York, pp. 153–172.

CARLSON, C. R., AND KAPLAN, R. S. 1976. A generalized access path model and its application to a relational data base system. In *Proceedings of the ACM-SIGMOD International Conference on Management of Data* (Washington, D.C., June 2–4). ACM, New York, pp. 143–154.

CERI, S., AND PELAGATTI, G. 1982. Allocation of operations in distributed database access. *IEEE Trans. Comput. C-31*, 2, 119–128.

CHAMBERLIN, D. D., ASTRAHAN, M. M., KING, W. F., LORIE, R. A., MEHL, J. W., PRICE, T. G., SCHKOLNICK, M., SELINGER, P. G., SLUTZ, D. R., WADE, B. W., AND YOST, R. A. 1981. Support for repetitive transactions and ad hoc queries in System R. *ACM Trans. Database Syst. 6*, 1 (Mar.), 70–94.

CHAN, A., AND NIAMIR, B. 1982. On estimating cost of accessing records in blocked database organizations. *Comput. J. 25*, 3, 368–374.

CHAN, A., DAYAL, U., FOX, S., GOODMAN, N., RIES, D. D., AND SKEEN, D. 1983. Overview of an Ada compatible distributed database manager. In *SIGMOD 83, Proceedings of the Annual Meeting* (San Jose, Calif., May 23–26). ACM, New York, pp. 228–237.

CHANDRA, A. K., AND HAREL, D. 1982a. Structure and complexity of relational queries. *J. Comput. Syst. Sci. 25*, 99–128.

CHANDRA, A. K., AND HAREL, D. 1982b. Horn clauses and the fixpoint query hierarchy. In *Proceedings of the ACM Symposium on Principles of Database Systems* (Los Angeles, Calif., Mar. 29–31). ACM, New York, pp. 158–163.

CHANDRA, A. K., AND MERLIN, P. M. 1977. Optimal implementation of conjunctive queries in relational data bases. In *Proceedings of the 9th Annual ACM Symposium on Theory of Computation* (Boulder, Colo., May 24). ACM, New York, pp. 77–90.

CHANG, C. L. 1978. DEDUCE 2: Further investigations of deduction in relational databases. In *Logic and Databases*, H. Gallaire and J. Minker, Eds. Plenum, New York, pp. 210–236.

CHANG, C. L. 1979. On evaluation of queries containing derived relations in a relational data base. IBM Res. Rep. RJ2667, IBM Research Laboratories, San Jose, Calif.

CHANG, J.-M. 1982. A heuristic approach to distributed query processing. In *Proceedings of the 8th International Conference on Very Large Data Bases* (Mexico City). VLDB Endowment, Saratoga, Calif., pp. 54–61.

CHEN, P. P. S., AND AKOKA, J. 1980. Optimal design of distributed information systems. *IEEE Trans. Comput. C-29*, 12, 1068–1080.

CHESNAIS, A., GELENBE, E., AND MITRANI, I. 1983. On the modeling of parallel access to shared data. *Commun. ACM 26*, 3 (Mar.), 196–202.

CHEUNG, T.-Y. 1982a. A method for equijoin queries in distributed relational databases. *IEEE Trans. Comput. C-31*, 8, 746–751.

CHEUNG, T.-Y. 1982b. Estimating block accesses and number of records in file management. *Commun. ACM 25*, 7 (July), 484–487.

CHIU, D. M., AND HO, Y. C. 1980. A methodology for interpreting tree queries into optimal semi-join expressions. In *Proceedings of the ACM—SIGMOD International Conference on Management of Data* (Santa Monica, Calif., May 14–16). ACM, New York, pp. 169–178.

CHIU, D. M., BERNSTEIN, P. A., AND HO, Y. C. 1981. Optimizing chain queries in a distributed database system. Tech. Rep. TR-01-81, Computer

Science Dept., Harvard University, Cambridge, Mass.

CHRISTODOULAKIS, S. 1981. Estimating selectivities in data bases. Tech. Rep. CSRG-136, Computer Science Dept., University of Toronto, Toronto, Canada.

CHRISTODOULAKIS, S. 1983. Estimating block transfers and join sizes. In *SIGMOD 83, Proceedings of the Annual Meeting* (San Jose, Calif., May 23–26). ACM, New York. pp. 40–54.

CHU, W. W., AND HURLEY, P. 1982. Optimal query processing for distributed database systems. *IEEE Trans. Comput. C-31,* 9, 835–850.

CLAUSEN, S. E. 1980. Optimizing the evaluation of calculus expressions in a relational database system. *Inf. Syst. 5,* 1, 41–54.

CODD, E. F. 1971. A database sublanguage founded on the relational calculus. In *Proceedings of the ACM-SIGFIDET Workshop, Data Description, Access, and Control* (San Diego, Calif., Nov. 11–12). ACM, New York, pp. 35–68.

CODD, E. F. 1972. Relational completeness of data base sublanguages. In *Courant Computer Science Symposia No. 6: Data Base Systems.* Prentice-Hall, New York, pp. 67–101.

DANIELS, D. 1982. Query compilation in a distributed database system. IBM Res. Rep. RJ3423, IBM Research Laboratories, San Jose, Calif.

DANIELS, D., SELINGER, S., HAAS, L., LINDSAY, B., MOHAN, C., WALKER, A., AND WILMS, P. 1982. An introduction to distributed query compilation in R*. In *Proceedings of the 2nd Symposium on Distributed Databases* (Berlin, FRG). Elsevier North-Holland, New York.

DAVIS, H. W., AND WINSLOW, L. E. 1982. Computational power in query languages. *SIAM J. Comput. 11,* 3, 547–554.

DAVIS, L. S., AND KUNII, T. L. 1982. Pattern databases. In *Data Base Design Techniques II,* S. B. Yao and T. L. Kunii, Eds. Springer, New York, pp. 357–399.

DAYAL, U. 1983a. Evaluating queries with quantifiers: A horticultural approach. In *Proceedings of the ACM Symposium on Principles of Database Systems* (Atlanta, Ga.). ACM, New York, pp. 125–136.

DAYAL, U. 1983b. Processing queries over generalization hierarchies in a multi-database system. In *Proceedings of the 9th International Conference on Very Large Data Bases* (Florence, Italy). VLDB Endowment, Saratoga, Calif., pp. 342–353.

DAYAL, U., AND GOODMAN, N. 1982. Query optimization for CODASYL database systems. In *Proceedings of the ACM-SIGMOD International Conference on Management of Data* (Orlando, Fla., June 2–4). ACM, New York, pp. 138–150.

DAYAL, U., GOODMAN, N., LANDERS, T. A., OLSON, K., SMITH, J. M., AND YEDWAB, L. 1981. Local query optimization in Multibase—A system for heterogeneous distributed databases. Tech. Rep. CCA-81-11, Computer Corporation of America, Cambridge, Mass.

DEMOLOMBE, R. 1980. Estimation of the number of tuples satisfying a query expressed in predicate calculus language. In *Proceedings of the 6th Conference on Very Large Data Bases* (Montreal, Oct. 1–3). IEEE, New York, pp. 55–63.

DEWITT, D. J. 1979. Query execution in DIRECT. In *Proceedings of the ACM-SIGMOD International Conference on Management of Data* (Boston, Mass., May 30–June 1). ACM, New York, pp. 13–22.

DOWNEY, P. J., SETHI, R., AND TARJAN, R. E. 1980. Variations on the common subexpression problem. *J. ACM 27,* 4 (Oct.), 758–771.

EGGERS, S. J., AND SHOSHANI, A. 1980. Efficient access of compressed data. In *Proceedings of the 6th International Conference on Very Large Data Bases* (Montreal, Oct. 1–3). IEEE, New York, pp. 205–211.

EPSTEIN, R., AND STONEBRAKER, M. 1980. Analysis of distributed data base processing strategies. In *Proceedings of the 6th International Conference on Very Large Data Bases* (Montreal, Oct. 1–3). IEEE, New York, pp. 92–101.

EPSTEIN, R., STONEBRAKER, M., AND WONG, E. 1978. Distributed query processing in a relational data base system. In *Proceedings of the ACM-SIGMOD International Conference on Management of Data* (Austin, Tex., May 31–June 2). ACM, New York, pp. 169–180.

ESCULIER, C., AND CLORIEUX, A. M. 1979. The SIRIUS-DELTA distributed DBMS. In *Proceedings of the International Conference on Entity-Relationship Approach,* P. Chen, Ed. Elsevier North-Holland, New York, pp. 543–551.

ESWARAN, K. P., GRAY, J. N., LORIE, R. A., AND TRAIGER, I. L. 1976. The notions of consistency and predicate locks in a database system. *Commun. ACM 19,* 11 (Nov.), 624–633.

FINKELSTEIN, S. 1982. Common expression analysis in database applications. In *Proceedings of the ACM-SIGMOD International Conference on Management of Data* (Orlando, Fla., June 2–4). ACM, New York, pp. 235–245.

FORKER, H. J. 1982. Algebraical and operational methods for the optimization of query processing in distributed relational database management systems. In *Proceedings of the 2nd International Symposium on Distributed Databases* (Berlin, FRG). Elsevier North-Holland, New York, pp. 39–59.

GARDARIN, G., VALDURIEZ, P., AND VIEMONT, Y. 1984. Predicate trees: An approach to optimize relational query operations. In *Proceedings of the IEEE COMPDEC Conference* (Los Angeles, Calif.). IEEE, New York.

GAVISH, B., AND SEGEV, A. 1982. Query optimization in distributed computer systems. In *Management of Distributed Data Processing,* J. Akoka, Ed. Elsevier North-Holland, New York, pp. 233–252.

GAVISH, B., AND SEGEV, A. 1983. Set query optimization in horizontally partitioned distributed databases. Working Paper QM8304, Graduate School of Management, University of Rochester, Rochester, N.Y.

GELENBE, E., AND GARDY, D. 1982. The size of projections of relations satisfying a functional dependency. In *Proceedings of the 8th International Conference on Very Large Data Bases* (Mexico City). VLDB Endowment, Saratoga, Calif., pp. 325–333.

GILLES, J. H., AND SCHUSTER, S. A. 1975. Query execution and index selection for relational data bases. Tech. Rep. CSRG-53, Computer Science Dept., University of Toronto, Toronto, Ontario.

GOODMAN, N., AND SHMUELI, O. 1980. Nonreducible database states for cyclic queries. Tech. Rep. TR-15-80, Computer Science Dept., Harvard University, Cambridge, Mass.

GOODMAN, N., AND SHMUELI, O. 1982. Tree queries: A simple class of relational queries. *ACM Trans. Database Syst. 7*, 4 (Dec.), 653–677.

GOTLIEB, L. R. 1975. Computing joins of relations. In *Proceedings of the ACM–SIGMOD International Conference on Management of Data* (San Jose, Calif., May 14–16). ACM, New York, pp. 55–63.

GOUDA, M. G., AND DAYAL, U. 1981. Optimal semijoin schedules for query processing in local distributed database systems. In *Proceedings of the ACM–SIGMOD International Conference on Management of Data* (Ann Arbor, Mich., Apr. 29–May 1). ACM, New York, pp. 164–175.

GRANT, J., AND MINKER, J. 1981. Optimization in deductive and conventional relational database systems. In *Advances in Database Theory*, H. Gallaire, J. Minker, and J.-M. Nicolas, Eds. Plenum, New York, pp. 195–234.

GRAY, P. M. D. 1981. Use of automatic programming and simulation to facilitate operations on CODASYL databases. In *Database*, M. P. Atkinson, Ed. Pergamon Infotech, London, pp. 315–369.

GRAY, P. M. D. 1984. Implementing the join operation on CODASYL DBMS. In *Databases: Role and Structure*, P. M. Stocker, Ed. Cambridge University Press, Cambridge, England.

GRIES, D. 1971. *Compiler Construction for Digital Computers.* Wiley, New York.

GRIFFETH, N. D. 1978. Nonprocedural query processing for databases with access paths. In *Proceedings of the ACM–SIGMOD International Conference on Management of Data* (Austin, Tex., May 31–June 2). ACM, New York, pp. 160–168.

GRIFFITHS, P. G., AND WADE, B. W. 1976. An authorization mechanism for a relational database system. *ACM Trans. Database Syst. 1*, 3 (Sept.), 242–255.

GRISHMAN, R. 1978. The simplification of retrieval requests generated by question-answering systems. In *Proceedings of the 4th International Conference on Very Large Data Bases* (West Berlin, FRG, Sept. 13–15). IEEE, New York, pp. 400–406.

GUDES, E., AND REITER, A. 1973. On evaluating Boolean expressions. *Softw. Pract. Exper. 3*, 345–350.

HALL, P. A. V. 1974. Common subexpression identification in general algebraic systems. Tech. Rep. UKSC 0060, IBM UK Scientific Center, Peterlee, England.

HALL, P. A. V. 1976. Optimization of single expressions in a relational data base system. *IBM J. Res. Devel. 20*, 3, 244–257.

HAMMER, M., AND NIAMIR, B. 1979. A heuristic approach to attribute partitioning. In *Proceedings of the ACM–SIGMOD International Conference on Management of Data* (Boston, Mass., May 30–June 1). ACM, New York, pp. 93–101.

HAMMER, M., AND ZDONIK, S. B., JR. 1980. Knowledge-based query processing. In *Proceedings of the 6th International Conference on Very Large Data Bases* (Montreal, Oct. 1–3). IEEE, New York, pp. 137–147.

HANANI, M. Z. 1977. An optimal evaluation of Boolean expressions in an online query system. *Commun. ACM 20*, 5 (May), 344–347.

HAWTHORN, P. 1982. Microprocessor assisted tuple access, decompression, and assembly for statistical database systems. In *Proceedings of the 8th International Conference on Very Large Data Bases* (Mexico City). VLDB Endowment, Saratoga, Calif., pp. 223–233.

HENSCHEN, L. J., AND NAQVI, S. A. 1984. On compiling queries in recursive first-order databases. *J. ACM 31*, 1 (Jan.), 47–85.

HEVNER, A. R. 1979. The optimization of query processing on distributed database systems. Ph.D. dissertation, Computer Science Dept., Purdue University, West Lafayette, Ind.

HEVNER, A. R., AND YAO, S. B. 1979. Query processing on a distributed database. *IEEE Trans. Softw. Eng. SE-5*, 3, 177–187.

HEVNER, A. R., AND YAO, S. B. 1981. Transaction optimization on a distributed database system. Tech. Rep. HR-81-257, Honeywell Corporate Computer Center, Bloomington, Minn.

HSIAO, D. K. 1979. Database machines are coming, database machines are coming. *IEEE Comput. 12*, 3, 7–9.

IBM CORPORATION 1966. Introduction to IBM direct-access storage devices and organization methods. Programming manual GC 20-1649-06,

IEEE 1982. Special issue on query optimization. *IEEE Database Eng. 5*, 3 (Sept.).

JARKE, M. 1984. Common subexpression isolation in multiple query optimization. In *Query Processing in Database Systems*, W. Kim, D. Reiner, and D. Batory, Eds. Springer, New York.

JARKE, M., AND KOCH, J. 1983. Range nesting: A fast method to evaluate quantified queries. In *SIGMOD 83, Proceedings of Annual Meeting* (San

Jose, Calif., May 23–26). ACM, New York, pp. 196–206.

JARKE, M., AND SCHMIDT, J. W. 1981. Evaluation of first-order relational expressions. Tech. Rep. 78, Fachbereich Informatik, Universitaet Hamburg, Hamburg, FRG.

JARKE, M., AND SCHMIDT, J. W. 1982. Query processing strategies in the PASCAL/R relational database management system. In *Proceedings of the ACM-SIGMOD International Conference on Management of Data* (Orlando, Fla., June 2–4). ACM, New York, pp. 256–264.

JARKE, M., AND VASSILIOU, Y. 1984. Coupling expert systems with database management systems. In *Artificial Intelligence Applications for Business*, W. Reitman, Ed. Ablex, Norwood, N.J., pp. 65–85.

JARKE, M., CLIFFORD, J., AND VASSILIOU, Y. 1984. An optimizing Prolog front-end to a relational query system. In *SIGMOD 84, Proceedings of Annual Meeting* (Boston, Mass., June 18–21). ACM, New York, pp. 296–306.

JOHNSON, D. S., AND KLUG, A. 1982. Testing containment of conjunctive queries under functional and inclusion dependencies. In *Proceedings of the ACM Symposium on Principles of Database Systems* (Los Angeles, Calif., Mar. 29–31). ACM, New York, pp. 164–169.

JOHNSON, D. S., AND KLUG, A. 1983. Optimizing conjunctive queries that contain untyped variables. *SIAM J. Comput. 12*, 4, 616–640.

JOHNSTON, H. R., SCHWEITZER, J. E., AND WARKENTINE, E. R. 1983. A DBMS facility for handling structured engineering entities. In *Proceedings of the Database Week Engineering Design Applications Conference* (San Jose, Calif.). ACM, New York, pp. 3–12.

KAMBAYASHI, Y., AND YOSHIKAWA, M. 1983. Query processing utilizing dependencies and horizontal decomposition. In *SIGMOD 83 Proceedings of the Annual Meeting* (San Jose, Calif., May 23–26). ACM, New York, pp. 55–67.

KAMBAYASHI, Y., YOSHIKAWA, M., AND YAJIMA, S. 1982. Query processing for distributed databases using generalized semi-joins. In *Proceedings of the ACM-SIGMOD International Conference on Management of Data* (Orlando, Fla., June 2–4). ACM, New York, pp. 151–160.

KATZ, R. H., AND WONG, E. 1982. Decompiling CODASYL DML into relational queries. *ACM Trans. Database Syst. 7*, 1 (Mar.), 1–23.

KELLOGG, C. 1982. A practical amalgam of knowledge and data base technology. In *Proceedings of the National Conference on Artificial Intelligence* (Pittsburgh, Pa.). AAAI, Menlo Park, Calif.

KERSCHBERG, L., TING, P. D., AND YAO, S. B. 1982. Query optimization in star computer networks. *ACM Trans. Database Syst. 7*, 4 (Dec.), 678–711.

KIM, W. 1980. A new way to compute the product and join of relations. In *Proceedings of the ACM-SIGMOD International Conference on Management of Data* (Santa Monica, (Calif., May 14–16). ACM, New York, pp. 179–187.

KIM, W. 1981. Query optimization for relational database systems. IBM Res. Rep. RJ3081, IBM Research Laboratories, San Jose, Calif.

KIM, W. 1982. On optimizing an SQL-like nested query. *ACM Trans. Database Syst. 7*, 3 (Sept.), pp. 443–469.

KIM, W. 1984. Global optimization of relational queries: A first step. In *Query Processing in Database Systems*, W. Kim, D. Reiner, and D. Batory, Eds. Springer, New York.

KIM, W., KUCK, D. J., AND GARSKI, D. 1981. A bit-serial/tuple-parallel relational query processor. IBM Res. Rep. RJ3194, IBM Research Laboratories, San Jose, Calif.

KING, J. J. 1979. Exploring the use of domain knowledge for query processing efficiency. Tech. Rep. STAN-CS-79-781, Computer Science Dept., Stanford University, Stanford, Calif.

KING, J. J. 1981. QUIST: A system for semantic query optimization in relational databases. In *Proceedings of the 7th International Conference on Very Large Data Bases* (Cannes, Sept. 9–11). IEEE, New York, pp. 510–517.

KLUG, A. 1980. Calculating constraints on relational expressions. *ACM Trans. Database Syst. 5*, 3 (Sept.), 260–290.

KLUG, A. 1982a. Equivalence of relational algebra and relational calculus query languages having aggregate functions. *J. ACM 29*, 3 (July), 699–717.

KLUG, A. 1982b. Access paths in the "ABE" statistical query facility. In *Proceedings of the ACM-SIGMOD International Conference on Management of Data* (Orlando, Fla., June 2–4). ACM, New York, pp. 161–173.

KLUG, A. 1983. Locking expressions for increased database concurrency. *J. ACM 30*, 1 (Jan.), 36–54.

KOCH, J., SCHMIDT, J. W., AND WUNDERLICH, V. 1981. Type derivation for first-order relational expressions. Tech. Rep. no. 79, Fachbereich Informatik, Universität Hamburg, Hamburg, FRG.

KOWALSKI, R. 1981. Logic as a database language. Unpublished manuscript, Computer Science Dept., Imperial College, London.

KUNIFUJI, S., AND YOKOTA, H. 1982. Prolog and relational databases for Fifth Generation Computer Systems. In *Proceedings of the Workshop on Logical Bases for Data Bases* (Toulouse, France). ONERA-CERT, Toulouse, France.

LAMERSDORF, W. 1984. Recursive data models for non-conventional database applications. In *Proceedings of the IEEE COMPDEC Conference* (Los Angeles, Calif.). IEEE, New York.

LANG, T., WOOD, C., AND FERNÁNDEZ, I. B. 1977. Database buffer paging in virtual storage systems. *ACM Trans. Database Syst. 2*, 4 (Dec.), 339–351.

LANGDON, G. G. 1979. Database machines: an introduction. *IEEE Trans. Comput. C-28*, 6, 381–383.

LEILICH, H.-O., STIEGE, G., AND ZEIDLER, H. C. 1978. A search processor for data base management systems. In *Proceedings of the 4th International Conference on Very Large Data Bases* (West Berlin, FRG, Sept. 13–15). IEEE, New York, pp. 280–287.

LIN, C. S., SMITH, D. C. P., AND SMITH, J. M. 1976. The design of a rotating associative memory for relational database applications. *ACM Trans. Database Syst. 1,* 1 (Mar.), 53–65.

LIU, J. W. S. 1976. Algorithms for parsing search queries in systems with inverted file organizations. *ACM Trans. Database Syst. 1,* 4 (Dec.), 299–316.

LUK, W. S. 1983. On estimating block accesses in database organizations. *Commun. ACM 26,* 11 (Nov.), 945–947.

MAEKAWA, M. 1982. Parallel join and sorting algorithms. In *Data Base Design Techniques II,* S. B. Yao and T. L. Kunii, Eds. Springer, New York, pp. 266–296.

MAHMOUD, S. A., RIORDON, J. S., AND TOTH, K. C. 1979. Database partitioning and query processing. In *Proceedings of the IFIP Working Conference on Database Architecture.* Elsevier North-Holland, New York, pp. 3–21.

MAIER, D. 1983. *The Theory of Relational Databases.* Computer Science Press, Rockville, Md.

MAIER, D., AND ULLMAN, J. D. 1983. Fragments of relations. In *SIGMOD 83, Proceedings of the Annual Meeting* (San Jose, Calif., May 23–26). ACM, New York, pp. 15–22.

MAIER, D., AND WARREN, D. S. 1981. Incorporating computed relations in relational databases. In *Proceedings of the ACM-SIGMOD International Conference on Management of Data* (Ann Arbor, Mich., Apr. 29–May 1). ACM, New York, pp. 176–187.

MAKINOUCHI, A., TEZUKA, M., KITAKAMI, H., AND ADACHI, S. 1981. The optimization strategy for query evaluation in RDB/V1. In *Proceedings of the 7th International Conference on Very Large Data Bases* (Cannes, Sept. 9–11). IEEE, New York, pp. 518–529.

MALL, M., REIMER, M., AND SCHMIDT, J. W. 1984. Data selection, sharing and access control in a relational scenario. In *On Conceptual Modeling. Perspectives from Artificial Intelligence, Databases, and Programming Languages,* M. Brodie, J. Mylopoulos, and J. W. Schmidt, Eds. Springer, New York, pp. 411–436.

MARBURGER, H., AND NEBEL, B. 1983. Natuerlichsprachlicher Datenbankzugang mit HAM-ANS: Syntaktische Korespondenz, natuerlichsprachliche Quantifizierung und semantisches Modell des Diskursbereichs. In *Sprachen fuer Datenbanken,* J. W. Schmidt, Ed. Springer-Verlag, Berlin, pp. 26–41.

MARCH, S. T. 1983. A mathematical programming approach to the selection of access paths for large multiuser data bases. *Decision Sci. 14,* 4, 564–587.

MARYANSKI, F. J. 1980. Backend database systems. *ACM Comput. Surv. 12,* 1 (Mar.), 3–25.

MENON, M. J., AND HSIAO, D. K. 1981. Design and analysis of a relational join operation for VLSI. In *Proceedings of the 7th International Conference on Very Large Data Bases* (Cannes, Sept. 9–11). IEEE, New York, pp. 44–55.

MERRETT, T. H. 1977. Database cost analysis: A top-down approach. In *Proceedings of the ACM-SIGMOD International Conference on Management of Data* (Toronto, Canada, Aug. 3–5). ACM, New York, pp. 135–143.

MERRETT, T. H. 1981. Why sort-merge gives the best implementation of the natural join. *SIGMOD Rec. 13,* 2, 39–51.

MERRETT, T. H., KAMBAYASHI, Y., AND YASUURA, H. 1981. Scheduling of page-fetches in join operations. In *Proceedings of the 7th International Conference on Very Large Data Bases* (Cannes, Sept. 9–11). IEEE, New York, pp. 488–498.

MINKER, J. 1975. Performing inferences over relation data bases. In *Proceedings of the ACM-SIGMOD International Conference on Management of Data* (San Jose, Calif., May 14–16). ACM, New York, pp. 79–91.

MINKER, J. 1978. Search strategy and selection function for an inferential relational system. *ACM Trans. Database Syst. 3,* 1 (Mar.), 1–31.

MINKER, J., AND NICOLAS, J.-M. 1983. On recursive axioms in deductive databases. *Inf. Syst. 8,* 1, 1–13.

MISSIKOFF, M., AND SCHOLL, M. 1983. Relational queries in domain based DBMS. In *SIGMOD 83, Proceedings of Annual Meeting* (San Jose, Calif., May 23–26). ACM, New York, pp. 219–227.

MONTGOMERY, A. I., D'SOUZA, D. J., AND LEE, S. B. 1983. The cost of relational algebraic operations in skewed data: Estimates and experiments. In *Information Processing 83.* Elsevier North-Holland, New York, pp. 235–241.

MUNZ, R. R. 1979. Gross architecture of the distributed database system. VDN. In *Proceedings of the IFIP Working Conference on Database Architecture.* Elsevier North-Holland, New York, pp. 23–34.

MUNZ, R. R., SCHNEIDER, H.-J., AND STEYER, F. 1979. Application of sub-predicate tests in database systems. In *Proceedings of the 5th International Conference on Very Large Data Bases* (Rio de Janeiro, Oct. 3–5). IEEE, New York, pp. 426–435.

MUTHUSWAMY, B., AND KERSCHBERG, L. 1983. Distributed query optimization using detailed database statistics. Unpublished manuscript, Computer Science Dept., University of South Carolina.

NAU, D. 1983. Expert computer systems. *IEEE Comput. 16,* 2 (Feb.), 63–85.

NEUHOLD, E. J., AND BILLER, H. 1977. POREL: A distributed data base on an inhomogeneous computer network. In *Proceedings of the 3rd Inter-*

*national Conference on Very Large Data Bases* (Tokyo, Oct. 6–8). IEEE, New York, pp. 380–395.

NG, P. 1982. Distributed compilation and recompilation of distributed queries. IBM Res. Rep. RJ3375, IBM Research Laboratories, San Jose, Calif.

NIEBUHR, K. E., AND SMITH, S. E. 1976. *N*-ary joins for processing Query by Example. *IBM Tech. Disclosure Bull. 19*, 6, 2377–2381.

NIEBUHR, K. E., SCHOLZ, K. W., AND SMITH, S. E. 1976. Algorithm for processing Query by Example. *IBM Tech. Disclosure Bull. 19*, 2, 736–741.

NIEVERGELT, J., HINTERBERGER, H., AND SEVCIK, K. C. 1984. The grid file: An adaptable, symmetric multikey file structure. *ACM Trans. Database Syst. 9*, 1 (Mar.), 38–71.

NILSSON, N. 1982. *Principles of Artificial Intelligence.* Springer, New York.

OTT, N. 1977. Interpretation of questions with quantifiers and negation in the USL system. IBM Tech. Rep. TR-77.10.005, IBM Scientific Center, Heidelberg, FRG.

OTT, N., AND HORLAENDER, K. 1982. Removing redundant join operations in queries involving views. IBM Tech. Rep. TR-82.03.003, IBM Scientific Center, Heidelberg, FRG.

OZKARAHAN, E. A. 1982. Database machine/computer based distributed databases. In *Proceedings of the 2nd International Symposium on Distributed Databases* (Berlin, FRG). Elsevier North-Holland, New York, pp. 61–80.

OZSOYOGLU, M. Z., AND OZSOYOGLU, G. 1983. An extension of relational algebra for summary tables. In *Proceedings of the 2nd Statistical Database Workshop* (Berkeley, Calif.). University of California, Berkeley.

OZSOYOGLU, M., AND YU, C. T. 1980. On identifying a class of database queries that can be processed efficiently. In *Proceedings of the IEEE COMPSAC Conference.* IEEE, New York, pp. 453–461.

PAIGE, R. 1982. Applications of finite differencing to database integrity control and query/transaction optimization. In *Proceedings of the Workshop on Logical Bases for Data Bases* (Toulouse, France). ONERA-CERT, Toulouse, France.

PALERMO, F. P. 1972. A data base search problem. In *Proceedings of the 4th Symposium on Computer and Information Science* (Miami Beach, Fla.). AFIPS Press, Reston, Va., pp. 67–101.

PARSAYE, K. 1983. Database management, knowledge base management, and expert system development in PROLOG. In *Proceedings of the Database Week Conference on Engineering Applications of Databases* (San Jose, Calif.). ACM, New York, pp. 159–178.

PECHERER, R. M. 1975. Efficient evaluation of expressions in a relational algebra. In *Proceedings of the ACM Pacific 75 Conference* (San Francisco, Calif., May 14–16). ACM, New York, pp. 44–49.

PECHERER, R. M. 1976. Efficient exploration of product spaces. In *Proceedings of the ACM–SIGMOD International Conference on Management of Data* (Washington, D.C., June 2–4). ACM, New York, pp. 169–177.

PIROTTE, A. 1979. Findamental and secondary issues in the design of non-procedural relational languages. In *Proceedings of the 5th International Conference on Very Large Data Bases* (Rio de Janeiro, Oct. 3–5). IEEE, New York, pp. 239–250.

PUTKONEN, A. 1979. On the selection of the access path in inverted database organizations. *Inf. Syst. 4*, 4, 219–225.

REIMER, M. 1983. Solving the phantom problem by predicative optimistic concurrency control. In *Proceedings of the 9th International Conference on Very Large Data Bases* (Florence, Italy). VLDB Endowment, Saratoga, Calif., pp. 81–88.

REITER, R. 1978. Deductive question-answering on relational data bases. In *Logic and Databases*, H. Gallaire and J. Minker, Eds. Plenum, New York, pp. 149–178.

RICHARD, P. 1981. Evaluation of the size of a query expressed in relational algebra. In *Proceedings of the ACM–SIGMOD International Conference on Management of Data* (Ann Arbor, Mich., Apr. 29–May 1). ACM, New York, pp. 155–163.

ROSENKRANTZ, D. J., AND HUNT, H. B. III. 1980. Processing conjunctive predicates and queries. In *Proceedings of the 6th International Conference on Very Large Data Bases* (Montreal, Oct. 1–3). IEEE, New York, pp. 64–72.

ROSENTHAL, A., AND REINER, D. 1982. An architecture for query optimization. In *Proceedings of the ACM–SIGMOD International Conference on Management of Data* (Orlando, Fla., June 2–4). ACM, New York, pp. 246–255.

ROSENTHAL, A., AND REINER, D. 1984. Querying relational views of networks. In *Query Processing in Database Systems*, W. Kim, D. Reiner, and D. Batory, Eds. Springer, New York.

ROTHNIE, J. B. 1974. An approach to implementing a relational data management system. In *Proceedings of the ACM–SIGMOD Workshop on Data Description, Access, and Control* (Ann Arbor, Mich., May 1–3). ACM, New York, pp. 277–294.

ROTHNIE, J. B., JR. 1975. Evaluating inter-entry retrieval expressions in a relational data base management system. In *Proceedings of the National Computer Conference* (Anaheim, Calif., May 19–22), vol. 44. AFIPS Press, Reston, Va., pp. 417–423.

ROTHNIE, J. B., AND GOODMAN, N. 1977. A survey of research and development in distributed database management. In *Proceedings of the 3rd International Conference on Very Large Data Bases* (Tokyo, Oct. 6–8). IEEE, New York, pp. 48–62.

ROUSSOPOULOS, N. 1982a. View indexing in relational databases. *ACM Trans. Database Syst. 7*, 2 (June), 258–290.

ROUSSOPOULOS, N. 1982b. The logical access path schema of a database. *IEEE Trans. Softw. Eng. SE-8*, 6, 563–573.

SACCO, G. M., AND SCHKOLNICK, M. 1982. A mechanism for managing the buffer pool in a relational database system using the hot set model. In *Proceedings of the 8th International Conference on Very Large Data Bases* (Mexico City). VLDB Endowment, Saratoga, Calif., pp. 257–262.

SACCO, G. M., AND YAO, S. B. 1982. Query optimization in distributed database systems. In *Advances in Computers*, vol. 21. Academic Press, New York, pp. 225–273.

SAGALOWICZ, D. 1977. IDA: An intelligent data access program. In *Proceedings of the 3rd International Conference on Very Large Data Bases* (Tokyo, Oct. 6–8). IEEE, New York, pp. 293–302.

SAGIV, Y. 1981. *Optimization of Queries in Relational Databases.* UMI Research Press, Ann Arbor, Michigan.

SAGIV, Y. 1983. Quadratic algorithms for minimizing joins in restricted relational expressions. *SIAM J. Comput. 12*, 2, 316–328.

SAGIV, Y., AND YANNAKAKIS, M. 1980. Equivalences among relational expressions with the union and difference operators. *J. ACM 27*, 4 (Oct.) 633–655.

SALTON, G., AND WONG, A. 1978. Generation and search of clustered files. *ACM Trans. Database Syst. 3*, 4 (Dec.) 321–346.

SCHEK, H.-J., AND PISTOR, P. 1982. Data structures for an integrated database management and information retrieval system. In *Proceedings of the 8th International Conference on Very Large Data Bases* (Mexico City). VLDB Endowment, Saratoga, Calif., pp. 197–207.

SCHENK, K. L., AND PINKERT, J. R. 1977. An algorithm for servicing multi-relational queries. In *Proceedings of the ACM-SIGMOD International Conference on Management of Data* (Toronto, Canada, Aug. 3–5). ACM, New York, pp. 10–20.

SCHKOLNICK, M. 1975. The optimal selection of indexes for files. *Inf. Syst. 1*, 4, 141–146.

SCHKOLNICK, M. 1982. Physical database design techniques. In *Data Base Design Techniques II*, S. B. Yao and T. L. Kunii, Eds. Springer, New York, pp. 229–252.

SCHMIDT, J. W. 1977. Some high level language constructs for data of type relation. *ACM Trans. Database Syst. 2*, 3 (Sept.), 247–261.

SCHMIDT, J. W. 1979. Parallel processing of relations: A single-assignment approach. In *Proceedings of the 5th International Conference on Very Large Data Bases* (Rio de Janeiro, Oct. 3–5). IEEE, New York, pp. 398–408.

SCHMIDT, J. W. 1984. Database programming: Language constructs and execution models. In *Programmiersprachen und Programmentwicklung*, U. Ammann, Ed. Springer-Verlag, Berlin, pp. 1–26.

SELINGER, P. G., AND ADIBA, M. 1980. Access path selection in distributed database systems. IBM Res. Rep. RJ2283, IBM Research Laboratories, San Jose, Calif.

SELINGER, P. G., ASTRAHAN, M. M., CHAMBERLIN, D. D., LORIE, R. A., AND PRICE, T. G. 1979. Access path selection in a relational database management system. In *Proceedings of the ACM-SIGMOD International Conference on Management of Data* (Boston, Mass., May 30–June 1). ACM, New York, pp. 23–34.

SEVERANCE, D. G., AND CARLIS, J. V. 1977. A practical approach to selecting record access paths. *ACM Comput. Surv. 9*, 4 (Dec.) 259–272.

SHMUELI, O. 1981. The fundamental role of tree schemas in relational query processing. Ph.D. thesis, Computer Science Dept., Harvard Univ., Cambridge, Mass.

SHNEIDERMAN, B. 1977. Reduced combined indexes for efficient multiple attribute retrieval. *Inf. Syst. 2*, 4, 149–154.

SHNEIDERMAN, B., AND GOODMAN, V. 1976. Batched searching of sequential and tree structured files. *ACM Trans. Database Syst. 1*, 3 (Sept.), 268–275.

SHOSHANI, A. 1982. Statistical database: Characteristics, problems, and some solutions. In *Proceedings of the 8th International Conference on Very Large Data Bases* (Mexico City). VLDB Endowment, Saratoga, Calif., pp. 208–222.

SHULTZ, R. K., AND ZINGG, R. J. 1984. Response time analysis of multiprocessor computers for database support. *ACM Trans. Database Syst. 9*, 1 (Mar.), 100–132.

SMITH, J. M., AND CHANG, P. Y. T. 1975. Optimizing the performance of a relational algebra database interface. *Commun. ACM 18*, 10 (Oct.), 568–579.

SMITH, J. M., BERNSTEIN, P. A., DAYAL, U., GOODMAN, N., LANDERS, T., LIN, K. W. T., AND WONG, E. 1981. MULTIBASE—Integrating heterogeneous distributed database systems. In *Proceedings of the AFIPS National Computer Conference* (Chicago, May 4–7), vol. 50. AFIPS Press, Reston, Va., pp. 487–499.

SOCKUT, G. H., AND GOLDBERG, R. P. 1979. Database reorganization—Principles and practice. *ACM Comput. Surv. 11*, 4 (Dec.) 371–395.

STONEBRAKER, M. 1975. Implementation of integrity constraints and views by query modification. In *Proceedings of the ACM-SIGMOD International Conference on Management of Data* (San Jose, Calif., May 14–16). ACM, New York, pp. 65–78.

STONEBRAKER, M., AND NEUHOLD, E. 1977. A distributed database version of INGRES. In *Proceedings of the 2nd Berkeley Workshop on Distributed Data Management and Computer Networks* (Berkeley, Calif.). University of California, Berkeley.

STONEBRAKER, M., WONG, E., KREPS, P., AND HELD, G. 1976. The design and implementation of INGRES. *ACM Trans. Database Syst. 1*, 3 (Sept.), 189–222.

STROET, J. W. M., AND ENGMANN, R. 1979. Manipulation of expressions in a relational algebra. *Inf. Syst. 4,* 4, 195–203.

SU, S. Y. W. 1979. Cellular-logic devices: Concepts and applications. *IEEE Comput. 12,* 3, 11–25.

SU, S. Y. W., AND LIPKOVSKI, G. 1975. CASSM: A cellular system for very large databases. In *Proceedings of the 1st International Conference on Very Large Data Bases* (Framingham, Mass., Sept. 22–24). ACM, New York, pp. 456–472.

SU, S. Y. W., AND MIKKILINENI, K. P. 1982. Parallel algorithms and their implementation in MICRONET. In *Proceedings of the 8th International Conference on Very Large Data Bases* (Mexico City). VLDB Endowment, Saratoga, Calif., pp. 310–324.

TANENBAUM, A. 1981. *Computer Networks.* Prentice-Hall, New York.

TEOREY, T. J., AND FRY, J. P. 1982. *Design of Database Structures.* Prentice-Hall, New York.

TODD, S. 1974. Implementing the join operator in relational data bases. IBM Scientific Center Tech. Note 15, IBM UK Scientific Center, Peterlee, England.

TSICHRITZIS, D. 1976. LSL: A link and selector language. In *Proceedings of the ACM–SIGMOD International Conference on Management of Data* (Washington, D.C., June 2–4). ACM, New York, pp. 123–133.

ULLMAN, J. D. 1982. *Principles of Database Systems.* Computer Science Press, Rockville, Md.

VALDURIEZ, P. 1982. Semi-join algorithms for multiprocessor systems. In *Proceedings of the ACM–SIGMOD International Conference on Management of Data* (Orlando, Fla., June 2–4). ACM, New York, pp. 225–233.

VALDURIEZ, P., AND GARDARIN, G. 1984. Join and semijoin algorithms for a multiprocessor database machine. *ACM Trans. Database Syst. 9,* 1 (Mar.), 133–161.

VAN DE RIET, R. P., WASSERMAN, A. I., KERSTEN, M. L., AND DE JONGE, W. 1981. High-level programming features for improving the efficiency of a relational database system. *ACM Trans. Database Syst. 6,* 3 (Sept.), 464–485.

VASSILIOU, Y., AND JARKE, M. 1984. Query languages—A taxonomy. In *Human Factors and Interactive Computer Systems,* Y. Vassiliou, Ed. Ablex, Norwood, N.J.

VASSILIOU, Y., AND LOCHOVSKY, F. 1980. DBMS transaction translation. In *Proceedings of the IEEE COMPSAC Conference.* IEEE, New York, pp. 89–96.

VASSILIOU, Y., CLIFFORD, J., AND JARKE, M. 1984. Access to specific declarative knowledge in expert systems: The impact of logic programming. *Decision Support Syst. 1,* 1.

VERHOFSTAD, J. S. M. 1978. Recovery techniques for database systems. *ACM Comput. Surv. 10,* 2 (June), 167–195.

WALKER, A. 1980. On retrieval from a small version of a large data base. In *Proceedings of the 6th International Conference on Very Large Data Bases* (Montreal, Oct. 1–3). IEEE, New York, pp. 47–54.

WARREN, D. H. D. 1981. Efficient processing of interactive relational database queries expressed in logic. In *Proceedings of the 7th International Conference on Very Large Data Bases* (Cannes, Sept. 9–11). IEEE, New York, pp. 272–281.

WELCH, J. W., AND GRAHAM, J. W. 1976. Retrieval using ordered lists in inverted and multilist files. In *Proceedings of the ACM–SIGMOD International Conference on Management of Data* (Washington, D.C., June 2–4). ACM, New York, pp. 21–29.

WHANG, K.-Y., WIEDERHOLD, G., AND SAGALOWICZ, D. 1983. Estimating block accesses in database organizations: A closed noniterative formula. *Commun. ACM 26,* 11 (Nov.), 940–944.

WILLIAMS, R., DANIELS, D., HAAS, L., LAPIS, G., LINDSAY, B., NG, P., OBERMARCK, R., SELINGER, P., WALKER, A., WILMS, P., AND YOST, R. 1982. R*: An overview of the architecture. In *Proceedings of the International Conference on Database Systems* (Jerusalem, Israel).

WONG, E. 1977. Retrieving dispersed data from SDD-1: A system for distributed databases. In *Proceedings of the Second Berkeley Workshop on Distributed Data Management and Computer Networks* (Berkeley, Calif.), pp. 217–235.

WONG, E. 1983. Dynamic rematerialization: Processing distributed queries using redundant data. *IEEE Trans. Softw. Eng. SE-9,* 3, 228–232.

WONG, E., AND KATZ, R. H. 1983. Distributing a database for parallelism. In *SIGMOD 83, Proceedings of the Annual Meeting* (San Jose, Calif., May 23–26). ACM, New York, pp. 23–29.

WONG, E., AND YOUSSEFI, K. 1976. Decomposition—A strategy for query processing. *ACM Trans. Database Syst. 1,* 3 (Sept.), 223–241.

XU, G. D. 1983. Search control in semantic query optimization. Tech. Rep. #83-09, Computer and Information Science Dept., University of Massachusetts, Amherst, Mass.

YANG, C.-S. 1977. Avoiding redundant accesses in unsorted multilist file organizations. *Inf. Syst. 2,* 4, 155–158.

YAO, S. B. 1977a. Approximating block accesses in database organizations. *Commun. ACM 20,* 4 (Apr.), 260–261.

YAO, S. B. 1977b. An attribute based model for database access cost analysis. *ACM Trans. Database Syst. 2,* 1 (Mar.), 45–67.

YAO, S. B. 1979. Optimization of query evaluation algorithms. *ACM Trans. Database Syst. 4,* 2 (June), 133–155.

YAO, S. B., AND DEJONG, D. 1978. Evaluation of database access paths. In *Proceedings of the ACM–SIGMOD International Conference on*

*Management of Data* (Austin, Tex., May 31–June 2). ACM, New York, pp. 66–77.

YOUSSEFI, K., AND WONG, E. 1979. Query processing in a relational database management system. In *Proceedings of the 5th International Conference on Very Large Data Bases* (Rio de Janeiro, Oct. 3–5). IEEE, New York, pp. 409–417.

YU, C. T., AND CHANG, C. C. 1983. On the design of a query processing strategy in a distributed database environment. In *SIGMOD 83, Proceedings of the Annual Meeting* (San Jose, Calif., May 23–26). ACM, New York, pp. 30–39.

YU, C. T., AND OZSOYOGLU, M. 1979. An algorithm for tree query membership of a distributed query. In *Proceedings of the IEEE COMPSAC Conference*. IEEE, New York, pp. 306–312.

YU, C. T., LUK, W. S., AND SIU, M. K. 1978. On the estimation of the number of desired records with respect to a given query. *ACM Trans. Database Syst. 3*, 1 (Mar.), 41–56.

ZANIOLO, C. 1979. Design of relational views over network schemas. In *Proceedings of the ACM-SIGMOD International Conference on Management of Data* (Boston, Mass., May 30–June 1). ACM, New York, pp. 179–190.

Received October 1983; final revision accepted April 1984.

# Principles of Transaction-Oriented Database Recovery

THEO HAERDER

*Fachbereich Informatik, University of Kaiserslautern, West Germany*

ANDREAS REUTER[1]

*IBM Research Laboratory, San Jose, California 95193*

In this paper, a terminological framework is provided for describing different transaction-oriented recovery schemes for database systems in a conceptual rather than an implementation-dependent way. By introducing the terms materialized database, propagation strategy, and checkpoint, we obtain a means for classifying arbitrary implementations from a unified viewpoint. This is complemented by a classification scheme for logging techniques, which are precisely defined by using the other terms. It is shown that these criteria are related to all relevant questions such as speed and scope of recovery and amount of redundant information required. The primary purpose of this paper, however, is to establish an adequate and precise terminology for a topic in which the confusion of concepts and implementational aspects still imposes a lot of problems.

Categories and Subject Descriptors: D.4.5 [**Operating Systems**]: Reliability—*fault tolerance*; H.1.0 [**Models and Principles**]: General; H.2.2 [**Database Management**]: Physical Design—*recovery and restart*; H.2.4 [**Database Management**]: Systems—*transaction processing*; H.2.7 [**Database Management**]: Database Administration—*logging and recovery*

General Terms: Databases, Fault Tolerance, Transactions

## INTRODUCTION

Database technology has seen tremendous progress during the past ten years. Concepts and facilities that evolved in the single-user batch environments of the early days have given rise to efficient multiuser database systems with user-friendly interfaces, distributed data management, etc. From a scientific viewpoint, database systems today are established as a mature discipline with well-approved methods and technology. The methods and technology of such a discipline should be well represented in the literature by systematic surveys of the field. There are, in fact, a number of recent publications that attempt to summarize what is known about different aspects of database management [e.g., Astrahan et al. 1981; Stonebraker 1980; Gray et al. 1981; Kohler 1981; Bernstein and Goodman 1981; Codd 1982]. These papers fall into two categories: (1) descriptions of innovative prototype systems and (2) thorough analyses of special problems and their solutions, based on a clear methodological and terminological framework. We are con-

[1] Permanent address: Fachbereich Informatik, University of Kaiserslautern, West Germany.

## CONTENTS



tributing to the second category in the field of database recovery. In particular, we are establishing a systematic framework for establishing and evaluating the basic concepts for fault-tolerant database operation.

The paper is organized as follows. Section 1 contains a short description of what recovery is expected to accomplish and which notion of consistency we assume. This involves introducing the transaction, which has proved to be the major paradigm for synchronization and recovery in advanced database systems. This is also the most important difference between this paper and Verhofstadt's survey, in which techniques for file recovery are described without using a particular notion of consistency [Verhofstadt 1978]. Section 2 provides an implementational model for database systems, that is, a mapping hierarchy of data types. Section 3 introduces the key concepts of our framework, describing the database states after a crash, the type of log information required, and additional measures for facilitating recovery. Crash recovery is demonstrated with three sample implementation techniques. Section 4 applies concepts addressed in previous sections on media recovery, and Section 5 summarizes the scope of our taxonomy.

## 1. DATABASE RECOVERY: WHAT IT IS EXPECTED TO DO

Understanding the concepts of database recovery requires a clear comprehension of two factors:

- the type of failure the database has to cope with, and
- the notion of consistency that is assumed as a criterion for describing the state to be reestablished.

Before beginning a discussion of these factors, we would like to point out that the contents of this section rely on the description of failure types and the concept of a transaction given by Gray et al. [1981].

### 1.1 What Is a Transaction?

It was observed quite early that manipulating data in a multiuser environment requires some kind of isolation to prevent uncontrolled and undesired interactions. A user (or process) often does things when working with a database that are, up to a certain point in time, of tentative or preliminary value. The user may read some data and modify others before finding out that some of the initial input was wrong, invalidating everything that was done up to that point. Consequently, the user wants to remove what he or she has done from the system. If other users (or processes) have already seen the "dirty data" [Gray et al. 1981] and made decisions based upon it, they obviously will encounter difficulties. The following questions must be considered:

- How do they get the message that some of their input data has disappeared, when it is possible that they have already finished their job and left the terminal?
- How do they cope with such a situation? Do they also throw away what they have done, possibly affecting others in turn? Do they reprocess the affected parts of their program?

```
FUNDS_TRANSFER: PROCEDURE;
  $BEGIN_TRANSACTION;
  ON ERROR DO;                                        /*in case of error*/
    $RESTORE_TRANSACTION;                             /*undo all work*/
    GET INPUT MESSAGE;                                /*reacquire input*/
    PUT MESSAGE ('TRANSFER FAILED');                  /*report failure*/
    GO TO COMMIT;
    END;
  GET INPUT MESSAGE;                                  /*get and parse input*/
  EXTRACT ACCOUNT_DEBIT, ACCOUNT_CREDIT,
      AMOUNT FROM MESSAGE;
  $UPDATE ACCOUNTS                                    /*do debit*/
    SET BALANCE = BALANCE - AMOUNT
      WHERE ACCOUNTS NUMBER = ACCOUNTS_DEBIT;
  $UPDATE ACCOUNTS                                    /*do credit*/
    SET BALANCE = BALANCE + AMOUNT
      WHERE ACCOUNTS NUMBER = ACCOUNTS_CREDIT;
  $INSERT INTO HISTORY                                /*keep audit trail*/
      <DATE, MESSAGE>;
  PUT MESSAGE ('TRANSFER DONE');                      /*report success*/
 COMMIT:                                              /*commit updates*/
$COMMIT_TRANSACTION;
   END;                                               /*end of program*/
```

**Figure 1.** Example of a transaction program. (From Gray et al. [1981].)

These situations and dependencies have been investigated thoroughly by Bjork and Davies in their studies of the so-called "spheres of control" [Bjork 1973; Davies 1973, 1978]. They indicate that data being operated by a process must be isolated in some way that lets others know the degree of reliability provided for these data, that is,

- Will the data be changed without notification to others?
- Will others be informed about changes?
- Will the value definitely not change any more?

This ambitious concept was restricted to use in database systems by Eswaran et al. [1976] and given its current name, the "transaction." The transaction basically reflects the idea that the activities of a particular user are isolated from all concurrent activities, but restricts the degree of isolation and the length of a transaction. Typically, a transaction is a short sequence of interactions with the database, using operators such as FIND a record or MODIFY an item, which represents one meaningful activity in the user's environment. The standard example that is generally used to explain the idea is the transfer of money from one account to another. The corresponding transaction program is given in Figure 1.

The concept of a transaction, which includes all database interactions between $BEGIN_TRANSACTION and $COMMIT_TRANSACTION in the above example, requires that all of its actions be executed *indivisibly*: Either all actions are properly reflected in the database or nothing has happened. No changes are reflected in the database if at any point in time before reaching the $COMMIT_TRANSACTION the user enters the ERROR clause containing the $RESTORE_TRANSACTION. To achieve this kind of indivisibility, a transaction must have four properties:

*Atomicity.* It must be of the all-or-nothing type described above, and the user must, whatever happens, know which state he or she is in.

*Consistency.* A transaction reaching its normal end (EOT, end of transaction), thereby committing its results, preserves the consistency of the database. In other words, each successful transaction by definition commits only legal results. This con-

```
BEGIN      BEGIN    BEGIN
READ       READ     READ
WRITE      WRITE    WRITE
READ       READ     READ
  :          :        :
WRITE      ABORT    ⇐SYSTEM ABORTS
COMMIT                TRANSACTION
```

**Figure 2.** Three possible outcomes of a transaction. (From Gray et al. [1981].)

dition is necessary for the fourth property, durability.

*Isolation.* Events within a transaction must be hidden from other transactions running concurrently. If this were not the case, a transaction could not be reset to its beginning for the reasons sketched above. The techniques that achieve isolation are known as *synchronization*, and since Gray et al. [1976] there have been numerous contributions to this topic of database research [Kohler 1981].

*Durability.* Once a transaction has been completed and has committed its results to the database, the system must guarantee that these results survive any subsequent malfunctions. Since there is no sphere of control constituting a set of transactions, the database management system (DBMS) has no control beyond transaction boundaries. Therefore the user must have a guarantee that the things the system says have happened have actually happened. Since, by definition, each transaction is correct, the effects of an inevitable incorrect transaction (i.e., the transaction containing faulty data) can only be removed by countertransactions.

These four properties, atomicity, consistency, isolation, and durability (ACID), describe the major highlights of the transaction paradigm, which has influenced many aspects of development in database systems. We therefore consider the question of whether the transaction is supported by a particular system to be the ACID test of the system's quality.

In summary, a transaction can terminate in the three ways illustrated in Figure 2. It is hoped that the transaction will reach its commit point, yielding the all case (as in the all-or-nothing dichotomy). Sometimes the transaction detects bad input or other violations of consistency, preventing a normal termination, in which case it will reset all that it has done (abort). Finally, a transaction may run into a problem that can only be detected by the system, such as time-out or deadlock, in which case its effects are aborted by the DBMS.

In addition to the above events occurring during normal execution, a transaction can also be affected by a system crash. This is discussed in the next section.

### 1.2 Which Failures Have to Be Anticipated

In order to design and implement a recovery component, one must know precisely which types of failures are to be considered, how often they will occur, how much time is expected for recovery, etc. One must also make assumptions about the reliability of the underlying hardware and storage media, and about dependencies between different failure modes. However, the list of anticipated failures will never be complete for these reasons:

- For each set of failures that one can think of, there is at least one that was forgotten.
- Some failures are extremely rare. The cost of redundancy needed to cope with them may be so high that it may be a sensible design decision to exclude these failures from consideration. If one of them does occur, however, the system will not be able to recover from the situation automatically, and the database will be corrupted. The techniques for handling this catastrophe are beyond the scope of this paper.

We shall consider the following types of failure:

*Transaction Failure.* The transaction of failure has already been mentioned in the previous section. For various reasons, the transaction program does not reach its normal commit and has to be reset back to its beginning, either at its own request or on behalf of the DBMS. Gray indicates that 3 percent of all transactions terminate abnormally, but this rate is not likely to be a constant [Gray et al. 1981]. From our own experiences with different application databases, and from Gray's result [Effelsberg et al. 1981; Gray 1981], we can conclude that

- Within one application, the ratio of transactions that abort themselves is rather constant, depending only on the amount of incorrect input data, the quality of consistency checking performed by the transaction program, etc.
- The ratio of transactions being aborted by the DBMS, especially those caused by deadlocks, depends to a great extent on the degree of parallelism, the granularity of locking used by the DBMS, the logical schema (there may be hot spot data, or data that are very frequently referenced by many concurrent transactions), and the degree of interference between concurrent activities (which is, in turn, very application dependent).

For our classification, it is sufficient to say that transaction failures occur *10–100 times per minute*, and that recovery from these failures must take place within the time required by the transaction for its regular execution.

*System Failure.* The system failures that we are considering can be caused by a bug in the DBMS code, an operating system fault, or a hardware failure. In each of these cases processing is terminated in an uncontrolled manner, and we assume that the contents of main memory are lost. Since database-related secondary (nonvolatile) storage remains unaffected, we require that a recovery take place in the same amount of time that would have been required for the execution of all interrupted transactions. If one transaction is executed within the order of 10 milliseconds to 1 second, the recovery should take no more than a few minutes. A system failure is assumed to occur *several times a week*, depending on the stability of both the DBMS and its operational environment.

*Media Failure.* Besides these more or less normal failures, we have to anticipate the loss of some or all of the secondary storage holding the database. There are several causes for such a problem, the most common of which are

- bugs in the operating system routines for writing the disk,
- hardware errors in the channel or disk controller,
- head crash,
- loss of information due to magnetic decay.

Such a situation can only be overcome by full redundancy, that is, by a copy of the database and an audit trail covering what has happened since then.

Magnetic storage devices are usually very reliable, and recovery from a media failure is not likely to happen more often than *once or twice a year.* Depending on the size of a database, the media used for storing the copy, and the age of the copy, recovery of this type will take on the order of 1 hour.

### 1.3 Summary of Recovery Actions

As we mentioned in Section 1.1, the notion of consistency that we use for defining the targets of recovery is tied to the transaction paradigm, which we have encapsulated in the "ACID principle." According to this definition, a database is consistent *if and only if* it contains the results of successful transactions. Such a state will hereafter be called *transaction consistent* or *logically consistent.* A transaction, in turn, must not see anything but effects of complete transactions (i.e., a consistent database in those parts that it uses), and will then, by definition, create a consistent update of the database. What does that mean for the recovery component?

Let us for the moment ignore transactions being aborted during normal execution and consider only a system failure (a crash). We might then encounter the situation depicted in Figure 3. Transactions T1, T2, and T3 have committed before the crash, and therefore will survive. Recovery after a system failure must ensure that the effects of all successful transactions are actually reflected in the database. But what is to be done with T4 and T5? Transactions have been defined to be atomic; they either succeed or disappear as though they had never been entered. There is therefore no choice about what to do after a system

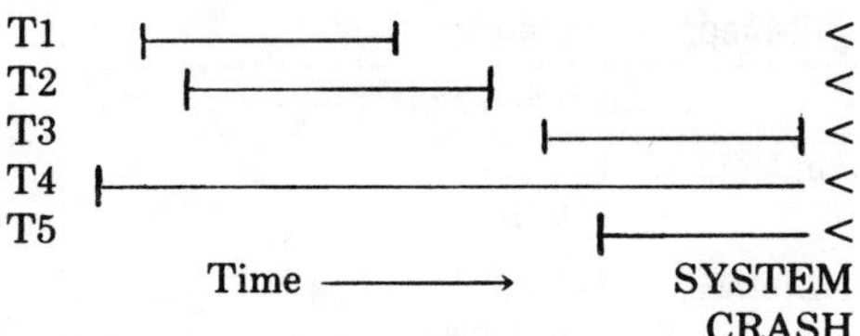


**Figure 3.** Scenario for discussing transaction-oriented recovery. (From Gray et al. [1981].)

failure; the effects of all incomplete transactions must be removed from the database. Clearly, a recovery component adhering to these principles will produce a transaction-consistent database. Since *all* successful transactions have contributed to the database state, it will be the *most recent* transaction-consistent state. We now can distinguish four recovery actions coping with different situations [Gray 1978]:

*Transaction UNDO.* If a transaction aborts itself or must be aborted by the system during normal execution, this will be called "transaction UNDO." By definition, UNDO removes all effects of this transaction from the database and does not influence any other transaction.

*Global UNDO.* When recovering from a system failure, the effects of all incomplete transactions have to be rolled back.

*Partial REDO.* When recovering from a system failure, since execution has been terminated in an uncontrolled manner, results of complete transactions may not yet be reflected in the database. Hence they must be repeated, if necessary, by the recovery component.

*Global REDO.* Gray terms this recovery action "archive recovery" [Gray et al. 1981]. The database is assumed to be physically destroyed; we therefore must start from a copy that reflects the state of the database some days, weeks, or months ago. Since transactions are typically short, we need not consider incomplete transactions over such a long time. Rather we have to supplement the copy with the effects of all transactions that have committed since the copy was created.

With these definitions we have introduced the transaction as the *only unit of recovery* in a database system. This is an ideal condition that does not exactly match reality. For example, transactions might be nested, that is, composed of smaller subtransactions. These subtransactions also are atomic, consistent, and isolated—but they are not durable. Since the results of subtransactions are removed whenever the enclosing transaction is undone, durability can only be guaranteed for the highest transaction in the composition hierarchy. A two-level nesting of transactions can be found in System R, in which an arbitrary number of save points can be generated inside a transaction [Gray et al. 1981]. The database and the processing state can be reset to any of these save points by the application program.

Another extension of the transaction concept is necessary in fields like CAD. Here the units of consistent state transitions, that is, the design steps, are so long (days or weeks) that it is not feasible to treat them as indivisable actions. Hence these *long* transactions are consistent, isolated, and durable, but they are not atomic [Gray 1981]. It is sufficient for the purpose of our taxonomy to consider "ideal" transactions only.

## 2. THE MAPPING HIERARCHY OF A DBMS

There are numerous techniques and algorithms for implementing database recovery, many of which have been described in detail by Verhofstadt [1978]. We want to reduce these various methods to a small set of basic concepts, allowing a simple, yet precise classification of all reasonable implementation techniques; for the purposes of illustration, we need a basic model of the DBMS architecture and its hardware environment. This model, although it contains many familiar terms from systems like INGRES, System R, or those of the CODASYL [1973, 1978] type, is in fact a rudimentary database architecture that can also be applied to unconventional approaches like CASSM or DIRECT [Smith and Smith 1979], although this is not our purpose here.

### 2.1 The Mapping Process: Objects and Operations

The model shown in Table 1 describes the major steps of dynamic abstraction from the level of physical storage up to the user

**Table 1.** Description of the DB-Mapping Hierarchy

| Level of abstraction | Objects | Auxiliary mapping data |
|---|---|---|
| Nonprocedural or algebraic access | Relations, views tuples | Logical schema description |
| Record-oriented, navigational access | Records, sets, hierarchies, networks | Logical and physical schema description |
| Record and access path management | Physical records, access paths | Free space tables, DB-key translation tables |
| Propagation control | Segments, pages | Page tables, Bloom filters |
| File management | Files, blocks | Directories, VTOCs, etc. |

interface. At the bottom, the database consists of some billions of bits stored on disk, which are interpreted by the DBMS into meaningful information on which the user can operate. With each level of abstraction (proceeding from the bottom up), the objects become more complex, allowing more powerful operations and being constrained by a larger number of integrity rules. The uppermost interface supports one of the well-known data models, whether relational, networklike, or hierarchical.

Note that this mapping hierarchy is virtually contained in each DBMS, although for performance reasons it will hardly be reflected in the module structure. We shall briefly sketch the characteristics of each layer, with enough detail to establish our taxonomy. For a more complete description see Haerder and Reuter [1983].

*File Management.* The lowest layer operates directly on the bit patterns stored on some nonvolatile, direct access device like a disk, drum, or even magnetic bubble memory. This layer copes with the physical characteristics of each storage type and abstracts these characteristics into fixed-length blocks. These blocks can be read, written, and identified by a (relative) block number. This kind of abstraction is usually done by the data management system (DMS) of a normal general-purpose operating system.

*Propagation*[2] *Control.* This level is not usually considered separately in the current database literature, but for reasons that will become clear in the following sections we strictly distinguish between *pages* and *blocks*. A page is a fixed-length partition of a linear address space and is mapped into a physical block by the propagation control layer. Therefore a page can be stored in different blocks during its lifetime in the database, depending on the strategy implemented for propagation control.

*Access Path Management.* This layer implements mapping functions much more complicated than those performed by subordinate layers. It has to maintain all physical object representations in the database (records, fields, etc.), and their related access paths (pointers, hash tables, search trees, etc.) in a *potentially unlimited* linear virtual address space. This address space, which is divided into fixed-length pages, is provided by the upper interface of the supporting layer. For performance reasons, the partitioning of data into pages is still visible on this level.

*Navigational Access Layer.* At the top of this layer we find the operations and objects that are typical for a procedural data manipulation language (DML). Occurrences of record types and members of sets are handled by statements like STORE, MODIFY, FIND NEXT, and CONNECT [CODASYL 1978]. At this interface, the user navigates one record at a time through a hierarchy, through a network, or along logical access paths.

*Nonprocedural Access Layer.* This level provides a nonprocedural interface to the

[2] This term is introduced in Section 2.4; its meaning is not essential to the understanding of this paragraph.

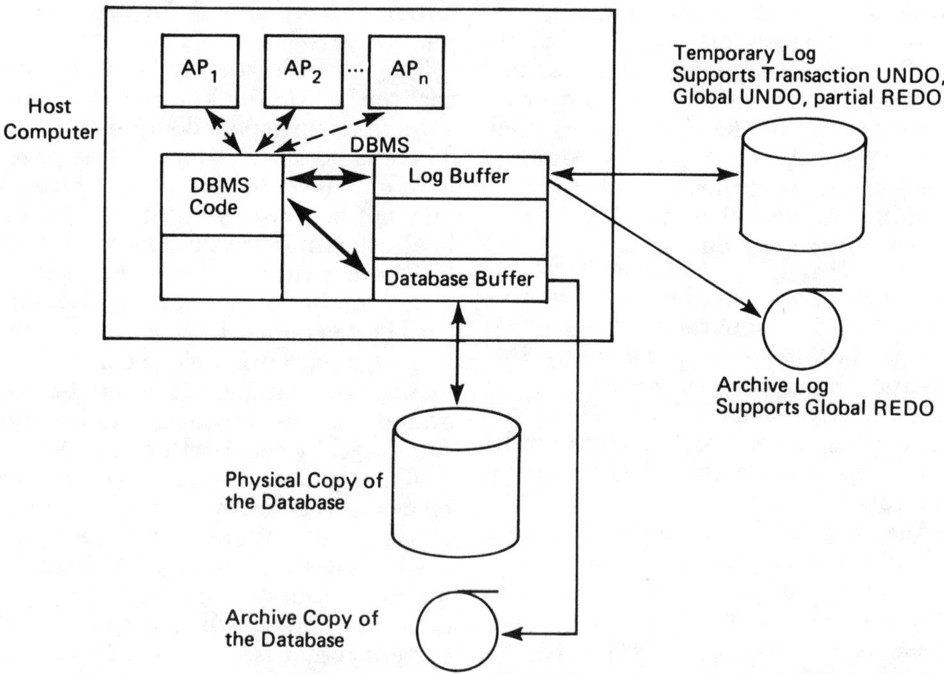


**Figure 4.** Storage hierarchy of a DBMS during normal mode of operation.

database. With each operation the user can handle sets of results rather than single records. A relational model with high-level query languages like SQL or QUEL is a convenient example of the abstraction achieved by the top layer [Chamberlin 1980; Stonebraker et al. 1976].

On each level, the mapping of higher objects to more elementary ones requires additional data structures, some of which are shown in Table 1.

### 2.2 The Storage Hierarchy: Implementational Environment

Both the number of redundant data required to support the recovery actions described in Section 1 and the methods of collecting such data are strongly influenced by various properties of the different storage media used by the DBMS. In particular, the dependencies between volatile and permanent storage have a strong impact on algorithms for gathering redundant information and implementing recovery measures [Chen 1978]. As a descriptional framework we shall use a storage hierarchy, as shown in Figure 4. It closely resembles the situation that must be dealt with by most of today's commercial database systems.

The host computer, where the application programs and DBMS are located, has a main memory, which is usually volatile.[3] Hence we assume that the contents of the database buffer, as well as the contents of the output buffers to the log files, are lost whenever the DBMS terminates abnormally. Below the volatile main memory there is a two-level hierarchy of permanent copies of the database. One level contains an on-line version of the database in direct access memory; the other contains an archive copy as a provision against loss of the on-line copy. While both are functionally situated on the same level, the on-line copy is almost always up-to-date, whereas the archive copy can contain an old state of the database. Our main concern here is database recovery, which, like all provisions for

[3] In some real-time applications main memory is supported by a battery backup. It is possible that in the future mainframes will have some stable buffer storage. However, we are not considering these conditions here.

fault tolerance, is based upon redundancy. We have mentioned one type of redundancy: the archive copy, kept as a starting point for reconstruction of an up-to-date on-line version of the database (global REDO). This is discussed in more detail in Section 4. To support this, and other recovery actions introduced in Section 1, two types of log files are required:

*Temporary Log.* The information collected in this file supports crash recovery; that is, it contains information needed to reconstruct the most recent database (DB) buffer. Selective transaction UNDO requires random access to the log records. Therefore we assume that the temporary log is located on disk.

*Archive Log.* This file supports global REDO after a media failure. It depends on the availability of the archive copy and must contain all changes committed to the database after the state reflected in the archive copy. Since the archive log is always processed in sequential order, we assume that the archive log is written on magnetic tape.

### 2.3 Different Views of a Database

In Section 2.1, we indicated that the database looks different at each level of abstraction, with each level using different objects and interfaces. But this is not what we mean by "different views of a database" in this section. We have observed that the process of abstraction really begins at Level 3, up to which there is only a more convenient representation of data in external storage. At this level, abstraction is dependent on which pages actually establish the linear address space, that is, which block is read when a certain page is referenced. In the event of a failure, there are different possibilities for retrieving the contents of a page. These possibilities are denoted by different views of the database:

The *current database* comprises all objects accessible to the DBMS during normal processing. The current contents of all pages can be found on disk, except for those pages that have been recently modified. Their new contents are found in the DB buffer. The mapping hierarchy is completely correct.

The *materialized database* is the state that the DBMS finds at restart after a crash *without* having applied any log information. There is no buffer. Hence some page modifications (even of successful transactions) may not be reflected in the on-line copy. It is also possible that a new state of a page has been written to disk, but the control structure that maps pages to blocks has not yet been updated. In this case, a reference to such a page will yield the old value. This view of the database is what the recovery system has to transform into the most recent logically consistent current database.

The *physical database* is composed of all blocks of the on-line copy containing page images—current or obsolete. Depending on the strategy used on Level 2, there may be different values for one page in the physical database, none of which are necessarily the current contents. This view is not normally used by recovery procedures, but a salvation program would try to exploit all information contained therein.

With these views of a database, we can distinguish three types of update operations—all of which explain the mapping function provided by the propagation control level. First, we have the *modification of page contents* caused by some higher level module. This operation takes place in the DB buffer and therefore affects only the current database. Second, there is the *write* operation, transferring a modified page to a block on disk. In general, this affects only the physical database. If the information about the block containing the new page value is stored in volatile memory, the new contents will not be accessible after a crash; that is, it is not yet part of the materialized database. The operation that makes a previously written page image part of the materialized database is called *propagation.* This operation writes the updated control structures for mapping pages to blocks in a safe, nonvolatile place, so that they are available after a crash.

If pages are always written to the same block (the so-called "update-in-place" operation, which is done in most commercial DBMS), writing implicitly is the equivalent

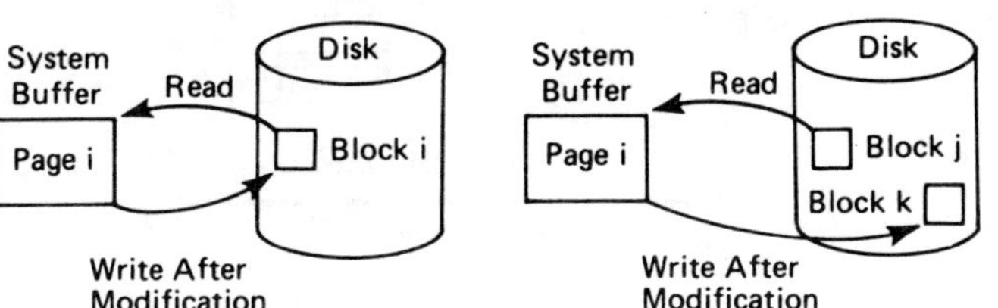


**Figure 5.** Page allocation principles.

of propagation. However, there is an important difference between these operations if a page can be stored in different blocks. This is explained in the next section.

### 2.4 Mapping Concepts for Updates

In this section, we define a number of concepts related to the operation of mapping changes in a database from volatile to nonvolatile storage. They are directly related to the views of a database introduced previously. The key issue is that each modification of a page (which changes the current database) takes place in the database buffer and is allocated to *volatile* storage. In order to save this state, the corresponding page must be brought to nonvolatile storage, that is, to the physical database. Two different schemes for accomplishing this can be applied, as sketched in Figure 5.

With *direct page allocation*, each page of a segment is related to exactly one block of the corresponding file. Each output of a modified page causes an update in place. By using an *indirect page allocation* scheme, each output is directed to a new block, leaving the old contents of the page unchanged. It provides the option of holding *n* successive versions of a page. The moment when a younger version definitively replaces an older one can be determined by appropriate (consistency-related) criteria; it is no longer bound to the moment of writing. This update scheme has some very attractive properties in case of recovery, as is shown later on. Direct page allocation leaves no choice as to when to make a new version part of the materialized database; the output operation destroys the previous image. Hence in this case writing and propagating coincide.

There is still another important difference between direct and indirect page allocation schemes, which can be characterized as follows:

- In *direct* page allocation, each single propagation (physical write) is interruptable by a system crash, thus leaving the materialized, and possibly the physical, database in an inconsistent state.
- In *indirect* page allocation, there is always a way back to the old state. Hence propagation of an arbitrary set of pages can be made uninterruptable by system crashes. References to such algorithms will be given.

On the basis of this observation, we can distinguish two types of propagation strategies:

*ATOMIC*. Any set of modified pages can be propagated as a unit, such that either all or none of the updates become part of the materialized database.

¬*ATOMIC*. Pages are written to blocks according to an update-in-place policy. Since no set of pages can be written indivisibly (even a single write may be interrupted somewhere in between), propagation is vulnerable to system crashes.

Of course, many details have been omitted from Figure 5. In particular, there is no hint of the techniques used to make propagation take place atomically in case of indirect page mapping. We have tried to illustrate aspects of this issue in Figure 6. Figure 6 contains a comparison of the current and the materialized database for the update-in-place scheme and three different implementations of indirect page mapping allowing for ATOMIC propagation. Figure 6b refers to the well-known shadow page

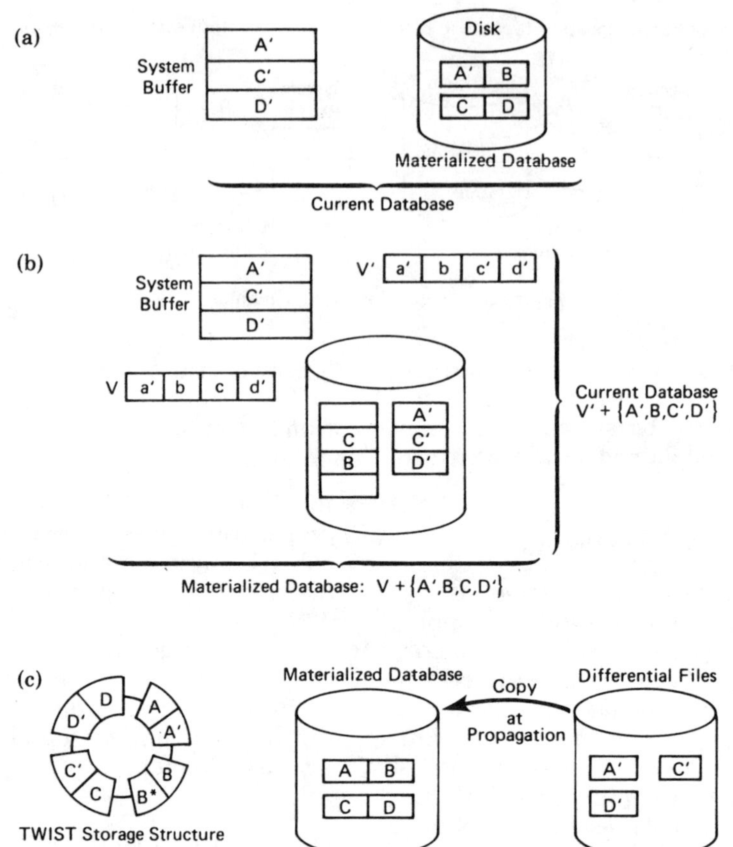


**Figure 6.** Current versus materialized database in ¬ATOMIC (a) and ATOMIC (b and c) propagation.

mechanism [Lorie 1977]. The mapping of page numbers to block numbers is done by using page tables. These tables have one entry per page containing the block number where the page contents are stored. The *shadow pages*, accessed via the shadow page Table V, preserve the old state of the materialized database. The current version is defined by the current page Table V′. Before this state is made stable (propagated), all changed pages are written to their new blocks, and so is the current page table. If this fails, the database will come up in its old state. When all pages have been written related to the new state, ATOMIC propagation takes place by changing one record on disk (which now points to V′ rather than V) in a way that cannot be confused by a system crash. Thus the problem of indivisibly propagating a set of pages has been reduced to safely updating one record, which can be done in a simple way. For details, see Lorie [1977].

There are other implementations for ATOMIC propagation. One is based on maintaining two recent versions of a page. For each page access, both versions have to be read into the buffer. This can be done with minimal overhead by storing them in adjacent disk blocks and reading them with chained I/O. The latest version, recognized by a time stamp, is kept in the buffer; the other one is immediately discarded. A modified page replaces the older version on disk. ATOMIC propagation is accomplished by incrementing a special counter that is related to the time stamps in the pages. Details can be found in Reuter [1980]. Another approach to ATOMIC propagation has been introduced under the name "differential files" by Severance and Lohman [1976]. Modified pages are written to a separate (differential) file. Propagating these updates to the main database is not ATOMIC in itself, but once all modifications are written to the differential file, propagation can be repeated as often as wished. In other words, the process of copying modified pages into the materialized database can be made to appear ATOMIC. A variant of this technique, the "intention list," is described by Lampson and Sturgis [1979] and Sturgis et al. [1980].

Thus far we have shown that arbitrary sets of pages can be propagated in an ATOMIC manner using indirect page allocation. In the next section we discuss how these sets of pages for propagation should be defined.

## 3. CRASH RECOVERY

In order to illustrate the consequences of the concepts introduced thus far, we shall present a detailed discussion of crash recovery. First, we consider the state in which a database is left when the system terminates abnormally. From this we derive the type of redundant (log) information required to reestablish a transaction-consistent state, which is the overall purpose of DB recovery. After completing our classification scheme, we give examples of recovery techniques in currently available database systems. Finally, we present a table containing a qualitative evaluation of all instances encompassed by our taxonomy (Table 4).

Note that the results in this section also apply to transaction UNDO—a much simpler case of global UNDO, which applies when the DBMS is processing normally and no information is lost.

### 3.1 State of the Database after a Crash

After a crash, the DBMS has to restart by applying all the necessary recovery actions described in Section 1. The DB buffer is lost, as is the *current database*, the only view of the database to contain the most recent state of processing. Assuming that the on-line copy of the database is intact, there are the *materialized database* and the *temporary log file* from which to start recovery. We have not discussed the contents of the log files for the reason that the type and number of log data to be written during normal processing are dependent upon the state of the materialized database after a crash. This state, in turn, depends upon which method of page allocation and propagation is used.

In the case of direct page allocation and ¬ATOMIC propagation, each write operation affects the materialized database. The decision to write pages is made by the *buffer manager* according to buffer capacity at points in time that appear arbitrary. Hence the state of the materialized database after a crash is unpredictable: When recent modifications are reflected in the materialized database, it is not possible (without further provisions) to know which pages were modified by complete transactions (whose contents must be reconstructed by partial REDO) and which pages were modified by incomplete transactions (whose contents must be returned to their previous state by global UNDO). Further possibilities for providing against this situation are briefly discussed in Section 3.2.1.

In the case of indirect page allocation and ATOMIC propagation, we know much more about the state of the materialized database after crash. ATOMIC propagation is indivisible by any type of failure, and therefore we find the materialized database to be exactly in the state produced by the most recent successful propagation. This state may still be inconsistent in that not all updates of complete transactions are visible, and some effects of incomplete transactions are. However, ATOMIC propagation ensures that a set of related pages is propagated in a safe manner by restricting propagation to points in time when the current database fulfills certain consistency constraints. When these constraints are satisfied, the updates can be mapped to the materialized database all at once. Since the current database is consistent in terms of the access path management level—where propagation occurs—this also ensures that all internal pointers, tree structures, tables, etc. are correct. Later on, we also discuss schemes that allow for transaction-consistent propagation.

The state of the materialized database after a crash can be summarized as follows:

*¬ATOMIC Propagation.* Nothing is known about the state of the materialized database; it must be characterized as "chaotic."

*ATOMIC Propagation.* The materialized database is in the state produced by the most recent propagation. Since this is bound by certain consistency constraints, the materialized database will be consistent (but not necessarily up-to-date) at least up to the third level of the mapping hierarchy.

In the case of ¬ATOMIC propagation, one cannot expect to read valid images for all pages from the materialized database after a crash; it is inconsistent on the propagation level, and all abstractions on higher levels will fail. In the case of ATOMIC propagation, the materialized database is consistent at least on Level 3, thus allowing for the execution of operations on Level 4 (DML statements).

### 3.2 Types of Log Information to Support Recovery Actions

The temporary log file must contain all the information required to transform the materialized database "as found" into the most recent transaction-consistent state (see Section 1). As we have shown, the materialized database can be in more or less defined states, may or may not fulfill consistency constraints, etc. Hence the number of log data will be determined by what is contained in the materialized database at the beginning of restart. We can be fairly certain of the contents of the materialized database in the case of ATOMIC propagation, but the result of ¬ATOMIC schemes have been shown to be unpredictable. There are, however, additional measures to somewhat reduce the degree of uncertainty resulting from ¬ATOMIC propagation, as discussed in the following section.

#### *3.2.1 Dependencies between Buffer Manager and Recovery Component*

*3.2.1.1 Buffer Management and UNDO Recovery Actions.* During the normal mode of operation, modified pages are written to disk by some replacement algorithm managing the database buffer. Ideally, this happens at points in time determined solely by buffer occupation and, from a consistency perspective, seem to be arbitrary. In general, even dirty data, that is, pages modified by incomplete transactions, may be written to the physical database. Hence the UNDO operations described earlier will have to recover the contents of both the materialized database and the external storage media. The only way to avoid this requires that the buffer manager be modified to prevent it from writing or propagating dirty pages under all circumstances. In this case, UNDO could be considerably simplified:

- If no dirty pages are propagated, global UNDO becomes virtually unnecessary that is, if there are no dirty data in the materialized database.
- If no dirty pages are written, transaction UNDO can be limited to main storage (buffer) operations.

The major disadvantage of this idea is that very large database buffers would be required (e.g., for long batch update transactions), making it generally incompatible with existing systems. However, the two different methods of handling modified pages introduced with this idea have important implications with UNDO recovery. We shall refer to these methods as:

*STEAL.* Modified pages may be written and/or propagated at any time.

*¬STEAL.* Modified pages are kept in buffer at least until the end of the transaction (EOT).

The definition of STEAL can be based on either writing or propagating, which are not discriminated in ¬ATOMIC schemes. In the case of ATOMIC propagation both variants of STEAL are conceivable, and each would have a different impact on UNDO recovery actions; in the case of ¬STEAL, no logging is required for UNDO purposes.

*3.2.1.2 Buffer Management and REDO Recovery Actions.* As soon as a transaction commits, all of its results must survive any subsequent failure (*durability*). Committed updates that have not been propagated to the materialized database would definitely be lost in case of a system crash, and so there must be enough redundant information in the log file to reconstruct these results during restart (partial REDO). It is conceivable, however to avoid this kind of recovery by the following technique.

During Phase 1 of EOT processing all pages modified by this transaction are propagated to the materialized database; that is, their writing *and* propagation are enforced. Then we can be sure that either the transaction is complete, which means that all of its results are safely recorded (no partial REDO), or in case of a crash, some updates are not yet written, which means that the transaction is not successful and must be rolled back (UNDO recovery actions).

Thus we have another criterion concerning buffer handling, which is related to the necessity of REDO recovery during restart:

*FORCE.* All modified pages are written and propagated during EOT processing.

*¬FORCE.* No propagation is triggered during EOT processing.

The implications with regard to the gathering of log data are quite straightforward in the case of FORCE. No logging is required for *partial REDO*; in the case of ¬FORCE such information is required. While FORCE avoids partial REDO, there must still be some REDO-log information for *global REDO* to provide against loss of the on-line copy of the database.

#### 3.2.2 Classification of Log Data

Depending on which of the write and propagation schemes introduced above are being implemented, we will have to collect log information for the purpose of

- removing invalid data (modifications effected by incomplete transactions) from the materialized database and
- supplementing the materialized database with updates of complete transactions that were not contained in it at the time of crash.

In this section, we briefly describe what such log data can look like and when such

**Table 2.** Classification Scheme for Log Data

| | State | Transition |
|---|---|---|
| Logical | — | Actions (DML statements) |
| Physical | Before images<br>After images | EXOR differences |

data are applicable to the crash state of the materialized database.

Log data are redundant information, collected for the sole purpose of recovery from a crash or a media failure. They do not undergo the mapping process of the database objects, but are obtained on a certain level of the mapping hierarchy and written directly to nonvolatile storage, that is, the log files. There are two different, albeit not fully orthogonal, criteria for classifying log data. The first is concerned with the *type* of objects to be logged. If some part of the physical representation, that is, the bit pattern, is written to the log, we refer to it as *physical logging*; if the operators and their arguments are recorded on a higher level, this is called *logical logging*. The second criterion concerns whether the *state* of the database—before or after a change—or the *transition* causing the change is to be logged. Table 2 contains some examples for these different types of logging, which are explained below.

*Physical State Logging on Page Level.* The most basic method, which is still applied in many commercial DBMSs, uses the page as the unit of log information. Each time a part of the linear address space is changed by some modification, insertion, etc., the whole page containing this part of the linear address space is written to the log. If UNDO logging is required, this will be done before the change takes place, yielding the so-called *before image*. For REDO purposes, the resulting page state is recorded as an *after image*.

*Physical Transition Logging on Page Level.* This logging technique is based also on pages. However, it does not explicitly record the old and new *states* of a page; rather it writes the *difference between them* to the log. The function used for computing the "difference" between two bit strings is the exclusive-or, which is both commutative and associative as required by the recovery algorithm. If this difference is applied to the old state of a page, again using the exclusive-or, the new state will result. On the other hand, applying it to the new state will yield the old state. There are some problems in the details of this approach, but these are beyond the scope of the paper.

The two methods of page logging that we have discussed can be compared as follows:

- Transition logging requires only one log entry (the difference), whereas state logging uses both a before image and an after image. If there are multiple changes applied to the same page during one transaction, transition logging can express these either by successive differences or by one accumulated difference. With state logging, the first before image and the last after image are required.
- Since there are usually only a small number of data inside a page affected by a change, the exclusive-or difference will contain long strings of 0's, which can be removed by well-known compression techniques. Hence transition logging can potentially require much less space than does state logging.

*Physical State Logging on Access Path Level.* Physical logging can also be applied to the objects of the access path level, namely, physical records, access path structures, tables, etc. The log component has to be aware of these storage structures and record only the changed entry, rather than blindly logging the whole page around it. The advantage of this requirement is obvious: By logging only the physical objects actually being changed, space requirements for log files can be drastically reduced. One can save even more space by exploiting the fact that most access path structures consist of fully redundant information. For example, one can completely reconstruct a B*-tree from the record occurrences to which it refers. In itself, this type of reconstruction is certainly too expensive to become a standard method for crash recovery. But if only the modifications in the records are logged, after a crash the corresponding B* tree can be recovered consistently, provided that an appropriate write discipline has been observed for the pages containing the tree. This principle, stating that changed nodes must be written bottom up, is a special case of the "careful replacement" technique explained in detail by Verhofstadt [1978]. For our taxonomy it makes no difference whether the principle is applied or not.

*Transition Logging on the Access Path Level.* On the access path level, we are dealing with the entries of storage structures, but do not know how they are related to each other with regard to the objects of the database schema. This type of information is maintained on higher levels of the mapping hierarchy. If we look only at the physical entry representation (*physical* transition logging), state transition on this level means that a physical record, a table entry, etc. is *added* to, *deleted* from, or *modified* in a page. The arguments pertaining to these operations are the entries themselves, and so there is little difference between this and the previous approach. In the case of physical state logging on the access path level, we placed the physical address together with the entry representation. Here we place the operation code and object identifier with the same type of argument. Thus physical transition logging on this level does not provide anything essentially different.

We can also consider *logical* transition logging, attempting to exploit the syntax of the storage structures implemented on this level. The logical addition, a new record occurrence, for example, would include all the redundant table updates such as the record id index, the free space table, etc., each of which was explicitly logged with the physical schemes. Hence we again have a potential saving of log space. However, it is important to note that the logical transitions on this level generally affect *more than one page*. If they (or their inverse operators for UNDO) are to be applied during recovery, we must be sure that all affected pages have the same state in the materialized database. This is not the case with direct page allocation, and using the more expensive indirect schemes cannot be

TRANSACTION LOG

| TRANSACTION DESCRIPTOR | ⇒ | RECORD ID, OLDVAL, NEWVAL |
|---|---|---|

**Figure 7.** Logical transition logging as implemented in System R. (From Gray et al. [1981].)

justified by the comparatively few benefits yielded by logical transition logging on the access path level. Hence logical transition logging on this level can generally be ruled out, but will become more attractive on the next higher level.

*Logical Logging on the Record-Oriented Level.* At one level higher, it is possible to express the changes performed by the transaction program in a very compact manner by simply recording the update DML statements with their parameters. Even if a nonprocedural query language is being used above this level, its updates will be decomposed into updates of single records or tuples equivalent to the single-record updates of procedural DB languages. Thus logging on this level means that only the INSERT, UPDATE, and DELETE operations, together with their record ids and attribute values, are written to the log. The mapping process discerns which entries are affected, which pages must be modified, etc. Thus recovery is achieved by reexecuting some of the previously processed DML statements. For UNDO recovery, of course, the inverse DML statement must be executed, that is, a DELETE to compensate an INSERT and vice versa, and an UPDATE returned to the original values. These inverse DML statements must be generated automatically as part of the regular logging activity, and for this reason this approach is not viable for network-oriented DBMSs with information-bearing interrecord relations. In such cases, it can be extremely expensive to determine, for example, the inverse for a DELETE. Details can be found in Reuter [1981].

System R is a good example of a system with logical logging on the record-oriented level. All update operations performed on the tuples are represented by one generalized modification operator, which is not explicitly recorded. This operator changes a tuple identified by its tuple identifier (TID) from an old value to a new one, both of which are recorded. Inserting a tuple entails modifying its initial null value to the given value, and deleting a tuple entails the inverse transition. Hence the log contains the information shown in Figure 7.

Logical transition logging obviously requires a materialized database that is consistent up to Level 3; that is, it can only be combined with ATOMIC propagation schemes. Although the number of log data written are very small, recovery will be more expensive than that in other schemes, because it involves the reprocessing of some DML statements, although this can be done more cheaply than the original processing.

Table 3 is a summation of the properties of all logging techniques that we have described under two considerations: What is the cost of collecting the log data during normal processing? and, How expensive is recovery based on the respective type of log information? Of course, the entries in the table are only very rough qualitative estimations; for more detailed quantitative analysis see Reuter [1982].

Writing log information, no matter what type, is determined by two rules:

- UNDO information must be written to the log file *before* the corresponding updates are propagated to the materialized database. This has come to be known as the "write ahead log" (WAL) principle [Gray 1978].
- REDO information must be written to the temporary and the archive log file *before* EOT is acknowledged to the transaction program. Once this is done, the system must be able to ensure the transaction's durability.

We return to different facets of these rules in Section 3.4.

**Table 3.** Qualitative Comparison of Various Logging Techniques[a]

| Logging technique | Level no. | Expenses during normal processing | Expenses for recovery operations |
|---|---|---|---|
| Physical state | 2 | High | Low |
| Physical transition | 2 | Medium | Low |
| Physical state | 3 | Low | Low |
| Logical transition | 4 | Very low | Medium |

[a] Costs are basically measured in units of physical I/O operations. Recovery in this context means crash recovery.

### 3.3 Examples of Recovery Techniques

#### 3.3.1 *Optimization of Recovery Actions by Checkpoints*

An appropriate combination of redundancy provided by log protocols and mapping techniques is basically all that we need for implementing transaction-oriented database recovery as described in Section 1. In real systems, however, there are a number of important refinements that reduce the amount of log data required and the costs of crash recovery. Figure 8 is a very general example of crash recovery. In the center, there is the temporary log containing UNDO and REDO information and special entries notifying the begin and end of a transaction (BOT and EOT, respectively). Below the temporary log, the transaction history preceding the crash is shown, and above it, recovery processing for global UNDO and partial REDO is related to the log entries. We have not assumed a specific propagation strategy.

There are two questions concerning the costs of crash recovery:

- In the case of the materialized DB being modified by incomplete transactions, to what extent does the log have to be processed for UNDO recovery?
- If the DBMS does not use a FORCE discipline, which part of the log has to processed for REDO recovery?

The first question can easily be answered: If we know that updates of incomplete transactions *can* have affected the materialized database (STEAL), we must scan the temporary log file back to the BOT entry of the *oldest* incomplete transaction to be sure that no invalid data are left in the system. The second question is not as simple. In Figure 8, REDO is started at a point that seems to be chosen arbitrarily. Why is there no REDO recovery for object A? In general, we can assume that in the case of a FORCE discipline modified pages will be written eventually because of buffer replacement. One might expect that only the contents of the most recently changed pages have to be redone—if the change was caused by a complete transaction. But look at a buffer activity record shown in Figure 9.

The situation depicted in Figure 9 is typical of many large database applications. Most of the modified pages will have been changed "recently," but there are a few hot spots like $p_i$, pages that are modified again and again, and, since they are *referenced* so frequently, have not been written from the buffer. After a while such pages will contain the updates of *many* complete transactions, and REDO recovery will therefore have to go back very far on the temporary log. This makes restart expensive. In general, the amount of log data to be processed for partial REDO will increase with the interval of time between two subsequent crashes. In other words, the higher the availability of the system, the more costly recovery will become. This is unacceptable for large, demanding applications.

For this reason additional measures are required for making restart costs independent of mean time between failure. Such provisions will be called *checkpoints*, and are defined as follows.

Generating a checkpoint means collecting information in a safe place, which has the effect of defining and limiting the amount of REDO recovery required after a crash.

Whether this information is stored in the log or elsewhere depends on which implementation technique is chosen; we give

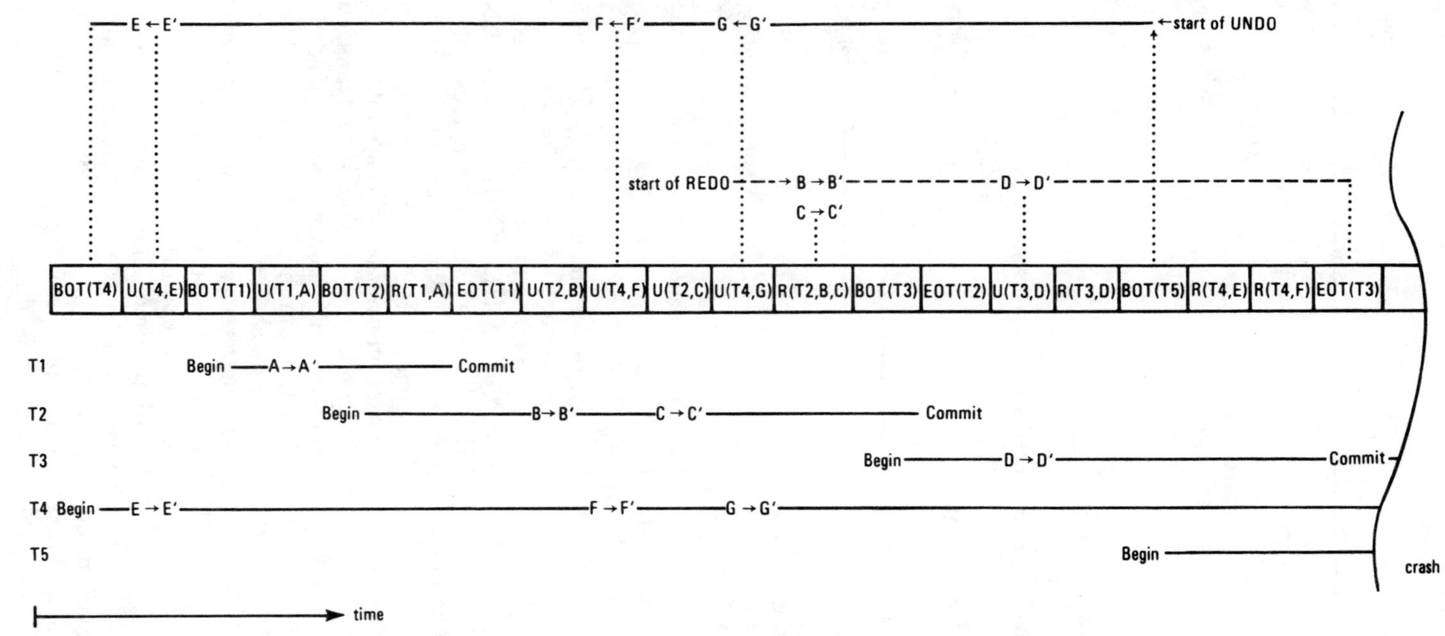


**Figure 8.** A crash recovery scenario.

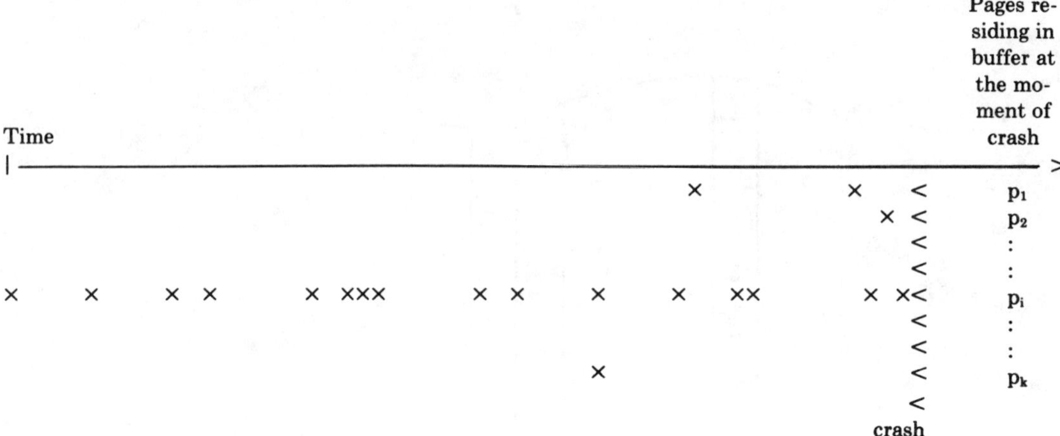


**Figure 9.** Age of buffer page modifications (×, page modification).

some examples in this section. Checkpoint generation involves three steps [Gray 1978]:

- Write a BEGIN_CHECKPOINT record to the temporary log file.
- Write all checkpoint data to the log file and/or the database.
- Write an END_CHECKPOINT record to the temporary log file.

During restart, the BEGIN-END bracket is a clear indication as to whether a checkpoint was generated completely or interrupted by a system crash. Sometimes checkpointing is considered to be a means for restoring the whole database to some previous state. Our view, however, focuses on transaction recovery. Therefore to us a checkpoint is a technique for optimizing crash recovery rather than a definition of a distinguished state for recovery itself. In order to effectively constrain partial REDO, checkpoints must be generated at well-defined points in time. In the following sections, we shall introduce four separate criteria for determining when to start checkpoint activities.

#### 3.3.2 Transaction-Oriented Checkpoints

As previously explained, a FORCE discipline will avoid partial REDO. All modified pages are propagated before an EOT record is written to the log, which makes the transaction durable. If this record is not found in the log after a crash, the transaction will be considered incomplete and its effects will be undone. Hence the EOT record of each transaction can be interpreted as a BEGIN_CHECKPOINT and END_CHECKPOINT, since it agrees with our definition of a checkpoint in that it limits the scope of REDO. Figure 10 illustrates transaction-oriented checkpoints (TOC).

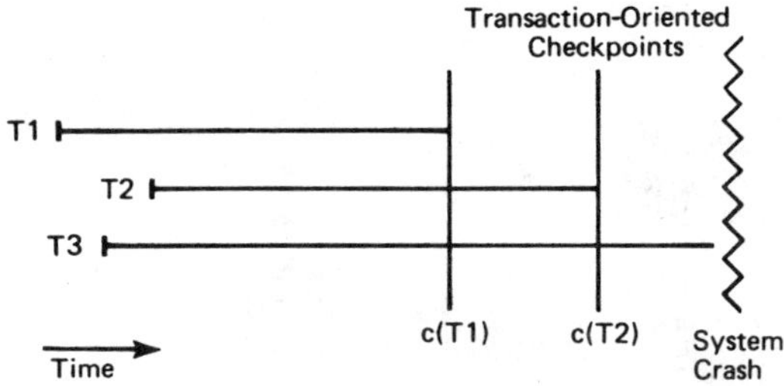


**Figure 10.** Scenario for transaction-oriented checkpoints.

As can be seen in Figure 10, transaction-oriented checkpoints are implied by a FORCE discipline. The major drawback to this approach can be deduced from Figure 9. Hot spot pages like $p_i$ will be propagated each time they are modified by a transaction even though they remain in the buffer for a long time. The reduction of recovery expenses with the use of transaction-oriented checkpoints is accomplished by imposing some overhead on normal processing. This is discussed in more detail in Section 3.5. The cost factor of unnecessary write operations performed by a FORCE discipline is highly relevant for very large

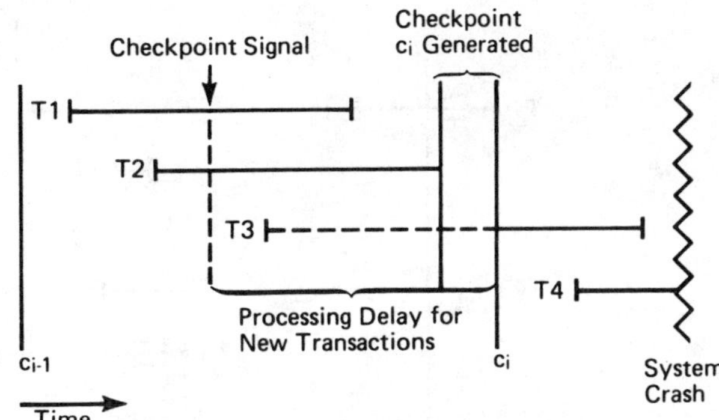


**Figure 11.** Scenario for transaction-consistent checkpoints.

database buffers. The longer a page remains in the buffer, the higher is the probability of multiple updates to the same page by different transactions. Thus for DBMSs supporting large applications, transaction-oriented checkpointing is not the proper choice.

### 3.3.3 Transaction-Consistent Checkpoints

The following transaction-consistent checkpoints (TCC) are *global* in that they save the work of all transactions that have modified the database. The first TCC, when successfully generated, creates a transaction-consistent database. It requires that all update activities on the database be quiescent. In other words, when the checkpoint generation is signaled by the recovery component, all incomplete update transactions are completed and new ones are not admitted. The checkpoint is actually generated when the last update is completed. After the END_CHECKPOINT record has been successfully written, normal operation is resumed. This is illustrated in Figure 11.

Checkpointing connotes propagating all modified buffer pages and writing a record to the log, which notifies the materialized database of a new transaction-consistent state, hence the name "transaction-consistent checkpoint" (TCC). By propagating all modified pages to the database, TCC establishes a point past which partial REDO will not operate. Since all modifications prior to the recent checkpoint are reflected in the database, REDO-log information need only be processed back to the youngest END_CHECKPOINT record found on the log. We shall see later on that the time between two subsequent checkpoints can be adjusted to minimize overall recovery costs.

In Figure 11, T3 must be redone completely, whereas T4 must be rolled back. There is nothing to be done about T1 and T2, since their updates have been propagated by generating $c_i$. Favorable as that may sound, the TCC approach is quite unrealistic for large multiuser DBMSs, with the exception of one special case, which is discussed in Section 3.4. There are two reasons for this:

- Putting the system into a quiescent state until no update transaction is active may cause an intolerable delay for incoming transactions.
- Checkpoint costs will be high in the case of large buffers, where many changed pages will have accumulated. With a buffer of 6 megabytes and a substantial number of updates, propagating the modified pages will take about 10 seconds.

For small applications and single-user systems, TCC certainly is useful.

### 3.3.4 Action-Consistent Checkpoints

Each transaction is considered a sequence of elementary actions affecting the database. On the record-oriented level, these actions can be seen as DML statements. Action-consistent checkpoints (ACC) can be generated when no update *action* is being processed. Therefore signaling an ACC means putting the system into quiescence on the action level, which impedes operation here much less than on the transaction level. A scenario is shown in Figure 12.

The checkpoint itself is generated in the very same way as was described for the

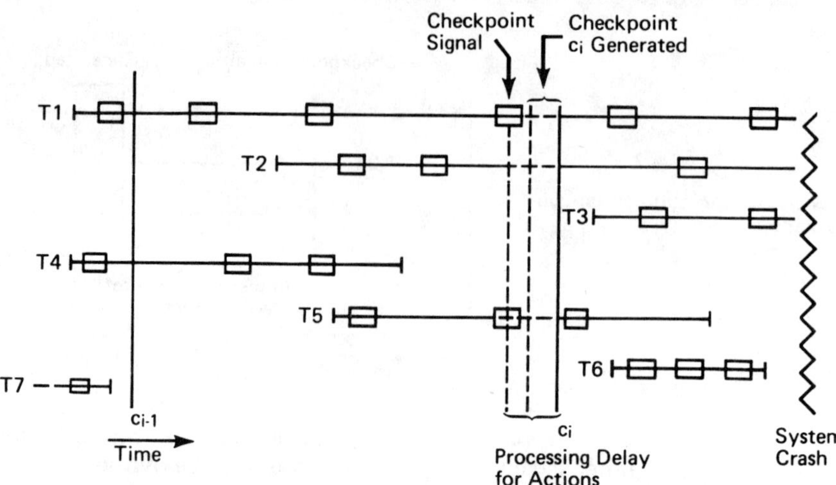


**Figure 12.** Scenario for action-consistent checkpoints.

TCC technique. In the case of ACC, however, the END_CHECKPOINT record indicates an action-consistent[4] rather than a transaction-consistent database. Obviously such a checkpoint imposes a limit on partial REDO. In contrast to TCC, it does not establish a boundary to global UNDO; however, it is not required by definition to do so. Recovery in the above scenario means global UNDO for T1, T2, and T3. REDO has to be performed for the last action of T5 and for all of T6. The changes of T4 and T7 are part of the materialized database because of checkpointing. So again, REDO-log information prior to the recent checkpoint is irrelevant for crash recovery. This scheme is much more realistic, since it does not cause long delays for incoming transactions. Costs of checkpointing, however, are still high when large buffers are used.

### 3.3.5 Fuzzy Checkpoints

In order to further reduce checkpoint costs, propagation activity at checkpoint time has to be avoided whenever possible. One way to do this is *indirect* checkpointing. Indirect checkpointing means that information about the buffer occupation is written to the log file rather than the pages themselves. This can be done with two or three write operations, even with very large buffers, and helps to determine which pages containing committed data were actually in the buffer at the moment of a crash. However, if there are hot spot pages, their REDO information will have to be traced back very far on the temporary log. So, although indirect checkpointing does reduce the costs of partial REDO, this does not in general make partial REDO independent of mean time between failure. Note also that this method is only applicable with ¬ATOMIC propagation. In the case of ATOMIC schemes, propagation always takes effect at one well-defined moment, which is a checkpoint; pages that have only been written (not propagated) are lost after a crash. Since this checkpointing method is concerned only with the temporary log, leaving the database as it is, we call it "fuzzy." A description of a particular implementation of indirect, fuzzy checkpoints is given by Gray [1978].

The best of both worlds, low checkpoint costs with fixed limits to partial REDO, is achieved by another fuzzy scheme described by Lindsay *et al.* [1979]. This scheme combines ACC with indirect checkpointing: At checkpoint time the numbers of all pages (with an update indicator) currently in buffer are written to the log file. If there are no hot spot pages, nothing else

[4] This means that the materialized database reflects a state produced by complete actions only; that is, it is consistent up to Level 3 at the moment of checkpointing.

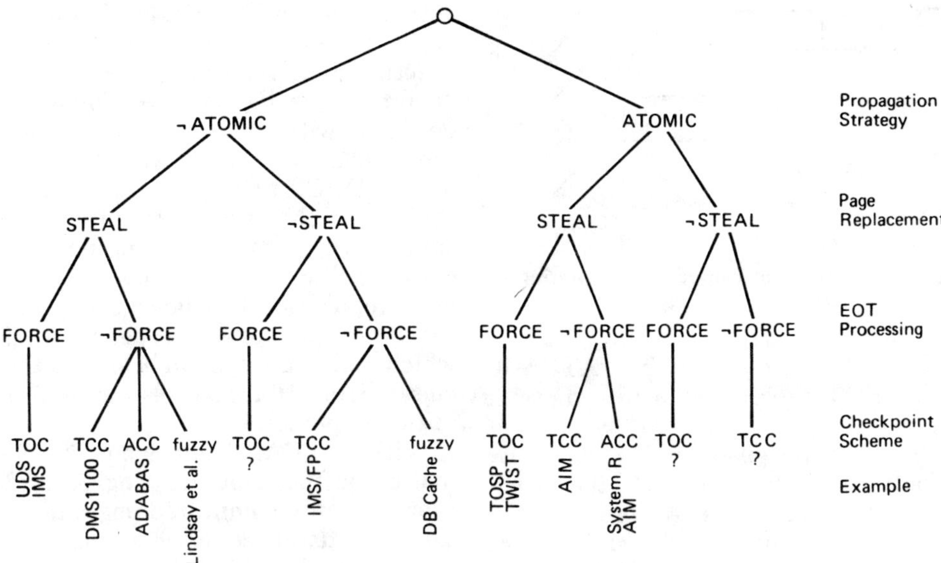


**Figure 13.** Classification scheme for recovery concepts.

is done. If, however, a modified page is found at two subsequent checkpoints without having been propagated, it will be propagated during checkpoint generation. Hence the scope of partial REDO is limited to two checkpoint intervals. Empiric studies show that the I/O activity for checkpointing is only about 3 percent of what is required with ACC [Reuter 1981]. This scheme can be given general applicability by adjusting the number of checkpoint intervals for modified pages in buffer.

Another fuzzy checkpoint approach has been proposed by Elhardt [1982]. Since a description of this technique, called database cache, would require more details than we can present in this paper, readers are referred to the literature.

### 3.4 Examples of Logging and Recovery Components

The introduction of various checkpoint schemes has completed our taxonomy. Database recovery techniques can now be classified as shown in Figure 13. In order to make the classification more vivid, we have added the names of a few existing DBMSs and implementation concepts to the corresponding entries.

In this section, we attempt to illustrate the functional principles of three different approaches found in well-known database systems. We particularly want to elaborate on the cooperation between mapping, logging, and recovery facilities, using a sample database constituting four pages, A, B, C, and D, which are modified by six transactions. What the transactions do is sketched in Figure 14. The indicated checkpoint $c_i$ is relevant only to those implementations actually applying checkpoint techniques. Prior to the beginning of Transaction 1 (T1), the DB pages were in the states A, B, C, and D, respectively.

#### 3.4.1 Implementation Technique: ¬ATOMIC, STEAL, FORCE, TOC

An implementation technique involving the principles of ¬ATOMIC, STEAL, FORCE, and TOC can be found in many systems, for example, IMS [N.d.] and UDS [N.d.]. The temporary log file contains only UNDO data (owing to FORCE), whereas REDO information is written to the archive log. According to the write rules introduced in Section 3.2, we must be sure that UNDO logging has taken effect before a changed page is either replaced in the buffer or

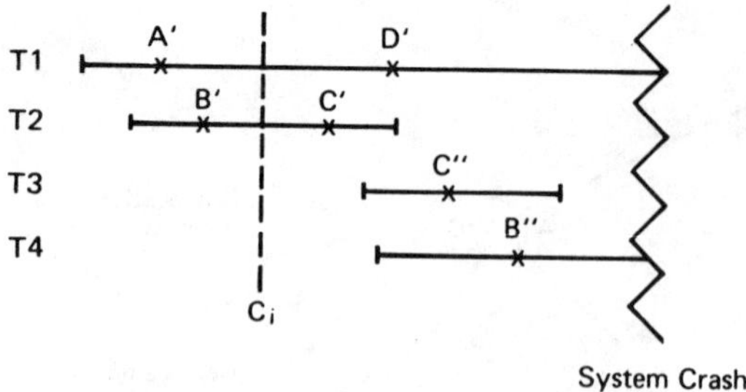


**Figure 14.** Transaction scenario for illustrating recovery techniques.

forced at EOT. Note that in ¬ATOMIC schemes EOT processing is interruptable by a crash.

In the scenario given in Figure 15, we need only consider T1 and T2; the rest is irrelevant to the example. According to the scenario, A′ has been replaced from the buffer, which triggered an UNDO entry to be written. Pages B′ and C′ remained in buffer as long as T2 was active. T2 reached its normal end before the crash, and so the following had to be done:

- Write UNDO information for B and C (in case the FORCE fails).
- Propagate B′ and C′.
- Write REDO information for B′ and C′ to the archive log file.
- Discard the UNDO entries for B and C.
- Write an EOT record to the log files and acknowledge EOT to the user.

Of course, there are some obvious optimizations as regards the UNDO data for pages that have not been replaced before EOT, but these are not our concern here. After the crash, the recovery component finds the database and the log files as shown in the scenario. The materialized database is inconsistent owing to ¬ATOMIC propagation, and must be made consistent by applying all UNDO information in reverse chronological order.

### 3.4.2 Implementation Technique: ¬ATOMIC, ¬STEAL, ¬FORCE, TCC

Applications with high transaction rates require large DB buffers to yield satisfactory performance. With sufficient buffer space, a ¬STEAL approach becomes feasible; that is, the materialized database will never contain updates of incomplete transactions. ¬FORCE is desirable for efficient EOT processing, as discussed previously (Section 3.3.2). The IMS/Fast Path in its "main storage database" version is a system designed with this implementation technique [IMS N.d.; Date 1981]. The ¬STEAL and ¬FORCE principles are generalized to the extent that there are no write operations to the database during normal processing. All updates are recorded to the log, and propagation is delayed until shutdown (or some other very infrequent checkpoint), which makes the system belong to the TCC class. Figure 16 illustrates the implications of this approach.

With ¬STEAL, there is no UNDO information on the temporary log. Accordingly, there are only committed pages in the materialized database. Each successful transaction writes REDO information during EOT processing. Assuming that the crash occurs as indicated in Figure 14, the materialized database is in the initial state, and, compared with the former current database, is old. Everything that has been done since start-up must therefore be applied to the database by processing the entire temporary log in chronological order. This, of course, can be very expensive, and hence the entire environment should be as stable as possible to minimize crashes. The benefits of this approach are extremely high transaction rates and short response times, since physical I/O during normal processing is reduced to a minimum.

The database cache, mentioned in Section 3.3, also tries to exploit the desirable properties of ¬STEAL and ¬FORCE, but, in addition, attempts to provide very fast crash recovery. This is attempted by implementing a checkpointing scheme of the "fuzzy" type.

### 3.4.3 Implementation Technique: ATOMIC, STEAL, ¬FORCE, ACC

ATOMIC propagation is not yet widely used in commercial database systems. This may result from the fact that indirect page mapping is more complicated and more expensive than the update-in-place technique. However, there is a well-known ex-

Before System Crash

After Restart

System Buffer

Currently Active:
T1: A′, D′
Committed:
T2: B′, C′

| D′ |
|---|
| C′ |
| B′ |

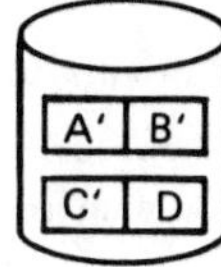


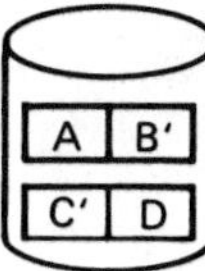


Log: UNDO(T1:A), REDO(T2:B′,C′)

**Figure 15.** Recovery scenario for ¬ATOMIC, STEAL, FORCE, TOC.

Before System Crash

After Restart

System Buffer

Currently Active:
T1: A′, D′
T4: B″

| A′ |
|---|
| B″ |
| C″ |
| D′ |

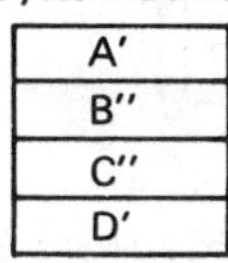


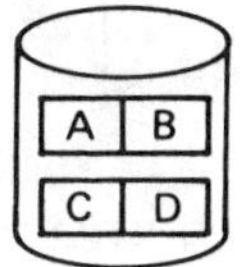


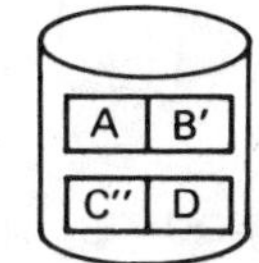

Log: REDO(T2:B′,C′), REDO(T3:C″)

**Figure 16.** Recovery scenario for ¬ATOMIC, ¬STEAL, ¬FORCE, TCC.

ample of this type of implementation, based on the shadow-page mechanism in System R. This system uses action-consistent checkpointing for update propagation, and hence comes up with a consistent materialized database after a crash. More specifically, the materialized database will be consistent up to Level 4 of the mapping hierarchy and reflect the state of the most recent checkpoint; everything occurring after the most recent checkpoint will have disappeared. As discussed in Section 3.2, with an action-consistent database one can use logical transition logging based on DML statements, which System R does. Note that in the case of ATOMIC propagation the WAL principle is bound to the propagation, that is, to the checkpoints. In other words, modified pages can be written, but not propagated, without having written an UNDO log. If the modified pages pertain to incomplete transactions, the UNDO information must be on the temporary log before the pages are propagated. The same is true for STEAL: Not only can dirty pages be written; in the case of System R they can also be propagated. Consider the scenario in Figure 17.

T1 and T2 were both incomplete at checkpoint. Since their updates (A′ and B′) have been propagated, UNDO information must be written to the temporary log. In System R, this is done with logical transitions, as described in Section 3.2. EOT processing of T2 and T3 includes writing REDO information to the log, again using logical transitions. When the system crashes, the current database is in the state depicted in Figure 17; at restart the materialized database will reflect the most recent checkpoint state. Crash recovery involves the following actions:

- UNDO the modification of A′. Owing to the STEAL policy in System R, incomplete transactions can span several checkpoints. Global UNDO must be applied to all changes of failed transactions prior to the recent checkpoint.
- REDO the last action of T2 (modification of C′) and the whole transaction T3 (modification of C″). Although they are committed, the corresponding page states are not yet reflected in the materialized database.
- Nothing has to be done with D′ since this has not yet become part of the materialized database. The same is true of T4. Since it was not present when $c_i$ was generated, it has had no effect on the materialized database.

### 3.5 Evaluation of Logging and Recovery Concepts

Combining all possibilities of propagating, buffer handling, and checkpointing, and

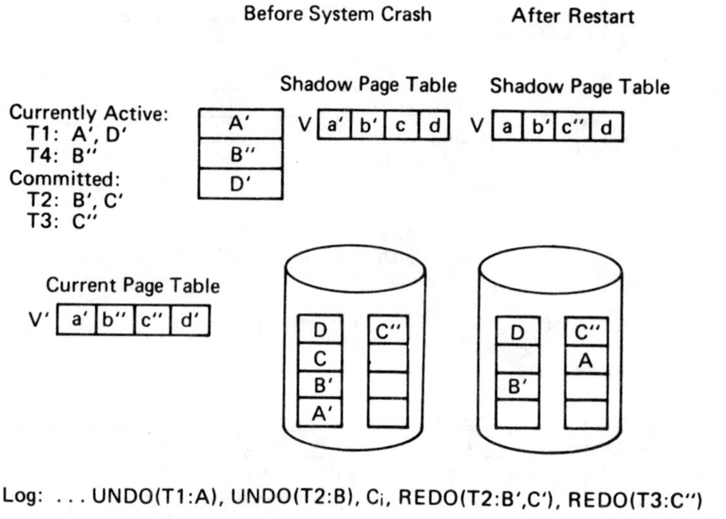

Before System Crash

After Restart

Currently Active:
T1: A', D'
T4: B''
Committed:
T2: B', C'
T3: C''

A'
B''
D'

Shadow Page Table
V | a' | b' | c | d |

Shadow Page Table
V | a | b' | c'' | d |

Current Page Table
V' | a' | b'' | c'' | d' |

D C B' A' | C''

D B' | C'' A

Log: . . . UNDO(T1:A), UNDO(T2:B), $C_i$, REDO(T2:B',C'), REDO(T3:C'')

**Figure 17.** Recovery scenario for ATOMIC, STEAL, ¬FORCE, ACC.

**Table 4.** Evaluation of Logging and Recovery Techniques Based on the Introduced Taxonomy

| propagation strategy | ¬ATOMIC | | | | | | | ATOMIC | | | | |
|---|---|---|---|---|---|---|---|---|---|---|---|---|
| buffer replacement | STEAL | | | | ¬STEAL | | | STEAL | | | ¬STEAL | |
| EOT processing | FORCE | ¬FORCE | | | FORCE | ¬FORCE | | FORCE | ¬FORCE | | FORCE | ¬FORCE |
| checkpoint type | TOC | TCC | ACC | FUZZY | TOC | TCC | FUZZY | TOC | TCC | ACC | TOC | TCC |
| materialized DB state after system failure | DC | DC | DC | DC | DC | DC | DC | TC | TC | AC | TC | TC |
| cost of transaction UNDO | + | + | + | + | -- | -- | -- | - | - | + | -- | -- |
| cost of partial REDO at restart | -- | - | - | + | -- | - | - | -- | - | - | -- | - |
| cost of global UNDO at restart | + | + | + | + | -- | -- | -- | -- | -- | + | -- | -- |
| overhead during normal processing | -- | -- | -- | -- | -- | -- | -- | + | + | + | + | + |
| frequency of check-points | + | - | - | - | + | - | - | + | - | - | + | - |
| checkpoint cost | + | ++ | ++ | - | + | ++ | + | + | ++ | ++ | + | ++ |

Notes:
Abbreviations: DC, device consistent (chaotic); AC, action consistent; TC, Transaction consistent.
Evaluation symbols: ––, very low; –, low; +, high; ++, very high.

considering the overall properties of each scheme that we have discussed, we can derive the evaluation given in Table 4.

Table 4 can be seen as a compact summary of what we have discussed up to this point. Combinations leading to inherent contradictions have been suppressed (e.g., ¬STEAL does not allow for ACC). By referring the information in Table 4 to Figure 13; one can see how existing DBMSs are rated in this qualitative comparison.

Some criteria of our taxonomy divide the world of DB recovery into clearly distinct areas:

- ATOMIC propagation achieves an action- or transaction-consistent materialized database in the event of a crash. Physical as well as logical logging techniques are therefore applicable. The benefits of this property are offset by increased overhead during normal processing caused by the redundancy required for indirect page mapping. On the other hand, recovery can be cheap when ATOMIC propagation is combined with TOC schemes.
- ¬ATOMIC propagation generally results in a chaotic materialized database in the event of a crash, which makes physical logging mandatory. There is almost no overhead during normal processing, but without appropriate checkpoint schemes, recovery will more expensive.
- All transaction-oriented and transaction-consistent schemes cause high checkpoint costs. This problem is emphasized in transaction-oriented schemes by a relatively high checkpoint frequency.

It is, in general, important when deciding which implementation techniques to choose for database recovery to carefully consider whether optimizations of crash recovery put additional burdens on normal processing. If this is the case, it will certainly not pay off, since crash recovery, it is hoped, will be a rare event. Recovery components should be designed with minimal overhead for normal processing, provided that there is fixed limit to the costs of crash recovery.

This consideration rules out schemes of the ATOMIC, FORCE, TOC type, which can be implemented and look very appealing at first sight. According to the classification, the materialized database will always be in the most recent transaction-consistent state in implementations of these schemes. Incomplete transactions have not affected the materialized database, and successful transactions have propagated indivisibly during EOT processing. However appealing the schemes may be in terms of crash recovery, the overhead during normal processing is too high to justify their use [Haerder and Reuter 1979; Reuter 1980].

There are, of course, other factors influencing the performance of a logging and recovery component: The granule of logging (pages or entries), the frequency of checkpoints (it depends on the transaction load), etc. are important. Logging is also tied to concurrency control in that the granule of logging determined the granule of locking. If page logging is applied, DBMS must not use smaller granules of locking than pages. However, a detailed discussion of these aspects is beyond the scope of this paper; detailed analyses can be found in Chandy et al. [1975] and Reuter [1982].

## 4. ARCHIVE RECOVERY

Throughout this paper we have focused on crash recovery, but in general there are two types of DB recovery, as is shown in Figure 18. The first path represents the standard crash recovery, depending on the physical (and the materialized) database as well as on the temporary log. If one of these is lost or corrupted because of hardware or software failure, the second path, archive recovery, must be tried. This presupposes that the components involved have independent failure modes, for example, if temporary and archive logs are kept on different devices. The global scenario for archive recovery is shown in Figure 19; it illustrates that the component "archive copy" actually depends on some dynamically modified subcomponents. These subcomponents create new archive copies and update existing ones. The following is a brief sketch of some problems associated with this.

Creating an archive copy, that is, copying the on-line version of the database, is a very expensive process. If the copy is to be consistent, update operation on the database has to be interrupted for a long time, which is unacceptable in many applications. Archive recovery is likely to be rare, and an archive copy should not be created too frequently, both because of cost and because there is a chance that it will never be used. On the other hand, if the archive copy is very old, recovery starting from such a copy will have to redo too much work and will take too long. There are two methods to cope with this. First, the database can be copied on the fly, that is, without inter-

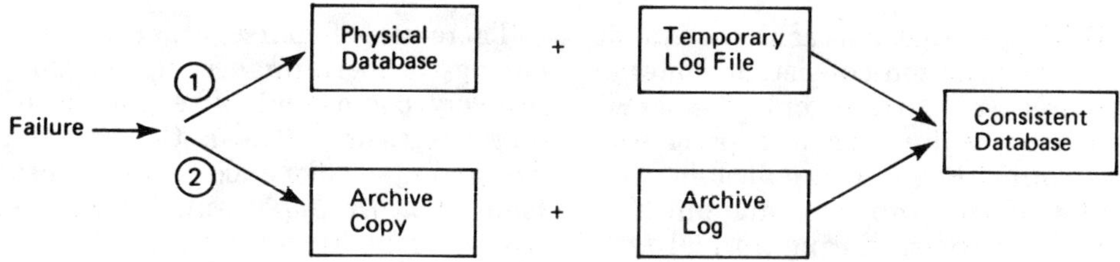


**Figure 18.** Two ways of DB recovery and the components involved.

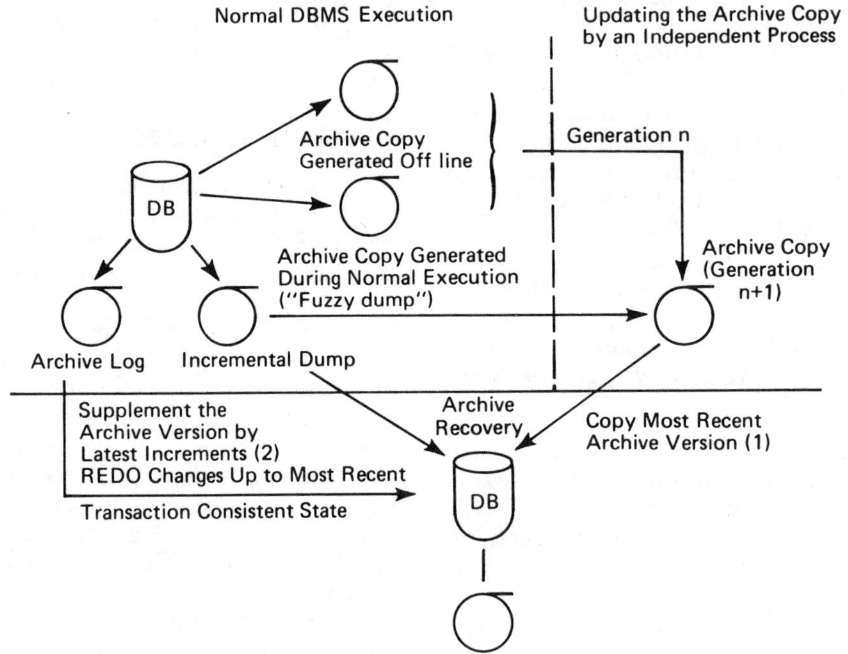


**Figure 19.** Scenario for archive recovery (global REDO).

rupting processing, in parallel with normal processing. This will create an inconsistent copy, a so-called "fuzzy dump."

The other possibility is to write only the changed pages to an incremental dump, since a new copy will be different from an old one only with respect to these pages. Either type of dump can be used to create a new, more up-to-date copy from the previous one. This is done by a separate off-line process with respect to the database and therefore does not affect DB operation. In the case of DB applications running 24 hours per day, this type of separate process is the only possible way to maintain archive recovery data. As shown in Figure 19, archive recovery in such an environment requires the most recent archive copy, the latest incremental modifications to it (if there are any), and the archive log. When recovering the database itself, there is little additional cost in creating an identical new archive copy in parallel.

There is still another problem hidden in this scenario: Since archive copies are needed very infrequently, they may be susceptible to magnetic decay. For this reason several generations of the archive copy are usually kept. If the most recent one does not work, its predecessor can be tried, and so on. This leads to the consequences illustrated in Figure 20.

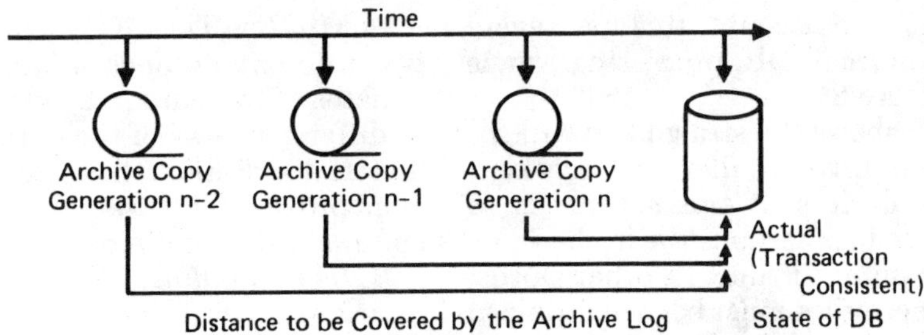


**Figure 20.** Consequences of multigeneration archive copies.

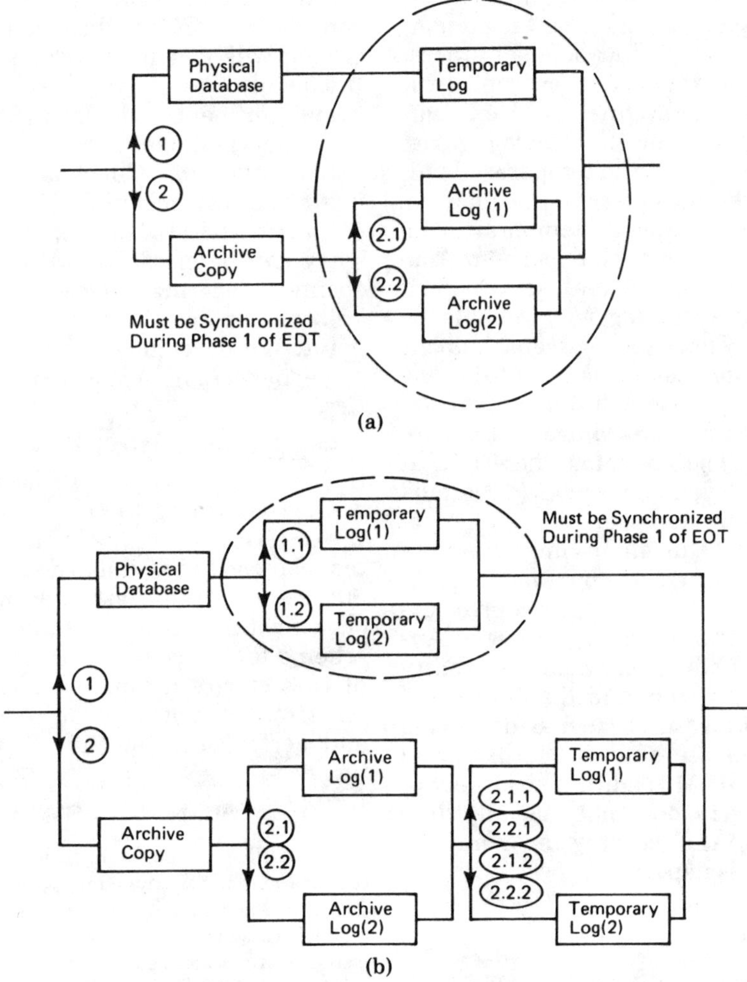


**Figure 21.** Two possibilities for duplicating the archive log.

We must anticipate the case of starting archive recovery from the *oldest* generation, and hence the archive log must span the whole distance back to this point in time. That makes the log susceptible to magnetic decay, as well, but in this case generations will not help; rather we have to duplicate the entire archive log file. Without taking storage costs into account, this has severe impact on normal DB processing, as is shown in Figure 21.

Figure 21a shows the straightforward solution: two archive log files that are kept on different devices. If this scheme is to work, all three log files must be in the same state at any point in time. In other words, writing to these files must be synchronized *at each EOT*. This adds substantial costs to normal processing and particularly affects transaction response times. The solution in Figure 21b assumes that *all log information* is written only to the temporary log during normal processing. An independent process that runs asynchronously then copies the REDO data to the archive log. Hence archive recovery finds most of the log entries in the archive log, but the temporary log is required for the most recent information. In such an environment, temporary and archive logs are no longer independent from a recovery perspective, and so we must make the temporary log very reliable by duplicating it. The resulting scenario looks much more complicated than the first one, but in fact the only additional costs are those for temporary log storage—which are usually small. The advantage here is that only two files have to be synchronized during EOT, and moreover—as numerical analysis shows—this environment is more reliable than the first one by a factor of 2.

These arguments do not, of course, exhaust the problem of archive recovery. Applications demanding very high availability and fast recovery from a media failure will use additional measures such as duplexing the whole database and all the hardware (e.g., see TANDEM [N.d.]). This aspect of database recovery does not add anything conceptually to the recovery taxonomy established in this paper.

## 5. CONCLUSION

We have presented a taxonomy for classifying the implementation techniques for database recovery. It is based on four criteria:

*Propagation.* We have shown that update propagation should be carefully distinguished from the write operation. The ATOMIC/¬ATOMIC dichotomy defines two different methods of handling low-level updates of the database, and also gives rise to different views of the database, both the materialized and the physical database. This proves to be useful in defining different crash states of a database.

*Buffer Handling.* We have shown that interfering with buffer replacement can support UNDO recovery. The STEAL/¬STEAL criterion deals with this concept.

*EOT Processing.* By distinguishing FORCE policies from ¬FORCE policies we can distinguish whether successful transactions will have to be redone after a crash. It can also be shown that this criterion heavily influences the DBMS performance during normal operation.

*Checkpointing.* Checkpoints have been introduced as a means for limiting the costs of partial REDO during crash recovery. They can be classified with regard to the events triggering checkpoint generation and the number of data written at a checkpoint. We have shown that each class has some particular performance characteristics.

Some existing DBMSs and implementation concepts have been classified and described according to the taxonomy. Since the criteria are relatively simple, each system can easily be assigned to the appropriate node of the classification tree. This classification is more than an ordering scheme for concepts: Once the parameters of a system are known, it is possible to draw important conclusions as to the behavior and performance of the recovery component.

## ACKNOWLEDGMENTS

We would like to thank Jim Gray (TANDEM Computers, Inc.) for his detailed proposals concerning the structure and contents of this paper, and his enlightening discussions of logging and recovery. Thanks are also due to our colleagues Flaviu Cristian, Shel Finkelstein, C. Mohan, Kurt Shoens, and Irv Traiger (IBM Research Laboratory) for their encouraging comments and critical remarks.

## REFERENCES

ASTRAHAN, M. M., BLASGEN, M. W., CHAMBERLIN, D. D., GRAY, J. N., KING, W. F., LINDSAY, B. G.,

LORIE, R., MEHL, J. W., PRICE, T. G., PUTZOLU, F., SELINGER, P. G., SCHKOLNICK, M., SLUTZ, D. R., TRAIGER, I. L., WADE, B. W., AND YOST, R. A. 1981. History and evaluation of System R. *Commun. ACM 24*, 10 (Oct.), 632–646.

BERNSTEIN, P. A., AND GOODMAN, N. 1981. Concurrency control in distributed database systems. *ACM Comput. Surv. 13*, 2 (June), 185–221.

BJORK, L. A. 1973. Recovery scenario for a DB/DC system. In *Proceedings of the ACM 73 National Conference* (Atlanta, Ga., Aug. 27–29). ACM, New York, pp. 142–146.

CHAMBERLIN, D. D. 1980. A summary of user experience with the SQL data sublanguage. In *Proceedings of the International Conference on Databases* (Aberdeen, Scotland, July), S. M. Deen and P. Hammersley, Eds. Heyden, London, pp. 181–203.

CHANDY, K. M., BROWN, J. C., DISSLEY, C. W., AND UHRIG, W. R. 1975. Analytic models for rollback and recovery strategies in data base systems. *IEEE Trans. Softw. Eng. SE-1*, 1 (Mar.), 100–110.

CHEN, T. C. 1978. Computer technology and the database user. In *Proceedings of the 4th International Conference on Very Large Database Systems* (Berlin, Oct.). IEEE, New York, pp. 72–86.

CODASYL 1973. *CODASYL DDL Journal of Development* June Report. Available from IFIP Administrative Data Processing Group, 40 Paulus Potterstraat, Amsterdam.

CODASYL 1978. CODASYL: Report of the Data Description Language Committee. *Inf. Syst. 3*, 4, 247–320.

CODD, E. F. 1982. Relational database: A practical foundation for productivity. *Commun. ACM 25*, 2 (Feb.), 109–117.

DATE, C. J. 1981. *An Introduction to Database Systems*, 3rd ed. Addison-Wesley, Reading, Mass.

DAVIES, C. T. 1973. Recovery semantics for a DB/DC System. In *Proceedings of the ACM 73 National Conference,* (Atlanta, Ga., Aug. 27–29). ACM, New York, pp. 136–141.

DAVIES, C. T. 1978. Data processing spheres of control. *IBM Syst. J. 17*, 2, 179–198.

EFFELSBERG, W., HAERDER, T., REUTER, A., AND SCHULZE-BOHL, J. 1981. Performance measurement in database systems—Modeling, interpretation and evaluation. In *Informatik Fachberichte 41*. Springer-Verlag, Berlin, pp. 279–293 (in German).

ELHARDT, K. 1982. The database cache—Principles of operation. Ph.D. dissertation, Technical University of Munich, Munich, West Germany (in German).

ESWARAN, K. P., GRAY, J. N., LORIE, R. A., AND TRAIGER, I. L. 1976. The notions of consistency and predicate locks in a database system. *Commun. ACM 19*, 11 (Nov.), 624–633.

GRAY, J. 1978. Notes on data base operating systems. In *Lecture Notes on Computer Science*, vol. 60, R. Bayer, R. N. Graham, and G. Seegmueller, Eds. Springer-Verlag, New York.

GRAY, J. 1981. The transaction concept: Virtues and limitations. In *Proceedings of the 7th International Conference on Very Large Database Systems* (Cannes, France, Sept. 9–11). ACM, New York, pp. 144–154.

GRAY, J., LORIE, R., PUTZOLU, F., AND TRAIGER, I. L. 1976. Granularity of locks and degrees of consistency in a large shared data base. In *Modeling in Data Base Management Systems.* Elsevier North-Holland, New York, pp. 365–394.

GRAY, J., MCJONES, P., BLASGEN, M., LINDSAY, B., LORIE, R., PRICE, T., PUTZOLU, F., AND TRAIGER, I. L. 1981. The recovery manager of the System R database manager. *ACM Comput. Surv. 13*, 2 (June), 223–242.

HAERDER, T., AND REUTER, A. 1979. Optimization of logging and recovery in a database system. In *Database Architecture*, G. Bracchi, Ed. Elsevier North-Holland, New York, pp. 151–168.

HAERDER, T., AND REUTER, A. 1983. Concepts for implementing a centralized database management system. In *Proceedings of the International Computing Symposium* (Invited Paper) (Nuernberg, W. Germany, Apr.), H. J. Schneider, Ed. German Chapter of ACM, B. G. Teubner, Stuttgart, pp. 28–60.

IMS/VS-DB N.d. IMS/VS-DB Primer, IBM World Trade Center, Palo Alto, July 1976.

KOHLER, W. H. 1981. A survey of techniques for synchronization and recovery in decentralized computer systems. *ACM Comput. Surv. 13*, 2 (June), 149–183.

LAMPSON, B. W., AND STURGIS, H. E. 1979. Crash recovery in a distributed data storage system. XEROX Res. Rep. Palo Alto, Calif. Submitted for publication.

LINDSAY, B. G., SELINGER, P. G., GALTIERI, C., GRAY, J. N., LORIE, R., PRICE, T. G., PUTZOLU, F., TRAIGER, I. L., AND WADE, B. W. 1979. Notes on distributed databases. IBM Res. Rep. RJ 2571, San Jose, Calif.

LORIE, R. A. 1977. Physical integrity in a large segmented database. *ACM Trans. Database Sys. 2*, 1 (Mar.), 91–104.

REUTER, A. 1980. A fast transaction-oriented logging scheme for UNDO-recovery. *IEEE Trans. Softw. Eng. SE-6* (July), 348–356.

REUTER, A. 1981. *Recovery in Database Systems.* Carl Hanser Verlag, Munich (in German).

REUTER, A. 1982. Performance Analysis of Recovery Techniques, Res. Rep., Computer Science Department, Univ. of Kaiserslautern, 1982. To be published.

SENKO, M. E., ALTMAN, E. B., ASTRAHAN, M. M., AND FEHBER, P. L. 1973. Data structures and accessing in data base systems. *IBM Syst. J. 12*, 1 (Jan.), 30–93.

SEVERANCE, D. G., AND LOHMAN, G. M. 1976. Differential files: Their application to the maintenance of large databases. *ACM Trans. Database Syst. 1*, 3 (Sept.), 256–267.

SMITH, D. D. P., AND SMITH, J. M. 1979. Relational database machines. *IEEE Comput. 12*, 3 28–38.

STONEBRAKER, M. 1980. Retrospection on a database system. *ACM Trans. Database Syst. 5*, 2 (June), 225–240.

STONEBRAKER, M., WONG, E., KREPS, P., AND HELD, G. 1976. The design and implementation of INGRES. *ACM Trans. Database Syst. 1*, 3 (Sept.), 189–222.

STURGIS, H., MITCHELL, J., AND ISRAEL, J. 1980. Issues in the design and use of a distributed file system. *ACM Oper. Syst. Rev. 14*, 3 (July), 55–69.

TANDEM. N.d. TANDEM 16, ENSCRIBE Data Base Record Manager, Programming Manual, TANDEM Computer Inc., Cupertino.

UDS, N.d. UDS, Universal Data Base Management System, UDS-V2 Reference Manual Package, Siemens AG, Munich, West Germany.

VERHOFSTADT, J. M. 1978. Recovery techniques for database systems. *ACM Comput. Surv. 10*, 2 (June), 167–195.

Received January 1980; Revised May 1982; final revision accepted January 1984

# The Performance of Alternative Strategies for Dealing with Deadlocks in Database Management Systems

*Rakesh Agrawal*

AT&T Bell Laboratories
Murray Hill, NJ 07974

*Michael J. Carey*
*Lawrence W. McVoy*

Computer Sciences Department
University of Wisconsin
Madison, WI 53706

**Abstract** — There is growing evidence that, for a fairly wide variety of database workloads and system configurations, locking is the concurrency control strategy of choice. With locking, of course, comes the possibility of deadlocks. Although the database literature is full of algorithms for dealing with deadlocks, very little in the way of practical performance information is available to a database system designer faced with the decision of choosing a good deadlock resolution strategy. This paper is an attempt to bridge this gap in our understanding of the behavior and performance of alternative deadlock resolution strategies. We employ a simulation model of a database environment to study the relative performance of several strategies based on deadlock detection, several strategies based on deadlock prevention, and a strategy based on timeouts. We show that the choice of the best deadlock resolution strategy depends upon the level of data contention, the resource utilization levels, and the types of transactions. We provide guidelines for selecting a deadlock resolution strategy for different operating regions.

**Index terms** — Database systems, concurrency control, transaction processing, deadlock, modeling and simulation.

## 1. INTRODUCTION

It was shown in a recent performance study that, for a fairly wide variety of database workloads and system configurations, a concurrency control algorithm based on two-phase locking [8], [9], [15], [18] will outperform concurrency control algorithms that use transaction restarts rather than blocking to resolve conflicts between transactions [2]. This result was found to be particularly true under models of realistic hardware configurations with limited physical resources. With two-phase locking, of course, comes the possibility of deadlock [8], [9], [18]. Since locking realizes consistency by blocking transactions whose lock requests cannot be granted, two (or more) transactions may hold locks needed by each other, consequently blocking each other's execution forever.

Given that locking is the concurrency control strategy of choice, it is imperative that the problem of deadlock and the performance of various deadlock resolution strategies be well understood. The database literature is full of algorithms that either detect and resolve deadlocks or somehow prevent deadlocks from happening [1], [5], [6], [7], [12], [13], [16], [17], [18], [22], [23], [25], [26], [27], [28], [29], [31], [32], [37], [39]. There have been several analytical studies devoted to estimating the probability of deadlocks [19], [33], [40], [41], but very little in the way of practical performance information is available to the database system designer who is faced with the decision of choosing a good deadlock resolution strategy. The only significant performance studies of deadlock resolution strategies that we have seen are an early study by Munz and Krenz [30] and a more recent study by Balter, Berard, and Decitre [5]. In [30], eleven methods for selecting a transaction to restart once a deadlock has been detected were compared. Although the study involved some 600 simulation runs, the paper contains little in the way of details about the simulation model and the range of parameters considered. In [5], five deadlock resolution strategies were com-

EH0252-7/87/0000/0311$01.00 © 1987 IEEE

pared using simulation. Their simulation model description is also somewhat vague, and no details are given regarding the simulation parameter values used in the study. In addition, they did not model disk and CPU resources or their limits in any detail in their simulation model. Instead, they simply assumed that all transactions can be processed in parallel in the absence of concurrency control conflicts, an assumption that has since been shown to have a significant influence on the conclusions of concurrency control performance studies [2]. We will look more closely at the results of these two studies later on.

The intent of this paper is to bridge the gap in our understanding of the behavior and performance of alternative strategies for dealing with the problem of deadlock in centralized database systems. We begin by establishing a reasonably complete simulation model of a database management system. Our model captures the main elements of a database environment, including both users (terminals, the source of transactions) and physical resources for storing and processing the data (disks and CPUs) in addition to the usual components used in models for studying deadlock (workload and database characteristics). We then study and compare the relative performance of three different classes of deadlock resolution strategies [8, 18], including several strategies based on deadlock detection, several strategies based on deadlock prevention, and a strategy that deals with the problem through the use of timeouts. Our study examines the relative performance of these strategies over a wide range of multiprogramming levels (and thus conflict probabilities), and both non-interactive and interactive workload types are considered.

The organization of the remainder of the paper is as follows. In Section 2 we describe the alternative deadlock resolution strategies that are examined in this paper. Our performance study is based on simulations of a closed queuing model of a single-site database system. The structure and characteristics of our simulator are described in Section 3. Section 4 presents the performance experiments and our results. Finally, Section 5 summarizes the main conclusions of this study.

## 2. DEADLOCK RESOLUTION STRATEGIES

Deadlocks are usually characterized in terms of a waits-for graph [14], [18], [21]. In a database context, a waits-for graph $G$ is a directed graph where each vertex represents a transaction; each edge of the form $T_i \rightarrow T_j \in G$ means that transaction $T_i$ is waiting for transaction $T_j$ (e.g., because $T_j$ owns a lock that $T_i$ wants). It has been shown that there exists a deadlock if and only if there is a cycle in the waits-for graph [14], [21].

We classify deadlock resolution strategies into three broad classes based on whether they require explicit maintenance of the waits-for graph and on whether or not a transaction that is not necessarily involved in a deadlock may be restarted for deadlock resolution purposes. These three classes of deadlock resolution strategies, *detection*, *prevention*, and *timeout* strategies, are described in more detail in this section. We also describe the particular instances of these three classes of strategies whose performance is studied in this paper. Before describing the various strategies of interest, however, we elaborate briefly on the issue of how waits-for information is maintained.

In addition to the waits-for graph described above, a typical lock manager maintains a lock table for keeping track of locks. This table contains an entry for every locked object, including such information as a list of its current lockers, the mode that it is locked in, and a queue of transactions that are waiting to obtain a lock on the object [18]. To illustrate how waits-for information is derived from these entries, suppose that transaction $T_1$ holds a read lock on $X$, $T_2$ is waiting for a write lock on $X$, $T_3$ and $T_4$ are waiting behind $T_2$ for read locks on $X$[1], and $T_5$ is at the back of the queue waiting for a write lock on $X$. This situation would be represented in the waits-for graph as the set of edges $\{T_2 \rightarrow T_1, T_3 \rightarrow T_2, T_4 \rightarrow T_2, T_5 \rightarrow T_3, T_5 \rightarrow T_4\}$. That is, each member of $X$'s waiting queue is waiting for the first transaction or group of transactions in front of it with which it conflicts.

### 2.1. Deadlock Detection

Strategies based on deadlock detection require that the waits-for graph be explicitly built and maintained. In *continuous detection*, the waits-for graph is always kept cycle-free by checking for (and breaking) cycles every time a transaction blocks. The connected component of the waits-for graph involving the newly blocked transaction is searched using a cycle detection algorithm [4]. In *periodic detection*, the graph is searched only periodically for cycles, and all connected components of the graph must be searched in this case. Selecting an appropriate time interval for periodic detection is a problem, and we will study the effects of different time intervals for periodic deadlock detection.

---

[1]Fairness dictates that, even though the lock requests from $T_3$ and $T_4$ are compatible with the current lock on $X$, they must wait until $T_2$'s request has been granted because their requests were made after $T_2$ made its request. Otherwise, read requests can lead to starvation of write requests [18].

An associated problem is that of selecting a transaction or set of transactions to restart in order to break any deadlock cycles that form. We will consider the following *victim selection* criteria:

(1) *Current Blocker*: Pick the transaction that blocked the most recently (i.e., the one that just blocked, the current blocker, in the case of continuous detection).

(2) *Random Blocker*: Pick a transaction at random from among the participants in the deadlock cycle.

(3) *Min Locks*: Pick the transaction that is holding the fewest locks.

(4) *Youngest*: Pick the transaction with the most recent initial startup time (i.e., the one that began running the most recently).

(5) *Min Work*: Pick the transaction that has consumed the least amount of physical resources (CPU + I/O time) since it first began running.

The first of these five victim selection criteria picks the most convenient transaction to restart in the continuous detection case, and the second criterion simply picks any transaction. The latter three criteria for victim selection attempt to restart the least expensive transaction, the difference among these criteria being the metric used by each to predict expensiveness. Following the lead in [30], we have not considered any victim selection criteria that selects the most expensive transaction, such as the transaction that is holding largest number of locks or that has consumed largest amount of physical resources. It was shown in [30] that the least expensive counterparts of these criteria always have better performance.

One detail needs to be mentioned at this point. It is possible that multiple cycles may be encountered in the waits-for graph, in which case more than one victim may be selected. Our implementation of deadlock detection follows the advice given by Gray in [18], which suggests repeatedly selecting a victim from each detected cycle according to the victim selection criteria until the graph is free of cycles. This approach was suggested by Gray (and adopted for our use) because the problem of selecting the least expensive set of transactions to break all cycles is NP-hard [18].

### 2.2. Deadlock Prevention

In deadlock prevention, the waits-for graph is not explicitly maintained. Deadlocks are prevented by never allowing blocked states that can lead to circular waiting. We consider the following set of deadlock *prevention* algorithms:

(1) *Wound-Wait*: If a lock request from transaction $T_i$ leads to a conflict with another transaction $T_j$, resolve the conflict as follows: If $T_i$ started running before $T_j$ did, then restart $T_j$ ("$T_i$ wounds $T_j$"); otherwise, block $T_i$ ("$T_i$ waits for $T_j$"). This algorithm is due to Rosenkrantz, Stearns, and Lewis [37]. Deadlocks cannot occur, as a transaction can be blocked only by an older transaction, and therefore cycles cannot form in the waits-for graph. Thus, wound-wait is a preemptive algorithm in which older transactions run through the system killing any younger ones that they conflict with, waiting only for older conflicting transactions.

(2) *Wait-Die*: If a lock request from transaction $T_i$ leads to a conflict with another transaction $T_j$, resolve the conflict as follows: If $T_i$ started up earlier than $T_j$, then block $T_i$ ("$T_i$ waits for $T_j$"); otherwise, restart $T_i$ ("$T_i$ dies"). This algorithm is also due to Rosenkrantz, Stearns, and Lewis [37]. Again, deadlocks are impossible because a transaction can only be blocked by an older transaction. Wait-die is a non-preemptive counterpart to the wound-wait deadlock prevention algorithm.

(3) *Immediate-Restart*: If a lock request from transaction $T_i$ leads to a conflict with another transaction $T_j$, then simply restart $T_i$. In this algorithm, due to Tay [40], [41], deadlocks are impossible because no transaction is ever blocked.

(4) *Running-Priority*: If a lock request from transaction $T_i$ leads to a conflict with another transaction $T_j$, resolve the conflict as follows: If $T_j$ is currently waiting due to some other conflict, then restart $T_j$ and grant $T_i$'s lock request; otherwise, if $T_j$ is active, then block $T_i$. This algorithm is due to Franaszek and Robinson [16], and the idea is not to allow blocked transactions to impede the progress of active transactions. In this algorithm, then, a transaction is blocked only when waiting for an active transaction — it is similar in nature to wound-wait, except that running (instead of older) transactions are favored. Deadlock cycles are impossible because no transaction ever waits for another waiting transaction.

Observe that in deadlock prevention, a restarted transaction is not necessarily involved in an actual deadlock cycle. Deadlock prevention policies are thus conservative in nature, trading more restarts for the purpose of preventing possible deadlocks.

## 2.3. Timeout

In the case of the *timeout* strategy for dealing with deadlocks, a transaction whose lock request cannot be granted is simply placed in the blocked queue. The transaction is later restarted if its wait time exceeds some threshold value. Thus, like the detection strategies, timeout will restart transactions that are actually involved in deadlocks; like the prevention strategies, timeout may also restart some transactions that are not involved in any cycle (when the transaction has been waiting a long time but no cycle of waiting transactions actually exists). As we will see in Section 4, selecting an appropriate threshold value is a problem with the timeout approach. We will examine the effect of different threshold values on the performance of this strategy.

# 3. SIMULATION MODEL

Our simulator for studying the performance of the deadlock resolution strategies is based on the closed queuing model of a single-site database system depicted in Figure 1. This model is the same simulation model that was used in [2], which is a model that has its origins in the models of [34], [35], [36] and [10], [11]. There are a fixed number of terminals from which transactions originate. There is a limit to the number of transactions allowed to be active at any time in the system, the multiprogramming level *mpl*. A transaction is considered active if it is either receiving service or waiting for service inside the database system. When a new transaction originates, if the system already has a full set of active transactions, it enters the *ready queue* where it waits for a currently active transaction to complete or abort (transactions in the ready queue are not considered active). The transaction then enters the *cc queue* (concurrency control queue) and makes the first of its lock requests. If the lock request is granted, the transaction proceeds to the *object queue* and accesses its first object. If more than one object is to be accessed, the transaction reenters the concurrency control queue and makes its next lock request prior to accessing the object. It is assumed for modeling convenience that a transaction performs all of its reads before performing any writes. We also examine the performance of deadlock resolution strategies under interactive workloads. The think path in the model provides an optional random delay that follows object accesses for this purpose.

If one of the transaction's lock requests leads to a lock conflict, the concurrency control module takes actions that are dependent upon the deadlock resolution strategy being used. For example, in the case of continuous deadlock detection, it checks whether blocking the current transaction will result in a cycle in the waits-for graph; if so, then the victim-selection criteria is applied to select the transaction(s) to be restarted. In the case of periodic deadlock detection, the transaction is simply added to the waits-for graph, with no check for cycles in the graph being made at this time. In the case of deadlock prevention, no waits-for graph is maintained; a decision is taken either to block the current transaction or to restart some transaction based on the prevention scheme being employed. In the case of timeout, the current transaction is always simply blocked.

If the result of a lock request is that the transaction must block, it enters the *blocked queue* until it is once again able to proceed. If a request leads to a decision to restart a transaction, the restarted transaction goes to the back of the ready queue after a restart delay period. It then begins making all of the *same* concurrency control requests and object accesses over again. The duration of the restart delay is exponential with a mean equal to the running average of the transaction response times — that is, the duration of the delay is *adaptive*, depending on the observed average response time. We chose to employ an adaptive delay after performing a sensitivity analysis that showed us that the performance of deadlock resolution strategies is sensitive to the restart delay time. Our experiments indicated that a delay of about one transaction time is best, and that throughput begins to drop off rapidly when the delay exceeds more than a few transaction times. To model periodic deadlock detection, an event is scheduled at fixed time intervals that checks for cycles in the waits-for graph and selects a victim (or victims) to break any and all cycles. To model timeouts, a timeout event is scheduled each time a transaction is blocked. If the blocked transaction is still blocked at the end of the threshold time period, it is restarted.

Eventually, when the transaction completes, one of two things happens. If the transaction is read-only, it is finished. If it has written one or more objects during its execution, however, the transaction first enters the *update queue* and writes its deferred updates into the database. Locks are released together at end-of-transaction after any deferred updates have been performed.

Underlying the logical model of Figure 1 are two physical resource types, CPU resources and I/O (disk) resources. Associated with the concurrency control, object access, and deferred update services in Figure 1 are some use of one or both of these two resource types. The amounts of CPU and I/O time per logical service are specified as simulation parameters. The physical queuing model is depicted in Figure 2, and Table 1 summarizes its associated simulation parameters. As shown, the physical model is a collection of terminals, CPU servers, and I/O servers. (While the model permits an arbitrary number of each class of server, as shown in Figure 2, our experiments will all be based on a configuration with one CPU server and two I/O servers. The sufficiency of this configuration for our purposes will be addressed in Section 4.) The delay paths for the think and restart delays are also reflected in the physical queuing model. Requests in the CPU queue are serviced FCFS (first-come, first-served), except that concurrency control requests have priority over all other service requests. Our I/O model is that of a database where the data is spread out evenly across all of the disks. There is a queue associated with each of the I/O servers; when a transaction needs service, it chooses an I/O server (at random, with all I/O servers being equally likely) and waits in the queue associated with the selected server. The service discipline for the I/O queues is FCFS.

The parameters *obj_io* and *obj_cpu* in Table 1 are the amounts of I/O and CPU time associated with reading or writing an object. Reading an object takes resources equal to *obj_io* followed by *obj_cpu*. Writing an object takes resources equal to *obj_cpu* at the time of the write request and *obj_io* at deferred update time, as it is assumed that transactions maintain deferred update lists in buffers in main memory. These parameters represent constant service time requirements rather than stochastic ones for simplicity. The *ext_think_time* parameter is the mean of an exponential time distribution which determines the time delay between the completion of a transaction and the initiation of a new transaction from a terminal. Finally, the *int_think_time* parameter is the mean of an exponential time distribution which determines the intra-transaction think time for the model (if any). To model interactive workloads, transactions can be made to undergo a thinking period between finishing their reads and starting their writes.

A transaction is modeled according to the number of objects that it reads and writes. The parameter *tran_size* is the average number of objects read by a transaction, the mean of a uniform distribution between *min_size* and *max_size* (inclusive). These objects are randomly chosen (without replacement) from among all of the objects in the database. The probability that an object read by a transaction will also be written is determined by the parameter *write_prob*. The size of the database is assumed to be *db_size*.

## 4. PERFORMANCE EXPERIMENTS

We ran a number of simulation experiments to study the performance of the alternative deadlock resolution strategies described in Section 2. We present the experiments and their results in this section. Experiment 1 examines the performance of the different victim selection criteria for continuous deadlock detection. Experiment 2 studies periodic deadlock detection, looking at how the detection interval size affects its performance and at how it compares to continuous deadlock detection. Experiment 3 examines the use of timeouts for handling deadlocks, looking at the question of how to choose an appropriate timeout interval. Finally, Experiment 4 compares the performance of the best deadlock detection alternative with that of the timeout strategy and the four deadlock prevention strategies (wound-wait, wait-die, immediate-restart, and running-priority). At the end of this section we discuss how our results on alternative deadlock resolution schemes compare with those reported by others.

Table 2 gives the simulation parameter values used for the experiments reported here. The database and transaction sizes were selected so as to jointly yield a region of operation which allows the interesting performance effects to be observed without necessitating impossibly long simulation times. These sizes are expressed in pages, as we equate objects and pages in this study. The multiprogramming level is varied between a limit of 5 transactions and a limit of the total number of terminals[2], set to 200 in this study, to allow a range of conflict probabilities to be investigated. The object processing costs were chosen based on our notion of roughly what realistic values might be. We employed a modified form of the batch means method [38] for our statistical data analyses, and each simulation was run for 20 batches with a large batch time to produce sufficiently tight 90% confidence intervals.[3] The actual batch time varied from experiment to experiment, but the throughput confidence intervals were typically in the range of plus or minus a few percent of the mean value, more than sufficient for our purposes. We discuss only the statistically significant performance differences when summarizing our results.

We investigated the performance of the algorithms in a configuration with one CPU server and two I/O servers. We considered two types of transaction workloads, a non-interactive workload, in which transactions have no intra-transaction think time, and an interactive workload, in which transactions perform a number of reads, then think for some period of time (their "internal think time", during which read locks are held), and then perform their writes. Besides being of interest in their own right, we found in [2] that an interactive transaction mix with a large intra-transaction (internal) think time causes a system with finite

[2]Keep in mind that the multiprogramming level simply serves to bound the number of active transactions in the system, not to strictly determine it. It is likely that fewer than *mpl* transactions will actually be ready to run when *mpl* = *num_terms* because of the external think time for the terminals.

[3] More information on the details of the modified batch means method may be found in [10].

| Parameter | Meaning |
|---|---|
| *db_size* | number of objects in database |
| *tran_size* | mean size of transaction |
| *max_size* | size of largest transaction |
| *min_size* | size of smallest transaction |
| *write_prob* | Pr(write X I read X) |
| *num_terms* | number of terminals |
| *mpl* | multiprogramming level |
| *ext_think_time* | mean time between transactions (per terminal) |
| *int_think_time* | mean intra-transaction think time (optional) |
| *obj_io* | I/O time for accessing an object |
| *obj_cpu* | CPU time for accessing an object |
| *num_cpus* | number of CPU servers |
| *num_disks* | number of I/O servers |

Table 1: Simulation Parameters.

physical resources (CPUs and disks) to behave as if the system had infinite resources. Based on the results in [2], it is safe to say that these two workload types are representative of the results that would be obtained over a wide range of resource configurations (i.e., numbers of CPU and I/O servers) and over a wide range of think times. Briefly, it was found that when the "useful" utilization[4] of the bottleneck resource type is moderately high (60-70% and above), the non-interactive workload results are good indicators of relative performance; for low utilizations (40-50% and below), interactive workloads with high intra-transaction think times are good indicators of relative performance (regardless of why the utilizations are low, whether due to an interactive workload or to large numbers of CPUs and disks). We chose the interactive transaction approach to approximating infinite resource behavior for this study because it is very expensive to run simulations for system configurations that have many CPU and I/O servers (or truly infinite resources).

We also found in [2] that for larger values of the database size (for 10,000 objects), conflicts became very rare; when conflicts are rare, all concurrency control algorithms perform alike (as shown in [2], [3], [10], [11] and a number of other studies). Since we were interested in investigating *differences* in the performance of alternative deadlock resolution strategies, we have not varied the size of the database as a simulation parameter. The size used here provides a wide range of conflict probabilities over the large range of multiprogramming levels used. Also, we feel that it is important to study workloads with non-negligible conflict levels in order to understand how the algorithms will perform under heavy conflict workloads or when "hot spots" exist in the database. Finally, we have also not varied transaction size as a simulation parameter here because varying the multiprogramming level for a fixed size database provides a similar range of conflict levels of interest.

| Parameter | Value |
|---|---|
| *db_size* | 1000 pages |
| *tran_size* | 8 page readset |
| *max_size* | 12 page readset (maximum) |
| *min_size* | 4 page readset (minimum) |
| *write_prob* | 0.25 |
| *num_terms* | 200 terminals |
| *mpl* | 5, 10, 25, 50, 75, 100, and 200 transactions |
| *ext_think_time (non-interactive)* | 1 second |
| *int_think_time (non-interactive)* | 0 seconds |
| *ext_think_time (interactive)* | 21 seconds |
| *int_think_time (interactive)* | 10 seconds |
| *obj_io* | 35 milliseconds |
| *obj_cpu* | 15 milliseconds |
| *num_cpus* | 1 |
| *num_disks* | 2 |

Table 2: Simulation Parameter Settings.

[4] We will explain the difference between total and useful resource utilization in Section 4.4.

### 4.1. Experiment 1: Continuous Detection

Our first experiment examined the effectiveness of the alternative victim selection criteria for continuous deadlock detection. Figures 3 and 4, respectively, show the throughputs (in transactions per second) obtained for the five criteria for the non-interactive type of transactions, where the resources are highly utilized, and for the interactive workload, where the resources have low utilizations. Although we also recorded the corresponding response time results, we omit them — they display the same relative trends, conveying no important additional information.

In both the non-interactive and interactive cases, for low levels of multiprogramming, the performance of the different victim selection criteria is almost identical. There are just not many deadlocks to differentiate the criteria. However, as the multiprogramming level is increased, the *random* selection criterion begins to lose out; so does the *current blocker* criterion, which is also a random selection in some sense. The *youngest*, *min locks*, and *min work* selection criteria, which attempt to restart the least expensive transaction, begin providing better performance as the multiprogramming level is increased. The reader may be surprised at first, as we were, by the superior performance of the *min locks* selection criterion as compared to the *min work* criterion. The explanation lies in the fact that a restarted transaction that is holding a large number of locks, although it may have consumed somewhat fewer resources as compared to some other transactions with fewer locks, would have to contend for all of its locks again — with the possibility of getting blocked or restarted at each lock request.[5] Figures 5 and 6 give the blocking ratio (the ratio of blocked lock requests to the number of transactions executed) and the restart ratio (the ratio of restarted transactions to the number of transactions executed) for the interactive workload case. Note that the *min locks* blocking and restart ratios are the lowest among all of the victim selection criteria. Similar trends were seen in the non-interactive workload case.

In examining the results of this experiment, we came to the conclusion that there are several *stability* properties that a given deadlock resolution mechanism might have, and we hypothesize that these properties are desirable ones:

*Guaranteed forward progress.* At any time, there is at least one transaction in the system that can be guaranteed to finish.

*No repeated restarts.* No one transaction may be restarted over and over again an indefinite number of times.

While having these properties will not guarantee superior performance for an algorithm, the absence of these properties may make an algorithm unstable and therefore likely to perform poorly in high conflict situations. Our results bear out this hypothesis, at least to some extent. Of the victim selection criteria studied here, only the *youngest* criterion has these two stability properties — the oldest transaction in the system is ensured of being able to finish without being restarted, and (by induction) every transaction will eventually become the oldest one and then finish. As a result, the *youngest* criterion performs moderately well. Both the *random* and *current blocker* criteria lack both stability properties. With these criteria, any transaction with at least one lock request remaining can be restarted when it makes the request, and they do nothing to protect a transaction from being repeatedly restarted (particularly if two or more transactions are attempting to read and then write the same object). Consequently, the *random* and *current blocker* criteria have inferior performance at high multiprogramming levels. The *min work* and *min locks* criteria don't have these stability properties in the strict sense. This is because it is possible for the transaction with the most locks or having consumed the most resources to be "passed" by another transaction. However, they do have *pseudo-stability* — the number of locks held and the amount of resources consumed are likely to be closely correlated with the age of the transaction. Also, they seem to be probabilistically stable; for example, the transaction with the most locks is unlikely to be passed by many other transactions, so it is fairly safe from being restarted using *min locks* (like an old transaction in the *youngest* policy).

---

[5] It should be noted here that all objects in our database model have the same granularity. In a system that supports granularity hierarchies, such as System R [18], the simple lock counting scheme would probably have to be modified to account for the number of objects associated with each lock.

### 4.2. Experiment 2: Periodic Detection

As was mentioned in Section 2, a problem with periodic deadlock detection is determining the time interval at which the detection algorithm should be periodically performed. Experiment 2 considered the choice of a deadlock detection interval and also compared the performance of periodic detection (with a good interval) to that of continuous detection. Based on the results of Experiment 1, we used the *min locks* victim selection policy here for for both continuous and periodic detection. We found in several preliminary experiments (not reported here) that the choice of the best victim selection criteria is independent of whether continuous or periodic detection is performed, which is not surprising.

#### 4.2.1. Deadlock Detection Interval

The deadlock detection interval selection portion of Experiment 2 was performed for a low level of multiprogramming (10) and for a high level of multiprogramming (100). Both the high resource utilization (non-interactive workload) and the low resource utilization (interactive workload) cases were considered. The throughput results are summarized in Figure 7. As the detection interval is increased, performance degrades significantly, particularly for large multiprogramming levels. This is because deadlocked transactions that are blocked while holding locks that are required by other transactions increase contention further if they are restarted later. In this experiment, we assumed that the waits-for graph is maintained in main memory,[6] and hence that cycle detection can be performed very efficiently. We also ignored the context-switching overhead involved in taking a timer interrupt, turning control over to the deadlock detection process, and then returning control to one of the transactions. This is why throughput does not suffer at all when the detection interval becomes quite small. In an actual system, throughput would probably decrease slightly for the smallest interval sizes due to the cost of context switching (which is probably about a millisecond or so in a typical system, for two context switches, associated transient cache misses, etc.). We will comment further on these cost modeling issues shortly.

#### 4.2.2. Periodic Versus Continuous Detection

The second half of Experiment 2 considered the performance of periodic versus continuous deadlock detection. Based on the preceding results, a time interval of 500 milliseconds was used for periodic detection in the non-interactive workload case, and a 1 second interval was used in the interactive case. The time interval for each class of workload was chosen by selecting the largest interval where neither the $MPL = 10$ nor the $MPL = 100$ throughput curves had dropped off significantly yet in Figure 7. This provides for a reasonable time gap between detections while not handicapping the periodic deadlock detection algorithm due to an overly large time interval for either class of workload.

Figures 8 and 9 show the throughput results obtained for the non-interactive and interactive workloads, respectively, and Figures 10 and 11 show the associated conflict ratios. As shown, the performance of continuous detection is generally slightly better than that of periodic detection. The difference is due to the fact that failure to detect deadlocks early results in somewhat longer blocking times for transactions, leading to higher blocking and restart ratios (as shown in Figures 10 and 11). The performance difference is more significant in the interactive case (Figure 9), where continuous deadlock detection outperforms periodic detection by about 10% at the highest multiprogramming levels. For most of the multiprogramming levels, however, the performance difference is fairly minimal.

Further discussion regarding detection costs is in order at this point. We chose not to include the cost of deadlock detection in our algorithm models for several reasons, not the least of which was that we did not believe we could model such an implementation-dependent cost realistically (so an attempt to do so would probably not lead to convincing results). However, we believe that continuous detection is probably cheaper than periodic detection for several reasons. In periodic detection, the high cost of context switching is likely to dominate the cost of running the detection routine itself — deadlock detection simply involves doing a depth-first search of each connected component of the waits-for graph, which costs $O(N^2)$ where $N$ is the number of blocked transactions [1]. $N$ is likely to be small, being just a fraction of the multiprogramming level. With continuous detection, no context switch is necessary — the blocking transaction is already inside the lock manager when detection is required. In addition, only the connected

[6] In System R and IMS, for example, the lock table is held in main memory [20].

component containing the current blocking transaction needs to be searched for continuous detection, so the worst-case cycle search cost is just $O(N)$ [1]. Thus, although continuous detection will involve more frequent checking, it appears likely to be less costly overall.[7]

### 4.3. Experiment 3: Timeout Interval

We performed a sensitivity analysis to examine the impact of the timeout interval on the performance of the timeout method for deadlock resolution, and also to see if we could discover a reasonable heuristic for selecting the timeout interval. The sensitivity analysis was performed for a low multiprogramming level (10) and a high multiprogramming level (100) both for the non-interactive and interactive workloads. Figure 12 summarizes the throughput results. As one would expect, the shape of the timeout throughput curve is convex. There is an optimal timeout value for a given level of multiprogramming and workload; smaller values degrade performance through too many restarts, and larger values degrade performance by blocking too many transactions for excessively long times. Note that the ideal timeout interval value varies with both the multiprogramming level and the nature of the workload.

One way of choosing the timeout interval would be to relate it in some way to the waiting time of a blocked request, $W$. The basis for this heuristic is that ideally the timeout interval should be just long enough to allow a blocked request to complete its waiting. We experimented with an adaptive version of the timeout algorithm where the timeout interval was dynamically adjusted to a running estimate of the value $avg(W) + k * \sigma(W)$, where $\sigma(W)$ is the standard deviation of the request waiting time. We ran simulations where $k$ was taken to be 0, 1, and 2. Figure 13 summarizes the throughput results from this experiment for these three values of $k$. The best overall results were obtained for the dynamically adjusted timeout interval of $avg(W) + \sigma(W)$ (i.e., for $k = 1$).

### 4.4. Experiment 4: Detection, Prevention, and Timeout Performance

In Experiment 4, the most important of the experiments that we ran, we compared the performance of continuous deadlock detection, the four deadlock prevention strategies (wound-wait, wait-die, immediate-restart, and running-priority), and the timeout algorithm. Based on the results of Experiment 1, *min locks* was chosen to be the victim selection criteria for continuous deadlock detection. Periodic deadlock detection is not included here since it has already been dealt with separately. The adaptive version of the timeout algorithm was used in this experiment, with the timeout interval being dynamically adjusted to a value equal to $avg(W) + \sigma(W)$. We ran this experiment for both the non-interactive and interactive workloads. We will discuss the results for the two workload types separately here, as their results are significantly different.

#### 4.4.1. The Non-Interactive Workload

The throughputs obtained with the alternative deadlock resolution strategies are summarized in Figure 14 for the non-interactive type of transactions. We again omit the response time results, as they display the same relative performance trends. For very low levels of multiprogramming, there are not enough lock conflicts to significantly differentiate between the alternative strategies. However, as the multiprogramming level is increased, differences begin to appear and a number of trends can be seen. Continuous detection emerges as the best strategy, and the immediate-restart algorithm has the worst performance of all. Wound-wait outperforms wait-die. For low levels of multiprogramming, running-priority provides somewhat better performance than wound-wait, but for high levels of multiprogramming, both wound-wait and wait-die perform significantly better than running-priority. The timeout strategy performs better than the immediate-restart strategy, but it performs worse than the other three deadlock prevention strategies. We analyze each of these trends in turn below.

The average utilization of the disks[8] (which happen to be the critical resource in our experiments) is

[7] We make this claim for a centralized system only, as message cost tradeoffs in the distributed case will make periodic detection cheaper there. We note that IBM's System R uses continuous detection, but that its distributed counterpart, System R*, uses periodic detection [24].

[8] Average disk utilization is used here because there are two disks in the simulated system; it is defined as the sum of their individual utilizations divided by two.

shown in Figures 15 and 16. The useful utilization is defined as the total utilization minus the fraction of the resource utilization that was used to process transactions that were later restarted. The figures show that, although the total disk utilization is nearly the same for all strategies, the useful utilization is strongly correlated with throughput. Figures 17 and 18 show the blocking and restart ratios for the alternative strategies. There are clearly a spectrum of blocking and restart ratios for the strategies, ranging from a combination of a zero blocking ratio and the highest restart ratio for the immediate-restart strategy to the highest blocking ratio combined with the lowest restart ratio for the continuous detection algorithm. The conclusion that one can draw is that, in a resource-limited situation, a deadlock resolution strategy that attempts to minimize the number of restarts (and hence to minimize the waste of physical resources) outperforms a strategy that relies exclusively on restarts. It is also the case that the immediate-restart strategy lacks the stability properties that were described in Section 4.1.

Both wound-wait and wait-die offer a balance between the extreme blocking and restart ratios, and each has intermediate performance. Note that wound-wait has both of the desirable stability properties described earlier — a restarted transaction will not be restarted again due to the same conflict, and the oldest transaction in the system is guaranteed to complete (and every transaction will eventually become the oldest). Wait-die has the first stability property (guaranteed progress), but it suffers from the possibility of repeated transaction restarts. A younger transaction may be repeatedly restarted by an older transaction in wait-die, whereas in wound-wait the younger transaction will wait for the older transaction to complete after being wounded by it. However, the severity of the repeated restarts problem is alleviated somewhat by the restart delay in our model. In both wound-wait and wait-die, the oldest transaction in the system is always guaranteed to finish. The restart ratios for wait-die are higher than the restart ratios for wound-wait in Figure 18, and wound-wait consequently has better performance.

The running-priority strategy is in some sense like continuous detection, but with the restriction that the wait-queue for each lock is limited to containing either one waiting writer or one set of waiting readers. It is thus not surprising that, for low multiprogramming levels where conflicts are rare and hence the average wait queue length is small, running-priority exhibits behavior like that of continuous deadlock detection. It has high blocking ratios and low restart ratios, and it outperforms wound-wait and wait-die in these cases. However, running-priority lacks the two stability properties. That is, a restarted transaction is basically random, being one that happened to be waiting at the time of a lock conflict rather than being chosen for age, lock count, or resource related reasons; consequently, no one transaction is assured of safely finishing, and there is no guarantee that an unlucky transaction will not be repeatedly restarted. For higher multiprogramming levels, then, running-priority is outperformed by wound-wait and wait-die because it lacks their stable, age-based selection of which transaction to restart.

The poor performance of the timeout strategy reflects the inherent problem of selecting a good timeout interval. Even with our adaptive version of the timeout algorithm, both the restart ratios and blocking ratios are much higher than those of wound-wait, wait-die, or running-priority, and consequently timeout has inferior performance. The timeout strategy also lacks the desired stability properties.

#### 4.4.2. The Interactive Workload

Figure 19 gives the throughput results for the alternative deadlock resolution strategies for the interactive workload case. As in the case of non-interactive transactions, the performance of the alternative strategies is not differentiable for low multiprogramming levels. As the multiprogramming level is increased, though, results very different from those for the non-interactive type workload are observed. Wound-wait emerges as the overall best strategy here, and the continuous deadlock detection strategy has the worst performance. Running-priority performs a little better than wait-die, and they both perform better than the timeout or immediate-restart algorithms. Timeout has slightly better performance than immediate-restart.

Figures 20 and 21 show the total and useful average disk utilizations for the alternative strategies, and Figures 22 and 23 give their blocking and restart ratios. On the average, transactions in our experiments require 150 milliseconds of CPU time and 350 milliseconds of disk time, so an internal think time of 10 seconds considerably reduces the average number of running (i.e., non-thinking) transactions. This reduces the demand on resources, and the resource utilizations decrease considerably. For high levels of multiprogramming, as the probability of conflicts increases, the blocking ratios increase; due to the fact that transactions think while holding locks, the lock waiting times also increase, which in turn further increases the amount of blocking. This excessive waiting in the system is the major reason for the degradation of the performance of continuous deadlock detection. Although its restart ratio increases due to deadlocks as the multiprogramming level is increased, blocking increases at much faster rate than deadlocks. The immediate-restart strategy, which is based purely on restarting a conflicting transaction, does somewhat better — because the resource utilizations are so low in this environment, the benefits attained through not blocking other transactions by waiting and holding locks outweigh the cost of wasted resources due to restarts (as reported by Tay in [40], [41]). Due to the restart delay, which is needed to prevent transactions from being restarted repeatedly in the immediate-restart algorithm, and due to the high number of restarts, a plateau is reached where increasing the multiprogramming level does not increase the number of active transactions because all other transactions are either in a think state or a restart delay state.

The best performance for the interactive workload case is achieved using a deadlock resolution strategy that balances the restart and blocking ratios, as is the case with the wound-wait strategy. Observe that the total and useful disk utilizations are also largest with this strategy (see Figures 20 and 21). Wait-die has higher restart ratios than wound-wait, causing wait-die to reach a plateau with fewer active transactions in the system than wound-wait. Running-priority attempts to limit waiting in the system by preempting blocked transactions in favor of active transactions. However, the blocking and restart ratios are much higher with running-priority compared to those for wound-wait, resulting in its relatively poorer performance. An analysis of simulation traces from running-priority and wound-wait runs showed that, in wound-wait, the major source of restarts is from write requests restarting conflicting younger read requests, which means that writers are pushing younger readers out of their way. In running-priority, however, it is common for a writer to block and wait for several active readers, and then to be subsequently restarted when a new reader arrives in the queue (since the reader will not wait for the blocked writer) — this leads to starvation of write requests under high conflicts. More restarts actually occur with wound-wait, but wound-wait has a lower restart ratio than running-priority because it also has many more commits (i.e., its restarts are productive ones). Running-priority has a higher blocking ratio because it blocks write requests before restarting them (as just described). Finally, timeout also has restart and blocking ratios which are higher than those of wound-wait, wait-die, and running-priority, explaining its lesser performance here.

### 4.5. Comparison With Other Results

It is interesting to compare our results on the performance of deadlock resolution strategies with the simulation results of Munz and Krenz [30] and those of Balter, Berard and Decitre [5]. We consider each of these studies in turn.

In [30], the relative performance of eleven victim selection algorithms was studied. They found the following three methods, each of which uses some sort of minimal cost criteria, to be considerably better than the other criteria examined — pick the transaction with the fewest locks, pick the transaction with the smallest number of exclusive locks, and pick the transaction that has done the least work (using a cost function based on CPU time, main storage occupation, and I/O activity). No clear winner among these algorithms was found. They also examined strategies where the current blocker and the most costly transaction were chosen as the victim. Our victim selection results for the non-interactive workload case concur well with theirs. For the interactive case, we found that the criterion based on the number of locks was by far the best, whereas it was just marginally best in the non-interactive case.

In [5], deadlock detection (with an unspecified victim selection algorithm), wound-wait, an "improved" version of wound-wait, wait-die, and a "modified deadlock detection" scheme were compared. The modified deadlock detection scheme was a non-preemptive version of the running-priority scheme that we have considered in this paper. It allows a transaction to wait only for an active transaction, restarting transactions that request locks that conflict with those held by waiting transactions. (Running-priority would restart the waiting transactions instead.) It was concluded that, under all conditions, for high multiprogramming levels, simple deadlock detection had the worst performance; wound-wait outperformed "improved" wound-wait and wait-die; and the modified deadlock detection performed the best of all algorithms studied. Unfortunately, the simulation model description in [5] is somewhat vague, and simulation parameter values were not specified.

Our conclusions regarding the relative performance of deadlock detection, wound-wait, and wait-die are similar to theirs under interactive workloads, but for transactions with no internal think times, our conclusions are very different. This is because Balter, Berard and Decitre did not include physical resources (disks and CPUs) in their model, effectively assuming them to be infinite by assuming that all active transactions can be processed in parallel. As explained in [2] and in Section 4, performance trends for interactive workloads that lightly load a database system are similar to those that arise when infinite resources are assumed. As for the overall better performance of the modified deadlock detection algorithm in their paper, we found in our interactive workload experiments that wound-wait consistently outperformed a similar algorithm, running-priority. Our result here also seems to contradict the result of Franaszek and Robinson that running-priority outperforms wound-wait [16]. The explanation lies in the lock modes considered in the studies — in our experiments, both read and write locks were used, whereas the studies by Balter et al and by Franaszek and Robinson considered only exclusive locks [5], [16]. The starvation problem that we described will not arise if transactions just use exclusive locks. Since real database systems usually provide both read locks and write locks, we feel that our results are probably more indicative of the real performance of the algorithms.

One further note on our performance results for wound-wait versus running-priority is in order. In our studies, all transactions were similar — they each read a number of objects, then wrote a subset of these objects, upgrading their read locks to write locks when making their write requests. Thus, virtually all transactions eventually needed to obtain one or more write locks, and write requests tended to be from older transactions than conflicting read requests. Wound-wait is favored by such a situation, and running-priority's starvation problem is particularly significant under these conditions. In order to rule out the possibility that our results were situation-specific, we ran another interactive workload experiment with two classes of transactions, pure readers and pure writers. We again found that wound-wait outperformed running-priority, but the difference was a little less pronounced in this case (wound-wait was 40% better than running-priority instead of 50% better at high multiprogramming levels). As a result of this experiment, we are quite confident that our results are indeed due to our having both read and write locks, and not to our particular choice of workload.

## 5. CONCLUSIONS

A major conclusion of this study is that the choice of the best deadlock resolution strategy is dependent upon the system's operating region. In a low conflict situation, the performance of all deadlock resolution strategies is basically identical. There are just not enough deadlocks in such situations to distinguish between the algorithms. In a situation where resources are fairly heavily utilized, continuous deadlock detection is the deadlock resolution strategy of choice. In this situation it is best to choose an algorithm that minimizes transaction restarts and hence wastes little in the way of resources. Such situations arise in database systems with physical resources and workloads such that a number of transactions tend to be competing for these resources at all times (i.e., primarily non-interactive workloads). If the transactions are primarily interactive, however, with long think times during which locks are held, then a deadlock detection strategy can cause excessive blocking and perform poorly. In such situations, an algorithm like wound-wait, which balances the blocking and restart ratios, provides the best performance. A deadlock resolution strategy such as immediate-restart, which exclusively relies on transaction restarts, was found to perform relatively poorly in both situations. Finally, continuous deadlock detection outperformed periodic deadlock detection due to the higher blocking and restart ratios associated with periodic detection, but the performance difference was generally quite small.

We presented two stability properties that we claim are desirable for deadlock resolution strategies, the first being that at any time there exists some transaction in the system that is guaranteed not to be restarted (*guaranteed progress*), and the second being that transactions cannot be restarted over and over many times (*no repeated restarts*). While having these properties will not guarantee superior performance for an algorithm, the absence of these properties may cause an algorithm to become unstable in high conflict situations. Among the victim selection criteria that we considered, the random and current victim selection criteria lack these properties, the youngest criteria has both of these properties, and the minimum locks and the minimum resources selection have approximately these stability properties. Consequently, the performance of the random and current criteria were found to be inferior to that of the other victim selection criteria. The minimum number of locks criterion was was found to be better than the other criteria because if a transaction that is holding a large number of locks is restarted, it has to contend for all of its locks again, increasing the probability of blocking and restarts. The wound-wait algorithm has both of the desired stability properties, whereas there may be repeated restarts with wait-die. Wound-wait was found to be consistently superior to wait-die. Running-priority has the nice property that it always chooses a blocked transaction in favor of a running transaction for restarting, but it lacks the stability properties. It thus has higher blocking and restart ratios as compared to wound-wait for high multiprogramming levels, resulting in inferior performance for high contention situations.

Our study highlighted the difficulty in choosing an appropriate timeout interval for the timeout strategy. It was demonstrated that the performance of timeout is sensitive to the timeout interval, and that the "right" timeout interval varies with the multiprogramming level and the transaction workload characteristics. We experimented with an adaptive version of the timeout strategy that outperformed the simple timeout strategy with its fixed timeout interval, but in no situation did timeout become the strategy of choice.

Several directions seem appropriate for future work. First, since our experiments were confined to the case of centralized database systems, an interesting open problem is the extent to which these results will extend to the distributed database case. The tradeoffs are less clear there, as message overhead adds a new dimension to the problem. Second, it would be useful to validate our simulation model by repeating the experiments in a real database system. This would require access to the source code for a real database system with an architecture that allows transactions to be blocked, restarted while blocked, and restarted while not blocked (i.e., preempted while running), as otherwise it would be necessary to rewrite much of the system's lock manager and recovery subsystem. Unfortunately, we do not currently have access to a system that meets these requirements. Finally, since our results indicate that the best choice for a deadlock resolution strategy depends on the system's level of resource utilization, which often varies over time, it would be both interesting and useful to develop criteria for dynamically choosing a deadlock resolution strategy.

## ACKNOWLEDGEMENTS

We wish to thank Rudd Canaday of AT&T Bell Laboratories for his encouragement and support of this work. The NSF-sponsored Crystal multicomputer project at the University of Wisconsin provided the many VAX 11/750 CPU-hours that were used in the course of this study.

## REFERENCES

[1] R. Agrawal, M. Carey and D. J. DeWitt, "Deadlock Detection Is Cheap", *ACM-SIGMOD Record* 13, 2 (Jan. 1983), 19-34.

[2] R. Agrawal, M. J. Carey and M. Livny, "Models for Studying Concurrency Control Performance: Alternatives and Implications", *Proc. ACM-SIGMOD 1985 Int'l Conf. on Management of Data*, May 1985, 108-121.

[3] R. Agrawal and D. J. DeWitt, "Integrated Concurrency Control and Recovery Mechanisms: Design and Performance Evaluation", *ACM Trans. Database Syst.*, 10, 4, (December 1985), 529-564.

[4] A.V. Aho, E. Hopcraft and J.D. Ullman, *The Design and Analysis of Computer Algorithms* (Chapter 5), Addison-Wesley, Reading, Mass., 1975.

[5] R. Balter, P. Berard and P. Decitre, "Why the Control of Concurrency Level in Distributed Systems is More Fundamental than Deadlock Management, *Proc. ACM SIGACT-SIGOPS Symp. on Principles of Distributed Computing*, Aug. 1982, 183-193.

[6] C. Beeri and R. Obermarck, "A Resource Class Independent Deadlock Detection Algorithm", *Proc. 7th Int'l. Conf. on Very Large Data Bases*, Sept. 1981.

[7] P. A. Bernstein, J. B. Rothnie, N. Goodman and C. H. Papadimitriou, "The Concurrency Control Mechanism of SDD-1: A System for Distributed Databases (The Fully Redundant Case)", *IEEE Trans. Software Eng.* SE-4, 3 (May 1978), 154-168.

[8] P. A. Bernstein and N. Goodman, "Concurrency Control in Distributed Database Systems", *ACM Computing Surveys* 13, 2 (June 1981), 185-221.

[9] P. A. Bernstein and N. Goodman, "A Sophisticate's Introduction to Distributed Database Concurrency Control", *Proc. 8th Int'l. Conf. on Very Large Data Bases*, Sept. 1982, 62-76.

[10] M.J. Carey, *Modeling and Evaluation of Database Concurrency Control Algorithms*, Computer Sciences Dept., Univ. California, Berkeley, Dec. 1983, Ph.D. Thesis.

[11] M.J. Carey and M.R. Stonebraker, "The Performance of Concurrency Control Algorithms for Database Management Systems", *Proc. 10th Int'l. Conf. on Very Large Data Bases*, Aug. 1984, 107-118.

[12] D. D. Chamberlain, R. F. Boyce and I. L. Traiger, "A Deadlock-Free Scheme for Resource Locking in a Data Base Environment", *Proc. IFIP 1974*, , 340-343.

[13] W. N. Chin, "Some Comments on 'Deadlock Detection is Cheap' in SIGMOD Record Jan. 83", *ACM-SIGMOD Record*, March 1984, 61-63.

[14] E. G. Coffman, M. J. Elphic and A. Shoshani, "System Deadlocks", *ACM Computing Surveys* 3, 2 (June 1971), 67- 78.

[15] K. P. Eswaran, J. N. Gray, R. A. Lorie and I. L. Traiger, "The Notions of Consistency and Predicate Locks in a Database System", *Commun. ACM* 19, 11 (Nov. 1976), 624-633.

[16] P. Franaszek and J.T. Robinson, "Limitations of Concurrency in Transaction Processing", *ACM Trans. Database Syst.*, 10, 1, (March 1985), 1-28.

[17] V. D. Gligor and S. H. Shattuck, "On Deadlock Detection in Distributed Systems", *IEEE Trans. Software Eng.* SE-6, 5 (Sept. 1980).

[18] J. N. Gray, "Notes on Database Operating Systems", in Lecture Notes in Computer Science 60, *Operating Systems: An Advanced Course*, R. Bayer, R.M. Graham and G. Seegmuller (ed.), Springer-Verlag, New York, 1979.

[19] J. N. Gray, P. Homan, H. Korth and R. Obermarck, *A Straw Man Analysis of the Probability of Waiting and Deadlock in a Database System*, Rep. RJ3066, IBM Research Lab., San Jose, California, Feb. 1981.

[20] J. N. Gray, personal communication to David DeWitt, April 1982.

[21] R. C. Holt, "Some Deadlock Properties of Computer Systems", *ACM Computing Surveys* 4, 3 (Sept. 1972), 179- 196.

[22] P. F. King and A. J. Collmeyer, "Database Sharing — An Efficient Method for Supporting Concurrent Processes", *Proc. AFIPS 1973 Nat'l. Computer Conf.*, 1973, 271-275.

[23] H. F. Korth, "Edge Locks and Deadlock Avoidance in Distributed Systems", *Proc. ACM SIGACT-SIGOPS Symp. on Principles of Distributed Computing*, Aug. 1982, 173-182.

[24] B. Lindsay, personal communication, May 1985.

[25] D. B. Lomet, "A Practical Deadlock Avoidance Algorithm for Data Base Systems", *Proc. ACM-SIGMOD 1977 Int'l Conf. on Management of Data*, Aug. 1977, 122-127.

[26] D. B. Lomet, "Deadlock Avoidance in Distributed Systems", *IEEE Trans. Software Eng.* SE-6, 3 (March 1980), .

[27] P. P. Macri, "Deadlock Detection and Resolution in a CODASYL Based Data Management System", *Proc. ACM-SIGMOD 1976 Int'l Conf. on Management of Data*, June 1976, 45- 49.

[28] D. A. Menasce and R. R. Muntz, "Locking and Deadlock Detection in Distributed Databases", *Proc. 3rd Berkeley Workshop on Distributed Data Management and Computer Networks*, Aug. 1978.

[29] D. Mitchell and M. J. Merritt, "Distributed Algorithm for Deadlock Detection and Resolution", *Proc. of ACM-SIGACT-SIGMOD Conf. on Principles of Distributed Computing*, Aug. 1984.

[30] R. Munz and G. Krenz, "Concurrency in Database Systems — A Simulation Study", *Proc. ACM-SIGMOD 1977 Int'l Conf. on Management of Data*, Aug. 1977, 111-120.

[31] G. Newton, "Deadlock Prevention, Detection and Resolution: An Annotated Bibliography", *ACM-SIGOPS Operating Systems Review* 13, 4 (April 1979), 33-44.

[32] R. Obermarck, "Distributed Deadlock Detection Algorithm", *ACM Trans. Database Syst.* 7, 2 (June 1982), .

[33] A. Reuter, *An Analytic Model of Transaction Interference in Database Systems*, IB 68/83, Univ. Kaiserslautern, West Germany, 1983.

[34] D.R. Ries and M.R. Stonebraker, "Effects of Locking Granularity in a Database Management System", *ACM Trans. Database Syst.*, 2, 3, (Sept. 1977), 233-246.

[35] D.R. Ries, *The Effects of Concurrency Control on Database Management System Performance*, Computer Sciences Dept., Univ. California, Berkeley, April 1979, Ph.D. Thesis.

[36] D.R. Ries and M.R. Stonebraker, "Locking Granularity Revisited", *ACM Trans. Database Syst.*, 4, 2, (June 1979), 210-227.

[37] D. J. Rosenkrantz, R. E. Stearns and P. M. Lewis, "System Level Concurrency Control for Distributed Database Systems", *ACM Trans. Database Syst.* 3, 2 (June 1978), 178-198.

[38] Sargent, R., "Statistical Analysis of Simulation Output Data", *Proc. 4th Annual Symp. on the Simulation of Computer Systems*, 1976.

[39] M. R. Stonebraker, "Concurrency Control and Consistency of Multiple Copies of Data in Distributed INGRES", *IEEE Trans. Software Eng.* SE-5, 3 (May 1979), 188-194.

[40] Y. C. Tay, *A Mean Value Performance Model for Locking in Databases*, Tech. Rep.-04-84, Harvard Univ., Cambridge, Mass., Feb. 1984. Ph.D. Thesis.

[41] Y. C. Tay, N. Goodman, and R. Suri, "Locking Performance in Centralized Databases", *ACM Trans. Database Syst.*, 10, 4, (December 1985), 415-462.


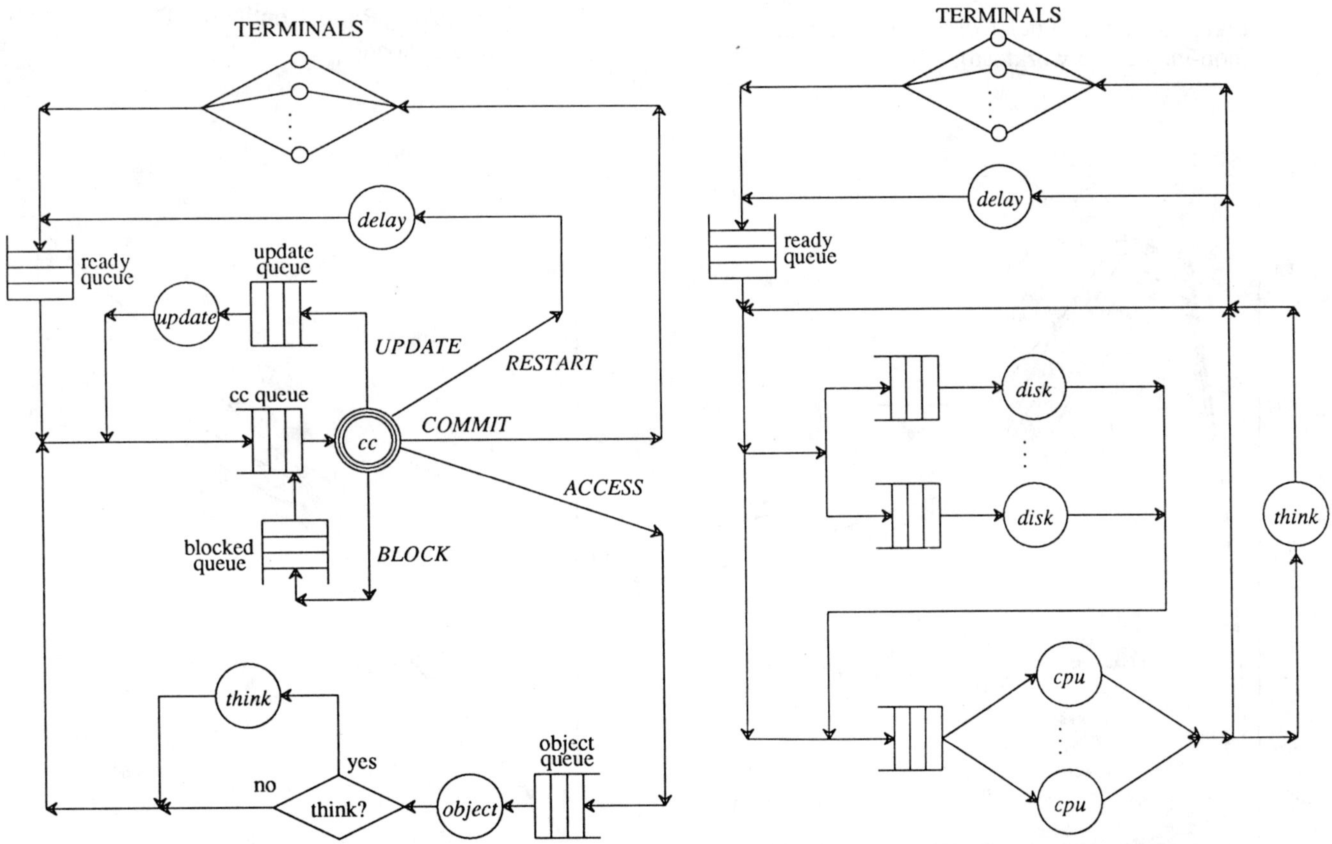


Figure 1: Logical Queuing Model.

Figure 2: Physical Queuing Model.

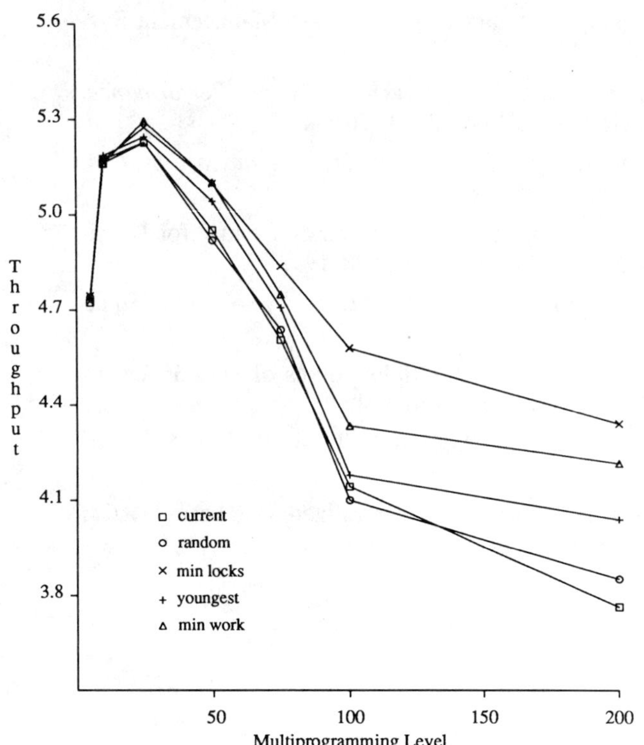


Figure 3: Throughput, Continuous Detection (non-interactive workload).

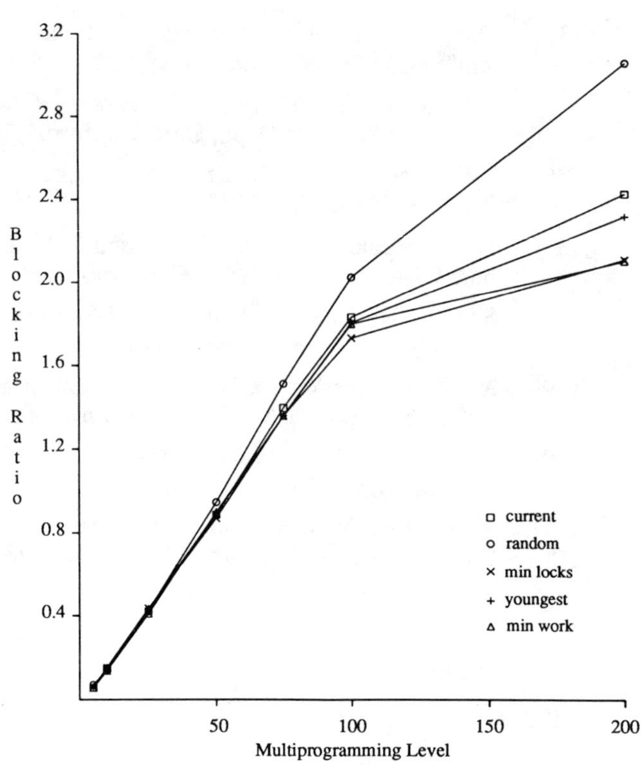


Figure 5: Blocking Ratio, Continuous Detection (interactive workload).

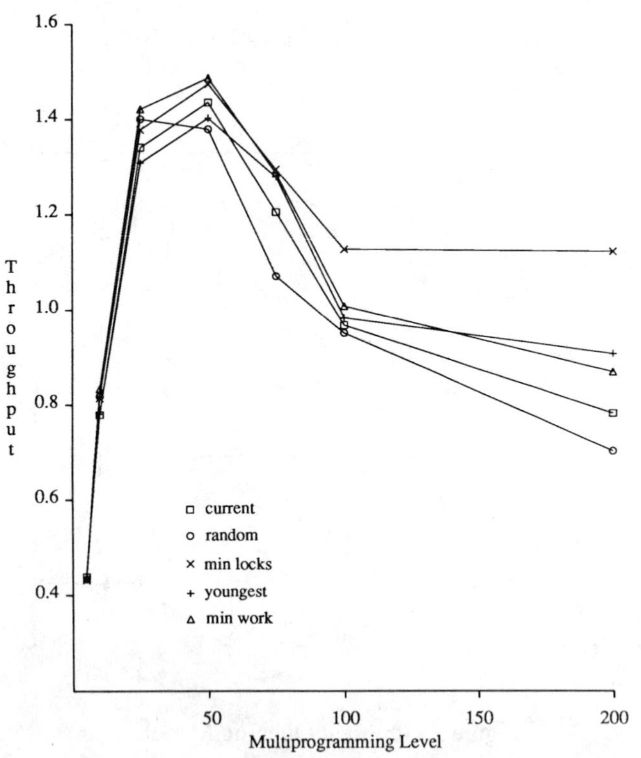


Figure 4: Throughput, Continuous Detection (interactive workload).

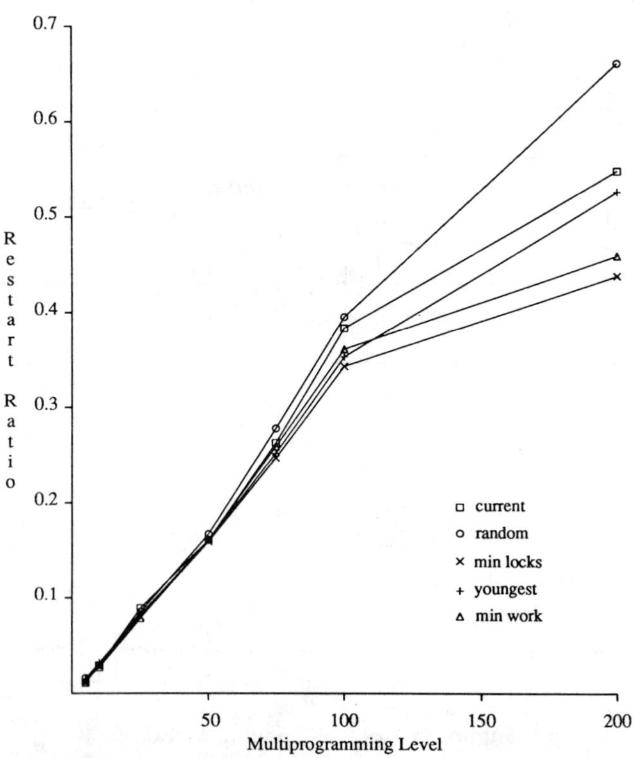


Figure 6: Restart Ratio, Continuous Detection (interactive workload).

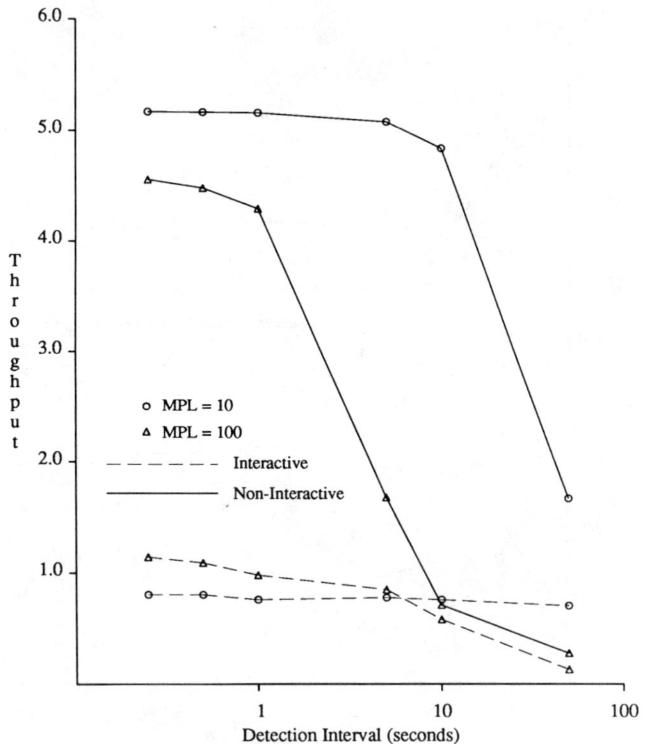


Figure 7: Throughput, Periodic Detection, Varying Detection Intervals.

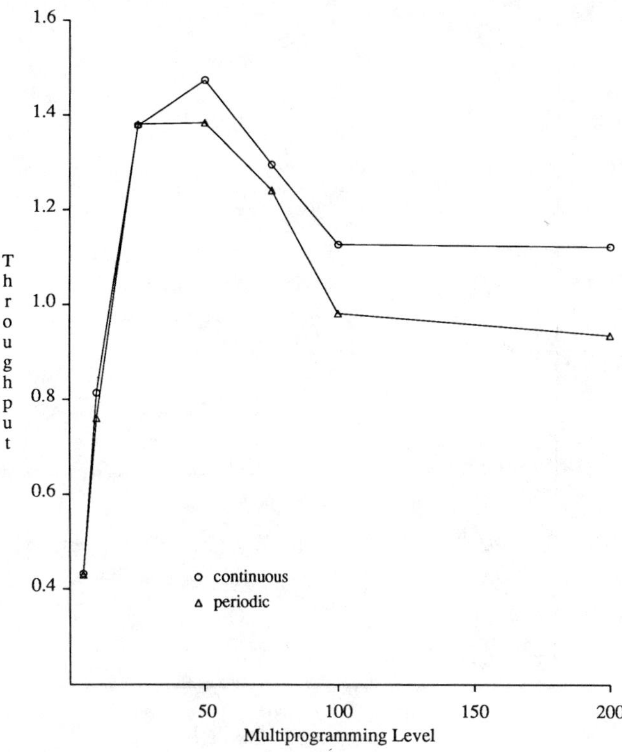


Figure 9: Throughput, Detection Alternatives (interactive workload).

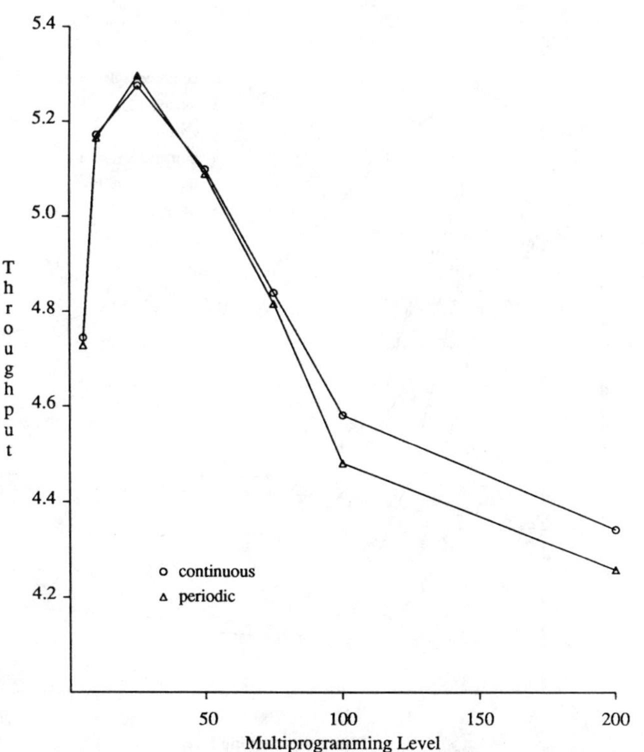


Figure 8: Throughput, Detection Alternatives (non-interactive workload).

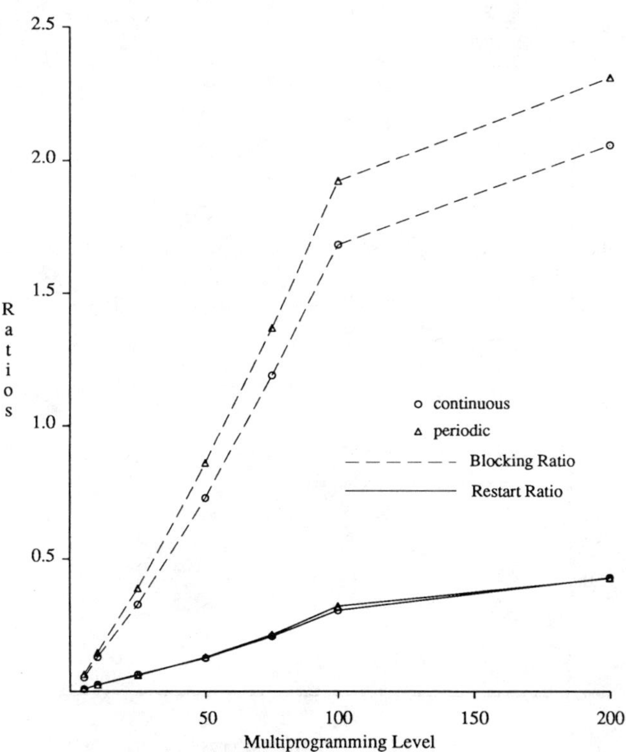


Figure 10: Blocking and Restart Ratios, Detection Alternatives (non-interactive workload).

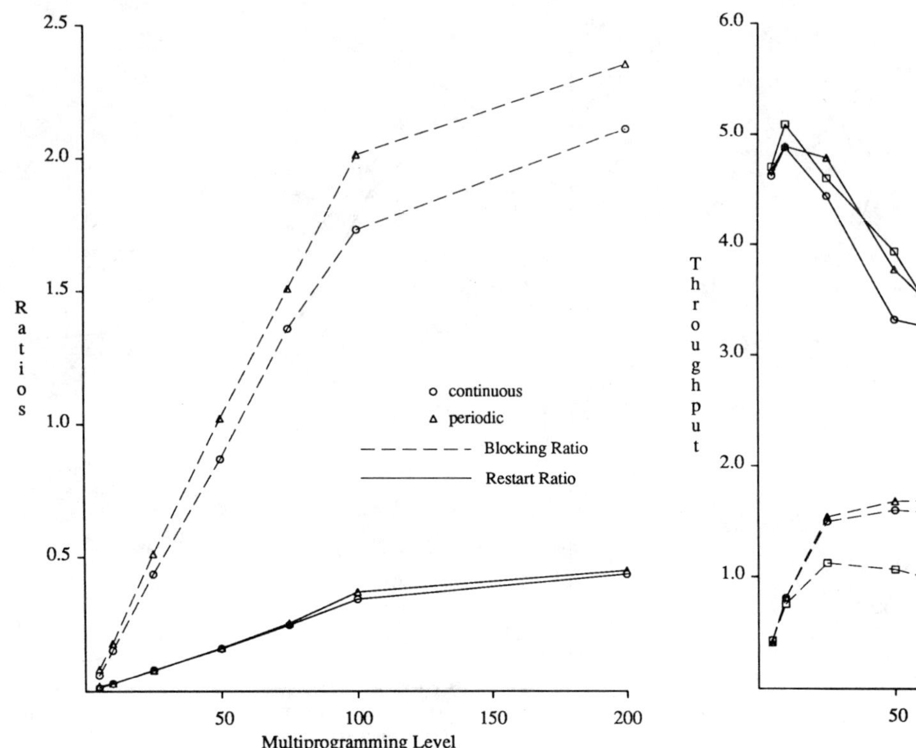


Figure 11: Blocking And Restart Ratios, Detection Alternatives (interactive workload).

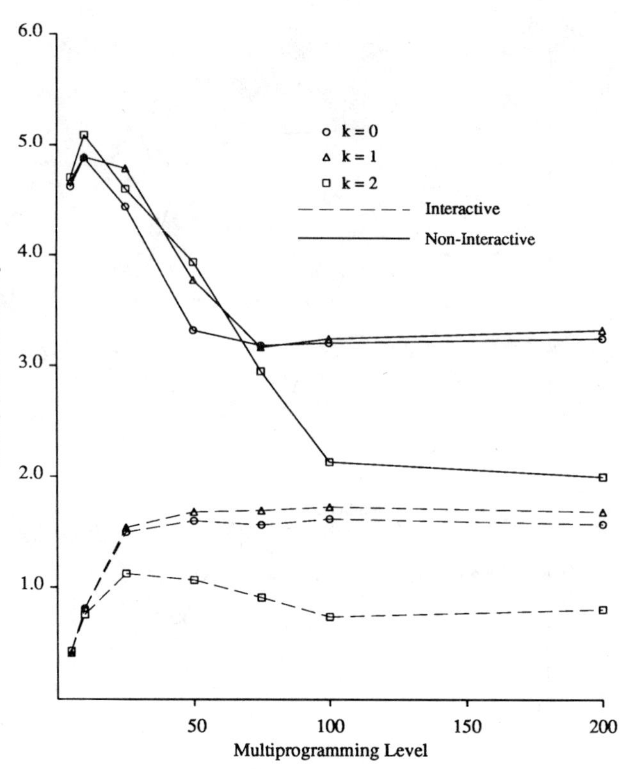


Figure 13: Throughput, Adaptive Timeout Algorithm.

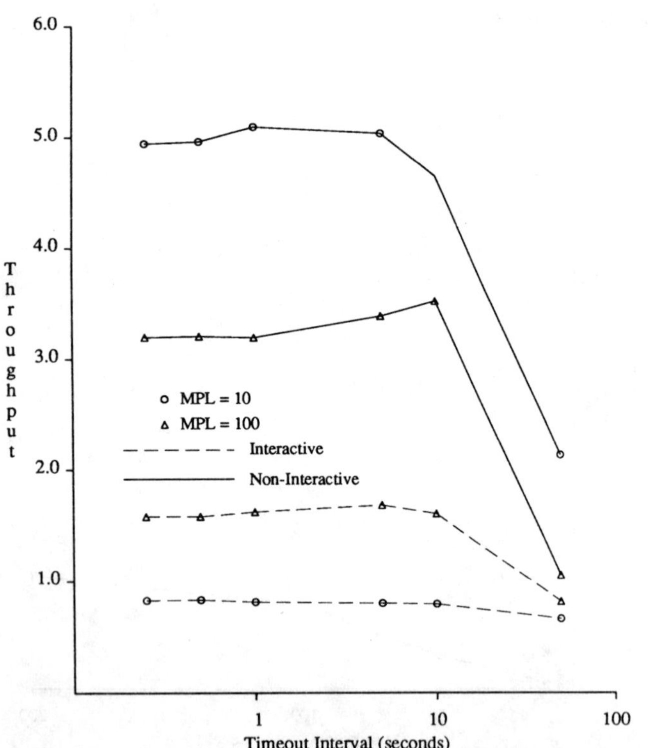


Figure 12: Throughput, Timeout Algorithm, Varying Timeout Intervals.

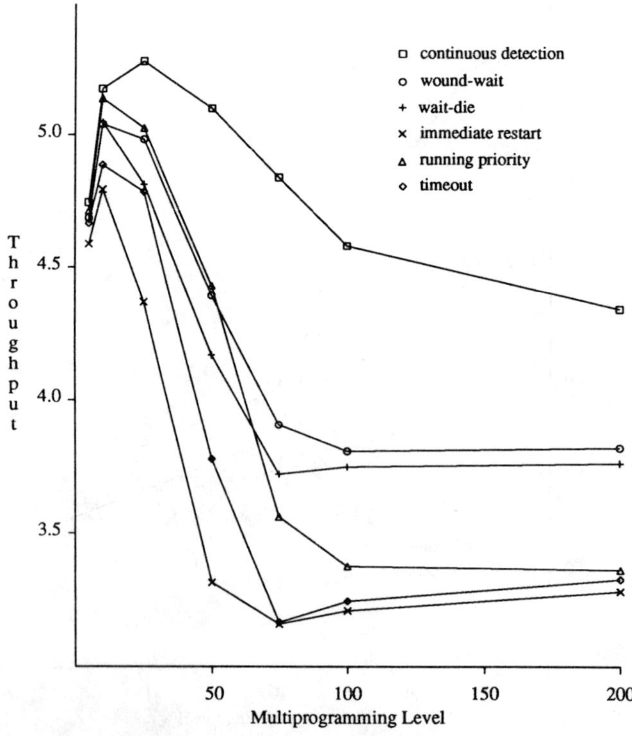


Figure 14: Throughput, Alternative Strategies (non-interactive workload).

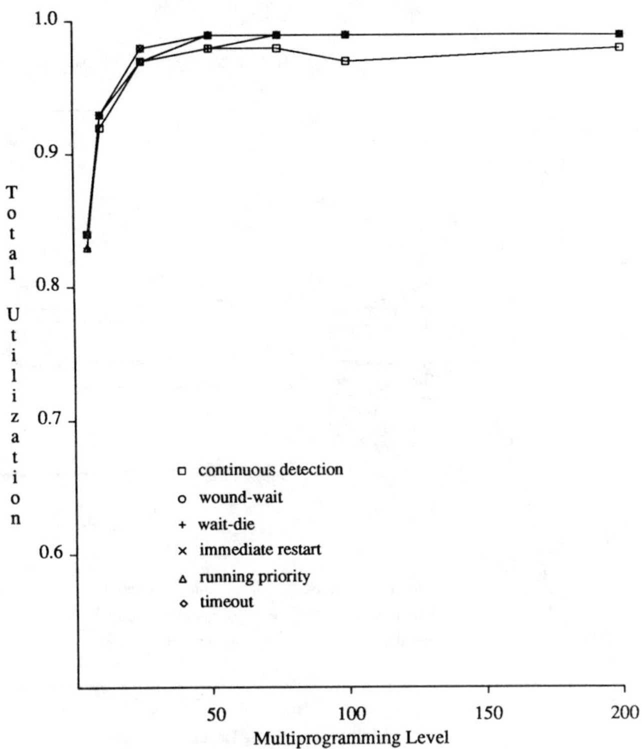


Figure 15: Total Disk Utilization, Alternative Strategies (non-interactive workload).

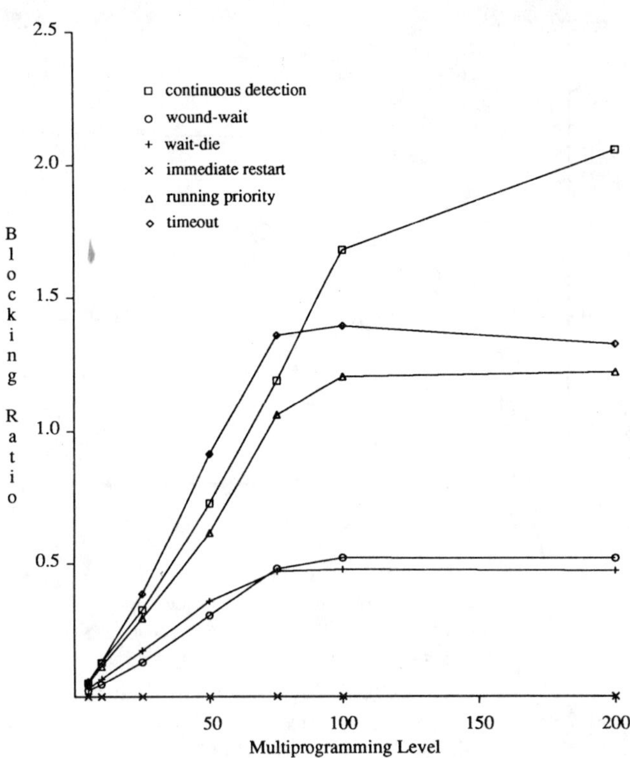


Figure 17: Blocking Ratio, Alternative Strategies (non-interactive workload).

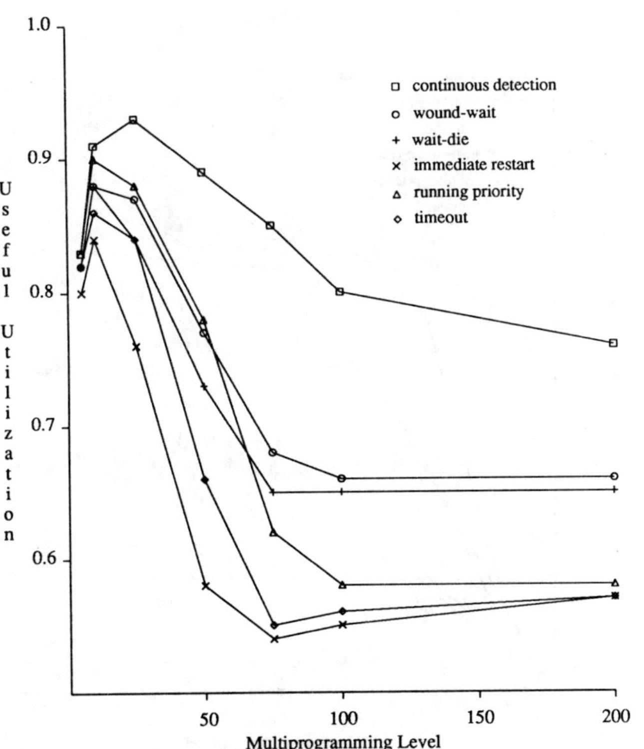


Figure 16: Useful Disk Utilization, Alternative Strategies (non-interactive workload).

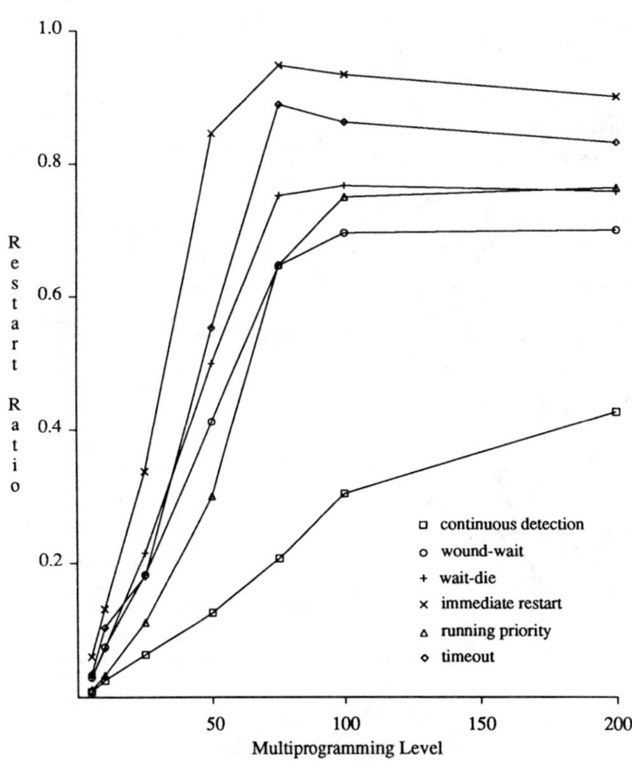


Figure 18: Restart Ratio, Alternative Strategies (non-interactive workload).

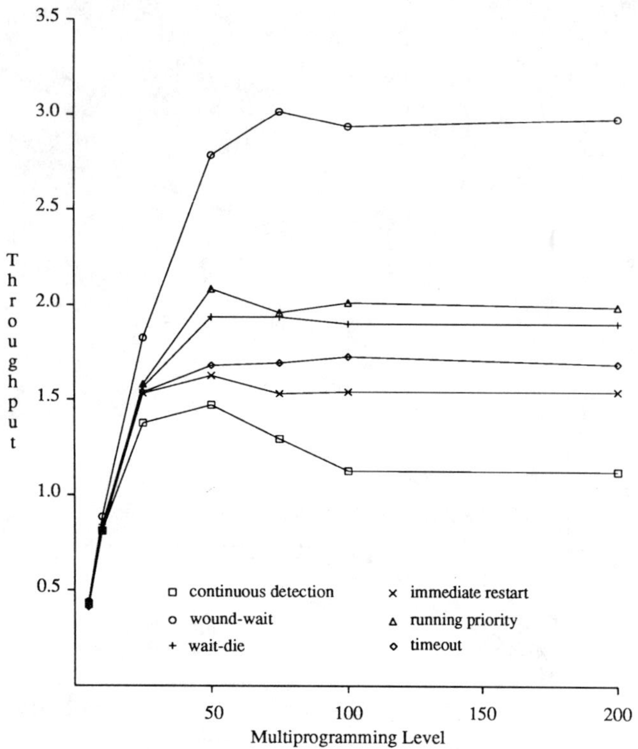


Figure 19: Throughput, Alternative Strategies (interactive workload).

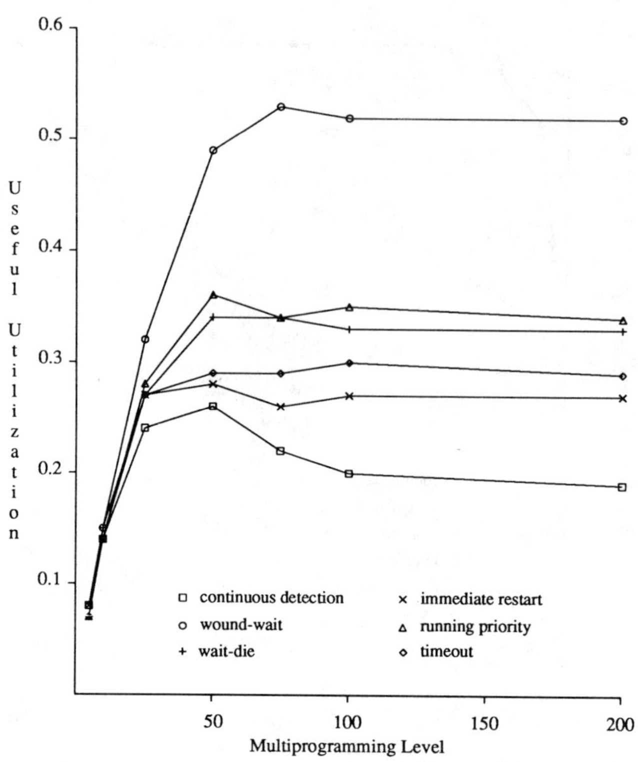


Figure 21: Useful Disk Utilization, Alternative Strategies (interactive workload).

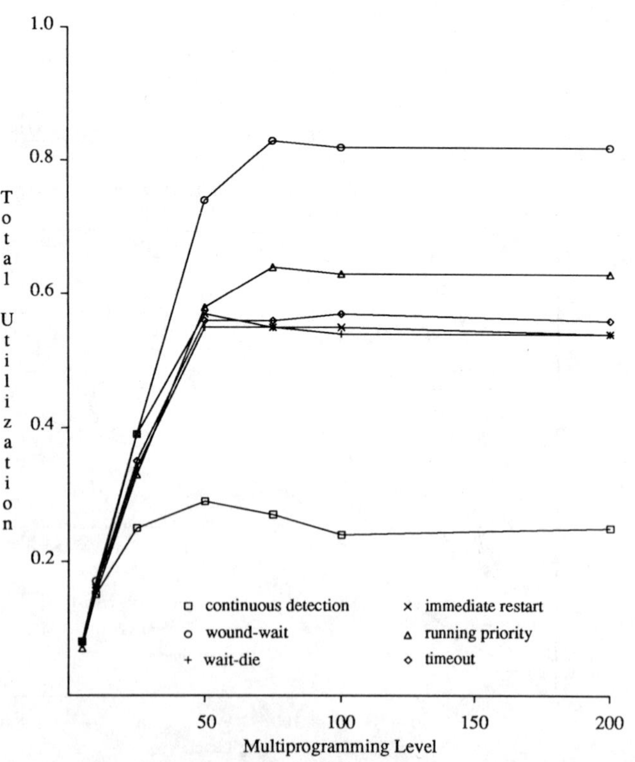


Figure 20: Total Disk Utilization, Alternative Strategies (interactive workload).

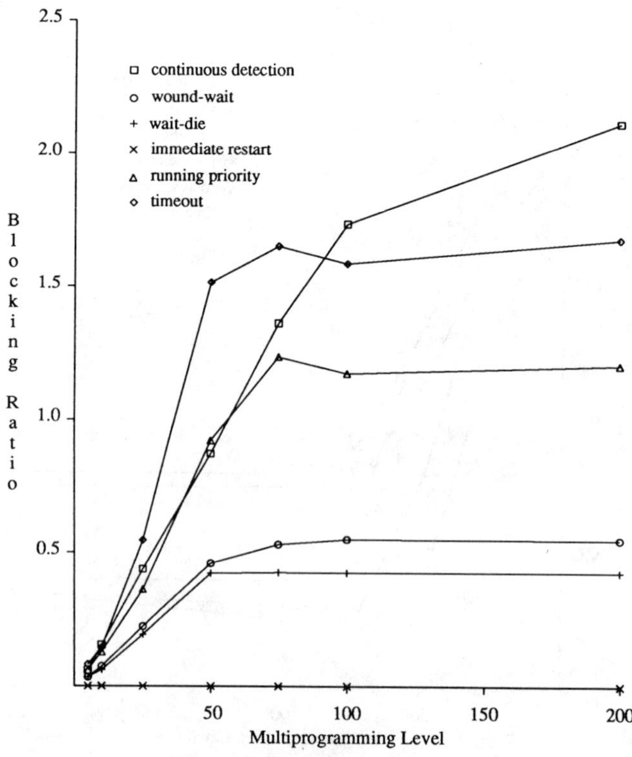


Figure 22: Blocking Ratio, Alternative Strategies (interactive workload).

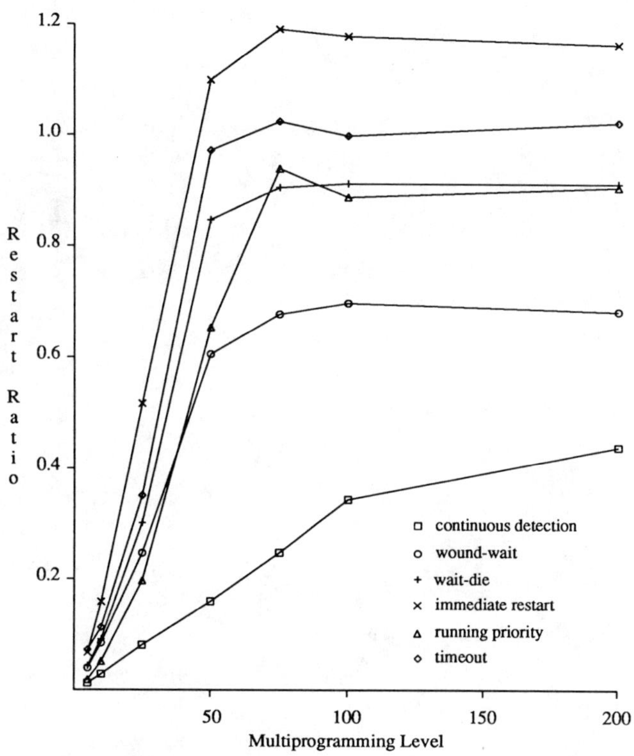


Figure 23: Restart Ratio, Alternative Strategies (interactive workload).

# Chapter 5: Recent Advances in Database Management Systems

Dramatic advances have been made in database management system technology in the past five years. Some of these advances are already beginning to find their way into commercial products. This chapter contains reprinted papers describing some of these exciting advances.

## 5.1: Theoretical Basis for Database Management Systems

Logic provides a useful formalism for studying classical database problems. The paper, "Logic and Databases: A Deductive Approach," by Gallaire, Minker, and Nicolas shows how logic applies to query languages, integrity modeling, maintenance, query evaluation, and database design through dependencies, representation and manipulation of deduced facts, and incomplete information.

## 5.2: Database Management Systems and Expert Systems

Recently, *expert systems*, systems that mimic the behavior of human experts solving complex problems, have been implemented. These expert systems need a database to store the facts and rules used in solving complex problems. The reprinted paper "The Transition from Data Management for Knowledge Management," by Kellogg discusses the transition from data management to knowledge management.

## 5.3: Object-Oriented Database Management Systems

Commercial database systems support a limited number of types of data. Object-oriented programming languages such as Smalltalk permit users to define new datatypes and the allowable operations on those data types. An object-oriented database management system would be very flexible in that it would allow the database administrator to define new types of data to be stored in the database. In a sense, the database administrator can design the data model for use in accessing the data. The reprinted paper, "Making Smalltalk a Database System," by Copeland and Maier describes such a system being developed by Servio Logic Corporation.

Design data management is a crucial feature of an integrated design system. Concurrent access must be controlled, the design data must be reliably sorted on secondary memory, the data must be kept well formed and consistent, and versions and alternatives must be maintained. The reprinted paper by Katz, in "Managing the Chip Design Database," describes such a database management system for designing integrated circuits.

## 5.4: Time in Databases

The need for supporting time varying information in databases has been recognized for quite some time. Two important aspects of time are that (1) *logical time* is characterized as the time that an event occurs in reality and that (2) *physical time* is characterized as the time when the data concerning the event was stored in the database. Examples of facts involving time include retroactive salary changes, release dates of engineering versions, scheduled events that have not yet occurred, and scheduled events that were supposed to occur, yet did not. The reprinted paper by Snodgrass and Ahn, "A Taxonomy of Time in Databases," presents a new taxonomy for representing time in a database and suggests extensions to a relational calculus language for dealing with these different aspects of time.

## 5.5: Highly Available Database Management Systems

As database management systems become more integrated into the daily activities of an enterprise, the enterprise comes to rely more and more on the availability of the database management system. For example, banking and airlines enterprises rely heavily on systems that, when not available, can cause major disruptions to the working of the enterprise. Database management systems that do not break down are needed.

Kim, in "Highly Available Systems for Database Applications," presents a survey and analysis of representative architectures and techniques that have been developed for constructing highly available systems for database applications. It also proposes a design of a distributed software subsystem that can serve as a unified framework for constructing database application systems that meet various requirements for high availability.

# Logic and Databases: A Deductive Approach

HERVE GALLAIRE

*Compagnie Générale d'Électricité Laboratoire de Marcoussis, Marcoussis, France*

JACK MINKER

*University of Maryland, Computer Science Department, College Park, Maryland*

JEAN-MARIE NICOLAS

*ONERA-CERT, Département d'Informatique, Toulouse, France*

The purpose of this paper is to show that logic provides a convenient formalism for studying classical database problems. There are two main parts to the paper, devoted respectively to conventional databases and deductive databases. In the first part, we focus on query languages, integrity modeling and maintenance, query optimization, and data dependencies. The second part deals mainly with the representation and manipulation of deduced facts and incomplete information.

Categories and Subject Descriptors: H.2.1 [**Database Management**]: Logical Design—*data models*; H.2.3 [**Database Management**]: Languages—*query languages*; H.2.4 [**Database Management**]: Systems—*query processing*

General Terms: Deductive Databases, Indefinite Data, Logic and Databases, Null Values, Relational Databases

## INTRODUCTION

As emphasized by Codd [1982], theoretical database studies form a fundamental basis for the development of homogeneous and sound database management systems (DBMS), which offer sophisticated capabilities for data handling. A comprehensive study of the many problems that exist in databases requires a precise formalization so that detailed analyses can be carried out and satisfactory solutions can be obtained. Most of the formal database studies that are under way at present are concerned with the relational data model introduced by Codd [1970], and use either a specially developed database theory [Maier 1983; Ullman 1982] or other formal theories such as mathematical logic as their framework. The purpose of this paper is to provide an overview and a survey of a subfield of logic as it is applied to databases. We are mostly concerned with the application of logic to databases, where logic may be used both as an inference system and as a representation language; we primarily consider relational type databases. Some important efforts in the application of other aspects of logic theory to databases (e.g., see Maier [1983], Ullman [1982], and the references provided there) or those that deal with nonrelational (i.e., hierarchical and network) databases (e.g., see Jacobs [1982] and Jacobs et al. [1982]) are not covered here.

The use of logic for knowledge representation and manipulation is primarily due to the work of Green [1969]. His work was the basis of various studies that led to so-called

Current address of Hervé Gallaire and Jean-Marie Nicolas: European Computer-Industry Research Centre (ECRC), Arabellastrasse 17, D-8000 München 81, FRG.

CONTENTS



question-answering systems, which are concerned mainly with a highly deductive manipulation of a small set of facts, and thus require an inferential mechanism provided by logic. Similar techniques have been adapted to databases to handle large sets of facts, negative information, open queries, and other specific database topics. These techniques have given rise to what is called deductive databases. However, the use of logic to study databases is not restricted to providing deductive capabilities in a DBMS; the pioneering work of Kuhns [1967, 1970] also uses logic for conventional databases to characterize answers to queries.

Aside from the introduction and conclusion to this paper, there are two main sections, which are devoted respectively to conventional databases and deductive databases. In this introduction we provide background material to familiarize the reader with the terminology used throughout the paper, introducing the reader to concepts in relational databases, to the area of mathematical logic, and to the basic relationships between logic and databases. Section 1 is an extended and revised version of material that appeared in Gallaire [1981]. This material shows how logic provides a formalism for databases, and how this formalism has been applied to conventional databases. Its use in query languages, integrity modeling and maintenance, query evaluation, and database schema analysis is described. In Section 2 we show how logic extends relational databases to permit deduction and describe how logic provides a sound basis for a proper treatment and understanding of null values and incomplete information.

In the remainder of this introduction, we first describe the main concepts of the relational data model. Following this, we specify what is meant by mathematical logic, focusing on logic relevant to databases rather than logic in general. Finally, we briefly introduce two ways in which databases can be considered from the viewpoint of logic.

### I.1 Relational Model

To define a relational model we need some concepts. A *domain* is a usually finite set of values. The *Cartesian product* of domains $D_1, \ldots, D_n$ is denoted by $D_1 \times \cdots \times D_n$ and is the set of all tuples $(x_1, \ldots, x_n)$ such that for any $i$, $i = 1, \ldots, n$ $(x_1 \in D_1)$. A *relation* is any subset of the Cartesian product of one or more domains. A database (instance) is a finite set of finite relations. By a finite relation we mean that the extension of the relation (i.e., the totality of all tuples that can appear in a relation) is finite. The arity of a relation $R \subseteq D_1 \times \cdots \times D_n$ is $n$. One may envision a relation to be a table of values. Names are generally associated with the columns of these tables; these names are called *attributes*. Values of an attribute associated with column $i$ of a relation are taken from domain $D_i$. A relation $R$ with attributes $A_1, \ldots, A_n$ defines a relation scheme denoted as $R(A_1, \ldots, A_n)$, whereas the specific relation $R$ (i.e., the relation with specified tuples) is said to be an *instance* or *extension* of the relation scheme.

Not all instances of a relation scheme have meaningful interpretations; that is, they do not correspond to valid sets of data according to the intended semantics of the database. One therefore introduces a set of constraints, referred to as *integrity constraints*, associated with a relation scheme to ensure that the database meets the intended semantics. Integrity constraints may involve interrelationships between relations.

To summarize, a database scheme consists of a collection of relation schemes together with a set of integrity constraints. A database instance, also called a database state, is a collection of relation instances, one for each relation in the database scheme. A database state is said to be valid if all relation instances that it contains obey the integrity constraints. In this paper, values in database/relation instances are referred to as elements, constants, or individuals, depending on the context.

To manipulate data in a relational database, a language is introduced. One may introduce an algebraic language based on algebraic operators, or a calculus language, which we discuss in the following section. In an algebraic language we need only two operators for our purposes: the project and join operators. Given a relation $R$, and $X$ a set of attributes of $R$, then the *projection* of $R$ on $X$ is $\{s[X] \mid s \in R\}$, where $s[X]$ is a tuple constructed from $s$ by keeping all and only those components that belong to attributes in $X$. Given two relations $R$ and $S$, the *natural join* $R * S$ is formed by computing the Cartesian product, $R \times S$, selecting out all tuples whose values on each attribute common to $R$ and $S$ coincide, and projecting one occurrence of each of the common attributes. For a more thorough presentation of the relational model, the reader is referred to Date [1977, 1981] and Ullman [1982]. See also Delobel [1980] and Maier [1983] for an overview and a survey of relational database theory.

### I.2 Mathematical Logic

As is true for any formal system, mathematical logic relies upon an object language, a semantics or interpretation of formulas in that language, and a proof theory.

As the *object language* we shall use a first-order language such as that of the first-order predicate calculus. Primitive symbols of such a language are (1) parentheses, (2) variables, constants, functions, and predicate symbols, (3) the usual logical connectors, $\neg$ (not), & (and), $\vee$ (or), $\rightarrow$ (implication), $\leftrightarrow$ (equivalence), and (4) quantifiers, $\forall$ (for all), $\exists$ (there exists). Throughout the paper we use lowercase letters from the start of the alphabet to represent constants $(a, b, c, \ldots)$, those from the end of the alphabet to represent variables $(u, v, w, x, y, z)$, and letters such as $(f, g, h, \ldots)$ to denote functions.

A *term* is defined recursively to be a constant or a variable, or if $f$ is an $n$-ary function and $t_1, \ldots, t_n$ are terms, then $f(t_1, \ldots, t_n)$ is a term. There are no other terms. We usually assume that a term in the context of databases is function free; that is, it is either a constant or a variable.

If $P$ is an $n$-ary predicate symbol and $t_1, \ldots, t_n$ are terms, then $P(t_1, \ldots, t_n)$ is an *atomic formula.* An atomic formula or its negation is a *literal. Well-formed formulas* (wffs) are defined recursively as follows. An atomic formula is a wff. If $w_1$ and $w_2$ are wffs, then $\neg(w_1)$, $(w_1) \vee (w_2)$, $(w_1)$ & $(w_2)$, $(w_1) \rightarrow (w_2)$, and $(w_1) \leftrightarrow (w_2)$ are wffs. A *closed* wff is one that does not contain any *free* variable (i.e., it contains only quantified variables and constants).

In dealing with wffs it is sometimes convenient to place them in a normal form. A wff is in *prenex normal form* if all quantifiers appear in front of the formula. The wff corresponding to the statement "Every teacher has a diploma" is

$$(1) \quad (\forall x\ \forall y)(\mathrm{TEACH}(x, y) \rightarrow (\exists z)\mathrm{DIPLOMA}(x, z)).$$

It is indeed possible to place all quantifiers in front of the formula to achieve the prenex normal form (see Chang and Lee [1973] for details). When this is done, formula (1) becomes formula (2):

$$(2) \quad (\forall x)(\forall y)(\exists z)(\neg\mathrm{TEACH}(x, y) \vee \mathrm{DIPLOMA}(x, z)).$$

Similarly, the prenex normal form of the wff

$$(3) \quad (\forall x)(\forall y)(((\exists z)(P(x, z) \;\&\; P(y, z))) \rightarrow (\exists u)Q(x, y, u))$$

is

$$(4) \quad (\forall x)(\forall y)(\forall z)(\exists u) (\neg P(x, z) \vee \neg P(y, z) \vee Q(x, y, u)).$$

A prenex formula is in *Skolem normal form* when all existential quantifiers are eliminated by replacing variables they quantify with arbitrary functions of all universally quantified variables that precede them in the formula. These functions are called Skolem functions; a Skolem function of 0 arguments is called a Skolem constant. A *clause* is a disjunction of literals, all of whose variables are implicitly universally quantified. The Skolem normal form of (2) is

$$(5) \quad \forall x\ \forall y(\neg \mathrm{TEACH}(x, y) \vee \mathrm{DIPLOMA}(x, f(x, y)),$$

where the existentially quantified variables are eliminated and replaced by Skolem functions. Similarly, the Skolem normal form of (4) is

$$(6) \quad (\forall x)(\forall y)(\forall z)(\neg P(x, z) \vee \neg P(y, z) \vee Q(x, y, g(x, y, z))),$$

where the existentially quantified variable $u$ has been eliminated and replaced by the Skolem function $g(x, y, z)$. When a wff is in Skolem normal form, all the quantifiers remaining in the front of the formula may be eliminated since all variables that remain are, by convention, universally quantified. Formula (5), above, may be replaced by

$$(7) \quad \neg \mathrm{TEACH}(x, y) \vee \mathrm{DIPLOMA}(x, f(x, y)).$$

Thus

$$\neg A_1 \vee \cdots \vee \neg A_m \vee B_1 \vee \cdots \vee B_n,$$

where the $A_1$ and the $B_j$ are positive literals, is a clause. We shall write a clause in an equivalent form as

$$A_1 \,\&\, \cdots \,\&\, A_m \rightarrow B_1 \vee \cdots \vee B_n.$$

In a clause, whenever $n$ is equal to 0 or 1, the clause is said to be a *Horn clause.* If both $m$ and $n$ are equal to 0, there are no atoms on the left- or right-hand side of the implication sign, and the clause is called the *empty clause.* A clause (a literal) in which no variables appear is called a *ground clause* (*ground literal*). Every closed, well-formed formula may be placed in clause form. We note that the transformation of a wff into prenex normal form preserves equivalence, but this is not the case for transformations into Skolem or clause form. The latter transformations only preserve satisfiability, which is sufficient for provability purposes.

Two complementary aspects of wffs are of interest. One deals with *semantics* (or *model theory*), the specification of truth values to wffs, whereas the other deals with *proof theory*, the derivation of a wff from a given set of wffs.

#### *I.2.1 Semantics: Model and Interpretation*

In semantics we are concerned with interpretations, where an *interpretation* of a set of wffs consists of the specification of a nonempty set (or domain) $E$, from which constants and variables are given values. Each $n$-ary function symbol is assigned a function from $E^n$ to $E$. Each $n$-ary predicate is assigned a relation on $E^n$.

In an interpretation with domain $E$, a closed wff is either true or false, whereas a (open) wff with $n$ ($n \geq 1$) free variables determines a set of $n$-tuples (i.e., a relation) on $E^n$. Each of these $n$-tuples is such that when its components are substituted for the corresponding free variables in the open wff, then in this interpretation, the closed wff that is obtained is true. If the set of $n$-tuples is empty, then the open wff is said to be false, and if the set of $n$-tuples coincides with $E^n$, then the open wff is said to be true. Broadly, the truth value of a closed wff is obtained as follows. If $R$ is the relation assigned to a $n$-place predicate symbol $P$, then $P(e_1, \ldots, e_n)$ evaluates to true if $\langle e_1, \ldots, e_n \rangle \in R$; otherwise it evaluates to false. Now, if $w_1$ and $w_2$ are closed wffs, $\neg w_1$ evaluates to true if $w_1$ is false; otherwise it evaluates to false. $w_1 \,\&\, w_2$ evaluates to true if both $w_1$ and $w_2$ are true; otherwise it evaluates to false. $w_1 \rightarrow w_2$ evaluates to true if either $w_1$ is false or $w_2$ is true; otherwise it evaluates to false. Well-formed formulas constructed using the other logical symbols may be evaluated similarly. Finally, if $x$ is a variable in $w$, $\forall x w(x)$ (respectively, $\exists x w(x)$) evaluates to true if for all elements $e_1$ in $E$ (respectively, there is an element $e_1 \in E$ such that) $w(e_1)$ is true; otherwise it evaluates to false.

A *model* of a set of wffs is an interpretation in which all wffs in the set are true. A wff $w$ is said to be a *logical consequence* of a set of wffs $W$ iff $w$ is true in all models of $W$. This is denoted by $W \models w$.

#### *I.2.2 Syntax: First-Order Theory*

*The first-order predicate calculus* is a formal system that has as object language a first-order language, a set of axiom schemas (the logical axioms), and two inference rules: *modus ponens* and *generalization.*

When other wffs are added as axioms, the formal system that is obtained is called a *first*-order theory. The new axioms are called *nonlogical* or (*proper*) axioms. A first-order theory is essentially characterized by its nonlogical axioms. A set of nonlogical axioms could be, for example,

Man(Turing),

$(\forall x)(\text{Man}(x) \rightarrow \text{Mortal}(x))$.

A *model* of a theory is an interpretation in which all axioms are true; logical axioms are, in fact, chosen to be true in all interpretations. For the above theory, setting

$$\text{Man(Turing)} = \text{True},$$

$$\text{Mortal(Turing)} = \text{True}$$

yields a model since it makes all statements in the above theory true. A wff $w$ is *derivable* from a set of wffs $W$ in a theory $T(W \vdash w)$ iff $w$ is deducible from $W$ and from the axioms of $T$ by a finite application of the inference rules.

Using the inference rule of modus ponens, which states that from $p$ and $p \rightarrow q$ one can conclude $q$, we obtain from the above theory the derived result: Mortal(Turing). If $W$ is empty, then $w$ is a *theorem* of $T$ ($\vdash_T w$, or equivalently $T \vdash w$). Whenever $T$ is clear, we shall write $W \vdash w$ for $W \vdash_T w$.

Inference rules other than modus ponens and generalization can be used to derive theorems; in fact most theorem-proving techniques are based on the inference rule termed the Robinson Resolution Principle [Robinson 1965], which applies to wffs in clausal form.

The Robinson Resolution Principle is a rule of inference that permits a new clause to be derived from two given clauses; further, the derived clause is satisfiable (i.e., has a model) if the two given clauses are satisfiable. In the context of databases assumed to be function free, the principle can be described in terms of the following example. From

C1: $\neg P(a, b, c) \vee Q(d, e)$, and

C2: $P(x, y, z) \vee R(x, y)$,

one obtains the derived clause

C3: $Q(d, e) \vee R(a, b)$.

The clause C3 is found by considering the literals in the two clauses that have the same predicate name, but one is negated and the other is not. The only predicate of this type is $P$. One then determines if the two atoms $\{P(a, b, c), P(x, y, z)\}$ can be made identical by some substitution to the variables, where $a$, $b$, and $c$ are assumed to be constants and $x$, $y$, and $z$ are assumed to be variables. The substitution $\{a/x, b/y, c/z\}$ is such a substitution, and is to be read: Substitute $a$ for $x$, $b$ for $y$, and $c$ for $z$. One then eliminates the two literals made identical by the substitution (said to be unified) from each clause, forms the disjunction of the remaining literals in the two clauses, and applies the unifying substitution to the remaining literals to obtain the derived clause. Thus in this example the clause C3 is derived.

The resolution principle is used mostly to carry out refutation proofs: In order to prove $W \vdash w$, one tries to show that $W$ and $\neg w$ are not simultaneously satisfiable. As resolution preserves satisfiability, if one can, by resolution from the clausal forms of $W$ and $\neg w$, derive the empty clause, then $W$ and $\neg w$ cannot simultaneously be satisfiable. For example, $\neg P(a, b, c)$ and

$P(x, y, z)$, where $x$, $y$, and $z$ are variables, would resolve to yield the empty clause.

A resolution proof consists of applying resolution to all clauses in the original set, adding those newly derived clauses to the set, and iterating the process.

The most important relationships between the semantic and the syntactic approaches are soundness and completeness. An inference system is *sound* iff for all $W$ and $w$, whenever $W \vdash w$, it implies that $W \models w$; it is *complete* iff for all $W$ and $w$, whenever $W \models w$, it implies that $W \vdash w$. The inference rules of modus ponens and generalization are complete and sound for the propositional calculus. Similarly, resolution refutation is complete and sound for first-order theories: The empty clause is derived if and only if the initial clause (which is negated to apply resolution) is a theorem in the theory. However, there is an element of undecidability; if the clause proposed to be proved is not a theorem, the inference process may never terminate. Resolution refutation is also complete and sound. The meaning of completeness and soundness is that the same results are obtained by using semantics, which deals with truth assignments, and provability, which deals with inference rules.

The reader should refer to Enderton [1972] and Mendelson [1978] for general background on logic and to Chang and Lee [1973] and Loveland [1978] for more material on the resolution principle.

### I.3 Databases Viewed through Logic

Before considering the formalization of databases in terms of logic, we shall mention some assumptions that govern query (and integrity constraint) evaluation of databases. On the one hand, these assumptions express a certain implicit representation of negative facts (e.g., "Paul is not the father of Peter:" ¬Father(Paul, Peter)) and, on the other hand, they make precise the universe of reference to which queries refer. There are three such assumptions:

(1) The *closed world assumption* (CWA), also called convention for negative information, which states that facts not known to be true are assumed to be false (i.e., $\neg R(e_1, \ldots, e_n)$ is assumed to be true iff the tuple $\langle e_1, \ldots, e_n \rangle$ fails to be found in relation $R$).
(2) The *unique name assumption*, which states that individuals with different names are different.
(3) The *domain closure assumption*, which states that there are no other individuals than those in the database.

Answers to "For all" queries or queries involving negation are obtained by using the above hypotheses. For example, the query, "Who is not a Full Professor?", addressed to a database whose current state consists of

Full-Prof.(Jean),
Full-Prof.(Paul),
Associate-Prof.(Andre),
Assistant-Prof.(Pierre),

will get as an answer {Pierre, Andre}. Indeed, the domain closure assumption restricts the individuals to be considered to the set {Jean, Paul, Pierre, Andre}. Furthermore, according to the unique name assumption, one gets the following: Pierre $\neq$ Jean, Pierre $\neq$ Paul. Consequently, Pierre $\notin$ Full-Prof., which, according to the closed world assumption, leads to ¬Full-Prof.(Pierre). The second element of the answer, ¬Full-Prof.(Andre), is obtained in a similar way.

We note that one way to avoid calling for the domain closure assumption is to consider as acceptable queries (and integrity constraints) only expressions that restrict their own reference domain. This is the case for any expression of the relational algebra and for the so-called class of definite (or safe, or range-restricted) logical formulas (see Section 1.1.1).

Although the query evaluation process in any DBMS (implicitly) works under the above hypotheses, these assumptions were made explicit and clearly understood only through a logical formalization of databases.

As first characterized by Nicolas and Gallaire [1978], a database can be considered from the viewpoint of logic in two different ways: either as an *interpretation* (of a first-order theory) or as a (first-order) *theory*. When considered from the viewpoint of interpretations, queries (and integrity constraints) are formulas that are to be evaluated on the interpretation using the semantic definition of truth. From the viewpoint of a theory, queries and integrity constraints are considered to be theorems that are to be proved. The interpretation viewpoint and the theory viewpoint respectively formalize the concepts of conventional and deductive databases.

Reiter [1984] and Kowalski [1981a] have investigated these two approaches more thoroughly. Reiter refers to the two approaches as the *model-theoretic view* and the *proof-theoretic view*, respectively, whereas Kowalski refers to them as the *relational structure view* and the *logic database view*.

The three terms "interpretation," "model," and "relational structure" are closely related. A model is an interpretation that makes all axioms true. The "relational structure" view means that queries are evaluated by assuming the database entries to be true. All these terms relate to the semantic definition of truth. We shall use the term "model-theoretic view" for these three terms throughout this paper. The three terms "theory," "proof theoretic," and "logic database" connote that, in order to determine answers to queries, one derives data from axioms. We use the term "proof theoretic" for these terms throughout the paper.

Both Kowalski and Reiter have shown that, although conventional databases are generally considered from a model-theoretic view, they can also be considered from the proof-theoretic view and can thus be considered as a particular logic database.

This section provides an intuitive characterization of these two views of a database through the perspective of logic. Further details are provided in Section 2 of this paper for the proof-theoretic view.

Let DB be an instance of a relational database. Then DB consists of a set of relations (i.e., a relation $R$ for each relation schema $R(A_1, \ldots, A_n)$) and a set of integrity constraints, IC. Let $D$ be the union of the underlying domains of all attributes that occur in the relation schema. Now define a first-order language $L$ to consist of an $n$-place predicate symbol $\mathbf{R}$ for each $n$-ary relation in DB and a set of constants, one for each element in $D$; the language is assumed to have no function symbols. DB can be seen as an interpretation of formulas of the language as defined in Section I.2, and the formulas of $L$ can be evaluated in this interpretation as follows: Variables range over the domain $D$, and $\mathbf{R}(e_1, \ldots, e_n)$ is true iff $\langle e_1, \ldots, e_n \rangle \in R$. The language can be extended to include arithmetic comparison operators ($<, =, >, \leq, \geq$) as particular predicate symbols, which are assigned their usual interpretation.

If the integrity constraints in IC are expressed as formulas of $L$, then the database DB will be a valid database state iff every constraint in IC evaluates to true in DB, that is, iff DB is a model of IC. We note that, according to the very definition of an interpretation, the evaluation of logical formulas (on an interpretation) is done in accord with the closed world, unique name, and domain closure assumptions stated at the beginning of this section.

The above constitutes a description of the model-theoretic view of a database. The proof-theoretic view of DB is obtained by constructing a theory $T$ that admits DB as a unique model. Then for any wff $w$ in $L$, $T \vdash w$ iff $w$ is true in DB.

The process of defining $T$ consists of making its (proper) axioms precise. The axioms (see Reiter [1984]) are of three kinds:

(1) *Assertions.* For any relation $R$ in DB and any tuple $\langle e_1, \ldots, e_n \rangle \in R$, an axiom $\mathbf{R}(e_1, \ldots, e_n) \in T$.

(2) *Particularization Axioms.* Particularization axioms explicitly state the evaluation hypotheses that, in the model-theoretic view, are conveyed by the notion of interpretation:

(i) *The completion axioms.* There is one such axiom for any relation $R$ in DB. If $\langle e_1^1, \ldots, e_i^n \rangle, \ldots, \langle e_p^1, \ldots, e_p^n \rangle$ are all the tuples in $R$, it is written as

$$\forall x_1 \cdots \forall x_n (R(x_1, \ldots, x_n) \rightarrow (x_1 = e_1^1 \,\&\, \cdots \,\&\, x_n = e_1^n) \vee \cdots \vee (x_1 = e_p^1 \,\&\, \cdots \,\&\, x = e_p^n)).$$

The completion axiom effectively states that the only values tuples that the relation $R$ can have are

$$\langle e_1^1, \ldots, e_1^n\rangle, \ldots, \langle e_p^1, \ldots, e_p^n\rangle.$$

(ii) *The unique name axioms.* If $e_1, \ldots, e_q$ are all the individuals in DB, the unique name axioms are

$$(e_1 \neq e_2), \ldots, (e_1 \neq e_q),$$
$$(e_2 \neq e_3), \ldots, (e_{q-1} \neq e_q).$$

(iii) *The domain closure axiom.* This is

$$\forall x((x = e_1) \vee (x = e_2) \vee \cdots \vee (x = e_q)).$$

(3) *Equality Axioms.* Equality axioms are needed since the axioms in (2) involve the equality predicate. These axioms specify the usual properties of equality:

- *reflexivity:*

$$\forall x(x = x).$$

- *symmetry:*

$$\forall x\, \forall y((x = y) \rightarrow (y = x)).$$

- *transitivity:*

$$\forall x\, \forall y\, \forall z((x = y)\ \&\ (y = z) \rightarrow (x = z)).$$

- *principle of substitution of equal terms:*

$$\forall x_1 \cdots \forall y_n(P(x_1, \ldots, x_n)\ \&\ (x_1 = y_1)\ \&\ \cdots\ \&\ (x_n = y_n) \rightarrow P(y_1, \ldots, y_n)).$$

Let us briefly give the underlying reason why $T$ admits DB as a unique model (up to an isomorphism). The only interpretation of $T$ in which the domain closure axioms and the unique name axioms are all satisfied is such that their individuals are in one-to-one correspondence with elements in $D$. Thus all the possible models of $T$ have the same domain as DB (up to an isomorphism). For any such model $M$, since its domain is fixed, in order to be different from DB, it must assign to at least one **R** a relation $R'$ different from $R$. But this is not possible. Indeed, if a tuple $\langle e_1, \ldots, e_n\rangle$ belongs to $R$ but not to $R'$, then $M$ does not satisfy one of the axioms in (1). Conversely, if $\langle e_1, \ldots, e_n\rangle$ belongs to $R'$ but not to $R$, then $M$ does not obey the completion axiom associated with **R**.

As defined above $T$ provides the proof-theoretic view of DB. According to this view, DB satisfies a constraint $w$ in IC iff $T \vdash w$. Furthermore, the answer to a query formulated as $W(x_1, \ldots, x_p)$—where $x_1, \ldots, x_p$ are the free variables in the formula $W$—consists of those $p$-tuples $\langle e_1, \ldots, e_p\rangle$ such that $T \vdash W(e_1, \ldots, e_p)$.

It is worth noting that, although according to this view query (and integrity constraint) evaluation calls for proof techniques, DB is and remains a conventional (i.e., nondeductive) database. No other (positive) facts than those explicitly stated in (1) can be derived from $T$.

At this stage one may notice that the above proof-theoretic view is not intended to be used directly as a basis for a DBMS implementation. The combinatorial complexity of the particularization axioms would lead to inefficient systems, but, as emphasized by Reiter [1984], the value of this view is found in the generalizations that it suggests for databases: (1) Add some disjunctive facts or existentially quantified literals among the assertions and one obtains a database with null values and incomplete information; (2) suppress from the set of ICs some of its formulas and add those formulas as axioms to the theory and one obtains a new theory that is a deductive database. However, the formulation of the completion axioms then has to be reconsidered, as is seen in Section 2. Except for work in deductive databases, the applications of logic to databases has mainly referred, either explicitly or implicitly, to the model-theoretic view. This work is reported upon in Section 1.

## 1. CONVENTIONAL DATABASES

The goal of Section 1 is to show how logic can provide formal support to study classical database problems, and in some cases, how logic can go further, helping to comprehend and then to solve them. We describe contributions published in the literature that relate to logic and databases with respect to query languages, integrity modeling and maintenance, query evaluation, and database schema analysis.

### 1.1 Query Languages

#### *1.1.1 Toward Relational Calculus*

One of the first impacts of logic on databases was the use of its language as a basis for defining assertional query languages. This can be done in any one of four ways [Pirotte 1976, 1978], depending on whether one-sorted or many-sorted languages [Enderton 1972] are used and whether tuples of relations or elements of domains are considered as primitive objects [Ullman 1980]. In fact, only two out of these four possibilities have been truly exploited: the so-called *domain relational calculus* (DRC, one sorted/elements of domains) and the *tuple relational calculus* (TRC, one sorted/tuples of relations). Both of these languages have the same expressive power [Ullman 1980]. The respective pioneering and fundamental efforts of Kuhns [1967] and Codd [1972] are shown in each of these two cases. We shall focus on the DRC.

As described in Section I.3, the reason for considering the language of logic as a basis for defining query languages is that a relational database (instance) can be viewed as an interpretation of a first-order language. Thus the answer to a formula $W(x_1, \ldots, x_p)$, where $x_1, \ldots, x_p$ are the free variables in $W$, considered as a query, is the set of $p$-tuples $\langle e_1, \ldots, e_p \rangle \in D^P$ such that $W(e_1, \ldots, e_p)$ is true. However, when considered as queries, some formulas may be "unreasonable" [Kuhns 1967], since their answer may be different in two database states, where the relations they refer to are the same. A typical example is the formula $\neg\mathbf{R}(x_1, \ldots, x_n)$, which characterizes all tuples in $D^n$ except those that are in $R$ as opposed to $P(x_1, \ldots, x_n)$ & $\neg\mathbf{R}(x_1, \ldots, x_n)$.

A semantic characterization of formulas that can be considered to be reasonable queries led to the notions of *definite* formulas [Kuhns 1967] and *safe* formulas [Ullman 1980]. Roughly, such formulas are domain independent since they self-restrict the range of the variables that they contain.[1] However, once these classes were defined, a new problem appeared, that of finding machine-recognizable criteria for determining whether a given formula is definite (or safe). Unfortunately, as proved by Di Paola [1969] and Vardi [1981], the decision problem for definite formulas is recursively unsolvable. Thus what remained to be done was to look for the largest of its subclasses that was recursive. This was one of the motivations for various authors who introduced purely syntactically defined subclasses of definite formulas such as "proper" [Kuhns 1970], range separable [Codd 1972], acceptable [Artaud and Nicolas 1974], range restricted [Nicolas 1979a, 1979b], and evaluable [Demolombe 1982] formulas.

Using many-sorted logic as a basis for defining query languages while considering elements of domains as primitive objects was exploited by Pirotte [1978] (see also Minker [1978b] and Reiter [1978b]). In such a case each sort is assigned to a database domain, and the well formedness of formulas is checked with regard to sort requirements. Languages obtained in this manner have the same expressive power as the preceding ones.

Many-sorted languages offer a more "precise" definition of the model, but they freeze to some extent any evolution of the application. In that respect one should note how important the issue of *knowledge representation* is to many applications, not only in the database field, but also in artificial intelligence and programming languages. An important workshop sponsored by SIGART, SIGMOD, and SIGPLAN brought to light many points common to these fields [Brodie and Zilles 1980] (see, e.g., papers by Codd [1980], Lacroix and Pirotte [1980], and Mylopoulos [1980]).

Two additional points indicating the importance of a relational calculus language are that Codd [1972] proposed it as a reference for measuring the "completeness"

[1] It turns out, and it is not fortuitous, that "reasonable" queries precisely correspond to formulas that avoid calling for the domain closure assumption (see Section I.3).

of query languages (discussed below), and query languages known to be "user friendly" (e.g., Query-by-example, Zloof [1977] and Quel, Stonebraker et al. [1976]) are based on it. However, improvements to user interfaces are still required, regardless of the query language.

### 1.1.2 Extensions to Query Languages

In this section we argue that logic supports powerful extensions to basic query languages in two directions: natural languages and programming languages. Logic languages are close to natural languages. In addition to Codd [1972], who used this argument to support the relational calculus as a yardstick to measure other languages, many linguists have also made this observation; thus querying databases using natural language has been and is a subject of active research [Colmerauer 1973; Colmerauer and Pique 1981; Dahl 1982; Moore 1981; Warren 1981; Woods 1967].

Several authors have questioned Codd's proposal to "define" completeness (i.e., expressiveness) of query languages with reference to a language (relational calculus) whose expressiveness had not been assessed from a semantic viewpoint. This proposal has also been questioned because some well-known operations on data such as the transitive closure of a relation [Aho and Ullman 1979] and aggregation operations used to compute sums, averages, and other operations are not expressible either in the relational calculus or in the relational algebra. This completeness notion has thus attracted much discussion.

Bancilhon [1978] and Paredaens [1978] have shown that, when restricted to finite relations, the relational calculus and the relational algebra are both complete in the sense that for a given database they can express all (and only those) relations whose extension is definable over the set of all domains of that database. This completeness definition is still restrictive as one cannot, for instance, express the transitive closure of a relation with a single expression independently of the extension of that relation. To attain such a capability, various authors proposed that the relational calculus or relational algebra be embedded in a host language [Aho and Ullman 1979; Chandra and Harel 1979, 1980]. Such an embedding will allow a simple expression (i.e., a program in the host language) to define an operator, for example, transitive closure, from the primitive constructs of the host language (such as iteration, recursion, or least fixed points). In some cases, all computable functions can be expressed; this is the ultimate notion of completeness.

Of course, the host language can be a logic programming language. Its expressive power attains completeness, according to Cooper [1980], or can be limited to subsets of computable functions. But logic offers an alternative way to provide extensions such as those that motivate the embedding of the query language (logic) in a host programming logic language. Indeed, the same effect is obtained by extending the representation and manipulation capabilities of the database system itself (rather than of the query language); this is precisely the idea of the deductive database system, where the database system is a theory, usually first order, with nonunit axioms (e.g., see Gallaire and Minker [1978]).

Accepting the view that a database system consisting of a theory that contains nonunit axioms is similar to extending the host language of a database system may not be entirely apparent. Harel [1980], in a review of the book edited by Gallaire and Minker [1978], attempts to refute the above view, but provides no convincing arguments. The database theory view has many theoretical advantages, if not practical ones, which are developed in Section 2 of the paper. Harel [1980] provided another critique of the work presented by Gallaire and Minker [1978], namely that some queries are not characterizable in first-order logic and hence the language must be extended to a higher order language. Although it is true that such extensions may yield answers to queries, that is, relation extensions that may not be first-order definable (e.g., the transitive closure of a relation), the query language remains precisely first order in the database-theoretic view, and may possibly remain first order in a model-theoretic view, depending on the choice of the host logic programming language. Thus the second critique need not apply. The possible failure to note the distinction between regarding a database an an interpretation or as a theory may have been the cause for the comments by Harel as conjectured by Kowalski [1981b].

#### 1.1.3 Null Values

Null values are a special case of the incomplete information problem that is addressed further in Section 2. Null values have been investigated in the ANSI/X3/SPARC [1975] report. Although many different meanings can be ascribed to missing or null values in the instance of a relation, most researchers have dealt primarily with "attributes applicable but values are unknown," whereas only a few deal with "value does not exist" [Zaniolo 1981]. An unknown value can be represented readily in a database, but problems arise with respect to its manipulation and interpretation in a query language.

A model-theoretic approach is to define a three-valued logic [Codd 1979], based on the truth values {true, false, undefined}. The logical connectors truth definition is extended appropriately: Should any component in a tuple be unknown, the corresponding literal has the truth value true, false, or undefined, depending on whether one obtains a literal that is systematically true, systematically false, or either true or false when substituting any value for unknown. This approach has been criticized by several authors [Grant 1977; Vassiliou 1979] because the theory does not provide for several unknown values. Some of the unknown values may be known to be equal even though their precise values are unknown. Furthermore, an expression should be evaluated globally, and not recursively in terms of its subexpressions, in order to infer some of the external knowledge from the incomplete internal knowledge. As a typical example, if the age of John is unknown, the expression

$$\exists x(\text{Age(John}, x) \ \& \ x < 60) \lor (\text{Age(John}, x) \ \& \ x \geq 60)$$

should receive the value true although both operands of the disjunction have value undefined.

Lipski [1979] defines information which *surely*, alternatively *possibly*, can be extracted from a database in the presence of unknown values. He then defines a query language that encompasses such modal operators. Although such an approach has been criticized on grounds of efficiency [Vassiliou 1980], where a denotational semantics approach is specified, Imielinski and Lipski [1981] improve upon Lipski's earlier approach and define systems capable of handling null values when subsets of the relational operators are used.

Where does logic stand in tackling this problem? As already noted, Codd's approach can be considered to be a model-theoretic approach. Other approaches that use logic as a basis and are more general encompass more forms of incomplete information such as indefinite data. Data are said to be indefinite if they are of the form $P(a) \lor Q(b)$, and it is unknown whether $P(a)$ is true, $Q(b)$ is true, or both are true. Reiter [1983, 1984] gives precise solutions to some of these issues on the basis of the proof-theoretic view of databases with null value and indefinite data. The theory that models such a database is obtained from the theory given for a standard database in Section I.3 by the addition of a new class of axioms that stand for facts with null values (Skolem constants in logical terms) and for indefinite data and by a reformulation of the particularization axioms that account for the presence of these new axioms. For details on these axioms see Reiter [1984]. Grant and Minker [1983] provide a precise algorithm to answer queries on such databases for a subclass of such data when null values are contained within the given domain of elements and only positive ground clauses are permitted.

Three additional approaches to the problem of null values use a tool from metalanguage techniques. In Levesque [1981] a language is defined that extends predicate calculus in that one can refer to the state of the database and thus to what is currently known. Both the semantics and proof theory are covered, cases where one can fall back on predicate calculus are studied, and connections with nonmonotonic logic (described in Section 2) are stressed and shown to yield a simpler semantics of the concept of nonmonotonicity. It becomes possible to specify that not all tuples of a relation are known and to query a database as to what is known and what is not known. A slightly different framework is provided by Konolige [1981], who uses a metalanguage based on first-order logic to describe information known about the domain of discourse (i.e., the actual world) and the database language. Queries are specified in the metalanguage. Some queries can be translated into a database language and hence can be evaluated. Others cannot be answered from the database; that is, they have no equivalent answer because of the incompleteness of the data. Both of these approaches can be dealt with within a general framework investigated by Bowen and Kowalski [1982]. They consider predicate logic as an object language and as a metalanguage where the provability relation of the object language can be formulated in the metalanguage. One can reason at the metalanguage level and at the same time provide answers at the object language level.

At this time the results discussed above tend to be more theoretical than practical. In the case of null values, a more practical solution combining logic and relational algebra has been studied by Biskup [1981], who also further investigates Codd's proposals, providing them with a sound foundation and arguing for their practical applicability [Biskup 1982]. In the case of more general incomplete information, we mention here the work by Bossu and Siegel [1981], where a promising approach based on model theory is taken, and the work by Minker [1982]. Finally, an interesting complement to logic for handling null values can be found in Siklossy and Lauriere [1982]. As mentioned above, work in artificial intelligence that deals with nonmonotonic logics is relevant to this topic. The interested reader is referred to papers in the 1980 special issue of the *Artificial Intelligence Journal* on nonmonotonic logic [AIJ 1980].

## 1.2 Integrity Constraints

### 1.2.1 Formulation and Enforcement

Database consistency is enforced by integrity constraints, which are assertions that database instances (states) are compelled to obey. Integrity constraints have been classified according to various criteria. The first criterion distinguishes between state constraints, which characterize valid database states, and transition constraints, which impose restrictions on the possible state transitions of a database. Among state constraints different subclasses can be isolated: for example, *type constraints*, which require the arguments of relations to belong to specified domains, or *dependency constraints*, which are discussed in Section 1.4.

As stated by Ullman [1980], a fundamental idea concerning integrity constraints is that query languages can be used to express them, although transition constraints require special attention [Casanova and Bernstein 1979; Florentin 1974; Nicolas and Yazdanian 1978]. It is therefore not surprising that various authors have used a first-order language to study integrity constraints and have appealed to both the model-theoretic and the proof-theoretic logical views.

The model-theoretic view is exploited by Nicolas and Yazdanian [1978] for characterizing those integrity constraints in a database that might be falsified by a given update, and must consequently be evaluated to determine whether the resulting database state is valid. Once such a constraint, say $C$, has been selected, one can take advantage of the fact that $C$ is known to be satisfied in the state before the update, in order to derive (according to the update) a simplified form of $C$, say $S(C)$, such that $S(C)$ is satisfied in the new database state iff $C$ is satisfied, and the evaluation cost of $S(C)$ is less than or equal to the evaluation cost of $C$. Then the evaluation of $S(C)$ can be substituted for the evaluation of $C$, thus reducing the cost of integrity constraint checking. Such a simplification method, which relies upon truth, preserving instantiations of formulas, is defined by Nicolas [1979a, 1979b] for constraints expressed in the domain relational calculus.

An implementation of this simplification method is reported upon by Homeier [1981]. A similar method was also introduced later by Blaustein [1981] for constraints expressed in the tuple relational calculus. Finally, in Casanova and Bernstein [1979] the same database logical view is used to define a data manipulation language with a logic system that permits one to prove whether or not a transaction preserves consistency (see Section 1.2.2).

In addition, Henschen et al. [1984] describe a technique for extracting integrity tests from database constraints expressed as first-order formulas. The tests can be generated at database design time and are applied when updates to the database appear. Of particular interest in this approach is that tests are applied before the update is made.

An alternative formulation of integrity constraints as first-order formulas has been exploited by McSkimin [1976], McSkimin and Minker [1977], Minker [1978b], and Reiter [1981]. Although their work was done in the context of deductive databases, it can be applied equally well to integrity checking in conventional databases. Both approaches consider a (principal) database augmented with a type database. Types are distinguished by unary relations (or Boolean combinations of them); a type database is a set of formulas (represented as a semantic graph in Minker [1978b]), expressing relations among types (e.g., inclusion, and disjointness) and also the inclusion of certain data values to a particular type. The connection between both databases is made via type integrity constraints that force arguments of relations to be of the same type.

Minker uses these integrity constraints to reject queries that are not well formed, such as a query that requires two relations to be joined on attributes that belong to disjoint types. A refutation-like procedure checks the well formedness of a query by using type constraints and the type database.

Reiter [1981] addresses the problem of detecting the violation of these constraints when the database is updated. Both insertions of data and of general laws are considered (integrity constraints on standard databases, axioms in a deductive database). The method relies upon a transformation of these general laws, which are universally quantified formulas, into a form for which simple criteria for the detection of type constraint violations are proposed.

#### 1.2.2 Proving Consistency of Transactions

It is clearly easier to prove the consistency of transactions when data is defined in a formal framework, and integrity constraints and database transactions (which retrieve, insert, delete, and update information) are stated formally and in the same language. Starting from a database state that complies with given constraints, consistency of transactions is proved when the state arrived at after the transaction has been executed also complies with these constraints. In order to prove consistency, a formal system can be provided whose objects are the transactions: A syntax, semantics, and proof theory for reasoning about objects are needed. A transaction is expressible in a programming language, including expressions used to define sets of data upon which the transaction acts; thus transaction languages include data definition languages. If the data definition language itself is endowed with a proof theory, the transaction formal system can use it. This is the case with the logic interpretation of databases.

Casanova and Bernstein [1979, 1980] offer an elegant, albeit theoretical, answer to these problems. The data definition language, viewed through its logic perspective, includes the integrity constraints as axioms of a first-order theory. The transaction language then is embedded in regular programs [Pratt 1976], supported by a formal system, first-order dynamic logic (DL). This embedding is accomplished by expressing the operations of retrieve, insert, delete, and update in terms of assignment, tests, random tuple selection, union, composition, and iteration operators, the semantics of which encompass that of all computable queries (Section 1.1.2). Regular first-order

DL [Harel 1979] then is extended to a system called modal dynamic logic (MDL) to reason about such programs. MDL is shown to have the necessary power to prove most essential database questions: consistency, transaction, and serializability of transactions. One should note that this work was also extended to deal with aggregate operators (Section 1.1.2). This approach obviously needs a more practical counterpart. Gardarin and Melkanoff [1979] offer a partial answer, using Hoare's logic rather than dynamic logic.

### 1.3 Query Optimization

Optimization of query evaluation, or improvement of query evaluation as it might better be termed, has been attacked in many different ways. A traditional approach is to use low-level information such as statistical information about various costs to access individual relations. Systems that have been implemented, for example, System R [Chamberlin et al. 1981; Selinger et al. 1979] and more experimental systems [Demolombe 1980; Grant and Minker 1981], have demonstrated that significant gains in efficiency can be achieved by using such information. However, it is clear that additional gains can be obtained by using higher level information, whether syntactic or semantic.

Syntactic transformations, yielding a logical equivalent of the initial query have been studied by Aho et al. [1979] and Chandra and Merlin [1976]. For example, the query

$$\begin{aligned}(\exists u, v, w, y, z)&R(x, v, w)\\ &\& \; R(x, z, w) \;\&\; S(u, w)\\ &\& \; S(u, v) \;\&\; S(y, w)\\ &\& \; S(y, v) \;\&\; S(y, z),\end{aligned}$$

where $x$ is a free variable, can be shown to be equivalent to

$$\exists u, v, w \; R(x, v, w) \;\&\; S(u, v).$$

But perhaps the most promising technique is found in the so-called semantic transformations. A first step in that direction was taken by McSkimin [1976] and McSkimin and Minker [1977], who used a form of integrity constraint that describes domains of relations and relates them to each other. Additional information, which takes into account the cardinality of intersections or unions of domains, is used to simplify queries and also to interrupt the process of extracting an answer whenever the additional information justifies it.

A more general approach, related to global problem-solving strategies [Kowalski 1979], is described by King [1981] and Hammer and Zdonik [1980], where the idea of query modification based on general rules is addressed. A set of general rules (integrity constraints and/or deductive laws—see Section 2) such as "a ship carries no more cargo than its rated capacity" or "the only ships whose deadweight exceeds 150 thousand tons are supertankers" [King 1981] can also be used to transform a query submitted by a user into a query less costly to evaluate, eliminating unnecessary relations or propagating constraints. This process then interacts with, and uses information from, a more classical optimizer, which can take into account such factors as indexing of attributes. Obviously a major problem is to control the derivation of queries from the original query. This is a classical problem in artificial intelligence systems, and has been studied by King, who derived a set of heuristics and specified and implemented a plan–generate–test process that gives interesting and practical results. Logic is seen at its best in such applications. Much remains to be done in this important area.

A different use of logic is reported by Warren [1981] in relation to the application of natural language database querying. The underlying database is relational, and logic is used to (1) write a translator from natural language input to an internal representation, (2) represent the internal form of queries as logic formulas, (3) write an optimizer of the querying process, which analyzes the query and uses the traditional type of statistical information already referred to above, to modify the query, and (4) evaluate the query (which could be interfaced to the access level of a standard database management system). The performance of the overall process is very acceptable; the interested reader is referred to Warren [1981] for further details. Warren's approach to optimization is similar to the approach taken by Selinger et al. [1979]. See Chakravarthy et al. [1982] for a discussion of how a logic database may be interfaced with a relational database and related work by Kunifuji and Yokota [1982] and Yokota et al. [1983].

Before leaving this extremely promising field, we note another use of constraints or general laws describing the domain of discourse in the query interpretation process. As discussed by Janas [1979, 1981], whenever a query has an empty answer, a reasonable set of subqueries can be constructed whose failure explains the empty answer of the original query; this reasonable set is obtained by taking particular integrity constraints into account. A reason for not having an answer is that no tuples that currently exist in the database satisfy the query, in which case the subquery that fails can be identified or the constraints of the database are such that no answers that satisfy the query will ever be possible from the database. Such information could be of considerable value to a user. See also Demolombe [1981] for related work.

## 1.4 Database Design

There is an area where logic plays an increasing role in the specification of data models. In general, there are several methods of formal specification and several formalisms for each method; databases are but one kind of object to formalize, and techniques developed for programming languages in general can be applied. We have seen in Section 1.2.2 how such a specification can be used for a precise purpose: proving the consistency of a transaction. Veloso et al. [1981] provide a comprehensive review of these techniques, for a large part on the basis of logic (see also Borgida and Wong [1981], where logic is used to define the formal semantics of the Taxis data model). Logic is a very important tool in this area, if only because it blends nicely with all the other tools described in this paper for different purposes.

We now turn to data dependencies, a concept central to database design. Data dependencies are special cases of integrity constraints that express structural properties of relations and permit relations to be decomposed, and retain certain properties described below. A number of dependencies of various kinds have been characterized and studied in the literature (see Delobel [1980] and Maier [1983] for comprehensive surveys on dependencies). In this section we see how logic has been used to study the properties of some of these dependencies and, in some cases, define them. We also note that special formal systems have been developed for that purpose (e.g., see Armstrong [1974]). This section is divided into two parts; the first is concerned with studies involving propositional logic, and the second with studies involving first-order logic.

### 1.4.1 Propositional Logic and Dependencies

Delobel, Fagin, Parker, and Sagiv [Delobel and Parker 1978; Sagiv and Fagin 1979; Sagiv et al. 1981] have shown that an equivalence exists between some dependencies and a fragment of the propositional logic. They have shown that functional dependencies (FDs) [Codd 1970] and multivalued dependencies (MVDs) [Fagin 1977b; Zaniolo 1976] can be associated with propositional logic statements. The equivalence developed between these dependencies and propositional logic extends earlier results of Fagin [1977a] and also Delobel and Casey [1973] that relate FDs to the theory of Boolean switching functions.

The above-mentioned equivalence provides new techniques for proving properties of FDs and MVDs, and for solving the membership problem for those dependencies. Additionally, shorter and simpler proofs have been obtained for important theorems about FDs and MVDs, and strategies developed for special-purpose theorem provers provide efficient algorithms for the membership problem. Furthermore, on the basis of a proof of this equivalence, a characterization of the dependency basis in terms of truth assignments has been given by Fagin [1977b]. This has led to the development of an efficient membership algorithm for FDs and MVDs by Sagiv [1980], which has been supplanted by a faster algorithm by Galil [1982]. As another application of this equivalence, Parker and Delobel [1979] have developed an algorithm to determine whether a set of attributes is a *key* for a relation, that is, whether a set of attributes uniquely determines a tuple in the relation and is itself not contained in any other set of attributes that uniquely determines a tuple.

The equivalence, first established for FDs, was extended later to include MVDs [Sagiv et al. 1981]. It has also been extended to other kinds of dependencies, for example, Boolean dependencies, which are expressions of attributes built using the Boolean operators &, $\vee$, $\neg$. For example, $A \vee (B \;\&\; \neg C)$ is a Boolean dependency whose meaning is "for every pair of tuples, either the two tuples agree on attribute $A$, or the two tuples agree on attribute $B$ and disagree on attribute $C$." However, although this shows that the equivalence can be extended to some generalization of FDs, it cannot be extended to embedded MVDs (MVDs that hold for a projection of a relation) or to mutual dependencies for which the inferential structure of propositional logic seems to be too weak [Delobel 1978]. Nicolas [1978] was the first to suggest that first-order logic be used. However, before considering first-order logic, we note a similar equivalence result between FDs obtained by Vassiliou [1980], who redefined a FDs interpretation in order to account for null values, and implicational statements of a model propositional logic system. Vassiliou exploited this equivalence, notably, for proving the completeness of a set of inference rules for those "newly interpreted" FDs.

#### 1.4.2 First-Order Logic and Dependencies

By considering dependencies as first-order formulas, one provides advantages similar to those sketched for propositional logic; results from proof theory and model theory can be used to study their properties.

Dependency statements can be expressed as first-order formulas. For example, given a relation scheme $R(ABCD)$, the FD $C \rightarrow D$ and the MVD $A \rightarrow\rightarrow B$ are, respectively, equivalent to the following two first-order formulas:

$$\forall x \cdots \forall v'(R(x, y, z, v) \;\&\; R(x', y', z, v') \rightarrow (v = v')),$$

$$\forall x \cdots \forall v'(R(x, y, z', v') \;\&\; R(x, y', z, v) \rightarrow R(x, y, z, v)).$$

New kinds of dependencies have been characterized and defined directly as particular first-order formulas. Typical of this are generalized dependency statements (GDs) and their embedded version (EGDs) [Grant and Jacobs 1982], implicational dependencies (IDs) and their embedded version (EIDS), and extended embedded IDs (XEIDs) [Fagin 1980, 1982], and tuple- and equality-generating dependencies [Beeri and Vardi 1980, 1981]. We briefly specify the main results related to these dependencies below.

Essentially, generalized dependencies are Horn clauses that contain no function symbols; they capture FDs, MVDs, JDs (join dependencies), IDs, and some other constraints. Horn clauses are defined in Section I.2 and in Section 2. After studying the implication problem for GDs, Grant and Jacobs [1982] proposed a decision procedure for determining whether a GD is a logical consequence of a set of GDs. This procedure is related to both techniques from automatic theorem proving and the "chase method," a decision procedure for dependencies described by Maier et al. [1979] on the basis of the tableau formalism of Aho and Ullman [1979].

Horn clauses were also used to define EIDs, which were studied to "help bring order to the chaos by presenting certain mathematical properties shared by all (the previously defined) dependencies" [Fagin 1980, 1982]. Among these properties are *domain independence*, which means that whether or not a dependency holds for a relation can be determined independently of the underlying domains of the attributes in the relation, *satisfiability on empty relations* (i.e., relations with no tuples), and *faithfulness* with regard to a version of the Cartesian product called direct product.

As principle results for EIDs, Chandra et al. [1981] have shown that any set $D$ of EIDs admits an Armstrong relation (i.e., a relation that obeys all dependencies in $D$—and their consequences—but no others) and that the decision problem for this class of dependencies is undecidable. However, a complete set of inference rules has been given for the equivalent class of algebraic dependencies [Yannakakis and Papadimitriou 1982].

On the basis of the formulation of dependencies as first-order formulas, Beeri and Vardi [1980, 1981] have studied the implication problem for a general class of dependencies, the tuple- and equality-generating dependencies (tgds and eqds), and for some of its subclasses. These dependencies, which, in fact, correspond to EIDs, intuitively require that, "if some tuples fulfilling certain conditions exist in the database, then either some other tuples (possibly with unknown values), fulfilling certain conditions, must also exist in the database (tgds), or some values in the given tuples must be equal (eqds)" [Beeri and Vardi 1980, 1981].

In the same work Beeri and Vardi proposed an extension to the chase method (see also Sadri and Ullman [1980, 1982]), which provides a proof procedure for these dependencies and a decision procedure for total dependencies (i.e., nonembedded). A decision procedure is guaranteed to terminate in any case, whereas a proof procedure is not guaranteed to terminate when $D$ does not imply $d$. It is worth noting that, when described in the formalism of logic, the chase method corresponds to a well-known theorem-proving procedure by refutation (using resolution and paramodulation) [Beeri and Vardi 1981].

We have described results by using logic that relates to conventional relational databases; in the following section, we describe how logic extends conventional databases to permit deduction and sheds new insight into problems concerning negative and incomplete information.

## 2. DEDUCTIVE DATABASES

A deductive database is a database in which new facts may be derived from facts that were explicitly introduced. We consider such databases here from a proof-theoretic viewpoint as a special first-order theory. In this framework, we focus upon several subjects: the manner in which *negative data* are to be treated in a database, the *null value* problem in which the value of a data item is missing, and *indefinite data* in which one knows, say $P(a) \vee P(b)$ is true, but one does not know if $P(a)$ is true, $P(b)$ is true, or both are true.

We first provide the background for defining deductive databases, and then treat two different kinds of deductive databases: definite and indefinite. It will be seen that assumptions generally made with respect to definite databases do not apply directly to indefinite databases. Finally, we briefly discuss other extensions to deductive databases and logic databases.

For additional material on the subjects of deductive databases or logic and databases not covered in this survey article, see Gallaire et al. [1984], the *Proceedings of the First Conference on Logic Programming* [1982], *the Logic Programming Workshop Proceedings* [1983], *the International Joint Conference on Artificial Intelligence* [1983], *the International Symposium on Logic Programming* [1984], and other conferences devoted to artificial intelligence and logic programming.

### 2.1 Definition of Deductive or Logic Databases

In general, we shall consider a database to consist of a finite set of constants, say $\{c_1 \cdots c_n\}$, and a set of first-order clauses without function symbols (see Section I.2). Functions are excluded in order to have finite and explicit answers to queries. Initially our theory precludes null values that arise in a database when one has statements such as $(\exists x)P(a, x)$, that is, linked to "$a$" in the predicate $P$ there is a value, but its precise value is unknown. When one skolemizes the formula $(\exists x)P(a, x)$ and places it in clause form, the clause $P(a, \omega)$ results, where $\omega$ is a Skolem constant (i.e., a constant whose value is otherwise unconstrained).

The general form of clauses that will represent facts and deductive laws is

$$P_1 \;\&\; P_2 \;\&\; \cdots \;\&\; P_k \rightarrow R_1 \vee \cdots \vee R_q.$$

It is equivalent to the clause

$$\neg P_1 \vee \cdots \vee \neg P_k \vee R_1 \vee \cdots \vee R_q.$$

The conjunction of the $P_i$ is referred to as the left-hand side of the clause and the disjunction of the $R_j$ as the right-hand side. Since the clauses that we will consider are function free, terms that are arguments of the $P_i$ and $R_j$ are either constants or variables. Whenever any variable that occurs in the right-hand side of a clause also occurs in the left-hand side, the clause is said to be *range restricted.* We shall briefly discuss various types of clauses depending on the respective values of $k$ and $q$, as in Minker [1983]:

*Type 1:* $k = 0$, $q = 1$. Clauses have the form

$$\rightarrow P(t_1, \ldots, t_m).$$

(a) If the $t_i$ are constants, $c_{i1}, \ldots, c_{im}$, then one has

$$\rightarrow P(c_{i1}, \ldots, c_{im}),$$

which represents an assertion or a fact in the database. The set of all such assertions for the predicate letter $P$ corresponds to a "table" in a relational database. The arrow preceding an assertion will generally be omitted.

(b) When some, or all, of the $t_i$ are variables, the clause corresponds to a general statement in the database. For example,

$$\rightarrow \text{Ancestor(Adam, } x),$$

states that Adam is an ancestor of all individuals in the database (the database consists only of human beings). Clearly, such data, which are not range-restricted clauses and therefore assume that all the individuals in the database are of the same "type," appear very seldom.

*Type 2:* $k = 1$, $q = 0$. Clauses have the form

$$P(t_1, \ldots, t_m) \rightarrow.$$

(a) When all of the $t_i$ are constants, then we have

$$P(c_{i1}, \ldots, c_{im}) \rightarrow,$$

which stands for a negative fact. Negative statements may seem peculiar since relational databases do not contain negative data. We shall return to this topic in a later section.

(b) Some of the $t_i$ are variables. This may either be thought of as an integrity constraint (as a particular Type 3 clause; see below), or as the "value does not exist" meaning for null values (see Section 1.1.3).

*Type 3:* $k > 1$, $q = 0$. Clauses have the form

$$P_1 \;\&\; \cdots \;\&\; P_k \rightarrow.$$

Such axioms may be thought of as integrity constraints. That is, data to be added to a database must satisfy the laws specified by the integrity condition to be allowed in the database. For example, one may specify an integrity law that states that "no individual can be both a father and a mother of another individual." This may be specified as

$$\text{FATHER}(x, y) \;\&\; \text{MOTHER}(x, y) \rightarrow.$$

If FATHER(JACK, SALLY) is already in the database, an attempt to enter MOTHER(JACK, SALLY) into the database should lead to an integrity violation. This does not rule out other kinds of integrity constraints.

*Type 4:* $k \geq 1$, $q = 1$. Clauses have the form

$$P_1 \;\&\; P_2 \;\&\; \cdots \;\&\; P_k \rightarrow R_1.$$

The clause may be considered to be either an integrity constraint or a definition of the predicate $R_1$ in terms of the predicates $P_1, \ldots, P_k$ (such a definition is a deductive law).

*Type 5:* $k = 0$, $q > 1$. Clauses have the form

$$\rightarrow R_1 \vee R_2 \vee \cdots \vee R_1.$$

If the $x_i$, $i = 1, \ldots, n$ are constants, then we have an *indefinite assertion.* That is, any combination of one or more $R_i$ is true, but we do not know which ones are true.

*Type 6:* $k \geq 1$, $q > 1$. Clauses have the form

$$P_1 \,\&\, P_2 \,\&\, \cdots \,\&\, P_k \rightarrow R_1 \vee R_2 \vee \cdots \vee R_q.$$

The clause may be interpreted as either an integrity constraint or the definition of indefinite data. An integrity constraint that states that each individual has at most two parents may be written as

$$P(x_1, y_1) \,\&\, P(x_1, y_2) \,\&\, P(x_1, y_3)$$
$$\rightarrow (y_1 = y_2) \vee (y_1 = y_3) \vee (y_2 = y_3).$$

As a general rule of deduction we might have

$$\text{Parent}(x, y) \rightarrow \text{Mother}(x, y) \vee \text{Father}(x, y).$$

This general law could also be interpreted as an integrity constraint.

Finally, a clause where $k = 0$, $q = 0$ (the empty clause) denotes falsity and should not be part of a database. Furthermore, we shall call a clause *definite* if its right-hand side consists of exactly one atom (i.e., Type 1b or Type 4).

All the types of clauses defined above, except ground facts (Type 1a), are treated as integrity constraints in conventional databases. In a deductive database some of them may be treated as deductive laws. We shall distinguish two classes of databases: definite databases in which no clauses of either Type 5 or Type 6 appear and indefinite databases in which such clauses do appear.

### 2.2 Definite Deductive Databases (DDDBs)

#### *2.2.1 A Formal Definition of DDDBs*

A definite deductive database is defined as a particular first-order theory (together with a set of integrity constraints). This theory is obtained from the theory given for conventional databases in Section I.3 by the addition of a new class of axioms, which stand for the deductive laws, and by a reformulation of the completion axioms, which account for the presence of these new axioms. More precisely, a definite deductive database consists of the following:

(1) *A theory T* whose proper axioms are

- Axioms 1 (the particularization axioms): the domain closure axiom, the unique name axioms, the equality axioms (as given in Section I.3), and the completion axioms (one for each predicate in $T$) whose formulation is given below.
- Axioms 2 (the elementary facts): a set of ground atomic formulas defined by clauses of Type 1a in Section 2.1.
- Axioms 3 (the deductive laws): a set of function-free definite clauses of Type 4 (or Type 1b) in Section 2.1.

(2) *A set of integrity constraints IC*, which consists of any closed formulas.

The completion axiom for a predicate $P$ is now not only built from the facts related to $P$ (which occur in Axioms 2), but also from the "only if" missing part of the definite clauses defining $P$ (which occur in Axioms 3). For example, let $P$ have the following assertions in $T$:

$$P(c_i, c_j),$$
$$P(c_p, c_q),$$

and let

$$Q(x, y) \,\&\, R(y, z) \rightarrow P(x, z),$$

and

$$S(x, y) \rightarrow P(x, y),$$

be all the clauses in Axioms 3 that imply $P$; then, the completion axiom for $P$ is

$$P(x, y) \rightarrow ((x = c_1) \,\&\, (y = c_j)) \vee ((x = c_p) \,\&\, (y = c_q)) \vee (Q(x, y) \,\&\, R(y, z)) \vee (S(x, y)).$$

Such a completion axiom permits one to derive a negative fact $\neg P(d, e)$ whenever $P(d, e)$ is neither in Axioms 2 nor derivable through Axioms 3. Thus from the database just specified we can derive $\neg P(c_i, c_p)$.

In such a deductive database the definition of answers to queries and of the satisfiability of integrity constraints is equivalent to their definition in a conventional database viewed from the proof-theoretic perspective. An answer to a query $W(x_1, \ldots, x_p)$, where $x_1, \ldots, x_p$ are free variables in $W$, is the set of tuples $\langle c_{i1}, \ldots, c_{ip} \rangle$ such that $T \vdash W(c_{i1}, \ldots, c_{ip})$. Now, a deductive database obeys the integrity constraints in IC iff for any formula $\phi$ in IC $T \vdash \phi$.

An alternative definition can be given for the satisfiability of integrity constraints: A deductive database obeys the integrity constraints in IC iff $T \cup$ IC (the axioms in $T$ together with the formulas in IC) is consistent [Kowalski 1979]. Since the theory $T$, as defined above for a definite deductive database, is complete (i.e., for any closed formula $W$, either $T \vdash W$ or $T \vdash \neg W$), both definitions are equivalent in that case. However, for more general deductive databases whose corresponding theory is not complete, the second definition is less stringent than the first and its impact is worth investigating.

Deductive laws (in Axioms 3) that imply a relation $R$ provide an extended definition for $R$. The tuples $\langle c_{i1}, \ldots, c_{im} \rangle$ that "satisfy" $R$ are not only those tuples such that $R(c_{i1}, \ldots, c_{im})$ is a fact in Axioms 2, but also those tuples such that $R(c_{i1}, \ldots, c_{im})$ is derivable through the deductive laws. Relations that are jointly defined by deductive laws and elementary facts in a deductive database, called derived relations, constitute a generalization of relations defined as "views" in a conventional database. A "view" is a relation, not stored in the database, that is defined in terms of database relations or other views by a relational algebra (or calculus) expression. A derived relation reduces to a view when

(i) there are no elementary facts in Axioms 2 related to this relation, and
(ii) no recursive deductive law or cycle appears among the deductive laws that imply this relation in Axioms 3.

In such a case, if $E_1 \rightarrow R, \ldots, E_q \rightarrow R$ are all the deductive laws that imply $R$, this derived relation corresponds to the view $V = E_1 \vee \cdots \vee E_q$. We note that Point (i) is not significant since two different names may be given to the "explicit part" and the "derived part" of a relation. However, Point (ii) has more impact. Some relations may be defined as derived relations, whereas strictly, they cannot be defined as views. A typical example is the Ancestor relation, which is the transitive closure of the Parent relation. Incidentally, we note that the relational calculus (or algebra) may be extended (or embedded into another language) in order to be able to define such a relation as a view. However, since from a model-theoretic viewpoint the transitive closure of a relation is not first-order definable, one has to call for languages that are more powerful than first-order language. But, in a (definite) deductive database defined from a proof-theoretic point of view as above, the Ancestor relation can easily be defined as a derived relation in terms of two deductive laws:

$$(\text{Parent}(x, y) \rightarrow \text{Ancestor}(x, y),$$
$$\text{Ancestor}(x, y) \;\&\; \text{Parent}(y, z) \rightarrow \text{Ancestor}(x, z)),$$

and strictly remain in the context of first-order logic (see Section 1.1.2).

Clearly, on considering the combinatorial complexity of the particularization axioms (Axioms 1), it would be quite inefficient to implement a (definite) deductive DBMS, while clinging to the formal definition of a DDDB given here, namely, to implement such a DBMS as a standard theorem prover that treats axioms in Axioms 1 in the same way as axioms in Axioms 2 or Axioms 3. The solution is similar to what is done for conventional DBMSs. It consists of substituting adequate metarules (or metaconventions) for the particularization axioms, thus obtaining a so-called operational definition of a DDDB. The following section is devoted to this issue.

#### 2.2.2 An Operational Definition of DDDBs

Particularization axioms may be eliminated for DDDBs in a way that is similar to conventional databases, thus providing a convenient way to implement corresponding systems. First, calling for the domain closure axiom may be avoided by dealing with range-restricted formulas for query, integrity constraint, and deductive law formulation (see Section 1.1.1). Then, as discussed by Kowalski [1978, 1979] and proved by Clark [1978], the unique name and completion axioms may be removed, provided that negation is interpreted as (finite) failure (see also Jaffar et al. [1983] for a stronger result). The metarule of *negation as failure* states that for any positive literal $P$, $\vdash \neg P$ iff $\nvdash P$; that is, failure to prove $P$ permits one to infer $\neg P$. Finite failure further requires that all proof attempts terminate. Finally, since the equality axioms were needed only for the presence of the equality predicate in the above axioms, they are no longer required.

To summarize, keeping in mind that any formula now has to be range restricted, from an operational point of view a DDDBs consists of the following:

(1) A set of axioms: Axioms 2 (elementary facts) ∪ Axioms 3 (deductive laws).
(2) A set of integrity constraints: IC.
(3) A metarule: negation as finite failure (nff).

Query answering and integrity constraint satisfiability remain defined as in Section 1.3.1 except that, now "$\vdash$" has to be interpreted as "provable under nff."

Negation as finite failure generalizes in the deductive databases case to the usual assumption underlying conventional databases for negative facts (see Section I.3). The use of this concept was discussed as the "convention for negative information representation" by Nicolas and Syre [1974] and Nicolas and Gallaire [1978], and also described as the "closed world assumption" (CWA)[2] by Reiter [1978a, 1980]. This concept is also used in the artificial intelligence languages PLANNER [Hewitt 1972] and PROLOG [Roussel 1975].

The syntactic definition (i.e., according to proof theory) of negation as failure given above has a semantic (i.e., according to model theory) counterpart. Let $G$ be the set of all possible ground (positive) atomic formulas constructible from the symbols in a given set of definite clauses. A Herbrand model for this set of clauses is a subset of $G$ that makes all the clauses true. It has been shown [Van Emden and Kowalski 1976] that the intersection of all such models is itself a model, and indeed is the minimal model (i.e., it contains the minimal number of atomic formulas). If one substracts the set of atomic formulas in the minimal model from $G$, the remaining set of atomic formulas is the set of all formulas whose negations may be assumed to be true. These are the same atomic formulas obtained by the CWA. This shows that the CWA and negation as failure assume complete knowledge, and there are no unknown facts. A discussion of the semantic definition of negation as failure can be found in Minker [1982] and Van Emden [1978].

Although the formal and operational definitions of a DDDB are equivalent in the sense that they will give the same answers to queries, they are in fact not strictly equivalent. The formal definition is stated in standard first-order logic, which is monotonic, whereas the use of negation as failure in the operational definition leads to a nonmonotonic logic. A logic is said to be *monotonic* if one is given a theory $T$ (i.e., a set of axioms) in which a formula $w$ can be proved (i.e., $T \vdash w$), then the addition to $T$ of an axiom $A$ still permits one to prove $w$; that is, $T \cup \{A\} \vdash w$. According to negation as failure, $\neg P(b)$ can be inferred from $\{P(a), Q(b)\}$ but not from $\{P(a), Q(b)\} \cup \{P(b)\}$; thus we have a nonmonotonic logic. For an analysis of the relation between predicate completion and work in artificial intelligence on nonmonotonic logic, the reader is referred to Reiter [1982].

Finally, we note that, as shown by Nicolas and Gallaire [1978] and formally proved by Reiter [1978a], a definite deductive database is always consistent under the CWA. The intuitive reason is that definite clauses preclude the derivation of positive facts from negative facts. We see in Section 2.3 that this is not the case when indefinite clauses are accepted as deductive laws.

#### *2.2.3 Deductive Laws and Integrity Constraints*

Both deductive laws in Axioms 3 and integrity constraints in IC correspond to general knowledge of the world modeled by the

[2] There is the open world assumption (OWA) corresponding to the CWA that provides a standard interpretation of negation as given with a full first-order theory.

database. Given such general knowledge, we might inquire as to the basis on which one can decide to consider a general rule as a deductive law, and thus incorporate it in Axioms 3, or as an integrity constraint, and thus incorporate it as part of the IC. There is no final answer to this (database design) question, but some suggestions are provided by Nicolas and Gallaire [1978] and Reiter [1978a, 1984]. They are briefly stated below.

(i) If one wants to obtain finite and explicit answers to queries (i.e., sets of tuples of elements in the database), deductive laws have to be function free. Thus general knowledge that corresponds to formulas that do not fulfill this constraint should be treated as integrity constraints. For example, the general knowledge "every teacher has a diploma,"

$$(\forall x\ \forall y(\text{TEACH}(x, y) \rightarrow (\exists z)\text{DIPLOMA}(x, z))),$$

should be treated as an integrity constraint since the clause form of the axiom contains a Skolem function.

(ii) In order to avoid inconsistency with the CWA, one retains as deductive laws only general knowledge that corresponds to definite clauses (and thus use the other clauses as integrity constraints). However, as we shall see in Section 2.3, there is another possibility, which consists of modifying the CWA.

(iii) Since purely negative clauses (i.e., clauses of Type 3 in Section 2.1) will never produce new facts (under the CWA), they need only be used as integrity constraints [Reiter 1978a].

(iv) General knowledge that implies instances of a relation that is completely defined independently of it will not, if used as a deductive law, produce any new valid facts and should be used as an integrity constraint.

For example, the general knowledge, "the age of any person is less than 150,"

$$(\forall x\ \forall y)(\text{Age}(x, y) \rightarrow (y < 150)),$$

used as a deductive law, would always produce facts which are either inconsistent (e.g., 180 < 150) or redundant (e.g., 35 < 150). A functional dependency statement such as

$$(\forall x\ \forall x'\ \forall y)(\text{Father}(x, y)\ \&\ \text{Father}(x', y) \rightarrow (x = x')),$$

is another example of this kind. Hence these rules are best used as integrity constraints.

In the two examples above, the implied relations are of a particular kind, and it is generally agreed that they are defined independently of any reference to a specific database. For more standard relations, it is a matter of choice (dependent upon database design) to decide what general knowledge and which assertions will participate in the complete definition of a relation. As an extreme case, in a conventional database it is (implicitly) assumed that every relation (other than views) is completely defined in terms of elementary facts (the tuples in the corresponding table), and thus all general knowledge is used as integrity constraints.

As noted by Kowalski [1979] and as we shall emphasize here, a deductive database can be viewed as a logic program that produces facts (the facts in the minimal model characterized in Section 2.2.2) and whose integrity constraints are the program properties. Modifications to the program (viz. database updates involving either deduction laws or elementary facts) must preserve those properties.

When general knowledge has been partitioned between deductive laws and integrity constraints, they have to be exploited conjointly. Integrity checking in a deductive context is discussed by Nicolas and Yazdanian [1978] and Reiter [1981], and a methodology for updating databases with integrity constraints and deductive laws was suggested by Fagin et al. [1983]. Further, query evaluation and update handling are uniformly treated by dos Santos et al.

[1981], where deduction provides either an analysis of a state of the database, that is, an answer to a query, or a plan, that is, a sequence of database modifications to reach a desired state. We now focus on deductive laws.

As mentioned in the preceding section, the theory that constitutes a definite deductive database admits a (unique) minimal model. This (minimal) model consists of a set of facts that connotes that these are the facts that are true. These facts constitute the conventional database (CDB) underlying the deductive database. Now, one can choose to exploit the deductive database in either of two ways. The underlying CDB can be kept implicit, in which case the deductive laws, or their compiled form (see Section 2.2.4.2), have to be run at query evaluation time to find the (implicit) deducible facts. The alternative consists of making the underlying CDB explicit. To do so, deductive laws have to be run when new facts are inserted into the database to make explicit the deducible facts. Then query evaluation can be done as in a conventional database. In the first case deductive laws are said to be used as derivation rules, whereas in the second case, they are said to be used as generation rules [Nicolas and Gallaire 1978]. The respective advantages of derivation and generation rules are discussed by Nicolas and Gallaire [1978] and Nicolas and Yazdanian [1982]. We only mention here that, as opposed to derivation paths, "generation paths" stop naturally even when recursive rules or cycles among the rules appear. The interested reader will find a description of a prototype deductive DBMS by using generation rules in Nicolas and Yazdanian [1982].

Finally, we note that exploiting deductive laws as generation rules can be viewed as an automatic revalidation of integrity constraints in a conventional database. This can also be viewed as providing a generalization of "concrete views" [Blaustein 1981], that is, views whose corresponding set of tuples is explicitly stored.

In the following section we focus on proof-theoretic techniques used for exploiting derivation rules.

#### 2.2.4 Inference Methods and Database Access

We shall describe two ways to perform the inference process: the interpretive and the compiled methods.

The *interpretive method* works with a problem solver, using the deductive laws and interleaves search of the extensional DB (which contains the elementary facts, i.e., Axioms 2). In the *compiled approach*, the problem solver uses all of the deductive laws until a point is reached at which either the problem is solved or all that remains is to search for facts in the extensional DB. Both methods work well when deductive laws are assumed to be free of cycles, that is, when there are no recursive axioms. Otherwise, both have difficulties handling the termination problem, that is, detecting at which point no new solutions will be found. However, it should be possible to find such termination conditions, as only a finite number of tuples can be generated as answers to any query to a definite deductive database (function free, with a finite set of constants and consisting of only definite clauses). This problem has been studied by a number of authors [Chang 1981; Kunifuji and Yokota 1982; Minker and Nicolas 1982; Naqvi and Henschen 1984; Reiter 1978c; Shapiro and McKay 1980; Yokota et al. 1983].

*2.2.4.1 Interpretive Method of Deduction.* We shall describe the interpretive method for the following simple database. Let the facts in the database (the extensional DB) be

| | | |
|---|---|---|
| $F(e, b_1)$ | $M(c, e)$ | $H(a, c)$ |
| $F(e, b_2)$ | $M(c, f)$ | |
| $F(e, b_3)$ | $M(c, g)$ | |
| | $M(g, d)$ | |

where F, M, and H stand, respectively, for Father, Mother, and Husband. Let the deductive laws be

$$(A_1)\quad M(x, y)\ \&\ M(y, z) \rightarrow GM(x, z),$$

$$(A_2)\quad M(x, y)\ \&\ F(y, z) \rightarrow GM(x, z),$$

$$(A_3)\quad GM(z, y)\ \&\ H(x, z) \rightarrow GF(x, y).$$

Relation GM (Grandmother) is said to be intensionally defined in terms of the extensional relations F and M. Relation GF (Grandfather) is intensionally defined in terms of the extensional relation H and intensional relation GM, and hence in terms of the extensional relations F and M as well. There is no loss of generality in assuming that no relation is hybrid; that is, all relations are either (purely) intensional or (purely) extensional (e.g., see Minker [1982]). We illustrate the interpretive approach, starting from a query $GF(a, y)$:

(1) $$GF(a, y),$$

and applying A3, using the Robinson Resolution Principle (Section I.2) yields

(2) $$GM(z, y) \ \& \ H(a, z)$$

as the subproblems to be solved. At this point a selection function could be used to provide advice to solve $H(a, z)$ first. The reason for selecting $H(a, z)$ first is that it contains a constant and is presumably easier to satisfy than the case where one arbitrarily looks for a tuple that satisfies $GM(z, y)$ and hopes that the value of $z$, when substituted into $H(a, z)$, will be in the database. By accessing the database, we find that $H(a, c)$ is in the database and $z$ is bound to $c$. Now, the subproblem

(3) $$GM(c, y)$$

remains to be solved. Since there are two ways to solve this last goal on the DB (Axioms $A_1$ and $A_2$), a choice is made to select Rule A2, yielding

(4) $$M(c, y_1) \ \& \ F(y_1, y),$$

which now must be solved. These subproblems may be solved in two steps, to obtain one answer, $\{b_1\}$. However, the process is not finished, and backtracking at previous choice points will yield $\{b_2, b_3, d\}$ as further answers. So, for the sake of efficiency, at each step one has to involve a selection function and a choice function. Some of the variants of this basic method have explored the idea of obtaining the whole set of answers at each access to the DB, rather than one at a time [Chakravarthy et al. 1982; Minker 1975a, 1975b, 1978a, 1978b]. Although no termination conditions are known in the general case, one should note that this problem also exists in logic programming, where it is left up to the skill of the programmer to specify a termination condition.

*2.2.4.2 Compilation Method of Deduction.* Access to the database is delayed in the deductive process until all the work remaining to be done for query evaluation is to access the database. This should allow the possibility for global optimizations of DB accesses. The method was basically described by Chang [1978], Furukawa [1977], Kellogg et al. [1978], Kellogg and Travis [1981], and Reiter [1978b]. Two possible techniques can be used. In the first technique, which could be called a pseudocompilation technique, only one path at a time is pursued. That is, a single expression involving only extensional relations is produced at a given time; backtracking then produces further expressions. This is clearly a source of redundant work. With the above deductive laws, first one would get the expression

$$M(z, y_1) \ \& \ M(y_1, y) \ \& \ H(a, z),$$

which would be passed over to the DB evaluator, and along a second path one might generate the expression

$$M(z, y_1) \ \& \ F(y_1, y) \ \& \ H(a, z),$$

which has obvious redundancies with the previous expression [Chakravarthy et al. 1982; Kunifuji and Yokota 1982]. The second technique aims at producing an iterative program that synthesizes the set of all retrieval expressions. Let us illustrate it by extending the deductive laws of our previous example to the following intensional recursive relation (Ancestor):

$$F(x, y) \ \& \ A(y, z) \rightarrow A(x, z),$$
$$M(x, y) \rightarrow A(x, y).$$

In this case, a method described by Naqvi and Henschen [1980, 1984] would produce the following program from an initial query $A(?, a)$.

```
z₂ := a
eval(F(y₂, y₁) & M(y₁, z₂))
                        /likely to access M first/
print(y₁)    /there may be several values of y₁/
enque(S, y₁)
  /put in set S those values not already put into
                                              it/
while(S ≠ empty) do
  y₂ := deque(S)          /take the first element/
  eval(F(y₃, y₂))
  print(y₃)
  enque(S, y₃)
  end
```

This method is general but suffers from some drawbacks in that some redundancy may still remain. The enque process may be time consuming and the program generated depends on the initial query.

### 2.3 Indefinite Deductive Databases (IDDDBs)

An indefinite deductive database differs from a definite deductive database (referring to its operational definition) in Axioms 3 and the metarule to handle negation. The difference in Axioms 3, although seemingly minor, will be seen to be substantial. We define Axioms 3′ as follows:

- Axioms 3′: a set of function-free definite or indefinite clauses. An indefinite clause is to the form given by Type 5 or Type 6 in Section 2.1, for example,

$$P(a, b) \vee Q(c, d, e),$$

or

$$R(x, y) \;\&\; T(y, z) \rightarrow P(x, z) \vee Q(x, y, z).$$

More precisely, an *indefinite deductive database* consists of

(1) A set of axioms $T$, where $T$ = Axioms 2 ∪ Axioms 3′.
(2) A set of integrity constraints IC.
(3) A metarule: generalized negation as failure, described below.

The addition of indefinite clauses changes matters radically. Methods and results that apply to definite deductive databases do not apply to indefinite deductive databases. For example, an indefinite database may be inconsistent under the CWA. Consider a database that consists of a single fact,

$$\text{cat(felix)},$$

and of a single deductive law,

$$\text{cat}(x) \rightarrow \text{black}(x) \vee \text{white}(x).$$

Since black(felix) cannot be proved, application of the CWA leads to

$$\vdash \neg\text{black(felix)}.$$

Similarly, one can also conclude

$$\vdash \neg\text{white(felix)}.$$

But the set

$$\{\text{cat}(x) \rightarrow \text{black}(x) \vee \text{white}(x), \text{cat(felix)}, \neg\text{black(felix)}, \neg\text{white(felix)}\}$$

is obviously inconsistent. Hence the closed world assumption (negation as failure) as defined for definite databases is not applicable to indefinite databases.

The concept of a CWA can be extended to achieve a *generalized closed world assumption* (GCWA) as follows. Let $E$ be the set of all purely positive (possibly empty) clauses not provable. Then assert $\neg P(x)$ iff $P(x) \vee C$ is not provable for any $C$ in $E$. We also refer to this as *generalized negation as failure.* As in the case of definite databases, one can obtain a semantic interpretation of generalized negation as failure. But, whereas in a definite database there is a unique minimal model, in an indefinite database a set of minimal models arises. The GCWA as defined above was introduced by Minker [1982]. In the case where no general axioms appear other than definite ground clauses, Grant and Minker [1983] have developed an algorithm on the basis of the GCWA to compute answers to queries. Although the GCWA provides a sound formal basis, this notion has not yet been shown to be sufficiently efficient when general axioms are permitted to be directly usable in practice. A variant that may be more promising from a practical point of view was introduced independently, and widely studied by Bossu and Siegel [1981].

The GCWA treats null values correctly, where it is meant here that the null value is among the constants already known in the database. Let the database consist of $\{P(\omega), Q(a), Q(b)\}$, where '$\omega$' is a null value, or Skolem constant that arises from the statement $\exists x P(x)$. If the domain $D$ consists only of $\{a, b\}$, then the existentially quantified statement corresponds to

$$(\exists x P(x)) \leftrightarrow P(a) \vee P(b).$$

Hence $P(\omega)$ is a shorthand notation for $P(a) \vee P(b)$. If one were to replace the entry $P(\omega)$ with $P(a) \vee P(b)$, and the database were treated under the GCWA, one could not conclude $\neg P(a)$ from this database. The null value is then treated correctly. A disadvantage to this approach is that of having to list a potentially long disjunction for a database with many constants in its domain.

Another major difference is that the deduction mechanism needs to be more complex for indefinite databases than for definite deductive databases. Indeed, proof strategies such as input resolution [Chang 1970] and LUSH resolution [Hill 1974], although complete for Horn clauses, are not complete for non-Horn clauses. When dealing with indefinite clauses, a complete proof strategy such as linear resolution [Loveland 1969, 1970; Reiter 1971], linear resolution with selection function (SL) [Kowalski and Kuehner 1971], or linear resolution with unrestricted selection function based on trees (LUST) [Minker and Zanon 1982] is required.

Answers in an indefinite deductive database are no longer definite. That is, if the entire database consists of the single entry $P(a) \vee P(b)$, then the answer to the query $P(x)$? is $x = a + b$, which denotes that either $x = a$ or $x = b$ or both satisfy the query. The problem of indefinite answers is addressed by Reiter [1978b] and Grant and Minker [1983].

Minker and Perlis [1983, 1984] treat a different kind of indefiniteness. Users may know that some of their facts are correct. They may also know that they are not willing to make statements about other facts. That is, the facts may or may not be true. In either a conventional or a deductive database there is no facility available to store facts and specify to the user that these facts may or may not be true. To account for this possibility Minker and Perlis have generalized the concept of circumscription developed by McCarthy [1980] to what they call protected circumscription. They have shown that the user can then obtain answers of the form yes, no, and unknown. Efficient computational techniques are required to make the approach practical. They have also developed a completeness and soundness result for protected circumscription in the case of finitary data, and hence for cases of interest to databases.

### 2.4 Logic Databases

The presentation of deductive databases given in the preceding sections essentially reflects a view from the perspective of conventional databases, that is, a "DB field" view. Starting with a conventional DB, one introduces some ad hoc deductive capabilities while keeping (as far as possible) the usual DB conventions. For example, only function-free formulas are retained, but clearly, authorizing functions allows more general forms of data to be manipulated (i.e., general terms instead of only constants and variables), which eventually give a different conceptual model to the user (e.g., semantic networks; see Deliyanni and Kowalski [1979] for a discussion as to how semantic networks can be represented in logic). We do not consider an (extended) deductive database as an unconstrained first-order theory because its implementation would be extremely inefficient.

Introducing functions into DB Horn clauses takes the deductive database field closer to the field of logic programming. It is thus not surprising to see the same enhancements carried out for both fields. Horn clauses augmented with negation as failure led to the PROLOG language, which has been demonstrated to be efficient [Roussel 1975]. A PROLOG program is quite similar to a definite deductive database (up to functions). However, this does not mean that a standard interpreter for such a language constitutes a DDBMS that must not only provide us with query facilities, but also with functions for integrity and maintenance of deduced facts. A logic database system would be obtained by combining the above-mentioned facilities with an efficient access method to a large number of facts. Such an integration can be realized in various ways (see Chakravarthy et al. [1982] and Gallaire [1983]). It should be clear that a logic database language could be continuously extended, by providing extensions to negation as failure, incorporating metalanguage capabilities and other capabilities. This could prove useful for databases, as argued by Kowalski [1981a].

## 3. CONCLUSION

We have attempted to cover results obtained within the framework of mathematical logic applied to databases mainly through the perspective of deductive databases. We have shown how logic applies to query languages, integrity modeling and maintenance, query evaluation, database design through dependencies, representation and manipulation of deduced facts, and incomplete information. However, the field of logic and databases, as it is called, is far from closed; logic provides an appropriate framework for many database problems that still need to be investigated thoroughly. We note some of these problems below. Many of the problems listed below as needing continued research have been drawn from a report to which the first and third authors of this paper contributed [Adiba et al. 1982] (see also Reiter [1984]):

- *Designing natural language query systems*, whatever "natural" means.
- *Optimizing query evaluation based on semantic knowledge*, which is needed, in general, for interactive access to databases and especially in a natural language context.
- *Finding criteria and methods for choosing, between equivalent sets of integrity constraints, a good set*, where "good" means constraint sets that are easy to check and to maintain.
- *Finding criteria to decide which relations should be base relations and which should be derived or hybrid relations*, in other words, what general knowledge should be used as integrity constraints and what should be used as deduction rules.
- *Finding more efficient means for detecting the violation of integrity constraints.*
- *Synthesizing a program preserving integrity from transaction specifications and integrity constraints*, both expressed in logic. Since such a program could also be written in logic (programming), the field of logic and databases appears to be particularly well suited here.
- *Relaxing some of the conditions for a formula to be an integrity constraint* and investigating the interest of such less stringent definitions.
- *Embedding data manipulation languages in programming languages.* In deductive databases one usually considers the deductive component to be part of the DBMS. However, it is possible to interface a (conventional or deductive) DBMS with a logic programming language, for example, PROLOG. Such an integration is accomplished most easily when the DBMS language is predicate calculus oriented; a full integration could result in which the DBMS appears as the part of the programming system specialized to the manipulation of facts.
- *Looking for practical solutions to handle general forms of incomplete information.* Although satisfactory solutions have been found for some incomplete information problems, major developments are needed to be able to handle practical problems. It will be necessary to investigate the concepts of circumscription and protected circumscription to expand their applicability to databases. The investigation of incomplete information is intimately connected with null value problems.
- *Investigating how logic can help in defining the so-called semantic models*, which appear as competitors to the relational model both for classical database applications and for more ambitious applications, where various types of data must be handled (e.g., text, computer-assisted design data, graphics). Such research will pursue problems identical to those in knowledge representation.

As we have attempted to demonstrate in this survey article, the field of logic and databases is important both to conventional and deductive databases. In this connection we note that "logic and databases" as have been described in this paper constitute the core of the work in Japan in the field of knowledge bases in their "Fifth-Generation Project."

Logic, we believe, provides a firm theoretical basis upon which one can pursue database theory in general. There are many research areas that remain to be investigated in addition to those listed above before a full understanding of databases is achieved. We believe that the field of logic and databases will contribute significantly to such an understanding. At the same time, we believe that logic databases may be made practical and efficient, as has been described by the many developments reported on in this survey.

## ACKNOWLEDGMENTS

We thank Bob Kowalski and Ray Reiter, whose work in the field of logic and databases has been very influential, and for the many discussions that we have had with them over the past several years. The comments of the referees, the ACM technical editor, and Joachim Biskup on an earlier version of this paper were greatly appreciated.

Support for the work on this paper was received by Hervé Gallaire from Compagnie Générale d'Électricité (CGE), by Jack Minker from the Air Force Office of Scientific Research (AFOSR) under Grant 82-0303, the National Aeronautics and Space Administration (NASA) under Grant NAG-1-51, and the National Science Foundation (NSF) under Grants MCS-7919418 and MCS-8305992, by Jean-Marie Nicolas from the Direction des Recherches, Études et Techniques d'Armements (DRET), the Centre National de la Recherche Scientifique (CNRS-APT Intelligence Artificielle), and the Institut National de la Recherche en Informatique et Automatique (INRIA). We gratefully acknowledge the support that made this work possible.

## REFERENCES

ADIBA, M., et al. 1982. Bases de donnes: Nouvelles perspectives. Rapport du groupe BD3 ADI-INRIA, Paris.

AHO, A. V., AND ULLMAN, J. D. 1979. Universality of data retrieval languages. In *Proceedings of the 6th ACM Symposium on Principles of Programming Languages* (San Antonio, Tex., Jan. 29–31). ACM, New York, pp. 110–120.

AHO, A. V., SAGIV, Y., AND ULLMAN, J. D. 1979. Equivalences among relational expressions. *SIAM J. Comput. 8*, 2 (May), 218–246.

ANSI/X3/SPARC 1975. Study Group on DBMS Interim Report. *SIGMOD FDT Bull. 7*, 2, 1975.

ARMSTRONG, W. W. 1974. Dependency structures of database relationships. In *Proceedings of IFIP 74*. Elsevier North-Holland, New York, pp. 580–583.

ARTIFICIAL INTELLIGENCE JOURNAL 1980. *13*, 1, 2; Special issue on nonmonotonic logic.

ARTRAUD, A., AND NICOLAS, J.-M. 1974. An experimental query system: SYNTEX. In *Proceedings of the International Computing Symposium 73*. Elsevier North-Holland, New York, pp. 557–563.

BANCILHON, F. 1978. On the completeness of query languages for relational databases. In *Proceedings of the 7th Symposium on Mathematical Foundations of Computer Science*. Springer-Verlag, Berlin and New York, pp. 112–123.

BEERI, C., AND VARDI, M. Y. 1980. A proof procedure for data dependencies. Tech. Rep., Computer Science Dept., Hebrew Univ., Jerusalem (Aug.).

BEERI, C., AND VARDI, M. Y. 1981. The implication problem for data dependencies. In *Proceedings of the 8th Colloquium on Automata, Languages, and Programming ACTC* (AKKO). Springer-Verlag, Berlin and New York, pp. 73–85.

BISKUP, J. A. 1981. A formal approach to null values in database relations. In *Advances in Database Theory*, vol. 1, H. Gallaire, J. Minker, and J.-M. Nicolas, Eds. Plenum, New York, pp. 299–341.

BISKUP, J. A. 1982. A foundation of Codd's relational maybe-operations. Tech. Rep., Computer Science Dept., Univ. of Dortmund, West Germany.

BLAUSTEIN, B. T. 1981. Enforcing database assertions: Techniques and applications, Ph.D. dissertation, Computer Science Dept., Harvard Univ., Cambridge, Mass. (Aug.).

BORGIDA, A., AND WONG, H. K. T. 1981. Data models and data manipulation languages: Complementary semantics and proof theory. In *Proceedings of the 7th Conference on Very Large Data Bases* (Cannes, France, Sept. 9–11). IEEE, New York, pp. 260–271.

BOSSU, G., AND SIEGEL, P. 1981. La saturation au secours de la non-monotonicite. These de 3eme Cycle, Départment d'Informatiques, Université d'Aix-Marseille-Luminy, Marseille, France (June).

BOWEN, K. A., AND KOWALSKI, R. A. 1982. Amalgamating language and metalanguage in logic programming. In *Logic Programming*, K. L. Clark and S. A. Tarnlund, Eds. Academic Press, New York, pp. 153–172.

BRODIE, M. L., AND ZILLES, S. N., Eds. 1980. *Proceedings of the Workshop on Data Abstraction, Databases and Conceptual Modeling* (Pingree Park, Colo., June). *ACM SIGMOD Rec. 11*, 2 (Feb.).

CASANOVA, M. A., AND BERNSTEIN, P. A. 1979. The logic of a relational data manipulation language. In *Proceedings of the 6th ACM Symposium on*

*Principles of Programming Languages* (San Antonio, Tex., Jan. 29–31). ACM, New York, pp. 101–109.

CASANOVA, M. A., AND BERNSTEIN, P. A. 1980. A formal system for reasoning about programs accessing a relational database. *ACM Trans. Program. Lang. Syst. 2,* 3 (July), 386–414.

CHAKRAVARTHY, U. S., MINKER, J., AND TRAN, D. 1982. Interfacing predicate logic languages and relational databases. In *Proceedings of the 1st Conference on Logic Programming* (Marseille, France, Sept.). Université d'Aix-Marseille-Luminy, Marseille, France, pp. 91–98.

CHAMBERLIN, D. D., ASTRAHAN, M. M., BLASGEN, M. W., GRAY, J. N., KING, W. F., LINDSAY, B. G., LORIE, R., MEHL, J. W., PRICE, T. G., PUTZOLU, F., SELINGER, P. G., SCHKOLNICK, M., SLUTZ, D. R., TRAIGER, I. L., WADE, B. W., AND YOST, R. A. 1981. A history and evaluation of System R. *Commun. ACM 24,* 10 (Oct.) 632–646.

CHANDRA, A. K., AND HAREL, D. 1979. Computable queries for relational data bases. In *Proceedings of the 11th ACM Symposium on Theory of Computing* (Atlanta, Ga., Apr. 30–May 2). ACM, New York, pp. 309–318.

CHANDRA, A. K., AND HAREL, D. 1980. Structure and complexity of relational queries. In *Proceedings of the 21st IEEE Symposium on Foundations of Computer Science* (Syracuse, N.Y., Oct.). IEEE, New York, pp. 333–347. Also in *J. Comput. Syst. Sci. 25,* 1 (Aug. 1982), 99–128.

CHANDRA, A. K., AND MERLIN, P. M. 1976. Optimal implementation of conjunctive queries in relational data bases. In *Proceedings of the 9th ACM Symposium on Theory of Computing* (Boulder, Colo., May 2–4). ACM, New York, pp. 77–90.

CHANDRA, A. K., LEWIS, H. R., AND MAKOWSKY, J. A. 1981. Embedded implicational dependencies and their inference problem. In *Proceedings of the 13th ACM Symposium on Theory of Computing* (Milwaukee, Wis., May 11–13). ACM, New York, pp. 342–354.

CHANG, C. L. 1970. The unit proof and the input proof in theorem proving. *J. ACM 17,* 4 (Oct.) 698–707.

CHANG, C. L. 1978. DEDUCE 2: Further investigations of deduction in relational databases. In *Logic and Databases,* H. Gallaire and J. Minker, Eds. Plenum, New York, pp. 201–236.

CHANG, C. L. 1981. On evaluation of queries containing derived relations in a relational database. In *Advances in Database Theory,* vol. 1, H. Gallaire, J. Minker, and J.-M. Nicolas, Eds. Plenum, New York, pp. 235–260.

CHANG, C. L., AND LEE, R. C. T. 1973. *Symbolic Logic and Mechanical Theorem Proving.* Academic Press, New York.

CLARK, K. L. 1978. Negation as failure. In *Logic and Databases,* H. Gallaire and J. Minker, Eds. Plenum, New York, pp. 293–322.

CODD, E. F. 1970. A relational model of data for large shared data banks. *Commun. ACM 13,* 6 (June), 377–387.

CODD, E. F. 1972. Relational completeness of database sublanguages. In *Data Base Systems,* R. Rustin, Ed. Prentice-Hall, New York, pp. 65–98.

CODD, E. F. 1979. Extending the relational database model to capture more meaning. *ACM Trans. Database Syst. 4,* 4 (Dec.), 397–434.

CODD, E. F. 1980. Data models in database management. In *Proceedings of the Workshop on Data Abstraction, Databases and Conceptual Modeling* (Pingree Park, Colo., June), pp. 112–114; *ACM SIGMOD Rec. 11,* 2 (Feb.).

CODD, E. F. 1982. Relational database: A practical foundation for productivity. *Commun. ACM 25,* 2 (Feb.), 109–117.

COLMERAUER, A. 1973. Un systeme de communication homme–machine en francais. Rapport, Groupe Intelligence Artificielle, Université d'Aix-Marseille-Luminy, Marseilles, France.

COLMERAUER, A., AND PIQUE, J. F. 1981. About natural logic. In *Advances in Database Theory* vol. 1, H. Gallaire, J. Minker, and J.-M. Nicolas, Eds. Plenum, New York, pp. 343–365.

COOPER, E. C. 1980. On the expressive power of query languages for relational databases. Tech. Rep. 14-80, Computer Science Dept., Harvard Univ., Cambridge, Mass.

DAHL, V. 1982. On database systems development through logic. *ACM Trans. Database Syst. 7,* 1 (Mar.), 102–123.

DATE, C. J. 1977. *An Introduction to Database Systems.* Addison-Wesley, Reading, Mass.

DATE, C. J. 1981. *An Introduction to Database Systems,* 3rd ed. Addison-Wesley, Reading, Mass.

DELIYANNI, A., AND KOWALSKI, R. A. 1979. Logic and semantic networks. *Commun. ACM 22,* 3 (Mar.), 184–192.

DELOBEL, C. 1978. Normalization and hierarchical dependencies in the relational data model. *ACM Trans. Database Syst. 3,* 3 (Sept.), 201–222.

DELOBEL, C. 1980. An overview of the relational data theory. In *Proceedings of IFIP 80.* Elsevier North-Holland, New York, pp. 413–426.

DELOBEL, C., AND CASEY, R. G. 1973. Decomposition of a database and the theory of Boolean switching functions. *IBM J. Res. Dev. 17,* 5 (Sept.), 484–485.

DELOBEL, C., AND PARKER, D. S. 1978. Functional and multivalued dependencies in a relational database and the theory of boolean switching functions. Tech. Rep. 142, Université de Grenoble, Grenoble, France (Nov.).

DEMOLOMBE, R. 1980. Estimation of the number of tuples satisfying a query expressed in predicate calculus language. In *Proceedings of the 6th International Conference on Very Large Data Bases* (Montreal, Oct. 1–3). IEEE, New York, pp. 55–63.

DEMOLOMBE, R. 1981. Assigning meaning to ill-defined queries expressed in predicate calculus language. In *Advances in Database Theory*, vol. 1, H. Gallaire, J. Minker, and J.-M. Nicolas, Eds. Plenum, New York, pp. 367–395.

DEMOLOMBE, R. 1982. Utilization du calcul des predicats comme langage d'interrogation des bases de données. These de doctorat d'état, ONERA-CERT, Toulouse, France (Feb.).

DI PAOLA, R. A. 1969. The recursive unsolvability of the decision problem for the class of definite formulas. *J. ACM 16,* 2 (Apr.), 324–327.

DOS SANTOS, C. S., MAIBAUM, T. S. E., AND FURTADO, A. L. 1981. Conceptual modeling of database operations. *Int. J. Comput. Inf. Sci. 10,* 5, 299–314.

ENDERTON, H. B. 1972. *A Mathematical Introduction to Logic.* Academic Press, New York.

FAGIN, R. 1977a. Multivalued dependencies and a new normal form for relational databases. *ACM Trans. Database Syst. 2,* 3 (Sept.), 262–278.

FAGIN, R. 1977b. Functional dependencies in a relational database and propositional logic. *IBM J. Res. Dev. 21,* 6 (Nov.), 534–544.

FAGIN, R. 1980. Horn clauses and data base dependencies. In *Proceedings of the 12th Annual ACM-SIGACT Symposium on Theory of Computing.* ACM, New York, pp. 123–134.

FAGIN, R. 1982. Horn clause and database dependencies. *J. ACM 29,* 4 (Oct.), 952–985.

FAGIN, R., ULLMAN, J. D., AND VARDI, M. Y. 1983. On the semantics of updates in databases. In *Proceedings of the 2nd ACM Symposium on Principles of Database Systems* (Atlanta, Ga., Mar. 21–23). ACM, New York, pp. 352–365.

FLORENTIN, J. J. 1974. Consistency auditing of data bases. *Comput. J. 17,* 1, 52–58.

FURUKAWA, K. 1977. A deductive question-answering system on relational databases. In *Proceedings of the 5th International Joint Conference on Artificial Intelligence* (Cambridge, Mass., Aug.), pp. 59–66.

GALIL, Z. 1982. An almost linear-time algorithm for computing a dependency basis in a relational database. *J. ACM 29,* 1 (Jan.), 96–102.

GALLAIRE, H. 1981. Impacts of logic on data bases. In *Proceedings of the 7th International Conference on Very Large Data Bases* (Cannes, France, Sept. 9–11). IEEE, New York, pp. 248–259.

GALLAIRE, H. 1983. Logic databases vs. deductive databases. *Logic Programming Workshop* (Albufeira, Portugal). University of Lisboa, Lisbon, Portugal, pp. 608–622.

GALLAIRE, H., AND MINKER, J., Eds. 1978. *Logic and Data Bases.* Plenum, New York.

GALLAIRE, H., MINKER, J., AND NICOLAS, J.-M., Eds., 1981a. *Advances in Data Base Theory,* vol. 1. Plenum, New York.

GALLAIRE, H., MINKER, J., AND NICOLAS, J.-M. 1981b. Background for advances in data base theory. In *Advances in Data Base Theory,* vol. 1, H. Gallaire, J. Minker, and J.-M. Nicolas, Eds. Plenum, New York, pp. 3–21.

GALLAIRE, H., MINKER, J., AND NICOLAS, J.-M., Eds. 1984. *Advances in Data Base Theory,* vol. 2. Plenum, New York.

GARDARIN, G., AND MELKANOFF, M. 1979. Proving consistency of database transactions. In *Proceedings of the 5th International Conference on Very Large Data Bases* (Rio de Janeiro, Oct. 3–5). IEEE, New York, pp. 291–298.

GRANT, J. 1977. Null values in a relational data base. *Inf. Process. Lett. 6,* 5, 156–157.

GRANT, J., AND JACOBS, B. E. 1982. On the family of generalized dependency constraints. *J. ACM 29,* 4 (Oct.), 986–997.

GRANT, J., AND MINKER, J. 1981. Optimization in deductive and conventional relational database systems. In *Advances in Data Base Theory,* vol. 1, H. Gallaire, J. Minker, and J.-M. Nicolas, Eds. Plenum, New York, pp. 195–234.

GRANT, J., AND MINKER, J. 1983. Answering queries in indefinite databases and the null value problem. Tech. Rep. 1374, Computer Science Dept., University of Maryland, College Park.

GREEN, C. 1969. Theorem proving by resolution as a basis for question-answering systems. In *Machine Intelligence 4,* B. Meltzer and D. Michie, Eds. Elsevier North-Holland, New York, pp. 183–205.

HAMMER, M. T., AND ZDONIK, S. B., JR. 1980. Knowledge-based query processing. In *Proceedings of the 6th International Conference on Very Large Data Bases* (Montreal, Oct. 1–3). IEEE, New York, pp. 137–147.

HAREL, D. 1979. First order dynamic logic. In *Lecture Notes in Computer Science,* vol. 68. Springer-Verlag, Berlin and New York.

HAREL, D. 1980. Review of *Logic and Databases,* H. Gallaire and J. Minker. *Comput. Rev. 21,* 8 (Aug.), 367–369.

HENSCHEN, L. J., MCCUNE, W. W., AND NAQVI, S. A. 1984. Compiling constraint checking programs from first order formulas. In *Advances in Database Theory,* vol. 2, H. Gallaire, J. Minker, and J.-M. Nicolas, Eds. Plenum, New York, pp. 145–169.

HEWITT, C. 1972. Description and theoretical analysis (using schemata) of PLANNER: A language for proving theorems and manipulating models in a robot. AI Memo No. 251, MIT Project MAC, Cambridge, Mass.

HILL, R. 1974. LUSH resolution and its completeness. DCS Memo, No. 78. University of Edinburgh, School of Artificial Intelligence.

HOMEIER, P. V. 1981. Simplifying integrity constraints in a relational database: An implementation. M.Sc. thesis, Computer Science Dept., University of California, Los Angeles.

IMIELINSKI, T., AND LIPSKI, W. 1981. On representing incomplete information in a relational database. In *Proceedings of the 7th International Conference on Very Large Data Bases* (Cannes,

France, Sept. 9–11). IEEE, New York, pp. 389–397.

INTERNATIONAL JOINT CONFERENCE ON ARTIFICIAL INTELLIGENCE 1983. August, 8–12, 1983, Karlsruhe, West Germany.

INTERNATIONAL SYMPOSIUM ON LOGIC PROGRAMMING 1984. Feb. 6–9, 1984, Atlantic City, N.J.

JACOBS, B. E. 1982. On database logic. *J. ACM 29,* 2 (Apr.), 310–332.

JACOBS, B. E., ARONSON, A. R., AND KLUG, A. C. 1982. On interpretations of relational languages and solutions to the implied constraint problem. *ACM Trans. Database Syst. 7,* 2 (June), 291–315.

JAFFAR, J., LASSEZ, J. L., AND LLOYD, J. 1983. Completeness of the negation by failure rule. In *Proceedings of the 8th International Joint Conference on Artificial Intelligence* (Karlsruhe, W. Germany, Aug.), pp. 500–506.

JANAS, J. M. 1979. Towards more informative user interfaces. In *Proceedings of the 5th International Conference on Very Large Data Bases* (Rio de Janeiro, Oct. 3–5). IEEE, New York, pp. 17–23.

JANAS, J. M. 1981. On the feasibility of informative answers. In *Advances in Data Base Theory,* vol. 1, H. Gallaire, J. Minker, and J.-M. Nicolas, Eds. Plenum, New York, pp. 397–414.

KELLOGG, C., AND TRAVIS, L. 1981. Reasoning with data in a deductively augmented data management system. In *Advances in Data Base Theory,* vol. 1, H. Gallaire, J. Minker, and J.-M. Nicolas, Eds. Plenum, New York, pp. 261–295.

KELLOGG, C., KLHAR, P., AND TRAVIS, L. 1978. Deductive planning and path finding for relational data bases. In *Logic and Databases,* H. Gallaire and J. Minker, Eds. Plenum, New York, pp. 179–200.

KING, J. J. 1981. QUIST: A system for semantic query optimization in relational databases. In *Proceedings of the 7th International Conference on Very Large Data Bases* (Cannes, France, Sept. 9–11). IEEE, New York, pp. 510–517.

KONOLIGE, K. 1981. A metalanguage representation of databases for deductive question-answering systems. In *Proceedings of the 7th International Joint Conference on Artificial Intelligence* (Vancouver, B.C., Aug.), pp. 469–503.

KOWALSKI, R. A. 1978. Logic for data description. In *Logic and Data Bases,* H. Gallaire and J. Minker, Eds. Plenum, New York, pp. 77–103.

KOWALSKI, R. A. 1979. *Logic for Problem Solving.* Elsevier North-Holland, New York.

KOWALSKI, R. A. 1981a. Logic as a data base language. In *Proceedings of the Advanced Seminar on Theoretical Issues in Data Bases* (Cetraro, Italy, Sept.).

KOWALSKI, R. A. 1981b. Personal communication.

KOWALSKI, R. A., AND KUEHNER, D. 1971. Linear resolution with selection function. *Artif. Intell. 2,* 3/4, 227–260.

KUHNS, J. L. 1967. Answering questions by computers—A logical study. Rand Memo RM 5428 PR, Rand Corp., Santa Monica, Calif.

KUHNS, J. L. 1970. Interrogating a relational data file: Remarks on the admissibility of input queries. Tech. Rep. TR-511-PR, Rand Corp., Santa Monica, Calif. (Nov.).

KUNIFUJI, S., AND YOKOTA, H. 1982. Prolog and relational databases for the fifth generation computer system. ICOT Rep. D02, Institute for New Generation Computer Technology, Tokyo.

LACROIX, M., AND PIROTTE, A. 1980. Associating types with domains of relational databases. In *Workshop on Data Abstraction, Databases and Conceptual Modeling* (Pingree Park, Colo., June). *ACM SIGMOD Rec. 11,* 2 (Feb.), 144–146.

LEVESQUE, H. J. 1981. The interaction with incomplete knowledge bases: a formal treatment. *Proceedings of the 7th International Joint Conference on Artificial Intelligence* (Vancouver, B.C., Aug.), pp. 240–245.

LIPSKI, W. 1979. On semantic issues connected with incomplete information systems. *ACM Trans. Database Syst. 4,* 3 (Sept.), 262–296.

LOGIC PROGRAMMING WORKSHOP PROCEEDINGS 1983. June 26–July, 1, 1983, Praia da Falesia, Algarve, Portugal. Dept. of Computer Science, University of Lisboa, Lisbon, Portugal.

LOVELAND, D. 1969. Theorem provers combining model elimination and resolution. In *Machine Intelligence,* vol. 4. B. Meltzer and D. Michie, Eds. Elsevier North-Holland, New York, pp. 73–86.

LOVELAND, D. 1970. A linear format for resolution. *Proceedings of the IRIA Symposium on Automatic Demonstration.* Springer-Verlag, Berlin and New York, pp. 147–162.

LOVELAND, D. 1978. *Automated Theorem Proving: A Logical Basis.* Elsevier North-Holland, New York.

MAIER, D. 1983. *The Theory of Relational Databases.* Computer Science Press, Rockville, Md.

MAIER, D., MENDELZON, A. O., AND SAGIV, Y. 1979. Testing implications of data dependencies. *ACM Trans. Database Syst. 4,* 4 (Dec.), 455–469.

MCCARTHY, J. 1980. Circumscription—A form of non-monotonic reasoning. *Artif. Intell. 13,* 27–39.

MCSKIMIN, J. 1976. Techniques for employing semantic information in question-answering systems. Ph.D. dissertation, Dept. of Computer Science, University of Maryland, College Park.

MCSKIMIN, J., AND MINKER, J. 1977. The use of a semantic network in a deductive question-answering system. In *Proceedings of the 5th International Joint Conference on Artificial Intelligence* (Cambridge, Mass., Aug.), pp. 50–58.

MENDELSON, E. 1978. *Introduction to Mathematical Logic,* 2nd ed. Van Nostrand-Reinhold, New York.

MINKER, J. 1975a. Performing inferences over relational data bases. In *ACM SIGMOD International Conference on Management of Data* (San Jose, Calif., May 14–16). ACM, New York, pp. 79–91.

MINKER, J. 1975b. Set operations and inferences over relational databases. In *Proceedings of the*

*4th Texas Conference on Computing Systems* (Nov.). Univ. of Texas, Austin, pp. 5A1.1–5A1.10.

MINKER, J. 1978a. Search strategy and selection function for an inferential relational system. *ACM Trans. Database Syst. 3,* 1 (Mar.), 1–31.

MINKER, J. 1978b. An experimental relational data base system based on logic. In *Logic and Databases*, H. Gallaire and J. Minker, Eds. Plenum, New York, pp. 107–147.

MINKER, J. 1982. On indefinite databases and the closed world assumption. In *Proceedings of the 6th Conference on Automated Deduction* (New York). Springer-Verlag Lecture Notes in Computer Science, No. 138. Springer-Verlag, Berlin and New York, pp. 292–308.

MINKER, J. 1983. On deductive relational databases. In *Proceedings of the 5th International Conference on Collective Phenomena* (July), J. L. Lebowitz, Ed., *Annals of the New York Academy of Sciences*, vol. 10. New York Academy of Science, New York, pp. 181–200.

MINKER, J., AND NICOLAS, J. M. 1982. On recursive axioms in deductive databases. *Inf. Syst. 8,* 1 (Jan.), 1–13.

MINKER, J., AND PERLIS, D. 1983. On the semantics of circumscription. Tech. Rep., Computer Science Dept., Univ. of Maryland, College Park.

MINKER, J., AND PERLIS, D. 1984. Applications of protected circumscription. In *Proceedings of the Conference on Automated Deduction 7* (Napa, Calif., May). Springer-Verlag, Berlin and New York, pp. 414–425.

MINKER, J., AND ZANON, G. 1982. An extension to linear resolution with selection function. *Inf. Process. Lett. 14,* 4 (June), 191–194.

MOORE, R. C. 1981. Problems in logical form. In *Proceedings of the 19th Annual Meeting of the Association for Computational Linguistics* (June). Association for Computational Linguistics, pp. 117–124.

MYLOPOULOS, J. 1980. An overview of knowledge representation. In *Proceedings of the Workshop of Data Abstraction, Databases, and Conceptual Modeling*, M. Brodie and S. N. Zilles, Eds. (Pingree Park, Colo., June). *ACM SIGMOD Rec. 11,* 2 (Feb.), 5–12.

NAQVI, S. A., AND HENSCHEN, L. J. 1980. Performing inferences over recursive data bases. In *Proceedings of the 1st Annual National Conference on Artificial Intelligence* (Stanford, Conn., Aug.). AAAI, Palo Alto, Calif., pp. 263–265.

NAQVI, S. A., AND HENSCHEN, L. J. 1984. On compiling queries in recursive first-order databases. *J. ACM 31,* 1 (Jan.), 47–85.

NICOLAS, J.-M. 1978. First order logic formalization for functional, multivalued and mutual dependencies. In *Proceedings of ACM-SIGMOD International Conference on Management of Data* (Austin, Tex., June 1, 2). ACM, New York, pp. 40–46.

NICOLAS, J.-M. 1979a. A property of logical formulas corresponding to integrity constraints on database relations. In *Proceedings of the Workshop on Formal Bases for Data Bases* (Toulouse, France). ONERA-CERT, Toulouse, France.

NICOLAS, J.-M. 1979b. Logic for improving integrity checking in relational databases. Tech. Rep. ONERA-CERT, Toulouse, France (Feb.). Also in *Acta Inf. 18,* 3 (Dec.), 227–253.

NICOLAS, J.-M., AND GALLAIRE, H. 1978. Database: Theory vs. interpretation. In *Logic and Databases*, H. Gallaire and J. Minker, Eds. Plenum, New York, pp. 33–54.

NICOLAS, J.-M., AND SYRE, J. C. 1974. Natural question answering and automatic deduction in the system SYNTEX. In *Proceedings of IFIP 1974.* North-Holland, Amsterdam, pp. 595–599.

NICOLAS, J.-M., AND YAZDANIAN, K. 1978. Integrity checking in deductive databases. In *Logic and Databases,* H. Gallaire and J. Minker, Eds. Plenum, New York, pp. 325–346.

NICOLAS, J.-M., AND YAZDANIAN, K. 1982. An outline of BDGEN: A deductive DBMS. Tech. Rep. TR-ONERA-CERT, Toulouse, France (Oct.). Also in *Proceedings of IFIP 83 Congress.* North-Holland, Amsterdam, 1983, pp. 711–717.

PAREDAENS, J. 1978. On the expressive power of relational algebra. *Inf. Process. Lett. 7,* 2 (Feb.), 107–111.

PARKER, D. S., AND DELOBEL, C. 1979. Algorithmic applications for a new result on multivalued dependencies. In *Proceedings of the 5th Conference on Very Large Data Bases* (Rio de Janeiro, Oct. 3–5). IEEE, New York, pp. 67–74.

PIROTTE, A. 1976. Explicit description of entities and their manipulation in languages for the relational database model. Thèse de doctorat, Université libre de Bruxelles, Brussells, Belgium (Dec.).

PIROTTE, A. 1978. High level data base query languages. In *Logic and Data Bases*, H. Gallaire and J. Minker, Eds. Plenum, New York, pp. 409–436.

PRATT, V. R. 1976. Semantical considerations on Floyd–Hoare logic. In *Proceedings of the 17th IEEE Symposium Foundations of Computer Science* (Oct.). IEEE, New York, pp. 409–120.

PROCEEDINGS OF THE 1ST CONFERENCE ON LOGIC PROGRAMMING 1982. Marseille, France (Sept.), Université d'Aix-Marseille-Luminy, Marseille.

REITER, R. 1971. Two results on ordering for resolution with merging and linear format. *J. ACM 18,* 4 (Oct.), 630–646.

REITER, R. 1978a. On closed world databases. In *Logic and Databases*, H. Gallaire and J. Minker, Eds. Plenum, New York, pp. 56–76.

REITER, R. 1978b. Deductive question-answering on relational databases. In *Logic and Data Bases*, H. Gallaire and J. Minker, Eds. Plenum, New York, pp. 149–178.

REITER, R. 1978c. On structuring a first-order database. In *Proceedings of the 2nd Canadian Society for Computer Science National Conference*, Canada (July).

REITER, R. 1980. Equality and domain closure in first-order databases. *J. ACM 27,* 2 (Apr.), 235–249.

REITER, R. 1981. On the integrity of first-order databases. In *Advances in Data Base Theory*, vol. 1, H. Gallaire, J. Minker, and J.-M. Nicolas, Eds. Plenum, New York, pp. 137–158.

REITER, R. 1982. Circumscription implies predicate completion (sometimes). In *Proceedings of the American Association for Artificial Intelligence 82 Conference* (Pittsburgh, Pa., Aug.). AAAI, Menlo Park, Calif., pp. 418–420.

REITER, R. 1983. A sound and sometimes complete query evaluation algorithm for relational databases with null values. Tech. Rep. 83-11, Computer Science Dept., University of British Columbia, Canada (June).

REITER, R. 1984. Towards a logical reconstruction of relational database theory. In *On Conceptual Modeling*, M. Brodie, J. Mylopoulos, and J. W. Schmidt, Eds. Springer-Verlag, Berlin and New York.

ROBINSON, J. A. 1965. A machine oriented logic based on the resolution principle. *J. ACM 12,* 1 (Jan.), 23–41.

ROUSSEL, P. 1975. PROLOG: Manuel de reference et d'utilisation. Tech. Rep., Département d'Informatiques, Université d'Aix-Marseille-Luminy, Marseille, France (Sept.).

SADRI, F., AND ULLMAN, J. D. 1980. A complete axiomatization for a large class of dependencies in relational databases. In *Proceedings of the 17th Annual ACM-SIGACT Symposium on Theory of Computing.* ACM, New York, pp. 117–122.

SADRI, F., AND ULLMAN, J. D. 1982. Template dependencies: A large class of dependencies in relational databases and its complete axiomatization. *J. ACM 29,* 2 (Apr.), 363–372.

SAGIV, Y. 1980. An algorithm for inferring multivalued dependencies with an application to propositional logic. *J. ACM 27,* 2 (Apr.), 250–262.

SAGIV, Y., AND FAGIN, R. 1979. An equivalence between relational database dependencies and a subset of propositional logic. Res. Rep. RJ2500, IBM Research Laboratories, San Jose, Calif. (Mar.).

SAGIV, Y., DELOBEL, C., PARKER, D. S., JR., AND FAGIN, R. 1981. An equivalence between relational database dependencies and a subclass of propositional logic. *J. ACM 28,* 3 (July), 435–453.

SELINGER, P. G., ASTRAHAN, M. M., CHAMBERLIN, D. D., LORIE, R. A., AND PRICE, T. G. 1979. Access path selection in a relational database management system. In *Proceedings ACM-SIGMOD International Conference on Management of Data* (Boston, May 30–June 1). ACM, New York, pp. 23–34.

SHAPIRO, S. E., AND MCKAY, D. P. 1980. Inference with recursive rules. In *Proceedings of the 1st Annual National Conference on Artificial Intelligence.* AAAI, Palo Alto, Calif.

SIKLOSSY, L., AND LAURIERE, J.-L. 1982. Removing restrictions in the relational database model: an application of problem solving techniques. In *Proceedings of the American Association for Artificial Intelligence 82 Conference* (Pittsburgh, Pa., Aug.). AAAI, Menlo Park, Calif., pp. 310–313.

Received February 1983; final revision accepted July 1984.

STONEBRAKER, M. R., WONG, E., AND KEEPS, P. 1976. The design and implementation of INGRES. *ACM Trans. Database Syst. 1,* 3 (Sept.), 189–222.

ULLMAN, J. D. 1980. *Principles of Database Systems.* Computer Science Press, Potomac, Md.

ULLMAN, J. D. 1982. *Principles of Database Systems,* 2nd ed. Computer Science Press, Potomac, Md.

VAN EMDEN, M. H. 1978. Computation and deductive information retrieval. In *Formal Description of Programming Concepts,* E. J. Neuhold, Ed. Elsevier North-Holland, New York, pp. 421–440.

VAN EMDEN, M. H., AND KOWALSKI, R. A. 1976. The semantics of predicate logic as a programming language. *J. ACM 23,* 4 (Oct.), 733–742.

VARDI, M. Y. 1981. The decision problem for database dependencies. *Inf. Process. Lett. 12,* 5 (Oct.), 251–254.

VASSILIOU, Y. 1979. Null values in data base management—A denotational semantics approach. In *Proceedings of the ACM-SIGMOD International Conference on the Management of Data* (Boston, May 30–June 1). ACM, New York, pp. 162–169.

VASSILIOU, Y. 1980. Functional dependencies and incomplete information. In *Proceedings of the 6th International Conference on Very Large Data Bases* (Montreal, Oct. 1–3). IEEE, New York, pp. 260–269.

VELOSO, P. A. S., DE CASTILHO, J. M. V., AND FURTADO, A. L. 1981. Systematic derivation of complementary specifications. In *Proceedings of the 7th International Conference on Very Large Data Bases* (Cannes, France, Sept. 9–11). IEEE, New York, pp. 409–421.

WARREN, D. H. D. 1981. Efficient processing of interactive relational database queries expressed in logic. In *Proceedings of the 7th International Conference on Very Large Data Bases* (Cannes, France, Sept. 9–11). IEEE, New York, pp. 272–281.

WOODS, W. A. 1967. Semantics for question-answering systems. Ph.D. dissertation, Rep. NSF-19, Aiken Computation Laboratory, Harvard University, Cambridge, Mass.

YANNAKAKIS, M., AND PAPADIMITRIOU, C. 1982. Algebraic dependencies. *J. Comput. Syst. Sci. 25,* 1 (Aug.), 2–41.

YOKOTA, H., KUNIFUJI, S., KAKUTA, T., MIYAZAKI, N., SHIBAYAMA, S., AND MURAKAMI, K. 1983. An enhanced inference mechanism for generating relational algebra queries. Tech. Rep. 026, ICOT Research Center, Institute for New Generation Computer Technology, Tokyo, Japan.

ZANIOLO, C. 1976. Analysis and design of relational schemata for data base system. Tech. Rep. UCLA Eng. 7769, Dept. of Computer Science, University of California, Los Angeles.

ZANIOLO, C. 1981. Incomplete database information and null values: An overview. In *Proceedings of the Advanced Seminar on Theoretical Issues in Data Bases* (Cetraro, Italy, Sept.).

ZLOOF, M. M. 1977. Query-by-example: A data base language. *IBM Syst. J. 16,* 4, 324–343.

# From Data Management to Knowledge Management

Charles Kellogg, Microelectronics and Computer Technology Corporation

Data management and artificial intelligence technologies can be combined to produce knowledge management systems that can analyze and evaluate massive databases.

During the last decade data management technology has produced storage and retrieval systems that can efficiently search large, complex databases. At the same time, artificial intelligence technology has created a number of expert systems, which use encoded knowledge to solve problems in a manner similar to that of a human expert.

Many present and future computer applications could benefit from an effective and efficient marriage of these two technologies. For example, managers and their staff associates could use a system that stores expertise about company policies, plans, finances, and product evaluation to intelligently access management information system databases. Similarly, command and control systems could exploit stored expertise in analyzing and evaluating masses of battlefield data to greatly aid military decision making.

Rising user expectations, the advancement of computer technology, and the impact of the continuing information explosion are combining to hasten the transition from current data management systems to future knowledge management systems. This article reviews some of the steps necessary to achieve this transition and describes the design and experimental use of a prototype knowledge manager.

## Background

Data management technology has progressed rapidly in recent years. We now have commercially viable data management systems that use hierarchical, network, and relational data models to effectively store and retrieve large quantities of data on anything from microcomputers, to mainframes, to specialized database machines. Meanwhile, artificial intelligence technology has made expert and knowledge-based systems more useful and practical.

For the most part, researchers in these two areas have developed their technologies independently. One exception is the work in logic-based systems. This activity, which includes

EH0252-7/87/0000/0367$01.00 © 1986 IEEE

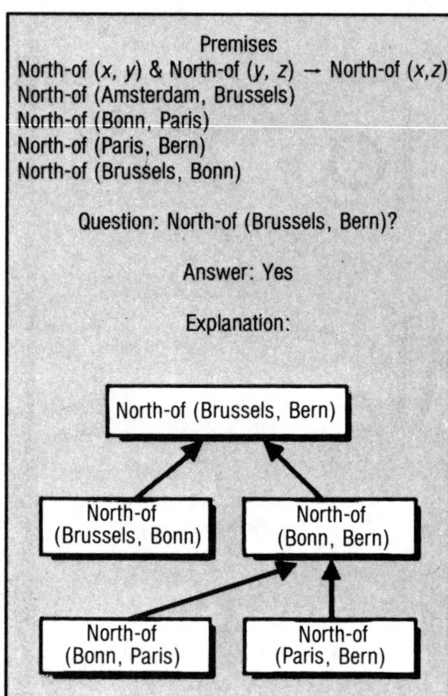


**Figure 1.** Logic for question answering.

research in logic and databases[1] and logic programming,[2] originated in Europe and the US, but has recently received worldwide attention because of the Japanese decision to adopt logic as a central formalism in their approach to the development of fifth-generation computer technology.[3]

But aside from research in logic-based systems, not much has been done to merge the two technologies. Moreover, there now exists a large and growing area of practical importance that neither current expert systems nor data management systems alone can satisfy. Existing expert systems, while they may use a few hundred or few thousand pieces for rule-based knowledge, lack a DMS's ability to efficiently search and exploit megabytes to gigabytes of data. Similarly, current DMSs, while they have been optimized to deal with masses of business and scientific data, were never designed to cope with the kinds of rule-based information we find in expert systems.

## Logic for question answering

**What is logic?** As succinctly stated by Robinson, "Logic deals with what follows from what."[4] It is fundamentally concerned with correct reasoning from a set of statements (the premises) to another statement (the conclusion). If we follow a line of correct reasoning, we say the conclusion is a logical consequence of the premises. To ensure that only correct conclusions are drawn from a series of premises, logic requires us to encode knowledge in a precise, unambiguous form. The logical formalism usually chosen for representing and reasoning with knowledge is the predicate calculus. It consists of atomic expressions (a predicate and a series of arguments) and molecular expressions that are truth functional (Boolean connective) combinations of atomic expressions. Predicates may be used to represent both the concepts typically found in expert systems and the relations used in modern data management systems. Arguments may be variables, constants, or functional terms.

Figure 1 provides a simple example of how the predicate calculus may be used in supporting deductive question answering. In a logic-based system, the answer to a user's query must be a logical consequence of the knowledge contained in a set of premises. An appropriate sequence of premises constitutes a proof of the correctness of the answer, and the structure of that proof explains how the answer was derived.

The figure contains a series of elementary premises: four atomic expressions and one molecular expression. The question, "Is Brussels north of Bern?" is answered affirmatively, since its assertional form is a logical consequence of several specific premises (atomic expressions) combined with several applications of a general premise (a molecular expression).

This example, as simple as it is, illustrates two important points about logic-based question answering:

(1) Recursive premises, such as the first premise in Figure 1, can be both expressively powerful (succinctly representing an important bit of knowledge) and a source of performance and control difficulties (since it may be difficult to determine just when to stop the recursion).

(2) If facts are stored separately then proof stategies involving recursive rules may sometimes be compiled into more efficient iterative data access strategies. In this example, the recursive premise could be compiled into a search routine to find the transitive closure of the north-of (Brussels, Bern) relation.

**Deductive augmentation of data management.** The development of efficient techniques for mechanizing the construction of proofs (theorem proving) has challenged computer scientists for more than 20 years. Only recently have inferencing techniques been developed that allow us to construct deductive processors or reasoning engines that can support the development of practical knowledge management systems. Figure 2 illustrates some of the interconnections between research in artificial intelligence and research in data management. (Barr and Feigenbaum[5] and Brodie et al.[6] provide overviews of relevant research in these areas.)

One of the earliest (1959) papers in artificial intelligence, John McCarthy's report on Advice Taker,[7] discusses the problem of using logic to support computer-based problem solving and question answering. Since that time, an extensive range of literature in mathematical theorem proving, program verification, problem solving, and deductive question answering has emerged.

The first system to use a general-purpose predicate calculus theorem prover in support of question answering was Cordell Green's QA3.5 system (1969).[8] Another pioneering effort in deductive question answering during the early 1970's was Jack Minker's Maryland Refutation Proof Procedure System, or MRPPS.[9]

These early systems demonstrated the general-purpose nature of mechanized logic but suffered from severe performance problems. Many AI researchers abandoned logic in the search for perhaps more limited, but more efficient techniques. This search led to the emergence of expert systems based on the use of production rules and other procedural knowledge representations.

Meanwhile, data management was undergoing its own evolution from the early file and record management techniques to hierarchical, then network, and finally to relational systems. In the last few years, a number of database researchers have developed semantic data models or systems that attempt to extend the relational approach to handle some limited forms of inferencing and knowledge structuring.

Logic-based systems research has produced a body of results and techniques that supports the view of logic as a unifying formalism for AI, data management, and programming. From the point of view of computational logic, a relational data management system mechanizes a finite conjunctive *model* —a set of concrete assertions or facts that represent a specific state of affairs in the real world. Facts are represented in an RDMS as instances (tuples) of a relation.

Deductive and expert systems, on the other hand, emphasize the processing of general assertions. These laws, judgments, and other forms of knowledge constitute, again from the point of view of logic, a *theory*—a representation and circumscription of a general state of affairs.

Logic itself is formalized in terms of proof theory and model theory. Proof theory provides formal specifications for correct reasoning with premises, while model theory prescribes how general assertions may be interpreted with respect to a collection of specific facts. Early investigations in deductively augmented data management carried out at System Development Corporation[10] were strongly influenced by these aspects of logic.

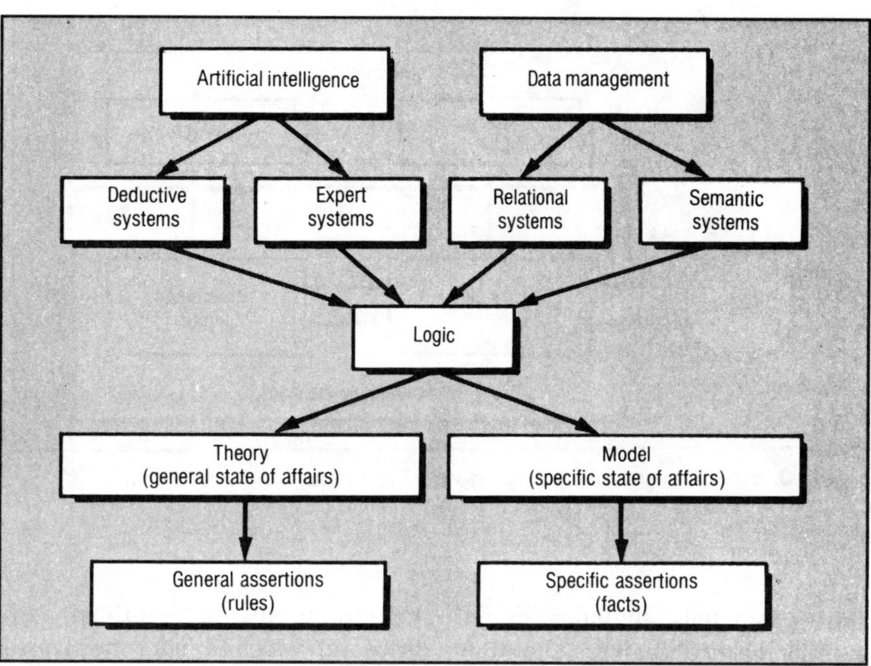


**Figure 2.** AI, data management, and logic.

## Reasoning with data

**Knowledge management.** Figure 3 illustrates the basic components of a knowledge management system. To a searching engine (an RDMS) and associated database of specific facts, we add a reasoning engine (a deductive processor) and a rule base of application-specific expertise. Communication with the KMS may be through a high-level graphical and English-like interface, or if an application program is calling the KMS, communication may be in some form of logical query language. In either case, the KMS must be able to accept knowledge and questions as input, update the knowledge base as necessary, and return answers and explanations for those answers as output.

**Benefits.** Many benefits can be expected from adding a rule base and reasoning engine to a DMS. The first is that a deductive processor permits the extraction of information that is not explicitly stored but that can be inferred by combining specific facts in the database with rule-based knowledge encoded in general assertions. This augmentation of the information-retrieval function can be especially important for very large database domains.

A deductive processor also allows a DMS's language to be extended and adapted to the needs of particular users. Thus, a user's language can be uncoupled from the particular terms and categories used in organizing a data file. This feature is essential if users are to work with a system without having a thorough knowledge of its file structure.

For example, a user should be able to ask whether the maternal grandfather of John Kennedy was richer

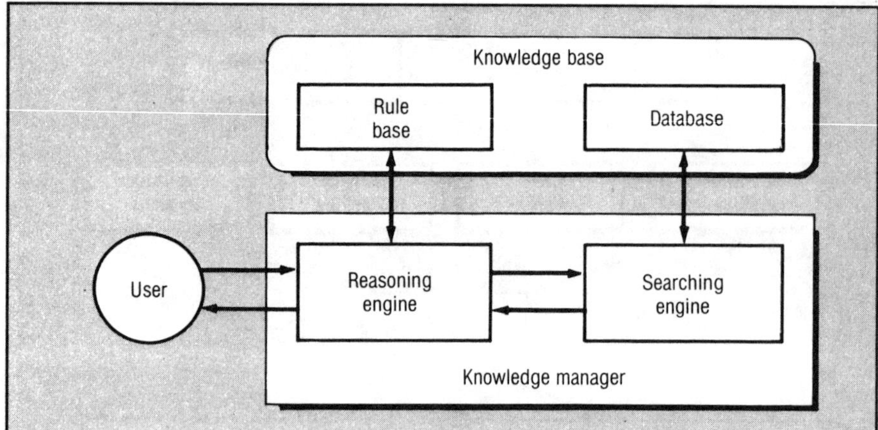


**Figure 3.** Basic components of a knowledge management system.

than his paternal grandfather without knowing the men's names or how the file is structured with respect to net worth. Relatively powerful inferential mechanisms are necessary to enable full use of such descriptive references.

Another benefit of adding a deductive processor to a DMS is that the processor not only generates answers to specific queries but also supplies evidence (lines of reasoning) for or against these answers. In some cases, the system may supply one argument leading to yes and another leading to no (indicating inconsistent information). In the real world of unreliable reports and uncertain facts, this kind of response will, in many cases, be much more valuable to a user than simple categorical answers.

While deduction is itself a precise and strict process, deductive arguments can use premises of differing degrees of plausibility. Since the plausibility of a conclusion (answer) is a function of the plausibility of the premises from which it is derived, deduction provides a basis for using soft information in a computer-based system. The important thing is that the system is able to show the user the evidence for a conclusion as well as the conclusion itself. Deduction can also be used to generate multiple distinct arguments for a conclusion, thereby supplying additional evidence with which to judge the plausibility of its answer.

Finally, a deductive processor can answer what-if and other kinds of high-level queries that are difficult if not impossible for present-day data management systems. It can also support the specification and enforcement of complex semantic integrity constraints.

## The KM-1 knowledge management system

There are many questions about how best to realize large-scale knowledge management systems. For example,

(1) How can a reasoning engine be designed to efficiently select (from a large rule base) only the small relevant subset of rules necessary to construct inferences for a specific question?

(2) How should the reasoning engine interface with and control the searching engine?

(3) How much information needs to be transferred from one machine to the other? When? How frequently?

(4) How can the results of rule-based deduction and data-based search be combined to generate answers and explanations?

Answers to these questions will become apparent only after much additional research. However, a prototype knowledge manager, KM-1,[11] has already demonstrated a level of KMS capability sufficient for some real-world applications.

The major components of the KM-1 are illustrated in Figure 4. KM-1 hardware consists of a Xerox 1100 Lisp machine, which serves as a user workstation and reasoning engine, and a Britton-Lee IDM-500 relational database machine, which searches large external (global) databases. Within the Lisp machine are the DADM (Deductively Augmented Data Management) deductive processor,[12,13] a resident (local) relational DMS, user interface software, and software to interface with the Britton-Lee. Lisp routines control the distribution of queries to, and the aggregation of data from, both local and external databases.

If external databases are preexisting, they may be augmented with rule-based expertise, or both databases and rule bases may be created as necessary for a new application. Local databases may be created by individual users of the system. For example, a manager might want to keep sensitive information, such as salary data, in his own local database.

In KM-1, if a user's query requires no deduction, it is translated directly from its English-like form to the query language of the underlying DMS, and the answer is obtained directly from that system and presented to the user. In this procedure, the *deduction by exception* principle is realized, which ensures that ordinary nondeductive queries incur no extra cost because of the reasoning engine.

If a user's query requires a modest amount of deduction (using the application-specific expertise encoded in the rule base), then short proof plans are produced. Consequently, modest-sized relational database queries are generated and executed, and the user again benefits from the searching efficiency of the underlying DMS.

As required deductions become deeper and more complex, the reasoning engine must operate for longer periods. Searches for specific facts are still, however, highly focused on obtaining just the data necessary to produce correct answers.

The DADM processor selects and combines rules, generates proof plans, and produces data access strategies that are sent to a distributor. The distributor then accesses either relational DMS or both as necessary and an aggregator combines the results of the data search into sets of tuples for return to the deductive processor. If computational procedures (consisting of Lisp functions) are needed during answer construction, they are obtained from a procedure library and automatically evaluated as necessary either before or after data retrieval. Results are sent to the DADM processor, which then constructs answers and associated proofs for display to the user.

Communication between the 1100 and the IDM-500 is via a serial RS-232 interface.

Software operating on the Xerox 1100 supports the following functions:

- generation of data access strategies in a compacted byte string, which is the basic form of commands and data accepted by the IDM-500;
- communication over the RS-232 port; and
- a multilevel protocol that activates the IDM-500 supports error detection and correction and converts IDM output into a Lisp compatible format.

KM-1's deductive processor is loosely coupled to the IDM-500. That is, the underlying database in the IDM-500 is accessed only once per proof plan. All data values necessary to generate answers for a plan are found by executing its associated data access strategy. This approach is in contrast to a tightly coupled one, in which many elementary data requests are generated for each proof plan. Tight coupling would require much more interaction and communication between the two processors and would suffer from the limited bandwidth of the serial interface.

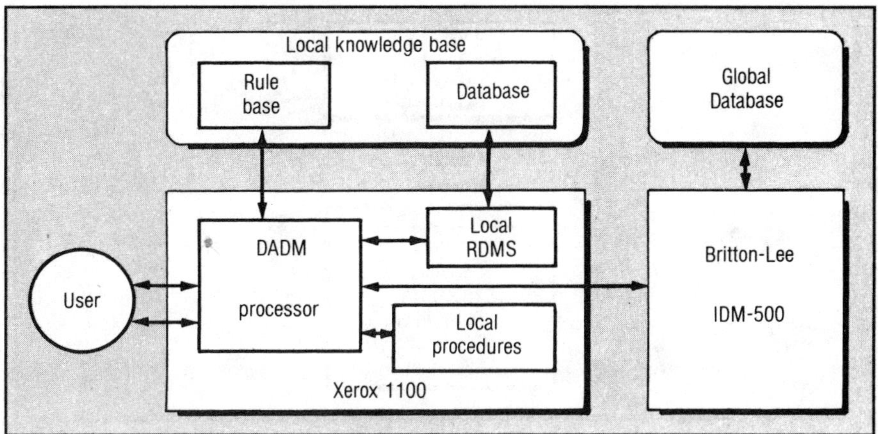


**Figure 4.** Components of the KM-1 prototype knowledge manager: DADM - Deductively Augmented Data Management; RDMS - relational data management system.

KM-1 has a knowledge-structuring component that categorizes objects, relations, and rules for efficient use by both the system and users. Hierarchies of object types, relations, and rules are automatically maintained as new knowledge is entered into the system.

Terminal object types such as Scientist and Laboratory point to entries in a type database. Objects in the type database are used during deductively-guided query formulation, while object types are checked for compatibility during deduction. Relations are currently categorized according to their type of support: deduce, search, or compute. Rules are grouped into classes according to function.

**The DADM processor.** Upon entry of a query, the DADM processor creates skeletal derivations or proof plans. A proof plan represents a possible structure for resolving the question posed by the user. User queries are decomposed into a series of subproblems for deductive, database, and compute support. All deductive problems are solved first by use of application-specific knowledge from the rule base and then by generation of data access/compute strategies, which are used to produce answers and answer explanations.

The DADM processor employs forward, backward, and bidirectional (middle-term) reasoning in the processing of three major types of queries: what-if, find, and given-find. A what-if query requires forward reasoning from the assumed or given relationships through the rule base and the database to the generation of answers. A find query uses backward reasoning from goal relationships toward rule and data support for that goal. Bidirectional reasoning is used in a given-find query, where both given and goal relationships occur.

To increase deductive searching efficiency the DADM processor constructs a predicate connection graph[14] from information abstracted from the rules. This graphical structure supports a process of global deductive planning.

In global planning, a representation is used in which proofs as a whole are explicit objects that can be

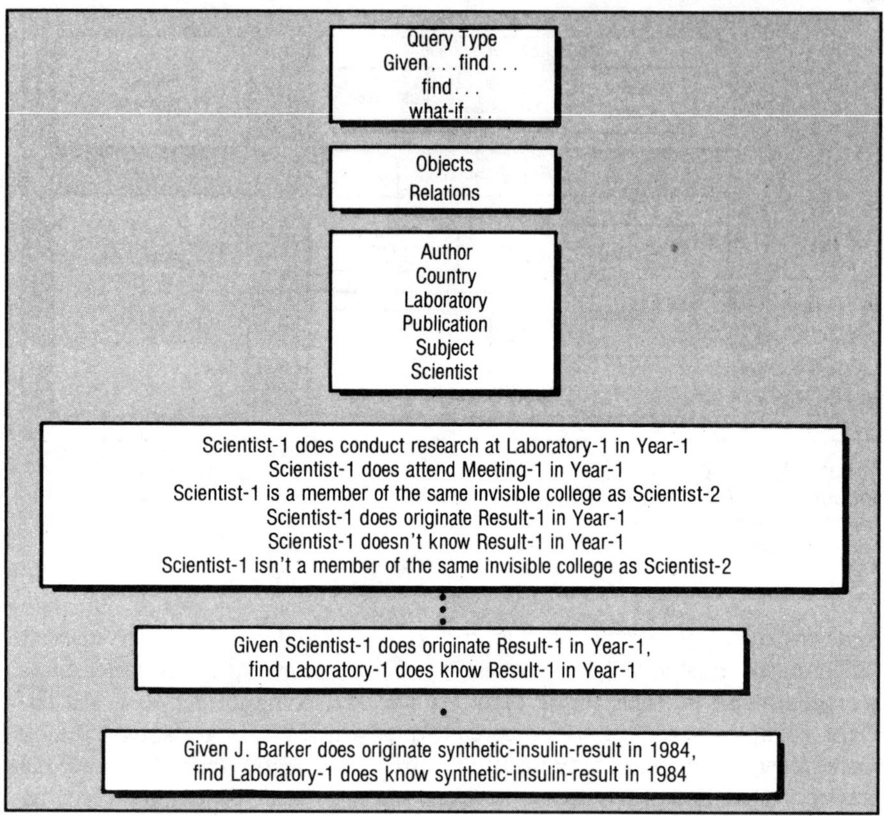


**Figure 5.** Deduction-aided query formulation.

analyzed and manipulated as the proofs are being articulated and developed. Consequently, there are more global strategies for determining what to try next. When exhaustive chaining is out of the question, as it is for most realistic premise sets, subselection strategies become crucial, and global strategies are better are better than local.

Most deductive systems use local criteria for deciding the order in which goals are selected for solution. For example, many Prolog implementations use depth-first expansion of goals followed by left-to-right sequencing as goals succeed. The advantage of such local strategies is greater speed in each step, since little context needs to be checked. This solution is appropriate for certain types of applications. For other applications—in particular, database retrieval—there are two significant problems.

First, a very nonlocal event may ultimately void a whole area of deductive development. Global planning in the DADM processor allows the failure of a goal in one deductive plan to be propagated to other plans that share the goal, thereby discarding many irrelevant deductive paths.

Second, strict, depth-first strategies do not take advantage of pseudoparallel or parallel development of proofs. Global planning, with its breadth-first orientation, supports the parallel development of many deductive plans (skeletal proofs) and the use of heuristic resource allocation guided by global criteria.

As the DADM processor proceeds, it produces a plan tree where the parent-child relation in the tree connotes that the child is a deductive extension of the parent with respect to subproblems in the parent that remain deductively open. The choose function (which decides what open deduction to work on next) scans the entire plan tree and selects a plan to work on next; within that plan, it selects an open subproblem to work on. Selection criteria consist of

- whether a plan is better than its parent (e.g., whether it has closed off subproblems or has caused additional subproblems to occur);
- whether previous attempts to extend a plan have consistently led to children that are unverifiable;
- what particular premises and/or middle-term relations have been used in a plan and whether they are advised;
- whether a plan is becoming unrealistically complex; and
- what plans have available paths to assumptions that are promising but so far unprocessed (promising in that they will not generate many, if any, additional subproblems).

For given-find queries, the predicate connection graph is used to find chains of middle-term predicates that deductively link the assumption and goal predicates.

The basic proof strategies of natural deduction, proof-by-contradiction, and proof-by-cases are automatically incorporated into global deductive planning (since the predicate dependency links reflected in the predicate connection graph are of the different kinds needed for all these strategies).[15]

The chain-generation process may be visualized as generating a series of expanding wave fronts from each assumption and goal predicate. These wave fronts represent deductively significant possible paths from each predicate. As the two wave fronts expand, intersections are taken to determine when an assumption wave front impinges on a goal wave front. When this happens, the system has discovered the beginning of a proof plan.

**Applications.** KM-1 has been used to implement several knowledge management applications including information specialist's assistant[16] and manager's assistant.[17]

*Information specialist's assistant.* This application was developed to experiment with deductively augmented access to a large bibliographic database. Bibliogaphic databases are in widespread use in several existing online information search systems such as SDC's Search Services and Lockheed's Dialog. These databases contain information about publications in scientific literature and typically support access by author, type and name of publication, subject, author affiliation, publication date, cited references, and index terms. Information specialists who use such services often devise rather complex and subtle information search strategies in seeking scientific and patent data for their clients.

To illustrate the use of KM-1 in this kind of activity, the notion of scientist membership in a clique, ingroup or invisible college* is formalized as a small set of rules, or microtheory. Examples of rules, expressed in KM-1's English-like logical formalism, that constitute such a microtheory are

- If Scientist-1 is an author of Publication-1 and Scientist-2 is an author of Publication-1, then Scientist-1 and Scientist-2 may be members of the same invisible college.
- If Scientist-1 cites Scientist-2 and Scientist-2 cites Scientist-1, then Scientist-1 and Scientist-2 are likely to be members of the same invisible college.
- If Scientist-1 knows Result-1 and Scientist-1 conducts research at Laboratory-1, then Laboratory-1 knows Result-1.

In these rules terms such as Scientist-1 stand for a variable of type Scientist. Modal terms such as "may" and "likely" map into a plausibility weight associated with a rule.

As a concrete example, suppose we work for a drug company and suspect that a competitor's scientist, Barker, has originated a new form of synthetic insulin. We are interested in finding out which laboratories might have learned about this result from members of Barker's invisible college before his result is published in the literature.

We could formulate a conditional or given-find query—a query consisting of an assumption that Barker originates a synthetic insulin result in 1984, and a goal expression requesting a list of laboratories that know about Barker's result.

Figure 5 illustrates how information in the KM-1 knowledge base may be exploited to guide a user in formulating a query. In the query-guidance mode, KM-1 presents a menu of basic query types to the user who, in this case, selects the given-find type.

Next, the user may choose Objects or Relations as a starting point in query formation. If Objects is selected, KM-1 uses its knowledge structure and predicate connection graph to produce a display of object types that can be used as assumptions. The user now selects Scientist, and KM-1 displays the relevant subset of relations that may be used as assumptions. In this case, we see that some relations may be used negatively (e.g., Scientist-1 Isn't—) as well as affirmatively.

The Originates template is chosen and the user continues in this manner to complete the development of a query skeleton, including a find part. The final step is to lead the user through a process in which he can replace some or all of the typed variables in his query with proper names. This last step is supported by the selective display of proper names from the database.

Top, line, and project managers were interviewed in a series of consultations designed to elicit their expertise and their information requirements.

Figure 6 illustrates the kind of graphical display that KM-1 generates to explain an answer. The line of reasoning followed by KM-1 is shown as a tree structure in a window that is both zoomable and scrollable. Individual nodes on the tree may be selected via the mouse for detailed display of either the facts supporting that node or the rule used to derive that node. For this question and evidence chain, nine separate facts had to be retrieved from the underlying database.

Most KM-1 users prefer the query guidance mode for constructing queries, but KM-1 may also be called from an application program. In this case, requests are expressed in logic and answers are returned as sets of derived tuples.

*Manager's assistant.* In this application, part of an actual corporate MIS database was brought up on the Britton Lee IDM-500. Standard knowledge engineering practice was then followed in constructing a rule base of managerial expertise. Top, line, and project managers were interviewed in a series of consultations

*Invisible college is used by sociologists of science to connote a group of scholars who regularly keep in touch with, and communicate new results to, each other through informal channels that are quicker and more efficient than formal publication.

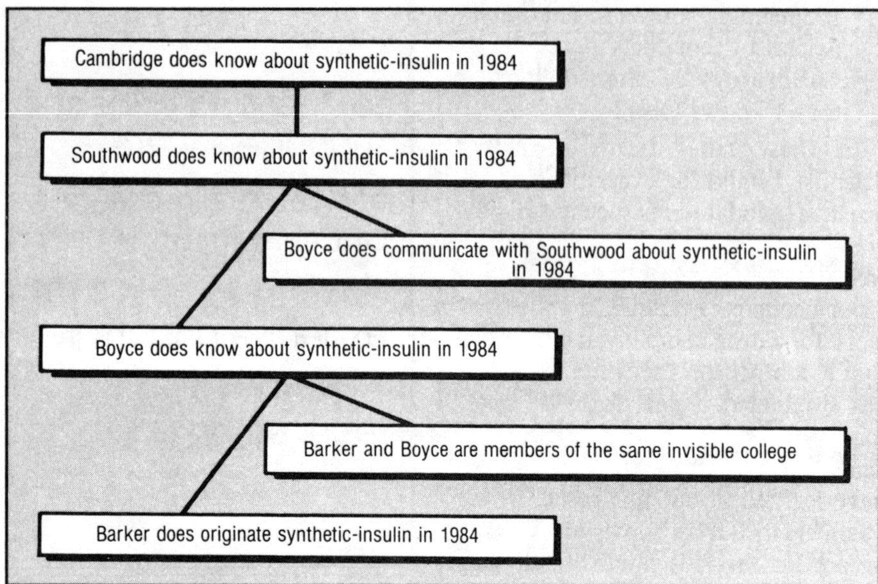


**Figure 6.** Graphical display of evidence chain.

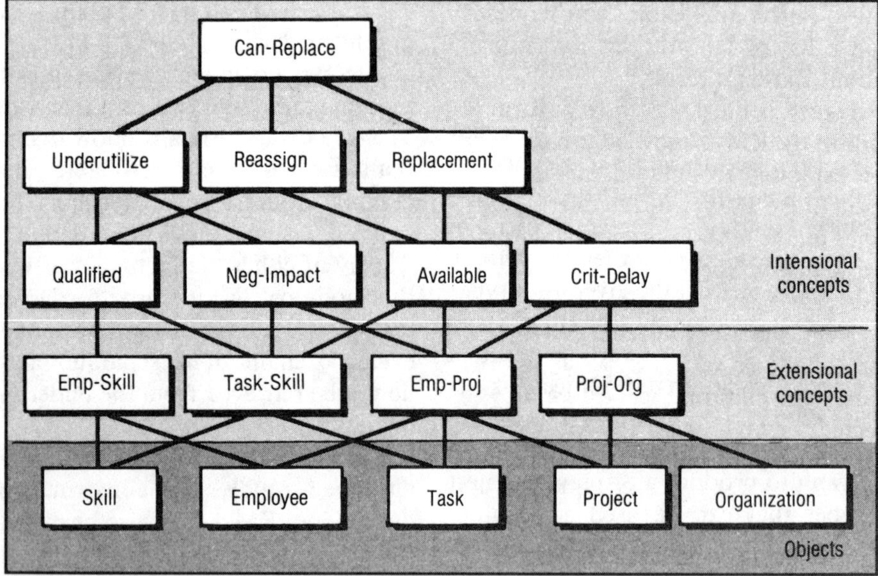


**Figure 7.** Managerial concepts.

designed to elicit their expertise and their information requirements.

Figure 7 shows the associations among a subset of managerial concepts developed as part of this process. Skill, employee, task, project, and organization are examples of basic object types from which extensional and intensional concepts are defined.

Extensional concepts, such as employee skill; task skill; and employee, project, and organization assignment, are represented by the tuple members of relations in the underlying database. Intensional concepts are expressed by means of rules, which, in this case, characterize expertise about the use and reassignment of personnel; critical delays in and negative impacts on the project; and other information useful in identifying projects that may be in trouble or require managerial action.

A typical manager's assistant query is one requesting the search for employees who may be qualified for a new project and who are not critical to an existing project. Hence, they would be likely candidates for reassignment.

A specific form of this query and a portion of a resulting evidence chain is shown in Figure 8. We see that Smith, who is currently assigned to the PV project, is a likely candidate for reassignment to CAM, since he has the requisite qualifications, PV is currently overstaffed, and he is not involved in a key activity on the PV project.

**User-knowledge-manager interaction.** In a user-KM-1 interactive session, the first step is *query formulation*. As discussed earlier, the system can guide a user through the possible query objects and relationships and enforce the development of syntactically correct and logically supported requests. Browsing or generalized navigation operations over the knowledge base are possible. For example, what-if queries are often useful in exploring the deductive consequences of a particular concept.

The next step is *plan generation*, in which KM-1 attempts to generate one or all possible proof/search/compute plans under user control. Where possible, it will generate the plans in order of their plausibility. If a complete plan cannot be generated, partial plans will be displayed.

In the *query explanation* step, a user may review plans before database search. Plans are displayed to a user in the same graphical format used in producing evidence chains. By visual inspection of proof plans, a user comes to understand the machine's interpretation of his request, and he may refine or abort his request on the basis of this understanding.

In *database search and answer generation,* responses include yes, no, don't know, a derived relation, and conditional answers. A conditional answer is produced when a strict categorical answer is not possible because of an incomplete database. Conditional answers are of the form Yes if--- or Information needed---, where dashes represent specific facts missing from the database that are necessary to complete a proof.

The last step in the user-KM-1 interactive session is *answer explanation.* When an answer tuple is selected by the user, its evidence chain will be displayed as illustrated in the previous examples. The user can then navigate through the explanation, requesting the display of additional facts or rules as desired.

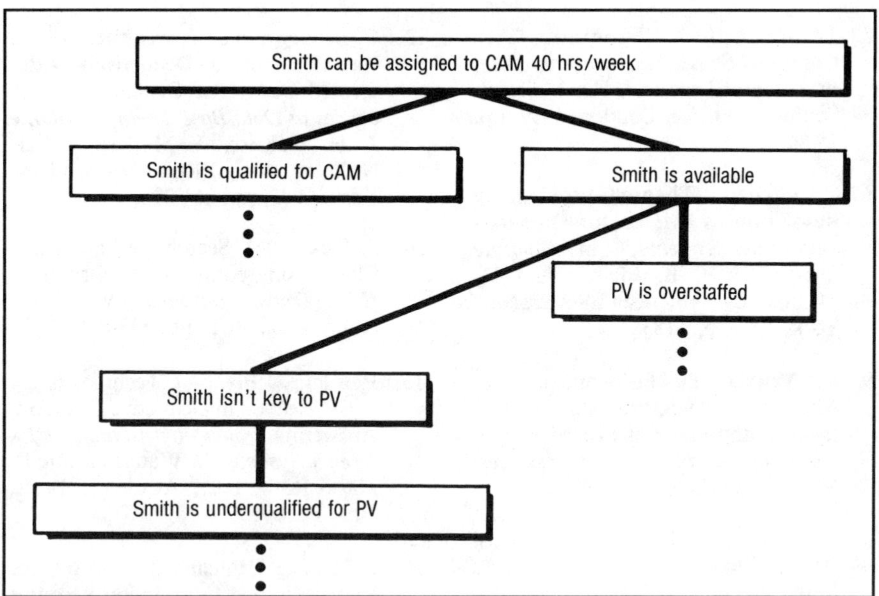


**Figure 8.** Find Employee-1 can be assigned to PV.

## The future of knowledge management

Much additional research is required in many areas, including knowledge representation, knowledge acquisition, and knowledge reasoning, to meet the expected demands for future KMSs. Achieving much higher levels of performance will be critical as knowledge base sizes increase by several orders of magnitude. An excellent summary of leading research issues in logic and databases is provided by Gallaire et al.[18]

Inference mechanisms can significantly enhance the power and usability of a data management system. They enable the compact storage of a large amount of information in the form of general assertions or rules, and they enable the combination of these assertions, with explicitly stored facts, to deduce facts that would otherwise not be available.

Perhaps just as important, a deductive adjunct to a data management system can extend the user language. The general assertions used by the deductive mechanisms can definitionally connect the concepts used by the DMS for organizing its database to different concepts more appropriate for a particular user community.□

## Acknowledgments


Research leading to the development of the DADM processor and the KM-1 prototype was carried out while I was employed at the System Development Corporation in Santa Monica, California. Larry Travis, at the University of Wisconsin, and Philip Klahr, now at The Rand Corporation, were major contributors in the design and construction of the DADM processor. Darrel Van Buer, Richard Whitney, and Dan Kogan at SDC provided many ideas and critical support in developing the software.


## References


1. *Logic and Data Bases,* H. Gallaire and J. Minker, eds., Plenum Press, New York, 1978.
2. R. Kowalski, *Logic for Problem Solving,* North-Holland, Amsterdam, 1979.
3. *Fifth Generation Computing Systems,* T. Moto-Oka, ed., North-Holland, Amsterdam, 1982.
4. J. Robinson, *Logic for Problem Solving,* North-Holland, Amsterdam, 1979.
5. A. Barr and E. Feigenbaum, *The Handbook of Artificial Intelligence,* HeurisTech Press, Stanford, Calif., 1981.
6. *On Conceptual Modeling,* M. Brodie, J. Mylopoulos, and J. Schmidt, eds., Springer-Verlag, New York, 1984.

7. J. McCarthy, "Programs with Common Sense," in *Mechanization of Thought Processes,* Her Majesty's Stationery Office, London, 1959, pp. 75-84.

8. C. Green, "Theorem-proving by Resolution as a Basis for Question-answering Systems," in *Machine Intelligence 4,* B. Meltzer and D. Michro, eds., American Elsevier, New York, 1969, pp. 183-205.

9. L. Minker, D. Fishman, and L. McSkimin, "MRPPS—An Interactive Refutation Proof Procedure," *J. Computers and Information Sciences,* Vol. 3, June 1974, pp. 105-122.

10. C. Kellogg, P. Klahr, and L. Travis, "A Deductive Capability for Data Management," in *Systems for Large Data Bases,* P. Lockemann and S. Neuhold, eds., North-Holland, Amsterdam, 1976.

11. C. Kellogg, "Knowledge Management: A Practical Amalgam of Knowledge and Data Base Technology," *Proc. Nat'l Conf. Artificial Intelligence,* Carnegie-Mellon University, Pittsburgh, Pa., 1982, pp. 306-309.

12. C. Kellogg, P. Klahr, and L. Travis, "Deductive Planning and Pathfinding for Relational Data Bases," in *Logic and Data Bases,* H. Gallaire and J. Minker, eds., Plenum Press, New York, 1978, pp. 179-199.

13. C. Kellogg and L. Travis, "Reasoning with Data in a Deductively Augmented Data Base System," in *Advances in Data Base Theory: Volume 1,* H. Gallaire, J. Minker, and J. Nicholas, eds., Plenum Press, New York, 1981, pp. 261-298.

14. S. Sickel, "A Search Technique for Clause Interconnectivity Graphs," *IEEE Trans. Computers,* Vol. C-25, No. 8, Aug. 1978, pp. 823-835.

15. P. Klahr, "Planning Techniques for Rule Selection in Deductive Question-Answering," in *Pattern-Directed Inference Systems,* D. Waterman and P. Hayes-Roth, eds., Academic Press, New York, 1978.

16. C. Kellogg, "Intelligent Assistants for Knowledge and Information Resource Management," *Proc. Eighth Int'l Joint Conf. Artificial Intelligence,* 1983, pp. 170-173.

17. D. Kogan, "The Manager's Assistant, An Application of Knowledge Management," *Proc. Int'l Conf. Data Engineering,* 1984, pp. 592-595.

18. H. Gallaire, J. Minker, and J. Nicholas, "Logic and Databases; A Deductive Approach," *ACM Computing Surveys,* Vol. 16, No. 2, June 1984, pp. 153-185.

**Charles Kellogg** is a senior member of the technical staff in the Advanced-Computer-Architecture Database Program at Microelectronics and Computer Technology Corporation, where he has worked since 1984. His current research focuses on logic-based knowledge representation and reasoning techniques, including predicate connection graphs to support rule and query compilation.

From 1962 to 1984, he was a research scientist at System Development Corporation in Santa Monica, California, where he carried out and directed research in natural-language access to databases, relational data management, and deductively augmented data management.

Kellogg received a BS in electrical engineering from the University of Florida. He is a member of IEEE, ACM, and the American Association of Artificial Intelligence.

His address is MCC, Echelon I, 9430 Research Blvd., Austin, TX 78759.

# Making Smalltalk a Database System

George Copeland
*Servio Logic Corporation*

David Maier
*Oregon Graduate Center*
and
*Servio Logic Corporation*

**Abstract**

To overcome limitations in the modeling power of existing database systems and provide a better tool for database application programming, Servio Logic Corporation is developing a computer system to support a set-theoretic data model in an object-oriented programming environment. We recount the problems with existing models and database systems. We then show how features of Smalltalk, such such as operational semantics, its type hierarchy, entity identity and the merging of programming and data language, solve many of those problems. Nest we consider what Smalltalk lacks as a database system: secondary storage management, a declarative semantics, concurrency, past states. To address these shortcomings, we needed a formal data model. We introduce the GemStone data model, and show how it helps to define path expressions, a declarative semantics and object history in the OPAL language. We summarize similar approaches, and give a brief overview of the GemStone system implementation.

## 1. Introduction

The areas of database systems, programming languages and artificial intelligence already have large overlaps in some areas [PP]. Designing a state-of-the-art system in one field means employing ideas from the other two fields. Databases require better integrated application programming interfaces, expert systems must deal with large collections of base facts, and programming languages need richer ways to model their data. Current database systems are primarily an effort to implement an abstract data type over the memory of a machine, rather than to support easy and natural modeling of real-world enterprises. They hide the complexities of file systems and indexing techniques, and provide a degree of physical data independence. The next generation of database systems will be knowledge management systems, with more support for data semantics, inferencing and general purpose programming [DE].



Servio Logic Corporation is designing a programming system for database applications, presently called GemStone, that avoids the restrictions and problems of current commercial database systems. The GemStone language, OPAL, incorporates ideas from knowledge representation, abstract data types, and object-oriented programming, as well as semantic data languages, set-theoretic data models, non-procedural query languages and temporal semantics. It provides rich data modeling facilities with a natural interface to a high-level programming language. This paper considers the choice of Smalltalk-80* [GR] as a basis for the OPAL language, and outlines the enhancements we made to Smalltalk to derive the OPAL language and GemStone system.

## 2. Shortcomings of Commercial Database Systems

We outline, in this section, the limitations of existing database systems in the areas of data modeling and programming interfaces. We also set forth the GemStone design goals that address each limitation.

**A. Type Definition Facilities:** Most database systems supply a fixed set of simple types--integer, real and character string--and perhaps a few specialized types, such as date or money. However, they lack the ability to define new simple types and to add operations to the existing types. We can't create a new "employee number" type with a non-standard ordering, or a new operator "nearest payday" on dates, without going outside the database system to an application programming language. The constructors for higher-level types are also limited. The relational model supports "tuple" and "set of homogeneous tuples" (relation). The hierarchical model supports "segment" and "tree of segments". The network model has "record" and "owned list of record" (CODASYL set). A value in a record itself cannot be a structured data item, except for limited support of repeating fields. The operations for higher-level types are induced by the type constructors and cannot be extended. The operations are similar in the three models: access or set a field in a tuple, segment or record; traverse a relation, tree or list in some order; select a record from a structured data item based on a Boolean condition. In addition, the relational model supports operations on entire relations, such as project and join. Even so, the set of operators can't be augmented within the database system.

A final point: Database systems don't separate

"Making Smalltalk a Database System" by G. Copeland and D. Maier from *SIGMOD '84 Proceedings*, 1984, pages 316-325. Copyright 1984, Association for Computing Machinery, Inc, reprinted by permission.

cleanly type definition from data declaration. For example, in relational systems, it is seldom possible to define a relation type (scheme) independently of declaring a relation to be of that type. Thus, redundant specification is necessary to declare several relations as instances of that type.

Some design goals of GemStone are to support arbitrary levels of data structuring, to allow definitions of operations on types, and to uniformly separate type definition from type instantiation.

**B. Artificial Restrictions:** Database systems abound with restrictions on legal database schemes and databases. The limitations often arise from implementation artifacts creeping into the data model. Examples are limits on field lengths, the number of fields in a record, number of files, number of relations in a query, number of indexable fields, number of records in a file and depth of repeating groups.

A design goal of GemStone is to avoid arbitrary limits on the sizes of schemes and data items. Only the size of secondary storage should impose size limits on data items.

**C. Structural Limitations:** The data structuring capabilities of current database systems do not adequately support the complexities and variations that occur in real data. Records (segments, tuples) of a given type must be identical in structure. Every record of a given type must have the same fields and a field must draw its values from the same type in each record. At best there is an allowance for null values or missing fields. Databases are less accommodating of an extra middle name or the possibility that a company car may be assigned to a department or to an individual employee. Current systems also have restrictions on how the data structuring operations may be applied. Tuples in relations are flat records of atomic values, with no repetition of fields. A set in the network model can't have owner and member records of the same type. In the hierarchical model, databases must be strict trees; segment instances can't share subsegments (except through logical pointers).

Dynamic modification of schemes is supported only in a few extant systems. Modifying a type, such as a relation scheme, requires reformatting an entire file.

GemStone design goals are to allow for variations in structured objects, to allow arbitrary data items as values, and to support modification of database schemes without database restructuring.

**D. Modeling Power:** Whenever data structures in a database system won't support the actual structure of information in the real world, then the form of the real-world information gets over-simplified in the database scheme, or it must be encoded into available data structures. If the structure of the real world is over-simplified, the utility and reliability of the data is compromised. For example, if a database scheme only allows for a single middle name, two people who are distinguishable by name might become indistinguishable in the database. When information is encoded, such as flattening a set-valued field into several tuples, application programs must deal with the encoding. Encoding information also means that a database needs extra integrity constraints to ensure that only legitimate encodings appear.

A data model provides *entity identity* if the data representing any entity can be referenced directly as a unit, and the entity may explicitly appear multiple places in a database without any pointer or other indirection mechanism visible to users. Lack of entity identity leads to inconvenience in modeling and proliferation of constraints. In the relational model, to reflect that two people have the same set of children requires either a relation representing named sets of children, or a rather complicated data dependency. In the first case, the indirect reference to the set is visible to users. In the second case, the set of children cannot be referenced as a unit. Entity identity also allows easier sharing of data between data items. In the relational model, two tuples for employees assigned to the same department must represent that commonality through logical pointers to the same department tuple. Logical pointing requires that the database designer find or create a key in the departments relation. Some update anomalies come about because names of entities are used for logical pointers. Consider the previous case when employee tuples use department name to indicate the link to a department. What happens when we want to change the department name? Object-based data models provide entity identity, but other data models can be adapted for entity identity. The trend in extending the relational model is adding surrogates for tuples [Cd]. The network model supports some degree of object identity, but not in an arbitrary manner. A record may belong to more than one set, but not to two instances of the same set type.

Commercial databases to date haven't supported a hierarchy of types. We can't exploit the similarities between, say, employees and managers. so as to define common operations. Type hierarchies are common in AI systems, have been suggested for data modeling by Smith and Smith [SS] and others, and provide the organizational framework in the TAXIS data model [MBW].

Another problem with current systems is that update commands are machine-oriented. Commands insert, delete and modify parts of data items. Such updates do not necessarily correspond to any possible change in the real world, such as changing an employee's birthdate. Changes in the state of the real world typically involve updates to several database objects. Hiring an employee could involve insertions in several relations. Furthermore, the database updates for a real-world change needn't be of the same sort. Changing the times a course meets could entail both insertions and deletions in a database. Being able to model real-world changes is a powerful capability for a database system. It can help in choosing implementations for data structures, and reduce the overhead in integrity checking, since updates can be made to preserve constraints. Applications are easier to write, because common operations on the database can be expressed succinctly. In those cases where some encoding of information is needed, say for time or space efficiency, the encoding and decoding can be hidden in the update operations.

A GemStone design goal is to provide powerful data modeling capabilities through both flexible data structuring and the ability to model real-world changes.

**E. Access to Past States of a Database:** A temporal extension to a data model provides historical access for users and an error recovery mechanism [Cp]. Although historical access is common in manual systems, it is usually not provided in automated database systems.

People are not only interested in the current state of systems. They are also interested in the events and trends that led to a particular state, to help decide what to do next. For example, accounting, legal, financial, manufacturing and engineering applications keep and use history for auditing, trend analysis, patent applications and management tracking. For databases to be useful as models for these systems, they must capture and provide access to history as well as current state. Temporal extensions of data models are a hot research topic of late, but the results of that research haven't reached commercial systems yet, except in the form of time series packages.

Deletion was invented as a means of reusing expensive on-line computer storage. However, the cost of on-line mass storage has been rapidly decreasing. Furthermore, several emerging technologies, such as write-once optical disk [Mi], vertical recording magnetic disks [El1] and rewritable magneto-optical disks [El2] promise a significant reduction in cost per bit of on-line storage. A temporal data model replaces deletion by maintaining object history, thereby exploiting this cost trend by offering historical access for users.

Most database systems do keep a history in the form of checkpoints and recovery logs, usually stored on removable media for error recovery. However, they provide no convenient or efficient way for users to access history. A temporal data model provides both historical access and error recovery.

A GemStone design goal is to explicitly capture the history of database states as part of the data model, and to support queries that access past states.

**F. Separation of Languages:** In the past, computer systems have placed more emphasis on programs than data. That focus manifests itself in the design of traditional programming languages, where data that exists for the life of the program (variables) is treated differently from data that persists after execution (files). Files generally provide for much less data structure than program variables, requiring user-generated encodings for structured values written to files. In the database world, data manipulation languages do not support arbitrary computations on database objects, necessitating an interface to a general-purpose programming language. One language must be embedded in the other, either the programming language in the database language, as in PRTV [To], or the more frequent situation of calls to the database system from the programming language.

The problem with having two languages is "impedance mismatch." One mismatch is conceptual--the data language and the programming languages might support widely different programming paradigms. One could be a declarative language while the other is strictly procedural. Sometimes even a third language is involved, the operating system command language, which further complicates database interaction. The other mismatch is structural--the languages don't support the same data types, so some structure is reflected back at the interface. For example, we can access a relational database using SQL from COBOL, but when the time comes to do some computation, COBOL can only operate at the tuple level. The relational structure is lost. The reflection problem is particularly severe for entity-based data models, where identity can be lost if an entity must be mapped to a character string, a record or whatever to be passed to an application program.

A GemStone design goal is to have a single language for data manipulation, general computation and system commands.

## 3. Our Strategy

Our task at Servio Logic was to design a database system that overcomes the limitations listed above. We wanted a more flexible data model, embedded in a general-purpose programming language. We began with a set-theoretic data model, designed a calculus and algebra for it, and developed an algorithm to translate queries from algebra to calculus. We chose Pascal as the point of departure for the OPAL programming language. That choice proved unsatisfactory. Pascal data type definitions do not support adding operations to a type, nor hierarchies of types. Also, the Pascal type definition paradigm is rigid about typing of subparts of structures, and does not support entity identity well. Multiple use of a data item only takes place through logical references, as in the relational model, or through explicit pointers, which clashed with GemStone design goals. In addition, we saw no clean way to add system commands to Pascal.

We wanted types to have a more operational semantics, and to support entity identity better. In trying to modify Pascal to accommodate our goals, we ended up with something resembling an object-oriented programming language. The resulting data language didn't look much like Pascal at all. We knew there would be user reluctance to switch to a database system that required learning a language dissimilar to any common programming language. We scrapped the Pascal-based version of OPAL, and to begin anew with an object-oriented language, Smalltalk-80 (ST80), as a basis. While ST80 does not have a wide following of users yet, we felt it was the direction of data languages of the future, and there was enough existing literature to acquaint potential users with the concepts of the language.

## 4. Smalltalk-80

### 4.1. A Short Description

ST80 is based on three concepts: *object*, *message*, and *class*. An object is essentially private memory with a public interface. The private memory is structured as a list of named or numbered *instance variables*. An object accepts messages that ask it to access, modify or return a portion of its private memory. So that each object does not have to carry around a list of messages it handles, objects are organized into classes. A class is a group of structurally similar objects that respond to the same set of messages. The class definition contains the procedures (*methods*) that its objects use to respond to messages. Classes are organized in a (strict) hierarchy, so that they can share common structure and methods in a superclass.

For example, an object of class **ArrayedCollection** has messages to put a value at a certain index, return the value at a certain index, create a textual display of its entire value, and "grow" itself to accommodate more values. We can define a class

**Employee**, with each instance having a name, a set of departments and a salary. Instances might accept messages to return the employee's name, change the employee's salary, or assign the employee to different departments. A subclass **Manager** of class **Employee** could define additional structure, such as the department managed, and additional messages, such as one to return a list of subordinate employees.

### 4.2. What it Brings

ST80 has a simple and elegant paradigm for general-purpose programming that meshed well with our data model. ST80 objects gave us entity identity; a single object can be a component of several other objects. ST80 also provides a clear distinction between identity and structural equivalence of entities. Two entities are identical if they are represented by the same object. Two entities can have equivalent structures (have all component values the same), but not be the same object. Thus, we can distinguish, say, two gates in a circuit that have all the same characteristics, but are not physically the same gate. While this identity-equivalence distinction is not present explicitly in other commercially used models, users should recognize it when modeling their enterprises. The distinction is most obvious during update, where if two objects share a component, updates to that component through one object are visible in the other object.

The class mechanism of ST80 handled our requirements for type definition. Messages and methods give us a means to define types with operations, and to hide encodings. The class mechanism provides a hierarchy of types, albeit a strict hierarchy, so that similar types an share operations. Classes give a means of controlling the updates that can be performed on a data object, through a class's message protocol. Also, classes make database schemes easy to modify, and new variants can be constructed easily with the subclass mechanism.

Finally, we note that ST80 treats system components as full-fledged objects, giving a natural and uniform way to issue system commands from within the ST80 language.

### 4.3. What it Lacks

The ST80 language met our needs for type definition and general computation within a data language. Why couldn't we take the ST80 system as is and use it as the basis of a database system? The first problem is that ST80 does not handle large numbers of data items or large data items. Only 32K objects are allowed in most implementations, and the maximum size for an object is 64K bytes. We need to handle more and larger data items for the databases we want to support, such as long documents and graphical images. There are also several arbitrary size limits in the ST80 system, such as the number of variables in a method, which could be exceeded in applications we anticipate. Being a single-user system, ST80 lacks the amenities of a production database system: concurrent access of data by multiple users, recovery mechanisms, and database administrator control over replication, authorization and auxiliary structures. Because ST80 is a strictly procedural language, it does not have any declarative constructs for data manipulation. We feel that associative access to subparts of an object is a necessary aid to application program design. Also, a declarative semantics allows more flexibility in evaluating queries, and that flexibility is needed to support reasonable optimization on queries involving large amounts of data.

The ST80 model of data, while meeting many of our requirements, does not have everything we want. It does not support object histories--past values of instance variables are not retained. We want optional instance variables, without a storage penalty in instances not containing the optional variables, and the ability to add new variables to existing instances, which ST80 does not provide. We also want a path syntax for navigating through objects, and to allow assignments to path expressions. That feature allows a user to circumvent the class protocol for updating objects, but sometimes it is the most natural way to define methods.

## 5. Enhancing Smalltalk as a Database Language

Our first concern in designing the GemStone system is to provide a database system with more modeling power and flexibility than is available currently in commercial systems. We actually developed a data model for GemStone before beginning the design of the OPAL language. We will first introduce the Set Theoretic Data Model (STDM), and discuss its advantages over previous models. STDM turned out to be a reasonable approximation of the object structure of ST80. The structure of all the classes provided with ST80 is too complex to provide the basis for a useful data model. STDM takes a more uniform view of objects, treating most as labeled sets, and that treatment allows a fairly simple path syntax and set calculus.

We then turn to a temporal extension of STDM, and indicate how histories of object states are structured and accessed. Finally in this section, we consider the merger of ST80 and the STDM, resulting in the OPAL language and a slightly modified model, the GemStone Data Model.

**5.1. A Short Description of STDM** STDM is based on labeled sets of heterogeneous values, which themselves can be sets or simple values. The model builds on the work of Childs [Chi], but is not identical to his model. A piece of an STDM database might look like

```
Acme: {Departments: {A12: {Name: 'Sales', Managers: {'Nathen', 'Roberts'},
                           Budget: 142,000},
                     A16: {Name: 'Research', Managers: {'Carter'},
                           Budget: 256,500},
                     ...},
       Employees: {E62: {Name: {First: 'Ellen', Last: 'Burns'}
                         Salary: 24,650, Depts: {'Marketing'}},
                   E83: {Name: {First: 'Robert', Last: 'Peters'},
                         Salary: 24,000, Depts: {'Sales','Planning'},
                         Phones:{3949, 3882}},
                   ...}}
```

(Examples in this section are not necessarily expressed in OPAL syntax.) STDM has *simple types*, generally subsets of number or character types, and *sets*. A set (denoted with {...}) has *elements*, each of which has an *element name* that labels the element and a *value*, which can be from a simple type or a set. In the sixth line of the database segment above, Name: {First: 'Ellen', Last: 'Burns'} is an element with element name **Name** and {First: 'Ellen', Last: 'Burns'} as the value. Essentially, elements function as identifier-value pairs. No two elements in a set may have the same element name.

For sets without labels, arbitrary aliases are used as element names. Presumably, the database system can generate unique aliases upon demand. In the database fragment above, the labels for department and employee sets (A12, A16,..., E62, E83,...) are aliases. In the example, we have elided element names for sets of simple values, such as {'Nathen', 'Roberts'}.

STDM uses a path syntax for accessing subparts of a set. If X is a variable whose value is the set above, then sample path expressions are X!Departments!A16!Managers and X!Employees!E62!Name.

We have developed a set-calculus query system for the STDM. As an example query, suppose we want to know employees and managers such that the employee is in the manager's department, and the employee's salary is more than 10% of the department's budget. The set-calculus expression for this query is

{{Emp: e, Mgr: m} where
(e ∈ X!Employees) and
(∃ d ∈ X!Departments) [(m ∈ d!Managers) and
(d!Name ∈ e!Depts) and (e!Salary > 0.10 * d!Budget)]}

Note that a declarative syntax is needed for easy navigation through sets with aliases as element names, such as Employees. We have developed a set algebra, and an algorithm to translate a set-calculus expression to a set-algebra expression.

### 5.2. Advantages of STDM

STDM is a more powerful modeling mechanism than data models supported in other commercial systems. Any place a simple value can occur, we can have a set of values, or a structured value. There is unlimited nesting of sets, so a single value can have arbitrarily detailed internal structure. STDM is also flexible: optional element names in a set are handled, and elements with new element names can be added to a set. The value associated with a particular element name is not restricted to a single type. For sets representing company cars, the element name AssignedTo could have a value that is an employee, a department or a set of departments.

The power and the flexibility of STDM allows closer and more direct modeling of real-world domains. Many standard data structures can be represented straightforwardly with STDM sets. Arrays may be represented by sets with numbers as element names:

{1: {'Anders', 'Roberts'},
2: {'Roberts', 'Ching'},
3: {'Albrecht', 'Ching'}}

The index set for an array need not be positive integers--with a little more set structure it could be an arbitrary type. Record structures, with arbitrary levels and types of subrecords, are represented naturally in STDM. A relation is represented as a set of tuples, where each tuple is a set with element names corresponding to attributes of the relation. For example, the relation

| A | B | C |
|---|---|---|
| 1 | 3 | 4 |
| 1 | 5 | 4 |

is represented by the set

{T1: {A: 1, B: 3, C: 4},
T2: {A: 1, B: 5, C: 4}}.

Data structured as in the hierarchical model have a direct representation in STDM, by modeling a segment as a set, with elements that are field values or sets of child segments. STDM can model arbitrary combinations of arrays, sets and records.

Some structures, handled readily in STDM, would require significant encoding to fit in the relational or hierarchical models. A set-valued attribute, such as children of an employee, has to be "flattened" into several tuples in the relational model, one per child. For example, the set structure

{Name: {First: 'Robert', Last: 'Peters'},
Children: {'Olivia', 'Dale', 'Paul'}}

comes out as a three-tuple relation:

| FirstName | LastName | Child |
|---|---|---|
| Robert | Peters | Olivia |
| Robert | Peters | Dale |
| Robert | Peters | Paul |

However, under such a representation, the set of children does not exist anywhere as a single object. An alternative would be to form an additional relation to represent sets of children. This alternative requires names for the sets of children, and introduces an artifact at the user level, requiring extra joins to bring the description of an employee together. There is unavoidable redundancy in either approach: Some value is going to be repeated three times. Operations on the set, other than insertions and deletions, are awkward to express. For example, stipulating one set is the subset of another set requires two quantifiers in relational calculus. STDM, while requiring some encoding for certain data items, at least preserves the integrity of entities. A set of children can be represented and manipulated as a single data item at some level. Reducing the amount of encoding to model real-world entities, and being able to preserve the integrity of those entities, makes data easier to understand and applications simpler to write.

The declarative syntax for STDM simplifies many application programs. It also allows much more access planning by the database system than with an equivalent query specified procedurally. The set calculus provides the basis for a declarative query syntax. A distinguishing feature of our calculus, as compared to relational calculus, is that variables can be bound to functions of other variables, rather than only to fixed database objects. Because a variable may assume a value that is a structured object, a condition such as

m ∈ d!Managers,

makes sense.

### 5.3. Adding History to Objects

#### 5.3.1. Transaction Time vs. Event Time

The first question to face when adding time to a data model is What kind of time to incorporate? *Transaction time* is the time when an event is recorded in the database. *Event time* is the time when an event occurs in the real world. GemStone uses transaction time to record history, rather than event time. We discuss that choice.

In many databases, transaction time and event time are either the same or close enough to be considered equivalent. Furthermore, as computer systems are used to more completely automate our real-world systems, databases are increasingly becoming more real-time, in which the official time of an event is the moment when the event is recorded in the database. Even though a database is a model of a real-world system, the database itself is a real-world system. Thus, the recording process itself is a significant real-world event whose event time is its transaction time.

Transaction time has a simple semantics that is application independent. Thus, transaction time is easily automated by a database system. In contrast, the semantics of event time is application dependent, so that event time is difficult for a database system to automate on behalf of users. Note that the use of transaction time to record history in GemStone does not imply that event time cannot be captured as user-defined data. In fact, the extendibility of classes that OPAL provides allows any semantics for time to easily be added by users. Since transaction time is system-generated, and cannot be modified by users, it provides high integrity. In contrast, event time must be modifiable by users when a discrepancy is discovered between the real world and its database model.

When we venture to extend the scope of computer science, we often have no empirical basis within our young field upon which to base our decisions. In the case of extending a data model to manage history, we do have some empirical basis in the fields of accounting and other recordkeeping disciplines. Accountants have dealt with the issue of transaction time vs. event time for many years, if not centuries. They have seen as fundamental the consideration of the recording process itself as a significant real-world event. Reed [Re1, Re2] argues that storing transaction time is useful for synchronizing concurrent transactions. This observation offers the possibility of sharing the overhead of generating and storing the transaction time over both functions.

#### 5.3.2. The Temporal Extension

In the data model presented so far, we represent each element of an object as an element name-value pair. We represent history in STDM by replacing an element's single value with a set of values. The element name is associated with each value via a transaction time. The binding between an element name and its associated value is indexed by time. For example, if E is a set representing an employee, then E!Salary is actually a mapping from transaction times to values giving the salaries of the employee in past and present states of the database. If T represents a point in time, then E!Salary@T gives the value of E's salary at time T. That is, E!Salary@T is the value that E!Salary had in the state of the database that existed at time T. The relationship between an element name and a particular value

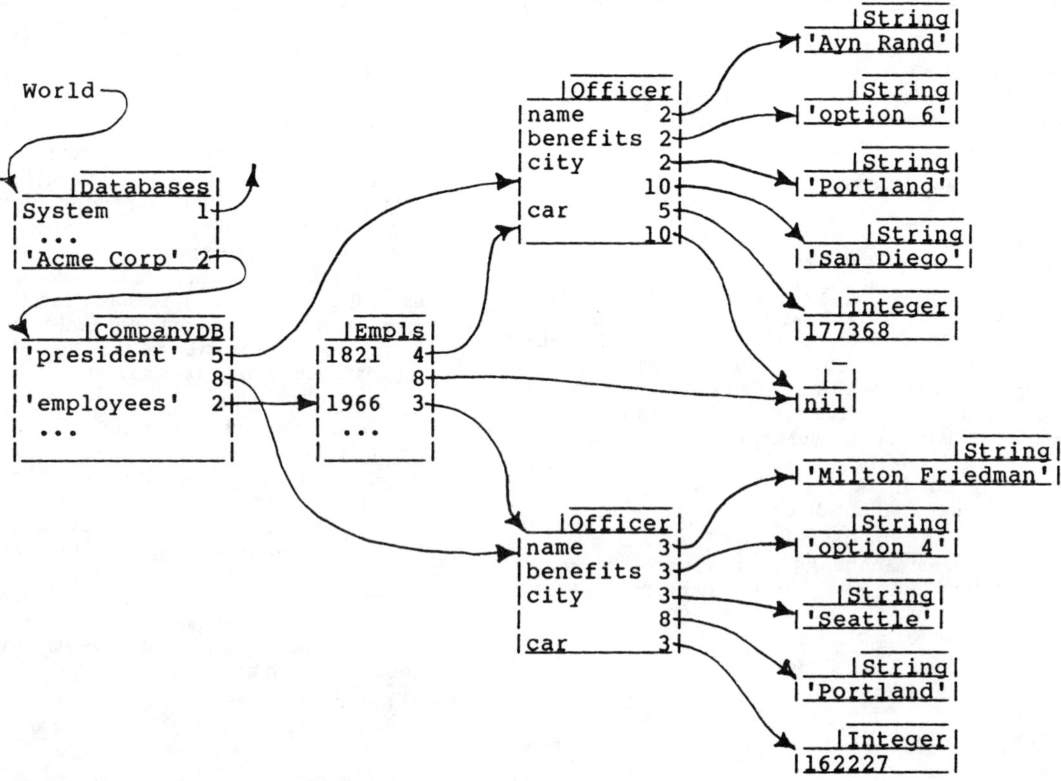


Figure 1: A Database with History

begins at the transaction time for the value, and ends when a new value is associated with the same element and a later transaction time. Objects themselves do not have time. Only their relationships with their elements are indexed by time.

The example in Figure 1 illustrates the temporal extension. The numbers at the right side of each box represent the transaction times of relationships. The example shows that at time 8, the company president was changed from 'Ayn Rand' to 'Milton Friedman'. The example represents a history of two presidents. Ayn was president from time 5 to 8. Milton was president from time 8 to the current time. Prior to this change, Milton had worked for the company in Seattle. His new appointment required a move to Portland. The example represents a history of Ayn as an employee from 2 to 8. The fact that Ayn left as an employee is indicated by the relationship in the employees object with her employee number 1821 as an element name and with time 8, whose value is the object nil. Shortly after leaving the company, Ayn moved to San Diego. She was allowed to continue to use her company car until her move at time 10.

A current transaction can access the new company president by the path expression

World!'Acme Corp'!'president'

or at a time in the recent past with the path expression

World!'Acme Corp'!'president'@10.

If the argument of @ were 7, then the previous president would be accessed. As another example, the previous president's current city, San Diego, can be accessed by the path

World!'Acme Corp'!'president'@7!city.

### 5.4. Merging ST80 and STDM

As we said, STDM was conceived before ST80 was chosen as the basis for OPAL. STDM provides the basis to add path syntax, set calculus and object history to ST80 to get OPAL. Conversely, there some deficiencies in STDM that ST80 helped overcome. While STDM is powerful and flexible, it did not provide all the modeling power we wanted. STDM does not support entity identity, except for simple, nonchangeable values. STDM sets are unlike mathematical sets, in that any set instance can be an element in at most one other set. In mathematical sets, of course, an element may be a member of several sets. If two sets represent two employees in the same department, they could have logical pointer to the same department set, or they could duplicate the department set as an element. Neither alternative is entirely satisfactory. The first requires navigating across data objects at the logical level; the second entails added complexity when updating a department description. Furthermore, without entity identity, STDM cannot capture network schemes directly, where a single record may be an element of several sets. STDM does not have a good type definition mechanism. We had a hard time deciding whether types should be associated with sets or elements, or both; how to describe types; how to specify operations on instances of a type; and how to factor element names from instances of a type. Also, we had no structure on types--there was no type hierarchy.

Definition of operations for a type was especially important to us, as certain real-world structures still required encoding. Thus, we needed a mechanism for information hiding, to make database objects appear and behave as their real-world counterparts. For example, to make a relation behave as a relation, we needed a tuple to appear as a mapping rather than a set. We also wanted to define subclasses of simple types with operators and orderings different from the parent type.

STDM does not provide a general programming interface. Set calculus is its only vehicle for describing set access and update. We needed a procedural language to support the set algebra. Further, we found many examples where procedural updates would be clearer and more succinct than the calculus equivalents. We also wanted to include general computations in the conditions of calculus expressions.

Merging STDM with ST80 to overcome these deficiencies is straightforward. We can identify sets and simple values in STDM with objects in ST80 and elements with instance variable-value pairs. Just as STDM induced changes in ST80 to get OPAL, ST80 dictated changes in STDM. We call the revised model the GemStone Data Model (GSDM). In STDM we had concentrated on names--path names and element names—in trying to assign types. In GSDM the focus became values (objects), and that is where typing went on. We still feel that some typing of element names could give us big performance advantages, such as more flexibility on access paths when processing declarative queries. and we are looking at this extension to OPAL, as are others [BI, Ha].

The switch from Pascal to ST80 as a basis for OPAL was propitious. We have a single language for general programming, data manipulation and system commands, with excellent support for data and operation definition. There is no impedance mismatch between application language and database language, which we noted is particularly troublesome for a database that tries to support entity identity. GSDM has true entity identity, not just entity integrity. GSDM retains the time dimension, path expressions and set calculus from STDM. We have been able to incorporate declarative statements in OPAL without departing from Smalltalk syntax. Thus, our realization of set calculus is particularly powerful, as it can *include* procedural parts, and can be *included in* procedural methods.

We have been careful to preserve entity identity in GSDM as regards time. Although entity identity is important in databases that do not model history, it is even more important when object history is modeled. Identity is a property of an object that spans time. When an object is instantiated, it is given a globally unique identity. It lives forever with that identity, although the value of its elements may change, and it may not be accessible from other objects in some states of the database. In OPAL, we have eschewed the !-@ notation for navigating through object histories in favor of a *time dial*. We feel that almost all navigation through history would be within a single past state of the database. Setting the time dial to time T is the same as appending @T to each component in a path expression. A useful feature of the time dial is the system variable SafeTime. A read-only transaction can set its time dial to SafeTime to get the most recent state for which no currently running transaction can make changes.

Support for views drops out almost for free. We can construct an object that provides a view, and that object can employ other objects, procedural statements and calculus expressions to define the extension of the view. Furthermore, since the view object can retain connections to the objects that contributed to the view, and since it can support its own methods for messages, view updates are more manageable than in other data models.

**6. Enhancing Smalltalk as a Database System**

The language extensions covered in the last section do not make ST80 into a database system. The problems of supporting concurrent access to large amounts of data, along with replication and recovery, remained to be solved. We have added classes and primitive methods to OPAL to provide transaction control, storage hints and requests for replication of data. Of course, the biggest requirement of the GemStone system is that it manage objects with all these database features efficiently. In this section we briefly cover the current implementation of GemStone.

The GemStone system is currently being implemented on special-purpose hardware, although we anticipate purely software versions to run on other vendors' hardware. We expect to obtain efficiency by having the database system control secondary storage directly, without an intervening operating system. A separate operating system would be somewhat oblivious to the storage needs and access patterns of the database system. Also, an independent operating system can play havoc with requirements on database consistency, security and recoverability. Disk access will always be by entire tracks, as a track is the natural unit of physical access for a disk. Also, by having a declarative query language, we have the latitude in processing queries to exploit fully secondary storage layout, directories, and special hardware.

Communication with GemStone is done in blocks of OPAL source code. Compilation and execution of those blocks is done entirely in the GemStone system.

The system structure of GemStone is similar to that of ST80, minus display and file system classes, but with additions for set calculus, path syntax, time, concurrency, authorization, recovery, replication and directories. The display part of ST80 is not currently needed, as our present implementation has GemStone running on its own hardware and communicating to user interface programs on host machines through a network link. We do envisage a stand-alone GemStone system eventually, which would support display control. All file system duties are assumed by the database system.

The GemStone system has two main parts, the *Executor* and the *Object Manager*. The Executor is responsible for controlling sessions in the GemStone system on behalf of users on host machines. The Executor handles communications between GemStone and host software: receiving blocks of code, returning results and error messages. It maintains a *Compiler* and *Interpreter* for each active user. The Interpreter is an abstract stack machine that executes *compiledMethods* consisting of sequences of *bytecodes*, much the same as the ST80 interpreter. It dispatches bytecodes, performs stack manipulations and some primitive methods, and makes calls to the Object Manager. The Compiler requires some modifications from the ST80 compiler. Most are small changes in syntax or for slightly different bytecodes, but a large addition is needed translate calculus expressions into procedural form.

The Object Manager performs the same operations as the ST80 object memory, but is quite different in structure. The Object Manager also handles operations related to concurrency and secondary storage management: transaction control, authorization, data replication, recovery and directory management. In addition, the Object Manager responds to messages to conduct its fetches in some previous state of the database. Each user session in the GemStone system has its own invocation of the Interpreter, and its own Object Manager with a private object space. Sessions have shared access to the permanent database through transactions.

In the standard implementation of the ST80 object memory, objects are represented as blocks of contiguous words of memory, with *object-oriented pointers* (OOPs) to the values of instance variables. Since GemStone objects retain history, they grow with time, and a fixed block of memory is not a feasible representation. In the GemStone Object Manager, the implementation of objects is based upon *associations*. An element is represented as an element name and a table of associations. The associations are pairs of transaction times and object pointers, each representing that the element acquired the object as its value at the time given by the transaction time. The mapping from arbitrary times to value for an element can easily be realized from this table. Objects are broken into elements and associations, which are organized into a linked list under a header for the object. A directory may be interposed between the object header and the participating elements. Such a directory is useful when an object has a long history, or it represents a set without labels, whose elements will likely be accessed associatively, rather than through element names. Between objects, pointers to elements are usually physical pointers, as we expect most of the data to be strict tree structures. Thus, physical access paths parallel logical access where objects aren't shared. Where an object is an element of more than one set, one logical path is chosen as the basis for the physical access path, and other references to the object use a *global object-oriented pointer* (GOOP). The GOOP is resolved through a *global object table* to get the primary logical path to the object, from which its physical access path can be deduced.

The Object Manager has several major subcomponents. The *Transaction Manager* is shared by all invocations of the Object Manager, and handles concurrent use of the permanent database in an optimistic manner. It records accesses to the database for each session, and validates them for consistency when a transaction commits. The *Directory Manager* creates and maintains directories. Directories use standard techniques modified to handle object histories. One headache has been that hints given in OPAL for structuring directories must be translated for use by the Object Manager. Another problem is using a nested element as a discriminator. Since that element may be different in different states of the database, its object may need to appear along two branches of the directory.

The *Linker* incorporates updates made by a transaction in the permanent database at commit time, calling for restructuring of directories as needed. The Linker is called by the *Boxer*, whose job it is to fit objects into tracks after database changes. The *Track Manager* schedules reads and writes of tracks. The *Commit Manager* provides *safe writing* for groups of tracks. Safe writing guarantees that all the tracks in the group get written, or none get written, and that the tracks in the group replace their old versions atomically.

The time dimension of GSDM leads to one simplification in the GemStone Object Manager over ST80 object memory. Database objects in the past never go away, as references exist to them in some state of the database, and, theoretically, all past states of a database are preserved. Thus, no garbage collection need be done on database objects. Temporary objects created by user sessions may have to be garbage collected. However, again the task is eased, as an entire session workspace can be discarded at the end of a session. A database administrator can explicitly move objects to other media, such as tape or write-only memory. Hence, while conceptually the entire history of the database exists, some objects in it may become temporarily or permanently inaccessible.

## 7. Similar Approaches

Others have attempted to make ST80 a better vehicle for database applications. Most of those efforts concentrate on supporting data in secondary storage. Probably the best-known extension to secondary storage is the Large Object-Oriented Memory (LOOM) [KK]. LOOM maintains a two-level object space in main memory and on disk. Objects are moved to main memory from disk as needed. LOOM does not meet our needs for four reasons. First, it is intended for a single user system. Second, while it allows many more objects than standard Smalltalk implementations, it retains the same maximum size for objects. Third, it uses the standard Smalltalk representation of objects. That representation is not suitable for us, as we have objects with a time dimension. For objects with a large history, we may want to bring only a fragment of the object into memory. Fourth, LOOM hasn't completely dealt with the problems of clustering and indexing in secondary storage.

Several recent data models undertake to solve many of the same problems that GSDM does. The Cypres database system [Ca] supports an entity-relationship-datum data model with a strong notion of object identity. However, Cypres does not provide general-purpose programming, nor operations definition for types. Morgenstern [Mo] describes the data model for the IM project at ISI. That model is also entity-based, and it provides a hierarchy of data types, but again, it doesn't provide operation definition. IM does address integrity constraints in greater depth than we have yet.

Programming language-data language integration has been tried in combinations other than a set-theoretic data model with an object-oriented language. Some of the first attempts were adding relations to highly-typed languages such as Pascal. Two examples are Pascal/R [Sch] and PLAIN [W+]. IBM has at least two efforts in the area. One is the EAS-E system [MMP], which provides a network data model in a structured-English programming language. The other is the IDE project at the Los Angeles Scientific Center [Ne], which uses an object-based data model. ADAplex [C+] combines the Daplex functional data model with the object-based language Ada. Beech [Be] describes IDL, which has an object-based data model, with a Formula type for defining operations on classes of objects. Finally, the combination of a relational database system with a logic programming language, such as Prolog, has gathered many adherents [Da, Pa1, Pa2, Wa].

## 8. Acknowledgements

Fred Boals did the initial work on the set calculus to set algebra translation algorithm, and Bob Johnson brought it to its current form. The adaptation of OPAL from ST80 was done for the most part by Alan Purdy and Jason Penney. The design of the Object Manager is due to Dave Schrader, Bob Bretl, Allen Otis, Walt Gorman, Pat Timlick and Lynn Nelson. Most of these people read earlier versions of this paper, and while the authors should accept responsibility for remaining errors themselves, they prefer to ascribe blame to the others.

## 9. Bibliography

[Be] D. Beech Introducing the integrated data model. Hewlett-Packard Computer Science Laboratory technical note CSL-15, January 1983. 2.

[Bl] A.H. Borning, D.H.H. Ingalls. A type declaration and inference system for Smalltalk. Univ. of Washington Computer Science TR 81-08-02a, November 1981.

[Ca] R.G.G. Cattell. Design and implementation of a relationship-entity-datum data model. Xerox PARC report CSL-83-4, May 1983.

[C+] A. Chan, et al. DDM: An Ada-compatible distributed database manager. Digest of Papers, COMPCON '83, February-March 1983, 422-425.

[Chi] D.L. Childs. Feasibility of a set-theoretic data structure based on a reconstituted definition of relation. IFIP '68, North-Holland, 1969, 162-172.

[Cd] E.F. Codd. Extending the database relational model to capture more meaning. *ACM TODS 4*, 4, December 1978, 397-434.

[Cp] G. Copeland. What if mass storage were free? *IEEE Computer 15*, 7, July 1982.

[Da] V. Dahl. On database systems development through logic. *ACM TODS 7* 1, March 1982, 102-123.

[DE] *Database Engineering 6*, 4, December 1983: issue on expert systems and database systems.

[El1] *Electronics 56*, 8. Perpendicular bits up density of prototype disk drives. April 1983.

[El2] *Electronics 56*, 14. Erasable optical disk system could be available by 1985. July 1983.

[GR] A. Goldberg, D. Robson. *Smalltalk-80: The Language and its Implementation*. Addison-Wesley, 1983.

[Ha] R. Hagmann. Preferred classes: a proposal for faster Smalltalk-80 execution. In *Smalltalk-80: Bits of History, Words of Advice*, G. Krasner, Ed., Addison-Wesley, 1983, 323-330.

[KK] T. Kaehler, T. Krasner. LOOM--Large object-oriented memory for Smalltalk-80 systems. In *Smalltalk-80: Bits of History, Words of Advice*, G. Krasner, Ed., Addison-Wesley, 1983, 251-272.

[MMP] A. Malhotra, H.M. Markowitz, D.P. Pazel. EAS-E: An integrated approach to application development. *ACM TODS 8*, 4, December 1983, 515-542.

[Mi] S.W. Miller, editor. Special issue on mass storage systems. *IEEE Computer 15*, 7, July 1982.

[Mo] M. Morgenstern. Active databases as a paradigm for enhanced computing environments. VLDB IX, Florence, Italy, October 1983.

[MBW] J. Mylopoulos, P.A. Bernstein, H.K.T. Wong. A language facility for designing database-intensive applications. *ACM TODS 5*, 2, June 1980, 185-207.

[Ne] P. Newman. Techniques for environment integration. Computer Science colloquium, Oregon Graduate Center, October 1983.

[Pa1] K. Parsaye. Database management, knowledge base management and expert system development in Prolog. ACM SIGMOD Database Week, Databases for Business and Office Applications, San Jose, May 1983, 159-178.

[Pa2] K. Parsaye. Logic programming in relational databases. In [DE], 20-29.

[PP] Proceedings of the Workshop on Data Abstraction, Databases and Conceptual Modeling, Pingree Park, Colorado. SIGMOD Record 11, 2, February 1981.

[Sch] J.W. Schmidt. Some high level constructs of data type relation. *ACM TODS 2*, 3, September 1977, 247-261.

[SS] J.M. Smith and D.C.P. Smith. Database Abstractions: Aggregation and Generalization. *ACM TODS 2*, 2, June 1977, 105-133.

[To] S.P.J. Todd. The Peterlee Relational Test Vehicle—a system overview. *IBM Systems Journal 15*, 4, December 1976, 285-308.

[Wa] D.H.D. Warren. Efficient processing of interactive relational queries expressed in logic. VLDB VII, Cannes, France, September 1981, 272-281.

[W+] A.I. Wasserman, et al. The data management facility of PLAIN. ACM SIGPLAN Notices 16, 5, May 1981, 59-80.

*A design data management system bridges the gap between design tools and database systems, creating an integrated tool environment.*

# Managing the Chip Design Database

Randy H. Katz, University of California, Berkeley

Because the Mead-Conway design method[1] made it possible for computer scientists to experiment with custom integrated circuits, a new generation of tools has developed. A partial list includes the Caesar[2] circuit editor, MacPitts datapath generator,[3] Esim and NL/RNL[4] design-rule checkers and switch-level simulators, as well as TV[5] and Crystal[6] timing analyzers.

But these are not *systems.* Tools created by different groups are difficult to integrate.[7] Cumbersome programs translate between the representations understood by individual tools. Standard interchange languages do not solve the problem, since each tool uses its own "escape hatches" for describing critical design information. For example, the Caltech Interchange Format[1] has no standard mechanism for associating symbolic names with geometric features of the layout. How to integrate the tools is still an open issue.

An integrated design database is needed before a collection of design tools can be formed into a design system (see Figure 1). The database organizes design information across representations, alternative implementations, and evolutionary versions. The system controls concurrent designer access and guarantees that the data can survive system crashes. Placing all design information under the responsibility of a single data management system makes the self-consistency of the design more easily maintained. When dependencies among parts of the design are explicit, ramifications of changes can be discovered and propagated in a controlled manner. Furthermore, the equivalence of all representations of the design can be verified economically.

Although design databases have long been of interest,[8-10] they have been largely ignored within the context of the new tools. Our purpose is to describe what design data management is and how it can integrate design tools. Our discussion focuses on unique data management requirements of design systems and conventional database facilities and their shortcomings for supporting design data. We also present the architecture of a prototype design management system in which designs are organized into a richly interconnected data structure, using an *object data model.* The structures of that system's storage, recovery, concurrency control, and design validation subsystems are also described as is a "browser" for interactively viewing design data.

## Basic terms

To better understand the systems presented later, a review of some basic VLSI design and database terms may be helpful. *Data structures* are logical organizations of data. Database systems typically support tabular (relational), tree (hierarchical), or graph (network) structures among records. For example, the Unix file system[11] supports a constrained graph structure among directories (internal vertices) and files (leaves). A link mechanism allows files to be incorporated in more than one directory.

*Storage structures* are implementations of data structures on secondary storage. A tree of design objects is a data structure, while its implementation as a balanced multi-directional tree on disk is a storage structure.

A *database* comprises the data describing the activities of an organization. For example, a chip design database contains information about how design objects are composed from primitives (such as geometries, transistors, and gates), how a design is described in different representations (such as layout, circuit, and logic), how the design has evolved over time, who is responsible for designing its parts, and so forth. Particular data structures selected to represent a specific database form a *database schema.*

A *database management system* manages databases stored on secondary storage and provides a standard inter-

EH0252-7/87/0000/0387$01.00 © 1983 IEEE



Reprinted from *Computer*, December 1983, pages 26-36. Copyright © 1983 by The Institute of Electrical and Electronics Engineers, Inc.

face for manipulating data. The data access operations are typically based on data structure rather than on storage structure, so the physical structure can be changed without affecting existing programs ("data independence"). The system protects the data from illegal actions, maintains data consistency, and ensures that changes can be recovered after a system crash. *Access methods* are storage-structure-specific routines for manipulating data on disk.

A *design data management system* chooses how to structure the design data within the database system. It provides a standard access interface for tools. Although the database system does not interpret the data it manages, a design management system understands how the structure of the data describes a design project. It enforces design data constraints. For example, part of the design data structure identifies equivalent objects across representations. The design data and the complex consistency constraints are normally what the design automation community mean by "database."

The major components of design data management include the storage component, reliably storing design data on disk; the recovery subsystem, saving incremental changes and ensuring resiliency to crashes either at workstations or database servers (that is, shared repositories of design data); the design librarian, supporting check-in/check-out of design parts from the database; the validation component, checking that design constraints remain in force after a change; the design transaction component, using the recovery subsystem, the design librarian, and the validation component to control the creation of new versions of design objects and the browser/chip assembler, providing an interactive front end for creating and viewing the design data structure.

A *design system* combines design tools, project management aids, and design data management facilities. The design tools create pieces of a design and validate correctness. The project management aids assist in planning the implementation effort. Design data management is responsible for structuring the design and exploiting the structure to keep the design consistent.

## What design systems need

Design applications need to structure design data hierarchically, support multiple design representations, maintain design versions and alternatives, help the designers cooperate and interact as a team, support remote design at workstations, with long-term storage at database servers, and maintain the consistency of the design.

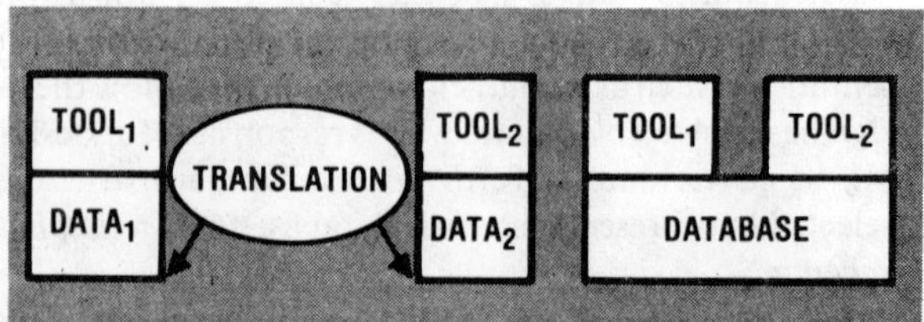


Figure 1. Design tools versus design systems.

Hierarchy and regularity are well-known tactics for reducing the complexity of a large design.[12,13] A design proceeds by a top-down decomposition of systems into subsystems and a bottom-up synthesis of building blocks from more primitive building blocks. The design is complete when all subsystems can be implemented by existing building blocks and primitives. The hierarchical structure of the design is mirrored in its data.

Design regularity reduces the size of the design database as well as the design effort. An object is designed once and used frequently, its description appearing once in the database. Additional data describe each use of the object, specifying how it is instantiated and placed within the design.

VLSI circuits are described in several representations, including geometric layouts, transistor networks, logic schematics, and functional descriptions. Each is appropriate for a different phase of design. Geometries are used for mask-making and geometric design rule-checking. Transistor, logic, and functional descriptions are used for electrical rule-checking, simulation, and timing verification at various levels of detail.

While the Mead-Conway style encourages a horizontal design partitioning, industrial designs are more typically partitioned vertically into architecture, logic, circuit, and layout. Different groups may be responsible for the detailed design of each representation. These must be shown to be equivalent.

**Design management must be provided in a distributed system of workstations and shared repositories of design data.**

Since much of design is evolutionary or exploratory, the database must support design versions and alternatives. *Versions* are improvements or corrections to a design object, while *alternatives* are different implementations of the same object with varying performance characteristics. Versions, providing insights into design approaches and rationale, are needed for documenting designs in the field as well as for legal reasons. Alternatives, especially within design libraries, enable designers to experiment with different implementations of the same function.

VLSI circuits are normally designed by teams. To help team members work harmoniously, design teams use check-out mechanisms, interface descriptions, and validation audit trails. Check-out mechanisms ensure that, at most, one designer is modifying an object at a time. The design data are made self-documenting by placing interface descriptions, dependency information, and design responsibility in the database. This helps a designer understand *how* an object is used, *where* it is used, and *who* is responsible for its design. The design validation subsystem helps to keep the design consistent, identifying the portions of the design affected by changes and maintaining an audit trail so responsibility can be assigned for incomplete or faulty validation.

Design management must be provided in a distributed system of workstations and database servers (shared repositories of design data). Designs are checked out to designers at workstations. Making the data resilient to system crashes is complicated by the lack of archival media at the workstations. Valuable design work can be lost unless efforts are made to frequently and automatically save changes on the servers. Allowing modified data to be checked back into the repository only when it has passed a lengthy validation process keeps the design database consistent.

A frequent error is the incomplete propagation of a change to all parts of the design that depend on it, a serious problem in design environments without integrated design management. An integrated design database must incorporate information about the dependencies across representations and design partitions.

## Why commercial databases are *not* like design databases

Database facilities have evolved to support both high-performance transaction processing and interactive use by nonprogrammers.[14,15] These include (1) structures for efficient access to data on secondary storage; (2) the concept of a transaction, collections of read and update operations treated as atomic units of database consistency; (3) protection and concurrency control mechanisms for controlled data-sharing; (4) automatic integrity maintenance; (5) crash recovery services; and (6) user-friendly interfaces (graphic or natural language) and high-level query languages.

Not all these services are valuable for design systems. For example, the database system can enforce only very simple integrity constraints automatically. Constraints on design data, however, are not easy to specify or enforce. Compare the constraint "salary must be greater than zero" with "the circuit must behave as specified with expected performance." Because of the large overhead for entering and leaving the system, a conventional database is best used as a shared, reliable repository. Large aggregates of design data are extracted and replaced as a unit. Data-sharing is controlled by not allowing more than one designer to update the same portion of the design at the same time. Recoverable update and archival mechanisms ensure that data are never lost because of a system crash.

Access to a conventional database is through transactions[16]—sequences of read and write actions that leave the database consistent. Interleaved transaction executions are permitted as long as the result is the same as some serial execution of the transactions. Transactions are atomic: all changes become visible at once (the transaction commits) or none become visible (the transaction aborts). They are durable: once a transaction has committed, its changes are permanently installed in the database.

Developed for the short-duration, simple units of work typically found in such transaction-processing environments as airlines reservations do not adequately model design interactions. A *design transaction* begins when a designer acquires exclusive access to a portion of the design, modifies it over a long period of time, and commits the changes only when they have been shown to be valid.[17,18]

Many database implementation issues are simplified in the design environment. Because of design teams and their strict partitioning of tasks, designer interference is rare. While many techniques have been proposed for controlling concurrent access, simple techniques are sufficient for resolving most conflicts in design applications. For example, negotiation usually resolves a conflict among designers needing the same data.

Design transactions are not atomic. In recovering from crashes, database systems undo the effects of incomplete transactions and redo the effects of completed transactions. If the duration of a transaction is from the time an object is checked out from the repository to when it is replaced, the system should never roll back the uncommitted design changes, since hours (or days) of work would be lost. The database should be restored to the most recent state possible, even past the last state "saved" by the designer.

While the effects of committed database transactions survive system crashes, design data live beyond subsequent transactions. Design transactions create new versions of the objects they update. However, conventional database systems provide no support for versions, even though this support greatly simplifies the implementation of concurrency control and recovery mechanisms.

Database systems for commercial applications, tuned for large volumes of regularly structured data, do not adequately handle the basic storage needs of design data. Design data are organized into complex structures with large numbers of interconnected files of relatively small size, although some design files are quite large. Therefore, design data are not easily formatted for storage in a conventional database.[19]

Obviously, there is a mismatch of what design tools need and what database systems provide. The rest of this article describes the structure of a system that can satisfy the data management needs of design tools.

## A system for design data management

Design systems provide a number of services necessary for designing integrated circuits. At the heart of such systems are design tools. However, many services are duplicated from tool to tool. If these services can be identified and implemented as stand-alone subsystems, future tools could be built much more easily. For example, menu and window packages are now available as stand-alone subsystems. What we are attempting to do is to implement such a system for design data management.

**System overview.** The system architecture (discussed in detail in the subsequent section on system structure) appears in Figure 2. The *storage component* stores design data on disk and guarantees that updates are atomic. A conventional database system can be used as a storage component,[19,20] although a suitably extended file system could be used instead.

The *object system* maps the design data, viewed as a collection of interrelated objects, into the files and structures supported by the storage component. A reliable object-oriented file system[21] can provide the facilities of both the storage component and the object system.

The *recovery subsystem* collects incremental changes made to objects, ensuring that they can be reconstructed after a crash.

The *design librarian* controls shared access to design objects. Although many designers can browse an object, only one at a time is allowed to create a new version of it.

The *design validation subsystem* interprets dependencies among design data to identify those portions that may be affected by a change.

Encompassing the design librarian, recovery, and design validation subsystems, the *design transaction* component ensures that designers create new consistent versions of design data with their tools. Design *transactions* bring data to the workstation, returning it as new versions. Design *tools* manipulate the data through operations supported by the object system at workstations.

The *browser/chip assembler* is the interactive interface to the design data management system.

**Data structures for specifying a design.** An object model defines the basic primitives from which the design data structure is formed. Methods of structuring a design for database storage have been described elsewhere.[18,20,22] Each method has an object rather than a record orientation, explicit representations of versions and alternatives, and support for subsystem interface descriptions. The motivation for our scheme is to make the design as self-describing as possible, enhancing the system's ability to keep it consistent.

*Objects.* Convenient aggregations of design information are called *design objects. Representation objects* describe a portion of the design in one of its representations, and they are of a particular type, such as layout, transistor, or logic. Furthermore, representation objects organize most of the information about the design. *Index objects* introduce auxiliary structures used by the browsing, configuration, and validation tools.

Each representation object is constructed from the composition of its primitives—such as geometries, transistors, and gates—and other objects of the same type. We call this hierarchical collection of design data a *representation hierarchy.* A *design hierarchy* is the data collection describing a full design, with additional structures linking together the representations and providing alternative groupings based on versions (configurations), alternative implementations, or common attributes. Representation objects have *interface descriptions* specifying their abstract behavior, usage information, and associated performance (speed, power, area). Design objects are not overwritten by design transactions. Instead, new object versions are created.

Indices group objects outside the normal decompositions within representations. The browser uses them to quickly find objects with particular attributes. For example, all ALU objects within a library may be grouped together by an index object. Indices can be composed in much the same way as representation objects. For example, the ALU index can be incorporated within an index of data-path pieces. Unlike representation objects, index objects do not have interfaces or versions.

The hierarchies are represented as directed acyclic graphs. Leaves are primitive objects, while internal vertices are composite objects. Although individual geometries or transistors could be primitive objects, they are more likely to be some simple function implemented with a small collection of these. A composite object is formed from the recursive composition of its graph descendants. Edges in the graph are directed from composite (parent) objects to component (child) objects.

**If design services can be identified and implemented as stand-alone systems, future tools could be built much more easily.**

The method for creating an instance of the component is associated with each edge. For some applications, such as simulation, the directed acyclic graph must be instantiated into a tree. Only information unique to an object's instance needs to be represented in the tree (see Figure 3).

While an object is defined by the composition of its components, each object can be updated independently. Whenever an object is updated, a new version is created. A new version of a composite object can be formed from new or existing versions of its components. Similarly, the components can evolve independent of the composites that reference them, since the composites refer to older versions (see Figure 4).

Representation hierarchies need not have identical decompositions. Beetem[23] and Mudge[24] have described more restricted approaches. The functional decomposition of a design may be quite different from its physical decompositions (see Figure 5). An *equivalency object* identifies equivalent objects across representations. For example, an ALU layout object and an ALU transistor object may be linked by an equivalency object to constrain them to be different representations of the same ALU, as enforced by the design validation component.

Defined by alternative and version objects, *generic* objects represent major subsystems undergoing frequent refinement. A *version* configures the subsystem by corelating versions of objects describing it in its different representations. Version objects are like equivalency ob-

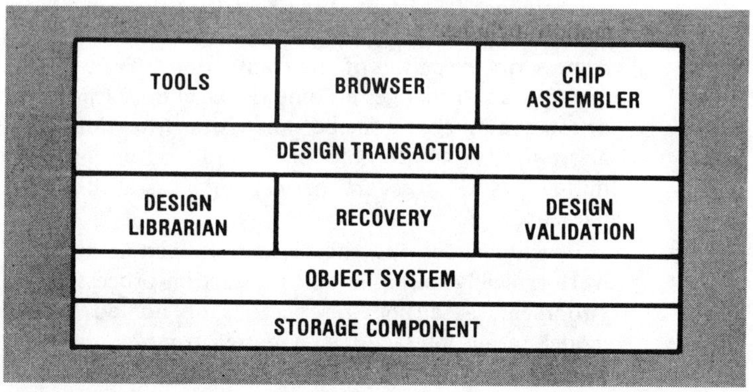

| TOOLS | BROWSER | CHIP ASSEMBLER |
|---|---|---|
| DESIGN TRANSACTION | | |
| DESIGN LIBRARIAN | RECOVERY | DESIGN VALIDATION |
| OBJECT SYSTEM | | |
| STORAGE COMPONENT | | |

Figure 2. System architecture.

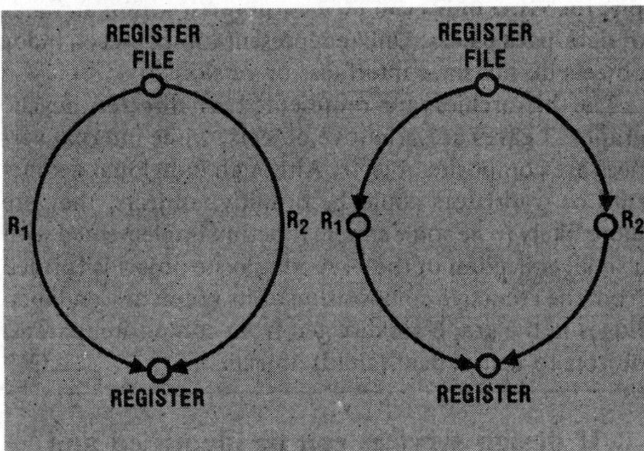


**Figure 3. Instantiated objects.**

jects since they group objects constrained to be equivalent. An *alternative* object is an index that groups version objects, representing different versions of the alternative. Finally, a generic object (see Figure 6) groups its alternatives together. Although each alternative has the same behavior as its parent, it has its own performance characteristics. For example, the generic object "the ALU" is composed of the alternative objects "fast ALU," "small ALU," and "low-power ALU." The "fast ALU" alternative consists of various version objects, such as "fast ALU/version 0.0" and "fast ALU/version 1.0." In turn, "fast ALU/version 1.0" consists of the representation objects describing it, such as "fast ALU/version 1.0/layout," "fast ALU/version 1.0/transistors," and "fast ALU/version 1.0/gates."

Generic objects are nested on a representation-by-representation basis (see Figure 7). An *implementation* is a version of a generic object's alternative. Nesting an ALU within a data path proceeds as follows. An ALU implementation is chosen for inclusion within a data-path implementation. Each of its representation objects that are grouped together—such as the layout, transistor, and gate objects—incorporates the object of corresponding type in the ALU's implementation.

*Interfaces.* Representation objects have interface descriptions. An interface contains enough information that an object can be used without a detailed understanding of its implementation. It documents the object and makes connectivity information explicit. Interface information includes:

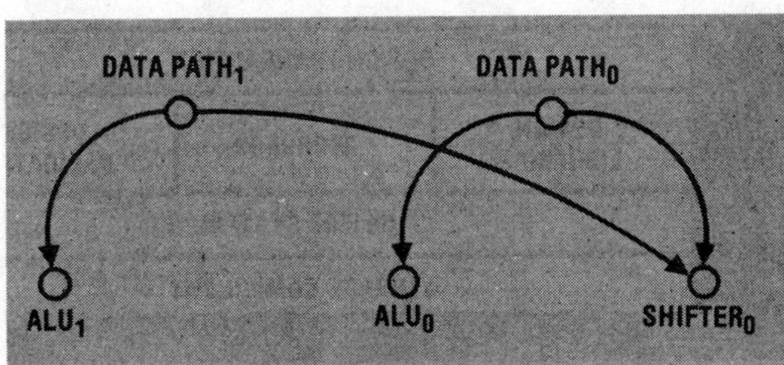


**Figure 4. A new data-path object with a new ALU.**

- *Name.* The name and version of the object are indicated.
- *Designer.* The designer responsible for the object's implementation is identified.
- *Description.* The object's behavior is detailed in, for example, an English-language description or a truth table describing outputs in terms of input combinations. Although this description is used primarily for documentation, it could eventually be used by validation tools.
- *Graphic representation.* An object is contained within a bounding polygon, specifying the "outline" of the object for viewing on a graphics terminal. Bounding polygons can be associated with any representation type.
- *Connectivity information.* Ports are I/O connection points. They are named, have types and directions, and are placed on the periphery of the bounding polygon. Ports with the same name must be connected by some signal path within the object. Ports are input, output, or bidirectional. The port type is representation-dependent. For example, for the layout representation, type information includes the interconnection layer and the logic level strength expected or supplied by the port.
- *Performance information.* The interface specifies constraints on power, area, and delay.

Port typing simplifies checking that compositions are well-formed. For Newkirk and his colleagues,[25] the four input types are 4:1 ratio (expects regenerated logic

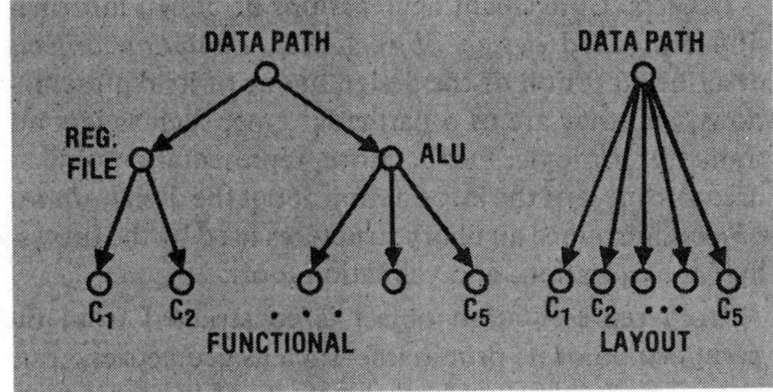


**Figure 5. Nonisomorphic representations.**

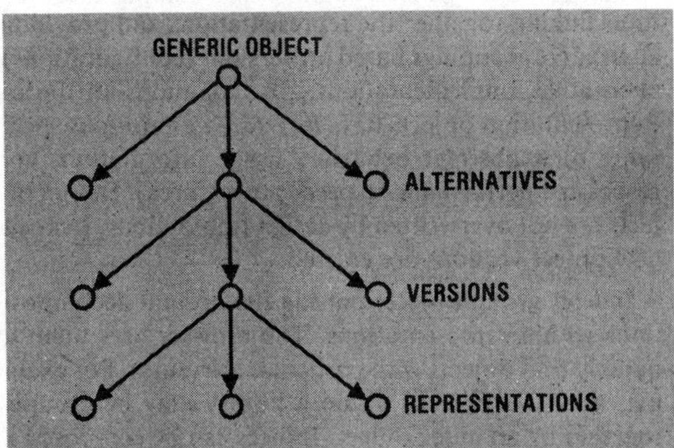


**Figure 6. Generic object data structure.**

levels), 8:1 ratio (does not expect regenerated levels), switch control (expects regenerated levels), and switched (does not expect regenerated levels). The four output types are gate (produces regenerated levels), superbuffer (produces regenerated levels), switch logic (produces unregenerated levels), and precharged (special). The compatibilities among the types are determined from a table, such as Table 1.

Port names are either local or global. Every port with the same global name is implicitly connected. Vdd and GND are typical global port names.

An interface description constrains the object's implementation. Checking that power and area are within constraints is straightforward. Associated with the layout representation, area can be determined from the bounding box of its geometries. The power constraint is also associated with the layout representation. The dc power consumption of a module can be determined by examining the width-to-length ratios of transistors. Much more difficult to specify, delay timing generally can be checked only through simulations.

There are several ways to describe an object's behavior. Truth tables are well-suited for combinatorial logic, and transition tables are appropriate for sequential logic. Many language-based functional simulators associate a program with an object to "simulate" its behavior. An approach suitable for functional/timing simulations describes behavior by input waveforms and expected output waveforms. The description portion of the interface must be general enough to support any of these approaches.

An object's implementations must agree with its interface. Types and directionality of ports as well as implied connectivity between ports must be verified. An "interface extractor" program could assist verification. Implementations do not need to be checked if these have been derived from their interfaces ("correctness by construction"), such as a PLA layout from Boolean equations.

*Composition and interface.* The general composition of objects can be viewed graphically. Placed within the composite's bounding polygon are the polygons of its components, composed by wiring together the component ports to form the ports of the composite object (see Figure 8).

Composition information is associated with both composites and components. Each component stores the names of objects that contain it. A composite object stores the names of its components. It gives unique names to component instances, describes how each is oriented and placed within its bounding polygon (for display purposes), and describes how the ports are wired.

*Objects as structured files.* Objects can be implemented as files extended with information describing the design data structure. The information relevant to the design management system is the object type, the interface specification, and the composition information (see Figure 9). The design tools—not the design data management system—determine representation details. We expect that new tools will be created that combine the creation of the interface, composition, and representation specifications. Existing design files can be referenced from within design object files to include their data in design data structure.

*System structure.* Designs are created at workstations connected by a high-speed network to a shared database server. Designers at the workstations transfer the relevant portions of the design to their local disks through the design transaction mechanism. Work proceeds independently at the stations with incremental changes spooled to the server, providing backup in case of a workstation crash. Changes are incorporated into the public database only after they have been shown to be valid.

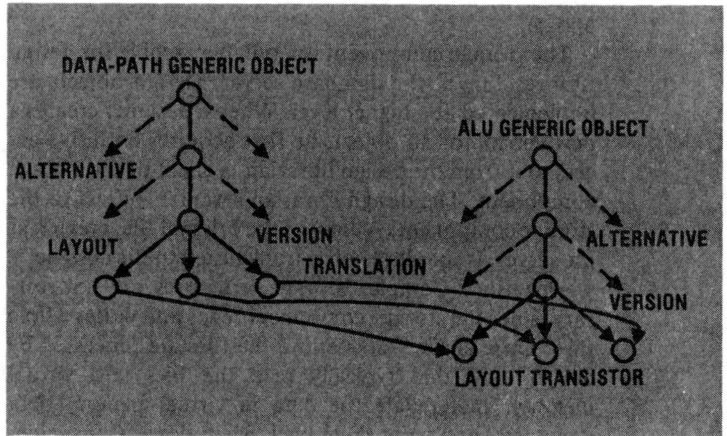


**Figure 7. Incorporating generic objects.**

**Table 1.**
**Compatibility of I/O types.**

| INPUTS | Gate | Superbuffer | Switch Logic | Precharged |
|---|---|---|---|---|
| | OUTPUTS | | | |
| 4:1 | OK | OK | NO | OK |
| 8:1 | OK | OK | OK | OK |
| Switch control | OK | OK | NO | OK |
| Switched | OK | OK | * | NO |

*OK, but charge-sharing problems are possible.

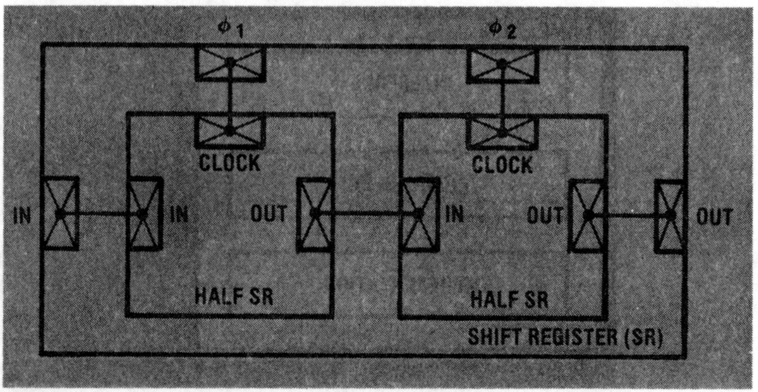


**Figure 8. Graphical compositions.**

The distributed database is actually more complicated than what we have outlined. Some validation can be performed at the workstation, but much is done on special-purpose hardware or high-performance machines. The database server must keep track of the location of design data at all times. In the discussion that follows, we concentrate on the interaction between the database server and workstations, but the ideas also apply to the general environment.

*Storage component.* The storage component manages design data on secondary storage. Although a conventional database system can serve as a storage component,[18,20] a transaction-based file system[18] also provides the required facilities. We are implementing our system on top of the Unix file system, which must be extended to provide atomic update.

The storage component is a reliable archive for design files residing at the database server. Design objects are implemented at a higher level. When a designer creates a new version of an object, he first acquires exclusive access to it from the design librarian, a client of the storage component. The design librarian serializes access to the storage component. A copy of the original file, created at the server, is simultaneously transmitted to the designer's workstation. Complex storage structures are unnecessary, since the storage component reads and writes whole files. Once at the workstation, the files are processed by design tools that typically read the files into virtual memory, manipulate the data in virtual-memory data structures, and write them back when done. Convenient mechanisms for mapping complex data structures on disk into virtual memory are still open research topics.[18,20]

The recovery subsystem supports save actions. Changes made to the files at the workstations are kept in special logs. At a save point, the logs are transmitted back to the storage component to be merged into the server's copy of the file. The merge operation is atomic, ensuring that files are never left with partially merged changes.

The merge is implemented as a conventional database transaction, if such transactions are supported by the storage component. Otherwise, the merge is made atomic by creating a temporary copy, merging the changes, renaming the temporary file, and removing the original.

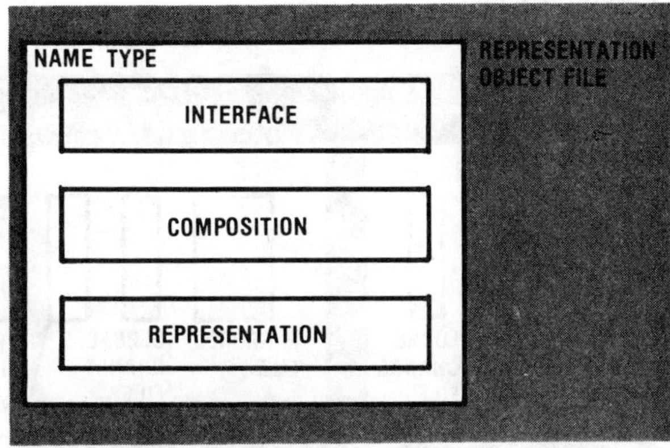


**Figure 9. Design objects as files.**

The merge can be restarted if a crash occurs. While the merge may appear time-consuming, it can be overlapped with continued activity at the workstation. Individual design files are relatively small, so the time to do a merge need not be excessive.

*Object system.* Design objects are files containing representational primitives and design management information, including the object's type, the objects that contain this object, the object's components and how they are composed, and the object's interface.

The object system maps the abstract notion of an "object" into the data describing it that are stored in storage component files. Design objects can be stored either as a single file, with combined representation and design management information, or as separate files. For representation types not known to the system, data are stored in a separate file referenced within the design object file. The object system can pass this "raw" representation data to existing design tools, thus acting as a conventional file system. The system uses the design management information for validation and browsing while traversing the complex structure of the design.

*Recovery subsystem.* The recovery manager ensures that as much data as possible survive a system crash. It accomplishes this by maintaining multiple copies with alternative failure modes: (1) the local working file, storing the object at the workstation; (2) the local change file, stored at the workstation and holding a log of changes since the last save point; (3) the mirrored file, storing the object in the database server; (4) the global change file, holding changes spooled to the server but not yet saved; and (5) the redo log, containing all saved changes since the last archive (see Figure 10). The local and global change files, containing the differences between the local file and its mirrored copy, protect data from being lost during workstation crashes. The redo log, containing the difference between the mirrored file and the original file, protects against losses during database server failure.

The recovery manager supports save points. Data and change file buffers are forced to disk by the workstation's buffer manager. The local change file is copied to the database server and atomically appended to the global change file. A background process copies the local change file entries to the global file, providing continuous recovery capability that guards against local crashes and reduces the latency of a save. To commit the changes, the storage component atomically merges the global change file into the mirrored file and appends the global change file to the redo log.

Recovery from a soft workstation crash proceeds as follows. The last save point is reconstructed by copying the database server copy back to the workstation. A more up-to-date version is optionally reconstructed by merging the local and global change files into the local file. Some updates will be lost because they were only in the local buffers, but updates written to disk since the last save can be restored.

A hard workstation crash loses data on the workstation's disk, and we assume that all local files are lost.

Copying the mirrored file back to the workstation restores the file to its last saved state. Alternatively, copying back the merged mirrored and global change files also restores the file to the last state known. The recovery subsystem determines what objects should be restored by asking the design librarian.

The database server employs more coventional techniques to ensure that its files are durable. The system is resilient to soft crashes because of the atomic operations supported by the storage component. Frequent archival dumps provide resiliency to hard crashes. The mirrored files can be restored to their last save point from the archive copy and the redo log. However, the recovery subsystem guarantees only that objects can be restored to their last save point, although every effort is made to restore beyond it. Spooled changes not yet saved are lost, since they are not normally logged. If the server loses the accumulated changes, it can always acquire the most up-to-date version of the file from the workstation. The global redo file should be duplexed to provide additional resiliency to hard crashes.

*Design librarian.* The librarian coordinates all access to shared design data, making design objects available to workstations. A designer acquires only one object at a time. The browser is used to navigate the hierarchies to find the object of interest. Checking out an object for update gives the designer the exclusive right to create its new version. The mirrored copies of design files, supported by the recovery subsystem on top of the storage component, become the new object versions when the changes are committed.

Several designers could simultaneously create new versions, but such a proliferation of versions is undesirable for effective project management. The design librarian employs check-out locks to guarantee that only one in-progress version exists for an object.

In the rare instance of one designer holding an object that another designer needs, the designer who has it is permitted to complete its revision, creating a new consistent version of the object. Afterwards, the requesting designer can acquire it, creating his new version based on any of its previous versions. That is, he is not restricted to creating a new version of the most up-to-date version, although this situation will be the most common.

Versions provide a flexible method for managing concurrent access to design objects. Previous versions can be browsed without regard to in-progress update activity. Simple locking protocols protect against the proliferation of versions. This is one example of how the design environment requires much simpler mechanisms than those needed in the general transaction-processing environment.

*Validation subsystem.* The validation subsystem helps designers keep track of what must be revalidated after a design change. Since validating the fully instantiated design is prohibitively expensive, the design's structure must be exploited to keep the validation effort reasonable.

A design is self-consistent if conformance, composition, and equivalence constraints are in force: (1) an object's implementation satisfies its interface (conformance constraints), (2) the composition of component objects is well-formed (composition constraints), and (3) objects specified as equivalent across representations are shown to be equivalent (equivalence constraints). Design transactions cannot complete until all constraints are satisfied.

We do not advocate a completely automatic approach for design validation. Frequently, designers will need to intervene to apply the appropriate validation tools and to interpret their results. The validation subsystem provides an audit capability, as in Noon, Robbins, and Roberts.[26] Designers report who they are, what constraints they have validated, and what tools have been used for the validation. If a design failure is traced to a particular design object, the designer responsible for its "validation" can at least be identified.

**A design is self-consistent if conformance, composition, and equivalence constraints are in force.**

Interface extraction is an obvious area for further tools development. Some parts of the interface—such as the location, type, and drive capability of ports—are easy to extract. However, performance aspects such as detailed delay information can be determined only through simulations performed by the design team, who then reports the results to the subsystem.

A composite object is well-formed if the interconnected ports of its components are type- and direction-compatible. That is, component ports connected to the composite object's ports must be type-compatible and must have the same direction.

Some objects are generated from other representations. For example, PLA layouts are generated from Boolean equations in the functional description. Equivalence in this case can be checked by analyzing the validation audit trail. If (1) the last update time of the PLA layout object is the same as when the generator was run, and not later, and (2) the last update time of the PLA functional object is before that time, the objects are known to be equivalent. Such equivalency constraints can be actively enforced by regenerating dependent objects on request.

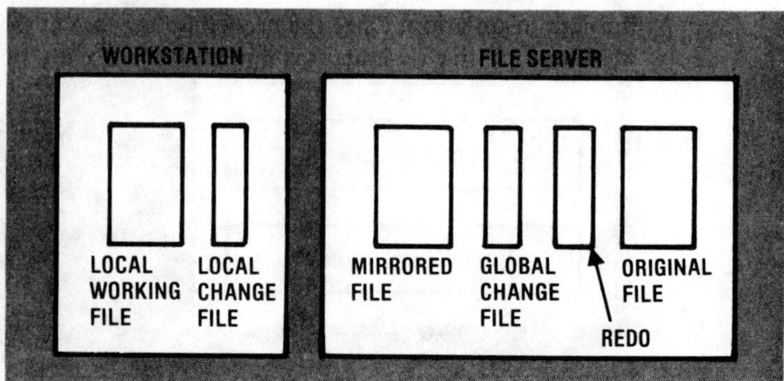


**Figure 10. Files associated with a checked-out object.**

Equivalency constraints reduce the effort needed to validate equivalence across representations. Suppose we must show equivalence between the layouts and transistor representations of a design. Normally, equivalence is checked by first extracting the layout into a transistor description, and then providing the same stimulus to simulations of both the extracted transistor description and the original transistor description. Ideally, only the changed portions of the layout description and parts of the design that depend on them should be extracted and simulated. If two objects in the different representations are already equivalent because they are connected by an equivalency object, the transistor object can be substituted for its counterpart in the extracted transistor description without further analysis. A multilevel simulator can simulate the object at this level without fully instantiating it.

**Design transactions are the mechanisms by which designers create new consistent versions of design objects.**

A design transaction cannot complete unless all newly created objects satisfy the three constraints discussed above. However, objects unaffected by changes do not have to be revalidated.

*Design transaction management.* Design transactions are the mechanisms by which designers create new consistent versions of design objects. Design transactions have *work, validation,* and *completion* phases. While work and validation phases can be intermixed, validation must be complete before a design transaction is allowed to enter the completion phase.

During the work phase, a designer requests design objects from the design librarian. If the object has not been granted to another designer, the request is honored and the appropriate files are transferred to the workstation's disk. Additional mirrored copies are made in the database server, providing redundant copies to be used for recovery.

If the object has been granted to another designer, the designer holding the object and the expected time of its return are identified. While deadlock is rare, it is nonetheless possible. Since designers can always determine who has what objects, a deadlock is resolved through negotiation. Once the needed objects are at the workstation, the designer manipulates them with his design tools.

Save points protect transactions from the loss of data due to local crashes. Since the changes are continuously being spooled to the server by a background process, most changes can be restored. Workstation activity can continue even though the connection to the server is broken (which fortunately is rare!), but it is not advisable, since it exposes the designer to a serious loss of data if a local crash occurs.

When design work is completed, the transaction enters a validation phase. Designers invoke verification programs to check that the modified design data are self-consistent. If validation fails, the inconsistencies must be located and corrected. The transaction reenters the work phase, and validation is attempted again. Checking is usually distributed throughout the lifetime of the transaction, so it need not occur only at the termination of design activity. The validation subsystem ensures that all relevant constraints have been enforced before a transaction is permitted to enter completion.

During the completion phase, the mirrored copies of design objects add their new versions. If part of an independent object, the new version is added to those objects pointed to by its appropriate alternative object. If a designer decides to abort this transaction, the global and local copies are destroyed and the original objects are made available again for check-out.

To see how a designer creates a new design, consider the following example (see Figure 11). A designer wishes to create a new version of a microprocessor with a revised register file design. He invokes a design transaction, acquires the register file object from the design librarian, and revises it, creating a new version. To create the new microprocessor, he must first create a new data-path object incorporating the new register file. He acquires the data-path object, and recomposes it from its original components and the new register file. Then, he acquires the microprocessor object and repeats the process. Next, the new microprocessor design, with revised data-path and register file, is validated. The design transaction can now complete successfully, with the new objects becoming permanent parts of the design database.

*Browser/chip assembler.* The browser and chip assembler are the interactive interfaces to the design management system.[24,27,28] The browser allows a designer to navigate through the complex design structures, making extensive use of graphics to present the data structure and menus to direct the navigation.

Interface descriptions provide on-line design documentation. Browsing through an object's versions provides insight into how the object has evolved over time. Alternatives within design libraries can be scanned to find a particular implementation suitable for use in a new design. A design can be browsed within a representation, across representations, at any level of composite object, or at the fully instantiated level of primitive objects. Several ways of browsing the design can be underway

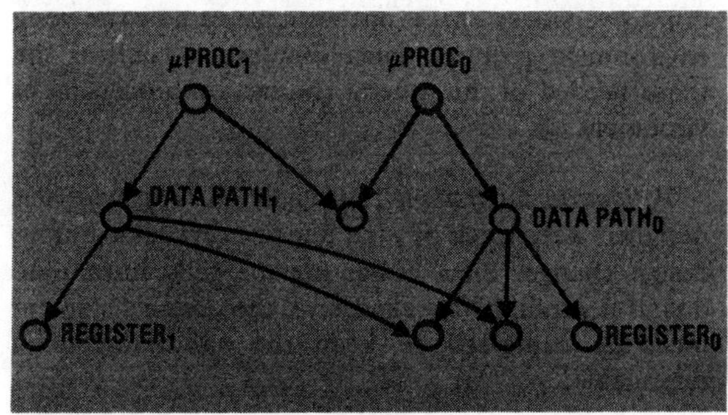


**Figure 11. Creating a new design.**

simultaneously, since each is presented within its own window.

The browser assists the designer in locating objects with particular attributes. Index objects group together those objects with similar attributes. For example, the ALU index object is composed of all generic ALU objects stored in the design database. Furthermore, the ALU index object can be included, for example, in a data-path index object, creating a hierarchy of indices.

The chip assembler takes data created by synthesis tools, such as graphic editors and data-path generators, and packages those data as objects for inclusion within the design database. In conjunction with the browser, the chip assembler provides an interactive front end for constructing the design data structure. It supports the interactive (1) composition of objects from more primitive objects, (2) specification of object interfaces, (3) identification of equivalences across representations, (4) construction of design configurations through version and alternative objects, and (5) creation and manipulation of index objects.

Chip assembly is the most data-intensive portion of the chip design task. Subsystems are constructed from component compositions. The interface information is examined to ensure that the compositions are well-formed. Interfaces also aid in understanding how pieces of the design interact and fit together, which is crucial for large design projects. Furthermore, since the assembly process creates a new configuration of the design, it must reflect an intimate concern for version control. Consequently, only the desired versions of design objects—selected by the designer with the aid of the browser—are used to build the chip. Invalid or out-of-date versions can be ignored.

Design data management is a crucial feature of an integrated design system. The design data must be reliably stored on disk, concurrent access must be controlled, versions and alternatives must be organized, and efforts must be made to keep the data well-formed and consistent within and across representation hierarchies. Existing design tools tackle design synthesis and validation problems, but the important design data management issues are frequently ignored. A design data management system provides these services to the ensemble of design tools, creating an environment in which tools are integrated to form a coherent design system.

We are in the process of implementing a system with many of the design management features described in this article. Since we could find no suitable database system for our storage component, we initially created our own data management system tailored for design applications (the Wisconsin Storage System). We have decided to redesign the storage and object components for use with the Unix file system, enhancing the transportability of our design management system. Efforts are underway to implement the object model, design librarian, browser, and chip assembler described in this article. ■

## Acknowledgments

This research was supported by NSF grant MCS-8201860. Work reported was done at the Computer Sciences Department, University of Wisconsin-Madison, Madison, WI 53706.

A number of students have been actively involved in the design and implementation of the design data management system. Ron Lunde and Shlomo Weiss helped define the object model. They are also working on the browser and chip assembler subsystem, collectively called Chipanzee. S. Bikkina, Greg Fischer, and Brian Rodgers implemented the reliable storage component on top of Unix and are currently working on the design librarian component. We call this portion of the system the Engineering Database Management System, or EDBMS.

## References

1. C. Mead and L. Conway, *Introduction to VLSI Systems,* Addison-Wesley, Reading, Mass., 1980.
2. J. K. Ousterhout, "Caesar: An Interactive Editor for VLSI Layout," *VLSI Design,* Fourth Quarter 1981.
3. J. M. Suskind et al., "Generating Custom High Performance VLSI Designs from Succinct Algorithmic Descriptions," in *Proc. Conf. Advanced Research in VLSI,* Paul Penfield, Jr., ed., Artech House, Dedham, Mass., 1982.
4. C. M. Baker and C. Terman, "Tools for Verifying Integrated Circuit Designs," *Lambda,* fourth quarter 1980, pp. 22-30.
5. N. P. Jouppi, "TV: An *n*MOS Timing Analyzer," *Proc. Third Cal Tech Conf. VLSI,* Computer Science Press, Rockville, Md, 1983.
6. J. K. Ousterhout, "Crystal: A Timing Analyzer for *n*MOS VLSI Circuits," *Proc. Third Cal Tech Conf. VLSI,* Computer Science Press, Rockville, Md., 1983.
7. R. H. Katz et al., "'Big Caesar and Little Caesar': Adventures in Modifying and Extending CAD Software," *VLSI Design,* Jan./Feb. 1983.
8. C. Eastman, "Database Facilities for Engineering Design," *Proc. IEEE,* Vol. 69, No. 10, Oct. 1981.
9. P. Losleben, "Data Structures, Data Base, and File Maintenance," in *Digital System Design Automation; Languages, Simulation & Data Base,* M. A. Breuer, ed., Computer Science Press, Woodland Hills, Calif., 1975.
10. P. Losleben, "Computer-Aided Design for VLSI," in *Very Large Scale Integration VLSI,* D. F. Barbe, ed., Springer Series in Electrophysics, Vol. 5, Springer-Verlag, Berlin, 1980.
11. K. Thompson, "UNIX Implementation," *Bell System Technical J.,* Vol. 57, No. 6, part 2, July/Aug. 1978.
12. A. R. Newton, "Computer-Aided Design of VLSI Circuits," *Proc. IEEE,* Vol. 69, No. 10, Oct. 1981.
13. C. H. Sequin, "Managing VLSI Complexity: An Outlook" *Proc. IEEE,* Vol. 71, No. 1, Jan. 1983.
14. C. J. Date, *An Introduction to Database Systems,* 3rd ed., Addison-Wesley, Reading, Mass., 1981.

15. C. J. Date, *An Introduction to Database Systems,* Vol. II, Addison-Wesley, Reading, Mass., 1982.

16. J. Gray, "The Transaction Concept: Virtues and Limitations," *Proc. Seventh Int'l Conf. Very Large Databases,* ACM, Washington, DC, 1981.

17. R. H. Katz and S. Weiss, "Design Transaction Management," to be submitted to 21st ACM/IEEE Design Automation Conference, Albuquerque, N.M., June 1984.

18. R. A. Lorie and W. Plouffe, "Complex Objects and Their Use in Design Transactions," *Proc. ACM Sigmod Conf. Databases for Engineering Design,* 1983.

19. R. L. Haskin and R. A. Lorie, "On Extending the Functions of a Relational Database System," *Proc. ACM Sigmod Conf.,* 1982.

20. R. H. Katz, "A Database Approach for Managing VLSI Design Data," *Proc. 19th ACM/IEEE Design Automation Conf.,* 1982.

21. D. Reed, "Implementing Atomic Actions on Decentralized Data," *ACM Trans. Computer Systems,* Vol. 1, No. 1, Feb. 1983.

22. D. McLeod et al., "An Approach to Information Management for CAD/VLSI Applications," *ACM Sigmod Conf. Databases for Engineering Design,* 1983.

23. J. F. Beetem, "Structured Design of Electronic Systems using Isomorphic Multiple Representations," PhD dissertation, Stanford University, Dec. 1981.

24. J. C. Mudge, "VLSI Chip Design at the Crossroads," in *VLSI 81: Very Large Scale Integration,* J. P. Gray, ed., Academic Press, London, 1981.

25. J. Newkirk et al., *"Standard nMOS Cell Library,"* tech. report TR 001, Stanford Informations Systems Laboratory, July 1981.

26. W. A. Noon, K. N. Robbins, and M. T. Roberts, "A Design System Approach to Data Integrity," *Proc. 19th ACM/IEEE Design Automation Conf.,* 1981.

27. R. H. Katz and S. Weiss, "Chip Assemblers: Concepts and Capabilities," *Proc. 20th ACM/IEEE Design Automation Conf.,* 1983.

28. J. C. Mudge, C. Peters, and G. M. Tarolli, "A VLSI Chip Assembler," in *Design Methodologies for Very Large Scale Integrated Circuits,* NATO Advanced Summer Institute, Belgium, 1980.

**Randy H. Katz** joined the faculty of the Electrical Engineering and Computer Science Department at the University of California, Berkeley, in 1983. Previously, he was a faculty member of the Computer Sciences Department at the University of Wisconsin-Madison. Current research interests include VLSI processor design, VLSI design tools, and applications of database technology to problems in CAD data management.

Katz is a member of the IEEE Computer Society, the ACM, the American Association for the Advancement of Science, the New York Academy of Sciences, Sigma Xi, and Phi Beta Kappa. He received an AB from Cornell University in 1976, and an MA and PhD in computer science from the University of California, Berkeley, in 1978 and 1980.

Katz's address is Computer Science Division, Electrical Engineering and Computer Science Department, University of California, Berkeley, CA 94720.

# A Taxonomy of Time in Databases

March, 1985

*Richard Snodgrass*†
*Ilsoo Ahn*

Department of Computer Science
University of North Carolina
Chapel Hill, NC 27514

## *Abstract*

***The need for supporting time varying information in databases has been recognized for quite some time. Many authors have proposed numerous schemes to satisfy this need by incorporating one or two time attributes in the database. Unfortunately, there has been confusion concerning the terminology and definition of these time attributes. This paper proposes a new taxonomy of three times for use in databases, one that is more cleanly defined, that may be conceptualized in a pictorial fashion, and that defines several kinds of databases differentiated by their ability to represent temporal information. The paper argues that future database management systems should support all three times to fully capture time varying behavior.***

## 1. Introduction

The need for recording time varying information in databases has been recognized for quite some time [Bubenko 1976]. There have been significant research activities in formulating a semantics of time at the conceptual level [Anderson 1982, Breutmann et al. 1979, Bubenko 1977, Hammer & McLeod 1981, Klopprogge 1981], developing a model for time varying databases analogous to the relational model for static databases [Clifford & Warren 1983, Codd 1979, Sernadas 1980], and the design of temporal query languages [Ariav & Morgan 1981, Ben-Zvi 1982, Jones & Mason 1980, Snodgrass 1982]. Recently, it has been argued that a single time attribute is insufficient, and that two time attributes are necessary to fully capture time-varying information. Unfortunately, there has been some confusion concerning terminology and the definition of these time attributes.

The next section will discuss the various characteristics attributed to the two times; the third section will illustrate the difficulties posed by the vague definition of these times. The fourth section will present a new taxonomy of time in databases to replace the two previous times. The new taxonomy consists of three distinct time concepts and four distinct kinds of database management systems (DBMS), differing in their support of the new time concepts. The final section will compare the new taxonomy with the old one.

## 2. Previous Characterizations

In this paper, we will use the terms *physical time* and *logical time* [Lum et al. 1984] to discuss the concepts as they appear in the literature. Physical time has also been called transaction time [Copeland & Maier 1984], registration time [Ben-Zvi 1982], data-valid-time-from/to [Mueller & Steinbauer 1983], and start/end time [Reed 1978]. Logical time has also been called event time [Copeland & Maier 1984], effective time [Ben-Zvi 1982], state [Clifford & Warren 1983], valid time [Snodgrass 1984], and start/end time [Jones et al.

† The work of this author was supported by NSF grant DCR-8402339 and by an IBM Faculty Development Award.

1979, Jones & Mason 1980]. Each paper has defined the terms in slightly different ways. There is general agreement on the definitions, but little consensus concerning the details. The differences identified by previous authors between physical and logical time may be characterized in terms of three related attributes. The purpose of this section is to discuss these attributes and to examine their contributions to the concepts of logical and physical time. We will proceed by stating the view presented in the literature, then follow in the next section with an analysis of this view. This summary is drawn primarily from the works of Copeland and Maier [Copeland & Maier 1984], Dadam et al. [Dadam et al. 1984], and Lum et al. [Lum et al. 1984], although others have also noticed that a single time stamp or a pair of time stamps is inadequate.

### 2.1. Reality versus Representation

The correspondence of the model stored in the database with reality is one aspect that is used to distinguish between logical and physical time. Logical time is characterized as the time that an event occurs in reality; physical time is characterized as the time when the data concerning the event was stored in the database. Examples include retroactive salary changes, release dates of engineering versions, scheduled events that have not yet occurred, and scheduled events that were suppose to occur, yet did not.

### 2.2. Update Flexibility

The types of update permitted to time values is another way that logical and physical time have been differentiated in the literature. A physical time value may be added to the database, yet once it has been added, it may not be changed. The concept of a non-stop running clock is evoked to indicate how the time values are generated. Logical time values, on the other hand, are always subject to change, since discrepancies between the history (a sequence of events or time intervals) as it actually occurred and the representation of the history as stored in the database will often be detected after the fact. The distinction then is between permitting only appends and permitting arbitrary modifications.

### 2.3. Application Dependency

The third attribute used to distinguish between physical and logical time is that of application dependency. Logical time is generally characterized in the literature as being application-dependent, while physical time is considered to be application-independent. While this attribute is the hardest to define precisely, it is usually equated with the control the user of the DBMS has over the value of a temporal domain in the database. If the value can be computed automatically by the DBMS, the value must necessarily be independent of any particular application and must have a simple semantics. An application-dependent time value, on the other hand, must have been defined explicitly by the user. Its value must also be specified by the user, and may thus be quite complex. The integrity of this data must be maintained by the user; the value must be modifiable by users when a discrepancy is discovered between the real world and the database model. Hence, the DBMS cannot guarantee the integrity of logical time values. The relationship between the types of time identified in the literature and their attributes is shown in Figure 1.

## 3. Comparison

Two of the attributes differentiating physical and logical time, those of reality versus representation and update flexibility, are reasonably precise concepts. They are also strongly related to each other, in that a time value that records when the data was stored cannot later be changed. The third attribute, that of application dependence, is unfortunately fraught with difficulties. It makes certain assumptions of which the most crucial is that all actions performed by the DBMS are application-independent. This assumption is not valid, at least to a certain degree. The database schema, which directs most actions by the DBMS, is certainly application-dependent. Many DBMS's allow the specification of integrity constraints, which are application-dependent, yet are interpreted automatically by the DBMS without user intervention. Application-dependent values can be handled by the DBMS if their semantics can be defined in terms the DBMS can interpret.

An example often cited of the distinction between application-independent and application-dependent time is a retroactive salary raise, where the time at which the raise was recorded (say, 12/1/83) is considered application-independent, as it is not under the user's control, whereas the time at which the raise was to take effect (say, 8/1/83) is considered application-dependent, as it is in some sense arbitrary and under the user's control.

Examining this situation more closely, however, can result in precisely the reverse semantics. In many commercial settings, salary updates are batched together and executed against the database only once or twice a month, whereas payments might be made at the last possible date to minimize cashflow problems, and hence may occur at arbitrary times during the month. That a salary update was performed by the DBMS on 12/1/83 may simply be an artifact of when salary updates are entered, which is application dependent. On the other hand, the user has no control over when the salary was changed, and hence the effective date is in this sense application-independent.

The point to be made is that characterizing a time value as being dependent or independent of an application involves fairly subtle issues of the semantics of that value, both as interpreted within the DBMS and as applied to the situation being modeled. Given these difficulties, this attribute appears to be less than ideal in differentiating physical and logical time.

| Reference | Terminology | Append -Only | Application Independent | Representation vs. Reality |
|---|---|---|---|---|
| [Ariav & Morgan 1982] | Time | Yes | Yes | Representation |
| [Ben-Zvi 1982] | Registration | Yes | Yes | Representation |
| | Effective | No | Yes | Reality |
| [Clifford & Warren 1983] | State | No | Yes | |
| [Copeland & Maier 1984] | Transaction | Yes | Yes | Representation |
| | Event (1) | No | No | Reality |
| [Dadam et al. 1984] & | Physical | (2) | Yes | Representation |
| [Lum et al. 1984] | Logical (1) | No | No | Reality |
| [Jones et al. 1979] & | Start/End | (2) | Yes | Reality |
| [Jones & Mason 1980] | User Defined | No | No | Reality |
| [Mueller & Steinbauer 1983] | Data-Valid-Time-From/To | (3) | Yes | Representation (4) |
| [Reed 1978] | Start/End | Yes | Yes | Representation |
| [Snodgrass 1984] | Valid Time | No | Yes | Reality |

Notes:

(1) Not actually supported by the system
(2) Can make corrections only
(3) Can make changes only in the future
(4) Reality is indicated only in the future

**Figure 1** : Types of Time

## 4. A New Characterization

The previous section argued that physical and logical time are not well defined, and that application time is particularly problematic. In this section we introduce a new taxonomy of time for use in databases. This taxonomy is more clearly defined, being based on reality versus representation, may be conceptualized in a pictorial fashion which aids understanding, and defines several kinds of databases differentiated by their ability to represent temporal information. Though the following discussion is based on the relational model, similar arguments also apply to hierarchical or network models. We will first discuss static databases, focusing on their representational inadequacies. We then define three new time concepts to replace the vaguely defined physical and logical time. We introduce each time concept by discussing the features associated with a particular kind of DBMS supporting that time concept.

### 4.1. Static Databases

Conventional databases model the real world, as it changes dynamically, by a snapshot at a particular point in time. A *state* or an *instance* of a database is its current contents, which does not necessarily reflect the current status of the real world.

Updating the state of a database is performed using data manipulation operations such as insertion, deletion or replacement, taking effect as soon as it is committed. In this process, past states of the database, and those of the real world, are discarded and forgotten completely. We term this type of database a *static database*.

In the relational model, a database is a collection of *relations*. Each relation consists of a set of *tuples* with the same set of *attributes*, and is usually represented as a 2-dimensional table (see Figure 2). As changes occur in the real world, changes are made in this table.

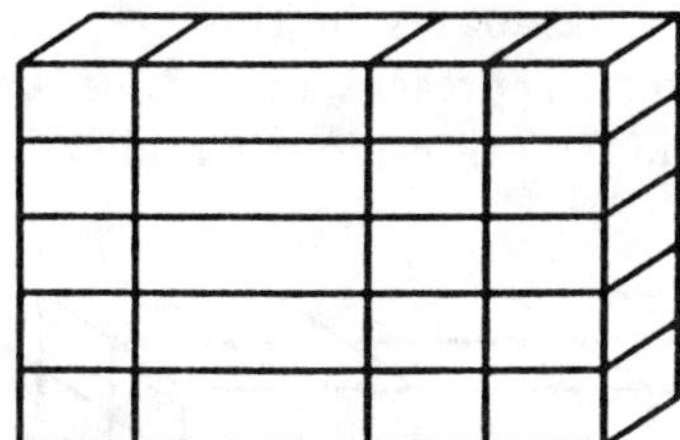

**Figure 2** : A Static Relation

For example, an instance of a relation 'faculty' at a certain moment may be

| name | rank |
|---|---|
| Merrie<br>Tom | full<br>associate |

and a query in Quel, a tuple calculus based language for the INGRES database management system [Held et al. 1975], requesting Merrie's rank,

**range of** f **is** faculty
**retrieve** (f.rank)
**where** f.name = "Merrie"

yields

| rank |
|---|
| full |

There are many situations where this static database relying on snapshots is inadequate. For example, it cannot answer queries such as

What was Merrie's rank 2 years ago? (historical query)
How did the number of faculty change over the last 5 years? (trend analysis)

nor record facts like

Merrie was promoted to a full professor starting last month. (retroactive change)
James is joining the faculty next month. (postactive change)

Without system support in this respect, many applications have had to maintain and handle temporal information in an ad-hoc manner.

### 4.2. Static Rollback Databases

One approach to resolve the above deficiencies is to store all past states, indexed by time, of the static database as it evolves. Such an approach requires a representation of *transaction time*, the time the information was stored in the database. A relation under this approach can be illustrated conceptually in three dimensions (Figure 3) with transaction time serving as the third axis. The relation can be regarded as a sequence of static relations indexed by time. By moving along the time axis and taking a vertical slice of the cube, it is possible to get a snapshot of the relation as of some time in the past (a static relation) and make queries upon it. The operation of taking a vertical slice is termed *rollback*, and a database supporting it is termed a *static rollback database*. Changes to a static rollback database may only be made to the most recent static state. The relation illustrated in Figure 3 had three transactions applied to it, starting from the null relation: (1) the addition of three tuples, (2) the addition of a tuple, and (3) the deletion of one tuple (entered in the first transaction) and the addition of another tuple. Each transaction results in a new static relation being appended to the front of the cube; once a transaction has completed, the static relations in the static rollback relation may not be altered.

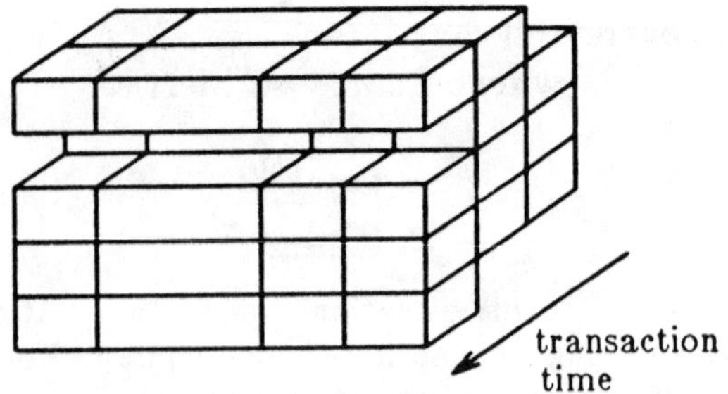


**Figure 3** : A Static Rollback Relation

One limitation of supporting transaction time is that the history of database activities, rather than the history of the real world, is recorded. A tuple becomes valid as soon as it is entered into the database as in a static database. There is no way to record retroactive/postactive changes, nor to correct errors in past tuples. Errors can sometimes be overridden (if they are in the current state) but they cannot be forgotten.

Implementing a static rollback relation in this way is impractical, due to excessive duplication: the tuples that don't change between states must be duplicated in the new state. Another approach that partially addresses this difficulty appends the start and end points of the transaction time to each tuple, indicating the points in time when the tuple was in the database. A typical relation in this approach looks like Figure 4. The double vertical bars separate the non-temporal domains from the DBMS-maintained temporal domains. The latter domains do not appear in the schema for the relation, but may rather be considered part of the overheads associated with each tuple. Note the fact that Merrie was previously an associate professor, a fact which could not be expressed in the example for a static database.

| name | rank | transaction time (start) | transaction time (end) |
|---|---|---|---|
| Merrie | associate | 08/25/77 | 12/15/82 |
| Merrie | full | 12/15/82 | ∞ |
| Tom | associate | 12/07/82 | ∞ |
| Mike | assistant | 01/10/83 | 02/25/84 |

**Figure 4** : A Static Rollback Relation

Any query language may be converted to one which may query a static rollback database by adding a clause effecting the rollback. TQuel (*Tem*poral *QUE*ry *L*anguage) [Snodgrass 1984, Snodgrass 1985], an extension of Quel for temporal databases, augments the retrieve statement with an *as of* clause to specify the relevant transaction time. The TQuel query

```
range of f is faculty
retrieve (f.rank)
        where f.name = "Merrie"
        as of "12/10/82"
```

on a 'faculty' relation shown in Figure 4 will find the rank of Merrie as of 12/10/82:

| rank |
|---|
| associate |

Note that the result of a query on a static rollback database is a pure static relation.

The concept of transaction time has appeared in several systems, including *GemStone* [Copeland & Maier 1984], *MDM/DB* (Model Data Management/Database) [Ariav & Morgan 1982], and the *SWALLOW* object store [Reed 1978, Svobodova 1981].

### 4.3. Historical Databases

While static rollback databases record a sequence of static states, *historical databases* record a single *historical state* per relation, storing the history as it is best known. As errors are discovered, they are corrected by modifying the database. Previous states are *not* retained, so it is not possible to view the database as it was in the past. There is no record kept of the errors that have been corrected. Historical databases are similar to static databases in this respect. Historical databases must represent *valid time*, the time that the stored information models reality.

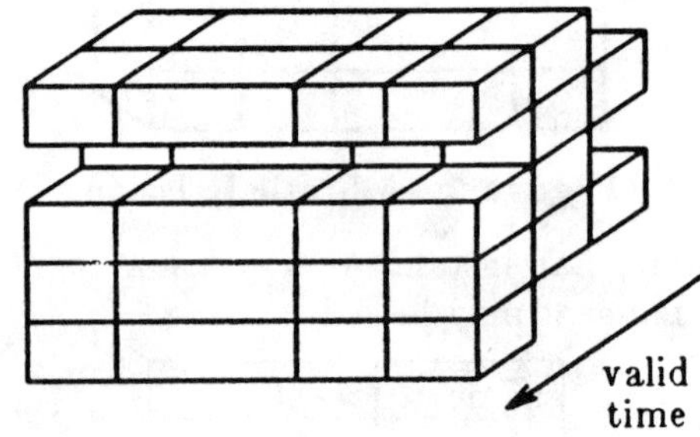


**Figure 5:** An Historical Relation

Historical databases may also be illustrated in three dimensions (see Figure 5). Though its illustration looks similar to one for the static rollback database (in fact, for many transaction sequences, it will be identical), the label of the time axis has been changed to valid time and the semantics are more closely related to reality, instead of update history. Therefore more sophisticated operations are necessary to manipulate the complex semantics of valid time adequately, compared to the simple rollback operation.

A second distinction between historical and static rollback databases is that historical DBMS's support arbitrary modification, whereas static rollback DBMS's only allow static states to be appended. The same sequence of transactions which resulted in the static rollback relation in Figure 3 also results in the historical relation in Figure 5. However, a later transaction (not possible on a static rollback relation) has removed an erroneous tuple inserted on the first transaction (compare Figures 3 and 5 closely). Static rollback DBMS's can rollback to an incorrect previous static relation; historical DBMS's can record the current knowledge about the past.

Historical databases also incorporate user-defined time, which will be discussed in the context of temporal databases. Both valid time and user-defined time concern modeling of reality, and so it is appropriate that they should appear together.

Historical databases require more sophisticated query languages. There have been two such languages developed: LEGOL 2.0 [Jones et al. 1979], based on the relational algebra, and TQuel [Snodgrass 1984], based on Quel [Held et al. 1975], a relational calculus query language. *LEGOL 2.0* [Jones & Mason 1980] was developed for writing complex rules such as those in legislation or high level system specification where the correct handling of time is important. It also attaches to each tuple two time attributes which delimit the period of existence for the associated member of the entity set.

TQuel supports the expression of historical queries by augmenting the *retrieve* statement with a *valid* clause to specify how the implicit time domain is computed, and a *when* predicate to specify the temporal relationship of tuples participating in a derivation. These added constructs handle complex temporal relationships such as *start of, precede,* and *overlap.*

As with static rollback databases, implementing a historical relation directly as above is impractical. Figure 6 illustrates an alternative: appending the endpoints of the valid time to each tuple, indicating the points in time when the tuple accurately modeled reality. Like the transaction time in static rollback databases, the valid time is not included in the relation schema.

| name | rank | valid time (from) | (to) |
|---|---|---|---|
| Merrie | associate | 09/01/77 | 12/01/82 |
| Merrie | full | 12/01/82 | ∞ |
| Tom | associate | 12/05/82 | ∞ |
| Mike | assistant | 01/01/83 | 03/01/84 |

**Figure 6** : A Historical Relation

The TQuel query requesting Merrie's rank when Tom arrived,

> **range of** f1 **is** faculty
> **range of** f2 **is** faculty
>
> **retrieve** (f1.rank)
> **where** f1.name = "Merrie"
> **and** f2.name = "Tom"
> **when** f1 **overlap start of** f2

on the historical relation 'faculty' in Figure 6 yields

| rank | valid time (from) | (to) |
|---|---|---|
| full | 12/01/82 | ∞ |

Note that the derived relation is also an historical relation, which may be used in further historical queries. While both this query and the example given for a static rollback relation seem to query Merrie's rank on 12/05/82, the answers are different. The reason is that Merrie was promoted on 12/01/82, but this information was recorded in the database two weeks later. Hence, the database was inconsistent with reality for that period of time. In the historical database, the error was corrected, but it is not possible to determine that, at least for a while, the database was inconsistent.

Historical databases have been the subject of several research efforts, including *CSL* (Conceptual Schema Language) [Breutmann et al. 1979], *TERM* (Time-extended Entity Relationship Model) [Klopprogge 1981], the intensional logic $IL_s$ [Clifford & Warren 1983], and *AMPPL-II* (Associative Memory Parallel Language II) [Findler & Chen 1971].

### 4.4. Temporal Databases

Benefits of both approaches can be combined by supporting both transaction time and valid time. While a static rollback database views tuples valid at some time as of that time, and a historical database always views tuples valid at some moment as of *now,* a temporal DBMS makes it possible to view tuples valid at some moment seen as of some other moment, completely capturing the history of retroactive/postactive changes.

We use the term ***temporal database*** to emphasize the need for both valid time and transaction time in handling temporal information. Since there are two time axes involved now, it should be illustrated in four dimensions (Figure 7 shows a *single* temporal relation). A temporal relation may be thought of as a sequence of historical states, each of which is a complete historical relation. The rollback operation on a temporal relation selects a particular historical state, on which an historical query may be performed. Each transaction causes a new historical state to be created; hence, temporal relations are append-only. The temporal relation in Figure 7 is the result of four transactions, starting from a null relation: (1) three tuples were added, (2) one tuple was added, (3) one tuple was added and an existing one deleted, and (4) a previous tuple was deleted (presumably it should not have been there in the first place).

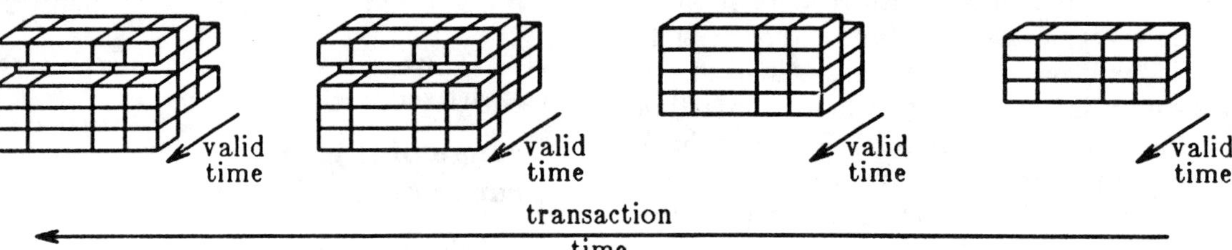


**Figure 7** : A Temporal Relation

| name | rank | valid time (from) | valid time (to) | transaction time (start) | transaction time (end) |
|---|---|---|---|---|---|
| Merrie | associate | 09/01/77 | ∞ | 08/25/77 | 12/15/82 |
| Merrie | associate | 09/01/77 | 12/01/82 | 12/15/82 | ∞ |
| Merrie | full | 12/01/82 | ∞ | 12/15/82 | ∞ |
| Tom | full | 12/05/82 | ∞ | 12/01/82 | 12/07/82 |
| Tom | associate | 12/05/82 | ∞ | 12/07/82 | ∞ |
| Mike | assistant | 01/01/83 | ∞ | 01/10/83 | 02/25/84 |
| Mike | assistant | 01/01/83 | 03/01/84 | 02/25/84 | ∞ |

**Figure 8** : A Temporal Relation

For example, the relation in Figure 6 will look like Figure 8 after adding transaction time. It shows that Merrie started working on 09/01/77, information that was entered into the database on 08/25/77 as a postactive data. Then she was promoted on 12/01/82, but the fact was recorded on 12/15/82 retroactively. Tom was entered into the database on 12/01/82 as joining the faculty as a full professor on 12/05/82; the fact that he was actually an associate professor was noted on 12/07/82. Mike left the faculty effective on 03/01/84, which was recorded on 02/25/84. Note all the details of history captured here, which were not expressible in other more restrictive databases. The TQuel query

> **range of** f1 **is** faculty
> **range of** f2 **is** faculty
>
> **retrieve** (f1.rank)
>     **where** f1.name = "Merrie"
>     **and** f2.name = "Tom"
>     **when** f1 **overlap start of** f2
>     **as of** "12/10/82"

on this relation determines Merrie's rank when Tom arrived, according to the state of the database as of 12/10/82. The result is

| rank | valid time (from) | (to) | transaction time (start) | (end) |
|---|---|---|---|---|
| associate | 09/01/77 | ∞ | 08/25/77 | 12/15/82 |

This derived relation is a temporal relation, so further temporal relations can be derived from it. If a similar query is made as of 12/20/82, the answer would be *full* because the fact was recorded retroactively by that time.

*TRM* (Time Relational Model) is another example of a temporal database [Ben-Zvi 1982]. However, the query language defined for TRM is not a temporal query language, because it can derive only static relations.

### 4.5. User-defined time

*User-defined time* [Jones & Mason 1980] is necessary when additional temporal information, not handled by transaction or valid time, is stored in the database. As an example, consider the 'promotion' relation shown in Figure 9. Since it is an event relation, only one valid time is necessary. The effective date is the date shown on the promotion letter that the promotion was to take effect; the valid date is the date the promotion letter was signed, i.e., the date the promotion was validated; and the transaction date is the date the information concerning the promotion was stored in the database. Merrie's retroactive promotion to full was signed four days before it was recorded in the database. The effective date is application-specific; it is merely a date which appears on the promotion letter. The values of user-defined temporal domains are not interpreted by the DBMS, and are thus the easiest to support; all that is needed is an internal representation and input and output functions. Such domains will then be present in the relation schema. Conventional DBMS's supporting application time include the ENFORM DBMS [Tandem 1983], Query-by-Example [Bontempo 1983], an experimental version of INGRES [Overmyer & Stonebraker 1982], and MicroINGRES [Relational 1984].

| name | rank | effective date | valid time (at) | transaction time (start) | (end) |
|---|---|---|---|---|---|
| Merrie | associate | 09/01/77 | 08/25/77 | 08/25/77 | ∞ |
| Merrie | full | 12/01/82 | 12/11/82 | 12/15/82 | ∞ |
| Tom | full | 12/05/82 | 12/05/82 | 12/01/82 | 12/07/82 |
| Tom | associate | 12/05/82 | 12/07/82 | 12/07/82 | ∞ |
| Mike | assistant | 01/01/83 | 01/01/83 | 01/10/83 | ∞ |
| Mike | left | 03/01/84 | 02/25/84 | 02/25/84 | ∞ |

**Figure 9** : A Temporal Event Relation

## 5. Conclusions

Three kinds of time, transaction time, valid time, and user-defined time, were introduced to replace the vague formulation of physical and logical time found in the literature. Database management systems may be categorized in terms of their support for handling temporal information. As shown in Figure 10, two orthogonal criteria are capabilities for rollback and historical queries. These criteria differentiate four types of databases: static, static rollback, historical and temporal. Support of the rollback capability requires the incorporation of transaction time, which concerns the representation; support of historical queries requires the incorporation of valid time, which is associated with reality (see Figure 11). DBMS's supporting rollback are append-only, whereas those not supporting rollback allow updates of arbitrary information. The attributes associated with the three kinds of time are illustrated in Figure 12, which should be compared to Figure 1.

The new time concepts may be loosely compared with those appearing previously in the literature. Transaction time is most closely associated with physical time, and valid and user-defined time with logical time. However, as we have shown in an earlier section, logical and physical time have not been precisely defined, whereas the new terms have been carefully defined by examining the aspects they model and the limitations they impose on the DBMS. Figure 13 classifies the time supported in existing or proposed systems according to the new taxanomy.

While fifteen years of research has focused on formalizing and implementing static databases, only a few researchers have recently studied the formalization of historical databases (e.g., [Clifford & Warren 1983]) and the implementation of static rollback databases (e.g., [Lum et al. 1984]). To the authors' knowledge, there has been nothing published on formalizing static rollback or temporal databases, nor implementing historical or temporal databases. The special opportunities promised by temporal databases are, at this time, matched by the challenges in supporting them.

| | No Rollback | Rollback |
|---|---|---|
| Static Queries | Static | Static Rollback |
| Historical Queries | Historical | Temporal |

**Figure 10** : Types of Databases

| | Transaction | Valid | User-defined |
|---|---|---|---|
| Static | | | |
| Static Rollback | √ | | |
| Historical | | √ | √ |
| Temporal | √ | √ | √ |

**Figure 11** : Attributes of the New Kinds of Databases

| Terminology | Append-Only | Application Independent | Representation vs. Reality |
|---|---|---|---|
| Transaction | Yes | Yes | Representation |
| Valid | No | Yes | Reality |
| User-defined | No | No | Reality |

**Figure 12** : Attributes of the New Kinds of Time

| Reference | System or Language | Transaction Time | Valid Time | User-defined Time |
|---|---|---|---|---|
| [Ariav & Morgan 1982] | MDM/DB | √ | | |
| [Ben-Zvi 1982] | TRM | √ | √ | |
| [Bontempo 1983] | QBE | | | √ |
| [Breutmann et al. 1979] | CSL | | √ | |
| [Clifford & Warren 1983] | $IL_s$ | | √ | |
| [Copeland & Maier 1984] | GemStone | √ | | |
| [Findler & Chen 1971] | AMPPL-II | | √ | |
| [Jones & Mason 1980] | LEGOL 2.0 | | √ | √ |
| [Klopprogge 1981] | TERM | | √ | |
| [Lum et al. 1984] | AIM | √ | | |
| [Relational 1984] | MicroINGRES | | | √ |
| [Mueller & Steinbauer 1983] | — | √ | | |
| [Overmyer & Stonebraker 1982] | INGRES | | | √ |
| [Reed 1978] | SWALLOW | √ | | |
| [Snodgrass 1985] | TQuel | √ | √ | √ |
| [Tandem 1983] | ENFORM | | | √ |
| [Wiederhold et al. 1975] | TODS | | √ | |

**Figure 13** : Time Support in Existing or Proposed Systems

## Bibliography


[Anderson 1982] Anderson, T. L. *Modeling Time at the Conceptual Level.* In *Improving Database Usability and Responsiveness,* Ed. P. Scheuermann. Jerusalem, Israel: Academic Press, 1982 pp. 273-297.

[Ariav & Morgan 1981] Ariav, G. and H. L. Morgan. *MDM: Handling the time dimension in generalized DBMS.* Technical Report. The Wharton School, University of Pennsylvania. May 1981.

[Ariav & Morgan 1982] Ariav, G. and H. L. Morgan. *MDM: Embedding the Time Dimension in Information Systems.* Technical Report 82-03-01. Department of Decision Sciences, The Wharton School, University of Pennsylvania. 1982.

[Ben-Zvi 1982] Ben-Zvi, J. *The Time Relational Model.* PhD. Diss. UCLA, 1982.

[Bontempo 1983] Bontempo, C. J. *Feature Analysis of Query-By-Example,* in Relational Database Systems. New York: Springer-Verlag, 1983. pp. 409-433.

[Breutmann et al. 1979] Breutmann, B., E. F. Falkenberg and R. Mauer. *CSL: A language of defining conceptual schemas,* in Data Base Architecture. Amsterdam: North Holland, Inc., 1979.

[Bubenko 1976] Bubenko, J. A., Jr. *The temporal dimension in information modeling.* Technical Report RC 6187 #26479. IBM Thomal J. Watson Research Center. Nov. 1976.

[Bubenko 1977] Bubenko, J. A., Jr. *The Temporal Dimension in Information Modeling,* in Architecture and Models in Data Base Management Systems. North-Holland Pub. Co., 1977.

[Clifford & Warren 1983] Clifford, J. and D. S. Warren. *Formal Semantics for Time in Databases. ACM Transactions on Database Systems,* 8, No. 2, June 1983, pp. 214-254.

[Codd 1979] Codd, E.F. *Extending the Database Relational Model to Capture More Meaning. ACM Transactions on Database Systems,* 4, No. 4, Dec. 1979, pp. 397-434.

[Copeland & Maier 1984] Copeland, G. and D. Maier. *Making Smalltalk a Database System.* In *Proceedings of the Sigmod '84 Conference,* June 1984 pp. 316-325.

[Dadam et al. 1984] Dadem, P., V. Lum and H.-D. Werner. *Integration of Time Versions into a Relational Database System.* In *Proceedings of the Conference on Very Large Data Bases,* 1984.

[Findler & Chen 1971] Findler, N. and D. Chen. *On the problems of time retrieval, temporal relations, causality, and coexistence.* In *Proceedings of the International Joint Conference on Artificial Intelligence,* Imperial College: Sep. 1971.

[Hammer & McLeod 1981] Hammer, M. and D. McLeod. *Database Description with SDM: A Semantic Database Model. ACM Transactions on Database Systems,* 6, No. 3, Sep. 1981, pp. 351-386.

[Held et al. 1975] Held, G.D., M. Stonebraker and E. Wong. *INGRES--A relational data base management system. Proceedings of the 1975 National Computer Conference,* 44 (1975) pp. 409-416.

[Jones et al. 1979] Jones, S., P. Mason and R. Stamper. *LEGOL 2.0: a relational specification language for complex rules. Information Systems,* 4, No. 4, Nov. 1979, pp. 293-305.

[Jones & Mason 1980] Jones, S. and P. J. Mason. *Handling the Time Dimension in a Data Base.* In *Proceedings of the International Conference on Data Bases,* Ed. S. M. Deen and P. Hammersley. British Computer Society. University of Aberdeen: Heyden, July 1980 pp. 65-83.

[Klopprogge 1981] Klopprogge, M. R. *TERM: An approach to include the time dimension in the entity-relationship model.* In *Proceedings of the Second International Conference on the Entity Relationship Approach,* Oct. 1981.

[Lum et al. 1984] Lum, V., P. Dadam, R. Erbe, J. Guenauer, P. Pistor, G. Walch, H. Werner and J. Woodfill. *Designing DBMS Support for the Temporal Dimension.* In *Proceedings of the Sigmod '84 Conference,* June 1984 pp. 115-130.

[Mueller & Steinbauer 1983] Mueller, T. and D. Steinbauer. *Eine Sprachschnittstele zur Versionenkontrolle in CAM-Datanbanken,* in Informatik-Fachberichte. Berlin: Springer, 1983. pp. 76-95.

[Overmyer & Stonebraker 1982] Overmyer, R. and M. Stonebraker. *Implementation of a Time Expert in a Database System. SIGMod Record,* 12, No. 3, Apr. 1982, pp. 51-59.

[Reed 1978] Reed, D. *Naming and Synchronization in a Decentralized Computer System.* PhD. Diss. M.I.T., Sep. 1978.

[Relational 1984] Relational Technologies, Inc. *MicroINGRES Reference Manual.* 1984.

[Sernadas 1980] Sernadas, A. *Temporal Aspects of Logical Procedure Definition. Information Systems,* 5 (1980) pp. 167-187.

[Snodgrass 1982] Snodgrass, R. *Monitoring Distributed Systems: A Relational Approach.* PhD. Diss. Computer Science Department, Carnegie-Mellon University, Dec. 1982.

[Snodgrass 1984] Snodgrass, R. *The Temporal Query Language TQuel.* In *Proceedings of the Third ACM SIGAct-SIGMOD Symposium on Principles of Database Systems,* Waterloo, Ontario, Canada: Apr. 1984 pp. 204-212.

[Snodgrass 1985] Snodgrass, R. *A Temporal Query Language.* 1985. (Submitted to *Transactions on Database Systems.*)

[Svobodova 1981] Svobodova, L. *A reliable object-oriented data depository for a distributed computer.* In *Proceedings of 8th Symposium on Operating Systems Principles,* Dec. 1981 pp. 47-58.

[Tandem 1983] Tandem Computers, Inc. *ENFORM Reference Manual.* Cupertino, CA, 1983.

[Wiederhold et al. 1975] Wiederhold, G., J. F. Fries and S. Weyl. *Structured organization of clinical data bases.* In *Proceedings of the National Computer Conference,* AFIPS. 1975.

# Highly Available Systems for Database Applications

WON KIM

*IBM Research Laboratory, San Jose, California 95193*

As users entrust more and more of their applications to computer systems, the need for systems that are continuously operational (24 hours per day) has become even greater. This paper presents a survey and analysis of representative architectures and techniques that have been developed for constructing highly available systems for database applications. It then proposes a design of a distributed software subsystem that can serve as a unified framework for constructing database application systems that meet various requirements for high availability.

Categories and Subject Descriptors: A.1 **[General Literature]**: Introductory and Survey; C.1.2 **[Processor Architectures]**: Multiple Data Stream Architectures (Multiprocessors)—*interconnection architectures*; C.4 **[Computer Systems Organization]**: Performance of Systems—*reliability, availability, and serviceability*; H.2.4 **[Database Management]**: Systems—*distributed systems, transaction processing*

General Terms: Reliability

Additional Key Words and Phrases: Database concurrency control and recovery, relational database

## INTRODUCTION

In this paper we examine major hardware and software aspects of highly available systems. Its scope is limited to those systems designed for database applications. Database applications require multiple paths from the processor to the disks, which gives rise to some difficult issues of system architecture and engineering. Further, they involve the software issues of concurrency control, recovery from crashes, and transaction management.

In a typical business data processing environment, a user message from a terminal invokes an application program. The application program interacts with a transaction manager to initiate and terminate (commit or abort) a transaction. Once a transaction has been initiated, the application program repeatedly interacts with a database manager to retrieve and update records in the database.

A transaction is a collection of reads and writes against a database that is treated as a unit [Gray 1978]. If a transaction completes, its effect becomes permanently recorded in the database; otherwise, no trace of its effect remains in the database. To support the notion of a transaction, undo log of data before updates and redo log of data after updates are used to allow a transaction to be undone or redone after crashes. The Write Ahead Log protocol often is used to ensure that the log is flushed to the disk before the updated database records are written to the disk.

The most fundamental requirement in constructing a highly available system for database applications is that each major hardware and software component must at least be duplicated. At minimum, the sys-

Author's current address: Microelectronics and Computer Technology Corporation, 9430 Research Boulevard, Austin, Texas 78759.



Computing Surveys, Vol. 16, No. 1, March 1984

CONTENTS



tem requires two processors. There may have to be two paths connecting the processors, and it is desirable to have at least two paths from the processors to the database, that is, two I/O subsystems consisting of a channel (I/O processor), controller, and disk drives. The disk controllers must be multiported, so that they may be connected to more than one processor.

On the software side, the system needs five essential ingredients: (1) a network communication subsystem, (2) a data communication subsystem, (3) a database manager (or a file system), (4) a transaction manager, and (5) the operating system.

The network communication subsystem must support interprocess(or) communication within a cluster of locally distributed processors. If the highly available system is a node on a geographically distributed system, the communication subsystem must also support internode communication.

The data communication subsystem is the terminal handler that receives user requests, invokes application programs, and delivers the results that it receives from the database/transaction manager.

The database manager must support the two fundamental capabilities of concurrency control and recovery. That is, it must guarantee that the database remains consistent despite interleaved reads and writes to the database by multiple concurrent transactions. Techniques such as locking and time stamping have been developed and extensively studied for this purpose [Bernstein and Goodman 1981; Kohler 1981].

The transaction/database manager must ensure that the database consistency is not compromised by system failures or transaction failures caused by software errors or deadlocks. In particular, it must be able to recover from transaction failures and soft crashes, which corrupt only the contents of the main memory, as well as from hard crashes, which destroy the contents of the disks. For recovery from soft crashes, the undo and redo logs of transactions are used [Gray et al. 1981; Haerder and Reuter 1983]. To recover from hard crashes, systems rely on periodic dumping of the database into archival storage.

The operating system is needed not only to run the other software components, but also to detect most of the common, low-level software/hardware errors that occur. Most computer systems rely on program checks (interrupts) and machine checks to detect such errors. Program checks are used to detect exceptions and events that occur during execution of the program [IBM 1980]. Exceptions include the improper specification or use of instructions and data, for example, arithmetic overflow or underflow, and addressing or protection violation. Machine checks are used to report machine malfunctions, such as memory parity errors, I/O errors, and missing interrupts. The hardware provides information that assists the operating system in determining the location of the malfunction and extent of the damage caused by it.

Most systems have been designed to survive the failure of a single software/hardware component. If a system is to be truly continuously operational, however, it must guarantee availability during multiple concurrent failures of software/hardware components, during on-line changes of such components, and during on-line physical reconfiguration of the database itself. To support the full range of high-availability requirements, the operating system must be supplemented with a software subsystem that can manage all software and hardware components of a system. Such a software subsystem will receive failure reports from the system components and reconfiguration requests from the system operator. It will analyze the status of all the resources it manages, and compute the optimal configuration of the system both in response to multiple concurrent failures of components and requests for load balancing. Further, it will initiate and monitor system reconfiguration, effecting mid-course correction of a reconfiguration that does not succeed. Finally, it will diagnose a class of failures that other components fail to recognize.

The systems introduced in the following paragraphs are often considered highly available, and are used as examples of various architectures and stratagems throughout the remainder of this paper, particularly in Sections 3 through 6. A certain number of these systems do not, in my opinion, meet the criteria for classification as highly available; these are discussed in Section 2.

Tandem Computers has been successful for several years in marketing fault-tolerant computer systems, which shield the users from various types of failures of the software and hardware components. Other companies have entered this market, including August Systems, Auragen Systems, Computer Consoles, Stratus Computer, Synapse Computer, Syntrex, Sequoia, Tolerant Systems, and others [Electronic Business 1981; IEEE 1983]. Of these, Auragen, Computer Consoles, Stratus, and Synapse have focused on transaction processing; August Systems aims at industrial and commercial process control.

A number of other systems address the issue of reliability and availability: Syntrex is marketing a local network file server called GEMINI; the MARK III Cluster File System, developed by General Electric, provides time-sharing services for its telephone-switching network users; and the Distributive Computing Facility developed by Bank of America automates the teller functions for accounts.

In addition, the late 1970s SRI SIFT project for aircraft control evoked the August Systems' products; Bolt Beranek and Newman (BBN) developed the PLURIBUS system for use as a highly reliable communications processor on ARPANET; and during the 1960s AT&T developed No. 1 ESS and No. 2 ESS (Electronic Switching System) for telephone switching services.

System D, a distributed transaction-processing system, was created as a prototype at IBM Research in San Jose with availability and modular growth as its major objectives, and there are other research projects currently under way at IBM Research to investigate availability and performance issues under various software/hardware structures.

The remainder of this paper is organized as follows. In Section 1, a taxonomy of system structures that has been used to construct highly available systems is developed, and a discussion is provided of the advantages and disadvantages of four possible structures. An intuitive set of criteria for highly available systems is given in Section 2. Systems belonging to each of the four system structures are surveyed and critiqued, where possible, in Sections 3 through 6. The discussions in these sections focus on various philosophies of system structure and transaction processing. In Section 7 the functions and structure of a software subsystem that provides a framework for high availability are described.

In view of the fact that such issues as concurrency control, recovery, transaction model, and network communications have been extensively addressed elsewhere, these aspects of highly available systems will not be given detailed treatment. Further, it is generally recognized that such mundane sources as downed telephone lines, careless computer operators, lack of defensive coding, and the way in which the operating system reacts to failures that it detects can seriously limit the availability of a system. Although important, such aspects are not within the scope of this paper.

## 1. MACHINE AND STORAGE ORGANIZATION TAXONOMY

Two fundamental decisions in constructing a multiple-processor system are the choice of machine organization and physical storage organization. The discussion in this section of the advantages and disadvantages of typical machine and storage organizations significantly benefits from Traiger [1983]. Two conventional techniques for organizing multiple processors are loosely coupled and tightly coupled multiprocessor organizations. In tightly coupled systems, two or more processors share main memory and disks, typically through an interconnection switch, and execute one copy of the operating system residing in the shared main memory. A local cache memory is usually associated with each processor to enhance access speed. In loosely coupled systems, each processor has not only a local cache memory but also its own main memory, and may or may not share disks with other processors. Each processor executes its own copy of the operating system from its own main memory. There are various ways to loosely couple the processors, including shared bus structures, cross-point switches, point-to-point links such as channel-to-channel adapters, and globally shared memories, as in Cm* [Swan et al. 1977].

Tightly coupled multiprocessor systems, such as the Synapse N+1 System, and BBN's PLURIBUS, offer important potential advantages. First, they naturally present a single-system image, since multiple processors execute one copy of the operating system and a common job queue. Second, the processors do not need to communicate via interprocessor messages, with their inherent overhead. However, this performance advantage may be offset by certain problems imposed by this architecture. First, there is contention among processors for the use of shared memory and other shared resources. This must somehow be reduced, especially if the cost/performance of the system is to keep up with its expansion as extra processors are added. Second, potentially complex techniques must be supported to ensure that the contents of each processor's cache memory are up-to-date.

In addition to these performance concerns, there is a potential availability problem with tightly coupled multiprocessors. All processors run the same operating system from shared main memory, and thus, when the operating system is corrupted or the shared memory system fails, the entire system must be restarted. Therefore application systems designed to run on a tightly coupled multiprocessor system must be able to restart very quickly in order to guarantee high overall availability.

Just as there are two techniques for organizing multiple processors, there are two ways to organize disks, and thus the database. One is to assign a set of disks to one processor and allow access to it only through that processor; the other is to have all of the processors share all the disks. The two techniques of organizing multiple processors and the two techniques of organizing disks are combined to give rise to four distinct system structures. The tightly coupled multiprocessor organization and the shared database organization results in a system structure that is called a tightly coupled system with a shared database. The loosely coupled multiprocessor organization gives rise to three other system structures. When a database is split into $N$ partitions and each partition is stored in one set of disks assigned to one of $N$ processors, the resulting system structure is called a loosely coupled multiprocessor with a partitioned database. When each of $N$ processors can directly access the entire database, stored in one set of disks, the system structure is called a loosely coupled multiprocessor with a shared database. When an entire database is replicated in each set of disk volumes attached to each of $N$ processors, and each processor computes the same user request in parallel, the resulting structure is called a loosely coupled multiprocessor with redundant computation.

The Tandem NonStop System, the Auragen System 4000, the Stratus Continuous Processing System, IBM's System D prototype (and its sequel, the Highly Available Systems project), Bank of America's Distributive Computing Facility, and AT&T's Stored Program Controlled Network are loosely coupled multiprocessors with partitioned databases. In this architecture, a database manager residing in each processor owns and manages the partition of the database assigned to that processor. Any user request (transaction) that requires access to more than one database partition is satisfied by message communication among the database managers that own the necessary partitions. Communication overhead is the single most significant disadvantage of the loosely coupled system with a partitioned database. There are two aspects to this interprocess(or) communication overhead: One is the messages sending requests to servers and receiving results from servers; another aspect is the messages and processing involved in the distributed commit protocol that ensures that the database, which is distributed across processors, is left in a globally consistent state when the transaction completes or aborts.

Some variation of the two-phase commit protocol described by Gray is used in committing or aborting a distributed transaction [Gray 1978]. One of the participating transaction managers is designated as the commit coordinator. During phase 1, the commit coordinator sends a "prepare to commit" message to all other participants. The participants reply with "yes" or "no" messages to the coordinator and enter phase 2. If the coordinator receives "yes" votes from all participants, it sends a "commit" message to all participants. If any participant replied with a "no" vote, the coordinator sends an "abort" message to all the participants. During phase 1 all participants retain the right to unilaterally abort the transaction. However, once they enter phase 2, they no longer can unilaterally abort the transaction; they must obey the decision of the commit coordinator.

Loosely coupled multiprocessor systems with shared database architecture, such as GE's MARK III Cluster File System, Computer Consoles' Power System, and IBM's AMOEBA research project [Traiger 1983], offer a potentially enhanced availability over a tightly coupled multiprocessor system, since the operating system is not shared among the processors. One disadvantage, however, is the lack of a single-system image; that is, system operators and system programmers must contend with multiple copies of the operating system. One important advantage of this architecture over a loosely coupled multiprocessor system with a partitioned database is that it avoids the difficult problem of deciding which partition of the database should be stored in which processors' disks. Processors may be added to the system without having to repartition the database, and new disk drives may be added without having to worry about which processors should own them.

However, contention on the shared disks is a potential problem, with each processor moving the disk arms to random positions. Further, algorithms for coordinating the global locking and logging of database updates must be carefully designed. A global locking technique in which all database managers must acquire and release locks through a single global lock manager will cause excessive communication overhead and create a bottleneck for performance and availability.

Loosely coupled multiprocessor systems with redundant computation, such as Syntrex's GEMINI file server, and SRI's SIFT (as well as its offspring, the Basic Controller of August Systems, Inc.), achieve fault tolerance by having more than one task perform the same computation and then comparing the results of the computation. In such applications as spacecraft control and process control in a nuclear power plant, correct results of computations are more critical than is the case in typical database applications. Further, the computations are well defined, and the results are often known in advance. For such applications, it makes sense to have multiple processors perform the same computations in order to detect and (even correct) conflicting results. But for office word-processing or transaction-processing applications, this approach may not be desirable.

For applications that require time-consuming computations and/or disk accesses, there tend to be ample opportunities for program checks and machine checks to detect low-level failures, and for time-outs or defensive coding to detect high-level failures. Unless the need for error detection and correction is highly critical, the redundant-computation approach appears to waste the processing power of the system. Further, the exchange of data and status information among the replicated tasks for each input and output is a considerable performance overhead.

## 2. INTUITIVE CRITERIA FOR HIGH AVAILABILITY

Now we must address the problem of what is meant by availability. The overall availability of a system may intuitively be defined as the ratio between the time when the end user and applications actually have access to all the database and the time when the end user and applications require access to the database. For example, if users require the system to be up for 8 hours a day and the system is actually up for 6 hours during the 8 hours, the availability of the system is $6/8 = .75$ during the 8-hour period.

It is more difficult to precisely define a single measure of availability. In the first place, it is not clear how to define the "mission duration" for the system. In spacecraft control applications, the mission duration is clearly defined: While the spacecraft is in orbit, the system must be available 24 hours per day. In business data processing applications, however, the mission duration can be several years. At what point in the life of a system, and for how long, should we measure availability? During one arbitrary month, a year after the installation of the system?

In the second place, should the entire database be available for access by authorized users during the entire duration? For example, when a single database partition becomes inaccessible in a loosely coupled multiprocessor architecture with a partitioned database, one may take the view that the system is no longer available. In fact, this is my view for the purposes of this paper. However, one may equally well take the more charitable view that the system is still largely available, since users may access other database partitions and perform useful work [Good 1983].

Similarly, in a geographically distributed environment, it is not entirely clear where to draw the line on availability, for example, when a node of the system cannot communicate with another node and consequently cannot access data owned and managed by the other node.

Very few vendors of the systems that we are considering have provided availability figures for public review. Suffice it to say here that, however one may define it, often a highly available system is expected to provide higher than 99 percent overall availability.

We use the following criteria to classify a system for database applications as highly available. The first three are hard criteria and provide the rationale for including and excluding detailed discussion of various systems in this paper. The last two are soft criteria, satisfied by very few existing systems and mainly included for future considerations.

(1) The system must support transaction-processing or file server capabilities, specifically concurrency control and recovery techniques, to maintain database consistency. A distributed database system must support a distributed commit protocol to ensure global consistency of the database.

BBN's PLURIBUS [Katsuki et al. 1978], SRI's SIFT design [Wensley et al. 1978], the Basic Controller system now being marketed by August Systems Inc. [Kinnucan 1981], and AT&T's No. 1 ESS and No. 2 ESS [Spencer and Vigilante 1969] do not satisfy this criterion, and will not be discussed in detail in the system survey portion of this paper.

(2) The system must support automatic takeover of full workload by a backup process when a primary process fails. This criterion excludes systems that rely on manual replacement of failed processors to survive a single failure.

The problem with the manual replacement approach is that (1) the responsibility of detecting failure often falls on users or the operators, and (2) the new processor is aware of either the database or the terminals and hence applications, and the system must be cold-started.

Japan National Railways' MARS train seat reservation system, a loosely coupled multiprocessor system with a partitioned database, does not support the concept of backup processes at the present time [Tsukigi and Hasegawa 1983]. Hence, when the processor that manages one partition of the database crashes, no user can access the database partition until the database manager that owns it can be restarted. This system is not given detailed treatment here.

IBM's Information Management System (IMS) with the data-sharing feature [Strickland et al. 1982] is a loosely coupled multiprocessor system with a shared database, with an IMS/VS system in two different processors, each able to access the database in shared disks. When one IMS/VS crashes, its terminals lose access to the database until it can be restarted, and the surviving IMS/VS is not aware of the transactions in process on the system that failed, and hence cannot abort or complete them. We do not consider this system highly available.

The Stratus system does not currently support the concept of primary–backup processes; however, in view of the great extent to which the system incorporates hardware fault tolerance and capabilities for on-line system reconfiguration, it is classified as a highly available system.

(3) The system must survive at least a single failure of such major components as processor, I/O channel, I/O controller, disk drives, and interprocessor communication medium. In particular, a single failure should not make any part of the database inaccessible to the users for beyond a reasonable recovery duration. A reasonable recovery duration may be 1 minute for a mini- and microprocessor system and perhaps 10 minutes for a mainframe, because of the larger number of terminals and applications dealt with by a mainframe system.

This criterion does not imply that a single point of failure is unacceptable, rather that when a single point of failure exists, it must not cause overall availability to suffer.

For example, the Synapse N+1 System has a single point of failure in its shared main memory, but is designed to recover quickly and provides high overall availability. System D has a single point of failure in the electronic switch that connects a pair of processors with the shared disks and terminals, but the probability of failure of such a switch is very low and hence does not severely compromise overall availability.

(4) The system should support on-line integration of repaired or new hardware/software components. Further, in the case of a partitioned database, the system should support on-line migration of the database from one disk system to another.

(5) Additional features aimed at making the component failures transparent to the users may be useful. One is the ability to automatically restart transactions in progress when system crash occurs, which may require the data communication subsystem to log the transaction request on the disk. Another is for the interprocessor communication subsystem to reroute messages originally targeted to a failed process to its backup. In view of the fact that transactions in typical business data processing are short-lived, that is, they complete within a few seconds, it does not appear that important to burden a system with these additional capabilities.

## 3. LOOSELY COUPLED SYSTEMS WITH A PARTITIONED DATABASE

This section provides overviews of architectures and transaction-processing strategies as employed in the Tandem NonStop System, Auragen System 4000, Stratus/32 Continuous Processing System, AT&T's Stored Program Controlled Network, Bank of America's Distributive Computing Facility, and System D.

It is noted that the Auragen, Stratus, AT&T, and Bank of America systems are actually loosely coupled clusters of processors, in which each cluster consists of two or more processors and manages one partition of the database. The cluster itself is not necessarily a loosely coupled multiprocessor architecture. Further, the Auragen, AT&T, and Bank of America systems currently do not support distributed on-line transaction processing: User requests are completely processed within one cluster,

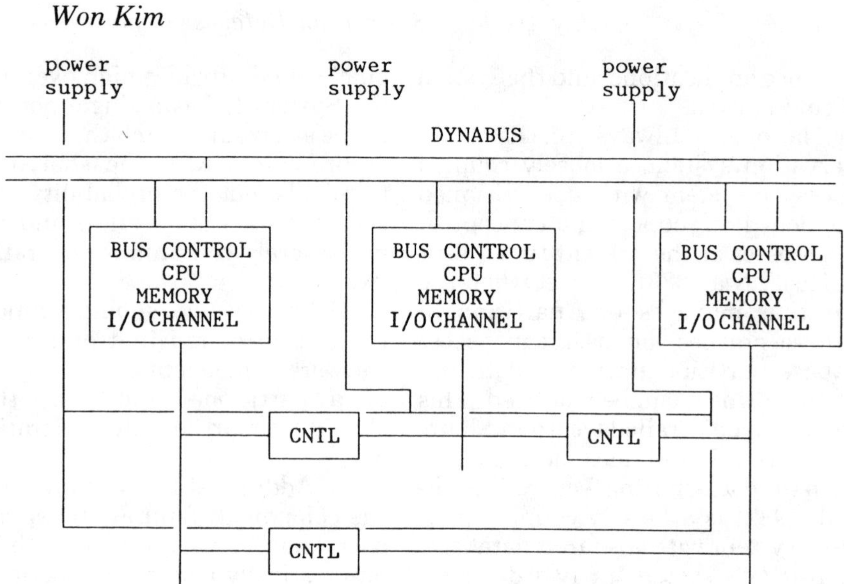


**Figure 1.** Tandem NonStop system architecture.

without requiring the participation of other clusters.

### 3.1 Tandem NonStop System

The NonStop System, developed by Tandem Computers about 1976, has made important contributions to the area of high availability [Bartlett 1978; Katzman 1977, 1978]. As shown in Figure 1, each processor module consists of a central processing unit (CPU), memory, interface to an interprocessor bus system called Dynabus, and an I/O channel. Each of the I/O controllers is connected to two processors via its dual-port arrangement, and each processor is connected to all other processors via a dual Dynabus. Further, as shown in Figure 2, each processor is connected to a pair of disk controllers, which in turn maintain a string of up to four pairs of (optionally) mirrored disk drives. Mirroring is supported in the I/O supervisor, which issues two disk writes for each page of data to be written to the disk. Thus it is clear that the system provides many paths to data, and hence the data are available to the user regardless of any single failure of a disk drive, disk controller, I/O channel, or processor.

The Tandem system was designed to continue operation through any single component failure, and also to allow the failure to be repaired without affecting the availability of the rest of the system. Each processor module has a separate power supply, which can be shut off to replace the failed module without affecting the rest of the system. Similarly, each I/O controller is powered by two power supplies associated with the two processors to which it is attached, and can be powered down by a corresponding switch, without affecting the rest of the system. Thus the I/O controllers survive a single power failure, and each I/O controller and processor module can be repaired without shutting down the rest of the system.

In order to detect a processor failure in the Tandem system, each processor broadcasts an "I-AM-ALIVE" message every 1 second and checks for an "I-AM-ALIVE" message from every other processor every 2 seconds [Bartlett 1978]. If a processor decides that another processor has failed to send the "I-AM-ALIVE" message, it initiates recovery actions, as described later. Although there is a possibility that different processors may reach different decisions as to which processor has crashed, the single-failure assumption precludes consideration (and prevention) of such a possibility.

This "active" failure-detection approach of the Tandem system helps to detect a processor failure soon after it occurs. However, it is not very useful to say that a

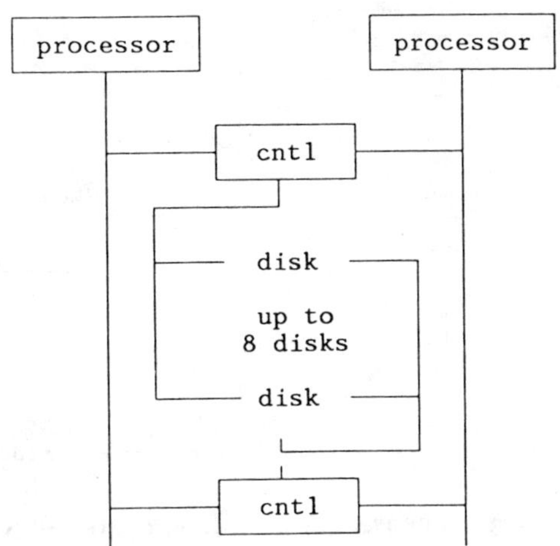


**Figure 2.** Tandem NonStop disk subsystem organization.

processor is "alive" simply because it can send the "I-AM-ALIVE" message, when tasks running in it may have crashed. Software failures must be detected by message time-outs.

The operating system that runs on the Tandem NonStop System is called Guardian. It is constructed of processes that communicate by using messages. Guardian provides high availability of processes by maintaining a primary–backup pair of processes, each in a different processor. The primary process periodically sends checkpoint information to its paired backup process, so that the backup will stand ready to take over as soon as the primary process fails. The checkpoint data from a primary I/O process contain information about the files that are opened and closed. The backup I/O process opens and closes the checkpointed files while the primary is still active, so that in the event of failure of the primary, the backup recovers and proceeds with normal processing without the time overhead of opening the files.

An "ownership" bit is associated with each of the two ports of an I/O controller, which indicates to each port whether it is the primary or backup. Only one port is active for the primary I/O process; the other is used only in the event of a path failure to the primary port, and any attempt to access data through the backup port is rejected. Upon detecting or being notified of the failure of the primary process, the backup process instructs Guardian to issue a TAKE OWNERSHIP command to the backup port. This command causes the I/O controller to swap its two ownership bits and do a controller reset.

The database/transaction manager that runs on the Tandem system is called ENCOMPASS [Borr 1981]. ENCOMPASS consists of four functional components: a database manager, a terminal manager, a transaction manager, and a distributed transaction manager. The ENCOMPASS database manager is implemented as a primary/backup I/O process (called the DISCPROCESS) pair per disk volume. In other words, a primary database manager in one processor and its backup in another processor own the partition of the database stored in the disk volume to which the two processors are connected. The primary database manager checkpoints to the backup, so that if the primary fails before completing a transaction, the backup may take over the disk volume and redo committed transactions and abort incomplete ones.

To run transactions against the database, the user provides two sets of programs: the Screen COBOL program and application server programs. The Screen COBOL program performs screen formatting and sequencing, data mapping, and field validation, and sends transaction requests to application server programs. The application server programs perform application functions against the database by invoking the database manager, the DISCPROCESS.

The Screen COBOL program is interpreted by the terminal management component of ENCOMPASS, called Terminal Control Process (TCP). TCP is also configured as a process pair; the primary TCP checkpoints the backup TCP with data extracted by the Screen COBOL program from input screens.

The transaction management component of ENCOMPASS, which implements the conventional model of transactions, is called Transaction Monitoring Facility (TMF). TMF consists of a lock manager, a log manager (called the AUDITPROCESS), and a recovery manager (called the BACKOUTPROCESS) to provide concurrency control and recovery of interleaved execution of concurrent transactions. The user's Screen COBOL program interfaces with TMF to indicate the beginning and end of a transaction. The Screen COBOL program receives a transaction identification from TMF at the beginning of a transaction, and attaches the transaction identification to all transaction request messages that it sends to the application server programs. When the Screen COBOL program notifies end of transaction, TMF initiates a transaction commit protocol to complete the transaction and make the effect of the transaction permanent. TMF does not support a global deadlock detection mechanism; deadlocks are detected by time-out, where the time limit is specified as part of lock requests.

### 3.2 AT&T's Stored Program Controlled Network

AT&T's Stored Program Controlled (SPC) Network [Cohen et al. 1983] consists of two key components: the Network Control Point (NCP) and the Action Point (ACP), as shown in Figure 3. The NCP is a database system which manages a database of customer records that is geographically distributed over a network of computers interconnected by the Common Channel Interoffice Signaling (CCIS) network. The ACP is a telephone call processing system, and is a highly reliable No. 4 ESS.

When a call is made to a customer of the expanded 800 services or Direct Services Dialing Capability (DSDC) services, the call is routed to an ACP. The ACP transmits the request to an NCP, which maintains the customer record. The NCP returns the response to the ACP, which in turn routes the call according to the response from the NCP. An administrative system called the User Support System (USS) is used to insert new customer records and update existing ones. The USS sends records to be inserted or updated through the Operations Support Network (OSN).

This system may require several NCPs, according to NCP capacity, performance requirements and market forecasts. The database is partitioned and each partition is assigned to two NCPs, one primary and

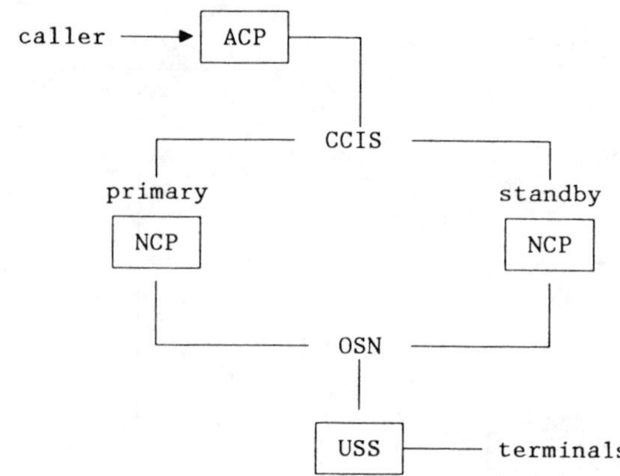


**Figure 3.** AT&T's Stored Program Controlled Network.

one backup, for call processing. A database partition is replicated in an NCP and its backup. One NCP may be a backup to another NCP with respect to one database partition, and a primary to that NCP with respect to another partition of the database. When a primary NCP fails and there are insufficient data at the site to restore its operation, its backup takes over while continuing to function as the primary for another database partition.

Each NCP is constructed using a 3B-20D processor [Mitze et al. 1983]. A 3B-20D consists of two identical processors: One component processor is active and the other is a standby at any given time. Each has its own main memory and control unit. Further, both processors share all the disks, and each processor has indirect access to the main memory of the other.

During normal operation, the active processor updates the main memory of the standby processor, which is ready at all times to take over if the primary should fail. At each NCP, the I/O channel, disk controller, and links to its standby NCP are duplicated. Further, the database partition managed by an NCP is quadruplicated, and stored in four separate sets of disk drives connected to the 3B-20D. The standby NCP in turn keeps four copies of the database partition.

For a customer record to be updated under normal conditions, a transaction is sent to the primary NCP with which the record is associated. The primary NCP checks the

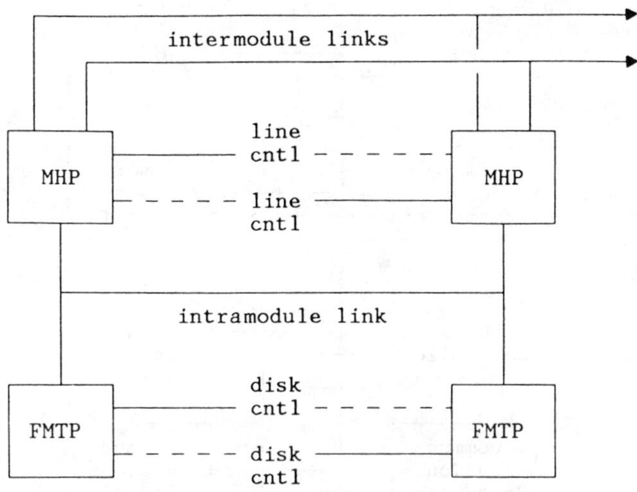


**Figure 4.** A module of Bank of America's DCF.

transaction for consistency and authorization; if it is valid, the primary NCP logs the transaction on the disk and sends an acknowledgment to the user. The primary NCP makes changes to its database and sends the update to its backup. The backup NCP applies the update to its database and acknowledges the primary, at which point the primary inserts a record in the transaction log and finishes the transaction. In the event of a network partition, when a primary NCP is disconnected from its backup NCP due to failure of the communication line, the primary updates its database without requiring agreement from its backup, but maintains a special history log of database changes, which it sends to its backup when communication is restored.

### 3.3 Bank of America's Distributive Computing Facility

Bank of America developed the Distributive Computing Facility (DCF) around 1978 to automate teller functions for customer checking and savings accounts [Good 1983]. By leased lines, branch offices access a customer accounts database in two data centers in Los Angeles and San Francisco. Each data center houses a DCF cluster, which consists of eight DCF modules interconnected by a local-area network. Each DCF module is a local-area network of four GA16/440 minicomputers, which manages one partition of the customer accounts database. Two of the four processors in a DCF module are communications front ends called Message Handling Processors (MHP). The other two are database back ends called File Management Transaction Processors (FMTP). The four processors communicate via a bus called the intramodule link.

As shown in Figure 4, each module is configured such that, under normal operation, each MHP is paired with one FMTP to operate on half the module's lines and database. When one MHP fails, the other takes control of all the lines. When one FMTP fails, the other takes control of the entire database of the module.

The DCF uses a simple scheme for detecting processor failures. Each processor has a watchdog timer, which it periodically resets. If the timer is not reset on schedule, the DCF module shuts the processor down and notifies the peer processor to assume full work load. When an MHP times out on a transaction request to an FMTP, it assumes that the FMTP is dead and starts sending subsequent transactions to the other FMTP. The transaction messages are not logged, and so any transaction in progress on a failed MHP or FMTP is lost.

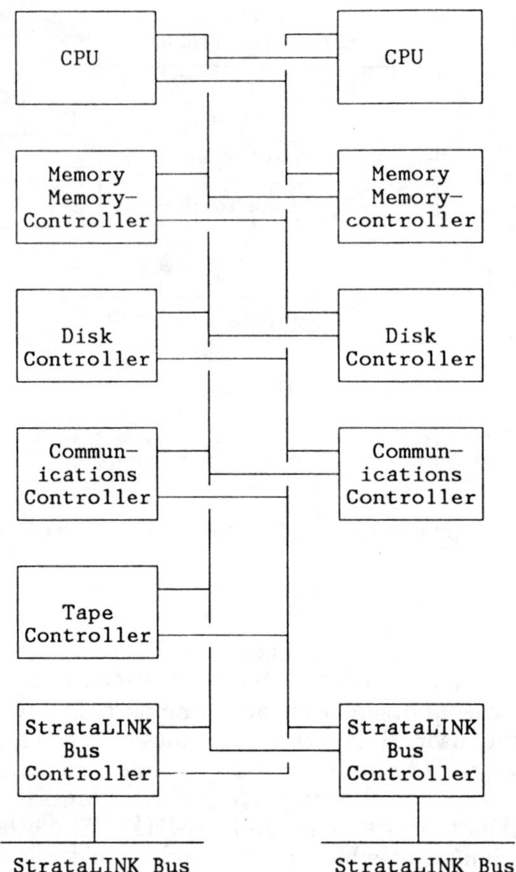


**Figure 5.** A Processing Module of Stratus/32.

### 3.4 Stratus/32 Continuous Processing System

The Stratus/32 Continuous Processing System [Kastner 1983; Stratus 1982] consists of 1–32 Processing Modules, where each Processing Module consists of duplicated CPU, memory, controller, and I/O as shown in Figure 5. The memory may be configured to be redundant or nonredundant, as the two memory subsystems are not paired with the two CPUs. In a redundant configuration, the CPUs read from and write to both memory subsystems simultaneously; in a nonredundant configuration, each memory subsystem becomes an independent unit and the memory capacity is doubled. Each Processing Module has duplicated power supplies. The Processing Modules are connected through a dual-bus system called the StrataLINK.

The duplicated components (CPU and controllers) of a Processing Module each perform the same computation in parallel. Each component (board), in turn, consists of two identical sets of hardware components on the same board. As shown in Figure 6 for a disk controller, a hardware logic compares the results of the computation by the duplicated boards. If the results are identical, they are sent to the bus or device. Otherwise, the results are not sent, the board is automatically disabled, and an interrupt signal is sent to the Stratus VOS operating system. However, processing continues with the duplexed board of the Processing Module.

All detected hardware malfunctions are reported to a maintenance software, which determines the cause and nature of the malfunction. The board is automatically restarted if the malfunction was caused by

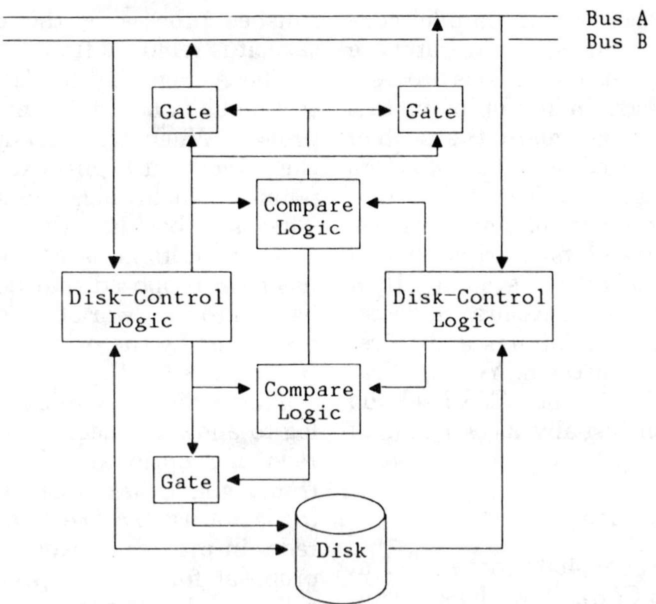


**Figure 6.** Self-checking disk controller in a Stratus/32.

a transient error, whereas permanent errors result in the board remaining out of service and a report being sent to an operator terminal.

The Stratus system supports optional mirroring of disk volumes. It also allows on-line removal and replacement of all duplexed boards and associated peripheral devices; in particular, it allows on-line integration of a new Processing Module. When a duplexed component is replaced, the new component is automatically brought to the same state as its partner. For example, the second disk in a dual-disk system is brought up-to-date while the first disk is used for normal processing. The VOS operating system accomplishes this by writing new blocks of pages to both disks and copying blocks from the first disk to the second concurrently with normal processing.

Further, the Stratus system allows the memory subsystems to be dynamically reconfigured to redundant or nonredundant mode, without taking the Processing Module off line.

The Stratus system supports transaction processing by providing a Transaction Processing Facility (TPF), VOS File System, the StrataNET network communications subsystem, and a Forms Management Facility. The system does not currently support a database management system; TPF invokes the File System to manipulate the database. TPF supports a two-phase commit protocol for on-line distributed transaction processing.

The Stratus system's continuous comparison of the results of computation from duplicated hardware components on the same board significantly reduces the probability of a hardware-induced error from propagating and corrupting the system and data integrity, provided that the hardware that compares the results does not malfunction. Further, the Stratus hardware and operating system provide protection against some system crashes induced by software errors, such as attempts by one user's program to cross another user's address space, to read or write into the operating system, to write into executable code, or to execute data.

The Stratus system does not currently support the concept of a backup subsystem, and hence applications running on Stratus may not survive software-induced crashes. The Stratus fault-tolerance philosophy is based on the view that the hardware can detect errors and automatically shut down a malfunctioning component while an identical component operating in parallel continues to function, thus ensuring database integrity and providing continuous processing of user requests. In my opinion, this approach does not safeguard the system against crashes induced by a class of errors that even the most sophisticated operating systems cannot cope with. For instance, IBM's System/370 and its Multiple Virtual System (MVS) operating system [IBM 1979] provide extensive measures to detect hardware and software failures and to repair and recover from them. Yet, applications running on MVS, and MVS itself, do occasionally crash, usually as a result of software failures.

### 3.5 Auragen System 4000

The Auragen System 4000, developed at Auragen Systems Corp., New Jersey, consists of 2–32 clusters of tightly coupled multimicroprocessors interconnected by a dual-bus system [Gostanian 1983]. Each cluster consists of three MC68000s, its own local memory, several types of I/O controllers, power supply, and battery backup. One of the 68000s is used exclusively to execute the operating system, whereas the other two are used to execute user tasks. Each cluster periodically broadcasts an "I-AM-ALIVE" message to detect failure of other clusters; the time-out mechanism is used to detect process failures. All peripheral devices are dual ported and are attached to two different clusters. The Auragen system allows disks to be configured in mirrored pairs, and mirroring may be specified on a file basis.

The Auragen database system, called AURELATE, is based on the ORACLE relational database system [Weiss 1980]. As in the Tandem system, Auragen 4000 supports a primary–backup pair of processes, implemented within the AUROS operating system, which is an enhanced version of UNIX III. To reduce the number of checkpoint messages, the AUROS operating system sends a collection of transaction messages to both the primary and the backup. After the primary has processed a predetermined number of these transaction messages, the backup is notified to process the checkpoint message. Once the backup finishes processing the checkpoint message, it is removed from the message queue.

The Auragen system's current recovery technique is based on the roll-forward approach. When the backup takes over for the primary, it begins execution at the last point of synchronization with the primary. That is, it begins with the last checkpoint message in its message queue. A technique has been proposed that does not allow the backup to redo work that already may have been done by the primary before the crash [Gostanian 1983].

The recovery technique requires an undo log to allow transaction abort. However, a redo log is optional and is used for recovery from a single disk crash, when disk mirroring is not used. Since a backup process will redo in-progress transactions, Auragen's proposal for commit processing does not call for the Write-Ahead Log protocol. However, this leaves the system unprotected from simultaneous failures of both the primary and backup processes.

### 3.6 System D Prototype

System D is a distributed transaction-processing system designed and prototyped at IBM Research, San Jose, as a vehicle for research into availability and incremental growth of a locally distributed network of computers [Andler et al. 1982]. The system was implemented on a network of Series/1 minicomputers interconnected with an insertion ring, and was the predecessor to the Highly Available Systems project currently under way at IBM Research, San Jose [Aghili et al. 1983; Kim 1982]. Although System D is not itself a highly available system, its rather novel transaction-processing and failure-diagnosis strategies warrant discussion here.

The System D transaction-processing software consists of three distinct types of modules: application, data manager, and storage manager modules. A module is a function that exists in a node and may consist of one or more processes called agents. The application module, called A, provides user interfaces for interactive users or application programmers. The data manager module, called D, transforms the record-level requests from the A module to

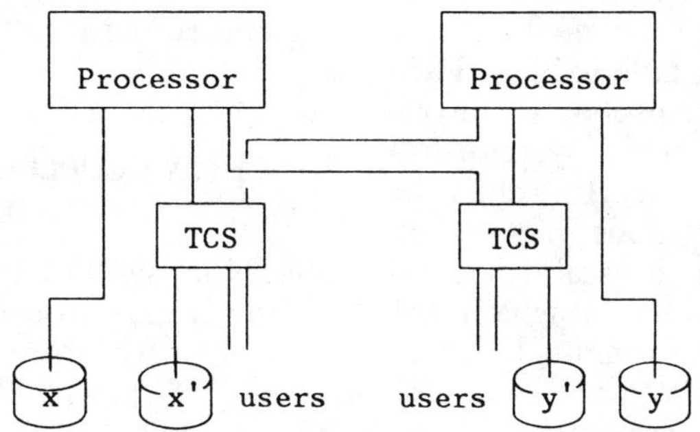


**Figure 7.** Processor pair in System D.

page-level requests for the storage module. All the changes made by an application are kept locally in the data manager module, which sends them to the storage manager only when the application commits the data changes to stable storage. The storage manager module, called S, supports multiple concurrent transactions against the physical database and database recovery from failures.

As shown in Figure 7, terminals and shared disks are connected to a pair of processors through an electronic switch, called a Two-Channel Switch (TCS). Only one of the processors has access to the shared disks and terminals at any given time. The processor periodically resets the timer in the TCS; if this does not occur on schedule, the TCS switches the shared disks and terminals over to the other processor. Thus, rather than requiring the processors to communicate with each other, System D gives the TCS the task of detecting the failure of a processor. Moreover, the TCS prevents a processor that is declared dead from writing to the disk.

System D provides a software subsystem called the Resource Manager (RM), which is responsible for diagnosing and taking appropriate actions to recover from the failures of modules and agents. The basic premise of its design is that the time-out mechanism detects all failures, including deadlock, agent or module crash, communication medium failure, or processor failure. Failures are detected only when service requests are sent.

Rather than the Tandem-like notion of primary and backup processes, System D supports multiple agents of a module running in the same processor. The Resource Manager attempts to bring down and restart failed agents, while normal service requests are handled by other agents. In the event of a processor failure, agents are brought up in the backup processor and all transactions in progress are aborted. The initial program load (IPL) of a low-end processor normally takes under 1 minute, which was considered a reasonable recovery duration, and System D was designed to avoid the overhead of maintaining synchronized pairs of primary and backup processes.

The failure-diagnosis logic described below was necessary because of the inadequate failure-detection capabilities of the operating system on which System D ran. The RM attempts to diagnose the problem by first attempting to establish communication with the node in which the agent is running. If the response is positive, the RM issues an "ABORT_TRANSACTION" command to the agent. The rationale here is that the service-request message may have experienced a data- or timing-dependent error that may not recur if the transaction is aborted and resubmitted. Successful processing of the "ABORT_TRANSACTION" command also indicates that the agent involved probably has not crashed.

If the transaction cannot be aborted, the RM attempts to bring down and restart the agent, since the code or the control structure of the agent may have been destroyed. If the agent cannot be brought down, the RM attempts to shut down and restart the module itself, since the control structures shared by the agents of the module may have crashed. If the RM fails to shut down and restart the module, probably the remote RM or the operating system has crashed, in which case an IPL must be executed remotely for the node in question.

Now, if the RM fails to establish communication with the node in which the resource resides or if the remote IPL was not successful, it will try to communicate with the RM in the backup node of the resource, since the TCS has probably switched. If the TCS has not switched over, the RM attempts to remotely execute an IPL for the node in which the resource resides. The reason is that initially it may have failed to communicate with the RM in that node because the RM, the CSS, or the operating system in that node may have crashed.

The standard two-phase commit protocol allows each node to unilaterally abort the transaction as long as the commit protocol has not entered the second phase. The design of System D recognizes that this privilege, often called site autonomy, is not so important in a locally distributed environment, and implements a different commit protocol [Andler et al. 1982]. In a sense, the System D protocol requires just a single phase and as soon as the commit coordinator decides to commit; no other node may abort the transaction.

In System D, actual updates to the database are not made until the transaction commits. At transaction commit, the transaction's log, maintained by the D module, is sent to the S module that is designated the commit coordinator, the first S module that receives page request from the D module. The commit coordinator writes the log to the disk and acknowledges the D module. The D module then sends "commit" messages to the other participating S modules. Each participant writes its log to the disk and then makes database changes.

The recovery procedure for this commit protocol is as follows. Upon restart, an S module re-DOes the changes in its local transaction log. The module then requests complete logs from any commit coordinators for transactions that are known to them but unknown to the recovering module, and runs these transactions serially in any order.

## 4. TIGHTLY COUPLED SYSTEMS WITH A SHARED DATABASE

The Synapse N+1 Computer System is an on-line transaction-processing system, developed by Synapse Computer Corporation [Jones 1983], which provides a dual path from a processor to the database stored in secondary storage devices. As Figure 8 shows, Synapse N+1 is a tightly coupled multiprocessor system with shared memory, in which processing is divided between general-purpose processors (GPP) and I/O processors (IOP), each of which is based on the Motorola 68000. Currently, up to 28 processors may be attached to a dual-bus system called the Synapse Expansion Bus.

GPPs execute user programs and most of the Synapse's Synthesis operating system from the shared memory. IOPs each manage up to 16 I/O controllers or communications subsystems. IOPs have direct memory access (DMA) capability to the shared main memory, but execute part of Synthesis from their own local memory. The Advanced Communications Subsystem (ACS) is a 68000-based communications controller, and the Multiple-Purpose Controller (MPC) is a controller for various devices. Whereas the Tandem NonStop system powers each processor with a separate power supply, the entire Synapse N+1 is powered by one set of duplicated power supplies.

Synapse enhances availability simply by having one additional processor, disk controller, and disk drive than what is necessary for satisfactory performance. This extra component is not an idle backup; it is used for normal transaction processing. When a component fails, the system sometimes has to restart, and reconfigure itself without the failed component.

The Synapse system also supports mirroring of disks. Mirroring is supported in the IOP, where two disk writes are issued for each page of data to be written to the disk. It is interesting that the Synapse system allows mirroring of disks on a logical volume basis, rather than physical volume.

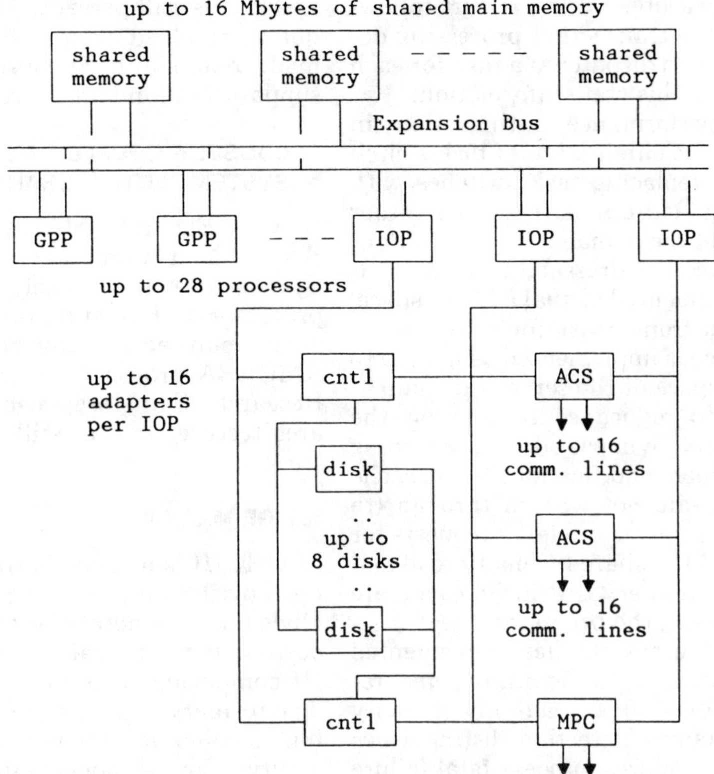


**Figure 8.** Synapse N+1 System architecture.

A logical volume may be all or part of a physical volume. Mirroring a logical volume is more flexible than mirroring a physical volume; for example, it allows storage on the same physical volume of a separate database that does not require high availability (and its associated overhead).

Synapse N+1 supports recoverable transactions using the Write-Ahead Log protocol. The Synapse database manager is a relational system. Further, the database may be migrated from one physical disk volume to another and may undergo structural changes without taking the applications off line.

The Synthesis operating system incorporates various techniques to optimize the performance of production transaction-processing systems. One is the placement of its database system directly above the kernel of Synthesis, rather than on top of the file system as has been the case with most database systems. The reason for this decision was to reduce the overhead associated with I/O requests from the database system to the operating system, both to retrieve data from disk, and to store the log of database changes after transaction processing.

An interesting side benefit of this approach is that higher levels of the Synthesis operating system can use the capabilities of the database system to query and manipulate data about operating system objects, such as files and devices. In particular, a higher level of the Synthesis operating system, called the transaction-processing domain, records the state of currently active applications in the database. An application consists of a number of programs; each program takes as input a screenful of information, processes it, and outputs a screen. The state information of an active application consists of a user identification, the identification of the current screen, the contents of its variable fields, and the next program to execute. During restart following a crash, the transaction-processing domain creates and dispatches a task for each terminal using this state information.

Another performance optimization in Synthesis is the elimination of task-switch overhead by replacing task switches with cross-domain (address space) calls. In other words, each of the domains (layers) of Synthesis has direct addressability to a partition of the segmented virtual address space, and a request from a task for an operating system service is implemented as a jump to the address space of the server's domain.

In order to reduce contention on the shared memory, Synapse adopted a caching scheme in which modifications to the cache in each GPP are not written through (to the shared memory), and fetch requests for the portion of the shared memory read and modified by another GPP in its cache are resolved between the processors.

The Synapse system has implemented failure detection, reconfiguration, and restart procedures in a read-only memory (ROM). Its failure detection distinguishes two classes of failures: process-fatal failure and system-fatal failure. A process-fatal failure causes the process and its associated transaction to be aborted and restarted, whereas a system-fatal failure results in a restart of the entire system.

The kernel of the operating system is capable of recognizing any failures caused by internal machine checks and is responsible for initiating the reconfiguration and restart of the system. In particular, it activates self-test code to verify whether each major hardware component is operational. After any failed components are configured out of the system, each domain (layer) of the operating system is reinitialized. Since the database system is a layer directly above the kernal operating system, transaction restart and recovery take place at this time.

Since the processing is divided between the GPPs and IOPs, and the IOPs run part of the operating system from their own local memories, the risk of total system failure due to corruption of the operating system is somewhat reduced. However, as long as the GPPs execute most of the operating system out of shared main memory, this risk is still present. This problem cannot be resolved even if shared memory is made redundant. Synapse N+1 does not support a redundant shared memory.

## 5. LOOSELY COUPLED MULTIPROCESSOR SYSTEM WITH A SHARED DATABASE

General Electric's MARK III Cluster File System and Computer Consoles' Power System use the loosely coupled multiprocessor architecture, in which each processor may access any of the disks. The AMOEBA project [Traiger 1983] at IBM Research, San Jose, also uses the same architecture, but is still in the research stage.

### 5.1 GE MARK III

MARK III is a time-sharing system developed by the Information Services Business Division of General Electric to provide its customers with local-call access to MARK III computing capabilities [Weston 1978]. The primary objectives of the system were high availability, reliability, and maintainability. Three supercenters (computing centers), located in Ohio, Maryland, and Amsterdam, provide computing power to the users. The computing facilities at a supercenter typically consist of front-end processors, MARK III foreground processors, and MARK III background processors, as shown in Figure 9.

The front-end processors are network front-end processors (central concentrators). The foreground processors support interactive users, whereas the background processors provide batch-processing capabilities. The foreground and background processors are interconnected via a Bus Adapter, which allows job and file movement between the foreground and background systems.

The Bus Adapter consists of a microprocessor, programmable read-only memory (PROM) control memory, and channel interfaces to the background systems. The microprocessor polls each of the channel interfaces for data transfer requests; each request is fully processed before the next request is serviced.

In 1975 GE developed new software to allow a single foreground processor of the

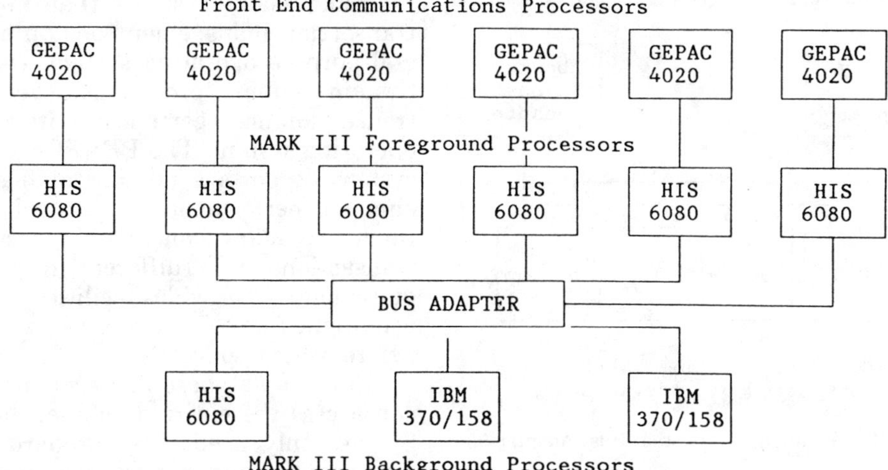


**Figure 9.** GE's MARK III Cluster File System architecture.

MARK III system to access more than one disk system at a time. This new system, called the Cluster File System, controls concurrent access to multiple-disk systems from multiple foreground processors by maintaining the access-conflict tables in one stable memory device accessible to all foreground processors. The Scratch Pad (SPAD) was developed to provide the high reliability, nonvolatility, and fast access time that such a memory device requires. All data transfers to and from the disk systems take place over normal I/O channels, but access-control decisions are made through use of the access tables in the SPAD.

Since the SPAD is the central point through which all requests are funneled, it was built with redundancy to prevent total failure of the cluster system resulting from the SPAD and Bus Adapter failure. As shown in Figure 10, the MARK III Cluster File System has two Bus Adapters, primary and secondary. Each foreground processor has access paths to both Bus Adapters. The memory and devices in SPAD dedicated to each disk system are themselves duplicated. Each of the Bus Adapters can access both the primary and backup elements of SPAD. The Bus Adapter was augmented to support the functions of, and dual access paths to, the SPAD, and the microcode in the Bus Adapter does dual read and write to the SPAD memory.

The SPAD contains 16 memory and logic devices (8 primary and 8 backup), each for a separate disk system. The Maryland supercenter supports seven disk systems. Each device contains the access-conflict table, which indicates whether a particular file in a disk system is in use and if so whether the file is sharable by other users.

One device, called the Cluster Control device (CLUSCON), is used for such global functions as processor status and recovery status. Each foreground processor periodically places its status in CLUSCON and checks to see if any other foreground processor has failed to do so in the previous interval. If it finds that another processor failed to update its status, it proceeds to clean up all resources belonging to the failed processor.

The MARK III Cluster File System is protected from single failures by redundancy in the interconnections between the front-end and foreground processors and between the foreground and background processors. The front-end processors (network central concentrators) are connected to remote concentrators, to which user terminals are connected. The connection between the central concentrators and remote concentrators is accomplished via redundant network-switching computers.

An obvious drawback of the MARK III Cluster File System is that the SPAD may become a performance bottleneck, espe-

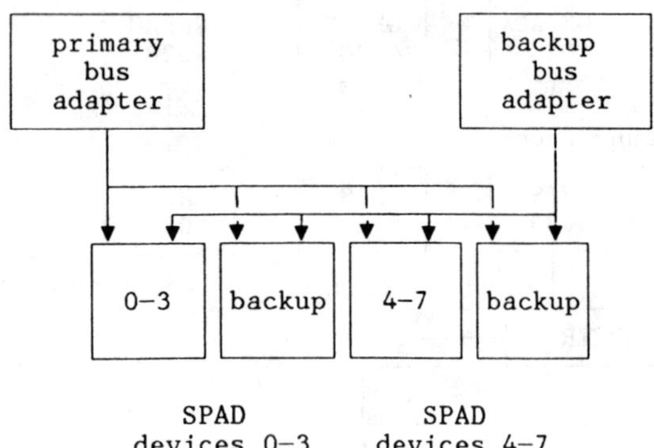


**Figure 10.** Redundancy in the Bus Adapter and SPAD.

cially with an expanded system, since each front-end processor must access it before accessing a shared file.

### 5.2 Computer Consoles' Power System

The Power Series systems have been developed at Computer Consoles, Inc., Rochester, New York [West et al. 1983]. The system is based on Motorola 68000s, and consists of a number of application processors and two coordination processors with front-end processors. The processors communicate via a dual-bus system called the Data Highway, as shown in Figure 11.

Each application processor (AP) is directly connected to all disks, and independently executes different user applications in parallel. The interprocessor coordination controllers (ICC) synchronize global operations among the APs, which consist mostly of lock requests to gain access to the shared database and system status changes due to reconfiguration. At any given time, one ICC is active and the other is a standby. The standby ICC is the only idle component of the system. The front-end processors (FEP) perform screen formatting, distribute transactions to APs, receive replies from APs, and assist in recovery from some system failures. Further, FEPs attempt to balance the load on the APs by distributing the transactions to the APs on the basis of application configuration and flow control information.

Unlike many systems that implement transaction management on top of a general-purpose operating system, the Power System combines process management and transaction management into its PERPOS operating system. The PERPOS operating system supports a number of features to enhance performance of critical applications. To allow concurrent execution of transactions with different response requirements, it provides facilities to fix critical applications in memory and run them before other applications.

Since the database manager in each AP can access the entire database, the Power System only needs the standard concurrency control and recovery techniques used for a central database. In particular, it does not need the coordinated commit protocol required by loosely coupled multiprocessors with partitioned databases.

Transaction recovery is done in a straightforward manner. The AP that receives the transaction from the FEP logs the transaction on the disk. When the FEP detects that the AP crashed, it requests another AP to abort the transaction and restart it from the log of the failed AP.

As in other systems, interprocessor message time-outs are used to detect processor failures. In addition, the primary ICC periodically polls the APs and FEPs to detect failures of processors that do not happen to be in communication with other processors. The ICC supports on-line system reconfiguration after a disk crash and on-line integration of new or repaired disks.

The primary ICC does not keep the standby up-to-date on the global lock table and the system configuration information. Rather, when the primary ICC fails, the standby requests status and lock information from all the APs and reconstructs the global lock table.

In order to reduce the communication overhead resulting from lock requests to the ICC, the system distinguishes shared files and nonshared files. When an AP opens a file for the first time, it considers the file nonshared, and does not make a lock request to the global lock manager in the ICC. When an AP opens a file currently owned by another AP, that file becomes a

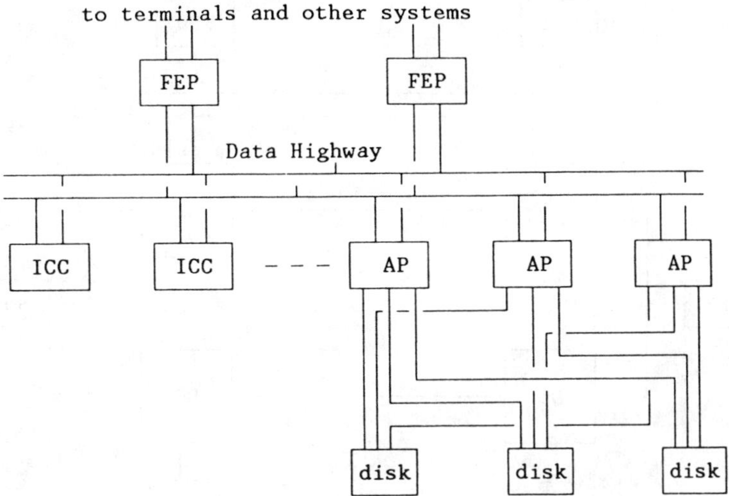


**Figure 11.** Power System architecture.

shared file under the jurisdiction of the global lock manager.

One potential drawback of the Power System architecture is that, as the number of APs increases, the ICCs may become a performance bottleneck. Further, the Power System's performance may be enhanced by generalizing its locking technique to the lock hierarchy technique similar to that found in IMS/VS [Strickland et al. 1982]. In this scheme, the database is logically partitioned, with each partition assigned to a different data manager that can acquire and release locks on data objects within its partition. The data manager consults the global lock manager only when it must lock and unlock objects outside its partition. This strategy potentially allows transfer of updated data pages from the buffer pool of one partition's data manager to another data manager. Traiger [1983] speculates on this in more detail.

## 6. REDUNDANT COMPUTATION SYSTEMS: SYNTREX'S GEMINI FILE SERVER

GEMINI is a file server developed by Syntrex, Inc., with the objective of uninterrupted operation, without backup, in the event of a single failure of any hardware or software component [Cohen et al. 1982]. Up to 14 workstations (word-processing terminals) connected to a GEMINI file server on a local-area network can share files and printers. A GEMINI system may be connected to other GEMINI systems through an Ethernet-like network.

As shown in Figure 12, GEMINI consists of two identical halves. Each half has the Aquarius interface (AI), a disk controller (DC), and a shared memory (SM), as well as a secondary storage system. The AI is a communications subsystem, implemented on an Intel 8088 microprocessor, that operates between GEMINI and the workstations, and between the AIs in each half. The DC, implemented on an Intel 8086, provides file storage and management for the workstations. Communication between an AI and a DC takes place through the shared memory (SM).

The two halves of GEMINI perform identical computations. Each half receives the same request from the workstations and retrieves and updates files in its secondary storage. When both halves are operational, one is designated the master and the other the slave. The only difference between them is that only the results from the master are returned to the workstations.

Each half continuously monitors the well-being of the other half. When one half

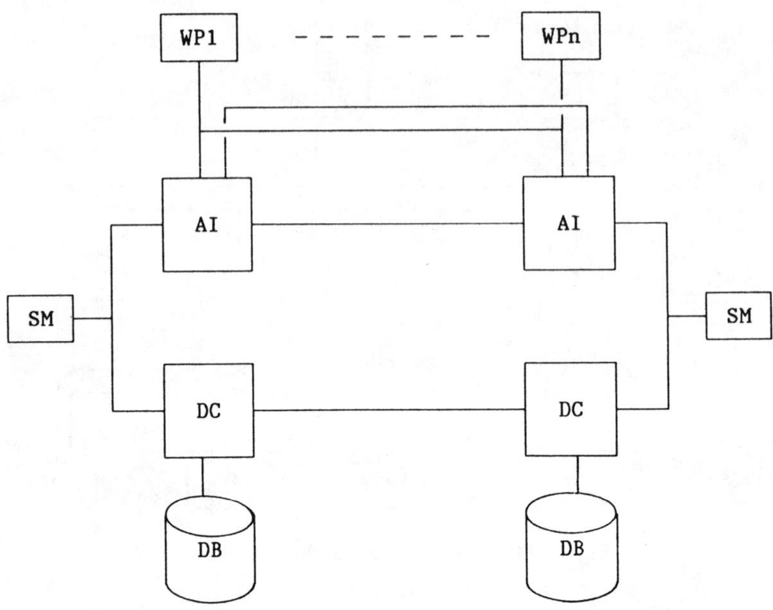


**Figure 12.** Syntrex's GEMINI file server architecture.

crashes, it is powered off and the other half continues as the master. While one half is down, its secondary storage system becomes out of date; when it is repaired, a utility is run to bring its secondary storage system up-to-date. The active system is suspended until copying is completed. Thus GEMINI does not support on-line reintegration of repaired components.

A time-out mechanism is used in the communication between the AIs of GEMINI and the workstations. If the workstation times out on its request, it retransmits the request; if GEMINI times out, it goes to receive mode and waits for the workstation to time out and retransmit the request. This means that the workstation time-out value is longer than the GEMINI time-out.

Another aspect of the reliability measures incorporated in the AI is the periodic self-checks, including auditing of input buffers, checking of the clock, memory tests, and testing of the DC and the communication link between the AIs. If any test fails, the AI logs the failure and, if possible, informs the other AI.

The heart of mutual checking in GEMINI is embedded in the AI–AI communications procedures. The availability and reliability of GEMINI critically depends on the assumption that the disk controllers (DC) of both halves receive and perform the same computation, and therefore that the two secondary storage systems are left with the same data at the end of computation. Since it is possible for one AI to receive a correctly transmitted request while the other receives the request with a transmission error, the two AIs are required to exchange status information about the requests that they received. The request is processed only when both AIs agree that they received the same request [without a character redundancy check (CRC) error].

Similarly, the AIs exchange information about the results of the computation to verify their correctness. It is possible for one AI to have completed a computation before the other is done. In such a situation, the slow half sends a notice that it is "working on the request," to prevent the other half from concluding that it is down. GEMINI takes precautions against an infinite sequence of "I am done" and "I am working on it" messages between the AIs. Since the results of computations may be too long, sometimes only the types of results are exchanged between the AIs. Therefore it appears that sometimes GEMINI may not detect conflicting results generated by the two AIs. Further, when GEMINI does detect conflicting results, it arbitrarily assumes that the master is correct. A meaningful vote really cannot be taken with less than three processors.

## 7. A FRAMEWORK FOR THE MANAGEMENT OF SYSTEM CONFIGURATION

It is clear from the preceding discussions that the design of existing systems has been guided by the single-failure assumption; that is, these systems can become unavailable if a software or hardware component fails while another related component has failed. Despite the general success of some of these systems, notably the Tandem system, the single-failure assumption may not be valid. Future systems may be required to tolerate multiple concurrent failures.

Most existing systems and those that are currently being developed are constructed with mini- and microcomputers. If relatively expensive medium- to high-end processors were to be used, it might not be economically feasible to keep spares around for use as replacements for malfunctioning processors. In that case, the mean time to repair such processors could be relatively long, increasing the probability that other subsystems or processors might go down before the failed processors are repaired.

In addition, the software in most existing systems was developed from scratch to run on minicomputers and to support only prospective new customers. Existing database and operating systems required by medium- to high-end processors tend to be complex, and the mean time between failures for these systems due to software-induced failures is expected to be shorter than that for simple transaction-processing systems that run under relatively simple operating systems.

If a system is to be continuously operational, it must guarantee availability not only during multiple concurrent failures of software and hardware components, but also during on-line changes of software and hardware components and on-line physical reconfiguration of the database and database backups. The latter problems do not appear to be properly addressed by most systems. Syntrex GEMINI, for example, requires system shutdown when a repaired processor is reintegrated into the system, and in general most systems force applications off line when the database is physically reorganized.

An architecture of a distributed software subsystem that can serve as a framework for constructing database application systems to meet most availability requirements is outlined in the remainder of this section. This software subsystem is called an *auditor*. The description of the functions and architecture of the auditor given here is based largely on my own research. A design based on this is currently being implemented for the Highly Available Systems project at IBM Research, San Jose [Aghili et al. 1983].

An auditor is a framework for total coherent management of software and hardware components of a highly available distributed system. It will serve as the repository of failure reports from various components of the system and reconfiguration requests from the system operator (for on-line changes). It will analyze the status of all resources it manages, and compute the optimal configuration of the system in response to multiple concurrent failures of components and requests for load balancing. Further, it will initiate system reconfiguration and monitor its progress in order to effect mid-course correction of a reconfiguration that does not succeed, and finally, it will diagnose a class of failures that other components fail to recognize.

From the discussions of the survey portion of this paper, it should have become clear to the reader that most systems provide many of the functions outlined for the auditor. All systems discussed support automatic detection of process and processor failures, followed by automatic switchover to a backup or notification to the service center. Many systems also support on-line integration of new or repaired software (process) and hardware components (processor, I/O controller, disk drives).

However, the implementation of the auditor functions in many systems suffers from two shortcomings. First, these functions have often been implemented as a loose collection of specialized routines, rather than as a single coherent subsystem. Second, the functions often are implemented to tolerate only a single failure of the system resources; as a result, the systems cannot cope with multiple failures, even when they have sufficient hardware redundancy.

Within this framework, one auditor will reside in each processor, but only one of the auditors may be designated as the audit coordinator. As pointed out by Garcia-Molina [1982], to allow each auditor to initiate reconfiguration may cause confusion or result in a less than optimal system configuration, and the notion of the audit coordinator is therefore central to the operation of the audit mechanism. If the coordinator crashes, a new coordinator must first be established, either by an election, as suggested by Garcia-Molina [1982], or by means of a dynamic succession list to which all the auditors have previously agreed [Kim 1982]. A succession list contains the system-wide unique rank for each auditor to indicate which subordinate auditor will take over the responsibilities of the audit coordinator once the corrent coordinator crashes. The authenticated version of the Byzantine consensus protocol proposed by Dolev and Strong [1982] and the version-number method discussed by Kim [1982] are possible techniques to ensure agreement on the succession list in the presence of failures of communication lines, processes, and processors.

The audit coordinator should be responsible for analyzing the states of all other subordinate auditors, analyzing the reports and initiating system reconfiguration, the replacement of failed subsystems or processors with their backups, and (re)integration of repaired (or new) subsystems or processors. The audit coordinator will also serve as the arbitrator of conflicting reports from different auditors, and is responsible for maintaining a stable configuration database which contains information about the status and physical location of each of the subsystems.

Such an auditor may be implemented as a collection of six asynchronous tasks: configuration-database task, audit task, reconfiguration task, state-report task, diagnose task, and operator-control task. The task structure of an auditor and the flow of control among the auditor tasks are illustrated in Figure 13.

The configuration-database task maintains a consistent and up-to-date configuration database. All queries and updates to the configuration database by other auditor tasks are directed to this task. Changes to the configuration database are exclusively handled by the configuration-database task of the audit coordinator. After each change, the configuration-database tasks of the subordinate auditors are given the most up-to-date copy of the configuration database. Although the configuration database viewed by a subordinate auditor may be temporarily out of date, consistency of the system configuration is not compromised since critical decisions can only be made by the audit coordinator.

The audit task is primarily responsible for coordinated surveillance of process and processor failures. The audit task of a subordinate auditor collects the local state reports from the state-report task, and delivers them to the audit task of the coordinator. The audit task of the coordinator receives these state reports from subordinate auditors, and analyzes them to determine whether any process or processor has failed.

One way for the audit coordinator to receive state reports is to periodically poll the subordinate auditors. An interesting alternative to polling by the audit coordinator is the approach proposed by Walter [1982], which requires each "auditor" to periodically send an "I-AM-ALIVE" message to its immediate neighbor on a virtual ring of "auditors." When an auditor does not receive the "I-AM-ALIVE" message within a certain time interval, it may request the audit coordinator to initiate reconfiguration.

When the audit task of the coordinator decides that a failure has occurred, or when it receives a reconfiguration request from the operator control task, it activates the reconfiguration task. Changes to system configuration are reflected in the configuration database after the reconfiguration task completes. The audit task of the coordinator is also responsible for preparing the succession list and securing its trans-

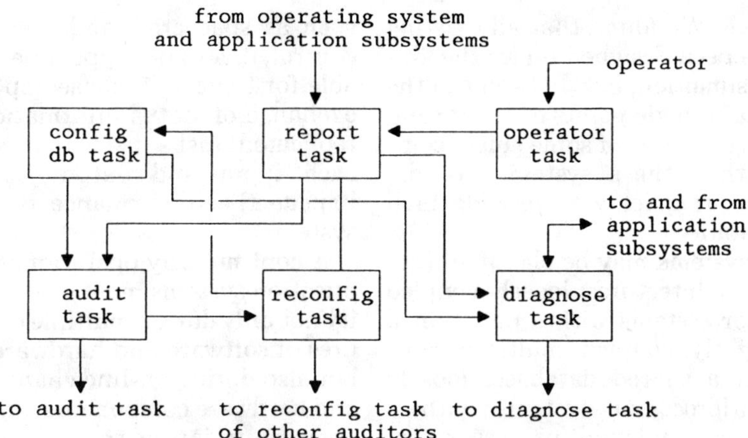


**Figure 13.** The task structure of an auditor.

mission to the audit tasks of subordinate auditors.

The reconfiguration task is responsible for processing the reconfiguration requests received from the audit task of the audit coordinator. Upon receiving a request, it initiates reconfiguration and monitors its successful completion. If the audit coordinator fails during a reconfiguration process, then the new coordinator completes the reconfiguration. Any change to the system configuration is stored in the configuration database. A report is sent back to the audit task of the coordinator upon completion of a reconfiguration request.

The state-report task receives state reports from the local database subsystems, interprocessor communication subsystem, and the operating system, as well as reconfiguration requests from the system operator. It manages this collection of state reports and makes it available to the local audit task and other auditor tasks.

The diagnose task is responsible for exposing process failures that may have gone undetected by the operating system or the process itself. It may also collect complaints from database subsystems about possible misbehavior of other subsystems (e.g., time-outs and lost messages). To establish availability or misbehavior of subsystems, it may resort to functional tests, such as checking if messages pass through queues, tracking down the messages exchanged by subsystems, and executing simple transactions whose results are known. This sometimes will require collaboration among the diagnose tasks of several auditors. Its findings are packaged into a state report and sent to a database subsystem (e.g., to report the loss of a message and the need for its retransmission) or to the state-report task (e.g., to report a subsystem crash that has remained undetected by the operating system).

The complexity of the diagnose task depends on the extent to which other software subsystems assist in identifying failures. If the operating system is capable of serving as a repository of hardware and program failures, and application software contains a reasonable amount of defensive code to detect impossible software states, the diagnose task can be quite simple. If this is not the case, the diagnose task may have to be designed in a manner similar to the Resource Manager of System D to expose the nature of failures.

The operator-control task is the auditor's interface to the system operator. By using this interface, the operator may query the system configuration or request a system reconfiguration.

## 8. CONCLUDING REMARKS

This paper has provided a survey and analysis of the architectures and availability techniques used in database application systems designed with availability as a primary objective. We found that all existing systems have been designed under the single-failure assumption, but that some of the systems contain single points of failure and cannot survive failures of some single components. Rather, these systems are designed to restart quickly to provide high overall availability.

All of the systems may be classified into four distinct architectures: loosely coupled multiprocessor systems with a partitioned database, tightly coupled multiprocessor systems with a shared database, loosely coupled multiprocessor systems with a shared database, and multiprocessor systems that perform redundant computations and compare the results. Of these, the loosely coupled multiprocessor with either a partitioned or shared database appears to offer the best framework for building a highly available system. Either architecture is conducive to incremental expansion and offers a natural boundary between data managers, which makes it difficult for a malfunctioning data manager to corrupt other data managers. Of course, both architectures require a low-overhead communications subsystem to process user requests that require access to more than one database partition. A difficult problem posed by the partitioned database, however, is that of deciding which database partition should be owned by which processor, so as to minimize the volume of processing requiring collaboration among more than one data manager. Potential drawbacks of the shared database approach are contention on shared disks and the difficulty of coordinating the global locking and the logging of database changes.

The tightly coupled multiprocessor architecture with a shared database compromises availability in favor of a potential performance advantage over the loosely coupled system with a partitioned database. However, before this potential advantage in performance can be realized, the problems of contention among processors for the use of shared memory and other shared resources, especially as more processors are added, must be resolved.

Although the redundant-computation approach may make sense for applications such as spacecraft and industrial process control, it does not appear particularly suitable for typical database applications. The exchange of status information among the replicated tasks to verify correctness of each input and output could seriously impede the performance of a production system.

A continuously operational database application systems must guarantee availability not only during multiple concurrent failures of software and hardware components but also during on-line changes of software and hardware components, on-line physical reconfiguration of the database, and generation of backup databases. An architecture was outlined in Section 7 of a distributed software subsystem called an auditor, which can serve as a framework for constructing database application systems to meet these requirements.

## ACKNOWLEDGMENTS

Irv Traiger (IBM Research, San Jose) read an initial version of this paper and made numerous valuable suggestions that helped to significantly improve the technical contents and presentation of the paper. John West of Computer Consoles, Richard Gostanian of Auragen Systems, Bob Good of Bank of America, Steve Jones of Synapse Computer, and Dave Cohen of AT&T Bell Labs kindly provided answers to various technical questions I had about their systems. The referees and Randy Katz made various constructive comments on an earlier version of this paper. Finally, a technical editor did a superb job of shaping the paper into publishable form.

## REFERENCES

AGHILI, H., ASTRAHAN, M., FINKELSTEIN, S., KIM, W., MCPHERSON, K., SCHKOLNICK, M., AND STRONG, M. 1983. A prototype for a highly available database system. IBM Res. Rep. RJ3755, IBM Research, San Jose, Calif., Jan. 17.

ANDLER, S., DING, I., ESWARAN, K., HAUSER, C., KIM, W., MEHL, J., AND WILLIAMS, R. 1982. System D: A distributed system for availability. In *Proceedings of the 8th International Conference on Very Large Data Bases* (Mexico City, Mexico D.F., Sept.), pp. 33–44.

BARTLETT, J. 1978. A nonstop operating system. In *Proceedings of the 1978 International Conference on System Sciences* (Honolulu, Hawaii, Jan.).

BERNSTEIN, P., AND GOODMAN, N. 1981. Concurrency control in distributed database systems. *ACM Comput. Surv. 13*, 2 (June), 185–221.

BORR, A. 1981. Transaction monitoring in ENCOMPASS (TM): Reliable distributed transaction processing. In *Proceedings of the 7th International Conference on Very Large Databases* (Cannes, France, Sept. 9–11). IEEE, New York, pp. 155–165. ACM, New York.

COHEN, D., HOLCOMB, J. E., AND SURY, M. B. 1983. Database management strategies to support network services. *IEEE Q. Bull. Database Eng. 6*, 2 (June), special issue on Highly Available Systems.

COHEN, N. B., HALEY, C. B., HENDERSON, S. E., AND WON, C. L. 1982. GEMINI: A reliable local network. In *Proceedings of the 6th Workshop on Distributed Data Management and Computer Networks* (Berkeley, Calif., Feb.), pp. 1–22.

DOLEV, D., AND STRONG, H. R. 1982. Polynomial algorithms for multiple processor agreement. In *Proceeding of the 14th ACM Symposium on Theory of Computing* (San Francisco, May 5–7). ACM, New York, pp. 401–407.

ELECTRONIC BUSINESS 1981. October issue.

GARCIA-MOLINA, H. 1982. Elections in a distributed computing system. *IEEE Trans. Comput. C-31*, 1 (Jan.), pp. 48–59.

GOOD, B. 1983. Experience with Bank of America's distributive computing System. In *Proceedings of the IEEE CompCon* (Mar.). IEEE Computer Society, Los Angeles.

GOSTANIAN, R. 1983. The Auragen System 4000. *IEEE Q. Bull. Database Eng. 6*, 2 (June), special issue on Highly Available Systems.

GRAY, J. N. 1978. Notes on data base operating systems. IBM Res. Rep. RJ2188, IBM Research, San Jose, Calif., Feb.

GRAY, J. N., MCJONES, P., BLASGEN, M., LINDSAY, B., LORIE, R., PRICE, T., PUTZOLU, F., AND TRAIGER, I. 1981. Recovery manager of a data management system. *ACM Comput. Surv. 13*, 2 (June), 223–242.

HAERDER, T., AND REUTER, A. Principles of transaction-oriented database recovery. *ACM Comput. Surv. 15*, 4 (Dec.), 287–317.

IBM 1979. OS/VS2 MVS multiprocessing: An introduction and guide to writing, operating, and recovery procedures. Form No. GC28-0952-1, File No. S370-34, International Business Machines.

IBM 1980. IBM System/370 principles of operation. Form No. GA22-7000-6, File No. S370-01, International Business Machines.

IEEE 1983. *IEEE Q. Bull. Database Eng. 6*, 2, (June), special issue on Highly Available Systems.

JONES, S. 1983. Synapse's approach to high application availability. In *Proceedings of the IEEE Spring CompCon* (Mar.). IEEE Computer Society, Los Angeles.

KASTNER, P. C. 1983. A fault-tolerant transaction processing environment. *IEEE Q. Bull. Database Eng. 6*, 2 (June), special issue on Highly Available Systems.

KATSUKI, D., ELSAM, E. S., MANN, W. F., ROBERTS, E. S., ROBINSON, J. G., SKOWRONSKI, F. S., AND WOLF, E. W. 1978. Pluribus—An operational fault-tolerant multiprocessor. *Proc. IEEE 66*, 10 (Oct.) 1146–1159.

KATZMAN, J. A. 1977. System architecture for NonStop computing. In *Proceedings of the CompCon* (Feb). IEEE Computer Society, Los Angeles. pp. 77–80.

KATZMAN, J. A. 1978. A fault tolerant computer system. In *Proceedings of the 1978 International Conference on System Sciences* (Honolulu, Hawaii, Jan.).

KIM, W. 1982. Auditor: A framework for highly available DB/DC systems. In *Proceedings of the 2nd Symposium on Reliability in Distributed Software and Database Systems* (Pittsburgh, Pa., July). *IEEE* Computer Society, Silver Spring, Md., pp. 76–84.

KINNUCAN, P. 1981. An industrial computer that 'can't fail.' *Mini-Micro Syst.* (Mar.), 29–34.

KOHLER, W. 1981. A survey of techniques for synchronization and recovery in decentralized computer systems. *ACM Comput. Surv. 13*, 2 (June), 149–183.

MITZE, R. W., ET. AL. 1983. The 3B-20D processor and DMERT as a base for telecommunications applications. *Bell Syst. Tech. J. Comput. Sci. Syst. 62*, 1 (Jan.), 171–180.

SPENCER, A. C., AND VIGILANTE, F. S. 1969. System organization and objectives, *Bell Syst. Tech. J.* (Oct.), 2607–2618, special issue on No. 2 ESS.

STRATUS 1982 *Stratus/32 System Overview.* Stratus Computers, Natick, Mass.

STRICKLAND, J. P., UHROWCZIK, P. P., AND WATTS, V. L. 1982. IMS/VS: An evolving system. *IBM Syst. J. 21*, 4, 490–510.

SWAN, R., FULLER, S. H., AND SIEWIOREB, D. P. 1977. Cm*—A modular, multi-microprocessor. In *Proceedings of the National Computer Conference* (Dallas, Tex., June 13–16), vol. 45. AFIPS Press, Reston, Va., pp. 637–644.

TRAIGER, I. 1983. Trends in systems aspects of database management. In *Proceedings of the British Computer Society 2nd International Conference on Databases* (Cambridge, England, Aug. 30–Sept. 2).

TSUKIGI, K., AND HASEGAWA, Y. 1983. The travel reservation on-line network system. *IEEE Q. Bull. Database Eng. 6*, 1 (Mar.), special issue on Database Systems in Japan.

WALTER, B. 1982. A robust and efficient protocol for checking the availability of remote sites. In *Proceedings of the 6th Workshop on Distributed Data Management and Computer Networks* (Berkeley, Calif., Feb.), pp. 45–68.

WEISS, H. M. 1980. The ORACLE data base management system. *Mini-Micro Syst.* (Aug.), 111–114.

WENSLEY, J. H., LAMPORT, L., GOLDBERG, J., GREEN, M., LEVITT, K., MELLIAR-SMITH, P. M., SHOSTAK, R., AND WEINSTOCK, C. 1978. SIFT: Design and analysis of fault-tolerant computer for aircraft control. *Proc. IEEE 66*, 10 (Oct.), 1240–1255.

WEST, J. C., ISMAN, M. A., AND HANNAFORD, S. G. 1983. Transaction processing in the PERPOS operating system. *IEEE Q. Bull. Database Eng. 6*, 2 (June), special issue on Highly Available Systems.

WESTON, J. 1978. General Electric's MARK III Cluster System. Presented to the American Institute of Industrial Engineers, Jan. 31.

Received April 1983; final revision accepted February 1984.

# Glossary and Term Index

*Aborted transaction:* A transaction that does not complete successfully. No permanent changes are made to a database by an aborted transaction. (Page 219)

*Accommodation:* The conversion of a schema to a data model that can be supported by a database management system. (Pages 165–167)

*After-image log:* A history of the new or modified values that result when transactions are applied to a database. (Page 222)

*Application generator:* A software program that accepts a specification expressed in a nonprocedural language and generates an equivalent procedural program. (Page 11)

*Attribute:* An interesting characteristic of an entity type; for example, the EMPLOYEE entity type has attributes NAME, AGE, and SALARY. (Page 161)

*Before-image log:* A history of the old values before modification when transactions are applied to a database. (Page 222)

*Canonical command translator:* A module in a database management system that converts canonical commands into physical commands to be executed by a runtime processor. (Pages 5–6)

*Category:* An object in an entity-category-relationship schema. A category is a subset of entities from an entity type. (Page 161)

*CODASYL data model:* See network data model. (Page 165)

*Column:* Attribute or field of a relation. (Page 93)

*Column designator:* A construct used in a programming language to access a column of a table (relation). (Page 96)

*Conceptual schema:* Description of types of data and their interrelationships that are useful to the enterprise as a whole. The ANSI/SPARC information architecture includes a conceptual schema. (Page 4)

*Commit:* When the results of a database transaction are made permanent in the database. (Page 219)

*Concurrent transactions:* Two transactions that overlap in time. (Page 220)

*Concurrency transparency:* The ability of a user to believe that he has sole access to the database even though the database management system can support several users simultaneously. (Page 6)

*Conflicting transactions:* One transaction needs to modify the data that another transaction needs to reference. (Page 220)

*Cursor:* A construct used to both define an SQL request in an embedded programming language and iterate over individual rows of the resulting table. A cursor is used in IBM products to access the results of a SQL request. (Page 97)

*Data dictionary:* A special database that contains data about data. The data dictionary may contain an internal representation of the various schemas used by a database management system. (Pages 7, 11)

*Data directory:* A catalog or directory that contains the location of data. A data dictionary almost always includes a data directory. (Page 11)

*Data model:* Style of describing and manipulating data in a database. Example data models include the hierarchical, network (CODASYL), and relational data models. (Page 2)

*Data independence:* See program-data independence. (Pages 5–6, 7–8, 90–92)

*Database:* Collection of data representing information of interest to an enterprise. In this tutorial, database will refer to that data that can be accessed electronically. (Page 1)

*Database administrator:* Person responsible for the organization of data in the database and also determines who may access that data. (Page 1)

*Database backup:* A complete copy of the database that may be used to restore the database if it is lost. (Page 221)

*Database management system:* Collection of computer software used to describe, insert, delete, modify, and retrieve data in a database. (Page 1)

*Database manipulation commands:* The commands accepted by a database management system that cause data to be stored, modified, deleted, and retrieved from the database. (Pages 9, 90–101)

*Database user:* Person who uses a database management system to insert, delete, modify, and retrieve data in the database according to the rules specified by the database administrator. (Page 1)

*DBTG data model:* See network data model. (Pages 3, 84–90, 165–166)

*Deadlock:* The situation when transactions have locked the data needed by each other. When deadlocked, the transactions cannot commit. (Pages 224–225)

*Deadlock detection:* An algorithm that determines if deadlocks exist among a set of active transactions. (Pages 224–225)

*Deadlock prevention:* A transaction scheduling algorithm that guarantees that a deadlock can never occur. (Pages 224–225)

*Differential file:* A special file that contains all of the changes made to a database. (Page 223)

*Domain:* Collection of values that attributes of entities may assume. (Page 93)

*Entity:* An object, event, thing, or concept that will be represented in a database. (Page 161)

*Entity type:* A class of homogeneous entities. (Page 161)

*Entity-Category-Relationship data model:* A data model frequently used during database design. The Entity-Category-Relationship data model can be used to capture a description of the object classes of a database without specifying implementation details. (Pages 161–165)

*External schema:* Description of data and their interrelationships of interest to one or more applications within an enterprise. The ANSI/SPARC information architecture contains several external schemas. (Page 4)

*Enterprise:* A group of people working toward a goal by using resources and tools held in common. (Page 1)

*Field:* A portion of a record that contains a value about some attribute of the entity represented by that record. For example, an EMPLOYEE record may contain NAME, AGE, and SALARY fields. (Page 83)

*File:* A collection of data stored on secondary storage. (Pages 83–84)

*File data model:* The data description and manipulation facilities provided by most operating systems that allow programmers to define and manipulate data stored permanently in files. The file data model is the most widely-used data model because most applications are written using files. (Pages 2–3, 83–84)

*File system:* A primitive type of database management system available with most operating systems. A file system allows the user to store data permanently in files so that the data can be accessed at a later time. (Pages 11, 83–84)

*Foreign key:* A column of one relation (table) that may contain only values that exist in the key column of another relation (table). (Pages 93, 166–167)

*Hierarchical data model:* A data model in which records of data are arranged in a hierarchy or tree structure. (Pages 2–3)

*Host language preprocessor:* A processor that accepts an application program written in a traditional programming language and produces a modified application program written in the same programming language. In the case of database management systems, the preprocessor replaces each database command by a call statement. (Page 7)

*Host programming language:* A traditional programming language such as FORTRAN or COBOL that has been extended to include database manipulation commands. (Pages 94–97)

*Information architecture:* Collection of schemas in a database management system and the relationship of those schemas. For example, the ANSI/SPARC information architecture consists of three schema types: external, conceptual, and internal. (Pages 3–5)

*Insertion option:* Semantic integrity constraint that can be specified for CODASYL sets and that describes rules for inserting new member records into a set. (Pages 88–89, 162, 165–166)

*Internal schema:* Description of the way in which data is stored and accessed on permanent storage devices. The ANSI/SPARC information architecture contains an internal schema. (Page 4)

*Live lock:* The situation in which a transaction is restarted and aborted over and over again. (Page 225)

*Lock:* A mechanism that can be set (or locked) by a user who wants to update data in a database. A lock guarantees that two users cannot update the same data at the same time. (Pages 223–225)

*Member record type:* A record type that participates in a CODASYL set. (Page 85)

*Meta data:* Data about data. The contents of a data dictionary can be thought of as meta data. A schema is an example of meta data. (Page 7)

*Multiple-record-per-command language:* See nonprocedural data manipulation language. (Pages 93–95)

*Network data model:* A data model in which records of data are arranged in a network structure. The network data model is also called the CODASYL data model and DBTG data model. (Pages 3, 84–90, 165–166)

*Nonprocedural data manipulation language:* A multiple-record-per command language in which a single command can manipulate many objects in the database. (Pages 9, 93–101)

*Owner record type:* A record type that participates as an owner of a CODASYL set. (Page 85)

*Procedural data manipulation language:* A single-record-per-command language in which the programmer can specify that several objects in the database be manipulated one at a time. (Pages 9, 90–93)

*Program-data independence:* The ability to restructure or reorganize the database without changing application programs. (Pages 5-6, 7–8, 90–92)

*Programming language:* Collection of rules for using words and phrases to describe and manipulate data in the program work space. Programming languages are often extended to include database manipulation commands that are used to access data residing permanently in a database. (Page 3)

*Query language:* Any database manipulation language that may be entered to a database management system at a terminal with the results displayed at the terminal in a short time. Originally, a query language could only retrieve data, but today most query languages can also update data. (Page 3)

*Query optimization:* The process of choosing the least expensive access paths and processing strategies to perform a query. (Page 3)

*Query-by-Example:* A nonlinear two-dimensional language developed by Moshe Zloof at IBM. (Pages 98–100)

*Range variable:* A variable used in relational calculus expressions to refer to a single row (tuple) of a table (relation). A range variable is similar to an iteration variable of a FOR loop in traditional programming languages. (Pages 95, 97)

*Record:* That piece of a file that represents a single entity. For example, an EMPLOYEE file may contain three records for the employees Jones, Smith, and Lewis. (Page 83)

*Record type:* The collection of records in a file that describe the same type of entity. Most files consist of only a single record type, although some files may contain more than one record type. (Page 83)

*Recursive set type:* A CODASYL set type in which the owner record type is also the member record type. (Page 87)

*Relation:* Relational term for entity class. (Page 93)

*Relational algebra:* A nonprocedural language used in some relational database management systems. The language has properties similar to the mathematical concept of an algebra. (Pages 94–95)

*Relational calculus:* A nonprocedural language used in some relational database management systems. The language has properties similar to the mathematical concept of predicate calculus. (Pages 94–95)

*Relational data model:* A data model in which the database user can access fields of a record that do not contain addresses of other records. All files appear as flat tables to the users. The relational data model is popular because of the nonprocedural interfaces associated with it. (Pages 3, 93–97, 166–167)

*Relationship set:* An object in an entity-category-relationship schema. A relationship associates entities from two or more entity classes. Not to be confused with relation, which is used in the relational data model. (Pages 161–165)

*Reorganization:* Process of moving data from one location to another. Data structures such as indexes may be adjusted or rebuilt. A database is reorganized to make better utilization of existing storage resources. (Page 7)

*Report generator:* Software program that accepts a description of the format and contents of a report and causes that report to be produced. A report generator usually has a greater range of output formating capabilities than does a query language. (Page 11)

*Restructure:* Process of adding or deleting from the database description; for example, inserting a new field into an existing file. (Page 7)

*Row:* A tuple (instance) of a relation (table). (Page 93)

*Row designator:* A construct in a programming language used to access a single row (tuple) of a table (relation). (Page 96)

*Runtime support processor:* A processor in a database management system that is responsible for accepting database requests and scheduling the processing of those requests. The runtime support processor is also responsible for concurrency control. (Pages 6–7)

*Relation:* Entity type in the relational data model; also called a table. (Page 93)

*Retention option:* Semantic integrity constraint that can be specified for CODASYL sets that describes rules for modifying and deleting existing member records in a set. (Pages 89, 162, 165–166)

*Schema:* Description of types of data and their interrelationships. (Pages 4–5)

*Set:* A data structure used in the CODASYL data model to represent one-to-many relationships between records. (Pages 84–90)

*Set key:* A specification used in the CODASYL data model to guarantee that no two members of a set occurrence have the same values for a record field. (Page 89)

*Set order:* The sequence of member record occurrences within a set. (Page 89)

*Select:* (1) A relational algebra function which returns some of the rows of a table in the database. Sometimes called RESTRICT (Pages 94–95); and (2) a keyword of the SQL language command used to retrieve data. (Page 95)

*Semantic integrity constraint:* Rules which data in the database must always obey. (Pages 8, 83, 88, 161)

*Serial transactions:* Transactions that do not overlap in time. (Page 220)

*Serializable history:* A history of two or more transactions that is equivalent to a serial history of the same transactions. (Pages 220–221)

*SEQUEL:* See SQL. (Pages 94, 95, 101)

*Single-record-per-command language:* See procedural data manipulation language. (Pages 91, 94)

*SQL:* Structured Query Language; a multiple-record-per-command language used in relational database management systems; also referred to as SEQUEL. (Pages 94, 95)

*Stand-alone data manipulation language:* A database manipulation language that can be used as a query language. A stand-alone data manipulation language can be used without being embedded into a programming language. (Page 3)

*Structural constraint:* Used in the entity-category-relationship data model to constrain the entities that can participate in a relationship. (Page 162)

*System architecture:* Description of the various processes and modules of a system and their interrelationships. (Pages 5–7)

*SYSTEM-owned set:* A CODASYL set type where there is exactly one instance, which is owned by a special record called SYSTEM. (Pages 88, 166)

*Table:* See relation. (Page 93)

*Table skeleton:* An icon used in Query-by-Example that displays the table name and column names of a table to be accessed. (Page 98)

*Timeout:* A mechanism for aborting transactions that might be deadlocked. After a prespecified time period, all transactions that are still waiting are aborted. (Page 225)

*Timestamp:* The value of a counter that is stored with a transaction or data item. (Page 225)

*Transaction:* Program code that may contain several database commands. (Pages 219–221, 223)

*Transaction atomicity:* A property of a transaction that requires that each transaction is either completely executed with any modifications made to the database permanently recorded or the transaction is aborted with no permanent change made to the database. (Pages 7, 219, 221)

*Transaction consistency:* The property of a transaction that transforms the database from one consistent state to another. (Pages 219, 221)

*Transaction durability:* The property of a transaction that guarantees that once committed, the results of a transaction will not be lost. (Pages 219, 221)

*Transaction log:* A history of the transactions applied to a database. (Pages 8, 221–223)

*Trigger:* An action that is automatically executed when the database satisfies a prespecified condition. (Page 93)

*Two-phase locking:* A protocol that guarantees that transaction histories are serializable. (Pages 224–225)

*User command translator:* A module of a database management system that accepts user requests expressed using one style of interface and converts the requests into a canonical format. (Page 5)

*Validation statements:* Statements in a program or schema which check if data satisfies predefined requirements; for example, a check to verify that a person's age is always a positive integer. (Page 8)

*View:* (1) A relational language request that has been stored and referenced in other relational language requests; and (2) a perception of the contents of a database for a single class of users. (Pages 161–165)

*View design:* The design and specification of a user's perception of the contents of a database. (Pages 161–165)

*View integration:* The integration or merging of two or more views. (Page 165)

*Well-formed transaction:* A transaction is well-formed if it locks data before using it and releases the locks after using the data. (Page 223)